ACCOUNTING

EIGHTH EDITION

Consulting Editor

Walter G. Kell, Ph.D., C.P.A.

Professor of Accounting
Syracuse University, Syracuse, N. Y.

PRINCIPLES

Howard S. Noble, **M.B.A., LL.D., C.P.A.**

Professor of Accounting, Emeritus
University of California, Los Angeles

C. Rollin Niswonger, **PH.D., C.P.A.**

Professor of Accounting
Miami University, Oxford, Ohio

Published by

South-Western Publishing Company

CINCINNATI 27 / CHICAGO 44 / DALLAS 2 / NEW ROCHELLE, N. Y. / BURLINGAME, CALIF.

Library of Congress Catalog Card Number 61-8600

K763

Printed in the United States of America

Preface

This eighth edition of *Accounting Principles* retains the basic framework of the early chapters of the seventh edition. An introduction to the role of accounting in the management of business enterprises is provided in the first chapter, together with a carefully integrated exposition of the relationship of business transactions to financial statements.

Procedural aspects of accounting have been de-emphasized throughout the book. Space hitherto devoted to alternative recording techniques is now occupied by new materials on internal controls, accounting concepts and principles, and the use of accounting data in decision making. This change in emphasis has been accomplished without slighting the hardcore basis of the introductory course. Regardless of their major field of interest, students should obtain an adequate grounding in the recording, classifying, and summarizing phases of accounting in order to proceed with the interpretation of accounting data.

Two new chapters have been added and others have been entirely rewritten. The first half of the book is more challenging than heretofore and should better prepare the student for the more specialized subjects of the latter half. The number of questions, exercises, and problems has been materially increased to provide greater flexibility, and the material is presented in the order of increasing difficulty. Problems for use in alternate years or sections of the course are provided in an appendix. They may also be assigned where supplementary or review problems are needed. Working papers provided for the end-of-chapter problems may also be used for the alternate problems.

The second half of the book is designed to permit selective omission of parts or chapters in order to satisfy varying requirements as to the length of the course, the level at which it is offered, the preferences of the teacher, and the needs of the students. As in earlier editions, this edition is planned for use in a basic course for (1) accounting majors, (2) majors in other areas of business administration, and (3) those whose major interest is in economics, political science, law, or other professional areas.

Three optional practice sets are available. The narrative of transactions and the instructions for the first set are presented in the textbook.

Data needed for the other two sets accompany the ruled forms. Demonstration problems, transparencies, study guides, and other teaching aids are also available.

The opinions and the preferences of many teachers were sought in anticipation of writing this edition. The response to our questionnaire of nearly two years ago was most gratifying. The criticisms and the commendations received were invaluable in preparing this edition. It would be impossible to list the names of all persons who over the years have contributed to the improvement of *Accounting Principles*. Special thanks are extended to the following who prepared extensive critiques of the seventh edition, submitted detailed suggestions for new materials, or read the manuscript: Professors John W. Anderson, University of Massachusetts; Horace Brock, North Texas State College; Arthur E. Carlson, Washington University; Thomas C. Hilliard, DePaul University; W. Asquith Howe, Temple University; Harold Q. Langenderfer, University of North Carolina; I. E. McNeill, University of Houston; Anka Ohman, City College of San Francisco; Harry R. Price, University of Miami; Silvan Tesoriere, Fordham University; P. B. Yeargan, University of Alabama.

The authors also acknowledge their indebtedness to Professor Walter G. Kell, Syracuse University, who served as consulting editor and in addition assumed major responsibility for portions of the manuscript. To the American Institute of Certified Public Accountants go our thanks for permission to use materials from their copyrighted publications.

HOWARD S. NOBLE

C. ROLLIN NISWONGER

Contents

CHAPTER   **PAGE**

Part 1 — Basic structure of accounting

1 Fundamental accounting relationships   **1**

Importance of accounting, 1; Specialized accounting fields, 2; Bookkeeping and accounting, 4; Need for business records, 4; Profession of accountancy, 6; Business transactions, 8; Property and business operations, 9; Accounting defined, 9; Business transactions and accounting values, 10; Assets, liabilities, and proprietorship, 11; Transactions and the accounting equation, 11; Summary of illustration, 15; Accounting statements, 15.

2 Accounting statements   **23**

Transactions and accounting statements, 23; Accounting period, 24; Classified balance sheet and income statement, 24; Classification of items on the balance sheet, 25; Standard forms of the balance sheet, 29; Balance sheet illustrated and analyzed, 30; Form of the income statement, 33; Classification of items on the income statement, 34; Income statement illustrated and analyzed, 36; Capital statement, 38; Interrelationship of accounting statements, 38.

Part 2 — Accounting cycle for a service enterprise

3 Accounts and the trial balance   **45**

Recording transactions, 45; Nature of an account, 45; Accounts and the balance sheet, 46; Debit and credit, 49; Arrangement of accounts in the ledger, 53; Illustration of a complete ledger, 53; Trial balance, 59; Proof provided by the trial balance, 59.

4 Journalizing and posting   **67**

Need for journals, 67; Two-column journal, 68; Standard form of the account, 69; Posting, 70; Chart of accounts, 70; Illustrations of the journal and the ledger, 72; Trial balance procedures, 77; Other journal forms, 78; Four-column journal illustrated, 80; Discovery of errors, 82; Correction of errors, 83.

5 Completion of the accounting cycle   **90**

Trial balance and accounting statements, 90; Mixed accounts and business operations, 91; Adjusting process, 91; Work sheet, 95; Financial statements, 99; Journalizing and posting adjusting entries, 101; Closing entries, 102; Ruling and balancing the accounts, 104; Post-closing trial balance, 108; Accounting cycle, 109; Interim statements, 110.

Part 3 — Accounting cycle for a merchandising enterprise

6 Sales and cash receipts   **117**

Need for special journals, 117; Merchandising, 117; Frequency of sales transactions, 118; Trade discounts, 119; Sales procedures, 119; Controlling accounts and subsidiary ledgers, 120; Sales journal, 121; Posting the sales journal, 122; Sales returns and allowances, 123; Using sales invoices as a sales journal, 126; Sources of cash receipts, 127; Credit terms, 127; Cash discounts, 127; Cash receipts journal, 128; Posting the cash receipts journal, 130; Accounts receivable control and subsidiary ledger, 131; Delivery of merchandise sold, 134.

7 Purchases and cash payments   141

Purchasing procedures, 141; Purchases journal, 142; Controlling account and subsidiary ledger, 143; Posting the purchases journal, 143; Purchases returns and allowances, 147; Using purchases invoices as a purchases journal, 149; Credit terms and cash discounts, 149; Cash payments journal, 150; Accounts payable control and subsidiary ledger, 152; Transportation on incoming shipments, 155.

8 Periodic summary   163

Outline of the periodic summary, 163; Merchandise inventory adjustments, 164; Adjustments and the work sheet, 165; Completing the work sheet, 167; Preparation of statements and supporting schedules, 170; Adjusting entries, 173; Closing entries, 174; Post-closing trial balance, 176; Reversing entries, 176; Errors of past periods, 180.

Practice Set 1, Greer Wholesale Shoes — Part 1   187

General ledger, 187; Subsidiary ledgers, 188; Journals, 189; Transactions for October, 189; Posting to the general ledger, 192; Data for adjustments, 192.

Part 4 — Notes, prepayments, and accruals

9 Notes and interest   193

Use of credit instruments in business, 193; Computing interest, 194; Determining the due date, 195; Notes payable, 196; Recording interest expense, 197; Notes receivable, 198; Recording interest income, 199; Discounting notes, 199; Dishonored notes, 204; Reporting interest on the income statement, 205.

10 Prepaid, unearned, and accrued items   211

Need for consideration, 211; Classification and terminology, 211; Prepaid expenses, 212; Unearned revenue, 215; Accrued liabilities, 219; Accrued assets, 221.

Part 5 — Receivables, inventory, and plant assets

11 Receivables and merchandise inventory   229

Classification of receivables, 229; Uncollectible accounts, 230; Direct write-off of uncollectible accounts, 230; Advance provision for uncollectible accounts, 231; Presentation of the allowance account in the balance sheet, 232; Charging uncollectible accounts to the allowance account, 233; Estimating losses from uncollectible accounts, 234; Importance of inventories, 236; Inventory systems, 237; Determining quantities in the inventory, 237; Determining the cost of inventory, 238; Valuation at cost or market, whichever is lower, 242; Retail method of inventory costing, 244; Presentation of merchandise inventory on the balance sheet, 245; Gross profit method of estimating inventories, 245.

CHAPTER   PAGE

12 Plant assets — depreciation   253

Nature of plant assets, 253; Determining initial costs, 254; Nature of depreciation, 254; Recording depreciation, 255; Depreciation methods, 257; Capital
and revenue expenditures, 260; Disposal of plant assets, 261; Subsidiary ledgers
for equipment, 265; Composite depreciation rates, 268; Plant assets on the
balance sheet, 268.

Practice Set 1, Greer Wholesale Shoes — Part 2   275

Transactions for November, 275; Posting to the general ledger, 279; Data for
adjustments, 279.

Part 6 — Accounting controls and concepts

13 Systems and controls   280

Accounting systems, 280; Internal control, 281; Using a bank account, 282;
Bank statement, 284; Bank reconciliation, 284; Entries based on bank recon-
ciliation, 288; Internal control of cash receipts, 288; Cash short and over, 289;
Special cash funds, 289; Supplementary records for notes, 293; Insurance, 293;
Alternative account forms, 296; Use of accounting machines, 297.

14 Voucher system   305

Control of cash payments, 305; Basic features of the voucher system, 305;
Preparation of vouchers, 307; Voucher register, 309; Unpaid voucher file, 310;
Check register, 311; Paid voucher file, 313; Comparison of controlling account
with unpaid vouchers, 313; Special problems, 314; Purchases discount, 317;
Remittance advice, 319; Voucher system and management, 320.

15 Concepts and principles   327

Need for concepts and principles, 327; Development of concepts and principles,
327; Business entity, 328; Going concern, 329; Unit of measurement, 330;
Accounting period, 331; Recognition of revenue, 332; Allocation of costs,
335; Consistency, 336; Adequate disclosure, 336; Materiality, 337; Conservatism, 338.

Part 7 — Payrolls and taxes

16 Payrolls — payroll taxes   346

Importance of payroll records, 346; Types of remuneration, 346; Employer-
employee relationship, 347; Computation of earnings, 347; Deductions from
earnings, 348; Calculation of net pay, 351; The payroll, 351; Entering the
payroll in the accounts, 355; Paying the payroll, 355; Employee's earnings
record, 357; Withholding statement, 359; Employer's payroll taxes, 360; Recording employer's payroll taxes, 361; Payment of payroll taxes, 362; Adjustments at the end of the fiscal period, 364; Completed payroll periods, 364.

17 Property, sales, and income taxes   371

Taxes in general, 371; Relationship to accounting, 371; Property taxes, 372;
Accounting for property taxes, 373; Delinquent taxes on property purchased,
375; Special assessments, 376; Sales taxes, 376; Sales taxes imposed upon the
purchaser, 377; Sales taxes imposed upon the seller, 378; Federal income tax,
379; Accounting methods, 379; Gross income, 381; Tax base, 382; Deductions
from gross income, 382; Adjusted gross income, 384; Deductions from adjusted

gross income, 384; Taxable income, 387; Capital gains and losses, 388; Income tax rates, 388; Credits against the tax, 390; Tax returns; payments, 390; Individual income tax problem illustrated, 391; Income tax records, 392.

Part 8 — Partnerships

18 Partnerships — organization and operation   401

Definition of partnership, 401; Characteristics, 401; Accounting in general, 403; Formation of a partnership, 403; Recording the investment, 404; Drawing accounts, 406; Division of income or loss, 406; Income division in arbitrary ratio, 407; Income division recognizing investment, 407; Income division recognizing services of partners, 411; Income division recognizing services of partners and investments, 412; Statements for a partnership, 413; Partnerships and federal income tax, 414.

19 Partnerships — dissolution and liquidation   421

Partnership dissolution, 421; Admission of a new partner, 421; Admission by purchase of interest from partners, 422; Admission by contribution of assets to the partnership, 423; Bonus or goodwill to former partners, 424; Bonus or goodwill to new partner, 426; Withdrawal of a partner, 428; Death of a partner, 430; Liquidation of a partnership, 430.

Practice Set 2, Clark & Madison — Part 1

The narrative for this practice set is supplied with the blankbooks that may be obtained from the publisher. In the first month of the set the business is operated as a partnership. It uses the voucher system and provides for the recording of both payroll and sales taxes.

Part 9 — Corporations

20 Corporations — nature and formation   441

Definition of a corporation, 441; Characteristics of a corporation, 442; Incorporation, 443; Working organization, 444; Stockholders and proprietorship, 445; Classes of stock, 447; Values of stock, 450; Authorized, issued, and outstanding stock, 452; Presentation of capital on the balance sheet, 452; Issuing stock at par for cash or other assets, 453; Incorporating a proprietorship or a partnership, 454; Organization costs, 456.

21 Corporations — capital stock   463

Premium and discount on capital stock, 463; No-par stock, 465; Subscriptions to capital stock, 466; Issuance of stock certificates, 467; Subscriptions and stock issuance illustrated, 467; Treasury stock, 469; Purchased treasury stock, 470; Donated treasury stock, 471; Redemption of preferred stock, 472; Records required by a corporation, 473.

22 Corporations — capital, earnings, and dividends   481

Corporation capital, 481; Paid-in capital, 481; Revaluation of assets, 483; Corporation earnings, 483; Corporation income taxes, 483; Retained earnings, 484; Appropriation of retained earnings, 485; Nature of dividends, 488; Cash dividends, 489; Stock dividends, 490; Stock split-up, 491; Corrections and unusual charges and credits, 492; Amortization and write-off of intangibles, 494; Retained earnings statement, 495.

23 Corporations — long-term obligations and investments 503

Financing corporations, 503; Bonds payable, 505; Bonds sold at a premium, 507; Bonds sold at a discount, 508; Extended illustration of accounting for bond premium, 509; Bond discount and bond premium on the balance sheet, 510; Bond sinking fund, 511; Restriction of dividends, 512; Redemption, 513; Long-term notes, 514; Investments in stocks and bonds, 514; Temporary investments, 515; Long-term investments, 516; Income from investments in stocks, 517; Income from investments in bonds, 517; Sale of investments, 518; Corporation balance sheet, 519.

Practice Set 2, Clark & Madison — Part 2

This part of Practice Set 2 is the second month of Practice Set 2, Part 1, but in this part the business is operated as a corporation.

Part 10 — Department, branch, and manufacturing operations

24 Departments and branches 527

Departmentalization, 527; Gross profit by departments, 528; Net operating income by departments, 528; Apportionment of operating expenses, 529; Work sheet, 531; Income statements, 534; Effect of discontinuing a department, 534; Branch operations, 535; Systems for branch accounting, 536; Reciprocal accounts in branch accounting, 537; Illustration of decentralized branch accounting, 539; Branch financial statements, 543; Combined statements for home office and branch, 543; Shipments billed at selling price, 546; Analyses of operations, 546.

25 Manufacturing 553

Manufacturing operations, 553; Asset and liability accounts, 553; Cost and expense accounts, 556; Controlling accounts and subsidiary ledgers, 557; Statement of cost of goods manufactured, 558; Adjusting and closing manufacturing accounts, 559; Work sheet of a manufacturing enterprise, 560; Statements, 564; Adjusting and closing entries, 567; Inventory determination, 567; Perpetual inventories and cost accounting, 568.

Practice Set 3, Dawson Manufacturing Company — Part 1

The narrative for this practice set is supplied with the blankbooks that may be obtained from the publisher. The business is operated as a corporation and uses the voucher system. The first month of the set deals with general accounting for manufacturing operations.

Part 11 — Cost accounting

26 Cost accounting — job order system 575

Cost accounting systems, 575; General accounting and job order cost accounting, 575; Flow of costs in perpetual inventory accounts, 576; Materials and supplies, 577; Factory labor, 578; Factory overhead, 579; Work in process, 581; Finished goods and cost of goods sold, 584; Sales, 585; Summary illustration of job order cost accounting, 586.

CHAPTER   **PAGE**

27   Cost accounting — process system; standard costs   597

Process cost systems, 597; Job order and process costs distinguished, 598; Service departments and process costs, 598; Processing departments, 599; Inventories of partially processed materials, 600; By-products, 603; Joint products, 603; Illustration of process cost accounting, 604; Process costs and business operations, 608; Fixed and variable costs, 610; Standard costs, 611.

Practice Set 3, Dawson Manufacturing Company — Part 2

This part of Practice Set 3 is the second month of Practice Set 3, Part 1, but in this part a job-order cost system is installed and maintained.

Part 12 — Additional accounting reports for management, creditors, and investors

28   Budgeting and internal reports   620

Accounting aids to management, 620; Nature of budgeting, 620; Budgeting and management, 621; Budgeting procedures, 622; Sales budget, 623; Production budget, 623; Operating expense budget, 624; Estimated income statement, 624; Cash budget, 626; Flexible budgets, 627; Nature of internal reports, 628; Essentials of effective internal reports, 628; Efficiency reports, 629; Trend reports, 630; Break-even analysis, 630; Alternative cost reports, 632; Acceptance of business at a special price, 633; Elimination of an unprofitable endeavor, 634; Make or buy, 635; Equipment replacement, 636.

29   Funds statement and other statements   647

Principal financial statements, 647; Comparative statements, 647; Funds statement, 648; Preparation of the funds statement, 648; Sources of funds, 652; Applications of funds, 654; Extended illustration of funds statement, 654; Consolidated statements, 659; Alternative forms of financial statements, 660; Rounding amounts, 662; Fiscal years, 663.

30   Statement analysis   669

Need for analysis, 669; Basic analytical procedures, 669; Horizontal analysis, 670; Vertical analysis, 674; Other analytical measures, 676; Current ratio, 677; Acid-test ratio, 677; Ratio of owners' equity to liabilities, 678; Ratio of plant assets to long-term liabilities, 679; Accounts receivable turnover, 679; Merchandise inventory turnover, 680; Ratio of sales to assets, 681; Ratio earned on total assets, 681; Rate earned on stockholders' equity, 682; Rate earned on common stockholders' equity, 682; Earnings per share on common stock, 683; Other measurements, 683.

Appendix

A — Alternative method of recording merchandise inventory   689

B — Specimen corporation statements   693

C — Alternate problems   713

Index   783

Fundamental accounting relationships

Importance of accounting

Accounting has been characterized as "the language of business."[1] The professional accountant must be expert in the use of this "language." Many persons engaged in other areas of business, such as finance, production, marketing, personnel, and general management, need not be expert accountants, but their usefulness is enhanced and their advancement is more assured if they have a good understanding of accounting principles. Everyone engaged in business activity, from the youngest employee to the manager and owner, comes into contact with accounting. The higher the level of authority and responsibility, the greater is the need for an understanding of accounting concepts and terminology.

Accounting has also been said to provide "the eyes and ears for management."[2] It is through accounting that the managers of an enterprise are informed of the operations of the organization. The accountant has the responsibility of keeping track of the essential dollars-and-cents information affecting the organization, of interpreting the information in terms of relative success or failure, and of helping to plan the course of future action.

Accounting always applies to an economic organization or unit in society. Economic units include profit-making businesses; governmental units, such as states, cities, and school districts; consumers, such as families and individuals; and other social organizations, such as churches, hospitals, and clubs. Each economic unit has business transactions that must be recorded, summarized, and interpreted. The accounting must therefore apply to each unit. For example, it is the particular automobile manufacturer, not the automobile industry as a whole, that has business transactions. This does not mean, of course, that accounting data for a particular unit cannot be combined with the data for other similar units to obtain an over-all picture. For example,

[1]Various publications (New York: American Institute of Certified Public Accountants).
[2]*Young Eyes on Accounting* (Madison, Wis.: American Accounting Association).

passenger revenue, passenger miles, and other operating data may be obtained for the entire airline industry; similarly, figures for national income and for the combined state and federal debt may be developed from the accounting records of many separate economic units.

In this text the emphasis will be placed on accounting principles applied to profit-making business enterprises. It should be kept in mind, however, that accounting principles can be applied to each unit in economic society.

In accounting, as in the physical and biological sciences, experimentation, development, and change are never-ending. Capable scholars devote their lives and their intellectual energies to analyzing accounting phenomena. Experienced professional accountants contribute their best thinking to the solution of problems forever confronting their clients or employers. One of the primary purposes of the several professional accounting associations is research. The studies and the deliberations of the special committees and staff members of these organizations result in pronouncements and recommendations that increase the usefulness of accounting.

Specialized accounting fields

As in many other areas of human activity in the twentieth century, accountants have developed a number of specialized fields. This tendency toward specialization has been caused in large measure by growth in size of business units, mounting taxes, and increasing regulation of business by law and by governmental agencies. These influences, together with rapid technological advances and accelerated economic growth, have created the need for a high degree of expertness in various specialties.

The term *general accounting* applies to the over-all accounting for an economic unit. It has to do with the recording of transactions for a business or other economic unit and the periodic preparation of statements from these records. The various general purpose and special purpose reports and statements prepared from the accounting records are used to impart useful information to managers, owners, creditors, government agencies, and the general public. The accounting principles and techniques that will be developed in this book are in large part included in general accounting.

Auditing represents a field of accounting activity that independently reviews general accounting. Auditing was the first service rendered by *public accountants* and is still one of their principal activities. These accountants examine records and statements and express an opinion regarding their fairness and accuracy. Large corporations with widely dispersed operations frequently employ their own staffs of *internal auditors.* One of the most important duties of internal auditors is to determine whether the various operating divisions observe the policies and procedures prescribed by management. Internal auditing has recently developed to the point of being considered a special field. The work programs of the public accountant and the internal audit staff are integrated so as to avoid needless duplication of effort.

Cost accounting emphasizes accounting for costs, particularly the cost of manufacturing processes and of manufactured products. It deals not only with actual or historical costs, but also with prospective costs and desired costs. One of the principal functions of the cost accountant is to assemble and interpret cost data for the use of management in controlling current manufacturing operations and in planning for the future.

Tax accounting includes the preparation of tax returns and the consideration of the tax consequences of proposed business transactions. Accountants specializing in this field must be familiar with the tax statutes affecting their employer or clients and also must keep up to date on administrative regulations and court decisions.

Accounting systems is the special field concerned with the creation of accounting and office procedures and with the designing of forms for particular enterprises or groups of similar enterprises. It seeks to devise the most efficient means of recording and reporting financial data. Accountants engaged in this field must be familiar with the uses and the relative merits of available accounting machines and electronic data processing equipment.

Budgetary accounting presents the plan of financial operations for a period and, through accounts and summaries, provides comparisons of actual operations with the predetermined plan. It is a combination of planning, coordinating, and controlling future operations.

Management services is a rapidly growing field of specialization. Accountants have only recently come to realize that their training and experience uniquely qualify them to advise management on policies and administration. Many public accountants customarily submit a confidential report to management as an extra service in performing an audit. They may also be engaged to study specific phases of business operations and to advise as to alternative courses of action.

Governmental accounting specializes in the transactions of political units, such as states and municipalities. It seeks to provide useful accounting information with regard to the business aspect of public administration, and it helps to control the expenditure of public funds according to law or legislative dictates.

Accounting instruction is perhaps the most obvious field of specialization. In addition to teaching, many accounting professors engage in auditing, tax accounting, or other areas of accounting on a part-time or consulting basis.

There is some overlapping among the various specialties, and leaders in any particular field are likely to be well versed in related fields. There is also some specialization within the specialized fields. For example, within the field of auditing one may become an expert in a particular classification such as department stores or public utilities; in tax accounting one may specialize in the problems of oil and gas producing companies; or in systems one may become expert in electronic data processing machines.

Bookkeeping and accounting

There is some confusion over the distinction between "bookkeeping" and "accounting." This is due in part to the fact that the two are related and that there is no universally accepted line of demarcation between them.

In general, *bookkeeping* is the recording of business data in a prescribed manner. A bookkeeper may be responsible for keeping all of the records of a business or only a small segment, such as a portion of the customers' accounts in a department store. Much of the work of the bookkeeper is clerical in nature.

Accounting is concerned with the design of the system of records, the preparation of reports based on the recorded data, and the interpretation of the reports. Some of the specialized fields of accounting were described in the preceding section. Accountants often direct and review the work of bookkeepers or of other accountants. The larger the firm, the greater is the number of gradations in responsibility and authority. The work of accountants at the beginning levels may include some bookkeeping. In any event, it is apparent that the accountant must possess a much higher level of knowledge and analytical skill than is required of the bookkeeper.

Need for business records

The purpose of business enterprise is to make a profit. Those who invest in business firms do so with the expectation that they will receive a return in the form of income. They also incur the risk of losing part or all of their investment. The managers of business enterprises are of necessity concerned with the same objective; they must constantly strive to maximize profits or minimize losses.

In order to appraise the degree of success achieved by management, it is necessary to have summaries of the effects of the transactions entered into by the business. The system of records must begin with the recording of each transaction. There are many different means of recording transactions, and a number of them can be used by a single business. The historical data thus accumulated provide the facts and figures from which various reports and statements are prepared.

Knowledge of the past performance of an enterprise is of additional value beyond its historical aspects; it is useful in planning future operations. By comparing summaries of the most recent month with the preceding month and with the comparable month of the preceding year, trends become apparent. Further study and analysis may develop the contributory causes of the trends and point the way to acceleration of those that are favorable and to halting those that are undesirable. For example, an increase in the volume of services or merchandise sold is a favorable indication. If the increase is accompanied by increases in costs and expenses of such magnitude that net income is decreased, the end result is, of course, unfavorable. Questions such as the following should be answered: Was the increased volume of sales attributable to excessive reductions in selling price? Did the cost of the merchandise increase without a comparable adjustment in selling price? Which expenses increased and what were the causes of the increases? Which increases were unavoidable and which ones can be reduced in the future without adverse effects?

A business that is contemplating expansion needs to give careful consideration to the probable effect of the added facilities on future volume of business and expenses. Will the return on the additional investment of cash justify the expansion? There may also be problems of financing. If money is to be borrowed, when can it be repaid? These are illustrations of the many problems that constantly confront business managers. Business records do not supply all of the answers and, of course, they do not take the place of good judgment. The data obtainable from the records are essential, however, as a partial basis for making decisions.

There are many other needs of a more routine nature served by records. For example, it is necessary to know the amount owed to each creditor and by each customer and the date each payment is due. Records of property are necessary in determining the amount and type of insurance that should be carried and in ascertaining the amount of any insured loss that may occur. Knowing when to place orders for merchandise and supplies, granting credit to customers, anticipating the amount of cash required at any particular time — these and many other essential items of information can be obtained in a timely and orderly fashion only if adequate records are maintained.

In addition to managers and owners, there are others who must be supplied with reports based on the business records. Banks customarily require periodic statements from businesses from which they have loans outstanding. It is customary to submit annual reports to credit-rating companies. Many branches of federal, state, and local governments require reports, particularly in connection with income, property, sales, social security, and other taxes. One of the prerequisites to the issuance of securities by corporations is the filing of detailed reports on business operations and financial position with governmental agencies. Stock exchanges also require periodic reports from corporations whose stocks are listed. The foregoing reasons for preparing accounting reports for outsiders are merely illustrative; there are many others.

Thus far consideration has been given only to business enterprises. Records are also needed by those engaged in professional pursuits and even by persons who have retired from active participation in a business or profession. Governmental units need records of their transactions; they are required to report to other units at a higher level of authority and also to the citizenry. In addition, performance in the past serves as a basis for future planning. Lodges, clubs, churches, educational institutions, labor unions, and other organizations need to maintain records of financial transactions.

In this text the records of commercial enterprises carried on for profit will be emphasized, but much of the discussion will be equally applicable to other economic units.

Profession of accountancy

Accountancy is a profession with stature comparable to that of law or engineering. The tremendous development of accounting theory and technique during the current century has been accompanied by an ever-increasing number of professionally trained accountants. Among the factors contributing to this growth have been the increase in number, size, and complexity of business corporations; the imposition of new and more complex taxes, especially since the adoption of the Federal Income Tax Amendment in 1913; and the restrictions imposed on business operations by governmental regulations.

Accountants who render accounting services on a fee basis, and staff accountants employed by them, are said to be engaged in *public accounting*. Accountants employed by a particular business firm, perhaps as chief accountant or controller, are said to be engaged in *private accounting*.

Recognizing the need for reliable professional accounting service, all the states have enacted laws providing for the licensing of certified public accountants, commonly called C.P.A.'s. Only those individuals who have met the qualifications and received a license may designate themselves as C.P.A.'s.

The qualifications required for the C.P.A. certificate differ among the various states. In most states the applicant must be a high-school graduate and must have had from one to three years' experience in public accounting or in accounting work considered equivalent. In some states accounting education at the college level may be substituted for all or part of the experience requirement. Several states require the completion of a collegiate course of study in accounting that is approved by their state board of accountancy. In all states candidates must successfully pass a series of examinations on the subjects of auditing, commercial law, theory of accounts, and accounting practice. All states use a uniform examination prepared by the American Institute of Certified Public Accountants, the national organization of C.P.A.'s. A few states also require candidates to pass an examination in an additional subject, such as business economics, governmental accounting, or taxation.

Although all states provide for the licensing of C.P.A.'s, many of them do not restrict the practice of public accounting to those so licensed. In the absence of express prohibition, any person may style himself as a public accountant, or P.A. A relatively recent development has been the enactment of regulatory laws, often referred to as "restrictive" or "two-class" legislation. Although details vary among states, this type of law requires the registration of self-styled public accountants within a definite time period following enactment. Those so registered may continue to practice public accounting, but after the deadline date no others may register. In time only those who are licensed as C.P.A.'s may practice on their own account. Details regarding the requirements of any specific state can be obtained from the state board of accountancy or other agency charged with administering the law.

The scope of activities and responsibilities of private accountants varies quite widely. Private accountants are concerned with the financial records of a particular business enterprise or nonprofit organization. They are frequently referred to as administrative or executive accountants, but they are sometimes called industrial accountants when they are employed by a manufacturing concern. Various branches of federal, state, and local governments also employ accountants in increasing numbers. Many C.P.A.'s are engaged in private and governmental accounting. The accounting division of business enterprises has long been recognized as a training ground for business executives, and many high positions in industry and government are held by professional accountants.

Business transactions

A business transaction is the occurrence of an event or of a condition that must be recorded. For example, an exchange of goods or services at an agreed price is a transaction. The payment of a monthly telephone bill of $25, the purchase of $500 of merchandise on account, and the acquisition of land and a store building for $100,000 are illustrative of the variety of business transactions.

The first two transactions are relatively simple, being a payment of money in exchange for a service and a promise to pay within a short time in exchange for commodities. The purchase of a building and the land on which it is situated is usually a more complex transaction. The total price agreed upon must be allocated between the land and the building, and the agreement usually provides for spreading the payment of a substantial part of the price over a period of years and the payment of interest on the unpaid balance. There may be other special provisions designed to safeguard the seller until the full price has been paid.

It can readily be seen that a particular business transaction may lead to an event or a condition that constitutes another transaction. For example, the purchase of merchandise on account referred to above will be followed by payment to the creditor, which is another transaction; and each time a portion of the merchandise is sold, another transaction occurs. Each of these events needs to be recorded. Each payment to the seller of the land and the building is a transaction, as is the payment of interest. The fact that the building will not last forever must also be given recognition in the records.

Most of the representatives of a business who enter into transactions with outsiders are not responsible for the accounting records. It is necessary, therefore, that some evidence of transactions be provided as a basis for the records. The form that this evidence takes varies with the nature of the transaction and the medium used. For example, a sale of merchandise for cash may be evidenced by a handwritten sales ticket or by depressing the appropriate keys on a cash register or other recording device. In addition to providing factual data for the recording of transactions, the supporting documents and other forms of evidence furnish a basis for subsequent review and verification of accounting records by certified public accountants and governmental auditors. Throughout this text a variety of supporting documents will be discussed and illustrated.

Property and business operations

The use of property is essential to the conduct of business. A place for the business must be provided in a building that is owned or rented; equipment adapted to the activities of the business must be owned or leased; if goods are sold, they must be purchased or manufactured and kept in stock prior to sale; if services are rendered, the equipment and the supplies used in rendering the services must be available for use. Wherever there is business, property is found.

Through the sale of commodities or services, business operations usually produce funds that may be used to purchase additional property as the business expands. These funds constitute an important element in the total property of the business. If a business is conducted in such a way that its total ownership increases, the business is said to be successful. In contrast, if its operations result in a decrease in its ownership, the business is considered to be unsuccessful.

An automobile-manufacturing business that grew from a one-man shop in the back lot of a Detroit residence to a huge corporation employing hundreds of thousands of people is an example of successful business operations and the accompanying increase in property. A five-and-ten-cent business that grew from a small store in a small town in Pennsylvania to a world-wide enterprise with departmentalized stores in every large city is another instance of expansion in business and property. Many of the large business firms in existence today began years ago as small enterprises. It should not be concluded, however, that only the giant enterprises are successful. Moderate-sized and small business enterprises often earn substantial income.

Accounting defined

In a general way, the purpose of accounting may be said to be to provide information concerning property and the rights to property, and to show how property and the rights to it have been affected by business operations. More specifically, accounting has been described as:

> ...The art of recording, classifying, and summarizing in a significant manner and in terms of money, transactions and events which are, in part at least, of a financial character, and interpreting the results thereof.[3]

Recording commits the transactions and events to writing. Various mechanical and electronic devices are used in recording accounting data, so that "writing" encompasses figures recorded in registers, holes punched in cards, magnetic impressions on tape, and other recording media.

---

[3] *Accounting Terminology Bulletin No. 1,* "Review and Résumé," 1953 (New York: American Institute of Certified Public Accountants), p. 9.

Classifying involves sorting the many transactions in an orderly and systematic manner. Special forms and procedures are devised to facilitate this process. A mass of isolated transactions conveys little meaning when considered individually; the data become useful only when sorted according to predetermined classes. Transactions must be understood before they can be classified. It is therefore of paramount importance that the student of accounting gain a thorough understanding of the effect of all types of transactions upon property and property rights.

Summarizing brings the accounting data together in a form that further enhances their usefulness. It is not the single business act but the sum of all the operations of a day, a week, a month, or a year that has the greatest significance. Therefore, summaries of operations and their effect on property and rights to property are prepared at intervals. These reports are made to the managers of the enterprise and to others who need the information. Some reports must be made frequently; others, only at longer intervals. For example, it may be desirable to have a daily summary of transactions affecting cash, while an annual report of transactions affecting buildings may be satisfactory.

Interpreting the results of operations, as summarized in the various reports, is an essential part of accounting. Interpretation is frequently in the form of percentage analyses and ratios. Comparison of operations for different periods may indicate important trends. From these ratios and trends, the most significant developments in the affairs of a business may be explained, emphasized, and directed.

Business transactions and accounting values

When properties or services are purchased by a business, the amount at which they are recorded is the price agreed upon in the business transaction. For example, if a business building is purchased for $50,000, that amount is used in the buyer's accounting records. The seller may have been asking $60,000 for the building up to the time of sale; the buyer may have initially offered $40,000 for it; the building may have been assessed at $35,000 for property tax purposes and insured for $45,000; and the buyer may have received an offer of $75,000 for the building the day after he acquired it. These values have no effect on the accounting records because they do not originate from an exchange transaction. The transaction price, or cost, of $50,000 determines the basis at which the building is recorded. Cost results from the actions of an informed buyer and an informed seller who are each attempting to obtain the most favorable price. It is an objective fact that can be verified from the evidence created by an exchange transaction; it is not a mere subjective opinion.

The offer of $75,000 for the building is an indication that it was a bargain at $50,000; but to record the building at $75,000 would give recognition to a fictitious profit of $25,000. If the purchaser accepts the offer of $75,000 and sells the building, there is a new accounting value for the new owner. The building would be entered on the accounting records of the new owner at his cost of $75,000 and, of course, the seller would realize a profit of $25,000 on the sale.

Accounting is essentially a process of accounting for costs; it is not a process of valuation. Only the amount agreed upon between buyer and seller in a transaction is sufficiently objective for accounting purposes. If upward and downward adjustments to properties were made on the basis of mere offers, appraisals, and opinions, accounting records would soon become so unstable and unreliable as to be meaningless.

Assets, liabilities, and proprietorship

The use of property in the operation of a business has been emphasized. It has also been pointed out that accounting deals with property and rights to property. For every business enterprise the sum of the properties owned is equal to the sum of the rights to the properties.

The properties owned by a business are called *assets*. The rights to the properties are called *equities*. The relationship between assets and equities may be stated as follows:

$$\text{Assets} = \text{Equities}$$

Equities may be subdivided into two principal types: the rights of creditors and the rights of owners. The equities of creditors are called *liabilities*, and the ownership equity is called *proprietorship* or *capital*. Expansion of the equation to give recognition to the two basic types of equities yields the following, which is known as the *accounting equation:*

$$\text{Assets} = \text{Liabilities} + \text{Proprietorship}$$

It is customary to place "Liabilities" ahead of "Proprietorship" in the accounting equation because creditors have preferential rights to the assets. The residual claim of the owner or owners is sometimes given greater emphasis by transposing liabilities, to yield:

$$\text{Assets} - \text{Liabilities} = \text{Proprietorship}$$

All business transactions, regardless of their complexity, can be stated in terms of their effect on the three basic elements of the accounting equation.

Transactions and the accounting equation

The effect of changes in assets, liabilities, and proprietorship on the accounting equation can be demonstrated by studying some typical transactions. As the basis of the illustration we will assume that John Reed establishes a new business under the name of Varsity Clothing. Each transaction or group of similar transactions during the first month of operations will be described and the effect on the accounting equation shown.

(a) Reed's first transaction is to deposit $8,000 in a bank account in the name of Varsity Clothing. The effect of this transaction is to increase the asset cash by $8,000 and to increase proprietorship, on the other side of the equation, by the same amount. After the transaction the equation for Varsity Clothing will appear as follows:

Assets		Proprietorship
Cash	=	John Reed, Capital
(a) 8,000		8,000

It should be noted that the equation applies only to the business enterprise. Reed's personal assets, such as his home and personal bank account, and his personal liabilities are excluded from consideration. Accounting is concerned only with the business as a separate entity.

(b) Reed's next transaction in establishing his business is to purchase display cases and other equipment, for which he pays $2,800 in cash. This transaction changes the composition of the assets but does not change the total. The items in the equation prior to this transaction, this transaction, and the new balances after the transaction are as follows:

Assets		Proprietorship
Cash + Equipment		John Reed, Capital
Bal. 8,000	=	8,000
(b) −2,800 +2,800		
Bal. 5,200 2,800		8,000

(c) During the month Reed purchases $4,900 of merchandise from various manufacturers, agreeing to pay in the near future. This type of transaction is called a purchase *on account* and the liability created is termed an *account payable*. In actual practice each transaction would be recorded as it occurred and a separate record would be maintained for each creditor. The effect of this group of transactions is to increase assets and liabilities by $4,900, as indicated below:

Assets		Liabilities + Proprietorship
Cash + Merchandise + Equipment		Accounts Payable + John Reed, Capital
Bal. 5,200 2,800	=	8,000
(c) +4,900		+4,900
Bal. 5,200 4,900 2,800		4,900 8,000

(d) During the month Reed pays $3,400 to his creditors on account, thereby reducing both assets and liabilities. The effect on the equation is as follows:

	Assets			Liabilities	+	Proprietorship
Cash	+ Merchandise	+ Equipment		Accounts Payable	+	John Reed, Capital
Bal. 5,200	4,900	2,800	=	4,900		8,000
(d) −3,400				−3,400		
Bal. 1,800	4,900	2,800		1,500		8,000

The principal objective of the proprietor of a business enterprise is to increase his proprietorship by earning a net income. For John Reed this means that the assets he acquires from the sale of merchandise must exceed the cost of the merchandise sold and the expenses of operating the business. The general term applied to the total charges to customers for goods or services sold is *revenue*.[4] More specifically, the revenue derived from the sale of merchandise in the ordinary operations of a business is called *sales*.

The excess of the revenue from sales over the cost of the goods that have been sold is termed *gross profit* or *margin*. For example, if merchandise that cost $2,000 is sold for $3,200, the gross profit is $1,200. If the operating expenses of the period are less than the gross profit, the remainder is *net income;* if the expenses exceed the gross profit, the excess is *net loss*.

In many businesses it is not feasible to determine and record the cost of the goods sold and the gross profit on each sale of merchandise. This would be the case in a retail grocery or a hardware business, for example. It is even more difficult, and usually impossible, to determine the amount of the operating expenses incurred in connection with each sale. It is quite satisfactory, however, to determine the gross profit and the net income or net loss for a selected period of time, such as a month or a year, rather than for each sale or small group of sales.

(e) Continuing with the illustration of transactions completed by John Reed, his records indicate that during the first month of operations he has sold merchandise for $3,000 in cash. The effect of these sales of merchandise is to increase cash by $3,000 and to yield revenue in the same amount. Although the revenue of $3,000 is not wholly an increase in proprietorship, it is customary to treat it as such. When the cost of the merchandise sold is determined, it will be offset against the revenue. Similarly, when expenses are incurred, they are treated as reductions of

---

[4] *Accounting Terminology Bulletin No. 2*, "Proceeds, Revenue, Income, Profit, and Earnings," 1955 (New York: American Institute of Certified Public Accountants).

proprietorship. In terms of the accounting equation the effect of the sales is presented as follows:

Assets				Liabilities	+	Proprietorship
Cash	+ Merchandise	+ Equipment		Accounts Payable	+	John Reed, Capital
Bal. 1,800	4,900	2,800	=	1,500		8,000
(e)+3,000						+ 3,000 Revenue
Bal. 4,800	4,900	2,800		1,500		11,000

Instead of requiring the payment of cash at the time goods are sold, a business may make sales *on account,* allowing the customer to pay later. In such cases the firm acquires an asset called *accounts receivable* and realizes revenue in exactly the same manner as though cash had been received. When the money is collected from the customer later, the asset Cash increases and the asset Accounts Receivable decreases.

(f) At the end of the month Reed determines that the cost of the merchandise on hand is $3,100 and, by deducting this amount from the merchandise of $4,900, that the cost of the goods sold is $1,800. There is, therefore, a reduction of $1,800 in merchandise and in proprietorship, which may be shown as follows:

Assets				Liabilities	+	Proprietorship
Cash	+ Merchandise	+ Equipment		Accounts Payable	+	John Reed, Capital
Bal. 4,800	4,900	2,800	=	1,500		11,000
(f)	−1,800					−1,800 Cost of goods sold
Bal. 4,800	3,100	2,800		1,500		9,200

(g) Various business expenses in the amount of $500 were incurred and paid during the month. The effect of this group of transactions is to reduce cash and to reduce proprietorship, as indicated below:

Assets				Liabilities	+	Proprietorship
Cash	+ Merchandise	+ Equipment		Accounts Payable	+	John Reed, Capital
Bal. 4,800	3,100	2,800	=	1,500		9,200
(g) − 500						− 500 Expenses
Bal. 4,300	3,100	2,800		1,500		8,700

(h) The final transaction to be considered is the withdrawal of $400 cash by Reed for personal use. This transaction has the same effect on the equation as the payment of expenses in transaction (g). It is different in one important particular, however; it is not a business expense and is therefore not considered in determining the net income from operations of the business. The balances in the equation, the withdrawal of $400, and the new balances are as follows:

	Assets		=	Liabilities	+ Proprietorship
Cash +	Merchandise +	Equipment		Accounts Payable +	John Reed, Capital
Bal. 4,300	3,100	2,800	=	1,500	8,700
(h) − 400					− 400 Drawing
Bal. 3,900	3,100	2,800		1,500	8,300

Summary of illustration

The business transactions of John Reed discussed in the preceding pages are summarized in tabular form below. The transactions are identified by letter, and the balance of each item in the equation is shown after each transaction. In studying the summary the following points should be noted:

   (1) The effect of all transactions can be stated in terms of increases or decreases in assets, liabilities, and proprietorship.

   (2) Equality between the two sides of the equation is always maintained.

		Assets		=	Liabilities	+ Proprietorship
	Cash +	Merchandise +	Equipment =		Accounts Payable +	John Reed, Capital
(a)	+8,000					+8,000
(b)	−2,800		+2,800			
	5,200		2,800			8,000
(c)		+4,900			+4,900	
	5,200	4,900	2,800		4,900	8,000
(d)	−3,400				−3,400	
	1,800	4,900	2,800		1,500	8,000
(e)	+3,000					+3,000 Revenue
	4,800	4,900	2,800		1,500	11,000
(f)		−1,800				−1,800 Cost of goods sold
	4,800	3,100	2,800		1,500	9,200
(g)	− 500					− 500 Expenses
	4,300	3,100	2,800		1,500	8,700
(h)	− 400					− 400 Drawing
	3,900	3,100	2,800		1,500	8,300

Accounting statements

The principal accounting statements are the *balance sheet* and the *income statement*. The balance sheet is a list of the assets, liabilities, and proprietorship of an economic unit as of a particular date, usually at the close of the last day of a month. The income statement is a summary of the revenues, cost of goods sold, and expenses for a particular period of time, such as a month or a year.

The summary of John Reed's transactions, presented in the preceding section, will be used to illustrate the basic characteristics of these

two accounting statements. In the illustration John Reed began operations by establishing a bank account of $8,000. By the end of the month
there were three kinds of assets in the business, and there were also
claims of creditors against the assets in addition to the claim of the
proprietor. The amounts of the various assets and of the liabilities and
proprietorship at the end of the month appear on the last line of the
summary. Minor rearrangements of these data yield the following
balance sheet:

```
                    Varsity Clothing
                    Balance Sheet
                    August 31, 1961
```

Assets		Liabilities	
Cash..............	$3,900	Accounts payable..	$1,500
Merchandise........	3,100		
Equipment..........	2,800	**Proprietorship**	
		John Reed, capital.	8,300
Total.............	$9,800	Total.............	$9,800

Reed's revenue, cost of goods sold, and expenses were recorded as
changes in proprietorship. These data are assembled in an orderly
manner to yield the following income statement:

```
                    Varsity Clothing
                    Income Statement
              For Month Ended August 31, 1961
```

Sales.............................	$3,000
Cost of goods sold...............	1,800
Gross profit on sales............	$1,200
Operating expenses...............	500
Net income.......................	$ 700

The net income of $700 reported in the income statement is an
increase in proprietorship. Comparison of the original capital of $8,000
with the capital of $8,300 appearing on the balance sheet at the end of
the month indicates an increase of only $300, however. The change in
proprietorship not reported on either statement is the reduction resulting
from the withdrawal of $400 in cash by the proprietor. All changes in
capital occurring between balance sheet dates are summarized in a
capital statement. Reed's changes in capital for the first month of operations
are presented in the following statement:

Varsity Clothing
Capital Statement
For Month Ended August 31, 1961

Capital, August 1, 1961................		$8,000
Net income for the month.............	$700	
Less withdrawals......................	400	
Increase in capital...................		300
Capital, August 31, 1961.............		$8,300

All financial statements should be identified by the name of the business, the title of the statement, and the date or period of time. The data presented in the balance sheet are for a specific date; the data presented in the income statement and the capital statement are for a period of time.

The financial history of a business enterprise may be depicted by a succession of balance sheets prepared at yearly intervals. The history of operations for the intervening periods is presented in a series of income statements. Serving as a connecting link between these two principal statements is the capital statement. If the life of a business enterprise is represented by a line moving toward the right, accounting statements may be diagrammed as follows:

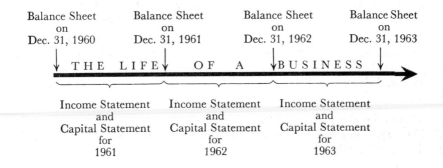

Balance Sheet on Dec. 31, 1960	Balance Sheet on Dec. 31, 1961	Balance Sheet on Dec. 31, 1962	Balance Sheet on Dec. 31, 1963

THE LIFE OF A BUSINESS

Income Statement and Capital Statement for 1961	Income Statement and Capital Statement for 1962	Income Statement and Capital Statement for 1963

Questions

1. Are accounting records useful to the proprietor or manager in planning future operations of a business? Discuss.

2. What is the primary source of information needed in preparing reports for (a) tax authorities and (b) creditors?

3. Why is a knowledge of accounting concepts and terminology useful to all individuals engaged in business activities?

4. Is it necessary for an accountant to be well grounded in general accounting before specializing in a particular field? Discuss.

5. Distinguish between public accounting and private accounting.

6. Describe in general terms the requirements that an individual must meet to become a C.P.A.

7. Explain briefly the recording, classifying, summarizing, and interpreting phases of accounting.

8. Distinguish between cost and value and explain their relative significance in accounting.

9. R. A. Star acquired for $25,000 land that had an assessed value for tax purposes of $18,000. Two years later Star was offered $40,000 for the land and the assessed valuation was $27,000. (a) At what amount should the land be recorded by Star at the time of acquisition? (b) What recognition should be given in the accounts to the values two years later? Discuss.

10. (a) Describe the three basic elements of the accounting equation. (b) Why must the equation always balance?

11. If the sum of the assets of a business is $15,000 and the liabilities total $5,000, what is the amount of the proprietorship?

12. A business incurs a liability of $4,000 for equipment purchased. What effect does the transaction have on proprietorship?

13. What are the possible effects on the three elements in the accounting equation of a transaction that:
   (a) Increases an asset.   (c) Increases a liability.
   (b) Decreases an asset.   (d) Decreases a liability.

14. The Ferndale Company sells hardware. Describe a transaction that will (a) increase an asset and decrease another asset, (b) increase an asset and increase a liability, (c) increase an asset and increase proprietorship, (d) decrease an asset and decrease a liability, (e) decrease an asset and decrease proprietorship.

15. George Bender sold for $5,000 a lot that he had originally purchased for $3,500. How did this transaction affect the total amount of (a) his assets? (b) his proprietorship?

16. During a month a business sold for $20,000 merchandise that it had purchased for $12,000. Its operating expenses for the period totaled $5,000. What was the amount of its (a) revenue? (b) cost of goods sold? (c) margin? (d) gross profit on sales? (e) net income?

17. Despite the fact that Midway Shoe Store earned a net income of $20,000 during the year, of which the proprietor withdrew $8,000, the total of the assets of the business at the end of the year was less than at the beginning. How was this possible?

18. Would it be safer to loan $10,000 to a business with a proprietorship of $100,000 than to one with a proprietorship of $50,000? Discuss.

Exercises

1. A list of transactions for the E. A. Brown Company is presented below. Indicate the increase or the decrease (+ or −) in assets, liabilities, and proprietorship resulting from each transaction. Tabulate your answers, using Assets, Liabilities, and Proprietorship as column headings.

(a) Purchase of equipment on account.
(b) Sale of land at a price in excess of cost.
(c) Payment of a liability.
(d) Additional investment of cash in the business by the proprietor.
(e) Purchase of a car on account for personal use of the proprietor.
(f) Payment of advertising expense.
(g) Sale of land at a loss.
(h) Withdrawal of cash by the proprietor for personal use.
(i) Return of defective equipment purchased on account (payment has not been made).

2. The following selected transactions were completed by Joy's Beauty Shop during the month of May:

(a) Paid rent for May, $75.
(b) Purchased beauty supplies on account, $115.
(c) Received $150 from cash customers.
(d) Paid creditors on account, $135.
(e) Purchased shop equipment for cash, $30.
(f) Paid miscellaneous expenses, $45.
(g) Withdrew $100 in cash for personal use.
(h) Charged customers for beauty services sold on account, $50.
(i) Received $75 from customers on account.
(j) Determined by taking an inventory that $105 of supplies had been used during the month.

Copy the following description of transactions and list after each the identifying letter of each of the above transactions that fits the description:

(1) Increase in one asset, decrease in another asset.
(2) Increase in an asset, increase in a liability.
(3) Increase in an asset, increase in proprietorship.
(4) Decrease in an asset, decrease in a liability.
(5) Decrease in an asset, decrease in proprietorship.

3. The total assets and the total liabilities of a business at the beginning and the end of a year were as follows:

	Assets	Liabilities
Beginning of year........	$20,000	$10,000
End of year............	30,000	15,000

(a) Determine the net income for the year, assuming that there were no additional investments and no withdrawals by the proprietor during the year.

(b) Determine the net income, assuming that the proprietor had withdrawn $7,000 during the year.

(c) Determine the net income, assuming that the proprietor had made no withdrawals but had made an additional investment of $4,000 during the year.

4. Summary financial data of Henry Morton's business on September 1 are presented in the equation below. Each line designated by a letter indicates the effect of a transaction on the equation. Transactions (d), (e), and (f) affect net income.

(1) Describe each of the transactions.

(2) What is the amount of the net income for the month?

(3) How much of the net income was retained in the business?

	Cash	+ Merchandise	+ Equipment	= Liabilities	+ Proprietorship
	3,000	6,000	1,500	500	10,000
(a)	− 500	+ 500			
	2,500	6,500	1,500	500	10,000
(b)	+ 300		− 300		
	2,800	6,500	1,200	500	10,000
(c)		+2,000		+2,000	
	2,800	8,500	1,200	2,500	10,000
(d)	+2,500				+2,500
	5,300	8,500	1,200	2,500	12,500
(e)		−1,800			−1,800
	5,300	6,700	1,200	2,500	10,700
(f)	− 300				− 300
	5,000	6,700	1,200	2,500	10,400
(g)	−1,500			−1,500	
	3,500	6,700	1,200	1,000	10,400
(h)	− 250				− 250
	3,250	6,700	1,200	1,000	10,150

5. James Foster manufactures a product at a unit cost of 60 cents and sells it at a unit cost of $1. His annual sales have averaged 1,000,000 units and his total operating expenses have been approximately $200,000. On the basis of experimentation in a particular region and of a careful study of costs and expenses it is concluded that (1) reduction of the selling price to 90 cents would result in a 50% increase in the number of units sold, (2) a 50% increase in production would result in a cost reduction of 5 cents a unit, (3) a 50% increase in volume would be accompanied by a 20% increase in operating expenses, and (4) the increased volume would not require the investment of additional funds in the business.

Assuming the correctness of the study, determine whether the reduction in price would yield a greater net income and, if so, how much.

Problems

1-1. Earl Cook has organized a dance band to play for various community organizations on Friday and Saturday nights. His transactions for the first month were as follows:

(a) Opened a bank account for use in his business enterprise by depositing $300.
(b) Purchased musical scores (music) for cash, $50.
(c) Purchased music stands and lights on account, $160.
(d) Received $175 from the Towers Club for services rendered.
(e) Paid $125 to members of the band.
(f) Purchased an amplifying system for $190 on account.
(g) Received $200 from Kenwood Country Club for services rendered.
(h) Paid $250 to creditors on account.
(i) Paid $140 to members of the band.
(j) Withdrew $50 from the bank account for personal use.

Instructions: (1) Record the transactions in tabular form, using the following headings:

Assets			=	Liabilities	+	Proprietorship
Cash +	Equipment +	Music		Accounts Payable	+	Earl Cook, Capital

Identify changes in proprietorship by placing the abbreviation R (revenue), E (expense), or D (drawing) at the right of each amount of increase or decrease in capital subsequent to the initial investment.

(2) Submit answers to the following questions:

(a) What was the amount of Cook's net income for the period?
(b) What was the amount of the increase in capital for the period in comparison with the original investment?

1-2. On August 1 of the current year, Ruth Ward established a women's clothing store called Sports Wear. Transactions completed during the month were as follows:

(a) Deposited $8,000 in cash in a bank account for Sports Wear.
(b) Purchased equipment for cash, $2,500.
(c) Purchased merchandise on account, $2,800.
(d) Paid salaries and other expenses, $400.
(e) Sold merchandise on account, $1,400.
(f) Purchased merchandise for cash, $900.
(g) Paid creditors on account, $1,900.
(h) Purchased equipment on account, $500.
(i) Sold merchandise for cash, $1,800.
(j) Received cash from customers on account, $800.
(k) Paid salaries and other expenses, $300.
(l) Withdrew cash for personal use, $200.
(m) Returned defective equipment purchased on account, $100.

(n) Determined by taking an inventory that the cost of the goods sold during the month was $2,000.

Instructions: (1) Record the transactions in tabular form, using the following headings:

Assets				=	Liabilities	+	Proprietorship
Cash +	Accounts Receivable	+ Merchandise +	Equipment	=	Accounts Payable	+	Ruth Ward, Capital

Identify changes in proprietorship by placing the abbreviation R (revenue), CGS (cost of goods sold), E (expense), or D (drawing) at the right of each amount of increase or decrease in capital subsequent to the initial investment.

(2) Prepare a balance sheet, an income statement, and a capital statement.

(3) Which of the statements present data for the specific date, August 31, and which for the entire month of August?

1-3. Carl Wynn operates a business known as Superior Drycleaners. The actual work of dry cleaning is done by another company at wholesale rates. The assets and the liabilities of the business on July 1 of the current year are as follows: Cash, $1,100; Accounts Receivable, $400; Supplies, $75; Delivery Equipment, $2,500; Furniture and Fixtures, $900; Accounts Payable, $620. His business transactions during July are summarized below.

(a) Paid rent for July, $100.

(b) Paid creditors on account, $540.

(c) Purchased supplies on account, $60.

(d) Received $900 from cash customers.

(e) Charged customers for dry cleaning services sold on account, $450.

(f) Received bill from cleaning company for $700.

(g) Received $510 from customers on account.

(h) Reimbursed a customer $25 for a garment lost by the cleaning company, which agreed to deduct the amount from the invoice received in transaction (f).

(i) Paid miscellaneous expenses, $125.

(j) Purchased an item of furniture on account, $50.

(k) Paid personal expenses by checks drawn on the business, $350, and withdrew $50 in cash for personal use.

(l) Determined by taking an inventory that $50 of supplies had been used during the month.

Instructions: (1) State the assets, liabilities, and proprietorship as of July 1 in equation form similar to that shown in this chapter.

(2) Record the transactions in tabular form, determining the new balances after each transaction. Identify changes in proprietorship by placing the abbreviation R (revenue), CSS (cost of services sold), E (expense), or D (drawing) at the right of each amount of increase or decrease in capital.

(3) Prepare a balance sheet, an income statement, and a capital statement.

Accounting statements

Transactions and accounting statements

The effect of transactions on assets, liabilities, and proprietorship was demonstrated in the preceding chapter by the use of the accounting equation. It should be readily apparent that revisions of the equation to record the effect of individual transactions or groups of similar transactions was illustrative only. Such a method of recording accounting data is not practicable. There is also no need to maintain a cumulative record such as that provided by the succession of equations. Before describing and illustrating the basic elements of a system for recording transactions, additional consideration should be given to the accounting statements that were introduced in Chapter 1. The statements represent an important part of the end product of the accounting records, and the information needed for the statements will have a material effect on the design of the accounting records.

Periodically the owner of a business should know the financial position of his business and the results of operations. If the proprietor has borrowed money from a bank or is heavily indebted to a supplier of merchandise, he may be required to present statements to such creditors at regular intervals. Credit rating bureaus, tax authorities, and other governmental agencies also require financial statements at least once each year and sometimes more frequently.

As indicated in Chapter 1, the two principal statements are the *balance sheet* and the *income statement*. The balance sheet provides information about the assets, liabilities, and proprietorship at a selected time, usually at the end of an accounting period. The revenues, costs, and expenses of an accounting period are summarized in the income statement. Neither the balance sheet nor the income statement reveals the changes that have occurred in proprietorship during the accounting period. Because of the importance attached to changes in the proprietor's equity, it is customary to summarize all such changes during the accounting period in a *capital statement*.

Accounting period

The interval of time between accounting statements varies among businesses. The maximum length of the accounting period is ordinarily one year, which includes a complete cycle of the seasons and of business activities. Income and property taxes are also based on yearly periods and thus require that annual reckonings be made.

The shortest accounting period is customarily one month. Many businesses prepare financial statements at the end of each month. In addition to the balance sheet as of the last day of the month and an income statement for the month, it is common practice to prepare an income statement for the entire period since the beginning of the year. For example, assuming that the business year begins on January 1, the following statements would be prepared during the first three months:

January: Balance sheet as of January 31
Income statement for January 1–31

February: Balance sheet as of February 28
Income statement for February 1–28
Income statement for January 1–February 28

March: Balance sheet as of March 31
Income statement for March 1–31
Income statement for January 1–March 31

The capital statements prepared to accompany the balance sheets and the income statements listed above could encompass either the most recent month or the entire period to date. It is ordinarily not necessary to prepare both single-month and cumulative capital statements.

The twelve-month accounting period adopted by an enterprise is known as its *fiscal year*. The fiscal year may coincide with the calendar year, January 1 to December 31, or it may begin with the first day of any particular month and end with the last day of the twelfth month. Any period for which an income statement is prepared, regardless of whether it is a year or some portion of a year, may be referred to as a *fiscal period*.

Classified balance sheet and income statement

Financial statements are prepared by accountants for the use of owners, managers, creditors, employees, and other interested persons. It is assumed that those who will read and study the statements have some knowledge of business and financial matters but that they are not necessarily experts in accounting and finance. Consequently, the format of the statements, the terminology used, and the sequence of the items should be such as to aid comprehension by the reader.

It is not unusual for large corporations to prepare several versions of their financial statements. Although the basic data are the same for each version, the different versions will vary as to the amount of detail and the terminology employed. Statements prepared for employees are usually condensed, with many items combined and only the summary figure presented; a phrase or an entire sentence may be used to describe an item. Statements prepared for stockholders are more formalized, with greater detail and briefer captions. Statements prepared for the Securities and Exchange Commission, the stock exchange, and the income tax authorities may all differ in the amount of detail, the groupings of the items, and the terminology employed.

In this book attention will be focused on statements suitable for the owners, creditors, and management. If the general form and the content of the statements are thoroughly understood, there should be no difficulty in understanding the many variations that may be encountered.

Classification of items on the balance sheet

The usual form of the balance sheet has three principal groupings that correspond to the three elements in the accounting equation: assets, liabilities, and proprietorship.

ASSETS. Any physical thing or any right that has a money value is an asset. Physical assets are *tangible* and rights are *intangible*. The dollar amount at which assets are shown is generally based on their cost. This is not always the case, however, as will be shown in later portions of the book. The classification most commonly applied to assets is: (1) *current assets* and (2) *plant assets*. These two categories and the specific items most commonly found in each are discussed in the paragraphs that follow. Additional classes of assets will be discussed in later chapters.

Current assets. Cash and other assets that may reasonably be expected to be realized in cash or sold or consumed in the near future through the normal operations of the business are called *current assets*. In addition to cash, the assets usually found in this group are notes receivable, accounts receivable, merchandise inventory, and prepaid expenses. They are customarily listed in that order, which is the order of their expected conversion into cash.

Cash. Cash includes bank deposits, currency, checks, bank drafts, and money orders. Any medium of exchange that a bank will accept at face value on deposit is usually shown on the balance sheet as cash. Most of the cash may be on deposit at the bank; some of it may be in the cash drawer or safe.

Notes receivable. A note receivable is a promissory note received from a debtor. A promissory note is a written promise to pay a certain sum in money at a definite time to the order of a specified person or to the bearer.

A note may be transferred by the business to some other person, or it may be transferred to a bank for cash. It represents a type of asset very readily convertible into cash.

Accounts receivable. An account receivable is a claim against a certain person or business. It usually arises from a sale of merchandise on account.

Merchandise inventory. Merchandise consists of goods purchased or produced for sale. Food offered for sale in a grocery store and clothing produced for sale in a clothing factory are examples. The merchandise on hand at any time is referred to as the *merchandise inventory*. The inventory is usually determined by a count of the merchandise on hand. Such a count of merchandise is known as a *physical inventory*.

Prepaid expenses. Supplies on hand and prepayments of expenses of a subsequent period are assets. Since they will be consumed in the near future in the normal operations of the business, they are considered to be current assets. Three of the more common types of prepaid expenses are described below.

(1) Store supplies include paper, twine, and similar items used in selling. They are consumed in the operation of the business and are considered as assets until they are consumed. The amount of such supplies on hand may be ascertained by taking a physical inventory on the date of the balance sheet.

(2) Office supplies include stationery, stamps, and similar items not used in selling but needed for the general operation of the business. Like store supplies, the amount on hand must be ascertained on the date of each balance sheet.

(3) Prepaid insurance consists of premiums paid in advance that will become an expense with the passage of time. The unexpired portion of the premiums at the balance sheet date represents a prepaid expense. Included are such types of property and casualty insurance as fire, windstorm, theft, compensation, and liability insurance.

Plant assets. Tangible assets used in the business that are of a relatively fixed or permanent nature are called *plant assets* or *fixed assets*. Such assets, with the exception of land, will gradually lose their usefulness with the passage of time. The expiration of usefulness, which is called *depreciation*, cannot be determined with the same degree of certainty that applies to the expiration of insurance or of other prepaid expenses. It is therefore customary to report both the original cost of plant assets and the *accumulated depreciation* on the balance sheet as illustrated on page 30.

The order of items within the plant asset classification is not uniform in practice. The shortest-lived plant assets may be listed first or the most permanent may be listed first. It is not feasible to adhere strictly to either order because the estimated life of individual items within a category (such as a steel safe and a typewriter, both of which are included in office equipment) often vary widely. In this book, insofar as practicable, the practice of presenting the shortest-lived plant assets first will be followed.

Delivery equipment. Delivery equipment includes trucks and other equipment used in delivering goods to customers.

Store equipment. Store equipment includes such long-lived assets as counters, showcases, window decorations, and any other items of furniture used directly in selling the goods.

Office equipment. Office equipment includes such assets as desks, typewriters, adding machines, and other items not used directly in selling the goods but needed for the general operation of the business.

Building. A building owned by a business may be used as a factory, a warehouse, a store, or an office. When a building is not owned by the business, it is rented or leased from its owner. In that case the building does not appear on the balance sheet of the business because the building is not property of the enterprise.

Land. The cost of the land on which a building is located is usually shown separately on the balance sheet. Although a building may no longer be valuable because of its age or its condition, the land still remains. Because of this difference, it is desirable to show land separately.

LIABILITIES. Liabilities are amounts owed by a debtor to his creditors. They are ordinarily payable in money but may be payable in goods or services. The number of liability items on the balance sheet is usually less than the number of asset items, but it is sufficiently large to justify classification. The classification used is similar to that used for assets, usually consisting of (1) *current liabilities* and (2) *long-term liabilities.*

Current liabilities. Liabilities that will be due within a short time and that are to be paid out of current assets are called *current liabilities.* For example, when a merchant purchases merchandise on account, he incurs a current liability. The general rule is that liabilities to be paid out of current assets within one year are classified as current liabilities.

Notes payable. A note payable is a promissory note given by the business. The business may give a note to a creditor from whom it has purchased merchandise or to a bank from which it borrows money.

Accounts payable. An account payable is a financial obligation usually arising from a purchase of merchandise on account. It is a liability for which a note has not been given.

Accrued liabilities. Amounts that are not yet due but that are owed to employees for salaries, to creditors for interest on notes, or to the government for taxes are called accrued liabilities. More complete explanations of accrued liabilities will be given in later chapters.

Unearned income. Collections received in advance for which goods or services will have to be given in future fiscal periods are classed as current liabilities. For example, subscriptions received in advance by a magazine publishing company would be called "unearned subscription income" and would be transferred to earnings as magazines are delivered.

Long-term liabilities. Liabilities that will not be due for a comparatively long time are called *long-term liabilities* or *fixed liabilities.* Such liabilities usually arise in the purchase of plant equipment items. Inasmuch as obligations due and payable within a year are classed as current liabilities, it follows that obligations not payable within a year are classed as long-term liabilities. For example, an obligation that is due and payable five years after it is incurred will be classed as a long-term liability until the end of the fourth year when it will become a current liability.

If the long-term liability is to be renewed at maturity rather than paid, it should continue to be classed as a long-term liability. When an obligation is to be paid in installments, that portion due within a year should be listed with the current liabilities and the remainder as a long-term liability.

Mortgage payable. A mortgage payable represents a debt owed by a business for which the creditor possesses a secured claim through a mortgage on an asset. If the amount owed is not paid by the debtor, this secured claim gives the creditor the right to bring court action that may result in the sale of the asset to satisfy the claim.

Bonds payable. Long-term obligations of corporations are commonly evidenced by formal certificates known as bonds. Bonds may or may not be secured by corporate assets. The claims and the rights of each bondholder are specified in the bond contract.

PROPRIETORSHIP. Proprietorship is the owner's equity in the business. It is a residual claim against the assets of the business after total liabilities are deducted. Other commonly used terms for proprietorship are *capital, stockholder's equity,* and *net worth.*

The capital of a business may be vested in two or more persons instead of in a sole proprietor. In such cases the business is known as a *partnership* or a *corporation,* depending upon the type of organization. The proprietary interest of each partner is shown separately on the partnership balance sheet. The sum of the interests of the various partners represents the capital of the partnership.

The identity of the owners of a corporation is not disclosed on the balance sheet. The interest of the stockholders as a group is divided into two amounts: (1) the amount invested by the stockholders in the corporation, and (2) the net earnings retained by the corporation since it was organized. The manner of reporting the different types of ownership interest on the balance sheet is illustrated below.

SOLE PROPRIETORSHIP

George B. Simmons, capital............................ $12,200

PARTNERSHIP

Robert T. Hart, capital......................	$14,450	
Harold R. Taylor, capital....................	18,150	
Total capital......................................		$32,600

CORPORATION

Capital stock..............................	$300,000	
Retained earnings.........................	186,400	
Total capital......................................		$486,400

In the sole proprietorship and the partnership the interests of the owners are designated by the names of the owners. In the corporation the stockholders' interests are represented by the sum of the *capital stock* (capital contributed) and the *retained earnings*. The nature of partnerships and corporations will be considered in later chapters.

Standard forms of the balance sheet

One of the commonly used forms of the balance sheet employs a single page divided vertically into two equal parts or two separate pages. Assets are listed on the left, and liabilities and proprietorship items are listed on the right. This form is called the *account form* because it is similar in design to an account, which is a basic record described in the next chapter. It also conforms to the equation $A = L + P$. The sum of the assets on the left is balanced by the sum of the liabilities and the capital on the right, hence the term "balance sheet."

In another form, called the *report form*, the liability and proprietorship sections are placed immediately below the asset section. The form selected in any particular case depends upon the number of items in the statement, the dimensions of the paper used, and other considerations of format and personal preference. In a variant of the report form the sum of the liabilities is deducted from the sum of the assets to yield the proprietorship $(A - L = P)$. There are still other variations in form that need not concern us at this point. There are also variations in title, such as *statement of financial position.*

Regardless of variations in form or title, the purpose of the statement is to disclose the types and the dollar amounts of the assets, the liabilities, and the proprietorship of a business on a specific date. A balance sheet would not be complete if it did not disclose the identity of the business and the date. It is customary to use a heading that states (1) the name of the business, (2) the name of the statement, and (3) the date, as in the illustration below. The particular time of the day need not be indicated in the heading since it is understood to be at the end of the day.

Balance sheet illustrated and analyzed

The account form of balance sheet is illustrated below. It is based on the records of George W. King's hardware business as of December 31, 1961. The use of indentions, captions, dollar signs, and rulings should be noted. They are employed to accentuate the several distinct sections and subsections of the statement.

Most items appearing on the balance sheet are of limited significance when considered individually. Even the total amount of a group of items, such as current assets, is not of particular significance by itself. It is through comparisons with other items or groups of items appearing on

King
Balance
December

Assets

Current assets:		
Cash.	$ 7,520.52	
Notes receivable.	2,500.00	
Accounts receivable	9,818.26	
Merchandise inventory..	31,112.18	
Store supplies.	326.10	
Office supplies	125.50	
Prepaid insurance	1,262.67	
Total current assets		$52,665.23
Plant assets:		
Delivery equipment. . . . . . . $ 6,500.00		
Less accumulated depreciation 2,384.50	$ 4,115.50	
Store equipment . . . . $ 8,651.80		
Less accumulated depreciation 5,239.52	3,412.28	
Office equipment. . . . . $ 2,694.37		
Less accumulated depreciation 1,469.26	1,225.11	
Building. $21,000.00		
Less accumulated depreciation 9,000.00	12,000.00	
Land.	3,500.00	
Total plant assets		24,252.89
Total assets.		$76,918.12

Balance sheet

the same balance sheet, or on earlier balance sheets, that judgments as to financial position can be formed. Such comparisons are often facilitated by the use of percentages and ratios. For example, King's cash balance of approximately $7,520 represents 14.3% ($7,520 ÷ $52,665) of his current assets and 9.8% ($7,520 ÷ $76,918) of his total assets.

One of the most commonly used ratios is that of current assets to current liabilities, called the *current ratio*. The current ratio for King Hardware at December 31, 1961, is 2.4 to 1, determined as follows:

$52,665 (current assets) ÷ $21,910 (current liabilities) = 2.4 to 1

The current ratio is an indication of the ability of a firm to pay its current liabilities as they come due. There are no arbitrary standards, however, as to what constitutes a satisfactory current ratio. Factors that need to be considered include the nature of the particular business, indications of improvement or retrogression in financial position and earnings, and general economic conditions and prospects.

Another indication of the adequacy of current assets in comparison with current liabilities is the excess of the former over the latter, which is called *net current assets* or *working capital*. It is the net amount available for use in the operation of the business. The working capital of King Hard-

```
Hardware
Sheet
31, 1961
```

Liabilities

Current liabilities:		
Notes payable	$ 3,100.00	
Accounts payable	15,842.80	
Mortgage payable (current portion)	1,500.00	
Taxes payable	642.53	
Salaries payable	450.00	
Interest payable	375.00	
Total current liabilities		$21,910.33
Long-term liabilities:		
Mortgage payable (due annually through 1966)		6,000.00
Total liabilities		$27,910.33

Proprietorship

George W. King, capital	49,007.79
Total liabilities and proprietorship	$76,918.12

—account form

ware on December 31, 1961, is $52,665 (current assets) − $21,910 (current liabilities), or $30,755. The amount of working capital is even less susceptible of comparison with arbitrary standards than the current ratio. Comparison of the amount of working capital at the current date with the amount at an earlier date will indicate the amount and the direction of change, which may be significant.

The foregoing brief introduction to the analysis of a balance sheet is an indication of the importance of the subject and its influence on the form of the statement. Further attention will be given to analysis and interpretation of accounting data in later chapters.

A report form of balance sheet is illustrated below. Except for the location of the liability and proprietorship sections, the statement is similar to the account form.

Martin's Shoes
Balance Sheet
September 30, 1961

Assets

Current assets:		
Cash	$ 1,625.81	
Accounts receivable.	1,262.15	
Merchandise inventory.	15,827.60	
Store supplies	182.00	
Office supplies.	75.30	
Prepaid insurance.	372.57	
Total current assets.		$19,345.43
Plant assets:		
Store equipment. . . . . $ 5,250.00		
Less accumulated depreciation. 1,740.00	$ 3,510.00	
Office equipment . . . . $ 575.00		
Less accumulated depreciation. 418.65	156.35	
Total plant assets.		3,666.35
Total assets		$23,011.78

Liabilities

Current liabilities:		
Accounts payable	$ 2,586.43	
Wages payable.	326.50	
Taxes payable.	297.36	
Total current liabilities		$ 3,210.29

Proprietorship

L. G. Martin, capital.		19,801.49
Total liabilities and proprietorship		$23,011.78

Balance sheet — report form

Form of the income statement

The principal items on the income statement were presented in Chapter 1 as revenue, cost, and expense, with net income emerging as the increase in proprietorship resulting from operations.

Revenue is the gross increase in proprietorship attributable to operating activities. It results from the sale of merchandise, the performance of services for a customer or a client, the rental of property, the lending of money, and other business and professional activities entered into for the purpose of earning income. The amount of revenue is measured by the charges made to customers for goods delivered or services rendered to them. More specific terms employed to identify the source of revenue include *sales, fees, commissions revenue,* and *interest income.*

Cost and *expense* are not mutually exclusive terms. The *cost* of a property or a service is the money expended or the liability incurred for it. The amount of a property or a service that has not been consumed is, of course, an asset, and may also be referred to as *unexpired* cost. Costs that have been consumed in the process of producing income are *expired* costs, or *expenses.* For example, merchandise inventory and prepaid insurance are unexpired costs, and the merchandise sold and the insurance used up during a period of time are expired costs. Although there is no rigid uniformity in the use of the term in the income statement, *cost* is customarily restricted to refer to the cost of properties sold, as in the caption "cost of goods sold." Other expired costs are termed *expense.*

There is considerable variation in the amount of detail presented in the income statement. For example, income statements prepared for stockholders of a large corporation are likely to be less detailed than income statements prepared for the managers or for the owner of a sole proprietorship.

There are also two general types of income statement, the "single-step" form and the "multiple-step" form. In the single-step form all revenue items are totaled, all costs and expenses are totaled, and the second total is deducted from the first total to yield net income. In the multiple-step form there are a number of groupings with intermediate balances, as illustrated on page 37. Throughout this book we will generally use the multiple-step form.

In all cases the amounts shown on the income statement must conform to the length of the accounting period. Thus on an income statement for the month of May, sales, purchases, cost of goods sold, rent, and all other items must apply to that month alone; none may apply to April, which has passed, or to June, which is to come.

As in the case of the balance sheet, the income statement should be properly identified. The heading should state (1) the name of the business, (2) the name of the statement, and (3) the exact period of time covered by the statement. The data appearing in an income statement have little meaning unless the reader is informed of the particular period that is being reported. One must know not only the length of the period, such as a month or a year, but also the particular month or year.

Other titles given to the income statement include *earnings statement, profit and loss statement,* and *statement of operations.*

Classification of items on the income statement

The various sections of a multiple-step income statement for a mercantile business are discussed in the subsections that follow.

Sales. The amount charged to customers for merchandise sold during the period is known as *sales.* No distinction is made between cash sales and charge sales, as revenue is recognized at the time of sale regardless of when the cash is received in payment.

Cost of goods sold. The *cost of goods sold* during the period is determined as follows:

(1) The cost of merchandise on hand at the beginning of the period and the cost of merchandise purchased during the period are added together to yield the cost of merchandise available for sale.

(2) The cost of merchandise on hand at the end of the period is deducted from the cost of merchandise available for sale to yield the cost of goods sold.

Gross profit on sales. When the cost of the merchandise sold is deducted from the sales revenue, the remainder represents the *gross profit on sales.* It is termed *gross* because all other expired costs, or expenses, for the period must be deducted to obtain the *net* operating income of the business. A synonym often used for gross profit is *gross margin* or *margin.*

Operating expenses. Commodities and services of various kinds are consumed in the operation of a business. The services of salesclerks are used in selling merchandise to customers, and the services of other employees may be used in delivering to customers the merchandise sold. Containers are used in preparing the merchandise for delivery to customers. Fuel and electricity are consumed in heating and lighting the building in which the business is conducted. Stationery and postage are consumed in carrying on correspondence with customers and suppliers.

The operating expenses of a business may be classified under a number of headings and subheadings. A large business with authority spread among many employees may use a rather elaborate classification as an aid in controlling expenses. In a small retail business of the kind that has been used for illustrative purposes, it is usually satisfactory to classify the operating expenses in two main groups.

Selling expenses. Expenses that are incurred directly and entirely in connection with the sale of merchandise are known as *selling expenses*. They include such things as salaries of the sales force, store supplies used, and advertising.

Small, unimportant selling expenses are reported under the heading "Miscellaneous selling expense." In general the best classification is one that keeps miscellaneous expense at a minimum. Whenever the total of the miscellaneous selling expense account is large, it should be analyzed and new expense classifications should be set up for the significant items.

The order in which the selling expenses are presented on the income statement varies among businesses. One of the arrangements commonly followed is to list them approximately in the order of size, beginning with the larger items. Miscellaneous selling expense is usually shown as the last item regardless of amount.

General expenses. Expenses incurred in the general operation of the business are known as *general expenses*. They include office salaries and office supplies used.

Expenses that are partly connected with selling and partly connected with the general operation of the business may be analyzed and reported in part as selling expenses and in part as general expenses. In a small business, however, such mixed expenses are commonly reported as general expenses. Examples of such expenses are rent, insurance, and taxes.

General expense items that are not of sufficient importance to justify their being reported separately are reported under the heading "Miscellaneous general expense." If the amount of the miscellaneous general expense account becomes large, the total should be analyzed and new expense classifications should be set up for the larger items.

As in the case of selling expenses, the order in which the general expenses may be listed is subject to considerable variation. Any particular system adopted is ordinarily applied to both classes, that is, to selling expenses and to general expenses.

Net income from operations. The difference between gross profit on sales and total operating expenses represents *net income from operations*. Other terms such as *net operating income, net trading profit,* and *net operating profit* are sometimes encountered. It is an important indicator of the efficiency of management and the profitability of an enterprise. If operating expenses exceed gross profit on sales, the amount is designated *net loss from operations.*

Other income. Minor sources of revenue are classified as *other income*. In a mercantile firm this category includes income from interest, rent, dividends, and gains resulting from the sale of plant assets.

Other expense. Expenses that cannot be associated directly or indirectly with operations are identified as *other expense*. Interest expense that results from financing activities and losses suffered in the disposal of plant assets are examples of items that should be shown in this section.

On an income statement, other expense items are offset against other income items. If other income exceeds other expense, the difference is added to net income from operations; if the reverse is true, the difference is subtracted from net income from operations.

Net income. The final figure on the income statement of an unincorporated enterprise is labeled *net income*. It is the net increase in proprietorship resulting from both operating and nonoperating activities. Net income indicates the over-all success of the business venture. If expenses exceed revenues during an accounting period, the caption *net loss* is used.

Income statement illustrated and analyzed

The income statement for King Hardware is shown on page 37. As in the balance sheet, captions, indentions, dollar signs, subtotals, and rulings are used to accentuate the several distinct sections and subsections of the statement.

The managers of a business enterprise are always vitally interested in comparing the results of operations of the current period with those of previous periods. For example, George W. King would compare the income statement on page 37 with the income statements for earlier years. If monthly statements are also prepared, the statement for December of the current year would be compared with that for the preceding month and also with the December statement for the preceding year.

In comparing operating data of the most recent period with that of earlier periods, it is useful to know the relationship of various items on the income statement to sales. For example, King Hardware's gross profit on sales for 1961 is 31.9% ($39,050 ÷ $122,441) of sales. If this percentage margin has declined materially from the preceding year, King should give serious consideration to his pricing and purchasing policies. The per cent of sales salary expense to sales is 7.4% ($9,120 ÷ $122,441); that of delivery expense to sales is 1.5% ($1,863 ÷ $122,441). The other expense items may be related to sales in similar fashion and the resulting percentages compared with those of the preceding year.

The per cent of net income from operations to sales is 14.4% ($17,612 ÷ $122,441). If this represents a significant change from preceding periods, it is advisable for the proprietor to make a careful study of the contributing factors. A later chapter will be devoted entirely to the analysis of financial statements.

King Hardware
Income Statement
For Year Ended December 31, 1961

Sales.			$122,440.60
Cost of goods sold:			
Merchandise inventory, January 1, 1961	$ 36,682.71		
Purchases.	77,820.37		
Merchandise available for sale	$114,503.08		
Less merchandise inventory, Dec. 31, 1961.	31,112.18		
Cost of goods sold			83,390.90
Gross profit on sales.			$ 39,049.70
Operating expenses:			
Selling expenses:			
Sales salary expense	$9,120.00		
Delivery expense	1,862.80		
Depreciation expense--delivery equipment.	1,375.00		
Advertising expense.	936.75		
Depreciation expense--store equipment.	761.15		
Store supplies expense	432.16		
Miscellaneous selling expense.	196.47		
Total selling expenses.		$ 14,684.33	
General expenses:			
Office salary expense.	$3,600.00		
Depreciation expense--building	840.00		
Utilities expense.	695.85		
Taxes expense.	610.34		
Insurance expense.	482.00		
Depreciation expense--office equipment.	219.44		
Office supplies expense.	121.60		
Miscellaneous general expense.	184.18		
Total general expenses.		6,753.41	
Total operating expenses			21,437.74
Net income from operations			$ 17,611.96
Other income:			
Rent income.	$ 600.00		
Interest income.	165.00	$ 765.00	
Other expense:			
Interest expense		650.00	115.00
Net income			$ 17,726.96

Income statement

Capital statement

A balance sheet should be accompanied by a report of the changes in the proprietor's capital that have occurred since the date of the preceding balance sheet. Increases in capital result from additional investments by the proprietor and from profitable operations. Withdrawals by the proprietor and operating losses reduce capital. The form of the report in which these details are presented is illustrated by the capital statement for King Hardware for the year ended December 31, 1961, below.

```
                        King Hardware
                      Capital Statement
                For Year Ended December 31, 1961
```

Capital, January 1, 1961		$43,280.83
Net income for the year.	$17,726.96	
Less withdrawals	12,000.00	
Increase in capital.		5,726.96
Capital, December 31, 1961		$49,007.79

Capital statement

If in the above illustration the withdrawals had exceeded the net income, the order of the two items would have been reversed and the difference between the two items, captioned "Decrease in capital," would have been deducted from the beginning capital.

The method of reporting an additional investment and a net loss from operations may be illustrated as follows:

Capital, January 1......................	$35,000.00	
Additional investment, July 1...........	6,000.00	
Total................................		$41,000.00
Net loss for the year....................	$ 8,000.00	
Withdrawals...........................	3,600.00	
Decrease in capital.....................		11,600.00
Capital, December 31...................		$29,400.00

The capital statement that accompanies the balance sheet of a partnership is basically the same as those illustrated above except that the changes in each individual partner's capital are shown. For a corporation the comparable report is called a *retained earnings statement*. It summarizes the changes during the period in the accumulated net income of a corporation.

Interrelationship of accounting statements

The three accounting statements discussed in this chapter are interrelated through proprietorship. The balance sheet shows assets, liabilities, and proprietorship at the close of business on the last day of the accounting period. It contains no information concerning operations or the effect of operations on capital. The income statement summarizes the revenues, expired costs, and expenses, and reports the net income or net loss for the accounting period. It does not disclose the amount of withdrawals or of additional investments made by the owner during the period.

These two statements are linked together by the capital statement, which begins with the amount of capital at the beginning of the accounting period and ends with the amount of capital at the close of the accounting period. Note that in the statements of King Hardware the net income of $17,726.96 reported on the income statement also appears as an addition in the capital statement. The ending balance of $49,007.79 on the capital statement is reported, in turn, as the amount of capital on the balance sheet.

Questions

1. What types of information should be presented in the heading of (a) the balance sheet? (b) the income statement? (c) the capital statement?

2. Identify the following as merchandise inventory, office equipment, or office supplies:

   (a) Stationery on the counters of a stationery store.
   (b) Stationery owned by a firm of attorneys.
   (c) Adding machines held for sale by an office equipment company.
   (d) Adding machines used by the accounting department of a furniture store.

3. John Maxwell acquired plant assets at a total cost of $20,000, paying $2,000 cash and giving a mortgage note for the remainder. The agreement provided that the debt be paid in monthly installments of $200 each. How should this liability be classified on his balance sheet on December 31 of the current year, at which time the amount still owed is $14,000?

4. The balance sheets of two firms on the same date list cash of $5,000 and $25,000, respectively. Both are engaged in the same type of business. Comment on the relative position of the two firms.

5. (a) What is meant by current ratio? (b) How is it computed?

6. Define working capital.

7. (a) What two items are added to obtain the cost of merchandise available for sale? (b) What is deducted from merchandise available for sale to determine the cost of goods sold?

8. A retail appliance store sold merchandise on account to a customer in January and received payment in February. The selling price was $300 and the cost was $200.

   (a) What was the amount of margin on the sale?

(b) What was the per cent of gross profit on the sale?

(c) What per cent of cost was added to $200 to obtain the selling price of $300?

(d) What was the effect of the February transaction on assets? on proprietorship?

9. Discuss unexpired and expired costs, giving examples of each.

10. Are both expired costs and expenses deducted from revenues in determining net income?

11. Classify the following as selling expense or general expense:

(a) Taxes on store equipment.

(b) Insurance on office equipment.

(c) Heating and lighting.

(d) Wages of driver of delivery truck.

(e) Payments to salesmen to reimburse them for their traveling expenses.

(f) Salary of a stenographer.

(g) Fee paid to a C.P.A. to audit the financial records.

(h) Rental paid for a billboard.

(i) Depreciation of store equipment.

12. (a) What is the significance of the percentage of gross profit on sales? (b) How is this percentage computed?

13. Name the item that appears on both of the statements of a mercantile business indicated below:

(a) Income statement and capital statement.

(b) Balance sheet and capital statement.

(c) Balance sheet and income statement.

14. James Miller's income statement for the month of September indicates a net income of $600. During the same period Miller withdrew $700 in cash from the business for personal use. Would it be correct to say that he incurred a *net loss* of $100 during the month?

15. The net income of Burton Shoe Store for the period is $14,620 and the capital at the end of the period is $39,460. On what financial statements prepared at the end of the period will these two amounts appear?

Exercises

1. At the beginning of the month the merchandise inventory was $35,000; during the month additional merchandise was purchased at a cost of $10,000; the physical inventory at the end of the month totals $37,000. (a) What is the cost of merchandise available for sale? (b) What is the cost of goods sold?

2. A premium of $648 is paid for a three-year property insurance policy, effective on July 1. (a) Determine the amount of premium expired and unexpired as of December 31 of the same year. (b) How much of the premium will appear on the income statement for the following year ending December 31? (c) How much of the premium will appear on the balance sheet as of December 31 of the following year?

3. The balance sheet of a business firm lists current assets of $20,000 and current liabilities of $8,000. (a) Determine the current ratio. (b) Determine the amount of working capital.

4. The firm in Exercise 3 borrows $10,000, giving a note payable in 90 days. Assuming that there have been no other transactions, determine (a) the current ratio and (b) the working capital.

5. The records of Gorman's Gift Shop reveal the following information regarding cash:

Cash balance at beginning of year, $6,000.
Received from customers on account during the year, $32,000.
Received from cash sales during the year, $28,000.
Paid to creditors on account during the year, $26,000.
Paid for expenses during the year, $22,000.

Assuming that there were no other cash transactions during the year, determine the cash balance at the end of the year.

6. The proprietorship of Ralph Moore increased $10,000 during the past fiscal year. Compute the amount of the income or the loss of his business enterprise under each of the following assumptions:

(a) There were no additional investments or withdrawals.
(b) There was an additional investment of $1,000; there were no withdrawals.
(c) There was an additional investment of $2,000; there were no withdrawals.
(d) There were withdrawals of $6,000; there were no additional investments.
(e) There was an additional investment of $2,000 and withdrawals of $4,000.
(f) There was an additional investment of $1,500 and withdrawals of $3,000.

7. From the following list of items select the current assets and prepare the current assets section of the balance sheet: cash, $12,000; accounts payable, $8,000; merchandise inventory, $25,000; building, $60,000; accumulated depreciation of building, $22,000; prepaid taxes, $1,000; insurance expense, $450; notes receivable, $3,000; prepaid insurance, $600; supplies, $390; unearned rent, $800; accounts receivable, $5,500.

Problems

2-1. On December 31 of the current year the business assets and liabilities of Henry Price, proprietor of Henry's Haberdashery, are as follows:

Accounts payable.	$ 9,840
Accounts receivable.	8,170
Building.	42,000
Accumulated depreciation — building.	8,000
Cash.	5,640
Furniture and fixtures.	8,500
Accumulated depreciation — furniture and fixtures.	3,200
Interest payable.	410
Land.	2,800
Merchandise inventory.	24,280
Notes payable.	10,500
Prepaid insurance.	1,320
Salaries payable.	340
Supplies.	850

All of the notes payable are due within one year except a mortgage note for $6,000, which is due two years and four months from the current December 31. At the beginning of the current year, Mr. Price's capital had been $54,470. He withdrew $600 in cash each month for personal use, and the net income for the year was $14,000.

Instructions: (1) Prepare a balance sheet in account form as of December 31 of the current year.

(2) Prepare a capital statement for the year ended December 31.

(3) Determine the following: (a) working capital, (b) current ratio, (c) per cent of net income for the year to capital at the beginning of the year.

2-2. At the beginning of the current fiscal year Booth's Appliances had a merchandise inventory of $38,200 and capital of $42,460. The physical inventory taken on September 30, the last day of the fiscal year, amounted to $33,500. The accounting records for the fiscal year reveal the following information:

Advertising expense....................................	$ 4,350
Depreciation expense — office equipment................	450
Depreciation expense — store equipment.................	1,000
Insurance expense.....................................	1,050
Interest expense......................................	200
Interest income......................................	650
Miscellaneous general expense.........................	1,270
Miscellaneous selling expense.........................	1,200
Office salary expense.................................	7,080
Office supplies expense...............................	1,650
Purchases..	170,300
Rent expense...	6,000
Sales..	250,000
Sales salary expense..................................	20,600
Store supplies expense................................	2,850
Withdrawals by the proprietor.........................	18,000

Instructions: (1) Prepare an income statement for the current fiscal year.

(2) Determine the percentage of the following items to sales: (a) cost of goods sold, (b) gross profit on sales, (c) total selling expenses, (d) total general expenses, (e) total operating expenses, (f) net income from operations.

(3) Prepare a capital statement for the current fiscal year (no additional investments were made during the year).

2-3. John Hardy, owner of Hardy Market, had a capital balance of $27,480 on January 1 of the current year. His merchandise inventory at the same date was $25,420. On March 1 he invested an additional $5,000 in the business. During the year he made withdrawals of $200 each week. The following asset and liability balances are as of December 31 of the current year; the revenue and expense amounts are for the current year ended on that date.

Accounts payable.....................................	$10,930
Accounts receivable..................................	3,150
Advertising expense..................................	1,520
Cash..	8,420
Depreciation expense — office equipment..............	380
Depreciation expense — store equipment...............	860

Insurance expense	$ 1,230
Interest expense	380
Merchandise inventory	31,350
Miscellaneous general expense	680
Miscellaneous selling expense	970
Notes payable	3,400
Office equipment	3,800
Accumulated depreciation — office equipment	1,100
Office salary expense	5,650
Office supplies	390
Office supplies expense	250
Prepaid insurance	2,160
Purchases	132,300
Rent expense	7,200
Sales	192,580
Salaries payable	260
Sales salary expense	22,920
Store equipment	10,400
Accumulated depreciation — store equipment	3,200
Store supplies	470
Store supplies expense	2,860
Taxes expense	910
Taxes payable	190
Utilities expense	1,420

Instructions: (1) Prepare an income statement for the current fiscal year.

(2) Prepare a balance sheet in report form as of December 31 of the current fiscal year.

(3) Prepare a capital statement for the current fiscal year.

2-4. On October 1 of the current year F. S. Walsh established a business enterprise. His transactions for the three months ending on December 31 are summarized below.

(a)	Deposited cash in a business bank account		$10,000
(b)	Purchased a going business known as Ace Parcel Delivery.		
	Assets acquired:		
	Accounts receivable	$ 2,200	
	Automotive supplies	500	
	Office supplies	100	
	Trucks	10,000	12,800
	Liabilities assumed:		
	Accounts payable		800
	Terms of payment:		
	Cash paid	$ 8,000	
	Note payable issued, due in four equal quarterly installments, with interest	4,000	12,000
(c)	Delivery service revenue charged to customers on account		9,000
(d)	Purchases on account:		
	Automotive supplies	$1,200	
	Office supplies	50	1,250
(e)	Receipts of cash from customers on account		9,700

(f) Payments of cash for the following purposes:

Creditors on account......................	$1,400	
Installment on note payable................	1,000	
Interest expense..........................	60	
Prepaid insurance.........................	1,200	
Prepaid taxes.............................	380	
Automotive supplies.......................	150	
Drivers' salary expense....................	3,600	
Rent expense.............................	300	
Utilities expense..........................	110	
Repairs expense...........................	240	
Withdrawals by proprietor.................	1,200	9,640
(g) Automotive supplies used.....................		1,300
(h) Depreciation of trucks.......................		650
(i) Insurance expired...........................		280
(j) Taxes expired...............................		80
(k) Office supplies used.........................		30

Instructions: (1) List the following captions in equation form, placing the first group across the top of the sheet and the second group across the middle of the sheet.

	Accounts	Automotive	Office	Prepaid	Prepaid	
Cash +	Receivable +	Supplies +	Supplies +	Insurance +	Taxes +	Trucks

Accumulated Depreciation,	Notes	Accounts	F. S. Walsh,	
− Trucks =	Payable +	Payable +	Capital	Capital Notations

(2) Record Walsh's original investment and the remaining transactions in the appropriate columns, identifying each by letter. Indicate increases by + and decreases by −. *Do not determine the new balances of the items after each transaction.* Indicate the nature of all changes in *capital* by notations at the right of each increase or decrease. The increase in accounts payable in (d) and the decrease in cash in (f) may be shown in one amount.

(3) Insert the final balances in each column and determine that Assets = Liabilities + Proprietorship at December 31, the end of the period.

(4) Prepare the following statements: (a) income statement (classify expenses as "operating expenses" and "other expenses"), (b) balance sheet in report form, (c) capital statement. (The name of the business was not changed.)

Accounts and the trial balance

Recording transactions

The transactions completed by a business during any fiscal period effect many changes in the various asset, liability, and capital items. In order to prepare periodic financial statements, it is necessary that the results of each transaction be recorded in a systematic manner. It is the purpose of this chapter to describe and illustrate the account, which is a basic record in the system known as double-entry accounting.

The effect of each transaction could be shown by the use of the accounting equation, as was done in Chapter 1, or the financial statements could be revised after each transaction. It is not necessary, however, that the owner or manager be informed of the effect of each individual transaction. Information showing him the effects of groups of similar transactions is usually sufficient for his purpose. Consequently, separate records are maintained for each item that appears on the financial statements. The individual records are then summarized at periodic intervals and the data thus obtained are presented in the balance sheet, the income statement, and the capital statement.

The form of record used for each item is appropriately called an *account*. A group of accounts is called a *ledger*. For example, an enterprise might have thirty accounts, each one being a record of a particular asset, liability, proprietorship, revenue, or expense item. The thirty accounts, which would ordinarily be kept together, would be referred to as the ledger.

Nature of an account

The simplest form of an account provides for three things: (1) a title, which is the name of the item recorded in the account; (2) a space for recording increases in the amount of the item, in terms of money; and (3) a space for recording decreases in the amount of the item, also in monetary terms. This form of an account, illustrated on page 46, is known as a T account because of its similarity to the letter T. Other

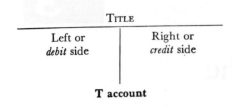

T account

forms of an account that provide spaces for recording additional information are illustrated later. Regardless of form, however, the three basic parts of the account are the title, a section for increases, and a section for decreases.

The left side of the account is called the *debit* side and the right side is called the *credit* side. The word *charge* is frequently used as a synonym for debit. Amounts entered on the left side of an account, regardless of the account title, are called *debits* or *charges* to the account, and the account is said to be *debited* or *charged*. Amounts entered on the right side of an account are called *credits*, and the account is said to be *credited*.

	CASH	
	3,000	500
	2,500	1,000
	4,000	2,500
4,300	*9,500*	300
		900
		5,200

In the illustration that appears at the left, the receipts of cash have been listed in vertical order on the debit side of the cash account. The cash payments have been listed in similar fashion on the credit side of the account. This arrangement for recording the increases and the decreases in cash facilitates the determination of the totals of each. The total of the cash receipts, $9,500, is shown in small pencil figures to distinguish it from debits to the account. The total of the cash payments, $5,200, is also shown in small pencil figures so that it will not be confused with the credits to the account. (The process of adding a formal column of figures and recording the temporary total is called *pencil footing*.) Finally, by subtracting $5,200, the sum of the credits, from $9,500, the sum of the debits, the difference of $4,300 is obtained. The difference between the total debits and the total credits in an account is termed the *balance*. In this case the cash account has a debit balance of $4,300. This temporary balance is placed on the debit side of the account beside the pencil footing. If a balance sheet were to be prepared at this time, the amount of cash to be reported thereon would be $4,300.

Accounts and the balance sheet

The relationship of accounts to the *account form of balance sheet* can be observed from a study of the following illustrations.

(a) On September 1, 1961, John Bell deposited $2,600 cash in a bank account for use in a business venture to be known as Bell TV Service.

Immediately after depositing the money, the balance sheet for the business would appear as follows:

Bell TV Service
Balance Sheet
September 1, 1961

Assets	*Proprietorship*
Cash...................... $2,600	John Bell, Capital.......... $2,600

The information could be recorded in accounts by debiting Cash and crediting John Bell, Capital as follows:

CASH		JOHN BELL, CAPITAL	
(a) 2,600			**(a)** 2,600

Note that the title of each account is written above the horizontal line. The title is descriptive of the data to be recorded in the account. It is not necessary to label the two sides of the accounts, inasmuch as the left side is *always* the debit side and the right side is *always* the credit side.

The amount of the asset Cash, which is on the left side of the account form of balance sheet, is recorded on the left or debit side of the cash account. The amount of the proprietorship, John Bell, Capital, which is on the right side of the account form of balance sheet, is recorded on the right or credit side of the account. Similarly, all other assets are entered on the left or debit side of appropriate accounts; all other proprietorship increases and all liabilities are entered on the right or credit side of appropriate accounts. The balances of all of the accounts can then be conveniently assembled to form a balance sheet, with the assets on the left and the liabilities and the proprietorship on the right.

(b) Bell TV Service purchased supplies for $700 in cash. This transaction results in the acquisition of a new asset, Supplies. The cost of this new asset, like that of any other asset, is recorded on the left or debit side of an account. The transaction also results in a decrease in the asset Cash. This decrease is entered on the right or credit side of the cash account. When all increases are entered on the debit side of the cash account and all decreases are entered on the credit side, the total of the receipts, the total of the payments, and the balance of the account may be found at any time in the manner illustrated on page 46. After this transaction is recorded, the ledger appears as follows:

CASH				JOHN BELL, CAPITAL	
(a)	2,600	(b)	700	(a)	2,600

SUPPLIES	
(b)	700

(c) Bell TV Service wished to purchase equipment from White &
Co. for $2,400, but reference to the cash account revealed that payment
of the entire amount would not be possible at this time. The business
therefore arranged with White & Co. to pay $1,500 in cash and the bal-
ance in 90 days. The effect of this transaction is to increase the asset
Equipment by $2,400, to reduce the asset Cash by $1,500, and to increase
the liability Accounts Payable by $900.

Liability accounts appear on the right side of the account form of
balance sheet; similarly, increases in liabilities are recorded on the right
or credit side of appropriate accounts. This transaction is therefore recorded as follows: Equipment is debited for $2,400 to record the cost of
this new asset; Cash is credited for $1,500 to record the decrease in this
asset; and Accounts Payable is credited for $900 to record this new
liability. The ledger of Bell TV Service now appears as follows:

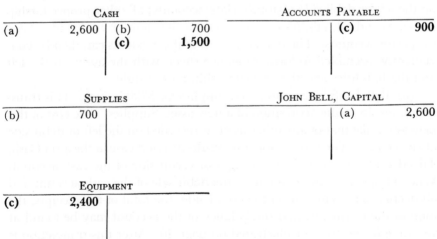

CASH				ACCOUNTS PAYABLE	
(a)	2,600	(b)	700	(c)	900
		(c)	1,500		

SUPPLIES				JOHN BELL, CAPITAL	
(b)	700			(a)	2,600

EQUIPMENT	
(c)	2,400

It is apparent that if there are a number of accounts payable, it would be necessary to maintain a separate record for each creditor. The method of accounting for each individual account payable will be presented in Chapter 7.

At this time the following balance sheet could be prepared from the accounts of Bell TV Service:

Bell TV Service
Balance Sheet
September 1, 1961

Assets		*Liabilities*	
Cash.........................	$ 400	Accounts payable.............	$ 900
Supplies.....................	700		
Equipment...................	2,400	*Proprietorship*	
		John Bell, capital.............	2,600
Total........................	$3,500	Total........................	$3,500

Debit and credit

Balance sheet accounts. In the preceding section it was observed that the left side of asset accounts is used for recording increases and the right side is used for recording decreases. It was also observed that the procedure is reversed for liability and proprietorship accounts, the right side being used to record increases and the left side to record decreases. The left side of all accounts, whether asset, liability, or proprietorship, is called debit and the right side is called credit. Consequently, a debit may signify either an increase or a decrease, depending on the nature of the account, and a credit may likewise signify either increase or decrease. The rules of debit and credit may therefore be stated as follows:

DEBIT signifies:	*CREDIT* signifies:
Increase in *asset* accounts	*Decrease* in *asset* accounts
Decrease in *liability* accounts	*Increase* in *liability* accounts
Decrease in *proprietorship* accounts	*Increase* in *proprietorship* accounts

The effect of transactions is ordinarily stated in terms of debit and credit rather than in terms of left and right, or increase and decrease. For example, the effect of the purchase of $700 of supplies for cash is stated as follows: debit Supplies for $700 and credit Cash for $700.

The rules of debit and credit may also be stated in relationship to the accounting equation and the account form of balance sheet. In the following diagram the symbols for plus and minus are used in place of "increase" and "decrease."

BALANCE SHEET

ASSETS		LIABILITIES	
ASSET ACCOUNTS		LIABILITY ACCOUNTS	
Debit +	Credit −	Debit −	Credit +

PROPRIETORSHIP

PROPRIETORSHIP ACCOUNTS	
Debit −	Credit +

A business transaction always affects at least two accounts. If only two accounts are affected, one of them must be debited and the other must be credited for a like amount. If more than two accounts are affected, the sum of the debits is always equal to the sum of the credits. This was demonstrated in the preceding section by the transaction involving the purchase of equipment, partly for cash and partly on account. The $2,400 debit to Equipment was equaled by the $1,500 credit to Cash plus the $900 credit to Accounts Payable. This equality of debit and credit for each transaction is inherent in the fundamental equation. It naturally follows that the sum of all the debit entries in the ledger equals the sum of all the credit entries.

Income statement accounts. The theory of debit and credit in its application to revenue and expense accounts is based on the relationship of these accounts to proprietorship. The net income or the net loss of a period, as revealed by the income statement, is the net increase or decrease in proprietorship resulting from operations. In order to collect efficiently the data that are needed to prepare the income statement, accounts are maintained in the ledger for each type of revenue and expense.

Revenue increases proprietorship; hence increases in revenues are recorded as credits to revenue accounts. Titles of such accounts vary with the source of the revenue. For example, the account used to record sales of merchandise or of business services is usually entitled "Sales," revenue from professional services may be called "Professional Fees," revenue from commissions may be called "Commissions Revenue," and revenue from lending money is usually termed "Interest Income."

All expired costs, which are generally called "expenses," must be deducted from revenue. They have the effect of decreasing proprietorship and are therefore recorded as debits to the various expense accounts, such as "Rent Expense," "Delivery Expense," and "Advertising Expense." Although debits to expense accounts signify *decreases in proprietorship*, they may also be referred to as *increases in expense*. The usual practice is to consider debits to expense accounts in the positive sense (increases in expense) rather than in the negative sense (decreases in proprietorship). The rules of debit and credit as applied to revenue and expense accounts are shown in the diagram below.

PROPRIETORSHIP ACCOUNTS

DEBIT − EXPENSE ACCOUNTS		CREDIT + REVENUE ACCOUNTS	
Debit +	Credit −	Debit −	Credit +

At the close of the fiscal period, the balances of the revenue and expense accounts are reported in the income statement. Their balances are then transferred to a summary account. The balance of the summary account, which is the net income or loss for the period, is then transferred to the capital account. Because of this periodic closing of the revenue and expense accounts, they are sometimes called *temporary proprietorship* or *nominal* accounts. The balance of each asset and each liability account and the balance of the proprietor's capital account are carried forward to succeeding fiscal periods. They are more permanent in nature and are sometimes referred to as *real* accounts.

Drawing account. The owner of a sole proprietorship customarily makes periodic withdrawals of cash from his business. This is particularly true if he devotes full time to managing the business or if it is his principal source of income. Such withdrawals reduce the capital of the business and could be recorded as debits to the capital account. It is preferable to record them in a separate *drawing* or *personal* account, however, in order that total withdrawals may more readily be determined at the end of the accounting period.

Debits to the drawing account may be considered either as decreases in capital or as increases in drawings. In this respect they are similar to debits to expense accounts, which record decreases in capital but increases in expense. Drawings differ from expenses, however, in that they do not represent expired costs allocable against revenue. Ordinarily the periodic withdrawals of the proprietor are made in anticipation of the business earning a net income. If withdrawals exceed net income, working capital is depleted and the operations of the enterprise are likely to suffer.

Normal balances. The account serves as a mathematical device for recording increases and decreases in monetary terms. Increases are placed on one side of the account and decreases are placed on the opposite side. The total of the increases can easily be found by adding all the items on the increase side; the total of the decreases can be similarly determined.

The sum of the increases in an account will customarily be equal to or greater than the sum of the decreases; consequently the normal balances of all accounts are positive rather than negative. When the balance of an account is to be determined, the smaller of the two totals is subtracted from the larger. For example, the total debits (increases) in an asset account will ordinarily be greater than the total credits (decreases); thus, asset accounts normally have debit balances. It is entirely possible, of course, for the debits and the credits in an account to be equal, in which case the account is said to be *in balance.*

The rules of debit and credit, and the normal balances of the various types of accounts, are summarized below. Note that drawing and expense accounts are considered in the positive sense. Increases in both types of accounts, which represent decreases in proprietorship, are recorded as debits.

Type of Account	Increase	Decrease	Normal Balance
Asset	Debit	Credit	Debit
Liability	Credit	Debit	Credit
Proprietorship			
Capital	Credit	Debit	Credit
Drawing	Debit	Credit	Debit
Revenue	Credit	Debit	Credit
Expense	Debit	Credit	Debit

When an account that normally has a debit balance actually has a credit balance, or vice versa, it is an indication of an error in recording or of an unusual transaction. A credit balance in the office equipment account, for example, could occur only through erroneous entries. On the other hand, a debit balance in an account payable account could result from paying an amount greater than that owed.

Arrangement of accounts in the ledger

It is customary to arrange accounts in the ledger in the order in which the items are presented in the balance sheet and the income statement. Current asset accounts come first, followed by plant assets, current liabilities, long-term liabilities, and proprietorship. The capital and drawing accounts are followed by the principal revenue accounts, the various operating expense accounts, and the other income and other expense accounts. There is one sheet for each account, and any new accounts needed as a result of a particular transaction can be readily inserted at the proper point.

Illustration of a complete ledger

The application of the rules of debit and credit will be illustrated by recording the transactions of an enterprise for the month of October. In the illustration, the accounts will be arranged to conform to the account form of the balance sheet, that is, asset accounts will be presented on the left side of the page and liability and proprietorship accounts, including revenue and expenses, will be presented on the right. The increase and decrease sides of each account will be indicated by + and − signs. The letter used to identify each transaction will be recorded in the accounts to facilitate cross-referencing. As an additional aid in identifying the effect of each transaction, the related debits and credits will be shown initially in bold type.

(a) James B. Hill, C.P.A., in opening a public accounting practice, invested $4,000 in cash, office equipment costing $500, and a library costing $800.

Analysis: The three asset accounts, Cash, Office Equipment, and Library, increase by the amounts indicated and are debited for $4,000, $500, and $800 respectively. Hill's claim against these assets is equal to the total of the three amounts; hence his capital account is credited for $5,300. The recognition of depreciation of the office equipment and other fixed assets will be considered in a later chapter.

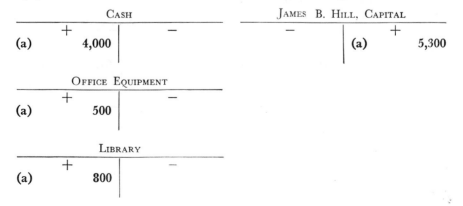

(b) Hill paid office rent for the month, $200.

Analysis: Rent is usually paid at the beginning of the month and is therefore an asset at the time of payment. But if the payment is made for one month only, at the end of the month it will be an expense. It is customary, therefore, to treat it as an expense at the time of payment. Expense accounts are subdivisions of proprietorship. Increases in expense are decreases in proprietorship; hence the rent expense account is debited for $200. The asset Cash is reduced by the transaction; therefore that account is credited for $200.

	Cash				Rent Expense	
	+		−		+	−
(a)	4,000	(b)	200	(b)	200	

(c) Purchased on account from Barton Equipment Co. additional office equipment for $600.

Analysis: Office Equipment increases and, in accordance with the rules of debit and credit, is debited for $600. The liability Accounts Payable increases and is credited for $600.

	Office Equipment				Accounts Payable	
	+		−		−	+
(a)	500				(c)	600
(c)	600					

(d) Purchased an automobile for business use from Alden Motors Corp., $2,800, paying $1,000 in cash and agreeing to pay the remainder in twelve monthly installments of $150 each.

Analysis: The asset account Automobile increases as a result of the transaction and is debited for $2,800. Another asset, Cash, decreases by $1,000 and is credited for that amount. Alden Motors Corp. acquires a claim of $1,800 against the business; hence Accounts Payable, a liability account, increases by $1,800 and is credited. The recording of the transaction may be expressed as follows: debit Automobile, $2,800; credit Cash, $1,000, and credit Accounts Payable, $1,800. Note that the one debit of $2,800 is equal to the two credits totaling $2,800.

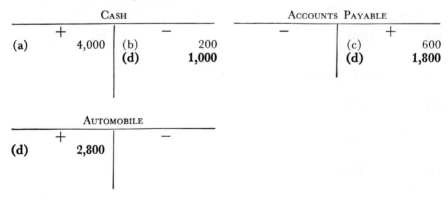

	Cash				Accounts Payable	
	+		−		−	+
(a)	4,000	(b)	200		(c)	600
		(d)	1,000		(d)	1,800

	Automobile		
	+		−
(d)	2,800		

(e) Purchased office supplies for cash, $100.

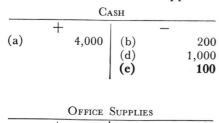

CASH			
+		**−**	
(a)	4,000	(b)	200
		(d)	1,000
		(e)	**100**

OFFICE SUPPLIES			
+		**−**	
(e)	**100**		

Analysis: This transaction represents the exchange of one asset, Cash, for another asset, Office Supplies. The office supplies account is debited for $100 to record the increase, and Cash is credited for $100 to record the decrease. Although the supplies will become an expense as they are used, it is proper to record them as an asset at the time of purchase. The problem of accounting for supplies consumed will be discussed in a subsequent chapter.

(f) Paid Barton Equipment Co. $300 on account.

Analysis: This payment reduces the liability account Accounts Payable, and that account is debited for $300. It also reduces the asset account Cash, which is credited for $300.

CASH					ACCOUNTS PAYABLE			
+		**−**			**−**		**+**	
(a)	4,000	(b)	200	**(f)**	**300**	(c)		600
		(d)	1,000			(d)		1,800
		(e)	100					
		(f)	**300**					

(g) Received $225 in payment of professional fees for services rendered a client.

Analysis: Cash is increased and is debited for $225. The revenue account Professional Fees, which is a subdivision of proprietorship, is increased and is credited for $225.

CASH					PROFESSIONAL FEES			
+		**−**			**−**		**+**	
(a)	4,000	(b)	200				**(g)**	**225**
(g)	**225**	(d)	1,000					
		(e)	100					
		(f)	300					

(h) Paid the premium for a three-year insurance policy on the equipment and the library, $75.

CASH			
+		**−**	
(a)	4,000	(b)	200
(g)	225	(d)	1,000
		(e)	100
		(f)	300
		(h)	**75**

Analysis: In this transaction the asset Prepaid Insurance is increased and the asset Cash is decreased by $75; Prepaid Insurance is debited for $75 and Cash is credited for $75. Consideration will be given in a later chapter to the problem of the gradual expiration of the prepaid insurance.

PREPAID INSURANCE			
+		**−**	
(h)	**75**		

(i) Paid biweekly salaries, $600.

Analysis: This transaction results in an increase in expense (decrease in proprietorship) and a decrease in cash; therefore Salary Expense is debited for $600 and Cash is credited for $600.

CASH					SALARY EXPENSE		
+		−			+		−
(a)	4,000	(b)	200	**(i)**	**600**		
(g)	225	(d)	1,000				
		(e)	100				
		(f)	300				
		(h)	75				
		(i)	**600**				

Transactions (j) through (p) are similar to those that have been analyzed and recorded above. Although each is not illustrated separately, the effect of all is shown in the accounts on page 58.

(j) Received $400 for professional services. [See transaction (g).]
Analysis: Debit Cash, $400; credit Professional Fees, $400.

(k) Paid a one-year insurance premium on the automobile, $90. [See transaction (h).]
Analysis: Debit Prepaid Insurance, $90; credit Cash, $90.

(l) Received a $150 fee for services. [See transaction (g).]
Analysis: Debit Cash, $150; credit Professional Fees, $150.

(m) Paid telephone and other miscellaneous expense bills, $290. [See transaction (b).]
Analysis: Debit Miscellaneous Expense, $290; credit Cash, $290.

(n) Paid biweekly salaries, $600. [See transaction (i).]
Analysis: Debit Salary Expense, $600; credit Cash, $600.

(o) Received a $300 fee for services. [See transaction (g).]
Analysis: Debit Cash, $300; credit Professional Fees, $300.

(p) Paid automobile expenses, $80. [See transaction (b).]
Analysis: Debit Automobile Expense, $80; credit Cash, $80.

(q) Hill withdrew $450 cash for personal use.
Analysis: This transaction results in a decrease in proprietorship and a decrease in cash. The decrease in proprietorship could be recorded as a debit to the capital account, but the more usual practice is to debit it to the proprietor's *drawing* account. Debits to the drawing account, which are decreases in proprietorship, are commonly referred to as increases in drawings. The transaction is recorded by a debit of $450 to James B. Hill, Drawing, and a credit of $450 to Cash.

	CASH				JAMES B. HILL, DRAWING	
	+		−		+	−
(a)	4,000	(b)	200	(q)	450	
(g)	225	(d)	1,000			
(j)	400	(e)	100			
(l)	150	(f)	300			
(o)	300	(h)	75			
		(i)	600			
		(k)	90			
		(m)	290			
		(n)	600			
		(p)	80			
		(q)	**450**			

(r) Sent invoices to clients for services rendered during the month, $1,400.

Analysis: The revenue of $1,400 has been earned but not received in cash during the month. The claims against the clients are recorded by a debit to the asset Accounts Receivable, and the revenue is recorded by a credit to the revenue account Professional Fees. (At the time cash is received in payment of an account, Cash will be debited and Accounts Receivable will be credited.)

	ACCOUNTS RECEIVABLE			PROFESSIONAL FEES		
	+		−	−		+
(r)	**1,400**				(g)	225
					(j)	400
					(l)	150
					(o)	300
					(r)	**1,400**

Hill's ledger, after all transactions for October have been recorded, appears on page 58. In order to recognize more easily the nature of each account, the accounts are grouped under the three major classifications of the fundamental accounting equation, with the drawing, revenue, and expense accounts appearing as subdivisions of proprietorship. In order to obtain the maximum benefit from the illustration, the statement of each transaction should be reviewed and the entries should be traced to the ledger.

The small italicized figures appearing in the accounts represent pencil footings and balances. Note that they are inserted only when they serve a purpose. For example, a pencil footing in accounts with a single debit or credit, such as Accounts Receivable and James B. Hill, Capital, would be superfluous. Similarly, the pencil footing below the two debits in Prepaid Insurance is sufficient to indicate the balance of the account as there are no credits.

Assets	=	Liabilities	+	Proprietorship

CASH

(a)	4,000	(b)	200
(g)	225	(d)	1,000
(j)	400	(e)	100
(l)	150	(f)	300
(o)	300	(h)	75
1,290	5,075	(i)	600
		(k)	90
		(m)	290
		(n)	600
		(p)	80
		(q)	450
			3,785

ACCOUNTS RECEIVABLE

(r)	1,400

OFFICE SUPPLIES

(e)	100

PREPAID INSURANCE

(h)	75
(k)	90
	165

AUTOMOBILE

(d)	2,800

OFFICE EQUIPMENT

(a)	500
(c)	600
	1,100

LIBRARY

(a)	800

ACCOUNTS PAYABLE

(f)	300	(c)	600
		(d)	1,800
		2,100	2,400

JAMES B. HILL, CAPITAL

(a)	5,300

JAMES B. HILL, DRAWING

(q)	450

Revenue

PROFESSIONAL FEES

(g)	225
(j)	400
(l)	150
(o)	300
(r)	1,400
	2,475

Expenses

SALARY EXPENSE

(i)	600
(n)	600
	1,200

RENT EXPENSE

(b)	200

AUTOMOBILE EXPENSE

(p)	80

MISCELLANEOUS EXPENSE

(m)	290

Trial balance

The debits resulting from each transaction should equal the credits from each transaction. This equality of debits and credits has been observed in recording the transactions in the preceding illustration; consequently, the sum of all the debits in the ledger should be equal to the sum of all the credits. A test of this equality is made at intervals, usually at the end of each month. Such a test is known as a *trial balance*.

The trial balance also serves to summarize the information shown in detail in the ledger. This summary is always prepared at the end of a fiscal period and provides much of the information needed to prepare the balance sheet and the income statement.

A trial balance of totals could be taken by listing in parallel columns the total of the debits and the total of the credits of each account in the ledger and then adding the two columns. If the equality of debits and credits had been maintained for each transaction and there were no arithmetical errors, the sum of the column of debit totals would equal the sum of the column of credit totals.

In preparing financial statements, however, it is the balance of each account that is needed rather than the total debits and the total credits of each account. Referring to the cash account in the ledger of James B. Hill, for example, it is the balance of $1,290 that will appear on the balance sheet, not the total debits of $5,075 and the total credits of $3,785. Therefore, a trial balance of balances is usually preferable to a trial balance of totals. If the sum of the debit balances equals the sum of the credit balances, it is evident that the debits and the credits in the ledger are equal. The trial balance of Hill's ledger, prepared according to the latter method, is illustrated at the top of page 60.

Proof provided by the trial balance

The trial balance does not provide complete proof of the accuracy of the ledger. It indicates only that the *debits* and the *credits* are *equal*. This is of value, however, because errors frequently affect the equality of debits and credits. If the two totals of a trial balance are not equal, it is probably due to one or more of the following types of errors:
  (1) Error in preparing the trial balance.
      (a) One of the columns was incorrectly added.
      (b) An account balance was omitted or incorrectly recorded on the trial balance.
  (2) Error in determining the account balances.
      (a) A balance was incorrectly computed.
      (b) A balance was entered on the wrong side of an account.
      (c) One side of an account was incorrectly computed.

James B. Hill, C.P.A.
Trial Balance
October 31, 1961

Cash	1290 00	
Accounts Receivable	1400 00	
Office Supplies	100 00	
Prepaid Insurance	165 00	
Automobile	2800 00	
Office Equipment	110 00	
Library	800 00	
Accounts Payable		210 00
James B. Hill, Capital		5300 00
James B. Hill, Drawing	450 00	
Professional Fees		2475 00
Salary Expense	1200 00	
Rent Expense	200 00	
Automobile Expense	80 00	
Miscellaneous Expense	290 00	
	9875 00	9875 00

Trial balance

(3) Error in recording a transaction in the ledger.
   (a) An erroneous amount was recorded as a debit or as a credit in an account.
   (b) A debit entry was recorded as a credit, or vice versa.
   (c) A debit or a credit entry was omitted.

Among the types of errors that will not cause an inequality in the trial balance totals are the following:

   (1) Failure to record a transaction.
   (2) Recording the same erroneous amount for both the debit and the credit parts of a transaction.
   (3) Recording the same transaction more than once.
   (4) Recording one part of a transaction in the wrong account.

It is readily apparent that in entering transactions in the ledger, care should be exercised in recording correct figures in the appropriate accounts. The desirability of accuracy in determining account balances and reporting them on the trial balance is equally obvious.

Questions

1. Distinguish between the terms *account* and *ledger*.

2. Do the terms "debit" and "credit" signify increase or decrease, or may they signify either? Explain.

3. On the basis of the rules for debiting and crediting asset, liability, and proprietorship accounts, explain why revenues are recorded as credits and expenses are recorded as debits.

4. (a) Why are withdrawals of cash or other assets by the proprietor recorded in a drawing account instead of in the capital account? (b) Are they recorded as debits or credits? Why?

5. Distinguish between real and nominal accounts.

6. Identify each of the following accounts as asset, liability, proprietorship, revenue, or expense, and state in each case whether the normal balance is a debit or a credit: (a) Cash, (b) Robert Jackson, Drawing, (c) Accounts Payable, (d) Accounts Receivable, (e) Office Equipment, (f) Robert Jackson, Capital, (g) Rent Expense, (h) Store Supplies, (i) Rent Income.

7. List the following accounts in the order in which they would appear in the ledger of Ralph Baker:

(a) Miscellaneous Expense
(b) Accounts Payable
(c) Salaries Payable
(d) Salary Expense
(e) Ralph Baker, Drawing
(f) Ralph Baker, Capital
(g) Sales
(h) Accounts Receivable
(i) Cash
(j) Prepaid Insurance

8. Explain how it would be possible for an account with a customer to have a credit balance. In such a case does the credit balance represent an asset, a liability, a proprietorship, an income, or an expense?

9. Joseph Ford deposits all cash receipts from his business in a bank account and makes all payments by check. The cash account at the end of the current fiscal period has a credit balance of $250 and there is no undeposited cash on hand. (a) Assuming that there were no errors in recording, what is the explanation of this unusual balance? (b) At this particular time is the cash account an asset, liability, proprietorship, revenue, or expense?

10. A business enterprise renders services to a customer for $500 in one fiscal period and receives payment from the customer in the following period. What accounts should be debited and credited in the period in which (a) the service was rendered and (b) the cash was received?

11. At the end of the month it is discovered that a payment of advertising expense was erroneously debited to Rent Expense. Would this error have caused the trial balance totals to be unequal?

12. At the beginning of the fiscal period George Crane's capital account had a credit balance of $6,000. During the period his withdrawals totaled $5,000 and he incurred a net loss of $3,000; he made no additional investments in the business. Assuming that there have been no recording errors, will the balance sheet prepared at this time balance?

13. During the month Central Service Station received $8,400 in cash and paid out $7,500 in cash. (a) How were the receipts and disbursements entered in the cash account? (b) Do the facts indicate that there was a net income of $900 for the month?

14. What is a trial balance and what does it prove?

15. In recording the payment of an insurance premium of $200, the cash account is erroneously debited instead of being credited. (Prepaid Insurance is debited for the correct amount.) Assuming no other errors and that the total of the debit column of the trial balance at the end of the month is $10,810, what is the total of the credit column?

16. Indicate which of the following errors, considered individually, would cause the trial balance totals to be unequal:

    (a) A payment of $150 for equipment was recorded as a debit of $156 to Equipment and a credit of $150 to Cash.
    (b) A withdrawal of $100 by the proprietor was recorded as a debit of $10 to Salary Expense and a credit of $10 to Cash.
    (c) A fee of $300 due from a client was not recorded because the cash had not been received.
    (d) A payment of $200 to a creditor was recorded as a credit of $200 to Accounts Payable and a credit of $200 to Cash.
    (e) A receipt of $120 from an account receivable was recorded as a debit of $120 to Cash and a credit of $120 to Sales.

Exercises

1. Record the following transactions in T accounts, identifying each debit and credit by the letter designating the transaction, and prepare a trial balance.

    (a) On March 1, Ralph Borden invested $800 in cash and $1,500 in equipment in a shoe repair shop that he will operate.
    (b) Purchased supplies, paying cash, $250.
    (c) Paid rent for March, $75.
    (d) Purchased additional equipment on account, $1,200.
    (e) Received cash for services rendered during the month, $900.
    (f) Paid assistant's salary for the month, $300.
    (g) Paid $200 on account for the equipment purchased.
    (h) Withdrew $350 for personal use.

2. Entries for the original investment and eight other transactions are recorded in the accounts at the top of page 63.

For each transaction indicate: (1) the type of account (asset, liability, capital, drawing, revenue, expense) debited, (2) whether the debit represents an increase or a decrease, (3) the type of account credited, and (4) whether the credit represents an increase or a decrease. Present your answers in the following form:

	(1)	(2)	(3)	(4)
(a)	asset	increased	capital	increased

CASH			
(a)	5,000	(b)	1,000
(e)	1,800	(c)	1,000
(i)	400	(d)	800
		(f)	1,000
		(g)	300

ACCOUNTS PAYABLE			
(c)	1,000	(b)	2,500
(f)	1,000		

SERVICE INCOME			
		(e)	1,800
		(h)	2,000

ACCOUNTS RECEIVABLE			
(h)	2,000	(i)	400

JOHN MASON, CAPITAL			
		(a)	5,000

OPERATING EXPENSES		
(d)	800	

EQUIPMENT	
(b)	3,500

JOHN MASON, DRAWING	
(g)	300

3. Assuming that during the month a business has a substantial number of transactions affecting each of the accounts listed below, state for each account whether it is likely to have (1) debit entries only, (2) credit entries only, (3) both debit and credit entries.

(a) Advertising Expense
(b) William Rice, Drawing
(c) Accounts Payable
(d) Salary Expense

(e) Professional Fees
(f) Accounts Receivable
(g) Miscellaneous Expense
(h) Cash

4. The totals of a trial balance are as follows: debit, $32,420; credit, $32,840. Assuming that the cause of the inequality is a single error in recording transactions, list two possible explanations, in each case stating the amount of the transaction.

5. The trial balance of Harne Company presented below does not balance. In reviewing the ledger and the records you discover that: (a) the debit and credit entries in the cash account total $12,250 and $7,850, respectively; (b) the balance of the delivery equipment account is $4,200; (c) a payment of $1,000 to a creditor on account was not recorded in the cash account. Prepare a corrected trial balance.

Harne Company
Trial Balance
December 31, 19--

Cash	4,500	
Accounts Receivable...........	1,750	
Prepaid Insurance.............		900
Delivery Equipment	2,400	
Accounts Payable		1,600
A. E. Harne, Capital		6,500
Salaries Payable	500	
Service Revenue		6,000
Advertising Expense...........	1,000	
Miscellaneous Expense..........		350
Salary Expense	3,000	
	13,150	15,350

Problems

3-1. James T. Meredith, architect, opened an office on September 1 of the current year. During the month he completed the following transactions connected with his professional practice:

   (a) Transferred cash from a personal bank account to an account to be used for the business, $3,000.
   (b) Paid September rent for office and workroom, $350.
   (c) Purchased used automobile for $1,500, paying $300 cash and giving a note for the remainder.
   (d) Purchased office and drafting room equipment on account, $2,000.
   (e) Paid cash for supplies, $210.
   (f) Received cash from a client for plans delivered, $400.
   (g) Paid cash for miscellaneous expenses, $25.
   (h) Paid cash for insurance policies on automobile and equipment, $180.
   (i) Paid cash to creditors on account, $800.
   (j) Recorded fee earned on plans delivered, payment to be made in following month, $860.
   (k) Paid salary of assistant, $425.
   (l) Received invoice for blueprint service, due in following month, $40.
   (m) Paid gas, oil, and repairs on automobile for September, $65.
   (n) Paid installment due on note payable, $200, and interest expense, $6.
   (o) Paid cash for miscellaneous expenses, $32.

Instructions: (1) Record the foregoing transactions in the following T accounts: Cash; Accounts Receivable; Supplies; Prepaid Insurance; Automobile; Equipment; Notes Payable; Accounts Payable; James T. Meredith, Capital; Professional Fees; Salary Expense; Rent Expense; Automobile Expense; Blueprint Expense; Miscellaneous Expense; Interest Expense. Record the letter identifying the transaction at the left of each debit and each credit in the accounts.

(2) Prepare a trial balance as of September 30 of the current year.

3-2. The accounts in the ledger of Henry L. Davis, physician and surgeon, are listed below, together with their balances as of January 1 of the current year: Cash, $4,200; Accounts Receivable, $6,100; Supplies, $250; Prepaid Insurance, $325; Equipment, $15,000; Accounts Payable, $500; Henry L. Davis, Capital, $25,375; Henry L. Davis, Drawing; Professional Fees; Salary Expense; Rent Expense; Laboratory Expense; Gas, Electricity, and Water Expense; Telephone Expense; Miscellaneous Expense.

Transactions completed during January were as follows:

   (a) Purchased equipment on account, $1,400.
   (b) Paid office rent for January, $500.
   (c) Received cash from debtors on account, $3,300.
   (d) Returned part of equipment purchased in (a), $150.
   (e) Purchased supplies on account, $90.
   (f) Paid laboratory expense, $175.
   (g) Paid cash for renewal of insurance policy, $120.
   (h) Sold X-ray film to another doctor at cost, as an accommodation, receiving cash, $25.
   (i) Paid salaries of receptionist and nurses, $1,200.
   (j) Received cash in payment of professional services rendered during January, $2,600.

(k) Paid cash to creditors on account, $900.

(l) Paid gas and electricity expense, $145.

(m) Paid miscellaneous expenses, $72.

(n) Recorded fees charged to customers on account for services rendered in January, $1,900.

(o) Paid cash from business bank account for personal expenses, $875.

(p) Paid telephone expense, $48.

(q) Discovered that a fee of $20 was erroneously charged to a patient in (n).

(r) Paid water expense, $18.

Instructions: (1) Set up a ledger of T accounts and record the balances as of January 1. Identify the balances by writing "Bal." to the left of the amount.

(2) Record the transactions for January. Identify each debit and each credit by the letter designating the transaction.

(3) Prepare a trial balance as of January 31 of the current year.

(4) If there were no other expired costs for January, such as depreciation and supplies expense, what would be the amount of net income for the month?

(5) What is the tentative amount of capital as of January 31, ignoring the effect of unrecorded expirations of cost?

3-3. The following trial balance for Williamson Company as of October 31 of the current year does not balance because of a number of errors.

Cash..	2,610	
Accounts Receivable..........................	1,420	
Supplies.......................................	415	
Prepaid Insurance.............................	230	
Equipment.....................................	5,350	
Notes Payable.................................		1,200
Accounts Payable..............................		1,410
R. G. Williamson, Capital.....................		4,703
R. G. Williamson, Drawing....................	100	
Sales..		4,600
Salary Expense................................	1,200	
Rent Expense..................................	325	
Advertising Expense...........................	29	
Utilities Expense..............................	98	
	11,777	11,913

In the process of comparing the amounts in the trial balance with the ledger, recomputing the balances of the accounts, and comparing the entries with the original evidences of the transactions, the following errors are discovered:

(a) The pencil footing of the debits to Cash is $4,200; the correct total is $4,300.

(b) A cash payment of $320 was recorded as a credit to Cash of $230.

(c) A credit of $150 to Accounts Receivable was not recorded.

(d) An insurance policy acquired at a cost of $60 was recorded as a credit to Prepaid Insurance.

(e) The pencil footings of $1,650 debit and $2,960 credit in Accounts Payable are correct but the balance was computed incorrectly.

(f) A debit of $300 for a withdrawal by the proprietor was recorded as a credit to the capital account.

(g) Sales was underfooted by $1,000.

(h) The balance of $290 in Advertising Expense was entered as $29 in the trial balance.

(i) Miscellaneous Expense was omitted from the trial balance. The account has a balance of $195.

Instructions: Prepare a corrected trial balance as of October 31 of the current year.

3-4. The following transactions were completed by Thomas R. Reynolds during April of the current year:

(a) Deposited cash in a bank account for use in acquiring and operating Stardust Drive-In Theatre, $15,000.

(b) Purchased the Stardust Drive-In Theatre for $16,000, allocated as follows: equipment, $4,000; buildings, $7,000; land, $5,000. Made a down payment of $8,000 and gave a mortgage for the balance.

(c) Paid for newspaper advertising, $350.

(d) Paid premiums for property and casualty insurance policies, $1,050.

(e) Purchased supplies, $200, and equipment, $500, on account.

(f) Cash receipts from admissions for the week, $1,800.

(g) Paid miscellaneous expenses, $45.

(h) Cash receipts from admissions for the week, $2,050.

(i) Paid semimonthly wages, $1,400.

(j) Paid miscellaneous expenses, $35.

(k) Granted concession for operation of refreshment stand at a rental of 12% of sales, but not less than $300 a month, payable in advance on the first of the month. Received $150 cash as advance payment for the second half of April.

(l) Cash receipts from admissions for the week, $1,700.

(m) Paid cash to creditors on account, $450.

(n) Purchased supplies for cash, $28.

(o) Paid semimonthly wages, $1,450.

(p) Paid for advertising, $150.

(q) Cash receipts from admissions for remainder of the month, $2,300.

(r) Paid utilities expenses, $285.

(s) Paid creditors on account, $150.

(t) Concessionaire reported sales of $2,100 for the second half of April. Received check for balance due.

(u) Withdrew cash for personal use, $500.

(v) Paid film rental for the month, $2,100.

(w) Paid installment, $500, and interest, $40, due on mortgage.

The accounts to be used in the ledger are as follows, arranged in alphabetical order: Accounts Payable; Admissions Income; Advertising Expense; Buildings; Cash; Concession Income; Equipment; Film Rental Expense; Interest Expense; Land; Miscellaneous Expense; Mortgage Payable; Prepaid Insurance; Thomas R. Reynolds, Capital; Thomas R. Reynolds, Drawing; Supplies; Utilities Expense; Wages Expense.

Instructions: (1) Set up T accounts for all of the accounts listed above, arranging them in appropriate sequence.

(2) Record the transactions for April. Identify each debit and each credit by the letter designating the transaction.

(3) Prepare a trial balance as of April 30 of the current year.

Journalizing and posting

Need for journals

The ledger is the basic record in which the effects of business transactions are classified and summarized. Each account in the ledger is a record of a particular asset, liability, or proprietorship item. In the preceding chapter the debits and the credits were recorded in appropriate accounts directly from informal descriptions of transactions. In actual practice, an initial record of each transaction, or of a group of similar transactions, is customarily evidenced by a business document such as a sales ticket, a check stub, or a cash register tape. On the basis of the evidence provided by the business documents, the transactions are analyzed in terms of their effect on the elements of the accounting equation and are then recorded in a *journal* or *book of original entry*. All entries in the journal are subsequently recorded in the ledger. The sequence of recording a transaction may be diagrammed as follows:

Transaction ⟶ Business document ⟶ Journal ⟶ Ledger

The record provided by a journal is useful in several ways. Each transaction is recorded in its entirety in one place, whereas in the ledger a portion of a transaction is recorded in one account and the remaining portion is recorded in one or more other accounts. It is therefore easier to determine from a journal the correctness of the analysis of a transaction. There is also more space in a journal for recording details or explanations of complex transactions.

The journal is a permanent chronological record of the debits and the credits resulting from transactions, together with all necessary explanations of the transactions. From time to time the debits and the credits are transferred to the accounts in the ledger, which in turn supply the cumulative data for financial statements and other reports for owners and managers.

Both journals and ledger accounts play indispensable roles in the recording of business transactions. Journals furnish the chronological record of the effect of individual transactions on the accounting equation. Ledger accounts provide for the classification and the summarization of the cumulative effects of all transactions on assets, liabilities, and proprietorship.

Two-column journal

There are various kinds of journals. The number and the type used in a particular business will depend upon the size of the business and the nature of its operations. The simplest form of journal has only two amount columns and may be used for recording all transactions of the business in chronological order.

JOURNAL   PAGE 6

DATE		DESCRIPTION	POST. REF.	DEBIT	CREDIT
July	1	Salary Expense		31000	
		Cash			31000
		Paid salaries for week.			
	1	Accounts Payable		35000	
		Cash			35000
		Paid Sims Supply Co. on account.			
	1	Cash		28600	
		Sales			28600
		Cash sales for the day.			

Standard form of the two-column journal

The process of recording a transaction in a journal is called *journalizing*. The procedures followed in journalizing are as follows:

(1) The year is written in small figures at the top of the first column. It is not written again on a page unless the year changes.

(2) The month of the first transaction is written on the first line in the first column. The name of the month is entered again only at the top of a new page or at the beginning of a new month.

(3) The day of each transaction is written in the second column on the first line used by each transaction. It is repeated for each transaction regardless of the number of transactions completed on the same day.

(4) The title of the account to be debited is written at the extreme left of the Description column, and the amount of the debit is entered in the left-hand or Debit amount column.

(5) The title of the account to be credited is written on the following line, indented about one-half inch, and the amount of the credit is entered in the right-hand or Credit amount column.

(6) The explanation is written on the next line, with an additional indention of about one-half inch. The explanation, while not necessarily limited to one line, should be as brief as possible without omitting essential information not readily apparent from reading the entry.

It should be noted that all transactions are recorded in terms of debits and credits to specific accounts in accordance with the rules of debit and credit discussed in the preceding chapter. The titles used in the entries should correspond to the titles of the accounts in the ledger. For example, a desk purchased for use in the office should be debited to Office Equipment, not to "desks purchased," and cash received should be debited to Cash, not to "cash received."

A blank line is left between each entry in order clearly to separate all entries. The column headed "Post. Ref." (posting reference) is not used at the time the entries are recorded in the journal. When the debits and the credits are transferred to the appropriate accounts in the ledger, the numbers identifying the accounts will be recorded in the posting reference column. The process of transferring the data to the ledger is explained later in the chapter.

Standard form of the account

The T accounts used in Chapter 3 were constructed in the simplest form possible. While such a form provides the basic elements of the account, it is used primarily for illustrative purposes. By adding special rulings to the basic T account form, the following standard form is obtained:

<table>
<tr><td colspan="9" align="center">Cash   ACCOUNT NO. 11</td></tr>
<tr><th>DATE</th><th>ITEMS</th><th>POST. REF.</th><th>DEBIT</th><th>DATE</th><th>ITEMS</th><th>POST. REF.</th><th>CREDIT</th></tr>
<tr><td>1961
July 1</td><td>Balance</td><td>✓</td><td>2 1 1 5 00</td><td>1961
July 1</td><td></td><td>5</td><td>3 1 0 00</td></tr>
<tr><td>1</td><td></td><td>6</td><td>2 8 6 00</td><td>1</td><td></td><td>6</td><td>3 5 0 00</td></tr>
<tr><td>3</td><td></td><td>6</td><td>3 1 9 00</td><td>3</td><td></td><td>6</td><td>1 1 0 00</td></tr>
<tr><td>3</td><td></td><td>6</td><td>2 6 0 00</td><td>3</td><td></td><td>6</td><td>1 9 00</td></tr>
<tr><td></td><td></td><td></td><td></td><td>3</td><td></td><td>7</td><td>1 2 5 00</td></tr>
</table>

Standard form of the account

Both sides of the account are identical except that the left side is used for debits and the right side is used for credits. The columns on each side provide for: (1) the date; (2) a brief explanation of the entry, if it is desired; (3) the page reference to the journal in which the transaction was recorded; and (4) the amount.

Both ledger and journal paper may be purchased either with or without the column headings printed as shown in the illustrations.

Posting

The process by which the entries in the journal are transferred to accounts is called *posting*. It consists in transferring each amount in the debit column of the journal to the debit side of an account and in transferring each amount in the credit column of the journal to the credit side of an account. The account to which each item is to be posted is determined from the account title stated in the journal. The debits and the credits may be posted in sequence as they appear in the journal or, if a considerable amount of posting is to be done at one time, all of the debits may be posted first, followed by the credits. The use of the latter procedure reduces the likelihood of posting items to the wrong side of accounts.

In some accounting systems much of the posting is done by machines designed for the purpose. However, when the posting is done manually, each debit and each credit is posted in the following manner:

(1) The date and the amount in the journal entry are recorded in the corresponding *account*. If the item appears as a debit in the journal, the posting will be to the debit side of the account; if it appears as a credit, the posting will be to the credit side of the account. The system of recording dates (year, month, and day) is similar to that employed in the journal.

(2) The number of the journal page from which the posting is made is recorded in the posting reference column of the *account*.

(3) The number of the account to which the posting has been made is recorded in the posting reference column of the *journal*. This procedure serves two purposes: first, it indicates that the item has been posted; and second, it completes the cross reference between the journal and the ledger.

The foregoing procedures are illustrated in the diagrams that appear on page 71.

Chart of accounts

The principal classes of accounts to be found in the ledger have been presented in earlier chapters. The number of accounts to be kept for a

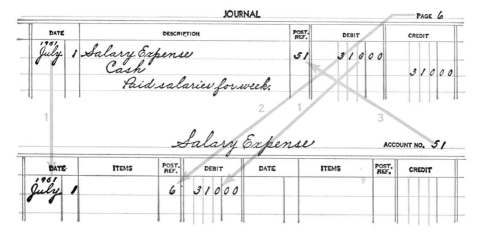

Diagram of the posting of a debit

Diagram of the posting of a credit

particular business will depend upon the nature of its operations, its volume of business, and the extent to which details are desired. In general, the account titles correspond to the descriptions used on the balance sheet and the income statement. For example, one particular enterprise may maintain separate accounts for light and power expense, heat expense, and telephone and telegraph expense, while another may combine all these expenses into a miscellaneous expense account.

Insofar as possible, the order of the accounts in the ledger should agree with the order of the items on the balance sheet and the income statement. The accounts are numbered to permit indexing and also for use as posting references in the journal. Accounts may be numbered consecutively like the pages of a book, or a system of indexing major classes and minor classes may be used.

One method used in the charting of accounts is reproduced below. All account numbers have two digits, the first digit indicating the major classification. Accounts beginning with 1 represent assets; 2, liabilities; 3, proprietorship; 4, revenue; and 5, expenses. This system has the further advantage of permitting the insertion of additional accounts in their proper sequence without disturbing the other account numbers. For a large enterprise with a number of departments or branches, it is not unusual for each account number to have four or more digits.

BALANCE SHEET ACCOUNTS

1. *Assets*

11. Cash
12. Accounts Receivable
14. Supplies
15. Prepaid Rent
18. Printing Equipment
19. Accumulated Depreciation[1]

2. *Liabilities*

21. Accounts Payable
22. Salaries Payable[1]

3. *Proprietorship*

31. David Hull, Capital
32. David Hull, Drawing
33. Expense and Revenue Summary[1]

INCOME STATEMENT ACCOUNTS

4. *Revenue*

41. Sales

5. *Expenses*

51. Salary Expense
52. Supplies Expense[1]
53. Rent Expense[1]
54. Depreciation Expense[1]
59. Miscellaneous Expense

Chart of accounts for Hull Print Shop

Illustrations of the journal and the ledger

David Hull operated a printing business in his home workshop on a part-time basis. He decided to move to rented quarters as of October 1 and to devote his full time to the business, which was to be known as Hull Print Shop. The following assets were invested in the enterprise: cash, $900; accounts receivable, $600; supplies, $400; and printing equipment, $3,200. This investment could have been recorded in the journal by four separate entries, each debiting one asset account for the amount of the asset and crediting David Hull, Capital for the same amount. The preferred method, however, is to journalize the entire transaction in a single entry, debiting the four asset accounts and

---

[1] The use of this account is explained and illustrated in Chapter 5.

crediting the capital account for the total, as illustrated below. An entry composed of three or more items is called a *compound entry*.

JOURNAL	PAGE *1*

DATE	DESCRIPTION	POST. REF.	DEBIT	CREDIT
1961 Oct. 2	Cash		900 00	
	Accounts Receivable		600 00	
	Supplies		400 00	
	Printing Equipment		3200 00	
	David Hull, Capital			5100 00
	Invested assets in Hull			
	Print Shop.			

Compound journal entry

If there had been any creditors' claims against the assets, such as accounts payable, the appropriate account title and amount would have been included in the opening entry as a credit. The amount of the credit to David Hull, Capital would have been correspondingly reduced.

The transactions completed by Hull Print Shop during the month of October are described below. As a means of limiting the length of the illustration and avoiding repetition of entries, some of the transactions will be stated as a summary of many transactions. For example, sales for cash will be recorded only at the middle of the month and at the end of the month. In actual practice they would be recorded each day. Similarly, all sales on account during the month will be summarized in one entry; in practice each sale would be recorded separately.

Oct. 2. Paid $600 cash on a lease rental contract, the payment representing three months' rental. (As only a part of this payment applied to the month of October, the asset account Prepaid Rent was debited.)

3. Purchased additional printing equipment on account from Blake Equipment Co. for $1,800.

4. Received $525 from customers in payment of their accounts.

6. Paid $40 for a newspaper advertisement.

10. Paid $400 cash to Blake Equipment Co. to apply on the $1,800 owed them.

13. Paid part-time assistants $240 for two weeks' salaries.

16. Received $920 cash from sales for the first half of October.

20. Paid $350 for additional supplies.

27. Paid part-time assistants $240 for two weeks' salaries.

31. Paid $20 for telephone bill for the month.

31. Paid $45 for electric bill for the month.

31. Received $850 cash from sales for the second half of October.

31. Sales on account totaled $510 for the month.

31. Withdrew $500 cash for personal use.

		JOURNAL			PAGE 1	
DATE		DESCRIPTION	POST. REF.	DEBIT	CREDIT	
1961 Oct.	2	Cash	11	900 00		
		Accounts Receivable	12	600 00		
		Supplies	14	400 00		
		Printing Equipment	18	3200 00		
		David Hull, Capital	31		5100 00	
		Invested assets in Hull Print Shop.				
	2	Prepaid Rent	15	600 00		
		Cash	11		600 00	
		Paid three months' rent.				
	3	Printing Equipment	18	1800 00		
		Accounts Payable	21		1800 00	
		On account from Blake Equipment Co.				
	4	Cash	11	525 00		
		Accounts Receivable	12		525 00	
		Received cash on account.				
	6	Miscellaneous Expense	59	40 00		
		Cash	11		40 00	
		Newspaper advertisement.				
	10	Accounts Payable	21	400 00		
		Cash	11		400 00	
		Blake Equipment Co.				
	13	Salary Expense	51	240 00		
		Cash	11		240 00	
		Biweekly salaries.				
	16	Cash	11	920 00		
		Sales	41		920 00	
		Cash sales for first half of month.				
	20	Supplies	14	350 00		
		Cash	11		350 00	
		Cash purchase of supplies.				

Journal — Hull Print Shop

JOURNAL   PAGE 2

DATE		DESCRIPTION	POST. REF.	DEBIT	CREDIT
1961 Oct.	27	Salary Expense	51	2 4 0 00	
		Cash	11		2 4 0 00
		Biweekly salaries.			
	31	Miscellaneous Expense	59	2 0 00	
		Cash	11		2 0 00
		October telephone bill.			
	31	Miscellaneous Expense	59	4 5 00	
		Cash	11		4 5 00
		October electric bill.			
	31	Cash	11	8 5 0 00	
		Sales	41		8 5 0 00
		Cash sales for second half of month.			
	31	Accounts Receivable	12	5 1 0 00	
		Sales	41		5 1 0 00
		Charge sales for month.			
	31	David Hull, Drawing	32	5 0 0 00	
		Cash	11		5 0 0 00
		Withdrew cash.			

Journal — Hull Print Shop (concluded)

The foregoing transactions are recorded in the journal that appears on this and the opposite page. Each entry should be studied in connection with the narrative of the transaction. The account numbers appearing in the posting reference column were not placed there at the time the entry was made; they were recorded in the journal as the final step in posting each item to the ledger.

After all of the entries for the month have been posted, the ledger will appear as shown on pages 76 and 77. Tracing each entry from the journal to the accounts in the ledger will give a clear understanding of the posting process.

Each account is on a separate page in the ledger. The accounts are numbered in accordance with the chart of accounts shown on page 72. Six accounts listed in the chart do not appear in the illustration of the ledger. They will be required in completing the work of the accounting cycle, which will be discussed in the next chapter.

Cash   ACCOUNT NO. 11

DATE	ITEMS	POST. REF.	DEBIT	DATE	ITEMS	POST. REF.	CREDIT
1961 Oct. 2		1	900 00	1961 Oct. 2		1	600 00
4		1	525 00	6		1	40 00
16		1	920 00	10		1	400 00
31	760.00	2	850 00 3195 00	13		1	240 00
				20		1	350 00
				27		2	240 00
				31		2	20 00
				31		2	45 00
				31		2	500 00 2435 00

Accounts Receivable   ACCOUNT NO. 12

DATE	ITEMS	POST. REF.	DEBIT	DATE	ITEMS	POST. REF.	CREDIT
1961 Oct. 2		1	600 00	1961 Oct. 4		1	525 00
31	585.00	2	510 00 1110 00				

Supplies   ACCOUNT NO. 14

DATE	ITEMS	POST. REF.	DEBIT	DATE	ITEMS	POST. REF.	CREDIT
1961 Oct. 2		1	400 00				
20		1	350 00 750 00				

Prepaid Rent   ACCOUNT NO. 15

DATE	ITEMS	POST. REF.	DEBIT	DATE	ITEMS	POST. REF.	CREDIT
1961 Oct. 2		1	600 00				

Printing Equipment   ACCOUNT NO. 18

DATE	ITEMS	POST. REF.	DEBIT	DATE	ITEMS	POST. REF.	CREDIT
1961 Oct. 2		1	3200 00				
3		1	1800 00 5000 00				

Accounts Payable   ACCOUNT NO. 21

DATE	ITEMS	POST. REF.	DEBIT	DATE	ITEMS	POST. REF.	CREDIT
1961 Oct. 10		1	400 00	1961 Oct. 3	1400.00	1	1800 00

Ledger — Hull Print Shop

David Hull, Capital   ACCOUNT NO. 31

DATE	ITEMS	POST. REF.	DEBIT	DATE	ITEMS	POST. REF.	CREDIT
				1961 Oct 2		1	5100 00

David Hull, Drawing   ACCOUNT NO. 32

DATE	ITEMS	POST. REF.	DEBIT	DATE	ITEMS	POST. REF.	CREDIT
1961 Oct. 31		2	500.00				

Sales   ACCOUNT NO. 41

DATE	ITEMS	POST. REF.	DEBIT	DATE	ITEMS	POST. REF.	CREDIT
				1961 Oct. 16		1	920 00
				31		2	850 00
				31		2	510 00
							2280 00

Salary Expense   ACCOUNT NO. 51

DATE	ITEMS	POST. REF.	DEBIT	DATE	ITEMS	POST. REF.	CREDIT
1961 Oct. 13		1	240 00				
27		2	240 00				
			450 00				

Miscellaneous Expense   ACCOUNT NO. 59

DATE	ITEMS	POST. REF.	DEBIT	DATE	ITEMS	POST. REF.	CREDIT
1961 Oct. 6		1	40 00				
31		2	20 00				
31		2	45 00				
			105 00				

Ledger — Hull Print Shop (concluded)

Trial balance procedures

As the first step in preparing the trial balance, the accounts having two or more debits or credits are footed. For accounts having both debits and credits the balance is also entered. Observe that in the cash account appearing on page 76 the debit and credit amount columns are added. The totals are entered in small pencil figures immediately below the last entry in each column so that they will not be mistaken for an entry nor interfere with an entry made on the following line. The balance is entered in small pencil figures in the Items column of the account on a line with and on the same side as the larger of the two footings. Observe that in the cash account the debit footing is larger than the credit footing and therefore the balance of $760 is entered in the Items column of the debit side. This balance is the amount that is to be entered on the trial balance.

The supplies, printing equipment, sales, salary expense, and miscellaneous expense accounts are also footed, but the balances are not entered in the Items columns as each account contains entries on one side of the account only and therefore the total is also the balance. Accounts having only one debit and one credit, such as the accounts payable account on page 76, are not footed, but the balance is entered in the Items column. Accounts that contain only one entry, such as the prepaid rent account, are not footed, and the balance is not entered in the Items column because the amount of the entry is the amount of the balance.

The trial balance taken from the ledger of Hull Print Shop on October 31 is shown below.

Hull Print Shop
Trial Balance
October 31, 1961

11	Cash	760 00	
12	Accounts Receivable	585 00	
14	Supplies	750 00	
15	Prepaid Rent	60 00	
18	Printing Equipment	5000 00	
21	Accounts Payable		1400 00
31	David Hull, Capital		5100 00
32	David Hull, Drawing	500 00	
41	Sales		2280 00
51	Salary Expense	480 00	
59	Miscellaneous Expense	105 00	
		8780 00	8780 00

Trial balance — Hull Print Shop

Other journal forms

The two-column journal provides for a chronological record of transactions. Its use also eliminates, for the most part, any need for explanations in the ledger accounts. It does not reduce the number of entries in the accounts, however, as each debit and each credit is posted individually to the ledger. Some of the unnecessary detail in the ledger can be eliminated by adding special columns to the journal. In any particular case, the number of columns to be added and the manner of their use depend upon the frequency of occurrence of different types of transactions.

For example, examination of the journal on pages 74 and 75 discloses that out of a total of fifteen transactions recorded during the month, thirteen included a receipt or a payment of cash. It was necessary to write "Cash" in the journal thirteen times, and it was also necessary to make thirteen postings to the cash account. It is possible to avoid the necessity of writing "Cash" in the Description column of the journal by adding two special columns, one for recording all debits to Cash and the other for recording all credits to Cash. An additional advantage of the special columns is that, instead of posting each individual debit and credit to the cash account, only the totals for the month need be posted. A four-column journal with special columns is illustrated below.

JOURNAL   PAGE 15

CASH		DATE	DESCRIPTION	POST. REF.	SUNDRY ACCOUNTS	
DEBIT	CREDIT				DEBIT	CREDIT
		1961				
		Sept. 12	Store Supplies		70 00	
			Accounts Payable			70 00
	380 00	13	Office Salary Expense		380 00	
940 00		14	Sales			940 00

Four-column journal

The two amount columns on the left side of the journal are used exclusively for debits and credits to Cash; the two amount columns on the right side, captioned "Sundry Accounts," are used for debits and credits to all other accounts. The Description column is used for the titles of accounts that are debited or credited in the sundry columns.

The procedure for recording a transaction that does not affect Cash is the same as that followed in the two-column journal. The title of the account to be debited is written at the extreme left of the Description column and the title of the account to be credited is written on the next line, indented about one-half inch. The amounts are entered in the Sundry Accounts Debit and Credit columns in the usual manner.

Each transaction affecting Cash and one other account is recorded on one line. The amount of the debit or the credit to Cash is entered in the proper column at the left. The title of the other account affected is written in the Description column, and the amount is entered in the

Sundry Accounts Debit or Credit column at the right. The account title may be written at the extreme left of the Description column, regardless of whether the account is being debited or credited.

It is customary to omit explanations of routine transactions in multi-column journals. The advantage of having an explanation after each entry is outweighed by the extra time and space required. In the relatively rare cases in which it becomes necessary to refer back to the explanation of a particular routine transaction, the details may usually be found in the supporting document used as the basis for the entry. For example, the evidence supporting disbursements of cash are the check stubs. If payments are made in currency, they are evidenced by paid-out slips, receipt forms, or other business papers. Invoices and copies of sales tickets are other types of supporting documents. In the event explanations are desired in the four-column journal, they are written in the Description column immediately below the entry.

It should be noted at this point that even though the four-column journal illustrated may be suitable for a particular business, it is merely one example. Other applications of the multicolumn technique are used in practice. The number and the arrangement of the columns in any selected case depend upon the specific needs of the business.

Four-column journal illustrated

In order to illustrate more fully the use of the journal with special columns for cash, it will be assumed that David Hull adopts it as of January 1 of the following year. The journal for the month is illustrated on page 81. It has been totaled and all postings have been made. The procedure for posting the items in the Sundry Accounts Debit and Sundry Accounts Credit columns is exactly the same as in the case of the two-column journal illustrated earlier. The procedures for totaling and proving the amount columns and posting to the cash account are as follows:

(1) Draw a single line across the money columns on the line below the last entry for the month.
(2) Add all four columns, inserting the totals below the ruled line.
(3) Prove the equality of debits and credits. This may be done on an adding machine tape or by a listing similar to the following:

	DEBIT	CREDIT
Cash Columns..............	$2,188.00	$1,462.00
Sundry Accounts Columns...	2,033.00	2,759.00
Total...................	$4,221.00	$4,221.00

The totals of debits and credits have no significance in the accounting process other than to serve as a proof of the debit-credit balance of the journal.

JOURNAL　　　　　　　　　　PAGE **9**

| CASH | | DATE | DESCRIPTION | POST. REF. | SUNDRY ACCOUNTS | |
DEBIT	CREDIT				DEBIT	CREDIT
		1962 Jan. 2	Printing Equipment	18	265 00	
			Accounts Payable	21		265 00
	30 00	2	Supplies	14	30 00	
290 00		5	Accounts Receivable	12		290 00
	240 00	9	Salary Expense	51	240 00	
		10	Accounts Receivable	12	250 00	
			Sales	41		250 00
	320 00	12	Accounts Payable	21	320 00	
	25 00	13	Miscellaneous Expense	59	25 00	
630 00		15	Sales	41		630 00
	150 00	16	David Hull, Drawing	32	150 00	
340 00		19	Accounts Receivable	12		340 00
	240 00	23	Salary Expense	51	240 00	
		26	Supplies	14	56 00	
			Accounts Payable	21		56 00
	93 00	29	Accounts Payable	21	93 00	
	22 00	31	Miscellaneous Expense	59	22 00	
	42 00	31	Miscellaneous Expense	59	42 00	
	300 00	31	David Hull, Drawing	32	300 00	
928 00		31	Sales	41		928 00
2188 00	1462 00				2033 00	2759 00
(✓)	(✓)				(✓)	(✓)

Four-column journal — Hull Print Shop

Cash　　　　　　　　　　ACCOUNT NO. **11**

DATE	ITEMS	POST. REF.	DEBIT	DATE	ITEMS	POST. REF.	CREDIT
1962 Jan. 1	Balance	✓	1038 61	1962 Jan. 31		9	1462 00
31		9	2188 00				

Cash account

(4) Below the totals draw double lines across all columns except the Description column.

(5) Place a check mark in parentheses below the Sundry Accounts Debit and Sundry Accounts Credit totals. The check mark indicates that these totals are not to be posted because the individual items in the columns are posted separately.

(6) Post the total cash debits to the cash account and record the number of the cash account in parentheses below the total. Follow the same routine for posting the total cash credits.

The use of the four-column journal does not alter the postings to any of the accounts except Cash. The saving in time required in posting to the cash account may be observed by tracing the posting of the cash columns in the illustrative four-column journal to the cash account, which is reproduced immediately below the journal. If the January transactions of Hull Print Shop had been recorded in a two-column journal, there would have been four debit postings and ten credit postings to Cash instead of only one debit and one credit.

The foregoing presentation of a four-column combination cash journal is suggestive of the flexibility in the form of records of original entry. Additional forms of specialized journals will be discussed in later chapters.

Discovery of errors

The existence of errors in the accounts may be ascertained in a variety of ways: through audit procedures, through chance discovery, or through the medium of the trial balance. As was emphasized in Chapter 3, there are some types of errors that are not disclosed by the trial balance. If the debit and the credit totals of the trial balance are unequal, however, the reason for the discrepancy must be found and the error must be corrected.

The amount of the difference between the two totals of the trial balance sometimes gives a clue to the location of the error. For example, if the difference between the totals is $450, it is possible that a debit or a credit posting of that amount was omitted; or, since the amount is evenly divisible by 2, there is a possibility that a debit entry for $225 was erroneously posted as a credit, or vice versa. Two other common types of posting errors are known as *transpositions* and *slides*. A transposition is the erroneous rearrangement of digits, such as writing $542 as $452 or $524. In a slide the entire number is erroneously moved one or more spaces to the right or the left, such as writing $542.00 as $54.20 or $5,420.00. If a single error of either type has occurred, the discrepancy between the trial balance totals will be evenly divisible by 9. If more than one error has occurred, the amount by which the trial balance does not balance will give no indication as to the possible nature of the error.

A preliminary examination along the lines suggested by the preceding paragraph will frequently disclose the error. If it does not, the general procedure is to retrace the various steps in the accounting process, beginning with the last step and working back to the original entries in the journal. While there are no rigid rules governing this check or audit, the following plan is suggested:

(1) Double check the totals that were obtained for the trial balance by re-adding the columns.

(2) Compare the listings in the trial balance with the balances shown in the ledger, making certain that no accounts have been omitted.

(3) Verify the accuracy of the account footings and balances by recomputing them.

(4) Trace the postings in the ledger back to the journal, placing a small check mark by the item in the ledger and also in the journal. If the error is not found, scrutinize each account to see if there is an entry without a check mark; do the same with the entries in the journal.

(5) Verify the equality of the debits and the credits in the journal.

Ordinarily, errors that affect the trial balance will be revealed before the foregoing procedures have been completed.

Correction of errors

It is inevitable that errors will occasionally be made in recording transactions in the journal and in posting to the accounts. Such errors should not be corrected by erasures, as erasures may arouse suspicions of dishonesty. The procedure for correcting errors varies with the nature of the error and the time of its discovery. If an incorrect account title or amount in a journal is discovered before the item has been posted, the correction is made by drawing a line through the error and by writing the correct title or amount immediately above. An incorrect amount posted to an account may be corrected in the same manner, by crossing out the incorrect amount and by writing the correct figure immediately above.

When an erroneous entry has been posted to the ledger, it is usually considered preferable to correct it by means of an entry in the journal. For example, if a disbursement of $50 for office equipment has been incorrectly journalized and posted as a debit to Office Supplies, a correcting entry should be made. Before attempting to record a correcting entry, it is helpful to set forth clearly (1) the erroneous entry and (2) the entry that should have been made. This may be done by the use of T accounts as in the example below.

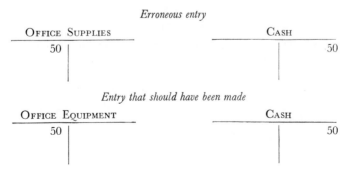

Erroneous entry

OFFICE SUPPLIES		CASH	
50			50

Entry that should have been made

OFFICE EQUIPMENT		CASH	
50			50

Comparison of the two sets of T accounts reveals that the erroneous debit of $50 to Office Supplies may be corrected by a $50 credit to that account and that Office Equipment should be debited for the same amount. The correcting entry is as follows:

Mar.	31	Office Equipment		50	
		Office Supplies			50
		To correct erroneous charge to			
		Office Supplies on March 5.			

Although there is some latitude in the methods employed to correct errors, the explanations should be sufficiently clear to be readily understood by anyone examining the records.

Questions

1. Why are journals sometimes called "books of original entry?"

2. Are the details of transactions more readily available in the journal or in the ledger?

3. To which record would you refer to determine the total sales of a preceding month, the journal or the ledger?

4. When must the bookkeeper analyze transactions, at the time of journalizing, at the time of posting, or at both times?

5. What is the general sequence of accounts in the ledger?

6. (a) When are account numbers recorded in the posting reference column of the journal? (b) What two things does the presence of a number in the posting reference column of the journal indicate?

7. Does the amount listed for Cash in the trial balance represent (a) the cash at the beginning of the period, (b) the receipts during the period, (c) the receipts minus the disbursements during the period, or (d) the balance of cash on the trial balance date?

8. At the end of August it is determined that cash of $78 received from William Stubbs on account was credited to Sales rather than to Accounts Receivable. (a) What effect would this error have on the trial balance totals? (b) When would such an error usually be discovered?

9. Give an example of (a) a transposition and (b) a slide.

10. In journalizing a check for $125.42 in payment for supplies, the amounts are recorded and posted as $152.42. (a) Would the error cause the trial balance to be out of balance? (b) Would your answer be the same if the entry had been journalized correctly but the debit to Supplies had been posted as $152.42?

11. Describe the three steps involved in posting the debit portion of the following journal entry (Equipment is Account No. 18):

Page 12

19--					
Dec.	10	Equipment		2,000	
		Accounts Payable			2,000

12. Are the totals of the Sundry Accounts Debit and Credit columns of a four-column journal posted to the ledger? Explain.

13. Would it be feasible to include enough special columns in a multicolumn journal to make Sundry Accounts Debit and Credit columns unnecessary?

14. Is it necessary to add the debit and the credit columns of a two-column journal at the end of the month? Explain.

15. An invoice is received for $500 of store equipment and $40 of store supplies purchased on account. Give the compound journal entry to record the transaction.

Exercises

1. The Nelson Employment Service has the following accounts in its ledger: Cash; Accounts Receivable; Supplies; Office Equipment; Accounts Payable; Mary Nelson, Capital; Mary Nelson, Drawing; Fees Income; Rent Expense; Advertising Expense; Utilities Expense; Miscellaneous Expense.

Record the following transactions completed during the month of June of the current year in a two-column journal:

June 1. Paid rent for the month, $100.
     3. Paid cash for supplies, $20.
     9. Collected accounts receivable, $175.
   15. Purchased office equipment on account, $250.
   20. Paid creditor on account, $75.
   24. Paid advertising, $25.
   29. Withdrew cash for personal use, $200.
   30. Paid telephone and electricity bills for the month, $42.
   30. Fees earned and billed for month, $525.

2. Record the transactions given in Exercise 1 in a four-column journal similar to the one on page 81.

3. A number of errors in posting from a two-column journal are described below. Assuming in each case that no other errors had occurred during the month, you are to indicate: (1) whether the trial balance at the end of the month would be out of balance; (2) if answer to (1) is "yes," the amount by which the trial balance totals would differ; and (3) which column of the trial balance would have the larger total. Use a tabular form for your answers, employing the following headings:

Error	(1) Out of Balance (yes or no)	(2) Difference (amount)	(3) Larger Total (Dr. or Cr.)

(a) A debit of $378 to Prepaid Insurance was posted as $738.
(b) A credit of $100 to Accounts Receivable was posted to Sales.
(c) A debit of $200 to Accounts Payable was not posted.
(d) A debit of $300 to Supplies was posted twice.
(e) A credit of $50 to Accounts Receivable was posted as a debit.
(f) An entry debiting Advertising Expense and crediting Cash for $30 was not posted.
(g) A credit of $1,400 to Cash was posted as $140.

4. A number of errors in recording transactions are described below. Present the necessary correcting entries in a two-column journal.

    (a) Cash of $540 received from a customer on account was recorded as a debit to Cash and a credit to Accounts Receivable for $450.

    (b) A $300 purchase of store supplies was charged to Advertising Expense.

    (c) Rent of $90 for the current month was recorded as a debit to Prepaid Rent and a credit to Cash.

    (d) A cash withdrawal of $250 was recorded as a debit to D. R. Jones, Capital and a credit to Cash.

    (e) Equipment of $1,000 purchased on account was recorded as a debit to Buildings and a credit to Cash.

Problems

4-1. The chart of accounts of Carson Decorating Co. includes the following accounts: Cash, 11; Accounts Receivable, 12; Supplies, 13; Prepaid Insurance, 14; Truck, 16; Equipment, 18; Notes Payable, 21; Accounts Payable, 22; A. R. Carson, Capital, 31; A. R. Carson, Drawing, 32; Sales, 41; Wages Expense, 51; Rent Expense, 53; Truck Expense, 54; Miscellaneous Expense, 59.

The enterprise completed the following transactions during September of the current year:

Sept. 16. The proprietor invested cash, $1,800, and equipment, $200, in the business.

     16. Purchased a truck for $3,200, paying $500 cash and giving a note payable for the remainder.

     17. Purchased supplies for cash, $160.

     17. Purchased additional equipment on account, $125.

     18. Paid rent for period of September 16 to end of month, $50.

     19. Received cash for job completed, $90.

     22. Purchased supplies on account, $315.

     23. Paid wages of employees, $420.

     25. Paid creditors on account, $230.

     26. Paid premiums on property and casualty insurance, $285.

     27. Recorded sales on account and sent bills to customers, $1,850.

     28. Received cash for job completed, $160. This sale had not been recorded previously.

     29. Paid miscellaneous expenses, $31.

     29. Received an invoice for truck expenses, to be paid in October, $43.

     30. Received cash from customers on account, $1,200.

     30. Paid wages of employees, $440.

     30. Withdrew cash for personal use, $250.

Instructions: (1) Open accounts in the ledger in accordance with the list presented above.

    (2) Record the transactions for September in a two-column journal.

    (3) Post from the journal to the ledger.

    (4) Take a trial balance of the ledger.

4-2. The ledger of Best Shoe Repairs includes the accounts listed below. The amounts shown for the asset, liability, and capital accounts are the balances as of January 1 of the current year.

Acct. No.	Account Title	Balance	Acct. No.	Account Title	Balance
11	Cash..............	$1,962.50	22	Accounts Payable.....	$ 569.40
12	Supplies............	637.00	31	J. R. Boone, Capital..	7,685.20
13	Prepaid Insurance....	58.90	32	J. R. Boone, Drawing.	———
14	Prepaid Rent........	———	41	Service Sales.........	———
16	Equipment..........	7,938.20	51	Wages Expense.......	———
17	Accumulated Depr....	2,342.00	52	Utilities Expense.....	———
21	Notes Payable.......	———	53	Advertising Expense...	———
			58	Miscellaneous Expense	———

The transactions completed by the business during January were as follows:

Jan.   2. Paid cash for advertising, $25.
       2. Paid rent for three months, $300.
       4. Purchased supplies on account, $126.50.
       5. Purchased repair equipment for $1,200, paying $300 cash and giving a note payable for the balance.
       6. Recorded cash sales for the week, $432.60.
       8. Paid premium on property insurance, $42.
      10. Paid creditors on account, $536.50.
      13. Paid biweekly wages, $420.
      13. Recorded cash sales for the week, $386.30.
      15. Paid cash for repairs to equipment, $73.50.
      16. Proprietor withdrew cash for personal use, $200.
      18. Purchased supplies on account, $215.90.
      20. Recorded cash sales for the week, $493.10.
      23. Returned supplies purchased on the 18th for credit, $22.30.
      26. Paid miscellaneous expenses, $12.60.
      27. Recorded cash sales for the week, $315.60.
      27. Paid biweekly wages, $430.
      30. Proprietor withdrew cash for personal use, $200.
      31. Paid utilities expenses for the month, $43.80.
      31. Recorded cash sales for the remainder of the month, $235.20.

Instructions: (1) Open an account in the ledger for each item listed above.

(2) Record the balances in the accounts under the date of Jan. 1, write "Balance" in the Items column, and place a check mark in the posting reference column.

(3) Record the transactions for January in a four-column general journal similar to that illustrated on page 81.

(4) Total and rule the journal. Prove the equality of debits and credits.

(5) Post to the ledger.

(6) Take a trial balance of the ledger.

(7) How many additional postings would have been required if a two-column journal had been used instead of a four-column journal?

4-3. The selected transactions and errors described below relate to the accounts of Paradise Valley Development Co., Morris L. Mills, proprietor, during the current fiscal year:

June 6. Proprietor invested cash of $6,000 and office equipment of $750 on which there was a balance owed of $200. The account payable is to be recorded on the books of the firm.

July 10. Discovered that cash of $350, received from a customer on account, had been journalized and posted as a debit to Cash and a credit to Commissions Earned.

Aug. 15. Received $510 as payment on a note receivable ($500) and interest ($10).

Sept. 9. Discovered that $50 of office equipment returned to the supplier for credit had been journalized and posted as a debit to Accounts Receivable and a credit to Office Supplies.

Oct. 4. Acquired land and a building to be used as an office at a total cost of $12,000, of which $3,000 was allocated to the land. The property was encumbered by a mortgage of $8,000. Paid $4,000 cash and agreed to assume the responsibility for paying the mortgage.

Nov. 4. Paid the installment due on the mortgage, $400, and interest, $40.

Dec. 1. Discovered that a cash payment of $10 for advertising had been journalized and posted as a debit to Miscellaneous Expense of $100 and a credit to Cash of $100.

Dec. 12. Discovered that a withdrawal of $500 by the proprietor had been charged to Office Salary Expense.

Instructions: Journalize the transactions and the corrections in a two-column journal. When there are more than two items in an entry, present the entry in compound form.

4-4. Henry Wheeler owns and manages Wheeler Realty, which acts as an agent in buying, selling, renting, and managing real estate. The trial balance of the ledger on May 31 of the current year is shown at the top of the following page.

The following transactions were completed by Wheeler Realty during the month of June:

June 1. Purchased office equipment on account, $350.

2. Paid rent for month, $250.

4. Purchased office supplies on account, $41.

10. Received cash from clients on account, $2,394.

12. Paid premium on automobile insurance, $195.

15. Paid salaries and commissions, $1,370.

15. Recorded revenue earned and billed to clients during first half of month, $2,340.

16. Returned for credit an item of office equipment purchased on June 1, $25.

18. Paid creditors on account, $552.

20. Received cash from clients on account, $1,986.

23. Paid advertising expense, $138.

24. Discovered that the amount stated for the transaction of June 4 was a transposition.

28. Paid automobile expenses, $76.

Wheeler Realty
Trial Balance
May 31, 19--

11	Cash..	2,314	
12	Accounts Receivable.........................	3,410	
13	Office Supplies..............................	115	
14	Prepaid Insurance...........................	249	
16	Automobile..................................	4,600	
17	Accumulated Depreciation — Automobile......		2,100
18	Office Equipment............................	2,530	
19	Accumulated Depreciation — Office Equipment..		990
21	Accounts Payable............................		186
31	Henry Wheeler, Capital......................		5,780
32	Henry Wheeler, Drawing.....................	5,000	
41	Revenue from Fees..........................		23,873
51	Salary and Commission Expense..............	12,400	
52	Rent Expense...............................	1,250	
53	Advertising Expense.........................	645	
54	Automobile Expense.........................	218	
59	Miscellaneous Expense.......................	198	
		32,929	32,929

June 28. Paid miscellaneous expenses, $48.

    29. Proprietor withdrew cash for personal use, $1,000.

    30. Recorded revenue earned and billed to clients during second half of month, $2,162.

    30. Paid salaries and commissions, $1,239.

Instructions: (1) Open an account in the ledger for each item listed in the trial balance of May 31.

(2) Record the balance in each account under the date of June 1, write the word "Balance" in the Items column, and place a check mark in the posting reference column.

(3) Record the transactions for June in a two-column journal.

(4) Post to the ledger.

(5) An error is discovered in billing the fees for the second half of the month. The amount is $2,126 instead of $2,162. Journalize the correcting entry and post.

(6) Take a trial balance of the ledger.

(7) What is the nature of the balance in Accounts Payable?

Completion of the accounting cycle

Trial balance and accounting statements

The trial balance prepared at the close of an accounting period provides much, but not all, of the information needed in preparing the financial statements. During the period all transactions between the enterprise and other companies or individuals were journalized and posted to the ledger. Barring errors, it might seem reasonable to assume that the account balances listed in the trial balance are the correct amounts for use in preparing the balance sheet, the income statement, and the capital statement. The assumption of correctness is valid for some accounts but not for others. For example, the balance of the cash account represents the amount of cash available on the last day of the period. On the other hand, the balance of the supplies account represents the cost of the supplies in stock at the beginning of the period plus the cost of those acquired during the period. Some of these supplies have been used during the period and consequently the balance of the account is greater than the cost of the supplies available at the end of the period.

Similarly, the balances in the prepaid insurance account and the other prepaid expense accounts will be greater than the cost of the unexpired assets remaining at the end of the period. Transactions between the enterprise and outsiders that affected these accounts were recorded as they occurred, but the day-by-day expirations of the assets have not been recorded.

Data in the trial balance may also be incomplete because of unrecorded revenue or expense of the period that will not be collected or paid until some later date. For example, salaries incurred between the last pay day and the end of the fiscal period would not be recorded in the accounts because salaries are customarily recorded only when they are paid. They are an expense of the period, however, because the services were rendered during the period, and they are a liability as of the last day of the period because they are owed to the employees.

The foregoing examples of unrecorded transactions of an internal nature evidence the need for additional accounting procedures that will provide correct data for the financial statements.

Mixed accounts and business operations

An account with a balance that is partly a balance sheet amount and partly an income statement amount is called a *mixed account*. For example, the balance of the supplies account, as listed on the trial balance, represents the cost of all supplies on hand at the beginning of the period plus those purchased during the period. It is known that some of the supplies have been used. Therefore, the trial balance amount is composed of two elements, the supplies on hand at the end of the period, which is an unexpired cost or an asset, and the supplies used during the period, which is an expired cost or an expense. It is for this reason that it is termed a mixed account. Before financial statements are prepared, it is necessary to determine the amount applicable to each type of cost. The amount of the asset can be determined by counting the quantity of each of the various commodities, multiplying each quantity by the unit cost of that particular commodity, and totaling the dollar amounts thus obtained. The resulting figure is the supplies inventory. The cost of the supplies consumed is then determined by deducting the amount of the inventory from the balance of the supplies account. On the basis of this information, the cost of the supplies used is transferred from the asset account to an expense account.

If it is known at the time of the expenditure that a payment for future services will become an expense in its entirety by the end of the accounting period, the charge may be made directly to an expense account. It will be a mixed account during the period, but it will be wholly expense at the end of the period. For example, if rent for March is paid on March 1, it is almost entirely an asset at the time of payment. The asset expires gradually from day to day, and at the end of the month the entire amount has become an expense. The payment may therefore be recorded as a debit to Rent Expense, as the true facts will be reflected at the close of the period without the necessity of an additional entry. On the other hand, if the period for which the rent is paid extends beyond the current fiscal period, the payment may be debited to the asset Prepaid Rent. At the end of the fiscal period it is then necessary to transfer the expired portion of the rent from Prepaid Rent to Rent Expense.

Adjusting process

The entries required at the end of a fiscal period to record internal transactions are called *adjusting entries*. In a broad sense they may be said to be corrections to the ledger. But the necessity for bringing the ledger up to date is a planned part of the accounting procedure; it is not caused by errors. The term "adjusting entries" is therefore more appropriate than "correcting entries."

The illustrations of adjusting entries that follow are based on the ledger of Hull Print Shop. T accounts are used in place of the standard form of accounts and the adjusting entries are shown in bold face type to differentiate them from the entries recorded during the month.

Prepaid expenses. According to Hull's trial balance appearing on page 78, the balance in the supplies account on October 31 is $750. Some of these supplies (paper, ink, etc.) have been used during the past month and some are still in stock. If the amount of either is known, the other can be readily determined. It is more economical to determine the cost of the supplies on hand at the end of the month than to keep a record of those used during the period. Assuming that the inventory of supplies on October 31 is $230, the amount to be transferred from the asset account to the expense account is determined as follows:

Supplies available (balance of account)............................. $750
Supplies on hand (inventory)..................................... 230
Supplies used (amount of adjustment)............................. $520

Increases in expense accounts are recorded as debits and decreases in asset accounts are recorded as credits. Hence the adjusting entry for supplies is a debit to Supplies Expense and a credit to Supplies of $520. After the $520 has been transferred to Supplies Expense, the asset account has a debit balance of $230 and the expense account has a debit balance of $520.

SUPPLIES				SUPPLIES EXPENSE	
Oct. 2	400	**Oct. 31**	**520**	**Oct. 31** **520**	
20	350				
	7 5 0				

Prepaid Rent is another mixed account that requires adjustment at the end of the accounting period. The debit balance in this account represents in part an expense of the current period and in part a prepayment of expense of future periods. The portion that is expense should be transferred to the expense account, Rent Expense. After this is done, the prepaid rent account and the rent expense account will accurately reflect the true situation.

The debit of $600 in the prepaid rent account represents payment of rent for three months, October, November, and December. At the end of October, the rent expense account should be increased (debited) and the prepaid rent account should be decreased (credited) for $200, the rental for one month.   The two accounts appear as follows after the adjusting entry has been recorded:

PREPAID RENT		RENT EXPENSE	
Oct. 2 600	Oct. 31 200	Oct. 31 200	

The prepaid rent account now has a debit balance of $400, which is an asset; the rent expense account has a debit balance of $200, which is an expense.

If adjustments for prepayments are not made, assets and proprietorship will be overstated on the balance sheet and net income will be overstated on the income statement.

Plant assets. All plant assets except land gradually lose their usefulness with the passage of time. This loss of usefulness, which is called *depreciation*, must be recorded at the end of each fiscal period. The adjusting entry is similar to those illustrated in the preceding section in that there is a transfer from an asset account to an expense account. The amount to be transferred to expense, however, must be based on estimate rather than on verifiable facts, as in the case of expiration of rent and other prepaid expenses. Because of this and the desire to present both the original cost and the accumulated depreciation on the balance sheet, the reduction of the asset is credited to an account entitled "Accumulated Depreciation."

The adjusting entry to record depreciation for October is illustrated in the T accounts below. The estimated amount of depreciation[1] for the month is $40.

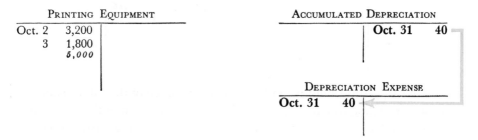

PRINTING EQUIPMENT		ACCUMULATED DEPRECIATION	
Oct. 2 3,200			Oct. 31 40
3 1,800			
5,000			
		DEPRECIATION EXPENSE	
		Oct. 31 40	

The accumulated depreciation account is a contra asset account. The $40 increase in the account represents a decrease in the printing equip-

---

[1]Methods of estimating depreciation will be presented in a later chapter.

ment account. The relationship of the two accounts is perhaps indicated best by the manner in which they are presented on the balance sheet, which is as follows:

Plant assets:
Printing equipment. $5,000
    Less accumulated depreciation. 40 $4,960

The difference between cost and accumulated depreciation represents the unexpired cost of the plant asset and is customarily referred to as *book value.*

Accrued expenses (liabilities). It is customary to pay for some types of services and commodities, such as insurance and supplies, in advance of their use. It is also customary to receive other services and commodities for which payment is not made until after they have been consumed. One of the most common examples is salaries. The expense accrues day by day and payment is made on a weekly, biweekly, or other regular basis. If the last day of a pay period does not coincide with the last day of the fiscal period, there is an expense and a liability that must be recorded in the accounts by an adjusting entry.

The data in the T accounts below were taken from the ledger of Hull Print Shop. The debits of $240 on October 13 and 27 in the salary expense account were biweekly payments on alternate Fridays for the payroll periods ended on those days. The salaries earned on Monday and Tuesday, October 30 and 31, amount to $48. This amount is an additional expense of October and it is therefore debited to the salary expense account. It is also a liability as of October 31 and it is therefore credited to Salaries Payable.

SALARIES PAYABLE				SALARY EXPENSE	
	Oct. 31	48	Oct. 13	240	
			27	240	
				480	
			31	**48**	

After the adjustment is made, the debit balance of the salary expense account is $528, which is the actual expense for the month; the credit balance of $48 in Salaries Payable is the liability for salaries owed as of October 31. If no adjustment were made for the accrued salaries, the net income would be overstated on the income statement, and the liabilities would be understated and the proprietorship overstated on the balance sheet.

Work sheet

Adjustments such as those just discussed must be considered in preparing the income statement and the balance sheet. But before the adjustments are actually recorded in the journal and posted to the ledger, it is usually customary to prepare a form known as a *work sheet*. Its use lessens the chance of overlooking an adjustment, provides a check on the accuracy of the work, and arranges data in a logical form for the preparation of the statements.

The work sheet for Hull Print Shop is presented on page 96. Note that there are three parts to the heading: (1) the name of the enterprise, (2) the title "Work Sheet," and (3) the period of time covered. It has columns for account numbers and titles and ten money columns, arranged in five pairs of debit and credit columns. The principal headings of the five sets of money columns are as follows:

1. Trial Balance
2. Adjustments
3. Adjusted Trial Balance
4. Income Statement
5. Balance Sheet

Trial Balance columns. The first step in the preparation of the work sheet is the trial balance. The trial balance may be prepared on another sheet first and then copied on the work sheet, or it may be prepared directly on the work sheet.

Adjustments columns. The adjustments required at the end of the period are recorded in the Adjustments columns. The order in which they are recorded is immaterial. Inasmuch as the debit and the credit portions of an adjustment are usually widely separated on the work sheet, it is customary to cross-reference them by inserting a letter at the left of each item. Some of the accounts requiring adjustment do not appear in the trial balance. In such cases the appropriate account titles are inserted below the trial balance as they are needed.

The adjusting entries for Hull Print Shop were discussed earlier in the chapter. It should be understood that the T accounts were used only for purposes of illustration. In practice the adjustments are recorded directly on the work sheet on the basis of inventory figures and other analyses prepared by the accounting department.

Adjusting entries recorded on the work sheet appearing on page 96 are as follows:

(a) *Supplies.* The supplies account has a debit balance of $750; the cost of the supplies on hand at the end of the period is $230; therefore, the supplies expense for October is the difference between the two amounts, or $520. The adjustment is entered by

Hull Print Shop
Work Sheet
For Month Ended October 31, 1961

ACCT. NO.	ACCOUNT TITLES	TRIAL BALANCE Dr.	TRIAL BALANCE Cr.	ADJUSTMENTS Dr.	ADJUSTMENTS Cr.	ADJUSTED TRIAL BALANCE Dr.	ADJUSTED TRIAL BALANCE Cr.	INCOME STATEMENT Dr.	INCOME STATEMENT Cr.	BALANCE SHEET Dr.	BALANCE SHEET Cr.
11	Cash	76000				76000				76000	
12	Accounts Receivable	58500				58500				58500	
14	Supplies	75000			(a) 52000	23000				23000	
15	Prepaid Rent	60000			(d) 20000	40000				40000	
18	Printing Equipment	500000				500000				500000	
21	Accounts Payable		140000				140000				140000
31	David Hull, Capital		510000				510000				510000
32	David Hull, Drawing	50000				50000				50000	
41	Sales		228000				228000		228000		
51	Salary Expense	48000		(e) 4800		52800		52800			
59	Miscellaneous Expense	10500				10500		10500			
		878000	878000								
52	Supplies Expense			(a) 52000		52000		52000			
53	Rent Expense			(d) 20000		20000		20000			
54	Depreciation Expense			(c) 4000		4000		4000			
19	Accumulated Depreciation				(c) 4000		4000				4000
22	Salaries Payable				(e) 4800		4800				4800
				80800	80800	886800	886800	139300	228000	747500	658500
	Net Income							88700			88700
								228000	228000	747500	747500

Ten-column work sheet

writing (1) *Supplies Expense* in the Account Titles column, (2) *$520.00* in the Adjustments Dr. column on the same line, and (3) *$520.00* in the Adjustments Cr. column on the line with Supplies.

(b) *Rent.* The prepaid rent account has a debit balance of $600, which represents a payment for three months beginning October 1; therefore, the rent expense for October is $200. The adjustment is entered by writing (1) *Rent Expense* in the Account Titles column, (2) *$200.00* in the Adjustments Dr. column on the same line, and (3) *$200.00* in the Adjustments Cr. column on the line with Prepaid Rent.

(c) *Depreciation.* Depreciation of the printing equipment for the month is estimated at $40. This expired portion of the cost of the equipment is a reduction in the asset and an expense. The adjustment is entered by writing (1) *Depreciation Expense* in the Account Titles column, (2) *$40.00* in the Adjustments Dr. column on the same line, (3) *Accumulated Depreciation* in the Account Titles column, and (4) *$40.00* in the Adjustments Cr. column on the same line.

(d) *Salaries.* Salaries accrued but not paid at the end of October amount to $48. This is an increase in expense and an increase in liabilities. The adjustment is entered by writing (1) *$48.00* in the Adjustments Dr. column on the same line with Salary Expense, (2) *Salaries Payable* in the Account Titles column, and (3) *$48.00* in the Adjustments Cr. column on the same line.

The final step in completing the Adjustments columns is to prove the equality of debits and credits by totaling and ruling the two columns.

Adjusted Trial Balance columns. The data in the Trial Balance columns and the Adjustments columns are now combined and entered in the Adjusted Trial Balance columns. This is done for each account title listed, beginning at the top of the sheet and proceeding with each account in order. In the illustration, Cash has a debit balance of $760 in the Trial Balance columns, and the Adjustments columns are blank; hence the $760 amount is carried over as a debit in the Adjusted Trial Balance columns. Similarly, the balance in Accounts Receivable is carried over. Supplies has a debit balance of $750 and a credit adjustment of $520, which yields an adjusted debit balance of $230.

This procedure is continued until all account balances, with or without adjustment as the case may be, have been entered in the Adjusted Trial Balance columns. Note that for accounts listed below the trial balance totals, the amount of the adjustment becomes the adjusted balance of the account. For example, Supplies Expense has an initial balance of zero and a debit adjustment of $520, yielding an adjusted debit balance of $520.

The Adjusted Trial Balance columns are completed by totaling and ruling the two columns to prove that the equality of debits and credits has been maintained.

Income Statement and Balance Sheet columns. Each amount entered in the Adjusted Trial Balance columns is extended to one of the remaining four columns. Asset, liability, and proprietorship items are extended to the Balance Sheet columns, and revenue and expense items are extended to the Income Statement columns. All debit balances in the Adjusted Trial Balance columns will then appear in either the Balance Sheet Dr. column or the Income Statement Dr. column, and all credit balances will likewise appear in the appropriate credit columns.

After all of the balances have been extended, the four columns are totaled. The amount of the net income or the net loss for the period is then determined by ascertaining the amount of the difference between the totals of the two Income Statement columns. If the credit column total is greater than the debit column total, the excess is the net income. For the work sheet presented on page 96, the computation is as follows:

Total of credit column (revenue).............................	$2,280.00
Total of debit column (expenses).............................	1,393.00
Net income (excess of revenue over expenses)...................	$ 887.00

The income statement accounts are temporary proprietorship accounts that are used to accumulate changes in proprietorship during the fiscal period. At the end of the fiscal period, the net balance of all of these accounts is transferred to proprietorship. In this case, the net credit balance of $887 is transferred to the credit side of a proprietorship account. The transfer is shown on the work sheet by a debit entry in the Income Statement Dr. column and a credit entry in the Balance Sheet Cr. column. The words "Net Income" are written in the Account Titles column as an explanation of this transfer.

The columns are then totaled and ruled in the manner shown on page 96. The totals of the two Income Statement columns are equal because the net income, $887, was obtained as the difference between the original totals of these columns. The totals of the Balance Sheet columns are also equal because, after the net income has been transferred to the proprietorship account, Assets = Liabilities + Proprietorship.

If total expenses of the period should exceed total revenue, the subtotal of the Income Statement Dr. column would be greater than the subtotal of the credit column. The difference between the two amounts

ACCT. NO.	ACCOUNT TITLES	INCOME STATEMENT DR.	INCOME STATEMENT CR.	BALANCE SHEET DR.	BALANCE SHEET CR.
11	Cash			760 00	
12	Accounts Receivable			585 00	
14	Supplies			230 00	
22	Salaries Payable				48 00
		1393 00	2280 00	7475 00	6588 00
	Net Income	887 00			887 00
		2280 00	2280 00	7475 00	7475 00

Income Statement and Balance Sheet columns
of the work sheet totaled and ruled

would be the net loss for the period. Losses decrease proprietorship; therefore the net loss would be entered in the Income Statement Cr. column and be transferred to the Balance Sheet Dr. column as a decrease in proprietorship.

The work sheet is a device employed by the accountant as the basis for preparing financial statements and recording adjusting and closing entries in the journal. It is not a formal statement and does not take the place of the formal balance sheet and income statement. Since it is not presented to the proprietor, manager, or others interested in the business, it is customarily prepared in pencil.

Financial statements

The income statement, balance sheet, and capital statement prepared from the work sheet of Hull Print Shop for October are as follows:

Hull Print Shop
Income Statement
For Month Ended October 31, 1961

Sales		$2280 00
Operating expenses:		
Salary expense	$528 00	
Supplies expense	520 00	
Rent expense	200 00	
Depreciation expense	40 00	
Miscellaneous expense	105 00	
Total operating expenses		1393 00
Net income from operations		$887 00

Income statement

Hull Print Shop
Balance Sheet
October 31, 1961

Assets			
Current assets:			
Cash	$ 760 00		
Accounts receivable	585 00		
Supplies	230 00		
Prepaid rent	400 00		
Total current assets			$1975 00
Plant assets:			
Printing equipment	$5000 00		
Less accumulated depreciation	40 00	4960 00	
Total assets			$6935 00
Liabilities			
Current liabilities:			
Accounts payable	$1400 00		
Salaries payable	48 00		
Total current liabilities			$1448 00
Proprietorship			
David Hull, Capital			5487 00
Total liabilities and proprietorship			$6935 00

Balance sheet

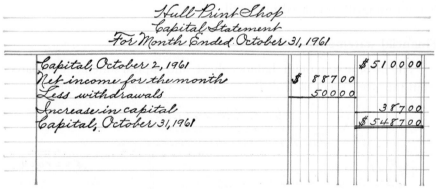

Hull Print Shop
Capital Statement
For Month Ended October 31, 1961

Capital, October 2, 1961			$5100 00
Net income for the month	$ 887 00		
Less withdrawals	500 00		
Increase in capital			387 00
Capital, October 31, 1961			$5487 00

Capital statement

All the accounting information for the income statement and the balance sheet is taken from the last four columns of the work sheet. In preparing the capital statement it is necessary to refer to the capital account in the ledger to determine the balance at the beginning of the period and the amount of any additional investments that may have been made during the period. In the illustration, the balance in the capital account remained unchanged during the period; hence the capital balance of $5,100 listed on the work sheet is the capital as of October 2. The amounts of net income and withdrawals for the period are taken from the Balance Sheet columns of the work sheet, and the balance of capital at the end of the period is determined arithmetically.

Journalizing and posting adjusting entries

After the financial statements have been prepared at the end of the fiscal period, the adjustments appearing on the work sheet are recorded in the accounts so as to bring the ledger into agreement with the financial statements.

As in the case of entries for transactions with outsiders, the adjusting entries must be recorded initially in the journal; they are then posted to the ledger. The entries are copied directly from the Adjustments columns of the work sheet, using the next available space in the journal. The entries are dated as of the last day of the accounting period, even though they are actually recorded at a later date. Each entry may be supported by an explanation, or the group may be identified by writing "Adjusting Entries" above the first entry in the series. The work sheet and supporting documents on adjustment data should be kept on file for future reference. The adjusting entries in the journal of Hull Print Shop appear below. The accounts to which the adjusting entries have been posted appear in the ledger beginning on page 105. All adjusting entries are identified in the items columns of the accounts as an aid to the student. It is not necessary that this be done in actual practice.

JOURNAL   PAGE 2

DATE	DESCRIPTION	POST. REF.	DEBIT	CREDIT
	Adjusting Entries			
31	Supplies Expense	52	5 2 0 00	
	Supplies	14		5 2 0 00
31	Rent Expense	53	2 0 0 00	
	Prepaid Rent	15		2 0 0 00
31	Depreciation Expense	54	4 0 00	
	Accumulated Depreciation	19		4 0 00
31	Salary Expense	51	4 8 00	
	Salaries Payable	22		4 8 00

Adjusting entries

Closing entries

As was explained earlier, the revenue, expense, and drawing accounts are temporary accounts employed in classifying and summarizing changes in proprietorship during the accounting period. At the end of the period the net effect of these accounts must be recorded in the capital account so that its balance will agree with the amount of capital shown on the balance sheet. The balances in the temporary proprietorship accounts must also be reduced to zero so that they can be used to record data for the ensuing accounting period. Both objectives are accomplished by a series of entries known as *closing entries*.

An account titled *Expense and Revenue Summary* is used for summarizing the data in the revenue and expense accounts. It is employed only at the end of the accounting period and is both opened and closed during the closing process. Various other titles are used for the account, including *Profit and Loss Summary* and *Income Summary*.

The entries required to close the temporary proprietorship accounts at the end of the period are as follows:

1. Debit each revenue account for the amount of its balance and credit Expense and Revenue Summary for the total revenue.

2. Credit each expense account for the amount of its balance and debit Expense and Revenue Summary for the total expense.

3. Debit Expense and Revenue Summary for the amount of its balance (net income) and credit the capital account for the same amount. (Debit and credit will be reversed for a net loss.)

4. Credit the drawing account for the amount of its balance and debit the capital account for the same amount.

After the foregoing series of entries are journalized and posted to the ledger, the balance in the capital account will agree with the amount shown on the balance sheet and the revenue, expense, and drawing accounts will be closed (zero balances). The closing entries for Hull Print Shop are illustrated in T accounts on page 103. The arrows indicate the direction in the data flow.

The account titles and amounts needed in journalizing the closing entries may be obtained from the work sheet, from the income and capital statements, or directly from the accounts in the ledger. An advantage of using the work sheet as the source is that all of the data appear on one sheet. The amounts appearing in the Income Statement columns correspond to the balances of the revenue and expense accounts in the ledger and are used for the first two closing entries. The amount of net income or loss appears at the bottom of the Income Statement and Balance Sheet

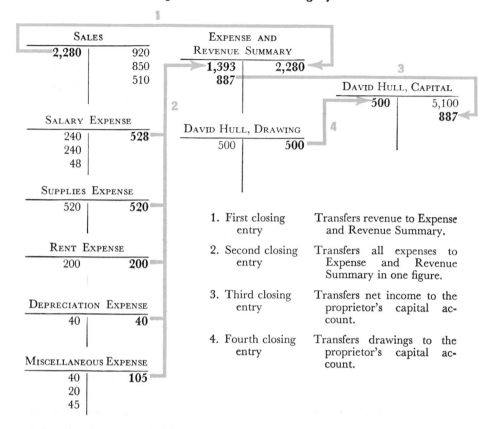

SALES	
2,280	920
	850
	510

SALARY EXPENSE	
240	528
240	
48	

SUPPLIES EXPENSE	
520	520

RENT EXPENSE	
200	200

DEPRECIATION EXPENSE	
40	40

MISCELLANEOUS EXPENSE	
40	105
20	
45	

EXPENSE AND REVENUE SUMMARY	
1,393	2,280
887	

DAVID HULL, DRAWING	
500	500

DAVID HULL, CAPITAL	
500	5,100
	887

1. First closing entry — Transfers revenue to Expense and Revenue Summary.

2. Second closing entry — Transfers all expenses to Expense and Revenue Summary in one figure.

3. Third closing entry — Transfers net income to the proprietor's capital account.

4. Fourth closing entry — Transfers drawings to the proprietor's capital account.

columns and is used for the third closing entry. Finally, reference to the balance of the drawing account appearing in the Balance Sheet Dr. column supplies the information needed for the fourth closing entry.

The data for the closing entries appearing in the journal on page 104 are taken from the work sheet for Hull Print Shop on page 96. Each journal entry may be supported by an explanation, or the group may be identified by writing "Closing Entries" above the first entry in the series. The entries are dated as of the last day of the accounting period, even though they are actually recorded at a later date.

The accounts to which these closing entries are posted are shown in the ledger of Hull Print Shop beginning on page 105. All closing entries are identified in the items columns of the accounts as an aid to the student. It is not necessary that this be done in actual practice.

A frequently used variant of the third closing entry is to close Expense and Revenue Summary to the drawing account instead of the capital account. The balance of the drawing account then represents the net increase or decrease in capital for the period, and in the final entry this balance is closed to the capital account.

JOURNAL   PAGE 3

DATE	DESCRIPTION	POST. REF.	DEBIT	CREDIT
	Closing Entries			
1961 Oct 31	Sales	41	2 2 8 0 00	
	Expense and Revenue Summary	33		2 2 8 0 00
31	Expense and Revenue Summary	33	1 3 9 3 00	
	Salary Expense	51		5 2 8 00
	Miscellaneous Expense	59		1 0 5 00
	Supplies Expense	52		5 2 0 00
	Rent Expense	53		2 0 0 00
	Depreciation Expense	54		4 0 00
31	Expense and Revenue Summary	33	8 8 7 00	
	David Hull, Capital	31		8 8 7 00
31	David Hull, Capital	31	5 0 0 00	
	David Hull, Drawing	32		5 0 0 00

Closing entries

Ruling and balancing the accounts

Following the completion of the closing process, the accounts in the ledger are prepared to receive entries for the ensuing fiscal period. This is done by ruling them in such a manner as to segregate entries of the old period just ended from entries of the new period just beginning. All of the procedures are illustrated in the ledger of Hull Print Shop beginning on page 105. As each procedure is explained, reference will be made to one of the accounts in the ledger that illustrates the procedure.

Temporary proprietorship accounts. After the revenue, expense, and drawing accounts have been closed, the debits in each account are equal to the credits in each account. To avoid the possibility of erroneously combining any of these entries with entries of the ensuing period, it is necessary to proceed as follows (see Sales):

1. Draw a single ruling across the amount columns immediately below the last figure in the longer of the two columns and on the same line of the shorter column.
2. Insert the total of each column below the single rulings.
3. Draw double rulings below the totals and across all columns except the Items columns.

If an account has only one debit and one credit (see Supplies Expense), there is no need to repeat the same figures as totals; the double rulings are drawn immediately below the entries.

Cash — ACCOUNT NO. 11

DATE	ITEMS	POST. REF.	DEBIT	DATE	ITEMS	POST. REF.	CREDIT
1961 Oct 2		1	900 00	1961 Oct 2		1	600 00
4		1	525 00	6		1	40 00
16		1	920 00	10		1	400 00
31	760.00	2	850 00 / 3 1 9 5 00	13		1	240 00
				20		1	350 00
				27		2	240 00
				31		2	20 00
				31		2	45 00
				31		2	500 00 / 2435 00
				31	Balance	✓	760 00
			3 195 00				3 195 00
Nov 1	Balance	✓	760 00				

Accounts Receivable — ACCOUNT NO. 12

DATE	ITEMS	POST. REF.	DEBIT	DATE	ITEMS	POST. REF.	CREDIT
1961 Oct 2		1	600 00	1961 Oct 4		1	525 00
31	585.00	2	510 00 / 1 1 1 0 00	31	Balance	✓	585 00
			1 1 1 0 00				1 1 1 0 00
Nov 1	Balance	✓	585 00				

Supplies — ACCOUNT NO. 14

DATE	ITEMS	POST. REF.	DEBIT	DATE	ITEMS	POST. REF.	CREDIT
1961 Oct 2		1	400 00	1961 Oct 31	Adjusting	2	520 00
20		1	350 00 / 7 5 0 00	31	Balance	✓	230 00
			750 00				750 00
Nov 1	Balance	✓	230 00				

Prepaid Rent — ACCOUNT NO. 15

DATE	ITEMS	POST. REF.	DEBIT	DATE	ITEMS	POST. REF.	CREDIT
1961 Oct 2		1	600 00	1961 Oct 31	Adjusting	2	200 00
				31	Balance	✓	400 00
			600 00				600 00
Nov 1	Balance	✓	400 00				

Ledger after the accounts have been adjusted, closed,
ruled, and balanced

Printing Equipment — ACCOUNT NO. 18

DATE	ITEMS	POST. REF.	DEBIT	DATE	ITEMS	POST. REF.	CREDIT
1961 Oct. 2		1	3200 00	1961 Oct. 31	Balance	✓	5000 00
3		1	1800 00				
			5000 00				5000 00
Nov. 1	Balance	✓	5000 00				

Accumulated Depreciation — ACCOUNT NO. 19

DATE	ITEMS	POST. REF.	DEBIT	DATE	ITEMS	POST. REF.	CREDIT
				1961 Oct. 31	Adjusting	2	40 00

Accounts Payable — ACCOUNT NO. 21

DATE	ITEMS	POST. REF.	DEBIT	DATE	ITEMS	POST. REF.	CREDIT
1961 Oct. 10		1	400 00	1961 Oct. 3	1200.00	1	1800 00
31	Balance	✓	1400 00				
			1800 00				1800 00
				Nov. 1	Balance	✓	1400 00

Salaries Payable — ACCOUNT NO. 22

DATE	ITEMS	POST. REF.	DEBIT	DATE	ITEMS	POST. REF.	CREDIT
				1961 Oct. 31	Adjusting	2	48 00

David Hull, Capital — ACCOUNT NO. 31

DATE	ITEMS	POST. REF.	DEBIT	DATE	ITEMS	POST. REF.	CREDIT
1961 Oct. 31	Closing	3	500 00	1961 Oct. 2		1	5100 00
31	Balance	✓	5487 00	31	Closing	3	887 00
			5987 00				5987 00
				Nov. 1	Balance	✓	5487 00

David Hull, Drawing — ACCOUNT NO. 32

DATE	ITEMS	POST. REF.	DEBIT	DATE	ITEMS	POST. REF.	CREDIT
1961 Oct. 31		2	500 00	1961 Oct. 31	Closing	3	500 00

**Ledger after the accounts have been adjusted, closed,
ruled, and balanced — continued**

Expense and Revenue Summary   ACCOUNT NO. 33

DATE	ITEMS	POST. REF.	DEBIT	DATE	ITEMS	POST. REF.	CREDIT
1961 Oct. 31	Closing	3	1393 00	1961 Oct. 31	Closing	3	2280 00
31	Closing	3	887 00				
			2280 00				2280 00

Sales   ACCOUNT NO. 41

DATE	ITEMS	POST. REF.	DEBIT	DATE	ITEMS	POST. REF.	CREDIT
1961 Oct. 31	Closing	3	2280 00	1961 Oct. 16		1	920 00
				31		2	850 00
				31		2	510 00
			2280 00				2280 00

Salary Expense   ACCOUNT NO. 51

DATE	ITEMS	POST. REF.	DEBIT	DATE	ITEMS	POST. REF.	CREDIT
1961 Oct. 13		1	240 00	1961 Oct. 31	Closing	3	528 00
27		2	240 00				
31	Adjusting	2	48 00				
			528 00				528 00

Supplies Expense   ACCOUNT NO. 52

DATE	ITEMS	POST. REF.	DEBIT	DATE	ITEMS	POST. REF.	CREDIT
1961 Oct. 31	Adjusting	2	520 00	1961 Oct. 31	Closing	3	520 00

Rent Expense   ACCOUNT NO. 53

DATE	ITEMS	POST. REF.	DEBIT	DATE	ITEMS	POST. REF.	CREDIT
1961 Oct. 31	Adjusting	2	200 00	1961 Oct. 31	Closing	3	200 00

Depreciation Expense   ACCOUNT NO. 54

DATE	ITEMS	POST. REF.	DEBIT	DATE	ITEMS	POST. REF.	CREDIT
1961 Oct. 31	Adjusting	2	40 00	1961 Oct. 31	Closing	3	40 00

Ledger after the accounts have been adjusted, closed,
ruled, and balanced — continued

Miscellaneous Expense   ACCOUNT NO. 59

DATE	ITEMS	POST. REF.	DEBIT		DATE	ITEMS	POST. REF.	CREDIT
1961 Oct. 6		1	40 00		*1961* Oct. 31	Closing	3	105 00
31		2	20 00					
31		2	45 00					
			105 00					105 00

Ledger after the accounts have been adjusted, closed,
ruled, and balanced — concluded

Assets, liabilities, and capital. The entries in each asset, liability, and capital account are summarized and the balance is recorded in the account as the first item for the new period. The procedure for balancing and ruling the accounts is as follows (see Cash):

1. Insert the balance of the account in the amount column of the first available line of the smaller of the two sides. Write "Balance" in the Items column, place a check mark in the Posting Reference column to differentiate it from posted entries, and write the last day of the period in the Date column.
2. Draw a single ruling across the amount columns immediately below the last figure in the longer of the two columns and on the same line of the shorter column.
3. Insert the totals of each column below the single rulings.
4. Draw double rulings below the totals and across all columns except the items columns.
5. Insert the balance in the amount column of the side that was originally the larger, write "Balance" in the Items column, place a check mark in the Posting Reference column, and write the first day of the new period in the Date column.

If an account has only one entry (see Salaries Payable) there is no need for formal balancing and ruling.

Post-closing trial balance

The final procedure of the accounting cycle is the preparation of a post-closing trial balance. Its purpose is to assure that debit-credit equality has been maintained in the ledger throughout the adjusting, closing, and balancing processes. All accounts and amounts appearing on the post-closing trial balance will correspond exactly with those shown on the balance sheet. This includes the capital account, since the net effect of all entries in the temporary proprietorship accounts during the past period has been transferred to the capital account through the closing process.

The post-closing trial balance for Hull Print Shop is presented below. A common practice is to proceed directly from the balances in the ledger to the preparation of adding machine listings, omitting the more formalized procedure. The adding machine tapes then become, in effect, the post-closing trial balance.

Hull Print Shop
Post-Closing Trial Balance
October 31, 1961

11	Cash	76000	
12	Accounts Receivable	58500	
14	Supplies	23000	
15	Prepaid Rent	40000	
18	Printing Equipment	500000	
19	Accumulated Depreciation		4000
21	Accounts Payable		140000
22	Salaries Payable		4800
31	David Hull, Capital		548700
		697500	697500

Post-closing trial balance

Accounting cycle

The principal accounting procedures of a fiscal period have been presented in this and the preceding chapter. The sequence of procedures is frequently called the *accounting cycle*. It begins with the analysis and the journalizing of transactions and ends with the post-closing trial balance. Although there are many possible variations in details, the basic outline of the cycle is fundamental to accounting practice.

An understanding of all phases of the accounting cycle is essential as a foundation for further study of accounting principles and the uses of accounting data by management. The following outline summarizes the basic steps of the cycle:

1. Analyze transactions.
2. Journalize transactions.
3. Post the journal entries to the ledger.
4. Prepare a trial balance.

5. Assemble the data needed to adjust the accounts.
6. Prepare a work sheet.
7. Prepare the financial statements.
8. Journalize and post the adjusting entries.
9. Journalize and post the closing entries.
10. Rule and balance the accounts.
11. Prepare a post-closing trial balance.

Interim statements

In the illustrative case of Hull Print Shop the accounting cycle was completed in one month. Most business enterprises close the temporary proprietorship accounts only at the end of the fiscal year rather than at the end of each month. Regardless of the length of the period, the closing procedures are the same. In order to restrict the number of transactions and the physical space requirements, a period of one month was used in the illustration.

When the books are closed annually, only Steps 1 through 4 of the accounting cycle need to be repeated monthly. The completion of posting and the preparation of a trial balance at the end of each month is customary regardless of when the books are closed. If interim financial statements are to be prepared monthly, Steps 5 through 7 of the accounting cycle, ending with the financial statements, must also be completed monthly.

If the books are not closed each time the statements are prepared, the revenue and expense data for the interim income statements will be cumulative. For example, assuming a fiscal year that begins on January 1, the amounts in the income statement columns of the February work sheet will be the cumulative totals for January and February; the revenue and expenses on the March work sheet will be the cumulative totals for January, February, and March; and so on. An income statement for each may be prepared, however, by determining the amount of the increase of each revenue and expense item on successive cumulative statements. Thus the excess of sales for the three-month period ended March 31 over sales for the two-month period ended February 28 represents the sales figure for March.

Questions

1. Differentiate between unexpired costs and expired costs, using examples.

2. (a) Name three mixed accounts. (b) Will they be mixed accounts immediately after the adjusting entries have been recorded?

3. Indicate whether each of the following goods and services is customarily paid for in advance or after it has been consumed: (a) property insurance, (b) services of salesmen, (c) water, (d) electric power, (e) rent, (f) office supplies, (g) store equipment.

4. Does every adjusting entry affect both an income statement account and a balance sheet account?

5. Do all adjusting entries have an effect on the amount of net income reported?

6. On September 1, R. T. Cannon pays the rent on his store building for the month of September. (a) At the time of payment does he acquire an asset or is he paying an expense? (b) What is the justification for debiting Rent Expense at the time of payment?

7. (a) Explain the purpose of the depreciation expense account and the accumulated depreciation account. (b) What is the normal balance of each account? (c) Is it customary for the balances of the two accounts to be equal? (d) On what financial statements, if any, will each of the accounts appear?

8. In preparing statements for the month of January (books are closed annually on December 31), accrued salaries of $800 for January 28–31 are completely overlooked. In preparing the statements for the two-month period January–February, the accrued salaries of $400 for February 27–28 are given proper recognition. (a) Is net income overstated, understated, or correct for January? for February? for the two-month period January–February? (b) What items would be overstated or understated on the balance sheet as of January 31? as of February 28?

9. Does the work sheet take the place of financial statements? Discuss.

10. What is the purpose of the expense and revenue summary account?

11. Name the accounts in the following list that should be closed to Expense and Revenue Summary at the end of the fiscal year: (a) Advertising Expense, (b) Cash, (c) Depreciation Expense, (d) Notes Payable, (e) Office Supplies, (f) Prepaid Rent, (g) Sales, (h) Store Supplies Expense, (i) Taxes Expense, (j) Accumulated Depreciation.

12. Adjusting and closing entries are dated as of the last day of a fiscal period. Does this indicate that they are journalized and posted on that specific date? Explain.

13. Name the accounts in the following list that will ordinarily appear in the post-closing trial balance: (a) Advertising Expense, (b) Accumulated Depreciation, (c) Cash, (d) Prepaid Insurance, (e) Building, (f) Accounts Payable, (g) J. Booker, Drawing, (h) Depreciation Expense, (i) Insurance Expense, (j) Sales.

14. How frequently are the books customarily closed?

Exercises

1. A business enterprise pays weekly office salaries of $1,500 on Friday for the five-day week ending on Friday. Journalize the necessary adjusting entry assuming that the fiscal period ends (a) on Monday and (b) on Wednesday.

2. On January 3 a business enterprise pays $240 to the city for annual license fees, charging the amount to Prepaid Taxes. By the end of January the same enterprise has incurred a tax expense of $105 that is payable to the state in April. (a) Journalize the two adjusting entries required to bring the accounts up to date as of January 31. (b) What is the amount of tax expense incurred thus far?

3. The balance in the prepaid insurance account at the end of the year is $1,420. Journalize the adjusting entry required under each of the following assumptions: (a) The insurance expired during the year was $310. (b) The unexpired insurance applicable to future periods is $960.

4. (a) Journalize the required closing entries for the following accounts:

Robert Price, Capital		Robert Price, Drawing	
	40,000	6,000	

Expense and Revenue Summary	
82,000	96,000

(b) What is the amount of Price's capital?

5. (a) Journalize the adjusting entries posted to the accounts appearing below. (b) Journalize the closing entries, parts of which are posted to the accounts appearing below. (c) Name any open accounts that should have been closed.

Salary Expense		Prepaid Insurance	
1,600	3,720	300	100
1,600		400	
520			

Store Supplies		Accumulated Depreciation	
350	50		1,200
			600

Salaries Payable		Store Supplies Expense	
	520	50	50

Insurance Expense		Depreciation Expense	
100	100	600	

Problems

5-1. The trial balance of Mountain View Launderette at December 31, the end of the current fiscal year, and data needed for year-end adjustments are presented below.

Mountain View Launderette
Trial Balance
December 31, 19 - -

Cash...	1,960	
Laundry Supplies..............................	1,650	
Prepaid Insurance.............................	324	
Laundry Equipment...........................	10,600	
Accumulated Depreciation......................		3,400
Accounts Payable..............................		280
Mary Vance, Capital...........................		6,812
Mary Vance, Drawing..........................	4,800	
Sales..		12,820
Wages Expense................................	2,318	
Rent Expense..................................	900	
Utilities Expense..............................	495	
Miscellaneous Expense.........................	265	
	23,312	23,312

Adjustment data:
(a) Laundry supplies on hand at December 31................. $ 220
(b) Depreciation for the year................................ 1,080
(c) Insurance expired during the year....................... 170
(d) Wages accrued at December 31.......................... 35

Instructions: (1) Record the trial balance on a ten-column work sheet.

(2) Complete the work sheet.

(3) Prepare an income statement, a capital statement (no additional investments were made during the year), and a balance sheet in report form.

(4) Record the adjusting entries in a two-column journal.

(5) Record the closing entries in a two-column journal.

(6) Compute the following:

(a) Per cent of net income to sales.

(b) Per cent of net income to the capital balance at the beginning of the year.

If the working papers correlating with this textbook are not used, omit Problem 5-2.

5-2. The ledger of Douglas Fixit Service, as of September 30 of the current year, is presented in the working papers. The books had been closed on August 31.

Instructions: (1) Prepare a trial balance of the ledger, listing only the accounts with balances, on a ten-column work sheet.

(2) Complete the ten-column work sheet. Data for the adjustments are as follows:

Supplies on hand at September 30............................	$670.00
Insurance expired during the month........................	35.66
Depreciation on trucks for the month.......................	110.00
Depreciation on equipment for the month.................	50.00
Salaries accrued at September 30..........................	150.00

(3) Prepare an income statement, a capital statement, and a balance sheet in report form.

(4) Record the adjusting entries in a two-column journal and post.

(5) Record the closing entries in a two-column journal and post.

(6) Rule the temporary accounts. Balance and rule the remaining accounts that contain more than one entry.

(7) Take a post-closing trial balance.

5-3. At the end of each month Bowl-Mor Lanes prepares a cumulative income statement for the year to date, an income statement for the month, and a balance sheet as of the close of the month. The books are closed annually on December 31. The trial balance at March 31 of the current year and the adjustment data needed at March 31 of the current year are presented below.

Bowl-Mor Lanes

Trial Balance

March 31, 19 - -

Cash..	4,560	
Prepaid Insurance............................	2,284	
Bowling Supplies.............................	1,540	
Equipment...................................	42,000	
Accumulated Depreciation — Equipment.........		12,600
Building.....................................	96,000	
Accumulated Depreciation — Building...........		7,200
Land..	11,500	
Accounts Payable............................		5,794
Mortgage Payable (Due 1980)................		88,000
Frank Morgan, Capital.......................		37,305
Frank Morgan, Drawing......................	1,200	
Bowling Fees...............................		13,260
Salaries Expense............................	2,050	
Utilities Expense............................	1,120	
Repairs Expense............................	880	
Advertising Expense.........................	780	
Miscellaneous Expense.......................	245	
	164,159	164,159

Adjustment data at March 31 are:

(a)	Inventory of bowling supplies............................	$ 600
(b)	Insurance expired for the period January 1–March 31.......	630
(c)	Depreciation on equipment for the period January 1–March 31	1,050
(d)	Depreciation on building for the period January 1–March 31	600
(e)	Accrued salaries......................................	150

The income statement for the two months ended February 28, 19--, is as follows:

Bowl-Mor Lanes

Income Statement

For Two Months Ended February 28, 19--

Bowling fees...............................		$8,620
Operating expenses:		
Salaries expense............................	$1,400	
Utilities expense...........................	730	
Depreciation expense — equipment.............	700	
Bowling supplies expense.....................	620	
Repair expense..............................	610	
Advertising expense.........................	515	
Insurance expense...........................	420	
Depreciation expense — building..............	400	
Miscellaneous expense.......................	150	
Total operating expenses....................		5,545
Net income.................................		$3,075

Instructions: (1) Record the trial balance on a ten-column work sheet.

(2) Complete the work sheet.

(3) Prepare an interim income statement for the three months ended March 31 and a balance sheet at March 31.

(4) Prepare an income statement for March.

(5) Compute the per cent of net income to revenue for:

    (a) The two-month period ended February 28.

    (b) The three-month period ended March 31.

    (c) The month of March.

5-4. The accounts and their balances in the ledger of Pioneer Photographic Studio on December 31, the end of the current fiscal year, before adjustments, are as follows:

11	Cash.......................................	$ 4,785
12	Accounts Receivable........................	946
13	Photographic Supplies......................	2,384
14	Office Supplies............................	320
15	Prepaid Insurance..........................	398
16	Photographic Equipment.....................	14,630
17	Accumulated Depreciation — Photographic Equipment.......	5,310
18	Office Equipment...........................	2,437
19	Accumulated Depreciation — Office Equipment.............	682
21	Notes Payable..............................	2,100
22	Accounts Payable...........................	515
23	Rent Payable...............................	
24	Salaries Payable...........................	
31	Robert Murray, Capital.....................	7,887
32	Robert Murray, Drawing.....................	8,400
33	Expense and Revenue Summary................	
41	Sales......................................	35,200

51	Salary Expense	$14,627
52	Photographic Supplies Expense	
53	Rent Expense	1,500
54	Depreciation Expense — Photographic Equipment	
55	Advertising Expense	738
56	Depreciation Expense — Office Equipment	
57	Office Supplies Expense	
58	Insurance Expense	
59	Miscellaneous Expense	529

The data needed for the year-end adjustments are as follows:

(a) Inventory of photographic supplies on December 31 ...... $ 320
(b) Inventory of office supplies on December 31 110
(c) Depreciation on photographic equipment for the year 1,410
(d) Depreciation on office equipment for the year 230
(e) Insurance expired during the year 165
(f) The lease provides for a rental of 5% of the total sales for the year, with a minimum of $1,500 payable in monthly installments of $125.
(g) Salaries accrued on December 31 175

Instructions: (1) Open an account in the ledger for each account listed. Enter the balances in the appropriate accounts under date of December 31.

(2) Prepare a trial balance on a ten-column work sheet, listing only the accounts with balances.

(3) Complete the work sheet.

(4) Prepare an income statement, a capital statement (there were no additional investments during the year), and a balance sheet in report form.

(5) Record the adjusting entries in a two-column journal and post to the ledger accounts.

(6) Record the closing entries and post to the ledger accounts.

(7) Rule the closed accounts, and balance and rule the remaining accounts having more than one entry.

(8) Determine the sum of the:

(a) Debit balances in the ledger.

(b) Credit balances in the ledger.

Sales and cash receipts

Need for special journals

All the transactions of an enterprise may be recorded in a single two-column journal. A considerable saving of time may be effected, however, both in journalizing and posting, by expanding the journal to include special columns. This was demonstrated in Chapter 4 by adding a column for recording debits to Cash and a column for recording credits to Cash. The journalizing and posting process may be facilitated further by the addition of other special columns, such as Accounts Receivable Debit, Accounts Receivable Credit, and Sales Credit. A single multi-column journal is often satisfactory for a business employing only one bookkeeper, but when the volume of transactions is such that a number of bookkeepers are required, it is not practicable for all of them to use a single journal.

The customary practice in medium-size and large businesses is to employ a number of special journals, each of which is designed to record a particular type of transaction. Obviously, special journals are needed only for transactions that occur frequently. For example, most accounting systems employ a special journal for recording cash receipts and a special journal for recording cash payments because in most businesses there are many transactions of both types. A business that extends credit might advantageously use a special journal to record sales on account. On the other hand, a business that does not extend credit would have no need for such a journal.

In addition to variations in the number of special journals used by different types of businesses, there are also many possible variations in the design of any particular journal. For example, the sources of revenue of a financial institution, such as a bank, are quite different from those of a merchandising business. Both would use a special journal for cash receipts, but their journals would be unlike in many respects.

Merchandising

Special journals suitable for a trading or merchandising business will be described and illustrated in this chapter and the succeeding chapter.

Although the accounting procedures applicable to an enterprise engaged in buying and selling commodities are different in some respects from those employed by a service type of business, there are also many similarities. Therefore much of the discussion will apply equally to both types of business activity.

Merchandising activities may ordinarily be classified as *wholesale* or *retail*. Manufacturers, producers, and importers usually sell their goods to wholesalers, brokers, or directly to retailers. Wholesale merchants sell to retailers and to large consumers, such as schools and hospitals. Retail merchants sell to consumers.

The number, purpose, and design of the special journals used in merchandising will of necessity vary, depending upon the needs of the particular enterprise. In the typical firm of moderate size the transactions that occur most frequently and the special journals in which they are recorded are as follows:

Transactions		*Special Journals*
Sales on account	*recorded in*	Sales journal
Cash receipts	*recorded in*	Cash receipts journal
Purchases on account	*recorded in*	Purchases journal
Cash payments	*recorded in*	Cash payments journal

Although most of the transactions of a typical business may be recorded in the foregoing special journals, every business has some transactions that are neither sales or purchases on account, nor receipts or payments of cash. The journal used for recording these miscellaneous transactions is known as a *general journal*. The most common form of the general journal is the two-column journal that is illustrated in Chapter 4.

Frequency of sales transactions

The principal source of revenue of a business appears as the first item on the income statement. For a merchandising business this item is sales of merchandise, which is usually shortened to *Sales*. The number of individual sales transactions to be recorded is usually large in relationship to other transactions and often ranks second only to cash transactions in order of frequency.

Some merchandising businesses sell goods only for cash, others sell largely on credit, and still others have many transactions of both types. *Cash sales* involve both a receipt of cash and a sale of merchandise, and it is customary to record them in the *cash receipts journal*. Sales of merchandise *on account*, and only such sales, are recorded in the *sales journal*.

Trade discounts

Manufacturers and wholesalers of certain types of commodities frequently grant substantial reductions from the *list price* quoted in their catalogs. Such reductions in price are called *trade discounts*. Trade discounts are a convenient method of making revisions in prices without the necessity of reprinting catalogs. As prices fluctuate, new schedules of discounts may be issued. Trade discounts may also be used to make price differentials among different classes of customers. For example, the schedule of discounts issued by a manufacturer to wholesalers may differ from that issued to retailers.

Trade discounts are not recorded in the books of account. They are used only as a means of arriving at the selling price. For accounting purposes it is the actual price, that is, the list price minus the trade discount, that is significant. For example, the seller of an article listed at $100 with a trade discount of $40 would record the transaction as a sale of $60. Similarly, the buyer would record the cost as $60. Since trade discounts are not recorded in the books of account, they are mentioned here merely to distinguish between them and the cash discounts discussed in later paragraphs.

Sales procedures

Every sale is made in response to an order received from a customer. An order given a retail store is usually oral; an order given a manufacturing, a wholesale, or a mail-order business is ordinarily written. There are many methods of handling orders and of recording sales, the routines varying with the type and the size of the business.

In a retail business a *sales ticket* is usually prepared for a sale on account. This sales ticket is made in duplicate or triplicate. One copy is given to the customer, one copy is sent to the accounting department for use as the basis of an entry in the sales record, and one copy may be used as the salesman's personal record of his sales or for other purposes as the organization of the business requires.

In a manufacturing, a wholesale, or a mail-order business a written order is received from a customer or from the salesman who obtained the order from the customer. After the order has been approved by the credit department, it is sent to the billing department, where the invoice is prepared. At least two copies of a *sales invoice* are made by the billing department. The original is sent to the customer, and the carbon copy is sent to the accounting department for use as the basis of an entry in the sales journal. Sometimes additional copies of the invoice are made for the use of different departments of the business. For example, the credit department may desire a copy for use in following up the payment of the invoice, or the shipping department may need a copy as authorization to pack and ship the goods.

One of the sales invoices used by Bennett Electrical Supplies is illustrated below.

BENNETT ELECTRICAL SUPPLIES	No. 615
813 Hamilton St. •• Allentown, Pa.	

Sold to E. A. Albertson
321 Dauphin St.
Philadelphia 20, Pa.

Date September 1, 1961

Terms 2/10,n/30

Shipped Via Express Collect

6	Transformers, Model 392 E	40.00	240.00
12	Switches, Model 719 J	5.00	60.00
50	Resistors, Model 420 K	1.00	50.00
			350.00

Sales invoice

Controlling accounts and subsidiary ledgers

In earlier chapters of this book, amounts debited and credited to customers on account have been recorded only in a single accounts receivable account. Consideration will now be given to the procedure for recording the amounts owed the business by each individual debtor.

Although it is possible to eliminate the accounts receivable account from the ledger and to substitute the individual customers' accounts, such a solution is not satisfactory if there is a substantial number of debtors. The inclusion of a large number of accounts with debtors would delay the preparation of the trial balance and the work sheet, and would make errors more difficult to find.

When a business has a large number of accounts that have a common characteristic, it is customary to segregate them in a special ledger called a *subsidiary ledger*. In order to differentiate between ledgers, the principal ledger that contains all of the balance sheet and income statement accounts is then referred to as the *general ledger*. A single account summarizing the many accounts in a subsidiary ledger must be maintained in the general ledger. This summarizing account is called a *controlling account* and may be said to *control* the related subsidiary ledger.

The *controlling account* for customers to whom sales are made on account is *Accounts Receivable;* it is located in the *general ledger.* The individual accounts with such customers comprise a *subsidiary ledger,* in this case called the *accounts receivable ledger* or *customers' ledger.*

The special journals in which numerous transactions affecting debtors are to be recorded are designed in such a way as to facilitate the posting of individual transactions to the customers' ledger and of monthly totals to the controlling account, Accounts Receivable. This technique is illustrated by the following flow chart of posting from a sales journal.

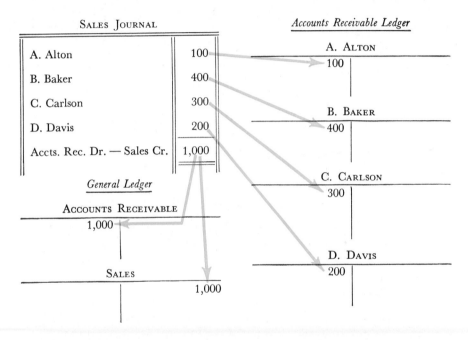

The debits to Alton, Baker, Carlson, and Davis recorded in the sales journal are posted to their respective accounts in the accounts receivable ledger. The total of the debits for the month, $1,000, is posted to the accounts receivable controlling account in the general ledger. It is evident that the sum of the debits to the four accounts in the subsidiary ledger is equal to the single debit to the controlling account.

Sales journal

The sales journal is used solely for recording *sales of merchandise on account.* Sales of merchandise for cash are recorded in the cash receipts journal. Sales of plant assets or other assets not a part of the stock in trade are recorded in either the cash receipts journal or the general journal. The restriction of the sales journal to sales of merchandise on

SALES JOURNAL   PAGE *35*

DATE	INVOICE NO.	ACCOUNT DEBITED	POST. REF.	ACCTS. REC. DR. SALES CR.
1961 Oct. 2	615	E. A. Albertson	✓	3 5 0 0 0
3	616	Quaker Supply	✓	6 0 4 0 0
5	617	James Owen	✓	3 0 5 0 0
9	618	E. A. Albertson	✓	1 3 9 6 0 0
10	619	Acme Co.	✓	7 5 0 0 0
17	620	R. E. Holt	✓	8 6 5 0 0
23	621	G. L. Bates	✓	5 0 2 0 0
26	622	Howard Strauss	✓	2 6 0 0 0
27	623	Quaker Supply	✓	9 0 8 0 0
31				5 9 4 0 0 0
				(113) (411)

Sales journal after posting

account is necessary because the journal total is posted as a debit to Accounts Receivable and a credit to Sales.

The sales journal of Bennett Electrical Supplies is illustrated above. Each invoice for a sale of merchandise on account is entered on a single line of the journal. The invoice number is indicated in the Invoice No. column to facilitate future reference to the supporting document if questions concerning the sale should arise. The customer's name is recorded in the Account Debited column, and the invoice total is recorded in the column at the right.

Posting the sales journal

Each entry in the sales journal is posted as a debit to the appropriate account in the accounts receivable ledger. The postings should be made at frequent intervals, preferably daily, so that the status of all customers' accounts can be readily determined at all times. The posting references inserted in the accounts should identify the sales journal by the letter "S" and the page on which the entry was recorded.

Customers' accounts are ordinarily arranged in alphabetical sequence in a loose leaf binder. New accounts are inserted at the proper point and inactive accounts can be removed at appropriate intervals. The assignment of code numbers to the accounts is therefore both impracticable and unnecessary. After each debit is posted to a customer's account, a check mark (√) is inserted in the posting reference column of the sales journal to indicate that the item has been posted.

Posting to a customer's account is illustrated below by the account with Acme Co. The complete ledger is presented later in connection with posting the cash receipts journal. Instead of the standard T form of account, Bennett Electrical Supplies uses a three-column form designed to show the balance of the account after each transaction.

NAME	Acme Co					
ADDRESS	118 James Street, Allentown, Pa.					
DATE	ITEMS	POST. REF.	DEBIT	CREDIT	BALANCE	
1961 Oct. 10		S35	750 00		750 00	

An account in the accounts receivable ledger

At the end of the month, the amount column of the sales journal is totaled, ruled, and posted. The sales on account recorded in the sales journal on page 122 amounted to $5,940. This total is posted as a debit to Accounts Receivable and a credit to Sales, and the respective account numbers are inserted below the total to indicate that the posting has been completed. The two accounts after posting are reproduced below.

Accounts Receivable   ACCOUNT NO. 113

DATE	ITEMS	POST. REF.	DEBIT	DATE	ITEMS	POST. REF.	CREDIT
1961 Oct. 1	Balance	v	4260 00				
31		S35	5940 00				

Sales   ACCOUNT NO. 411

DATE	ITEMS	POST. REF.	DEBIT	DATE	ITEMS	POST. REF.	CREDIT
				1961 Oct. 1	Balance	✓	98236 00
				31		S35	5940 00

Accounts receivable and sales accounts in the general ledger
after posting the sales journal

Sales returns and allowances

Goods sold on account may be returned by the customer or, because of defects or for other reasons, the customer may be allowed a reduction from the original price at which the goods were sold. In such cases the seller usually issues to the customer a *credit memorandum* showing the amount of the credit and the reason therefor. A typical credit memorandum is illustrated on the following page.

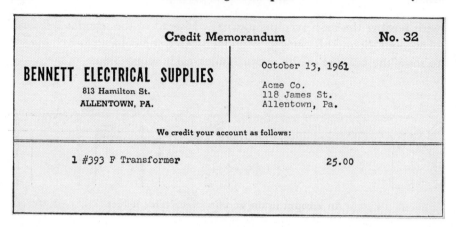

Credit memorandum

The effect of a sales return or allowance is a reduction in sales and a reduction in accounts receivable. If the sales account is debited, however, the balance of the account at the end of the period will represent net sales, and the volume of returns and allowances will not be disclosed. Because of the loss in revenue resulting from allowances, and the various expenses (transportation, unpacking, repairing, etc.) related to returns, it is advisable that management be informed of the magnitude of such transactions. It is therefore preferable to debit an account called *Sales Returns and Allowances.* The remainder of the transaction is recorded by a credit to the accounts receivable (controlling) account in the general ledger and to the customer's account in the accounts receivable (subsidiary) ledger.

Bennett Electrical Supplies issued two credit memorandums during the month. They were recorded in the general journal as shown below.

GENERAL JOURNAL   PAGE *18*

DATE		DESCRIPTION	POST. REF.	DEBIT	CREDIT
1961 Oct.	13	Sales Returns and Allowances	412	25 00	
		Accounts Receivable—Acme Co.	113 ✓		25 00
		Credit Memo No. 32.			
	28	Sales Returns and Allowances	412	45 00	
		Accounts Receivable—G. L. Bates	113 ✓		45 00
		Credit Memo No. 33.			

General journal entries for sales returns

Note that in each transaction both the controlling account and the customer's account are credited. A diagonal line should be placed in the posting reference column *at the time the entry is recorded in the general journal.* It serves as an indication that the amount must be posted to both the general ledger and the subsidiary ledger. When the credit is posted to the customer's account, a check mark is placed to the right of the diagonal line. The number of the accounts receivable controlling account is entered at the left in accordance with the usual routine of posting to that account in the general ledger. After the posting has been completed, the accounts receivable account and the sales returns and allowances account in the general ledger and the customers' accounts in the subsidiary ledger appear as follows:

GENERAL LEDGER

Accounts Receivable   ACCOUNT NO. 113

DATE	ITEMS	POST. REF.	DEBIT	DATE	ITEMS	POST. REF.	CREDIT
1961 Oct. 1	Balance	✓	4 2 6 0 00	1961 Oct. 13		J18	2 5 00
				28		J18	4 5 00

Sales Returns and Allowances   ACCOUNT NO. 412

DATE	ITEMS	POST. REF.	DEBIT	DATE	ITEMS	POST. REF.	CREDIT
1961 Oct. 13		J18	2 5 00				
28		J18	4 5 00				

ACCOUNTS RECEIVABLE LEDGER

NAME Acme Co

ADDRESS 118 James Street, Allentown, Pa.

DATE	ITEMS	POST. REF.	DEBIT	CREDIT	BALANCE
1961 Oct. 10		S35	7 5 0 00		7 5 0 00
13		J18		2 5 00	7 2 5 00

NAME G. L. Bates

ADDRESS 1211 State St., Trenton 3, N.J.

DATE	ITEMS	POST. REF.	DEBIT	CREDIT	BALANCE
1961 Oct. 23		S35	5 0 2 00		5 0 2 00
28		J18		4 5 00	4 5 7 00

Accounts receivable account, sales returns and allowances account, and customers' accounts after the posting of sales returns

If sales returns and allowances are of frequent occurrence, special columns for Sales Returns and Allowances Debit and for Accounts Receivable Credit may be inserted in the general journal, or a special sales returns and allowances journal similar to the one illustrated below may be used. The recording and posting routines for this special journal are the same as those that apply to the sales journal.

SALES RETURNS AND ALLOWANCES JOURNAL					PAGE 6
DATE	CR. MEMO. NO.	ACCOUNT CREDITED	POST. REF.	SALES RET. & ALLOW. DR. ACCTS. REC. CR.	
1961 July	2	12	Francis Arnold	√	142 00
	6	13	James T. Cliff	√	150 00
	29	26	Robert A. Lehman	√	13 00
	31				1,762 50
					(412) (113)

Sales returns and allowances journal

It should be noted that in all of the foregoing illustrations the customer's account was credited for the amount of a return or allowance. When a return or allowance occurs after the account has been paid, the seller may make a cash refund, in which case the transaction would be recorded as a debit to Sales Returns and Allowances in the cash payments journal, which is discussed in Chapter 7.

Using sales invoices as a sales journal

Businesses that make a large number of sales on account frequently use duplicate copies of their sales invoices as a sales journal. Under this system, the postings to the customers' accounts are made directly from the duplicate invoices. At the end of the month an adding machine listing of all the invoices is made. The total thus obtained is the basis for an entry in the general journal debiting Accounts Receivable and crediting Sales.

When the volume of transactions is large, the use of the invoices as a journal may effect material savings in bookkeeping expenses. The need for writing the name of the customer and the amount of the sale in the sales journal is eliminated. The system also lends itself to a division of labor, as the duplicate copies can be divided alphabetically by customers and several persons can post to the particular group of accounts assigned to them. Furthermore, the elimination of the intermediate step of recording each sale in the sales journal reduces the possibility of errors.

The same system can be employed with equal effectiveness in handling returns and allowances, the credit memorandums becoming in effect the sales returns and allowances journal.

Sources of cash receipts

All transactions that increase the amount of cash are recorded in a cash receipts journal. Cash may be received from a variety of sources, such as investments in the business by the owner, receipts from cash sales, collections from customers to whom sales have been made on account, and collections of principal and interest on notes receivable. In a typical merchandising business the sources of cash receipts of most frequent occurrence are likely to be cash sales and collections from customers on account.

Before describing the form and use of the cash receipts journal, it is necessary that consideration be given to the nature of the agreement between the business enterprise and its customers.

Credit terms

The arrangements agreed upon by the seller and the buyer as to when payments for goods are to be made are called the *credit terms*. If payment is required immediately upon delivery of the goods, the terms are said to be "cash" or "net cash." Otherwise, the buyer is allowed a period of time, known as the *credit period*, in which to pay.

There is considerable variation in credit periods. Retailers may require that all purchases by customers in one month be paid for by a particular date in the succeeding month. They sometimes stipulate that purchases made after the twenty-fifth will not be included in the billing for that month but will be carried over to the succeeding month. They may also have special "budget" terms and "lay-away" terms.

Among manufacturers and wholesalers it is usual for the credit period to begin with the date of the sale as evidenced by the date of the invoice. If payment is due within a stated number of days after the date of the invoice, for example 30 days, the terms are said to be "net 30 days," which may be written as "n/30." If payment is due by the end of the month in which the sale was made, it may be expressed as "n/eom."

Cash discounts

As a means of encouraging payment before the expiration of the credit period, a cash discount may be offered for early payment. Thus, the expression "2/10, n/30" means that, while the credit period is 30 days, the debtor may deduct 2% of the amount of the bill if payment is made in 10 days from the date of the invoice. This deduction is known as a *cash discount*.

For example, assume a sales invoice totaling $500 dated July 6, with credit terms of 2/10, n/30. If the buyer mails his check on or before

July 16, he may deduct $10 from the invoice and pay $490. If he wishes to wait the full credit term, payment of the full amount should be made on or before August 5.

From the seller's point of view, cash discounts are known as *sales discounts;* the purchaser refers to them as *purchases discounts*. At one time cash discounts were considered to be similar to interest for the use of money and were accordingly treated as an expense by the seller and as revenue by the buyer. Today, however, when cash discounts are offered by the seller, it is with the expectation that the customer will pay within the discount period. In effect the seller is offering to make the sale for the invoice price reduced by the amount of the discount. In accordance with this interpretation it is customary for the seller to view discounts as a deduction from sales and for the buyer to consider them as a deduction from the quoted price of the commodity purchased.

Cash receipts journal

As was demonstrated in Chapter 4, journalizing and posting can be expedited by the use of special columns for accounts frequently debited or credited. Inasmuch as all transactions involving receipts of cash, and only such transactions, are recorded in the cash receipts journal, it should have a special column entitled Cash Dr. Receipts of cash by Bennett Electrical Supplies that occur most frequently are from cash sales to consumers and collections from retailers to whom sales have been made on 2/10, n/30 terms. There are also infrequent receipts of cash from miscellaneous sources. Accordingly, the cash receipts journal of Bennett Electrical Supplies illustrated on page 129 has columns entitled (1) Sundry Accounts Cr., (2) Sales Cr., (3) Accounts Receivable Cr., (4) Sales Discount Dr., and (5) Cash Dr.

The Sundry Accounts Cr. column is used to record credits to any account for which there is no special column. For example, on October 2 Bennett Electrical Supplies collects $150 on a note receivable. The transaction is recorded by writing the account title "Notes Receivable" in the space provided, and $150 in the Sundry Accounts Cr. column and the Cash Dr. column. The posting reference column is left blank until the credit is posted.

The Sales Cr. column is used for recording sales of merchandise for cash. Each individual sale is recorded on a cash register or some other automatic device, and the totals thus accumulated are entered in the cash receipts journal daily, weekly, or at other regular intervals. This is illustrated by the entry of October 7 recording weekly sales of $1,200. The account title "Sales" is written in the space provided for Account

CASH RECEIPTS JOURNAL   PAGE *14*

DATE	ACCOUNT CREDITED	POST. REF.	SUNDRY ACCOUNTS CR.	SALES CR.	ACCOUNTS RECEIVABLE CR.	SALES, DISCOUNT DR.	CASH DR.
1961 Oct. 2	Notes Receivable	112	15000				15000
5	E. A. Albertson	✓			80000	1600	78400
6	John B. Deatrick	✓			62500	1250	61250
7	Sales	✓		120000			120000
10	James Owen	✓			60000	1200	58800
13	Quaker Supply	✓			60400	1208	59192
14	Sales	✓		163200			163200
17	Acme Co.	✓			72500	1450	71050
19	R. E. Holt	✓			185000		185000
21	Sales	✓		192030			192030
23	Purchases Ret. and Allow.	513	3620				3620
24	O. L. Tanner	✓			20000		20000
27	R. E. Holt	✓			86500	1730	84770
28	Sales	✓		158600			158600
31	Sales	✓		42340			42340
31			18620	676170	626900	8438	1313252
			(✓)	(411)	(113)	(413)	(111)

Cash receipts journal after posting

Credited and $1,200 is entered in the Sales Cr. and Cash Dr. columns.
Inasmuch as the total of the Sales Cr. column will be posted at the end
of the month, a check mark is inserted in the posting reference column to
indicate that the $1,200 item needs no further attention.

Credits to customers' accounts for payment of invoices are recorded
in the Accounts Receivable Cr. column. The amount of the cash discount
granted, if any, is recorded in the Sales Discount Dr. column and the
amount of cash actually received is recorded in the Cash Dr. column.
The entry on October 5 illustrates the use of these columns. The title
of the account in the subsidiary ledger, E. A. Albertson, is written
in the Account Credited space, the amount of the invoice for which payment is received, $800, is entered in the Accounts Receivable Cr. column,
the 2% cash discount of $16 is entered in the Sales Discount Dr. column,
and the $784 received is entered in the Cash Dr. column. The posting
reference column is left blank until the credit is posted to the customer's
account.

It should be noted that when a debtor has returned merchandise or
has received an allowance, the discount should be computed on the
amount of the invoice less the amount of the credit memorandum. For
example, on October 17 a check for $710.50 is received from Acme Co.

in settlement of an invoice of $750, less a credit of $25 for merchandise returned. The discount granted is 2% of $725, or $14.50.

Posting the cash receipts journal

Each amount in the Sundry Accounts Cr. column of the cash receipts journal is posted to the appropriate account in the general ledger at any time during the month and the posting is indicated by writing the account number in the posting reference column. At regular intervals the amounts in the Accounts Receivable Cr. column are posted to the customers' accounts in the subsidiary ledger and check marks are placed in the posting reference column to indicate that they have been posted. None of the individual amounts in the remaining three columns of the cash receipts journal is posted.

At the end of the month the several columns are footed and ruled as shown in the illustration. To check the accuracy of the footings, the equality of debits and credits should be proved by a listing similar to the following:

DEBIT TOTALS		CREDIT TOTALS	
Sales Discount..........	$ 84.38	Sundry Accounts........	$ 186.20
Cash..................	13,132.52	Sales.................	6,761.70
		Accounts Receivable......	6,269.00
	$13,216.90		$13,216.90

The total of the Sundry Accounts Cr. column is not posted, as the amounts in this column have been posted individually to general ledger accounts. A check mark may be inserted below the total to indicate that no further action is necessary. The totals of the other four columns are posted to the appropriate accounts in the general ledger and their account numbers are inserted below the totals to indicate that the posting was completed.

In terms of posting procedures, there are three distinct types of columns in the cash receipts journal. They may be described as follows:

(1) Items posted individually to general ledger accounts, column total not posted:
      Sundry Accounts Cr. column
(2) Items not posted individually, column total posted to a general ledger account:
      Sales Cr. column
      Sales Discount Dr. column
      Cash Dr. column
(3) Items posted individually to subsidiary ledger accounts, column total posted to the corresponding general ledger controlling account:
      Accounts Receivable Cr. column

Accounts receivable control and subsidiary ledger

During October the following postings were made to Accounts Receivable in the general ledger of Bennett Electrical Supplies:

DEBITS
Oct. 31 (Total sales on account, from sales journal)....... $5,940.00

CREDITS
Oct. 13 (A sales return, from general journal)............   25.00
Oct. 28 (A sales return, from general journal)............   45.00
Oct. 31 (Total credits resulting from cash received on account, from cash receipts journal)..............   6,269.00

The controlling account with its opening balance, the foregoing postings, and memorandum totals and balance is shown below.

Accounts receivable account in the general ledger
at the end of the month

As was indicated in the discussion of posting the sales journal, postings to the customers' accounts in the subsidiary ledger should be made daily. In order to answer inquiries from customers about the status of their account and in approving sales for additional credit, it is imperative that all customers' accounts be up to date. There is also an obvious advantage in spreading the posting over the month rather than allowing it to accumulate until the end of the month.

The accounts receivable ledger of Bennett Electrical Supplies after posting all entries for the month is shown on the following pages.

The sum of the balances of the accounts in the customers' ledger should be compared periodically with the balance of the accounts receivable account in the general ledger. This is customarily done at the end of each month at the same time that the trial balance is prepared. If the subsidiary ledger and the controlling account are not in agreement, the error must be found and corrected. As in the case of the trial balance, however, arithmetic equality is not an absolute guarantee of correctness. For example, the erroneous posting of a credit for cash received from a

NAME *Acme Co.*

ADDRESS *118 James Street, Allentown, Pa.*

DATE	ITEMS	POST. REF.	DEBIT	CREDIT	BALANCE
1961					
Oct. 10		S35	750 00		750 00
13		J18		25 00	725 00
17		CR14		725 00	

NAME *E. A. Albertson*

ADDRESS *321 Dauphin St., Philadelphia 20, Pa.*

DATE	ITEMS	POST. REF.	DEBIT	CREDIT	BALANCE
1961					
Sept. 27		S34	800 00		800 00
Oct. 2		S35	350 00		1150 00
5		CR14		800 00	350 00
9		S35	1396 00		1746 00

NAME *G. L. Bates*

ADDRESS *1211 State St., Trenton 3, N.J.*

DATE	ITEMS	POST. REF.	DEBIT	CREDIT	BALANCE
1961					
Oct. 23		S35	502 00		502 00
28		J18		45 00	457 00

NAME *John B. Deatrick*

ADDRESS *46 First Ave., Allentown, Pa.*

DATE	ITEMS	POST. REF.	DEBIT	CREDIT	BALANCE
1961					
Sept. 28		S34	625 00		625 00
Oct. 6		CR14		625 00	

Accounts receivable ledger at the end of the month

NAME *R. E. Holt*

ADDRESS *1213 River Road, Easton, Pa.*

DATE	ITEMS	POST. REF.	DEBIT	CREDIT	BALANCE
1961					
Sept 19		S34	1850 00		1850 00
Oct 17		S35	865 00		2715 00
19		CR14		1850 00	865 00
27		CR14		865 00	—

NAME *James Owen*

ADDRESS *1619 Washington St., Allentown, Pa.*

DATE	ITEMS	POST. REF.	DEBIT	CREDIT	BALANCE
1961					
Sept 29		S34	600 00		600 00
Oct 5		S35	305 00		905 00
10		CR14		600 00	305 00

NAME *Quaker Supply*

ADDRESS *907 Barr St., Reading, Pa.*

DATE	ITEMS	POST. REF.	DEBIT	CREDIT	BALANCE
1961					
Oct 3		S35	604 00		604 00
13		CR14		604 00	—
27		S35	908 00		908 00

NAME *Howard Strauss*

ADDRESS *192 Ember St., Narberth, Pa.*

DATE	ITEMS	POST. REF.	DEBIT	CREDIT	BALANCE
1961					
Oct 26		S35	260 00		260 00

NAME *O. L. Tanner*

ADDRESS *1014 Slauson Ave., Reading, Pa.*

DATE	ITEMS	POST. REF.	DEBIT	CREDIT	BALANCE
1961					
Aug 24		S33	385 00		385 00
Oct 24		CR14		200 00	185 00

Accounts receivable ledger at the end of the month—concluded

particular customer as a credit to another customer's account would not be revealed by this comparison.

The balances in the subsidiary ledger accounts may be summarized by use of an adding machine, or a schedule of accounts receivable similar to the one illustrated below may be prepared. Note that the total of the schedule, $3,861, is in agreement with the balance of the accounts receivable account appearing on page 131.

Bennett Electrical Supplies
Schedule of Accounts Receivable
October 31, 1961

E. A. Albertson	1 746 00
G. L. Bates	4 57 00
James Owen	3 05 00
Quaker Supply	9 08 00
Howard Strauss	2 60 00
O. L. Tanner	1 85 00
Total Accounts Receivable	3 861 00

Schedule of accounts receivable

Delivery of merchandise sold

The terms of a sales agreement include an implied or express provision concerning the cost of delivering the goods to the buyer. If the seller is to assume the cost of transportation, the terms are said to be *FOB* (free on board) *destination;* if the buyer is to absorb the cost, the terms are stated as *FOB shipping point.*

When the seller agrees to absorb the costs of delivering the merchandise, the amount paid to railways, trucking companies, etc. is debited to Delivery Expense or Freight-Out, which is classified as a selling expense.

When the buyer agrees to absorb the delivery costs and pays the carrier directly, the seller's responsibility ceases when the merchandise is turned over to the carrier. However, a not infrequent practice is for the seller to pay the carrier even though the terms are FOB shipping point. It is not practicable to do otherwise for postal shipments. When shipment is by other agencies, the seller may nevertheless pay the transportation charges as a convenience to the buyer. In all such cases the delivery costs are added to the sales invoice and are charged to the customer's account.

A sales journal designed to accommodate such transactions is illustrated below. The selling price of the merchandise sold to Whitney Corp. was $800, to which was added transportation costs of $30, making a total charge of $830 to the customer. At the time the seller pays the carrier for charges on outgoing merchandise, the amount is debited to Delivery Expense regardless of who is to bear the transportation costs. When the total of the Delivery Expense Cr. column of the sales journal is posted at the end of the month, the delivery expense account will automatically be reduced by the amount of the charges that have been passed on to customers; thus any balance remaining will represent the amount of delivery expense borne by the seller.

SALES JOURNAL   PAGE 63

DATE	SALE NO.	ACCOUNT DEBITED	POST. REF.	ACCOUNTS RECEIV- ABLE DR.	DELIVERY EXPENSE CR.	SALES CR.
1961 Nov. 1	2477	Whitney Corp.	√	830 00	30 00	800 00

Sales journal designed for charging
prepaid transportation costs to customers

When delivery costs are prepaid as an accommodation and the sales are subject to a cash discount, the discount should be computed on the sale price only; it does not apply to the transportation charges advanced by the seller. For example, assuming that the sale to Whitney Corp. in the foregoing illustration is subject to a discount of 2%, the discount would amount to $16 (2% of $800), and the amount to be paid would be $814 ($800 − $16 + $30). In order to have the basis for the discount readily available, the amount of the transportation charge may be recorded in the items section of the customers' accounts at the time of posting.

Questions

1. Ralph Mason, a retail hardware merchant, makes about 350 charge sales each month. Each sale is recorded in a two-column general journal. If a sales journal were used, how much work would be saved (a) in recording and (b) in posting these transactions?

2. The Hale Department Store has about 600 customers that buy merchandise on account. If the customers' accounts were kept in the general ledger, approximately how many additional items would appear in the trial balance?

3. Distinguish between trade discounts and cash discounts.

4. Describe the two related transactions recorded in the T accounts below.

CASH	ACCOUNTS RECEIVABLE	SALES	SALES DISCOUNT
(b) 1,568	(a) 1,600 | (b) 1,600	(a) 1,600	(b) 32

5. The following errors were made in recording transactions in a single-column sales journal or in posting therefrom. How will each error be discovered?

(a) A sale of $50 was recorded as $500.

(b) A sale to Robert L. Barker was recorded as a sale to Robert L. Baker.

(c) An entry of $100 was posted to the customer's account as $10.

(d) The sales journal for the month was underfooted by $1,000.

6. As an accommodation, Henry Norton sells some of his office supplies to a customer on account. Should this transaction be recorded in the sales journal or in the general journal? Why?

7. The Bell Tractor Co. maintains a subsidiary ledger for accounts receivable. In posting the journal entry given below, the bookkeeper failed to post the credit to the controlling account. How will this error be discovered?

June 26 Sales Returns and Allowances.......... 412   100.00
                Accounts Receivable — Edward Adams   ✓   100.00

8. Why is it advisable to maintain an account for sales returns and allowances when the same net result may be obtained by debiting them directly to the sales account?

9. After receiving full payment for a sale of merchandise on account, the buyer returns a portion of the shipment for credit and the seller credits the buyer's account. What is the nature of the credit balance in the customer's account?

10. After paying an invoice of $100, terms 2/10, n/30, within the discount period, the buyer returns the merchandise with the consent of the seller. What is the amount of the refund to which the buyer is entitled?

11. Who bears the transportation costs when the terms of sale are (a) FOB destination, (b) FOB shipping point?

12. Is the buyer entitled to a discount on prepaid freight, assuming that the terms are FOB shipping point and that he pays the invoice within the discount period? Give a reason for your answer.

13. Wholesale Merchandise Co. makes a sale of $2,000 to Dayton Home Store on account, FOB shipping point, 2/10, n/30, paying the freight charges of $35. Dayton Home Store returns $100 of merchandise for credit and remits the correct amount in full settlement within the discount period. What is the amount of the check received by Wholesale Merchandise Co.?

14. Will the amounts in the Delivery Expense Cr. column of the sales journal illustrated on page 135 be posted individually or in total?

Exercises

1. (a) Determine the amount to be recorded as the sale for each of the following invoices:

Invoice Date	List Price	Trade Discount	Credit Terms	Date Paid
(1) June 8	$ 400	50%	2/10, eom	July 9
(2) June 17	550	30%	2/10, n/30	June 27
(3) June 20	900	40%	2/10, n/30	July 2
(4) June 28	700	25%	2/10, 1/20, n/60	July 17
(5) June 30	1,200	50%	n/30	July 30

(b) What is the amount to be paid in each of the above cases?

2. George White uses his sales invoices as a sales journal. The adding machine listing of the 973 invoices for September totals $92,420.

(a) Journalize the entry to record this information.

(b) What is the source for posting debits to the customer's ledger?

3. James Burton sells merchandise to Briggs Co. on October 10 for $800, terms FOB shipping point, 1/10, n/30. Burton prepays freight of $25. On October 16 Burton issues a credit memorandum for $75 for goods returned, and on October 20 he receives a check for the amount due on the invoice. Present Burton's entries, in general journal form, to record (a) the sales invoice, (b) the credit memorandum, and (c) the receipt of cash.

4. The Monarch Co. sells razors and razor blades to dealers on account, FOB shipping point, 2/10, n/30. Two accounts are maintained for sales, Razor Sales and Blade Sales. In some cases the delivery costs are prepaid and charged to the customer. List the captions of the amount columns needed in their sales journal. After each caption indicate (1) whether each individual item or the column total is to be posted and (2) the ledger to which it is to be posted.

5. A two-column general journal is to be expanded by the addition of special columns to record credit memorandums to customers. List the exact caption of each of the four amount columns in the revised journal.

6. Present the general journal entries necessary to correct each of the errors described below. Assume that the incorrect entries had been posted and that the errors are discovered in the same fiscal period in which they occurred.

(a) A cash sale of $50 was recorded as a sale to Henry Roberts on account.

(b) A $500 sale to William Ward on account, FOB shipping point, with prepaid delivery expense of $28, was recorded as a $528 debit to Ward (and Accounts Receivable) and a $528 credit to Sales.

(c) A cash receipt of $490 ($500 less 2% discount) from George Adams was recorded as a $490 debit to Cash and a $490 credit to Adams (and Accounts Receivable).

(d) A cash refund of $25 received for an overcharge on an insurance premium was recorded as a sale of merchandise for cash.

Problems

6-1. Specialty Sales Co. was established early in August of the current year. During the remainder of the month its sales of merchandise on account and related returns and allowances were as listed below. All sales were subject to terms of n/30, FOB shipping point.

Aug. 16. Sold merchandise on account to Warner Corporation, Sale No. 1, $320.
   17. Sold merchandise on account to A. D. Collins, Sale No. 2, $450.
   18. Sold merchandise on account to Miller & Co., Sale No. 3, $800.
   19. Sold merchandise on account to Hill & Matthews, Sale No. 4, $750.
   20. Issued Credit Memorandum No. 1 for $20 to A. D. Collins for merchandise returned.
   23. Sold merchandise on account to Miller & Co., Sale No. 5, $380.
   24. Issued Credit Memorandum No. 2 for $80 to Warner Corporation for merchandise returned.
   25. Sold merchandise on account to J. R. Altman Co., Sale No. 6, $530.
   26. Sold merchandise on account to Superior Distributors, Inc., Sale No. 7, $620.
   27. Sold merchandise on account to A. D. Collins, Sale No. 8, $260.
   30. Issued Credit Memorandum No. 3 for $30 to J. R. Altman Co. for damages to merchandise caused by faulty packing.
   31. Sold merchandise on account to Hill & Matthews, Sale No. 9, $110.

Instructions: (1) Record the above transactions, using a sales journal similar to the one illustrated on page 122 and a two-column general journal.

(2) Open the following accounts in the general ledger, using the account numbers indicated: Accounts Receivable, 113; Sales, 411; Sales Returns and Allowances, 412.

(3) Open the following accounts in the accounts receivable ledger: J. R. Altman Co., A. D. Collins, Hill & Matthews, Miller & Co. Superior Distributors, Inc., Warner Corporation.

(4) Post the journals to the accounts receivable ledger and the accounts in the general ledger.

(5) (a) What is the sum of the balances of the subsidiary accounts? (b) What is the balance of the controlling account?

6-2. Transactions related to sales and cash receipts completed by John Ross Co. during April of the current year are described below. The terms of all sales on account are 2/10, n/30, FOB destination.

April 1. Sold merchandise on account to Thomas & Co., Invoice No. 428, $1,785.
   7. Sold merchandise on account to Morley & Larson, Inc., Invoice No. 429, $850.
   8. John Ross invested additional cash in the business, $2,000.
   9. Issued to Morley & Larson, Inc. a credit memorandum for merchandise returned, $50.
   12. Sold merchandise on account to J. D. Baker Co., Invoice No. 430, $2,400.
   13. Received cash for store supplies returned to the manufacturer, $25.

April 14. Sold merchandise on account to Morley & Larson, Inc., Invoice No. 431, $1,250.
   15. Cash sales for April 1 to 15, $9,625.
   16. Received cash from Morley & Larson, Inc. for the $800 due on Invoice No. 429, less discount.
   19. Sold merchandise on account to J. D. Baker Co., Invoice No. 432, $2,100.
   22. Received cash from J. D. Baker Co. for Invoice No. 430, less discount.
   23. Received cash from Morley & Larson, Inc. for Invoice No. 431, less discount.
   27. Sold merchandise on account to Morley & Larson, Inc., Invoice No. 433, $2,328.
   29. Received cash for a note receivable due today, $500.
   30. Received cash from Thomas & Co. for Invoice No. 428.
   30. Cash sales for April 16 to 30, $8,127.

Instructions: (1) Open the following accounts in the general ledger:

111 Cash	311 John Ross, Capital
112 Notes Receivable	411 Sales
113 Accounts Receivable	412 Sales Returns and Allowances
116 Store Supplies	413 Sales Discount

(2) Open the following accounts in the accounts receivable ledger: J. D. Baker Co., Morley & Larson, Inc., Thomas & Co.

(3) Record the transactions for the month in a sales journal similar to the one illustrated on page 122, a cash receipts journal similar to the one illustrated on page 129, and a two-column general journal. Immediately after recording a transaction affecting a customer's account, post to the *subsidiary ledger.*

(4) Add the columns of the special journals and post all three journals to the general ledger.

(5) Prepare a schedule of accounts receivable.

(6) What is the balance of the accounts receivable account?

6-3. Transactions related to sales and cash receipts completed by Marion Distributors during November of the current year are described below. The terms of all sales on account are 2/10, n/30, FOB shipping point. All delivery charges are prepaid and charged to the customer.

Nov. 2. Received cash from Robert R. Marsh for the balance due on his account, less discount.
   4. Issued Invoice No. 642 to Walsh & Taylor, $750; delivery, $15; total, $765.
   6. Issued Invoice No. 643 to Robert R. Marsh, $320; delivery, $10; total, $330.
   6. Received cash from Adamson Co. for the balance due on their account, less discount.

Post all journals to the accounts receivable ledger.

   9. Issued Invoice No. 644 to M. L. Scott, Inc., $455; delivery, $13; total, $468.
  10. Issued Credit Memo No. 39 to Robert R. Marsh, $20.
  12. Issued Invoice No. 645 to Walsh & Taylor, $2,400; delivery, $42; total, $2,442.

Nov. 13. Received cash from Adamson Co. in payment of a note receivable, $2,100.
13. Received cash from Walsh & Taylor for Invoice No. 642, less discount.

Post all journals to the accounts receivable ledger.

16. Received cash from Robert R. Marsh for balance due on Invoice No. 643, less discount.
16. Recorded cash sales for first half of the month, $3,640.
17. Received cash from M. L. Scott, Inc. for the balance on November 1; no discount.
18. Issued Invoice No. 646 to Adamson Co., $1,893; delivery, $53; total, $1,946.
22. Received cash from Walsh & Taylor for Invoice No. 645, less discount.
24. Issued Credit Memo No. 40 to Adamson Co., $43.

Post all journals to the accounts receivable ledger.

25. Issued Invoice No. 647 to Walsh & Taylor, $1,520; delivery, $33; total $1,553.
26. Received cash refund for a premium overcharge on property insurance, $45.
28. Received cash from Adamson Co. for the balance due on Invoice No. 646, less discount.
28. Issued Invoice No. 648 to Robert R. Marsh, $1,420; delivery, $38; total, $1,458.
30. Recorded cash sales for the second half of the month, $4,890
30. Issued Credit Memo No. 41 to Robert R. Marsh, $65.

Post all journals to the accounts receivable ledger.

Instructions: (1) Open the following accounts in the general ledger, inserting the balance as of November 1 in the accounts receivable account:

111 Cash	411 Sales
112 Notes Receivable	412 Sales Returns and Allowances
113 Accounts Receivable, $2,780	413 Sales Discount
117 Prepaid Insurance	615 Delivery Expense

(2) Open the following accounts in the accounts receivable ledger, inserting the balances indicated, as of November 1: Adamson Co., $825, including a delivery charge of $25; Robert R. Marsh, $1,285, including a delivery charge of $35; M. L. Scott, Inc., $670, including a delivery charge of $20; Walsh & Taylor.

(3) Record the transactions for the month in a sales journal similar to the one illustrated on page 135, a sales returns and allowances journal similar to the one illustrated on page 126, and a cash receipts journal similar to the one illustrated on page 129. Post to the accounts receivable ledger at the points indicated in the narrative of transactions.

(4) Add the columns of the journals and post to the general ledger accounts.

(5) (a) What is the sum of the balances of the accounts in the subsidiary ledgers? (b) What is the balance of the controlling account?

7

Purchases and cash payments

Purchasing procedures

The procedures followed in purchasing activities vary considerably among business firms. In a small retail store the proprietor may do all of the buying, in many cases placing orders with salesmen or by telephone. Large concerns may maintain a purchasing department that is responsible for determining best sources of supply, investigating quality, knowing market prices and their likely trends, placing orders, and doing all other things necessary to assure the efficient operation of all buying activities.

To avoid misunderstanding, all orders for merchandise, equipment, supplies, or other goods should be in writing. An order may be written on a form supplied by the vendor, or the buyer may use his own forms. The original of the purchase order is sent to the supplier; it is his authorization to deliver the items listed at the prices specified. A duplicate copy of the order should be retained as evidence of what was ordered and of the other terms stipulated.

The vendor usually mails an invoice to the buyer at about the time the goods are shipped. From the viewpoint of the seller, the invoice is a sales invoice; the buyer refers to it as a purchase invoice. An invoice should contain the names and the addresses of both the buyer and the seller; the date of the transaction; the terms; the method of shipment; and the quantities, descriptions, and prices of the goods. An invoice from Allied Electronics Supply in response to a purchase order of Bennett Electrical Supplies is shown on the following page.

The invoice form illustrated is a standard form recommended by the National Association of Purchasing Agents. It is divided into three distinct sections: (1) upper left section for miscellaneous details of the terms of the transaction; (2) lower section for quantity, description, unit price, and amount; and (3) upper right section for use by the purchaser as a record that various comparisons and verifications have been made.

		FOR CUSTOMER'S USE ONLY	
ALLIED ELECTRONICS SUPPLY		Register No.	Voucher No.

ALLIED ELECTRONICS SUPPLY
405 Murray Street
CHICAGO 15, ILLINOIS

F. O. B. Checked	
Terms Approved	Price Approved
	W X

Customer's Order No. & Date	412	Refer to Invoice No.	106-8

Requisition No.

Calculations Checked	
C. R. S.	

Contract No.		Invoice Date	Oct. 11, 1961

Transportation

Vendor's Nos.	

Freight Bill No.	Amount

SOLD TO   Bennett Electrical Supplies
813 Hamilton Street
Allentown, Pennsylvania

Material Received			
10/13 19*61*	*M.A.S.*	*Rec. Cl.*	
Date	Signature		Title

Shipped to and Destination   Same

Satisfactory and Approved

Adjustments

Date Shipped	Oct. 11, 1961	From	Chicago	Prepaid or Collect?
Car Initials and No.		F. O. B.	Allentown	Prepaid

Accounting Distribution

How Shipped and Route   Eastern Trucking Co.

Audited	Final Approval
J.H.C.	*K.C.*

Terms	2/10, n/30	Made in U. S. A.

QUANTITY	DESCRIPTION	UNIT PRICE	AMOUNT
10 ✓	392E Transformers	30.00 ✓	300.00 ✓
50 ✓	719J Switches	2.50 ✓	125.00 ✓
20 ✓	406P Capacitors	4.00 ✓	80.00 ✓
5 ✓	215J Reactors	10.00 ✓	50.00 ✓
			555.00 ✓

Invoice

The supporting document for recording a purchase is an invoice. However, before a purchase invoice is approved for payment, the following verifications should be made: (1) that the billing is in accordance with the provisions of the purchase order, (2) that the goods have been received in good condition, and (3) that all quantitative details (such as price extensions) have been checked. The invoice usually arrives in advance of the goods, and it is sometimes recorded in the journal before the shipment is received. Terms, quantities, prices, and other details on the invoice should be compared with the corresponding items on the copy of the purchase order. When the goods arrive, they should be counted and inspected. This work is ordinarily done by the receiving department, which may check the quantities received against those indicated on the invoice or may make an independent report to the purchasing department of quantities received. In the latter case the purchasing department will compare the receiving report with the invoice, thus affording better internal check over the receiving operations of the business.

Purchases journal

A wide variety of assets may be purchased by a business enterprise. Property most frequently purchased on account by a trading concern is of the following types: (1) merchandise for resale to customers, (2) supplies for use in conducting the business, and (3) plant assets. Because of the variety of assets acquired on credit terms, the purchases journal should be designed to accommodate the recording of all purchases on account. The number and the purpose of the special columns provided in the journal depend upon the nature of the business and the frequency of purchases of the various assets. The form used by Bennett Electrical Supplies is illustrated on pages 144 and 145.

For each transaction recorded in the purchases journal, the credit is entered in the Accounts Payable Cr. column. The next three columns are used in accumulating debits to the particular accounts most frequently affected.

The Purchases Dr. column is for merchandise bought for resale. A more exact title for the column and the account to which the total is posted would be "Merchandise Purchases." It is customary, however, to refer to goods bought for resale as just "Purchases." The purpose of the Store Supplies Dr. and Office Supplies Dr. columns is readily apparent. If supplies of these two categories were bought only infrequently, the two columns could be omitted from the journal.

The final set of columns, under the principal heading Sundry Accounts Debit, is used to record purchases on account of items not provided for in the special debit columns. The title of the particular account in the general ledger is entered in the Account column, the amount of the debit is recorded in the Amount column, and the number of the account is written in the Post. Ref. column at the time of posting.

Controlling account and subsidiary ledger

The necessity for maintaining a separate account for each creditor is evident. Although it would be possible to keep these accounts in the general ledger, it is ordinarily preferable to segregate them in a subsidiary ledger. The account in the general ledger that summarizes the debits and credits to the individual accounts is entitled Accounts Payable. It is a *controlling account*. The subsidiary ledger may be referred to as the *accounts payable ledger* or the *creditors' ledger*.

Posting the purchases journal

At frequent intervals, usually daily, throughout the month the amounts in the Accounts Payable Cr. column are posted to the creditors' accounts in the subsidiary ledger. As each posting is completed, a check mark is placed in the posting reference column of the purchases journal at the left of the item.

PAGE *19*   PURCHASES JOURNAL

	DATE	ACCOUNT CREDITED	POST. REF.	ACCOUNTS PAYABLE CR.	
1	1961 Oct. 2	United Parts Wholesalers	✓	6 1 9 0 0	1
2	3	Queen Electronics	✓	4 0 6 0 0	2
3	7	Reed Supplies, Inc.	✓	5 7 0 0	3
4	9	Queen Electronics	✓	2 0 8 0 0	4
5	11	Black Electric Corp.	✓	6 2 3 0 0	5
6	13	Allied Electronics Supply	✓	5 5 5 0 0	6
7	14	Wilson Manufacturing Co.	✓	9 1 0 0 0	7
8	16	Office Equipment Distributors	✓	5 7 0 0 0	8
9	19	State Distributors	✓	1 0 0 0 0 0	9
10	21	Wilson Manufacturing Co.	✓	1 6 5 0 0	10
11	25	Reed Supplies, Inc.	✓	3 2 0 0	11
12	27	Black Electric Corp.	✓	3 7 5 0 0	12
13	31			5 5 2 0 0 0	13
14				(211)	14
15					15
16					16

Purchases journal, left page

The three-column account form ordinarily used for the accounts payable ledger is designed to show at all times the balance owed each creditor. The accounts are arranged alphabetically so as to permit easy access. A loose-leaf binder is used to facilitate the insertion of new accounts and the withdrawal of pages that have been completely filled.

As each item is posted to a creditor's account, the source of the entry is recorded in the posting reference column of the account by the letter "P" and the page number of the purchases journal. The account with Allied Electronics Supply, taken from the accounts payable ledger of Bennett Electrical Supplies, is presented below as an example.

NAME *Allied Electronics Supply*
ADDRESS *405 Murray St., Chicago 15, Ill.*

DATE	ITEMS	POST. REF.	DEBIT	CREDIT	BALANCE
1961 Oct. 13		P19		5 5 5 00	5 5 5 00

An account in the accounts payable ledger

At the end of the month the purchases journal is totaled and ruled in the manner illustrated on pages 144 and 145. Before posting, the equality of the debits and the credits should be verified by comparing the total of all of the debit columns with the total of the credit column.

PURCHASES JOURNAL　　　　PAGE *19*

	PURCHASES DR.	STORE SUPPLIES DR.	OFFICE SUPPLIES DR.	SUNDRY ACCOUNTS DEBIT			
				ACCOUNT	POST. REF.	AMOUNT	
1	6 1 9 00						1
2	4 0 6 00						2
3		3 6 00	2 1 00				3
4	2 0 8 00						4
5	6 2 3 00						5
6	5 5 5 00						6
7	9 1 0 00						7
8				*Office Equipment*	122	5 7 0 00	8
9	1 0 0 0 00						9
10				*Store Equipment*	121	1 6 5 00	10
11		1 8 00	1 4 00				11
12	3 7 5 00						12
13	4 6 9 6 00	5 4 00	3 5 00			7 3 5 00	13
14	(511)	(115)	(116)			(✓)	14
15							15
16							16

Purchases journal, right page

This may be done on an adding machine tape or by a listing similar to the following:

DEBIT TOTALS		CREDIT TOTALS	
Purchases................	$4,696.00	Accounts Payable.........	$5,520.00
Store Supplies............	54.00		
Office Supplies...........	35.00		
Sundry Accounts..........	735.00		
	$5,520.00		$5,520.00

The total of the Accounts Payable Cr. column is posted to the accounts payable account in the general ledger and the posting reference is indicated below the column total. The totals of the Purchases Dr., Store Supplies Dr., and Office Supplies Dr. columns are posted in a similar manner. Each individual amount in the Sundry Accounts section is posted to the appropriate account in the general ledger, the posting reference being entered at the left of the amount. The total of the column is not posted. A check mark is therefore placed below the $735 total to indicate this fact.

Postings were made to six accounts in the general ledger of Bennett Electrical Supplies. Three of the accounts are presented on page 146. The debit of $570 to Office Equipment was posted from the Sundry Accounts Dr. column of the purchases journal; the credit of $5,520 to Accounts Payable and the debit of $4,696 to Purchases were posted as totals from the Accounts Payable Cr. and Purchases Dr. columns, respectively.

Office Equipment   ACCOUNT NO. 122

DATE	ITEMS	POST. REF.	DEBIT	DATE	ITEMS	POST. REF.	CREDIT
1961 Oct. 1	Balance	✓	4600 00				
16		P19	570 00				

Accounts Payable   ACCOUNT NO. 211

DATE	ITEMS	POST. REF.	DEBIT	DATE	ITEMS	POST. REF.	CREDIT
				1961 Oct. 1	Balance	✓	6275 00
				31		P19	5520 00

Purchases   ACCOUNT NO. 511

DATE	ITEMS	POST. REF.	DEBIT	DATE	ITEMS	POST. REF.	CREDIT
1961 Oct. 1	Balance	✓	49218 00				
31		P19	4696 00				

General ledger accounts after posting from purchases journal

The relationship between the purchases journal and the ledger of Bennett Electrical Supplies is shown in a flow diagram below.

PURCHASES JOURNAL

DATE	ACCOUNT CREDITED	P. R.	ACCOUNTS PAYABLE CR.	PURCHASES DR.	STORE SUPPLIES DR.	OFFICE SUPPLIES DR.	SUNDRY ACCOUNTS DEBIT		
							ACCOUNT	P. R.	AMOUNT
xx	xxx		619	619					
xx	xxx		406	406					
xx	xxx		57		36	21			
xx	xxx		570				Office Equipment	122	570
xx	xxx		165				Store Equipment	121	165
xx	Totals		5,520	4,696	54	35			735

ACCOUNTS PAYABLE LEDGER

Each individual item is posted to the credit of an account in the accounts payable ledger, making a total of $5,520.

GENERAL LEDGER

Purchases	Store Supplies	Store Equipment
4,696	54	165

Accounts Payable	Office Supplies	Office Equipment
5,520	35	570

Relationship between the purchases journal and the ledgers

Two points in particular should be noted: (1) the purchases journal is the source of postings to both ledgers and (2) the sum of the *individual* postings to creditors' accounts in the subsidiary ledger is equal to the *columnar total* posted to Accounts Payable in the general ledger.

Purchases returns and allowances

When merchandise purchased on account is returned or an allowance is requested, the purchaser usually informs the seller of the circumstances in writing. If such transactions are of frequent occurrence, the debtor may use his own *debit memorandum* forms. This form, illustrated below, is a convenient medium for informing the vendor of the amount being debited to his account on the buyer's books and the reasons therefor.

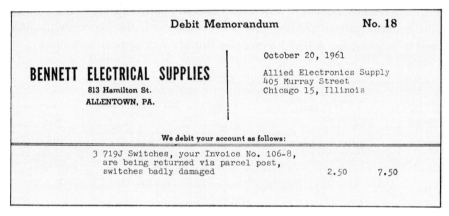

Debit memorandum

Regardless of the form in which the request is made, the creditor usually issues a *credit memorandum*. Either form may be used by the debtor as the basis for an entry debiting the creditor's account and crediting Purchases Returns and Allowances. If the volume of returns and allowances is negligible, they may be credited directly to the purchases account. It is ordinarily advisable, however, for management to know both the total amount of purchases and the total amount of purchases returns and allowances, and the most efficient procedure for obtaining the information is to have a separate account for each. If the volume of returns and allowances in relationship to purchases becomes excessive, it is an indication that purchasing procedures are faulty and that remedial action should be taken by management.

On October 20 Bennett Electrical Supplies issued a debit memorandum to Allied Electronics Supply for merchandise returned. The entry could be recorded in a two-column general journal as follows:

GENERAL JOURNAL   PAGE 18

DATE	NAME OF ACCOUNT	POST. REF.	DEBIT	CREDIT
Oct. 20	Accounts Payable—Allied Electronics Supply	211/✓	7 50	
	Purchases Returns and Allowances	512		7 50
	Debit Memo No. 18.			

General journal entry for a purchases return

Note that the debit is posted to the accounts payable account, which is Account No. 211 in the general ledger, and to the creditor's account in the subsidiary ledger. The necessity for posting this item to two different accounts is indicated by placing the diagonal line in the posting reference column when the transaction is recorded; the account number and the check mark are written in when the respective postings are made. When this general journal posting has been completed, the accounts payable ledger account for Allied Electronics Supply will appear as follows:

NAME Allied Electronics Supply
ADDRESS 405 Murray St., Chicago 13, Ill.

DATE	ITEMS	POST. REF.	DEBIT	CREDIT	BALANCE
1961 Oct. 13		P19		5 55 00	5 55 00
20		J18	7 50		5 47 50

A creditor's account in the accounts payable ledger
after posting a debit for a purchases return

When goods other than merchandise held for resale are returned, or an allowance is granted on such goods, the credit in the journal is made directly to the account that was originally debited. For example, if office equipment is returned to the vendor, the controlling account and the subsidiary account payable would be debited in the usual manner and Office Equipment would be credited. Similarly, when store supplies are returned to the vendor, Store Supplies would be credited for the amount of the return. The number of such returns is usually so small that no significant information would be obtained by maintaining separate accounts for these returns.

If merchandise purchases returns and allowances are of frequent occurrence, special columns for Accounts Payable Debit and Purchases Returns and Allowances Credit may be inserted in the general journal, or a special purchases returns and allowances journal similar to the one illustrated on page 149 may be used.

PURCHASES RETURNS AND ALLOWANCES JOURNAL   PAGE 5

DATE		ACCOUNT DEBITED	POST. REF.	ACCTS. PAY. DR. PUR. R. & A. CR.
1961				
Nov.	1	Standard Paint Corp.	√	33 00
	2	Goodman Hardware Wholesalers	√	93 20
	30	Merkle Builders Supplies, Inc.	√	229 50
	30			923 80
				(211) (512)

Purchases returns and allowances journal

During the month the individual items in the amount column are posted daily to the debit of the creditors' accounts in the subsidiary ledger. At the end of the month the total of the column is debited to Accounts Payable and credited to Purchases Returns and Allowances in the general ledger.

In all of the foregoing examples the creditor's account was debited. When the return or the allowance is granted after the invoice has been paid, the settlement may be made in cash. In such cases the transaction would be recorded in the cash receipts journal as a debit to Cash and a credit to Purchases Returns and Allowances.

Using purchases invoices as a purchases journal

Many businesses treat the invoices themselves as a journal, thus eliminating the intermediate step of recording each invoice in the purchases journal. When this is done, the amount of each invoice is posted from the invoice direct to the creditor's account in the subsidiary ledger. At the end of the month an adding machine list may be made of all the invoices. If some of the purchases are for goods other than merchandise, separate adding machine lists are made for each kind of purchase. An entry is then made in the *general journal* debiting the appropriate general ledger accounts and crediting the accounts payable account. For example, if the adding machine lists show purchases of merchandise, $8,612, office supplies, $340, store supplies, $218, and office equipment, $670, the general journal entry would be as follows:

Nov.	30	Purchases..................		8,612		
		Office Supplies..............		340		
		Store Supplies..............		218		
		Office Equipment...........		670		
		Accounts Payable.........			9,840	

Credit terms and cash discounts

The credit terms quoted on purchases of stock in trade and other assets ordinarily differ among various suppliers. Some may sell on a net cash basis and others may grant credit for varying periods of time. The payment of accounts as they become due is an important factor in maintaining a good credit rating. It is also important that advantage be taken of all available cash discounts, even though it may be necessary to borrow money to do so. For example, assume a purchase invoice for $800, with terms of 2/10, n/30. The obligation could be discharged within 10 days by payment of $784, representing a savings of $16. In contrast, the interest expense incurred by borrowing $784 for the remaining 20 days of the credit period would be $2.61, assuming an interest rate of 6%. The net savings accruing to the purchaser would thus be the difference between the cash discount of $16 and the interest expense of $2.61, or $13.39.

There are various systems designed to assure payment within the discount period or on the last day of the credit period. A simple but effective method is to file unpaid invoices according to the dates when payment should be considered. The file is composed of a group of folders numbered from 1 to 31, the numbers representing dates. Each invoice is first filed by its discount date. For example, a purchase invoice dated October 10, with terms of 2/10, n/30, should be considered for payment on October 20, the last day of the discount period. It is therefore placed in the folder numbered "20." On October 20 this invoice, together with all other invoices requiring consideration on that date, will be taken from the folder by the treasurer or other person responsible for making disbursements. Each invoice in the folder will then either be paid or be refiled in the appropriate folder. For example, if the October 10 invoice is not paid on October 20, it should be considered again on November 9, the last day of the credit period, and it should accordingly be refiled in the "9" folder.

Cash payments journal

The criteria for determining the special columns to be provided in the cash payments journal are the same as for other journals illustrated earlier, namely, the nature of the transactions to be recorded and the frequency of their occurrence. It is necessary, of course, to have a Cash Cr. column. Payments to creditors on account are usually sufficiently frequent to require columns for Accounts Payable Dr. and Purchases Discount Cr. The cash payments journal illustrated on page 151 has these three columns and an additional column for Sundry Accounts Dr. If payments for one or more specific operating expenses were sufficiently numerous, other special columns could be added to the journal.

All payments by Bennett Electrical Supplies are made by check and the check stubs serve as the written evidence of the transactions. As

CASH PAYMENTS JOURNAL   PAGE 16

DATE	CHK. NO.	ACCOUNT DEBITED	POST. REF.	SUNDRY ACCOUNTS DR.	ACCOUNTS PAYABLE DR.	PURCHASES DISCOUNT CR.	CASH CR.
1961 Oct. 2	312	Purchases	511	195 00			195 00
4	313	Office Equipment	122	270 00			270 00
12	314	Queen Electronics	✓		406 00	4 06	401 94
12	315	Sales Salaries	611	380 00			380 00
12	316	Office Salaries	711	160 00			160 00
14	317	Misc. General Expense	715	26 40			26 40
16	318	Prepaid Insurance	117	84 00			84 00
18	319	Queen Electronics	✓		208 00	2 08	205 92
20	320	Moore Wholesalers	✓		1850 00		1850 00
21	321	Sales Returns and Allow.	412	62 00			62 00
23	322	United Parts Wholesalers	✓		1600 00		1600 00
23	323	Purchases	511	89 20			89 20
24	324	State Distributors	✓		2300 00		2300 00
24	325	Wilson Manufacturing Co.	✓		525 00		525 00
26	326	Sales Salaries	611	380 00			380 00
26	327	Office Salaries	711	160 00			160 00
26	328	Allied Electronics Supply	✓		547 50	10 95	536 55
26	329	Advertising Expense	613	86 00			86 00
27	330	Misc. Selling Expense	617	41 50			41 50
28	331	John Bennett, Drawing	312	500 00			500 00
31				2434 10	7436 50	17 09	9853 51
				(✓)	(211)	(513)	(111)

Cash payments journal after posting

each transaction is recorded in the cash payments journal, the related check number is entered in the column at the right of the date column. The check numbers facilitate the control of cash payments, since a review of this column will indicate whether all checks have been recorded.

The Sundry Accounts Dr. column is used to record debits to any account for which there is no special column. For example, on October 2 Bennett Electrical Supplies paid $195 for a cash purchase of merchandise. The transaction was recorded by writing the account title "Purchases" in the space provided and $195 in the Sundry Accounts Dr. and the Cash Cr. columns. The posting reference was inserted later, at the time the debit was posted.

Debits to creditors' accounts for invoices paid are recorded in the Accounts Payable Dr. column. If there is no cash discount, the amount recorded in the Cash Cr. column will be equal to the debit to the creditor. If a discount is allowed, the credit to Cash will be correspondingly less. Cash discounts taken on merchandise purchased for resale are recorded in the Purchases Discount Cr. column. For example, the payment to Queen Electronics on October 12 was recorded as a debit to Accounts Payable of $406.00, a credit to Purchases Discount of $4.06, and a credit to Cash of $401.94.

At frequent intervals during the month, the amounts entered in the Accounts Payable Dr. column are posted to the debit of creditors' accounts in the accounts payable ledger. The source of the entries is indicated by inserting "CP" and the appropriate page number in the posting reference column of the accounts. Check marks are placed in the posting reference column of the cash payments journal to indicate that the amounts have been posted. The items in the Sundry Accounts column are also posted to the appropriate accounts in the general ledger at frequent intervals and the posting is indicated by writing the account numbers in the posting reference column of the cash payments journal.

At the end of the month the cash payments journal is ruled, each of the money columns is footed, and the equality of debits and credits is determined as follows:

Debit Totals		Credit Totals	
Sundry Accounts (net)....	$2,434.10	Purchases Discount.......	$ 17.09
Accounts Payable........	7,436.50	Cash..................	9,853.51
	$9,870.60		$9,870.60

A check mark is placed below the total of the Sundry Accounts Dr. column to indicate that it is not posted. As each of the totals of the other three columns is posted to a general ledger account, the appropriate posting references are inserted below the column totals.

Accounts payable control and subsidiary ledger

During October the following postings were made to Accounts Payable in the general ledger of Bennett Electrical Supplies:

CREDITS

Oct. 31 (Total purchases on account, from purchases journal).... $5,520.00

DEBITS

Oct. 20 (A purchases return, from general journal)............   7.50
     31 (Total debits resulting from payments on account, from cash payments journal).........................   7,436.50

The controlling account with its opening balance, the foregoing postings, and memorandum totals and balance is shown below.

				Accounts Payable						ACCOUNT NO. 211				
DATE	ITEMS	POST. REF.			DEBIT		DATE	ITEMS		POST. REF.			CREDIT	
1961 Oct. 20		J18			7 50		1961 Oct. 1	Balance		✓		6 2 7 5 00		
31		CP16	7 4 3 6 50				31		4351.00	P19		5 5 2 0 00		
			7 4 4 4 00								1 1 7 9 5 00			

Accounts payable account in the general ledger at the end of the month

Although the column totals in the cash payments journal are posted only at the end of the month, it is advisable to post to the creditors' accounts each day. Daily posting distributes the work load more evenly over the month and also makes it possible to determine easily the status of any creditors' account at any time.

The accounts payable ledger of Bennett Electrical Supplies, after posting all entries for the month, is shown on this and the following page.

NAME *Allied Electronics Supply*
ADDRESS *405 Murray St., Chicago 15, Ill.*

DATE	ITEMS	POST. REF.	DEBIT	CREDIT	BALANCE
1961					
Oct. 13		P 19		5 5 5 00	5 5 5 00
20		J 18	7 50		5 47 50
26		CP 16	5 47 50		—

NAME *Black Electric Corp.*
ADDRESS *42-46 N. Randolph, Pittsburgh 4, Pa.*

DATE	ITEMS	POST. REF.	DEBIT	CREDIT	BALANCE
1961					
Oct. 11		P 19		6 23 00	6 23 00
27		P 19		3 75 00	9 98 00

NAME *Moore Wholesalers*
ADDRESS *370 Third St., Trenton 5, N.J.*

DATE	ITEMS	POST. REF.	DEBIT	CREDIT	BALANCE
1961					
Sept. 21		P 18		1 8 50 00	1 8 50 00
Oct. 20		CP 16	1 8 50 00		—

NAME *Office Equipment Distributors*
ADDRESS *2113 Elwood St., Cincinnati 2, Ohio*

DATE	ITEMS	POST. REF.	DEBIT	CREDIT	BALANCE
1961					
Oct. 16		P 19		5 70 00	5 70 00

Accounts payable ledger at the end of the month

NAME *Queen Electronics*
ADDRESS *1215 College St., Cleveland 5, Ohio*

DATE	ITEMS	POST. REF.	DEBIT	CREDIT	BALANCE
1961 Oct. 3		P19		406 00	406 00
9		P19		208 00	614 00
12		CP16	406 00		208 00
18		CP16	208 00		

NAME *Reed Supplies, Inc.*
ADDRESS *2811 N. High St., Reading, Pa.*

DATE	ITEMS	POST. REF.	DEBIT	CREDIT	BALANCE
1961 Oct. 7		P19		57 00	57 00
25		P19		32 00	89 00

NAME *State Distributors*
ADDRESS *10231 Fortieth St., Pittsburgh 12, Pa.*

DATE	ITEMS	POST. REF.	DEBIT	CREDIT	BALANCE
1961 Sept. 26		P18		2300 00	2300 00
Oct. 19		P19		1000 00	3300 00
24		CP16	2300 00		1000 00

NAME *United Parts Wholesalers*
ADDRESS *1319 Hyde Place, Chicago 9, Ill.*

DATE	ITEMS	POST. REF.	DEBIT	CREDIT	BALANCE
1961 Sept. 25		P18		1600 00	1600 00
Oct. 2		P19		619 00	2219 00
23		CP16	1600 00		619 00

NAME *Wilson Manufacturing Co.*
ADDRESS *3636 Chestnut St., Philadelphia 6, Pa.*

DATE	ITEMS	POST. REF.	DEBIT	CREDIT	BALANCE
1961 Sept. 28		P18		525 00	525 00
Oct. 14		P19		910 00	1435 00
21		P19		165 00	1600 00
24		CP16	525 00		1075 00

Accounts payable ledger at the end of the month—concluded

After all posting has been completed for the month, the sum of the balances in the creditors' ledger should be compared with the balance of the accounts payable account in the general ledger. If the controlling account and the subsidiary ledger are not in agreement, the error or errors must be located and corrected. The balances of the individual creditors' accounts may be summarized on an adding machine tape, or a schedule like the one below may be prepared. The total of the schedule, $4,351, agrees with the balance of the accounts payable account shown on page 152.

Bennett Electrical Supplies Schedule of Accounts Payable October 31, 1961		
Black Electric Corp.		998 00
Office Equipment Distributors		570 00
Reed Supplies, Inc.		89 00
State Distributors		1 000 00
United Parts Wholesalers		619 00
Wilson Manufacturing Co.		1 075 00
Total Accounts Payable		4 351 00

Schedule of accounts payable

Transportation on incoming shipments

The cost of merchandise acquired includes the transportation charges for delivery of the goods. Similarly, the cost of fixed assets, supplies, and other items purchased includes transportation costs. This is true, in general, regardless of whether the seller or the buyer agrees to bear the cost of transporting the goods from the shipping point to the destination. Businesses that quote prices FOB destination must, of necessity, consider the transportation costs in establishing their prices.

When assets are purchased on an FOB shipping point basis, the related freight, express, postage, or other transportation costs should be charged to the same account to which the commodities were charged. Thus, transportation charges on merchandise should be debited to Purchases, transportation charges on store equipment should be debited to Store Equipment, etc. If the buyer pays the transportation agency, the debit is recorded when the bill is paid. If the shipper pays the delivery costs and adds them to the invoice, the entire amount of the invoice, including transportation, is debited to the appropriate account.

Some businesses maintain a separate account entitled *Freight-In* or *Transportation-In* to which they charge delivery costs on merchandise purchased. The account is then presented on the income statement as an addition to Purchases. This is not ordinarily necessary, however, as the relationship of the total amount of freight-in to the total amount of merchandise purchases for a period is not significant. The important thing is to buy at the best possible delivered price, which means that the purchasing department must consider list price and transportation and discount terms in placing each order.

Questions

1. Explain how an invoice can be both a purchase invoice and a sales invoice.

2. (a) Name two business papers described in this chapter that are used as the basis for accounting entries. (b) Name one business paper that facilitates but does not represent a completed business transaction.

3. The receiving department of A Co. is provided with the purchase invoice for use in reporting the receipt of goods purchased. B Co. provides a carbon copy of the purchase order on which quantities and prices do not appear and requires that the receiving department insert the quantities of the various goods received. Comment on the relative merits of the two systems.

4. Describe the three related transactions recorded in the T accounts below:

CASH		ACCOUNTS PAYABLE	
(c) 1,078	(b) 100	(a) 1,200
	(c) 1,100	

PURCHASES RET. & ALLOW.		PURCHASES DISCOUNT	
(b) 100		(c) 22

PURCHASES	
(a) 1,200	

5. The following errors were made in recording transactions in the purchases journal or in posting therefrom. How will each error be brought to the attention of the bookkeeper other than by chance discovery?

(a) An invoice for office supplies of $50 was recorded as $5.

(b) The accounts payable column is overfooted by $100.

(c) An invoice for merchandise of $500 from Miller Corp. was recorded as having been received from Mills Corp., another supplier.

(d) A credit of $700 to J. B. Baker, Inc. was posted as $70.

6. Would you recommend the use of sales and purchases journals for the following businesses: (a) a cafeteria, (b) a wholesale drug company, (c) a retail drugstore doing a cash business, (d) a gardener who raises vegetables and sells them in a neighboring city?

7. At the end of the month the accounts payable and cash columns in the cash payments journal were unknowingly underfooted by $1,000. (a) Assuming no other errors in recording or posting, what effect will the error have on the trial balance? (b) Will the creditors' ledger agree with the accounts payable account?

8. Why should management be interested in keeping the volume of purchases returns to a minimum?

9. When a debit or credit to the account of a customer or creditor is entered in a two-column general journal, it is advisable to insert a diagonal line in the posting reference column on the same line. What is the reason for this procedure?

10. In recording a cash payment the bookkeeper enters the correct amount of $600 in the Accounts Payable Dr. column and the correct amount of $594 in the Cash Cr. column but omits the entry for Purchases Discount. How will this error be brought to his attention other than by chance discovery?

11. Central Appliance Co. purchases 20 automatic washers for $150 each, FOB shipping point, 2/10, n/30. The transportation charges on the shipment amount to $90. Assuming that the invoice is paid within the discount period, what is the net unit cost of the washers?

Exercises

1. Benton Market uses its purchases invoices as its purchases journal. At the end of June, adding machine lists show the following totals for the various kinds of purchases on account: merchandise purchases, $24,674; store supplies, $850; office supplies, $70; office equipment, $175. Prepare the general journal entry that should be made on the basis of this information.

2. Determine the amount to be paid in full settlement of each of the following invoices, assuming that credit for returns and allowances was received prior to payment and that all invoices were paid within the discount period.

Purchase Invoice			Returns and
Merchandise	Transportation	Terms	Allowances
(a) $1,000	—	FOB shipping point, 2/10, n/30	$100
(b) 1,500	$50	FOB shipping point, 1/10, n/30	—
(c) 900	—	FOB destination, n/30	50
(d) 1,200	60	FOB shipping point, 2/10, n/30	80
(e) 600	—	FOB destination, 1/10, n/30	200

3. Robert Conrad purchases $500 of merchandise from Jacobs Corp., FOB shipping point, 2/10, n/30. Jacobs Corp. adds transportation charges of $20 to the invoice. Conrad returns merchandise for which he receives credit for $60 and then pays the amount due within the discount period. Present Conrad's entries, in general journal form, to record (a) the invoice, (b) the debit memorandum, and (c) the payment.

4. Jensen Fabrics Co. purchased $600 of merchandise on account from Meredith Mills, 2/10, n/30, paying the invoice within the discount period. They subsequently discovered that some of the fabrics were not color fast and with the permission of the creditor returned items with an invoice price of $400. Present Jensen Fabrics Co. entries in general journal form to record the return (a) assuming they receive a cash refund and (b) assuming they elect to have Meredith Mills credit their account. (c) Assuming that they elect (b) and subsequently purchase $400 of merchandise subject to the same discount terms, present the entry, in general journal form, to record the purchase.

Problems

7-1. Purchases on account and related returns and allowances completed by The Bookshelf during June of the current year are described below.

June 2. Purchased merchandise on account from Wallace Cards, Inc., $223.80.
4. Purchased merchandise on account from Stuart Publishers, $651.
7. Received a credit memorandum from Wallace Cards, Inc. for merchandise returned, $27.60.
10. Purchased office supplies on account from Lamson Supply Co., $38.50.
14. Purchased store equipment on account from Inland Furniture Co., $674.80.
15. Purchased merchandise on account from Wallace Cards, Inc., $124.10.
17. Purchased merchandise on account from Beacon Publishing Co., $452.70.
18. Received a credit memorandum from Lamson Supply Co. for office supplies returned, $8.40.
21. Purchased merchandise on account from Dayton Press, Inc., $394.
23. Received a credit memorandum from Stuart Publishers as an allowance for damaged merchandise, $110.
24. Purchased store supplies on account from Lamson Supply Co., $48.20.
25. Purchased merchandise on account from Beacon Publishing Co., $580.30.
29. Purchased office supplies on account from Lamson Supply Co., $14.70.

Instructions: (1) Open the following accounts in the general ledger and enter the balances as of June 1:

114 Store Supplies	$ 265.00	511 Purchases		$22,695.20
115 Office Supplies	177.50	512 Purchases Returns		
121 Store Equipment	6,720.00	and Allowances		741.50
211 Accounts Payable	1,622.10			

(2) Open the following accounts in the accounts payable ledger and enter the balances in the balance columns as of June 1: Beacon Publishing Co., $832.40; Dayton Press, Inc.; Inland Furniture Co.; Lamson Supply Co.; Stuart Publishers, $474.00; Wallace Cards, Inc., $315.70.

(3) Record the transactions for June, using a purchases journal similar to the one illustrated on pages 144 and 145, and a two-column general journal. Post to the subsidiary ledger account immediately after recording each transaction.

(4) Post the journals to the general ledger.

(5) (a) What is the sum of the balances of the accounts in the subsidiary ledger?

(b) What is the balance of the controlling account?

7-2. Modern Clothiers was established in October of the current year. Transactions related to purchases, returns and allowances, and cash payments during the remainder of the month are described below.

Oct. 16. Purchased store equipment on account from Glendale Merchants Supply, $4,500.

16. Purchased merchandise on account from Rochester Clothing, Inc., $2,300.

17. Issued check No. 1 in payment of rent for October, $250.

18. Issued check No. 2 in payment of office supplies, $22, and store supplies, $48.

18. Purchased merchandise on account from Adams & Co., $1,600.

19. Purchased merchandise on account from Walsh Brothers, $950.

20. Received a credit memorandum from Adams & Co. for returned merchandise, $100.

Post the journals to the accounts payable ledger.

24. Issued check No. 3 to Rochester Clothing, Inc., in payment of invoice of $2,300, less 2% discount.

25. Issued check No. 4 to Glendale Merchants Supply in payment of invoice of $4,500.

26. Received a credit memorandum from Walsh Brothers for defective merchandise, $45.

26. Issued check No. 5 to a cash customer for merchandise returned, $23.

27. Issued check No. 6 to Adams & Co. in payment of the balance owed, less 2% discount.

27. Purchased merchandise on account from Walsh Brothers, $1,980.

Post the journals to the accounts payable ledger.

30. Purchased the following from Glendale Merchants Supply on account: store supplies, $18; office supplies, $29; office equipment, $850.

30. Issued check No. 7 to Walsh Brothers in payment of the invoice of $950 less the credit of $45.

30. Purchased merchandise on account from Rochester Clothing, Inc., $1,420.

31. Issued check No. 8 in payment of transportation charges on merchandise purchased, $124.

31. Issued check No. 9 in payment of sales salaries, $480.

Post the journals to the accounts payable ledger.

Instructions: (1) Open the following accounts in the general ledger, using the account numbers indicated:

111 Cash	412 Sales Returns and Allowances
116 Store Supplies	511 Purchases
117 Office Supplies	512 Purchases Returns and Allowances
121 Store Equipment	513 Purchases Discount
122 Office Equipment	611 Sales Salaries
211 Accounts Payable	712 Rent Expense

(2) Open the following accounts in the accounts payable ledger: Adams & Co.; Glendale Merchants Supply; Rochester Clothing, Inc.; Walsh Brothers.

(3) Record the transactions for October, using a purchases journal similar to the one illustrated on pages 144 and 145, a purchases returns and allowances journal similar to the one illustrated on page 149, and a cash payments journal similar to the one illustrated on page 151. Post to the accounts payable ledger at the points indicated in the narrative of transactions.

(4) Post to the general ledger.

(5) Prepare a schedule of accounts payable.

If the working papers correlating with the textbook are not used, omit Problem **7-3.**

7-3. Fieldcrest Supply Co. uses carbon copies of its sales invoices as a sales journal, posting to the accounts receivable ledger directly from the invoices. At the end of the month the invoices are totaled and the appropriate entry is recorded in the general journal. Purchases on account are handled in a similar manner, the invoices being used as a purchases journal. Sales and purchases on account during January of the current year were as follows:

Sales

Jan.	5.	No. 681 Edward Allen Corp.	$2,300
	6.	No. 682 Nelson and Co.	1,650
	10.	No. 683 Fred Collins	1,350
	16.	No. 684 Tucker and Walsh	450
	17.	No. 685 Fred Collins	2,712
	22.	No. 686 Nelson and Co.	563

Purchases

Jan.	2.	Walker Corp.: store supplies, $130; office supplies, $24	$ 154
	3.	Lewis Manufacturing Co., merchandise	2,475
	11.	James Bell, Inc., merchandise	1,900
	18.	Stewart-Barnes Co., office equipment	1,225
	19.	Johnson & Co., merchandise	862
	29.	Walker Corp., store supplies	36
	31.	James Bell, Inc., merchandise	1,119

Other transactions completed during the month were recorded in a 4-column general journal, a cash receipts journal, and a cash payments journal, all of which are presented in the working papers. The subsidiary ledgers and the general ledger accounts affected by transactions of the month are also presented in the working papers.

Instructions: (1) Summarize the sales invoices and the purchases invoices listed above and record the appropriate entries in the 4-column general journal.

(2) Post all items affecting the *subsidiary* ledgers, in the following order: sales invoices, purchases invoices, general journal, cash receipts journal, cash payments journal. When postings are made daily, which is the usual practice, the entries in customers' and creditors' accounts will appear in chronological order. The fact that in this problem postings to some of the accounts will not be in perfect date sequence is immaterial.

(3) Post all items recorded in the Sundry Accounts Dr. and Sundry Accounts Cr. columns of the journals, in the following order: general journal, cash receipts journal, cash payments journal.

(4) Foot and rule the general journal; post the columnar totals of the journals, following the same sequence as in instruction (3).

(5) Prepare a trial balance.

(6) What is the sum of the balances in the

    (a) Accounts receivable ledger?

    (b) Accounts payable ledger?

7-4. The transactions completed by Selby's during July, the first month of the current fiscal year, were as follows:

July 1. Issued check No. 647 for July rent, $500.

     2. Purchased merchandise on account from Winters Co., $2,120.

     3. Purchased equipment on account from Pearce Supply Co., $1,500.

     3. Issued invoice No. 722 to Arnold & Morris, $700.

     5. Received check for $882 from George Little in payment of $900 invoice, less discount.

     5. Issued check No. 648 in payment of miscellaneous selling expense, $115.

     5. Received credit memorandum from Winters Co. for merchandise returned to them, $70.

     8. Issued invoice No. 723 to Ross Corp., $1,650.

     9. Issued check No. 649 for $2,156 to Carson-Knox Corp. in payment of $2,200 balance less discount.

     9. Received check for $1,519 from Arnold & Morris in payment of $1,550 invoice, less discount.

   10. Issued check No. 650 to Pearce Supply Co. in payment of invoice of $1,500; no discount.

Post all journals to the accounts receivable ledger and the accounts payable ledger.

   10. Issued invoice No. 724 to George Little, $2,680.

   11. Issued check No. 651 to R. T. Harris in payment of account, $720; no discount.

   12. Received check from John Weston on account, $780; no discount.

   15. Issued credit memorandum to George Little for damaged merchandise, $30.

   15. Issued check No. 652 for $2,009 to Winters Co. in payment of $2,050 balance less discount.

   16. Cash sales for July 1–16, $4,621.

   17. Purchased merchandise on account from Carson-Knox Corp., $1,870.

   18. Received check for return of merchandise that was originally purchased for cash, $24.

   18. Issued check No. 653 in payment of miscellaneous general expense, $96.

   22. Purchased the following on account from Pearce Supply Co.: store supplies, $43; office supplies, $21.

   22. Issued check No. 654 in payment of advertising expense, $210.

Post all journals to the accounts receivable ledger and the accounts payable ledger.

   23. Issued invoice No. 725 to John Weston, $960.

   25. Purchased the following on account from Reed Manufacturing Co.: merchandise, $840; store supplies, $12.

   26. Issued invoice No. 726 to Ross Corp., $1,020.

   29. Issued check No. 655 to Reed Manufacturing Co. in payment of account, $1,350; no discount.

July 30. Received check for $2,597 from George Little in payment of $2,650 balance less discount.

30. Issued check No. 656 to David Selby as a personal withdrawal, $600.

31. Issued check No. 657 for monthly salaries as follows: sales salaries, $750; office salaries, $400.

31. Cash sales for July 17–31, $3,924.

31. Issued check No. 658 for transportation on commodities purchased during the month as follows: merchandise, $112; equipment, $27.

Post all journals to the accounts receivable ledger and the accounts payable ledger.

Instructions: (1) Open the following accounts in the general ledger, entering the balances indicated as of July 1:

111	Cash.................$ 6,412	411	Sales
113	Accounts Receivable... 3,230	412	Sales Returns and Allowances
114	Merchandise Inventory 25,620	413	Sales Discount
115	Store Supplies........ 320	511	Purchases
116	Office Supplies....... 115	512	Purchases Returns and Allow-
117	Prepaid Insurance..... 584		ances
121	Equipment.......... 14,280	513	Purchases Discount
121.1	Accumulated Deprecia-	611	Sales Salaries
	tion.............. 6,322	612	Advertising Expense
211	Accounts Payable..... 4,270	619	Miscellaneous Selling Expense
311	David Selby, Capital.. 39,969	711	Office Salaries
312	David Selby, Drawing.	712	Rent Expense
		719	Miscellaneous General Expense

(2) Open the following accounts in the accounts receivable ledger, entering the balances as of July 1 in the balance columns: Arnold & Morris, $1,550; George Little, $900; Ross Corp.; John Weston, $780.

(3) Open the following accounts in the accounts payable ledger, entering the balances as of July 1 in the balance columns: Carson-Knox Corp., $2,200; R. T. Harris & Co., $720; Pearce Supply Co.; Reed Manufacturing Co., $1,350; Winters Co.

(4) Record the transactions for July, using a sales journal (as on page 122), a purchases journal (as on pages 144 and 145), a cash receipts journal (as on page 129), a cash payments journal (as on page 151), and a 2-column general journal. The terms of all sales on account are FOB shipping point, 2/15, n/60. Post to the subsidiary ledgers at the points indicated in the narrative of transactions.

(5) Post all journals to the general ledger.

(6) Prepare a trial balance.

(7) Prepare a schedule of accounts receivable and a schedule of accounts payable.

Periodic summary

Outline of the periodic summary

Twelve months is the standard maximum length of the fiscal period. At yearly intervals throughout the life of a business enterprise it is necessary to summarize the operating and financial data, prepare statements for owners, creditors, and other interested persons, and prepare the accounts for entries of the ensuing year. Interim statements may have been prepared at the end of each month, but it is necessary to record adjusting and closing entries at the end of the year.

Although it is possible to vary the sequence of procedures to a limited extent, the accounting department of a business firm must perform the following year-end tasks:

1. Prepare a trial balance of the general ledger.
2. Determine that each subsidiary ledger is in agreement with the related controlling account in the general ledger.
3. Review the accounts to determine which ones should be adjusted, and compile the data necessary for making the adjustments.
4. Prepare a work sheet from the trial balance and the data for the adjustments.
5. Prepare financial statements from the data in the work sheet.
6. Record the adjusting entries in the journal.
7. Record the closing entries in the journal.
8. Post the adjusting and closing entries, rule the closed accounts, and balance and rule other accounts.
9. Prepare a post-closing trial balance of the general ledger.
10. Record the reversing entries necessary to prepare the accounts for entries of the ensuing year.
11. Post the reversing entries, and rule the accounts that are in balance.

The foregoing outline is similar to the outline presented in Chapter 5 except for the addition of the comparison of controlling accounts with related subsidiary ledgers and the addition of reversing entries. The added procedures apply both to service and merchandising businesses. The illustration of the periodic summary that follows includes two adjusting entries that are different in nature from those previously considered. Both are related to the merchandise inventory and the determination of the cost of the merchandise sold.

Merchandise inventory adjustments

The entry to record a sale of merchandise is a debit to Cash or Accounts Receivable and a credit to Sales. Assuming that the goods are sold at a price in excess of cost, the credit to Sales is composed of two elements: (1) reduction in merchandise and (2) gross profit. In most businesses it is impractical to attempt to determine and record these two elements separately. For example, if an item that cost $6.00 is sold for $8.20, the effect of the transaction is to decrease merchandise by $6.00 and to increase gross profit by $2.20. It is customary to ignore these details for the time being by recording the entire $8.20 as a credit to Sales.

At the end of the accounting period it is necessary to determine the total cost of the goods sold during the period. The cost may then be deducted from the sales revenue to yield the gross profit on sales. If there were no inventories on hand at the beginning or end of the period, the cost of the goods sold would be the same as the net purchases. This is not the usual situation, however. The procedure for determining the cost of the goods sold is illustrated in the following tabulation:

Merchandise inventory, beginning of year			$10,000
Purchases		$64,000	
Less: Purchases returns and allowances	$1,200		
Purchases discount	800	2,000	
Net purchases			62,000
Merchandise available for sale			$72,000
Less merchandise inventory, end of year			12,000
Cost of goods sold			$60,000

In the foregoing tabulation the amounts shown for the merchandise inventory at the beginning of the year, the purchases, the purchases returns and allowances, and the purchases discounts were taken from the trial balance; they are the balances of the respective accounts in the ledger. The beginning inventory of $10,000 had been debited to Merchandise Inventory at the close of the preceding year and there were no other debits or credits to the account during the current year. The amount of the ending inventory, $12,000 was obtained from a physical inventory of the goods on hand on the last day of the year.

It is necessary to replace the old balance of $10,000 in Merchandise Inventory with the new amount, $12,000. It is also necessary to use both figures in determining the cost of goods sold. These objectives are accomplished by transferring $10,000 from the merchandise inventory account to the expense and revenue summary account and transferring $12,000 from the expense and revenue summary account to the merchandise inventory account, by the following adjusting entries:

Dec.	31	Expense and Revenue Summary........	10,000	
		Merchandise Inventory............		10,000
Dec.	31	Merchandise Inventory..............	12,000	
		Expense and Revenue Summary.....		12,000

After the two entries have been posted, the merchandise inventory account will have a debit balance of $12,000, which is the amount of the asset at the end of the year. The entries in the expense and revenue summary account will automatically adjust the purchases, purchases returns and allowances, and purchases discount that will be closed to the account as a part of the closing process, to yield the cost of the merchandise sold.

The effect of the inventory adjustments may also be shown in T accounts as follows:

MERCHANDISE INVENTORY

Jan. 1 Beginning inventory	10,000	Dec. 31 Beginning inventory 10,000
Dec. 31 Ending inventory	12,000	

EXPENSE AND REVENUE SUMMARY

Dec. 31 Beginning inventory	10,000	Dec. 31 Ending inventory 12,000

Adjustments and the work sheet

After all journals have been posted at the end of the year, the balance of each account in the general ledger is determined and a trial balance is prepared. The sum of the balances of the accounts in each subsidiary ledger should also be determined and compared with the balance of the related controlling account. Any errors revealed should be corrected before the work sheet is completed.

The trial balance for Bennett Electrical Supplies as of December 31, 1961, appears in the first two columns of the work sheet illustrated on pages 168 and 169. The data needed for adjusting the accounts are obtained from various sources and set forth in a compilation similar to the one at the top of the following page.

The procedures for recording adjustments on the work sheet of a merchandising company are similar to those described for a service enterprise in Chapter 5. The adjustments in the work sheet on pages 168 and 169 are briefly described in the paragraphs that follow.

DATA FOR ADJUSTMENTS, DECEMBER 31, 1961

Merchandise inventory as of December 31, 1961............		$18,200
Inventories of supplies as of December 31, 1961:		
Store supplies.......................................		690
Office supplies......................................		340
Insurance expired during 1961:		
On merchandise and store equipment..................	$420	
On office equipment and building....................	296	716
Depreciation during 1961:		
On store equipment.................................		1,000
On office equipment................................		340
On building..		700
Salaries and commissions accrued on December 31, 1961:		
Sales salaries.....................................	$152	
Office salaries....................................	60	212
Sales commissions.................................		564

Merchandise inventory. The $16,600 balance of merchandise inventory appearing in the trial balance represents the amount of the inventory at the close of the preceding year. It is a part of the merchandise available for sale during the year and is hence transferred to Expense and Revenue Summary, where it will be combined with the cost of merchandise purchased during the year. (Entry (a) on the work sheet.)

The cost of the merchandise on hand at the end of the current year, as determined by a physical inventory, is $18,200. It is an asset and must be debited to the asset account Merchandise Inventory. It must also be deducted from the cost of the merchandise available for sale (beginning inventory plus net purchases) to yield the cost of the goods sold. These objectives are accomplished by debiting Merchandise Inventory and crediting Expense and Revenue Summary. (Entry (b) on the work sheet.)

Supplies. The $1,270 balance of the store supplies account in the trial balance is the sum of the inventory on hand at the close of the preceding year and net purchases of store supplies during the current year. The physical inventory at the end of the year indicates store supplies on hand totaling $690. The difference of $580 ($1,270 − $690) is therefore the amount of store supplies consumed. The accounts are adjusted by debiting Store Supplies Expense and crediting Store Supplies for $580. (Entry (c) on the work sheet.) The adjustment for office supplies consumed is determined in the same manner. (Entry (d) on the work sheet.)

Prepaid insurance. The adjustment for insurance expired is similar to the adjustment for supplies consumed. The balance in Prepaid Insurance is the sum of the amount prepaid at the beginning of the year and additional premiums paid during the year. Analysis of the various insurance policies reveals that a total of $716 in premiums have expired, of which $420 is applicable to merchandise and store equipment, and $296 is applicable to office equipment and building. Insurance Expense — Selling is debited for $420, Insurance Expense — General is debited for $296, and Prepaid Insurance is credited for $716. (Entry (e) on the work sheet.)

Depreciation of plant assets. The expired cost of plant assets is debited to a depreciation expense account and credited to an accumulated depreciation account. A separate account for the expense and for the accumulation is maintained for each plant asset account. Thus, the adjustment for depreciation of the store equipment is recorded by a debit to Depreciation Expense — Store Equipment and a credit to Accumulated Depreciation — Store Equipment for $1,000. The adjustments for depreciation of the office equipment and the building are recorded in a similar manner. (Entries (f), (g), and (h) on the work sheet.)

Salaries and commissions payable. The liability for the salaries earned by employees but not paid is recorded by a credit of $212 to the liability account Salaries Payable. The appropriate expense accounts are debited, Sales Salaries for $152 and Office Salaries for $60. (Entry (i) on the work sheet.) Similarly, commissions earned but not paid are recorded by a credit to the liability account Commissions Payable and a debit to the expense account Sales Commissions. (Entry (j) on the work sheet.)

Completing the work sheet

After all necessary adjustments are entered on the work sheet, the two columns are totaled to prove the equality of the debits and credits.

The amounts in the Trial Balance section are then combined with those in the Adjustments section. In the work sheet illustrated in Chapter 5 the amounts were extended to the appropriate columns of the Adjusted Trial Balance section and the arithmetical accuracy of the computations was verified by totaling the columns. Many accountants prefer to omit this intermediate step and extend the trial balance amounts, after adjustment, directly to the Income Statement and Balance Sheet sections. This latter plan is followed in the illustration on pages 168 and 169.

The most efficient procedure for extending the amounts to the statement sections is to begin at the top of the work sheet and dispose of each item in sequential order. Nothing is gained by extending only the income statement items or the balance sheet items first and then going over the

Bennett Electrical Supplies
Work Sheet
For Year Ended December 31, 1961

ACCT. NO.	ACCOUNT TITLES	TRIAL BALANCE DR.	TRIAL BALANCE CR.	ADJUSTMENTS DR.	ADJUSTMENTS CR.	INCOME STATEMENT DR.	INCOME STATEMENT CR.	BALANCE SHEET DR.	BALANCE SHEET CR.
111	Cash	967500						967500	
113	Accounts Receivable	890000						890000	
114	Merchandise Inventory	1660000		(b)1820000	(a)1660000			1820000	
115	Store Supplies	127000			(c)58000			69000	
116	Office Supplies	58000			(d)24000			34000	
117	Prepaid Insurance	152000			(e)71600			80400	
121	Store Equipment	1200000						1200000	
122	Accumulated Depr.—Store Equip.		470000		(f)100000				570000
123	Office Equipment	340000						340000	
124	Accumulated Depr.—Office Equip.		68000		(g)34000				102000
125	Building	2800000						2800000	
126	Accumulated Depr.—Building		350000		(h)70000				420000
127	Land	300000						300000	
211	Accounts Payable		927000						927000
221	Mortgage Payable		800000						800000
311	John Bennett, Capital		4375100						4375100
312	John Bennett, Drawing	1200000						1200000	
411	Sales		16457400				16457400		
412	Sales Returns and Allowances	315000				315000			
413	Sales Discount	131400				131400			
511	Purchases	10392000				10392000			
512	Purchases Returns and Allow.		264000				264000		

Account	Trial Balance Dr	Trial Balance Cr	Adjustments Dr	Adjustments Cr	Income Statement Dr	Income Statement Cr	Balance Sheet Dr	Balance Sheet Cr
513 Purchases Discount		185700				185700		
611 Sales Salaries	1451000		(i) 15200		1466200			
612 Sales Commissions	686700		(j) 56400		743100			
613 Advertising Expense	258000				258000			
615 Delivery Expense	96300				96300			
618 Miscellaneous Selling Expense	72400				72400			
711 Office Salaries	506400		(i) 6000		512400			
712 Legal Expense	176200				176200			
717 Miscellaneous General Expense	69300				69300			
911 Interest Expense	48000				48000			
	2389 7200	2389 7200						
313 Expense and Revenue Summary			(a) 1660000 (b) 1820000		1660000	1820000		
616 Store Supplies Expense			(c) 58000		58000			
715 Office Supplies Expense			(d) 24000		24000			
617 Insurance Expense—Selling			(e) 42000		42000			
716 Insurance Expense—General			(e) 29600		29600			
614 Depreciation Expense—Store Equip.			(f) 100000		100000			
713 Depreciation Expense—Office Equip.			(g) 34000		34000			
714 Depreciation Expense—Building			(h) 70000		70000			
213 Salaries Payable				(i) 21200				21200
212 Commissions Payable				(j) 56400				56400
			3915200	3915200	14297900	18727100	9700900	7277100
Net Income					2422200			2422200
					18727100	18727100	9700900	9700900

list again and extending the remaining amounts to the other section. To do so requires more time, and errors are more likely.

Both of the adjustments to Expense and Revenue Summary for merchandise inventory are extended to the Income Statement sections of the work sheet. The debit adjustment of $16,600 for the beginning inventory is entered in the debit column of the Income Statement section and the credit adjustment of $18,200 for the ending inventory is entered in the credit column of the Income Statement section. Substitution of the excess credit of $1,600 ($18,200 credit − $16,600 debit) for the debit and credit would not affect the computation of the net income at the bottom of the work sheet. The $1,600 variation in the inventory is not used, however, in preparing the income statement. When both inventory amounts are extended, the statement can be prepared completely from the data appearing in the Income Statement section of the work sheet.[1]

After all of the items have been extended into the statement sections of the work sheet, the four columns are totaled and the net income or loss is determined. In the illustration the difference between the credit and debit columns of the Income Statement section is $24,292, the amount of the net income. The difference between the debit and credit columns of the Balance Sheet section is also $24,292, the increase in proprietorship resulting from net income. Agreement between the two balancing amounts is evidence of debit-credit equality and arithmetical accuracy.

Preparation of statements and supporting schedules

The income statement, capital statement, and balance sheet are now prepared, using the data appearing in the statement sections of the work sheet. The items in the work sheet are generally in the order in which they appear in the two principal statements, except for those that are listed below the trial balance totals. Account numbers serve as a guide to the sequence of the items. In preparing the capital statement it is necessary to refer to the capital account in the general ledger to determine whether there have been investments or reductions during the year.

Formal schedules of accounts receivable and payable are sometimes prepared from the respective subsidiary ledgers. They may be useful to management in reviewing customer accounts for credit purposes and in preparing statements for credit rating agencies.

When there are several statements and supporting schedules included in a financial report, each may be designated by a letter or number.

---

[1]An alternative method of recording merchandise inventories on the work sheet is presented in Appendix A.

Although there are many possible variations in the system, the designations employed in the statements illustrated below and on pages 172 and 173 are satisfactory.

```
                    Bennett Electrical Supplies              Exhibit A
                         Income Statement
                    For Year Ended December 31, 1961
```

Revenue from sales:			
Sales.			$164,574
Less: Sales returns and allowances.	$ 3,150		
Sales discount.	1,314	4,464	
Net sales.			$160,110
Cost of goods sold:			
Merchandise inventory, January 1, 1961		$ 16,600	
Purchases.	$103,920		
Less: Purchases returns and allowances $2,640			
Purchases discount. 1,857	4,497		
Net purchases.		99,423	
Merchandise available for sale		$116,023	
Less merchandise inventory, December 31, 1961.		18,200	
Cost of goods sold			97,823
Gross profit on sales.			$ 62,287
Operating expenses:			
Selling expenses:			
Sales salaries	$ 14,662		
Sales commissions.	7,431		
Advertising expense.	2,580		
Depreciation expense--store equipment.	1,000		
Delivery expense	963		
Store supplies expense	580		
Insurance expense--selling	420		
Miscellaneous selling expense.	724		
Total selling expenses		$ 28,360	
General expenses:			
Office salaries.	$ 5,124		
Taxes expense.	1,762		
Depreciation expense--office equipment	340		
Depreciation expense--building	700		
Office supplies expense.	240		
Insurance expense--general	296		
Miscellaneous general expense.	693		
Total general expenses		9,155	
Total operating expenses			37,515
Net income from operations			$ 24,772
Other expense:			
Interest expense			480
Net income			$ 24,292

Income statement

Bennett Electrical Supplies   Exhibit B
Balance Sheet
December 31, 1961

Assets
Current assets:

Cash	$ 9,675	
Accounts receivable - Schedule 1	8,900	
Merchandise inventory.	18,200	
Store supplies	690	
Office supplies.	340	
Prepaid insurance.	804	
Total current assets		$38,609

Plant assets:

Store equipment.	$12,000		
Less accumulated depreciation.	5,700	$ 6,300	
Office equipment	$ 3,400		
Less accumulated depreciation.	1,020	2,380	
Building	$28,000		
Less accumulated depreciation.	4,200	23,800	
Land		3,000	
Total plant assets			35,480

Total assets	$74,089

Liabilities
Current liabilities:

Accounts payable - Schedule 2.	$ 9,270	
Mortgage payable (current portion)	1,000	
Commissions payable.	564	
Salaries payable	212	
Total current liabilities.		$11,046

Long-term liabilities:	
Mortgage payable (due annually through 1968) . . .	7,000

Total liabilities.	$18,046

Proprietorship

John Bennett, capital - Exhibit C.	56,043

Total liabilities and proprietorship	$74,089

Balance sheet

Bennett Electrical Supplies   Exhibit C
Capital Statement
For Year Ended December 31, 1961

Capital, January 1, 1961		$43,751
Net income for the year - Exhibit A.	$24,292	
Less withdrawals	12,000	
Increase in capital.		12,292
Capital, December 31, 1961		$56,043

Capital statement

Bennett Electrical Supplies   Exhibit B
Schedule of Accounts Receivable   Schedule 1
December 31, 1961

Acme Co.	$ 460
E. A. Albertson.	1,890
G. L. Bates.	716
John B. Deatrick	602
R. E. Holt	1,140
James Owen	865
Quaker Supply.	146
Howard Strauss	1,383
O. L. Tanner	750
Otto Wright.	948
Total accounts receivable	$8,900

Schedule of accounts receivable

Bennett Electrical Supplies   Exhibit B
Schedule of Accounts Payable   Schedule 2
December 31, 1961

Allied Electronics Supply.	$2,419
Black Electric Corporation	1,298
Office Equipment Distributors.	415
Queen Electronics.	1,132
Reed Supplies, Inc., ...	89
State Distributors	1,677
Wilson Manufacturing Company	2,240
Total accounts payable	$9,270

Schedule of accounts payable

Adjusting entries

After the financial statements have been prepared, the adjusting entries appearing in the Adjustments columns of the work sheet are journalized and posted to the ledger. The analysis necessary in formulating the adjusting entries was completed in preparing the work sheet, hence no further consideration need be given to the supporting data for the adjustments. After the posting is completed, the accounts will agree with the details reported in the financial statements. The adjusting entries for Bennett Electrical Supplies are presented on page 174.

GENERAL JOURNAL   PAGE 28

DATE	NAME OF ACCOUNT	POST. REF.	DEBIT	CREDIT
	Adjusting Entries			
31	Expense and Revenue Summary	313	16600 00	
	Merchandise Inventory	114		16600 00
31	Merchandise Inventory	114	18200 00	
	Expense and Revenue Summary	313		18200 00
31	Store Supplies Expense	616	580 00	
	Store Supplies	115		580 00
31	Office Supplies Expense	715	240 00	
	Office Supplies	116		240 00
31	Insurance Expense—Selling	617	420 00	
	Insurance Expense—General	716	296 00	
	Prepaid Insurance	117		716 00
31	Depreciation Expense—Store Equip.	614	1000 00	
	Accumulated Depreciation—Store Equip.	122		1000 00
31	Depreciation Expense—Office Equip.	713	340 00	
	Accumulated Depreciation—Office Equip.	124		340 00
31	Depreciation Expense—Building	714	700 00	
	Accumulated Depreciation—Building	126		700 00
31	Sales Salaries	611	1520 0	
	Office Salaries	711	600 0	
	Salaries Payable	213		2120 0
31	Sales Commissions	612	5640 0	
	Commissions Payable	212		5640 0

Adjusting entries

Closing entries

The closing entries are recorded in the general journal immediately following the adjusting entries. The effect of the closing entries is to reduce the balances of all temporary proprietorship accounts to zero and to transfer the net increase or decrease in proprietorship to the capital account. The four closing entries for Bennett Electrical Supplies, which are illustrated on page 175, may be described as follows:

GENERAL JOURNAL　　　　　　　　PAGE 29

DATE	NAME OF ACCOUNT	POST. REF.	DEBIT	CREDIT
	Closing Entries			
1961 Dec. 31	Sales	411	16 4 5 7 4 00	
	Purchases Returns and Allowances	512	2 6 4 0 00	
	Purchases Discount	513	1 8 5 7 00	
	Expense and Revenue Summary	313		16 9 0 7 1 00
31	Expense and Revenue Summary	313	14 6 3 7 9 00	
	Sales Returns and Allowances	412		3 1 5 0 00
	Sales Discount	413		1 3 1 4 00
	Purchases	511		103 9 2 0 00
	Sales Salaries	611		14 6 6 2 00
	Sales Commissions	612		7 4 3 1 00
	Advertising Expense	613		2 5 8 0 00
	Delivery Expense	615		9 6 3 00
	Miscellaneous Selling Expense	618		7 2 4 00
	Office Salaries	711		5 1 2 4 00
	Taxes Expense	712		1 7 6 2 00
	Miscellaneous General Expense	717		6 9 3 00
	Interest Expense	911		4 8 0 00
	Store Supplies Expense	616		5 8 0 00
	Office Supplies Expense	715		2 4 0 00
	Insurance Expense—Selling	617		4 2 0 00
	Insurance Expense—General	716		2 9 6 00
	Depreciation Expense—Store Equip.	614		1 0 0 0 00
	Depreciation Expense—Office Equip.	713		3 4 0 00
	Depreciation Expense—Building	714		7 0 0 00
31	Expense and Revenue Summary	313	2 4 2 9 2 00	
	John Bennett, Capital	311		2 4 2 9 2 00
31	John Bennett, Capital	311	1 2 0 0 0 00	
	John Bennett, Drawing	312		1 2 0 0 0 00

Closing entries

(1) The first entry closes all income statement accounts with *credit* balances by transferring the total to the *credit* side of Expense and Revenue Summary.

(2) The second entry closes all income statement accounts with *debit* balances by transferring the total to the *debit* side of Expense and Revenue Summary.

(3) The third entry closes Expense and Revenue Summary by transferring its balance to John Bennett, Capital.

(4) The fourth entry closes John Bennett, Drawing by transferring its balance to John Bennett, Capital.

After the foregoing closing entries have been posted, the expense and revenue summary account will have three debits and two credits. The first debit and the first credit in the account, which is reproduced below, were posted from the two entries adjusting the merchandise inventory account.

DATE	ITEMS	POST. REF.	DEBIT	DATE	ITEMS	POST. REF.	CREDIT
1961				1961			
Dec. 31		J28	16600 00	Dec. 31		J28	1820 00
31		J29 146379 00		31		J29 169071 00	
31		J29 24292 00					
			187271 00				187271 00

Expense and revenue summary account

After the adjusting entries and the closing entries have been posted to Bennett's ledger, the accounts are balanced and ruled. Only the asset accounts, the liability accounts, and the proprietor's capital account remain open. The balances of these accounts correspond exactly with the amounts on the balance sheet on page 172.

Post-closing trial balance

At the end of a fiscal period the equality of the debits and the credits in the ledger is determined by means of a trial balance. The adjusting and the closing entries are then made. If these entries are recorded and posted correctly, the equality of the debits and the credits in the ledger is not disturbed because the entries consist of equal debits and credits. A post-closing trial balance is therefore taken to determine whether the debit-credit equality has been maintained. The trial balance may be composed of an adding machine listing of the debit balances in the ledger and another of the credit balances, or the details may be recorded in more formal fashion, as illustrated at the top of the following page.

Reversing entries

Some adjusting entries recorded at the close of the fiscal period affect the recording of otherwise routine transactions in the following period. A typical example of such a situation is the adjusting entry for salaries accrued at the end of the period. Ordinarily the payment of salaries is recorded by a debit to Salary Expense (or various salary expense accounts) and a credit to Cash. If salaries are paid weekly, this type of

Bennett Electrical Supplies
Post-Closing Trial Balance
December 31, 1961

111	Cash	9 6 7 5 0 0	
113	Accounts Receivable	8 9 0 0 0 0	
114	Merchandise Inventory	1 8 2 0 0 0 0	
115	Store Supplies	6 9 0 0 0	
116	Office Supplies	3 4 0 0 0	
117	Prepaid Insurance	8 0 4 0 0	
121	Store Equipment	1 2 0 0 0 0	
122	Accumulated Depreciation—Store Equip.		5 7 0 0 0 0
123	Office Equipment	3 4 0 0 0	
124	Accumulated Depreciation—Office Equip.		1 0 2 0 0 0
125	Building	2 8 0 0 0 0 0	
126	Accumulated Depreciation—Building		4 2 0 0 0 0
127	Land	3 0 0 0 0 0	
211	Accounts Payable		9 2 7 0 0 0
212	Commissions Payable		5 6 4 0 0
213	Salaries Payable		2 1 2 0 0
221	Mortgage Payable		8 0 0 0 0 0
311	John Bennett, Capital		5 6 0 4 3 0 0
		8 5 0 0 9 0 0	8 5 0 0 9 0 0

Post-closing trial balance

transaction would occur 52 to 53 times during the year. When there are accrued salaries at the end of the year, however, the amount owed will be included in the first payroll for the ensuing year. Unless some special provision is made, it will be necessary to debit Salaries Payable for the amount owed for the earlier year and Salary Expense for the portion of the payroll that represents expense for the later year.

In order to illustrate the situation the following facts will be assumed for an enterprise that pays salaries weekly and closes its books on December 31:

(1) Salaries are paid on Friday for the five-day week ending on Friday.
(2) The balance in Salary Expense as of Friday, December 27, is $62,500.
(3) Salaries accrued for Monday and Tuesday, December 30 and 31, total $500.
(4) Salaries paid on Friday, January 3, of the ensuing year total $1,200.

The foregoing facts are presented in diagrammatic form at the top of the following page.

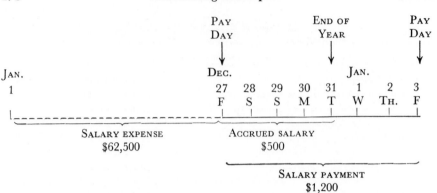

SALARY EXPENSE
$62,500

ACCRUED SALARY
$500

SALARY PAYMENT
$1,200

The entry to adjust the salary expense account and the salaries payable account is as follows:

| Dec. | 31 | Salary Expense...................... | 611 | 500 | |
| | | Salaries Payable.................. | 213 | | 500 |

After the adjusting entry for accrued salaries has been posted, Salary Expense will have a debit balance of $63,000 ($62,500 + $500) and Salaries Payable will have a credit balance of $500. After the accounts are closed, Salary Expense will be in balance and Salaries Payable will still have a credit balance of $500. As matters now stand it will be necessary to record the $1,200 payroll on January 3 as a debit of $500 to Salaries Payable and a debit of $700 to Salary Expense. This means that the employee who records payroll entries must record this particular payroll in a different manner from the other payrolls for the year, and also that he must refer to the adjusting entries in the journal or to ledger accounts to determine the amounts to be debited to the liability and expense accounts.

The necessity of referring back to earlier entries and splitting the debit between two accounts when recording the first payroll of the fiscal period may be avoided by a simple technique known as a *reversing* or *readjusting* entry. As the terms imply, such an entry is the exact reverse of the adjusting entry; the same account titles and amounts are used but the debits and credits are reversed. Reversing entries are recorded after the accounts have been ruled and balanced; they are dated as of the first day of the new fiscal period. For the example above, the reversing entry would be as follows:

| Jan. | 1 | Salaries Payable.................... | 213 | 500 | |
| | | Salary Expense.................. | 611 | | 500 |

The effect of this entry is to transfer the liability from the salaries payable account to the credit side of the salary expense account. When the payroll is paid on January 3, the usual entry would be made debiting Salary Expense and crediting Cash for $1,200. After posting, the salary expense account will then have a debit balance of $700, which is the amount of the expense for the first three days of January. The entries are also illustrated in the accounts below.

SALARY EXPENSE   ACCOUNT No. 611

19--					19--					
Jan.	5		CP36	1,240	Dec.	31	Closing	J9	63,000
Dec.	6		CP80	1,300					
	13		CP81	1,450					
	20		CP83	1,260					
	27		CP84	1,350					
	31	Adjusting	J8	500					
				63,000					63,000
19--					19--				
Jan.	3		CP85	1,200	Jan.	1	Reversing	J9	500
		(*Balance $700*)							

SALARIES PAYABLE   ACCOUNT No. 213

19--					19--				
Jan.	1	Reversing	J9	500	Dec.	31	Adjusting	J8	500

The adjusting entries for salaries and commissions recorded on the books of Bennett Electrical Supplies are reversed as of January 1 so that at the time of payment the entire amounts may be charged to the appropriate expense accounts. The reversing entries are as follows:

GENERAL JOURNAL   PAGE 29

DATE	NAME OF ACCOUNT	POST. REF.	DEBIT	CREDIT
	Reversing Entries			
1962 Jan. 1	Salaries Payable	213	2 1 2 0 0	
	Sales Salaries	611		1 5 2 0 0
	Office Salaries	711		6 0 0 0
1	Commissions Payable	212	5 6 4 0 0	
	Sales Commissions	612		5 6 4 0 0

Reversing entries

After the two reversing entries have been posted, the accounts Salaries Payable and Commissions Payable will have a balance of zero and should be ruled. The liability for salaries and commissions will now appear as credits in the respective expense accounts. As salaries and commissions are paid in the new period, *the entire amount paid* will be debited to the appropriate expense accounts. The balances of the expense accounts will then automatically represent the expense of the new period.

Errors of past periods

Various procedures for correcting errors in journal and ledger entries were described in Chapter 4. In all of the situations considered, the errors were discovered and corrected in the same period in which they had occurred. The manner in which an error is corrected is affected in some cases by the closing of the books in the interim between the occurrence of the error and its discovery. In other cases, such as errors affecting only asset or liability accounts, the entry to correct the error will be the same regardless of the time of discovery. For example, if the cost of a delivery truck was recorded as a debit to Office Equipment, the correction would be a debit to Delivery Equipment and a credit to Office Equipment regardless of when the error was discovered.

Errors resulting in a misstatement in the amount of net income of a period for which the books have been closed cannot be corrected by an entry in a revenue or expense account of a later period. The effect of the error in the earlier period has already been transferred to the capital account. For example, assume that at the close of the preceding period the following adjustment was recorded:

Dec.	31	Insurance Expense..................	716	425	
		Prepaid Insurance...............	116		425

Early in the current year it is discovered that the amount of insurance expired was $625 instead of $425. The $200 understatement of expenses of the preceding period resulted in an overstatement of $200 in the amount of net income transferred to the capital account. The correcting entry would therefore be as follows:

Jan.	21	Alvin Carter, Capital..............	311	200	
		Prepaid Insurance...............	116		200
		To correct error in adjusting entry of Dec. 31.			

All corrections to the capital account should be presented in the capital statement, as otherwise the effect of the errors on past income statements will not be disclosed. Assuming that in addition to the error in insurance expense there had been a $750 overstatement of repairs expense in the preceding year, the corrections would be presented on the capital statement in the following manner:

Alvin Carter
Capital Statement
For Year Ended December 31, 1961

Capital, January 1, 1961.		$52,000
Corrections applicable to past period:		
Add — Overstatement of repair expense in 1960.	$ 750	
Deduct — Understatement of insurance expense in 1960.	200	550
Capital, January 1, 1961, as corrected.		$52,550
Net income for the year	$22,600	
Less withdrawals.	15,000	
Increase in capital.		7,600
Capital, December 31, 1961.		$60,150

There are differences of opinion among accountants as to whether a misstatement of net income of a period should be corrected through the capital account or whether it should be reflected in the net income of the period in which the error is discovered. For the present, all corrections of income of prior years will be made directly to the capital account. The alternative of disclosing the correction in the income statement will be considered in Chapter 22.

Questions

1. Assuming that merchandise is sold at a price above cost, explain the nature of the credits to Sales.

2. The merchandise inventory appearing on the unadjusted trial balance at the end of the period represents the inventory as of what date?

3. (a) Identify the debit and credit amounts extended into the Income Statement columns opposite "Expense and Revenue Summary" in the illustration on page 169. (b) What is the reason for extending both amounts into the Income Statement columns instead of the net difference between the amounts?

4. Does the omission of the Adjusted Trial Balance columns of the work sheet affect the purpose or use of the work sheet? Discuss.

5. Discuss the purpose of (a) adjusting entries, (b) closing entries, and (c) reversing entries.

6. Salary Expense before adjustment at the end of the fiscal year has a balance of $90,000. The amount accrued is $600. Give the (a) adjusting entry, (b) closing entry, (c) reversing entry.

7. Assume that the first payroll in the ensuing period (Question 6) amounts to $1,100. (a) Give the entry to record payment of the payroll. (b) What is the balance of Salary Expense immediately after the entry?

8. After the closing entries have been posted and the accounts have been ruled, it is discovered that an advertising expense item of $300 was erroneously debited to Miscellaneous General Expense. Would revision of the income statement for the period be sufficient to correct this error or should a correcting entry be made in the general journal? Discuss.

9. Immediately after the work of the periodic summary has been completed at the end of the year, Taxes Expense has a *credit* balance of $430. Assuming that there have been no errors, what is the nature of this balance?

10. Accrued wages of $650 are ignored at the end of the year and no adjusting entry is made. The amount of the first payroll of the succeeding year is $900, which includes the accrual from the preceding year. (a) Was net income of the first year overstated or understated and by what amount? (b) Was the net income of the second year (assuming no correcting entry) overstated or understated, and by what amount? (c) Was the net income of the two years combined overstated or understated, and by what amount?

Exercises

1. On the basis of the following data, journalize the necessary adjusting entries:
- (a) Merchandise Inventory: January 1, $17,920; December 31, $14,560.
- (b) Store supplies physical inventory, December 31, $92.50; store supplies account balance before adjustment $285.60.
- (c) Office salaries are uniformly $1,000 for a five-day work week. The last payday was Friday, December 26.
- (d) The prepaid insurance account before adjustments on December 31 has a balance of $850. An analysis of the policies indicates that $390 has expired during the year.

2. The fiscal year of Murray Motors ends on December 31. The errors described below, applicable to the past year, were discovered in February of the current year. Present the general journal entries (with explanations) required to correct the errors.
- (a) Merchandise inventory taken on December 31 was understated by $6,500.
- (b) A receipt of cash of $250 from J. B. Martin was erroneously credited to J. B. Morton.
- (c) Expired rent expense of $800 had not been recorded. Payments had been debited to Prepaid Rent.
- (d) No adjustment was made for office supplies consumed, the office supplies account with a balance of $420 being closed to Expense and Revenue Summary. The inventory of office supplies at December 31 was $190.

3. At the beginning of the current year the balance of the proprietor's capital account on the books of Murray Motors in Exercise 2 was $65,000 (before giving effect to the correcting entries). The net income for the year was $28,000 and the withdrawals totaled $18,000. Prepare a capital statement for the year.

4. A portion of the salary expense account of an enterprise is presented at the top of the following page. The fiscal year of the firm ends on December 31. (a) Describe each transaction identified by letter. (b) Present, in general journal form, each entry from which the items identified by letter were posted.

SALARY EXPENSE

19-- Jan.	6		CP11	2,100	19-- Dec.	31	(d)	J9	99,600

	28	(a)	CP31	2,000					
	31	(b)	J8	400					
				99,600					99,600
19-- Jan.	4	(c)	CP32	1,900	19-- Jan.	1	(e)	J9	400

5. The accounts listed below were selected from the Income Statement and Balance Sheet columns of a work sheet for the year ended October 31 of the current year. (a) Prepare an income statement for the year. (b) Journalize the closing entries.

Sales....................	$210,000	Purchases Discount	$1,900
Merchandise Inventory 11/1	46,900	Accumulated Depreciation —	
Purchases...............	143,400	Building	6,800
Merchandise Inventory		Purchases Returns and	
10/31................	54,600	Allowances..............	2,100
Selling Expenses (total) ...	35,200	Sales Returns and Allowances	1,800
General Expenses (total) ..	19,400	A. B. Jordan, Drawing......	9,000
Salaries Payable.........	700	Prepaid Insurance	600
Sales Discount	1,200		

6. Two or more items are omitted in each of the following tabulations of income statement data. Determine the amounts of the missing items, identifying them by letter.

Sales	Sales Returns	Net Sales	Beginning Inventory	Purchases	Purchases Returns	Ending Inventory	Cost of Goods Sold	Gross Profit
$40,000	(a)	$38,000	$ 7,000	$42,000	$ 3,000	(b)	$32,000	$ 6,000
(c)	$ 4,000	46,000	(d)	50,000	5,000	$25,000	35,000	11,000
72,000	6,000	66,000	20,000	(e)	4,000	15,000	(f)	10,000
50,000	3,000	(g)	12,000	40,000	(h)	14,000	38,000	(i)
80,000	(j)	78,000	15,000	70,000	7,000	(k)	(l)	12,000

Problems

8-1. The account balances in the ledger of the Watson Company on December 31 of the current year are as follows:

Cash....................	$15,000	Sales....................	$142,000
Accounts Receivable.......	14,300	Sales Discount...........	4,000
Merchandise Inventory.....	22,700	Purchases................	94,000
Supplies.................	800	Purchases Discount........	3,000
Prepaid Insurance........	2,400	Sales Salaries............	15,000
Store Equipment..........	7,500	Rent Expense.............	4,800
Accumulated Depreciation..	2,500	Advertising Expense.......	1,300
Accounts Payable.........	14,000	Delivery Expense.........	1,200
Paul Watson, Capital......	28,700	Miscellaneous Expense....	7,200

The data needed for year-end adjustments on December 31 are as follows:

Merchandise inventory on December 31...............	$20,500
Supplies inventory on December 31...................	550
Insurance expired during the year...................	1,100
Depreciation for current year.......................	1,000
Accrued salaries on December 31....................	700

Instructions: (1) Prepare an eight-column work sheet for the fiscal year ended December 31.

(2) Record the adjusting entries in a general journal.

(3) Record the closing entries in a general journal.

8-2. During the past fiscal year ending on December 31, a number of errors were made in the accounts of Valley Hardware Co., owned by John Wright. The errors, which are described below, were not discovered until after the books had been closed and year-end financial statements had been prepared.

(a) Prepaid rent at December 31 was understated $600.

(b) Merchandise inventory at December 31 was overstated $2,000.

(c) The amount of expired insurance for the past year was understated $800.

(d) Advertising expense for the past year included $400 of delivery expense.

(e) Accrued sales commissions payable on December 31 of the past year were understated $350.

(f) Miscellaneous office expense for the past year included a $300 debit for the cost of a typewriter, purchased on July 1, that should have been debited to office equipment.

(g) Depreciation expense was understated $15 because of the error in recording the typewriter. (See item (f).)

Instructions: (1) Present the necessary correcting entries in the current year, using the identifying letters in place of dates.

The balance in the capital account on December 31 of the past fiscal year was $17,000. During the current year, charges to the drawing account totaled $4,800, and net income closed from Expense and Revenue Summary to the capital account was $9,000.

(2) On the basis of the facts given above and the correcting entries recorded during the year, prepare a capital statement for the current year.

If the working papers correlating with this textbook are not used, omit Problem 8-3.

8-3. C. B. Henshaw owns and operates the Plaza Variety Shop. The general ledger balances at the beginning of the twelfth month and the journals for the twelfth month of the current year are presented in the working papers.

Instructions: (1) Post the journals to the general ledger accounts. An assistant has made all postings to the accounts in the subsidiary ledgers.

(2) Take a trial balance at December 31 on an eight column work sheet, listing only the accounts with balances.

(3) Complete the work sheet. Adjustment data are:

Merchandise inventory at December 31	$7,800.00
Supplies on hand at December 31...............	187.50
Insurance expired during the year..............	240.00
Depreciation for the current year on	
Store equipment...........................	625.00
Office equipment...........................	150.00
Accrued taxes at December 31.................	200.00

(4) Prepare an income statement, a balance sheet in report form, and a capital statement. There were no additional investments of capital by the owner during the year.

(5) Record the adjusting entries in the general journal and post to the ledger.

(6) Record the closing entries and post to the ledger.

(7) Rule and balance the accounts that have two or more postings.

(8) Prepare a post-closing trial balance.

(9) Record the reversing entry or entries on January 2, post to the ledger, and rule the additional account or accounts that are now in balance.

8-4. The accounts and their balances in the ledger of Norton Wholesale Co. on June 30 of the current year are as follows:

111	Cash	$ 28,800	412	Sales Ret. and Allow.	8,600
112	Accounts Receivable	40,100	511	Purchases	215,600
113	Merchandise Inv.	48,200	512	Purchases Returns	
114	Store Supplies	2,100		and Allowances	7,300
115	Office Supplies	1,800	513	Purchases Discount	2,600
116	Prepaid Rent	5,600	611	Sales Salaries	16,400
117	Prepaid Insurance	3,600	612	Delivery Expense	11,900
121	Store Equipment	12,000	613	Rent Expense—Selling	——
121.1	Acc. Depreciation—		614	Insur. Exp. — Selling	——
	Store Equipment	3,600	615	Store Supplies Exp.	——
122	Office Equipment	4,000	616	Depreciation Exp. —	
122.1	Acc. Depreciation—			Store Equipment	——
	Office Equipment	1,200	617	Misc. Selling Exp.	400
211	Accounts Payable	29,700	711	Office Salaries	11,400
212	Salaries Payable	——	712	Rent Exp.—General	——
221	Mortgage Payable		713	Insur. Exp.—General.	——
	(due 1970)	15,000	714	Office Supplies Exp.	——
311	Leo Norton, Capital	70,500	715	Depreciation Exp. —	
312	Leo Norton, Drawing	9,000		Office Equipment	——
313	Expense and Revenue		716	Misc. General Exp.	300
	Summary	——	911	Interest Expense	900
411	Sales	290,800			

The data for year-end adjustments on June 30 are as follows:

Merchandise inventory on June 30		$49,800
Inventory of supplies on June 30		
Store supplies		700
Office supplies		960
Rent expired during year		
Allocable as selling expense	$2,880	
Allocable as general expense	1,920	4,800
Insurance expired during year		
Allocable as selling expense	$1,440	
Allocable as general expense	960	2,400
Depreciation		
Store equipment		1,200
Office equipment		400
Salaries payable on June 30		
Sales salaries	$ 500	
Office salaries	300	800

Instructions: (1) Enter the accounts in an eight-column work sheet in proper sequence, including those that do not have balances.

(2) Complete the work sheet.

(3) Prepare an income statement (Exhibit A), a balance sheet in report form (Exhibit B), and a capital statement (Exhibit C).

(4) Record the adjusting entries in a general journal.

(5) Record the closing entries.

(6) Record the reversing entries on July 1.

(7) Compute the following: (a) working capital, (b) current ratio, (c) percentage of gross profit to net sales, and (d) percentage of net income to net sales.

8-5. On February 15 of the current fiscal year the following errors were discovered in the books of the Evergreen Mart, Paul Root, proprietor:

(1) Merchandise inventory at the end of the preceding year was understated $2,500.

(2) Three purchases returns and allowances totaling $750 were erroneously recorded as credits to sales returns and allowances in December of the preceding year.

(3) The adjusting entry for store supplies at the end of the preceding year transferred $530 to the expense account. The amount should have been $350.

(4) A home freezer costing $450, purchased by Root on December 31 for his wife, was debited to store equipment.

(5) No provision was made at the end of the preceding year for accrued sales salaries payable, $800.

(6) Additional land costing $10,000 was purchased for the construction of a new building. The building account was debited in error; and, in addition, $400 of depreciation was incorrectly recorded on this acquisition during the preceding year.

Instructions: (1) Record the journal entries required by the foregoing errors.

(2) Open the capital account. Enter the beginning balance, $25,000, as of January 1 of the current year. Post the corrections that affect the capital account.

(3) On December 31 of the current year journalize the entries to close the expense and revenue summary account (credit balance, $12,500) and the drawing account (debit balance, $6,000).

(4) Post the closing entries to the capital account.

(5) Prepare a capital statement for the current year.

(6) Rule and balance the capital account.

Practice set 1

Part 1
Greer Wholesale Shoes

The transactions in this practice set were completed by Greer Wholesale Shoes, owned and operated by Thomas R. Greer. Although the transactions deal with the operations of a wholesale shoe business, they illustrate general principles of accounting rather than the techniques of the accounting system of a particular business.

Part 1, which is given on the following pages, applies the principles and the methods developed in the first eight chapters. Part 2, which follows Chapter 12, applies additional principles and methods developed in Chapters 9 through 12. Both parts of the practice set may be recorded in a single set of books of account.

General ledger

The chart of general ledger accounts is as follows:

111	Cash	312	Thomas R. Greer, Drawing
112	Notes Receivable	313	Expense and Revenue Summary
113	Accounts Receivable	411	Sales
113.1	Allowance for Uncollectible Accounts	412	Sales Returns and Allowances
		413	Sales Discount
114	Interest Receivable	511	Purchases
115	Merchandise Inventory	512	Purchases Returns and Allowances
116	Store Supplies	513	Purchases Discount
117	Office Supplies	611	Sales Salaries
118	Prepaid Insurance	612	Advertising Expense
119	Prepaid Interest	613	Store Supplies Expense
121	Store Equipment	614	Depreciation Expense — Store Equipment
121.1	Accumulated Depreciation — Store Equipment		
		615	Miscellaneous Selling Expense
122	Office Equipment	711	Office Salaries
122.1	Accumulated Depreciation—Office Equipment	712	Rent Expense
		713	Depreciation Expense — Building
123	Building	714	Bad Debts Expense
123.1	Accumulated Depreciation—Building	715	Insurance Expense
		716	Office Supplies Expense
124	Land	717	Depreciation Expense — Office Equipment
211	Notes Payable		
212	Accounts Payable	718	Miscellaneous General Expense
213	Interest Payable	811	Interest Income
214	Salaries Payable	812	Rent Income
215	Unearned Rent	911	Interest Expense
221	Mortgage Payable	912	Loss on Disposal of Plant Assets
311	Thomas R. Greer, Capital		

187

Instructions: (1) The general ledger is included in the materials that may be obtained for this practice set. If these materials are not used, open the foregoing general ledger accounts in the order in which they are given, allowing at least twelve lines for each account. Some of the accounts will not be used during the first month of the practice set, but all should be opened at this time.

The post-closing trial balance of Greer Wholesale Shoes as of September 30 of the current year is as follows:

Greer Wholesale Shoes
Post-Closing Trial Balance
September 30, 19—

111	Cash.............................	6,846 85	
113	Accounts Receivable................	4,631 23	
115	Merchandise Inventory..............	34,926 87	
116	Store Supplies.....................	208 67	
117	Office Supplies....................	79 83	
118	Prepaid Insurance..................	425 90	
121	Store Equipment...................	5,235 00	
121.1	Accum. Depreciation — Store Equip...		1,686 40
122	Office Equipment..................	2,327 50	
122.1	Accum. Depreciation — Office Equip...		532 60
212	Accounts Payable..................		3,562 90
311	Thomas R. Greer, Capital...........		48,899 95
		54,681 85	54,681 85

Instructions: (2) The account balances listed on the post-closing trial balance are recorded in the general ledger included in the materials that may be obtained for this practice set. If these materials are not used, record the foregoing balances in the appropriate accounts as of October 1 of the current year.

Subsidiary ledgers

The accounts in the accounts receivable ledger and their balances on September 30 are as follows:

Arnold Shoe Store, 2140 High St., Hamilton............	
Central Department Store, 623 Fairview St., Middletown...	$1,775.80
Finch Bootery, 465 Bedford St., Middletown............	
T. L. Jordan, Inc., 410 S. Central Ave., Springfield......	
Macon & Elder, 8231 Western Blvd., City.............	526.90
Parker & Son, 396 N. Spruce St., Hamilton............	895.78
Town & Country, Inc., 1462 Second Ave., City........	
Varsity Shop, 186 E. Campus Ave., City...............	1,432.75
	$4,631.23

The accounts in the accounts payable ledger and their balances on September 30 are as follows:

Barton Shoe Corp., 142 S. Malden St., Cincinnati........
Fashion Shoes, Inc., 3658 River Rd., Cincinnati.......... $1,782.90
Merchants Supply Co., 496 N. Main St., City........... 98.00
Ross & Co., 841 Erie Ave., Marion....................
Stride-Rite Shoe Co., 1324 E. High St., St. Louis........ 1,682.00
Western Manufacturing Co., 2120 W. Jefferson St., Ports-
mouth...

$3,562.90

Instructions: (3) The subsidiary ledgers, with the balances recorded, are included in the materials that may be obtained for this practice set. If these materials are not used, open accounts for the accounts receivable and the accounts payable in the order in which they are given, allowing at least twelve lines for each account, and record the balances in the appropriate accounts as of October 1.

Journals

The journals used by Greer Wholesale Shoes are as follows: purchases journal like that illustrated on pages 144 and 145; sales journal like that illustrated on page 122; sales returns and allowances journal like that illustrated on page 126; cash receipts journal like that illustrated on page 129; cash payments journal like that illustrated on page 151; general journal with two amount columns. (Because of their infrequent occurrence, purchases returns and allowances are recorded in the general journal.)

Instructions: (4) The journals described above are included in the materials that may be obtained for this practice set. *Before recording any transactions,* number the pages of each journal, beginning with the following numbers: purchases journal, 11; sales journal, 17; sales returns and allowances journal, 4; cash receipts journal, 15; cash payments journal, 19; general journal, 21. If the materials are not used, construct the various journals and number the pages as indicated above.

Transactions for October

Instructions: (5) Record the following transactions in the appropriate journals. In practice it is customary to post to the accounts in the *subsidiary* ledgers daily, but because of the comparatively small number of transactions, such posting will be done at the end of each week and at the end of the month. When instructed to post to the subsidiary ledgers, post from the journals in the following sequence: (a) purchases journal, (b) sales journal, (c) sales returns and allowances journal, (d) cash receipts journal, (e) cash payments journal, and (f) general journal. The fact that postings to some of the accounts will not be in perfect date sequence is immaterial.

Post to the accounts in the *general* ledger *only at the end of the month.*

Oct. 2. Issued Check No. 701 for $575 for rent of building for October.
     2. Made the following purchases on account:
        Fashion Shoes, Inc., merchandise, $2,201.
        Barton Shoe Corp., merchandise, $1,427.50.
     3. Made the following sale on account:
        Sale No. 1161, Town & Country, Inc., $1,259.

Oct. 3. Issued checks as follows:
     Check No. 702 for $215 for newspaper advertising.
     Check No. 703 for $98 to Merchants Supply Co. in payment of its
        invoice for $98.
    4. Sale No. 1160 for $1,775.80 on September 29 was incorrectly charged
     to the account of Central Department Store when it should have been
     charged to the account of Arnold Shoe Store.
    4. Issued Check No. 704 for $45 for cash purchase of store supplies.
    5. Made the following purchases on account:
     Merchants Supply Co., office supplies, $35.75; store supplies, $119.80.
    5. Issued check No. 705 for $1,747.24 to Fashion Shoes, Inc. in payment
     of its invoice for $1,782.90 less 2% discount.
    6. Issued Credit Memo No. 105 for $115.50 to Town & Country, Inc.
     for the return of merchandise on the sale of October 3.
    6. Issued Check No. 706 for $1,648.36 to Stride-Rite Shoe Co. in pay-
     ment of its invoice for $1,682 less a 2% discount.
    6. Received checks as follows:
     A check for $516.36 from Macon & Elder in payment of our invoice
       for $526.90 less a 2% discount.
     A check for $877.86 from Parker & Son in payment of our invoice
       for $895.78 less a 2% discount.
    6. Made the following sales on account:
     Sale No. 1162, Parker & Son, $347.50.
     Sale No. 1163, Finch Bootery, $1,364.
    6. Received $2,186.50 from cash sales for October 2–6.

Instructions: (6) Post to the *subsidiary* ledgers (see Instruction 5).

Oct. 9. Received checks as follows:
     A check for $1,740.28 from Arnold Shoe Store in payment of our in-
       voice for $1,775.80 less a 2% discount.
     A check for $1,404.09 from Varsity Shop in payment of our invoice for
       $1,432.75 less a 2% discount.
    9. Issued Check No. 707 for $35.50 for cash purchase of office supplies.
    9. Made the following purchases on account:
     Stride-Rite Shoe Co., merchandise, $1,270.
     Barton Shoe Corp., merchandise, $700.74.
   10. Issued Check No. 708 for $61.75 for a miscellaneous selling expense.
   10. Made the following sales on account:
     Sale No. 1164, Central Department Store, $1,736.
     Sale No. 1165, Macon & Elder, $558.40.
   10. Issued checks as follows:
     Check No. 709 for $2,156.98 to Fashion Shoes, Inc. in payment of its
       invoice for $2,201 less a 2% discount.
     Check No. 710 for $1,398.95 to Barton Shoe Corp. in payment of its
       invoice for $1,427.50 less a 2% discount.
   11. Issued Check No. 711 for $575.95 for a cash purchase of merchandise.
   12. Received a credit memorandum for $125.74 from Barton Shoe Corp.
     for the return of merchandise on its invoice of October 9.
   12. Received checks as follows:
     A check for $1,120.63 from Town & Country, Inc. in payment of our
       invoice for $1,259, less the credit of $115.50, less a 2% discount.
   13. Purchased merchandise on account from Western Manufacturing Co.,
     $2,220.

Oct. 13. Issued Check No. 712 for $2,770 for biweekly salaries divided as follows: sales salaries, $1,850; office salaries, $920.
13. Received $1,650 from cash sales for October 9–13.

Instructions: (7) Post to the *subsidiary* ledgers.

Oct. 16. Issued Check No. 713 for $300 to Thomas R. Greer for personal use.
16. Received checks as follows:
A check for $340.55 from Parker & Son in payment of our invoice for $347.50 less a 2% discount.
A check for $1,336.72 from Finch Bootery in payment of our invoice for $1,364 less a 2% discount.
17. Made the following purchases on account:
Merchants Supply Co., office supplies, $50, and miscellaneous general expense, $68.75.
Barton Shoe Corp., merchandise, $3,076.80.
17. Issued Check No. 714 for $563.50 to Barton Shoe Corp. in payment of its invoice for $700.74 less the return of $125.74 less a 2% discount.
18. Received a check for $42 for the return of merchandise that had been purchased for cash.
18. Issued Check No. 715 for $52 for a cash purchase of store supplies.
19. Issued Credit Memo No. 106 for $20 to Central Department Store for merchandise returned on the sale of October 10.
20. Made the following sales on account:
Sale No. 1166, Varsity Shop, $2,768.
Sale No. 1167, Finch Bootery, $592.30.
Sale No. 1168, T. L. Jordan, Inc., $1,900.90.
20. Issued Check No. 716 for $2,175.60 to Western Manufacturing Co. in payment of its invoice for $2,220 less a 2% discount.
20. Received checks as follows:
A check for $1,681.68 from Central Department Store in payment of our invoice for $1,736 less the return of $20, less a 2% discount.
A check for $547.23 from Macon & Elder in payment of our invoice for $558.40 less a 2% discount.
20. Received $1,890.22 from cash sales for October 16–20.

Instructions: (8) Post to the *subsidiary* ledgers.

Oct. 24. Made the following sales on account:
Sale No. 1169, Town & Country, Inc., $1,520.20.
Sale No. 1170, Parker & Son, $2,940.85.
25. Issued Check No. 717 for $3,015.26 to Barton Shoe Corp. in payment of its invoice for $3,076.80 less a 2% discount.
26. Issued Credit Memo No. 107 for $32.85 to Parker & Son for damaged merchandise returned on the sale of October 24.
27. Issued Check No. 718 for $2,800 for biweekly salaries divided as follows: sales salaries, $1,900; office salaries, $900.
27. Purchased merchandise on account from Western Manufacturing Co., $3,068.90.
27. Received $2,003.45 from cash sales for October 23–27.

Instructions: (9) Post to the *subsidiary* ledgers.

Oct. 30. Purchased store supplies on account from Ross & Co., $85.
30. Issued Credit Memo No. 108 for $42.20 to Town & Country, Inc. for the return of merchandise on the sale of October 24.

Oct. 30. Issued Check No. 719 for $124 in payment of utilities.   (Charge
      Miscellaneous General Expense.)
   30. Received a check for $1,862.88 from T. L. Jordan, Inc. in payment of
      our invoice for $1,900.90 less a 2% discount.
   31. Made the following sale on account: Sale No. 1171, Arnold Shoe
      Store, $1,946.20.
   31. Issued checks as follows:
      Check No. 720 for $360.35 for freight charges on merchandise pur-
      chased.
      Check No. 721 for $400 to Thomas R. Greer for personal use.
   31. Received $2,157.25 from cash sales for October 30–31.

Instructions: (10) Post to the *subsidiary* ledgers.

Posting to the general ledger

Instructions: (11) Total each column of the various special journals. Prove
the equality of debits and credits in each journal. Make the following computation to determine the cash balance at October 31: cash balance, October 1, plus
debits to cash, minus credits to cash. The balance obtained should be $7,086.11.

(12) Post all items that need to be *individually* posted to the general ledger,
beginning with the purchases journal and proceeding through the other
journals in the order indicated in instruction (5).

(13) Rule the journals, and post totals to the appropriate accounts in the
general ledger.

(14) Prepare a trial balance on eight column paper, listing only the accounts with balances.

Data for adjustments

The additional data required to complete the work sheet are as follows:

Merchandise Inventory on October 31................	$31,447.34
Inventories of supplies on October 31:	
Store supplies.....................................	327.92
Office supplies....................................	162.75
Insurance expired during October.....................	39.40
Depreciation for October:	
Store equipment..................................	43.20
Office equipment.................................	21.15
Salaries payable on October 31:	
Sales salaries....................................	380.00
Office salaries...................................	175.00

(15) Prepare an income statement, a balance sheet, a capital statement, and
schedules of accounts receivable and accounts payable, employing the exhibit
the schedule designations illustrated on pages 171 through 173.

(16) Complete the work of the periodic summary for the month of October,
following the outline on page 163. Do not overlook the recording and posting
of the reversing entry as of November 1.

*Part 2 of this practice set, containing the narrative of transactions for November,
appears at the end of Chapter 12. The journals and ledgers used for October will also be
used in recording the transactions for November.*

Notes and interest

Use of credit instruments in business

The extension of credit plays an important role in the operations of many business enterprises. Credit may be granted on open account or on the basis of a formal instrument of credit such as a *promissory note*. The use of the latter is customary for credit periods in excess of 60 days, as in sales on the installment plan, and for transactions of relatively large dollar amounts. Credit instruments may also be used in settlement of an open account and in borrowing or lending money.

From the point of view of the creditor a claim evidenced by a credit instrument has some advantages over a claim in the form of an account receivable. By signing the instrument the debtor acknowledges the debt and agrees to pay it in accordance with the terms specified. It is therefore a stronger legal claim in the event of court action. It is also more liquid than an open account as it can be transferred to a creditor in settlement of a debt or to a bank in exchange for cash.

A promissory note, frequently referred to simply as a *note*, is a written promise to pay a certain sum of money at a fixed or determinable future time. As in the case of a check, it must be payable to the order of a particular person or firm, or to bearer. It must also be signed by the person or firm that makes the promise. The one to whose order the note is payable is called the *payee*, and the one making the promise is called the *maker*. In the illustration at the top of the following page, James Otis is the payee and Frank Long is the maker.

The person or firm owning a note refers to it as a *note receivable* and records it at its face amount in the asset account Notes Receivable. The maker of a note refers to it as a *note payable* and records it at its face amount in the liability account Notes Payable. Thus, the note in the illustration would appear in Otis' notes receivable account at $1,600 and in Long's notes payable account at $1,600.

A note that provides for the payment of interest for the period between the issuance date and the due date is called an *interest-bearing note*.

193

```
 $1,600.00          Detroit, Michigan, October 2                    19 61
 -----------------Sixty days-----------------AFTER DATE___ I ___ PROMISE TO PAY TO
 THE ORDER OF__James Otis_____
  One Thousand Six Hundred 00/100--------------------------------------- DOLLARS
 PAYABLE AT_First National Bank_____
 VALUE RECEIVED WITH INTEREST AT----6---%
 No._14___  DUE December 1, 1961 _____        Frank Long
```

Interest-bearing note

If the note makes no provision for interest, the note is said to be *non-interest-bearing*. In such cases, however, interest may be charged at the legal rate for any time that the note remains unpaid after it is due. The interest that a business is obliged to pay is an expense and is called *interest expense*. The interest that a business is entitled to receive is income and is called *interest income*.

Computing interest

Rates of interest are usually stated in terms of a period of one year. Thus, the interest on a $1,500, 1-year, 6% note would amount to 6% of $1,500, or $90. If, instead of one year, the term of the note was six months, the interest would amount to one half of $90, or $45.

Notes covering a period of time longer than a year ordinarily provide that the interest be paid annually, semiannually, or at some other stated interval. The time involved in commercial credit transactions is usually less than a year, and the interest provided for by the note is payable at the time the note is paid. In computing interest for a period of less than a year, agencies of the federal government use the actual number of days in the year; for example, 90 days is considered to be 90/365 of a year. The usual commercial practice is to use 360 as the denominator of the fraction; thus 90 days is considered to be 90/360 of a year. The commercial practice will be followed in this book.

The basic formula for computing interest is as follows:

$$\text{Principal} \times \text{Rate} \times \text{Time} = \text{Interest}$$

To illustrate the application of the formula, assume a note for $800, payable 15 days from date, with interest at 6%. The interest would be $2.00, computed as follows:

$$\$800 \times \frac{6}{100} \times \frac{15}{360} = \$2.00 \text{ interest}$$

There are a number of short-cut methods of computing interest. One that is commonly used is called the 60-day, 6% method. This method is based on the fact that interest at the rate of 6% per year is equal to 1% for 60 days or 1/6 of a year. The interest on any amount for 60 days at 6% can be determined, therefore, by moving the decimal point in the principal two places to the left. Thus for 60 days, the interest at 6% for $1,342 is $13.42; for $264, the interest is $2.64; and for $982.73, the interest is $9.83.

The interest on $800 for 66 days at 6% may be determined as follows:

$800 for 60 days (1% of $800)...........................	$8.00
$800 for 6 days (1/10 of $8.00)...........................	.80
Interest for 66 days at 6%................................	$8.80

It is often necessary to compute the interest for a certain period at a rate greater or smaller than 6%. In such a case the interest for the period at 6% is determined first. The proper amount to be added to or subtracted from this amount is then computed, and the interest at the given rate is thus ascertained. For instance, the interest on $924 for 81 days at 4% may be calculated in the following manner:

$924 for 60 days at 6%....................................	$ 9.24
$924 for 15 days at 6% (1/4 of $9.24).....................	2.31
$924 for 6 days at 6% (1/10 of $9.24).....................	.92
Interest for 81 days at 6%................................	$12.47
$924 for 81 days at 2% (1/3 of $12.47)....................	4.16
Interest for 81 days at 4%................................	$ 8.31

The method used in computing interest is a matter of individual preference. In the illustration above, for example, solving by the basic formula might require less time and afford less opportunity of arithmetic error.

When the term of a note is expressed in months, each month may be considered as being 1/12 of a year, or, alternatively, the actual number of days in the term may be counted. For example, the interest on a 3-month note dated June 1 could be computed on the basis of 3/12 of a year or on the basis of 92/360 of a year. It is the usual commercial practice to employ the first method, while banks usually charge interest for the exact number of days. For the sake of uniformity, the commercial practice will be followed here.

Determining due date

The period of time between the issuance date and the maturity date of a short-term note may be expressed either in days or months. When the term of a note is expressed in days, the due date is the specified number of days after the issuance date of the note. The due date may be determined in the following manner:

(1) Subtract the date of the note from the number of days in the month in which it is dated.
(2) Add as many full months as possible without exceeding the number of days in the note, counting the full number of days in these months.
(3) Subtract the total days obtained in (1) and (2) from the number of days in the note.

Assuming a 90-day note dated March 16, the due date is determined as follows:

```
        Term of the note.................  90
        March (days)..............  31
        Date of note..............  16
                                    ──
            Remainder................  15
        April (days)..................  30
        May (days)..................  31
                                    ──
        Total........................  76
                                         ──
        Due date, June..................  14
                                         ══
```

When the term of a note is expressed as a specified number of months after the issuance date, the due date is determined by counting the number of months from the issuance date. Thus, a 3-month note dated June 5 would be due on September 5. In those cases in which there is no date in the month of maturity that corresponds to the issuance date, the due date becomes the last day of the month. For example, a 2-month note dated July 31 would be due on September 30.

Notes payable

Notes payable are ordinarily issued to a relatively small number of creditors; consequently, all notes may be recorded in a single account in the general ledger. A carbon copy or other memorandum record is maintained for each note. A subsidiary ledger for notes payable may be employed, but there is usually no advantage in doing so.

When a note is issued to a creditor in payment of an account, the liability Accounts Payable is decreased and the liability Notes Payable is increased. These facts are recorded by debiting the accounts payable account and the account of the creditor to whom the note was issued, and by crediting the notes payable account.

For example, if a business requests an extension of time for payment of an invoice, the creditor may require that the debtor issue a note for the period involved. Assume that on June 6 George Burke gave a 30-day, non-interest-bearing note for $900 to F. B. Murray on account. The transaction was recorded in Burke's general journal as follows:

June	6	Accounts Payable — F. B. Murray..........	213/√	900 00	
		Notes Payable.........................	211		900 00
		Issued a 30-day, non-interest-bearing note.			

The payee may hold the note until July 6, the due date, or he may transfer it by endorsement to one of his creditors or to his bank. Regardless of who holds the note at maturity, when the maker pays the note his liability Notes Payable decreases and his asset Cash decreases. The payment of the note is recorded in the cash payments journal in the following manner:

CASH PAYMENTS JOURNAL   PAGE 16

DATE	CHECK NO.	ACCOUNT DEBITED	POST. REF.	SUNDRY ACCTS. DR.	ACCTS. PAY. DR.	PUR. DISC. CR.	CASH CR.
1961 July 6	318	Notes Payable	211	900 00			900 00

Recording interest expense

Like all other expenses, interest expense represents a deduction from proprietorship. It is recorded as a debit in an account entitled Interest Expense.

For example, on October 5 George Burke gave a creditor, John Davis, a note for $600, due in 60 days and bearing interest at the rate of 6%. On December 4 Burke gave Davis a check for $606 in payment of the note and the interest. The issuance of the note was recorded in Burke's general journal and the payment of the note and the interest was recorded in his cash payments journal as follows:

Oct.	5	Accounts Payable — John Davis.............	213/√	600 00	
		Notes Payable.........................	211		600 00
		Issued a 60-day, 6% note.			

CASH PAYMENTS JOURNAL   PAGE 20

DATE	CHECK NO.	ACCOUNT DEBITED	POST. REF.	SUNDRY ACCTS. DR.	ACCTS. PAY. DR.	PUR. DISC. CR.	CASH CR.
1961 Dec. 4	421	Notes Payable	211	600 00			606 00
		Interest Expense	911	6 00			

All of the examples considered thus far have involved notes issued to a creditor on account. A business may also issue notes in borrowing money from a bank. For example, on September 19 George Burke borrowed $4,000 from the First National Bank, the loan being evidenced by a note payable in 90 days, with interest at the rate of 6%. The entries made by Burke in his cash receipts and cash payments journals to record the loan and its payment were as follows:

CASH RECEIPTS JOURNAL   PAGE 9

DATE		ACCOUNT CREDITED	POST. REF.	SUNDRY ACCTS. CR.	SALES CR.	ACCTS. REC. CR.	SALES DISC. DR.	CASH DR.
1961 Sept.	19	Notes Payable	211	4,000 00				4,000 00

CASH PAYMENTS JOURNAL   PAGE 20

DATE		CHECK NO.	ACCOUNT DEBITED	POST. REF.	SUNDRY ACCTS. DR.	ACCTS. PAY. DR.	PUR. DISC. CR.	CASH CR.
1961 Dec.	18	432	Notes Payable	211	4,000 00			4,060 00
			Interest Expense	911	60 00			

Notes receivable

The typical retail enterprise makes most of its sales for cash or on account. If the account of a customer becomes past due, the seller may insist that the account be converted into a note. In this way the debtor may be given an extension of time and if the creditor needs additional funds he may endorse and transfer the note to his bank. Notes may also be received by retail firms that sell merchandise on long-term credit. For example, a dealer in household appliances may require a down payment at the time of sale and accept a note or a series of notes for the remainder. Such arrangements usually provide for monthly payments. Wholesale firms and manufacturers are likely to receive notes more frequently than retailers, although here, too, much depends upon the nature of the product and the length of the credit period.

When a note is received from a customer to apply on his account, the asset Notes Receivable is increased and the asset Accounts Receivable is decreased. These facts are recorded by debiting the notes receivable account and by crediting the accounts receivable account and the account of the customer from whom the note is received. It is not necessary to maintain a subsidiary ledger for notes receivable because the notes themselves provide adequate information. The amount due from each customer on a note can be ascertained by examining the notes on hand. The due date, the interest terms, and other details can be determined in the same manner. However, if numerous notes are received, it may be desirable to summarize the details of all notes in a supplementary record. Such a record is described in a later chapter.

For example, assume that the account of T. J. Cole on the books of George Burke has a debit balance of $300. The account is past due. On October 19 Burke received Cole's note for $300, dated October 18 and due 20 days after the date of issue, bearing interest at the rate of 6%. The receipt of the note was recorded in Burke's general journal as follows:

Oct.	19	Notes Receivable..........................	113	300 00	
		Accounts Receivable — T. J. Cole.........	115/√		300 00
		Received a 20-day, 6% note dated October 18.			

The debit entry would be posted to the notes receivable account in the general ledger. The credit entry would be posted to the accounts receivable controlling account in the general ledger and to the account of T. J. Cole in the subsidiary ledger.

If notes are received quite frequently, the time consumed in recording and posting such transactions could be reduced by the addition of a Notes Receivable Dr. column and an Accounts Receivable Cr. column to the general journal.

Recording interest income

Revenue earned for money loaned or credit granted to others is recorded as a credit in an account entitled Interest Income. To illustrate the recording of the collection of the principal and interest on a note receivable, assume that George Burke received payment from T. J. Cole for the $300, 20-day, 6% note dated October 18. The transaction was recorded in the cash receipts journal as follows:

CASH RECEIPTS JOURNAL   PAGE 12

DATE		ACCOUNT CREDITED	POST. REF.	SUNDRY ACCTS. CR.	SALES CR.	ACCTS. REC. CR.	SALES DISC. DR.	CASH DR.
1961 Nov.	7	Notes Receivable	113	300 00				301 00
		Interest Income	811	1 00				

Discounting notes

A note that makes no provision for the payment of interest for the period from the date of issuance to the date of maturity is called a non-interest-bearing note. It does not necessarily follow that there can be no interest charge involved in issuing or transferring such a note. In making loans to customers, banks sometimes prefer non-interest-bearing notes, deducting the interest charge from the face of the note and paying cash or crediting the depositor's account for the remainder. This procedure is referred to as *discounting a note*. The rate used in computing the interest is sometimes called the *discount rate*, the deduction made for interest is referred to as the *discount*, and the net amount available to the customer is called the *proceeds*.

Discount on a note is computed in the same manner as interest is computed on an interest-bearing note except that the discount rate is always applied to the maturity value of the note. For a non-interest-bearing note, the maturity value is the same as the face value. The significant difference between *interest* and *discount* is that discount is deducted in advance.

Notes payable. To illustrate the discounting of a note payable, assume that on September 11 George Burke issued a $3,000, 60-day, non-interest-bearing note to the First National Bank. The bank charged a discount rate of 5%, making the discount $25 and the proceeds $2,975. The transaction with the bank was recorded in the cash receipts journal as follows:

CASH RECEIPTS JOURNAL   PAGE **9**

DATE		ACCOUNT CREDITED	POST. REF.	SUNDRY ACCTS. CR.	SALES CR.	ACCTS. REC. CR.	SALES DISC. DR.	CASH DR.
1961 Sept.	11	Notes Payable	211	3,000 00				2,975 00
		Interest Expense	911	(25 00)				

The interest expense was recorded in the Sundry Accounts Credit Column and circled to identify it as a debit. A circled or red ink entry in any journal identifies the item as being the opposite of the debit or credit designation at the top of the column.

An additional sundry accounts column may be inserted in any special journal to provide greater flexibility. The foregoing transaction recorded in a cash receipts journal with a Sundry Accounts Dr. column is illustrated below.

CASH RECEIPTS JOURNAL   PAGE **9**

DATE		ACCOUNT	POST. REF.	SUNDRY ACCOUNTS DR.	SUNDRY ACCOUNTS CR.	SALES CR.	ACCTS. REC. CR.	SALES DISC. DR.	CASH DR.
1961 Sept.	11	Notes Payable	211		3,000 00				2,975 00
		Interest Expense	911	25 00					

The posting of the transaction is the same in both illustrations. It should be observed that the note payable is recorded at the face amount of $3,000 and the discount of $25 is debited to Interest Expense. The adjusting entry that may be required for prepaid interest at the close of the fiscal period will be considered in Chapter 10.

On November 10 Burke paid the bank $3,000, the maturity value of the note. The transaction was recorded as follows:

CASH PAYMENTS JOURNAL PAGE 11

DATE	CHECK NO.	ACCOUNT DEBITED	POST. REF.	SUNDRY ACCTS. DR.	ACCTS. PAY. DR.	PUR. DISC. CR.	CASH CR.
1961 Nov. 10	391	Notes Payable	211	3,000 00			3,000 00

Non-interest-bearing notes receivable. One of the advantages of a note receivable over an account receivable is that a note may be readily converted into cash at any time. Instead of holding notes until maturity the owner may transfer them to a bank by endorsement. The bank charges interest from the date of the transfer to the maturity date of the note. The discount is computed on the maturity value of the note, and the remainder, or proceeds, is paid by the bank.

For example, on August 21 George Burke received from a customer, R. L. Davis, the latter's 90-day, non-interest-bearing note for $1,340 to apply on his account. This transaction was recorded as follows:

Aug..	21	Notes Receivable......................	113	1,340 00			
		Accounts Receivable — R. L. Davis.......	115/√		1,340 00		
		Received a 90-day, non-interest-bearing note.					

Thirty days later, on September 20, Burke needed additional cash and therefore discounted this note at his bank. From the bank's standpoint, the note was not worth $1,340, inasmuch as that amount could not be collected from the maker of the note until 60 days later; consequently it deducted discount, or interest, on $1,340 for 60 days. The bank rate of discount was 6% and the amount of the discount was $13.40. Burke therefore received proceeds of $1,326.60 ($1,340 − $13.40). The transaction with the bank was recorded in the cash receipts journal as follows:

CASH RECEIPTS JOURNAL PAGE 9

DATE		ACCOUNT	POST. REF.	SUNDRY ACCOUNTS DR.	SUNDRY ACCOUNTS CR.	SALES CR.	ACCTS. REC. CR.	SALES DISC. DR.	CASH DR.
1961 Sept.	20	Notes Receivable	113		1,340 00				1,326 60
		Interest Expense	911	13 40					

Interest-bearing notes receivable. The note in the preceding illustration did not bear interest and therefore its maturity value was the same as its face value. When an interest-bearing note receivable is discounted, its maturity value must be computed before the amount of the discount and the proceeds can be determined. To illustrate, assume that on November 8 Burke received from John Mason a 90-day note for $1,800 bearing interest at 5%. The transaction was recorded in the general journal as follows:

Nov.	8	Notes Receivable.......................	113	1,800 00	
		Accounts Receivable — John Mason......	115/✓		1,800 00
		Received a 90-day, 5% note.			

Ten days later, on November 18, the note is discounted at the bank at a discount rate of 6%. The amount that the maker of the note promised to pay in 90 days was the face amount, $1,800, plus interest of $22.50, or a total of $1,822.50. The bank therefore used $1,822.50 as the basis for computing the discount. Since the bank must wait for 80 days to collect the note, the maturity value of $1,822.50 was discounted for 80 days at the bank discount rate of 6%, yielding a discount of $24.30. This amount, $24.30, was subtracted from the maturity value, $1,822.50, to determine the proceeds of $1,798.20. These computations may be tabulated as follows:

Face value of note........................	$1,800.00
Interest on note — 90 days at 5%...........	22.50
Maturity value of note....................	$1,822.50
Discount on maturity value — 80 days at 6%..	24.30
Proceeds of note.........................	$1,798.20

The same information is presented graphically below. In reading the data, follow the direction of the arrows.

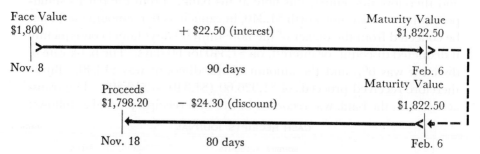

The note that Burke discounted had been recorded on his books at $1,800, its face value. The proceeds of the note amounted to $1,798.20. The difference between these two amounts, $1.80, was interest expense.

The transaction with the bank was recorded in the cash receipts journal as follows:

CASH RECEIPTS JOURNAL   PAGE 12

DATE		ACCOUNT	POST. REF.	SUNDRY ACCOUNTS		SALES CR.	ACCTS. REC. CR.	SALES DISC. DR.	CASH DR.
				DR.	CR.				
1961 Nov.	18	Notes Receivable	113		1,800 00				1,798 20
		Interest Expense	911	1 80					

In the foregoing example the proceeds of the discounted note were less than the face value, resulting in an interest expense. The proceeds obtained from discounting a customer's interest-bearing note are not always less than the face value of the note, however. For example, if a note receivable bearing interest at the rate of 7% were discounted at the rate of 6%, the proceeds would be greater than the face value. This would be true even though the note was discounted on the same day that it was issued. Another determining factor is the time elapsed between the issuance date and the discount date as compared to the time between the discount date and the maturity date.

For example, if Burke had discounted Mason's note (at the same discount rate) on December 28, 40 days before the note became due, the discount would have amounted to $12.15 and he would have received proceeds of $1,810.35. The $10.35 excess of the proceeds over the face of the note would have been interest income and the entry in the cash receipts journal would have been as follows:

CASH RECEIPTS JOURNAL   PAGE 12

DATE		ACCOUNT	POST. REF.	SUNDRY ACCOUNTS		SALES CR.	ACCTS. REC. CR.	SALES DISC. DR.	CASH DR.
				DR.	CR.				
1961 Dec.	28	Notes Receivable	113		1,800 00				1,810 35
		Interest Income	811		10 35				

Contingent liability. When a note receivable is discounted, it is necessary for the owner to endorse the note. By endorsing the note, the endorser becomes responsible to the bank or other endorsee for its payment if the note is not paid by the maker at maturity. Discounting a note therefore results in the creation of a possible future obligation that is known as a *contingent liability*. The liability is contingent rather than real. If the maker pays the note at maturity, which is probable, the contingent liability is discharged without any action on the part of the endorser. If, on the other hand, the note is not paid by the maker at maturity and the endorser is notified of the fact, the liability becomes a real one.

In preparing a balance sheet the total amount of discounted notes receivable that are not yet due at the balance sheet date should be disclosed. Disclosure may be made by a note in the liability section or at the bottom of the balance sheet, somewhat along the following lines: "The company is contingently liable for notes receivable discounted in the amount of $16,420." The amount of the contingent liability can be determined from a memorandum record of amounts, due dates, disposition, etc. of all notes receivable.

An alternative procedure is to maintain a current record of the contingent liability in the ledger. This is done by crediting Notes Receivable Discounted at the time the note is discounted. As each discounted note matures it is then necessary to debit Notes Receivable Discounted and credit Notes Receivable. The notes receivable on hand at any time is the excess of the debit balance in Notes Receivable over the credit balance in Notes Receivable Discounted. The procedure is seldom used in practice because of the many additional entries required and the ease of obtaining the same information from supplementary records. It should be noted that it is only the amount of the unmatured notes discounted on the balance sheet date that is significant; the number of such notes is usually a small fraction of the total number of short-term notes discounted during the year.

Dishonored notes

A note that is not paid when it becomes due is said to be *dishonored*. When a note receivable held by a business is dishonored, the note is no longer negotiable. For this reason the amount due should ordinarily be transferred to the accounts receivable account. For example, if the $300, 20-day, 6% note received and recorded on October 19 (page 199) had been dishonored at maturity, the entry to charge the note back to the customer's account would have been as follows:

Nov.	7	Accounts Receivable — T. J. Cole..........	115/√	301	00		
		Notes Receivable.......................	113			300	00
		Interest Income.......................	811			1	00
		Dishonored note and interest.					

If there had been some assurance that Cole would pay the note within a few days after maturity, the foregoing entry could have been omitted. In extending credit to the customer in the future, however, it is desirable that his account disclose the fact that the note was dishonored.

In the event that a customer's note that has been discounted is dishonored, the bank will notify the endorser. The latter will then have to pay the note and any interest accrued. For example, if the note that was discounted on November 18 (page 202) is dishonored, Burke, the endorser, will have to pay the bank the face of the note, $1,800, plus interest of $22.50. The entire amount of the payment would be charged to the maker's account, as shown in the following entry:

CASH PAYMENTS JOURNAL   PAGE 23

DATE	CHECK NO.	ACCOUNT DEBITED	POST. REF.	SUNDRY ACCTS. DR.	ACCTS. PAY. DR.	PUR. DISC. CR.	CASH CR.
1961 Feb. 6	572	Accts. Rec. — John Mason	115/ √	1,822 50			1,822 50

In some cases the bank submits to the endorser a notarized statement of the facts of the dishonor. The fee paid by the bank for obtaining this statement, known as a *protest fee*, is charged to the endorser, who in turn charges it to the maker of the note. For example, if there had been a protest fee of $2 in connection with the dishonor and the payment recorded above, the debit to the maker's account and the credit to Cash would have been $1,824.50.

Reporting interest on the income statement

Interest income is usually reported on the income statement as *other income;* interest expense, as *other expense.*

Items listed on the statement under the headings "Other Income" and "Other Expense" affect the net income or the net loss of the enterprise, but they are considered apart from items representing the ordinary operations of the business and are therefore usually placed at the end of the statement. A common method of reporting interest on the income statement is illustrated below.

Net income from operations..................................		$9,823.56
Other income:		
Interest income................................	$90.60	
Other expense:		
Interest expense...............................	43.20	47.40
Net income..		$9,870.96

Partial income statement showing treatment of interest items

If the total other expense is greater than the total other income, the order may be reversed and the difference deducted from the net income from operations to obtain the net income.

Questions

1. Why are claims evidenced by credit instruments more liquid than accounts receivable?

2. Is the interest rate stated on a note the rate for the term of the note or for a year?

3. What is the basic formula for computing interest?

4. (a) What is the amount of interest on $1,000 for 60 days at 6%? (b) The amount of interest computed in (a) is what per cent of $1,000?

5. (a) What is the face value of a $1,000, 90-day, 6% note? (b) What is the maturity value of the note in (a)?

6. Under what circumstances will the face value of a note be the same amount as the maturity value of a note?

7. When face value and maturity value of a note differ, which amount is recorded in the notes receivable or notes payable account?

8. What is the meaning of (a) discounting a note, (b) discount rate, (c) proceeds, (d) dishonored note?

9. Does the maker of a note incur a contingent liability when he discounts a note at his bank?

10. The payee of a $2,000, 60-day, 6% note discounts the note at his bank. The note is dishonored and the payee pays the bank the face amount, $20 for interest, and $2 for protest fee. To what account or accounts should the $2,022 be charged? Explain.

11. During the year Bennett Home Appliances discounted $60,000 of notes receivable. At December 31, the end of the fiscal year, discounted notes in the amount of $14,000 have not matured. (a) What is the amount of the contingent liability? (b) How should the contingent liability be disclosed?

12. The series of five transactions recorded in the following T accounts were incident to a sale to a customer. Describe each transaction briefly.

CASH		NOTES RECEIVABLE		ACCOUNTS RECEIVABLE	
(c) 602.97	(d) 606.00	(b) 600.00	(c) 600.00	(a) 600.00	(b) 600.00
(e) 609.03				(d) 606.00	(e) 606.00

SALES		INTEREST INCOME	
	(a) 600.00		(c) 2.97
			(e) 3.03

Exercises

1. John Burton issued to Henry Wheeler on account the note illustrated at the top of the following page.

(a) Name the payee. (b) Name the maker. (c) Give Burton's general journal entry to record the issuance of the note. (d) Give Wheeler's general journal entry to record receipt of the note. (e) What is the due date of the note? (f) What is the amount of interest to be paid at maturity? (g) Give Burton's entry, in general journal form, to record the payment of the note and the interest at maturity. (h) Give Wheeler's entry, in general journal form, to record receipt of payment at maturity.

```
$800.00 _____          _Phoenix, Arizona, August 10,_ _____ 19_62_

_____Ninety days_____AFTER DATE____I____ PROMISE TO PAY TO

THE ORDER OF_ Henry Wheeler _____

_Eight hundred 00/100_____ DOLLARS

PAYABLE AT_City Bank and Trust Company_____

VALUE RECEIVED WITH INTEREST AT _--6---_%

No._18 ___                              John Burton
```

2. Use the 60-day, 6% method to compute the interest for the following:

AMOUNT OF NOTE	DAYS	INTEREST RATE
(a) $ 175.40	83 days	5%
(b) 2,350.00	36 days	6%
(c) 1,934.50	67 days	$5\frac{1}{2}$%
(d) 876.25	9 days	7%
(e) 1,142.37	59 days	4%

3. In negotiating a 60-day loan, Arnold Carey has the option of either (1) issuing a $10,000, non-interest-bearing note that will be discounted at the rate of 6%, or (2) issuing a $10,000 note bearing interest at the rate of 6% that will be accepted at face value. (a) What would be the amount of his interest expense in each case? (b) What would be the amount of the proceeds in each case? (c) Which of the two alternatives is more favorable to Carey? (d) Assuming that he adopts the first alternative, give the entry, in general journal form, at the time the note is issued and at the time the note is paid.

4. Gordon Runyon holds a 90-day, 5% note for $600, dated June 14, that he has received from a customer on account. On July 14 he discounts the note at his bank at the rate of 6%. (a) What is the maturity value of the note? (b) How many days are there in the discount period? (c) What is the amount of the discount? (d) What is the amount of the proceeds? (e) Give the entry, in general journal form, to record the transaction on July 14.

5. Record the following transactions, each in general journal form, on the books of Roy Taylor:

June 1. Received a $2,400, 60-day, 5% note dated June 1 from Thomas Meeker on account.
July   1. Discounted the note at First National Bank, discount rate 6%.
July 31. The note is dishonored; paid the bank the amount due on the note plus a protest fee of $2.50.
Aug. 30. Received amount due on the dishonored note plus interest at 6% on the amount outstanding since July 31.

6. On the basis of the following data applicable to the Rako Company for the current fiscal year ended December 31, prepare the section of the income statement beginning with net income from operations and ending with net income:

Net income from operations.............................. $25,420
Interest income..   796
Interest expense.......................................   1,084

Problems

9-1. The following were selected from among the transactions completed by Johnson Co. during the current year:

Jan. 10. Purchased merchandise on account from Adams & Co., $650.
     20. Paid Adams & Co. for the invoice of January 10, less 1% discount.
Feb. 2. Purchased merchandise on account from J. R. Beckett, $900.
Mar. 4. Issued a 30-day, 6% note for $900 to J. R. Beckett on account.
Apr. 3. Paid J. R. Beckett the amount owed on the note of March 4, $904.50.
May 12. Borrowed $2,000 from Valley National Bank, issuing a 60-day, 6% note for that amount.
July 11. Paid Valley National Bank the $20 interest due on the note of May 12 and renewed the loan by issuing a new 30-day, 6% note for $2,000.
Aug. 10. Paid Valley National Bank amount due on note of July 11, $2,010.
Sept. 5. Issued a 60-day, non-interest-bearing note for $5,000 to Hamilton National Bank, receiving proceeds of $4,950.
Nov. 4. Paid Hamilton National Bank amount due on note of September 5.
     6. Purchased store equipment from Prescott Co. for $4,000, paying $1,000 in cash and issuing a series of six 6% notes for $500 each, coming due at 30-day intervals.
Dec. 6. Paid the amount due Prescott Co. on the first note in the series issued on November 6, $502.50.

Instructions: Record the transactions in general journal form, using a two-column general journal.

9-2. The following were selected from among the transactions completed by Bergman & Co. during the current year:

Jan. 6. Sold merchandise on account to Frost Co., $850, charging an additional $10 for prepaid transportation costs.
    16. Received from Frost Co. the amount due on the invoice of January 6, less 2% discount.
Feb. 4. Sold merchandise on account to White & Barker, $600.
    14. Accepted a 30-day, 8% note for $600 from White & Barker on account.
Mar. 16. Received from White & Barker the amount due on the note of February 14, $604.
Apr. 2. Sold merchandise on account to A. T. Lewis, Inc., $900.
May 2. Accepted a 60-day, 8% note for $900 from A. T. Lewis, Inc., on account.
    22. Discounted the note from A. T. Lewis, Inc., at the Bank of Douglas at 6%, receiving proceeds of $905.92.
July 2. Received notice from Bank of Douglas that A. T. Lewis, Inc., had dishonored its note. Paid the bank the amount of the face of the note, $900, interest of $12, and a protest fee of $3.
    31. Received from A. T. Lewis, Inc. the amount owed on the dishonored note, plus additional interest of $6.10.
Aug. 12. Loaned $200 to John Fairchild, a customer, receiving a 30-day, 6% note.
Sept. 11. Received interest of $1 from John Fairchild and a new 30-day, 6% note, as a renewal of the loan.
Oct. 11. Received from John Fairchild the amount due on his note, $201.

Instructions: Record the transactions in general journal form, using a two-column general journal.

9-3. The following were selected from among the transactions completed by Corbett Co. during the current fiscal year:

June   3. Purchased merchandise on account from Marshall Co., $650.
     10. Sold merchandise on account to G. B. Harris, Invoice No. 684, $500.
     18. Discounted a 30-day, non-interest-bearing note payable for $5,000 at First National Bank; discount rate, 6%.
     20. Received cash from G. B. Harris for the invoice of June 10, less 1% discount.
     21. Sold merchandise on account to J. Miller, invoice No. 701, $700.
     29. Sold merchandise on account to W. T. Scott Co., invoice No. 715, $1,200.

July   3. Issued a 60-day, 7% note for $650 to Marshall Co. on account.
     5. Purchased merchandise on account from Whitney & Co., $850.
    15. Issued check No. 842 to Whitney & Co. for the amount due on the purchase of July 5, less 2% discount.
    18. Issued check No. 848 to First National Bank for the amount due on the note dated June 18.
    21. Received from J. Miller on account a 60-day, 6% note for $700, dated July 21.
    22. Sold merchandise on account to Carlton Co., invoice No. 820, $800.
    29. Received from W. T. Scott Co. on account a 1-month, 6% note for $1,200, dated July 29.

Aug.   1. Received from Carlton Co. on account a 30-day, 6% note for $800, dated August 1.
    10. Discounted J. Miller's $700 note, dated July 21, at Security National Bank, discount rate 6%.
    29. Received cash from W. T. Scott Co. for the amount owed on note dated July 29.
    31. Carlton Co. dishonored its note dated August 1. Charged the dishonored note to their account.

Sept. 1. Issued check No. 923 to Marshall Co. in payment of the note dated July 3.
    19. Received notice from Security National Bank that J. Miller had dishonored his note dated July 21. Issued check No. 941 in payment of the amount due; no protest fee.
    29. Received cash from J. Miller for the principal and interest on his dishonored note, plus additional interest at 8% on the total amount from September 19.

Instructions: Record the transactions, using the following journals: sales journal (as illustrated on page 122); purchases journal (with only one money column, headed Purchases Dr. and Accts. Pay. Cr.); cash receipts journal (as illustrated on page 199); cash payments journal (as illustrated on page 205); two-column general journal.

9-4. The following transactions were completed by Barton Wholesalers during the current fiscal year:

Jan.   4. Received from Frontier Market a 90-day, non-interest-bearing note for $4,000, dated January 3, on account.
    23. Issued to K. C. Packing Co. a 2-month, 5% note for $5,000, on account.

Feb. 12. Discounted at the Union Trust Co. at 6% the note received from Frontier Market, dated January 3.

Mar. 23. Issued check No. 531 to K. C. Packing Co. in payment of the note issued on January 23.

Apr. 10. Discounted a 60-day, non-interest-bearing note payable for $10,000 at the Union Trust Co.; discount rate, 6%.

May 10. Received from C. B. Shaw a 90-day, 5% note for $800, dated May 8, on account.

16. Purchased land for a building site from Progressive Development Co. for $30,000, issuing check No. 610 for $5,000 and a 7% mortgage note for the balance. The contract provides for payments of $2,500 of principal plus accrued interest at intervals of six months.

June 9. Issued check No. 648 to Union Trust Co. for the amount due on the note payable issued on April 10.

15. Discounted at the Union Trust Co. at 6% the note received from C. B. Shaw, dated May 8.

Aug. 7. Received notice from the Union Trust Co. that C. B. Shaw had dishonored the note due on August 6. Issued check No. 719 to the bank for the amount due on the note, plus a protest fee of $4.

Sept. 16. Received from Campus Food Center a 90-day, 5% note for $700, dated September 15, on account.

Oct. 6. Received from C. B. Shaw the amount due on the note dishonored on August 6, including interest at 6% from August 6 to October 5 on the maturity value of the note plus protest fee.

Nov. 16. Issued check No. 873 for installment due on mortgage note, together with interest on $25,000 for six months.

Dec. 14. Campus Food Center dishonored its note dated September 15. Charged the dishonored note to their account.

Instructions: Record the transactions, using the following journals: cash receipts journal (as illustrated on page 201); cash payments journal (as illustrated on page 201, except for an additional column for Sundry Accounts Cr.); two-column general journal.

9-5. The Payson Contracting Co. received the notes described below during the three month period October 1 to December 31. Notes (a), (b), (c), and (d) were discounted at Williams State Bank on the dates indicated; discount rate 6%.

	Date	Face Amount	Term	Interest Rate	Date Discounted
(a)	Oct. 5	$1,000	90 days	6%	Oct. 6
(b)	Oct. 24	4,200	30 days	—	Nov. 2
(c)	Nov. 8	3,000	2 months	6½%	Dec. 1
(d)	Nov. 17	940	60 days	7%	Dec. 17
(e)	Dec. 13	1,250	6 months	6%	

Instructions: (1) Determine for each note (a) the due date and (b) the amount of interest due at maturity, identifying each note by letter.

(2) Determine for each of the first four notes (a) the maturity value, (b) the discount period, (c) the discount, (d) the proceeds, and (e) the interest income or interest expense, identifying each note by letter.

(3) Present, in general journal form, the entries to record the discounting of note (b) and note (d).

Prepaid, unearned, and accrued items

Need for consideration

Reports on the financial position and the results of operations of business enterprises are prepared at regular intervals. The data on financial position are presented in the balance sheet, and the summary of operations is presented in the income statement. The maximum interval of time between these periodic summaries is one year. It is also customary to prepare interim reports at quarterly or monthly intervals.

Procedures employed in preparing the financial statements and summarizing the ledger at the end of the fiscal year have been described in earlier chapters. The necessity for recording cost allocations has been emphasized as an important part of the periodic summary. There are many situations in which adjusting entries are required to bring the ledger into agreement with the true state of affairs. Some of them have been described and illustrated in earlier chapters. For example, the cost of prepaid insurance expires from day to day, but it is not until financial statements are to be prepared that the expired cost is recorded. At that time the expired cost of the entire period is transferred from the asset account to an appropriate expense account. Similar provisions must be made to assure that all revenues and expenses are recorded for the period and that all assets and liabilities are fairly stated as of the last day of the period.

Classification and terminology

There are various kinds of prepaid, unearned, and accrued items and there is also some variation in the terms used to describe them. This chapter is devoted to a discussion of the following four classes:

1. *Prepaid expenses;* also called prepayments, or deferred charges.
   Items in this category are classified as assets, usually current assets.
2. *Unearned revenues;* also called income collected in advance, or deferred credits.
   Items in this category are classified as liabilities, usually current liabilities.

3. *Accrued liabilities;* also called accrued payables.
   Items in this category are classified as current liabilities.
4. *Accrued assets;* also called accrued receivables.
   Items in this category are classified as current assets.

Prepaid expenses

Prepaid expenses are commodities and services that have been purchased for consumption, but which are unconsumed at the end of the accounting period. The portion of the asset that has been used during the period has become an expense; the remainder will become an expense in the future. It is because of this deferment of benefits to the future that prepaid expenses are sometimes termed *deferred charges.* Prepaid expenses include such items as prepaid insurance, prepaid rent, prepaid advertising, prepaid interest, and various types of supplies.

Two methods of accounting for prepaid expenses will be explained. Prepaid insurance will be used to illustrate the first method, and prepaid interest, the second method. It should be understood that either of the alternative methods may be employed in any particular case.

Prepaid expenses recorded initially as assets. When prepaid insurance or other consumable services or supplies are purchased, they may be charged to an asset account. Although it is known at the time of purchase that part of the services or supplies will be consumed during the accounting period, the determination of the amount is postponed until the statements are prepared.

The expired insurance may be analyzed according to the various types of property insured, so that the amount allocable to selling expense and the amount allocable to general expense can be determined. For example, expired insurance on merchandise and store equipment is considered a selling expense; that on office equipment and building, a general expense.

To illustrate, assume that the prepaid insurance account has a balance of $814 at the close of the year. This amount represents the unexpired insurance at the beginning of the year plus the total of premiums paid during the year. It is ascertained that $506 of insurance has expired during the year, of which $426 represents selling expense and $80 represents general expense. The adjusting entry to record the expired insurance appears as follows:

Dec.	31	Insurance Expense — Selling..........	615	426	
		Insurance Expense — General.........	716	80	
		Prepaid Insurance.................	118		506

After this entry has been posted, the three accounts affected appear as follows:

PREPAID INSURANCE   Acct. No. 118

1961					1961				
Jan.	1	Balance	√	430	Dec.	31	Adjusting	J17	506
Mar.	18		CP6	220					
Aug.	26		CP16	100					
Nov.	11		CP21	64					
				814					

INSURANCE EXPENSE — SELLING   Acct. No. 615

1961				
Dec.	31	Adjusting	J17	426

INSURANCE EXPENSE — GENERAL   Acct. No. 716

1961				
Dec.	31	Adjusting	J17	80

After $506 of expired insurance is transferred to the expense accounts, the balance of $308 remaining in Prepaid Insurance represents the premiums on various policies that apply to future periods. It is an asset and is shown on the balance sheet. The amounts transferred to the two expense accounts appear on the income statement.

Prepaid expenses recorded initially as expenses. In the foregoing illustration the prepaid expenses were originally charged to the asset account. An alternative is to charge them directly to the appropriate expense account as they are acquired. This method is frequently used in recording the discount on notes issued to banks, which are ordinarily for a period of from 30 to 90 days. If the prepaid interest is charged to Interest Expense at the time the funds are borrowed and if the notes are paid by the end of the fiscal year, no adjusting entry is necessary. When one or more discounted notes are still outstanding on the last day of the year, however, the portion of the interest applicable to the ensuing period should be deducted from the expense account and transferred to the asset account in an adjusting entry.

To illustrate this alternative method, assume that during the year four non-interest-bearing notes payable were discounted and that in each case the discount was debited to Interest Expense. Three of the notes became due and were paid during the year. The fourth, a $12,000, 90-day note, had been issued on December 1 at a discount of $180.

As of December 31, the last day of the fiscal year, only 30 days of the term of the $12,000 note have elapsed. Therefore only 30/90 of the $180 discount is an expense of the year; the remaining 60/90 will become an expense during the first 60 days of the following year. The adjusting entry to transfer the prepaid portion of the interest ($120) to the asset account is as follows:

| Dec. | 31 | Prepaid Interest.................... | 117 | 120 | |
| | | Interest Expense................. | 911 | | 120 |

After this entry has been posted, the prepaid interest account and the interest expense account appear as follows:

PREPAID INTEREST   Acct. No. 117

| 1961 | | | | | | | | | |
| Dec. | 31 | Adjusting | J17 | 120 | | | | | |

INTEREST EXPENSE   Acct. No. 911

1961					1961				
Feb.	5		CR3	50	Dec.	31	Adjusting	J17	120
May	15		CR8	144					
June	10		CR10	105					
Dec.	1		CR20	180					
				479					

The remaining balance of $359 ($479 − $120) in Interest Expense is the amount of expense for the year; it will be reported in the income statement. The balance of $120 in Prepaid Interest is a current asset and will be reported in the balance sheet. In the process of closing the books the debit balance of $359 in Interest Expense will be closed to Expense and Revenue Summary.

As of the first day of the following year the balance in Prepaid Interest is transferred back to Interest Expense by the following *reversing* entry:

| Jan. | 1 | Interest Expense.................... | 911 | 120 | |
| | | Prepaid Interest................. | 117 | | 120 |

After the reversing entry has been posted, the prepaid interest account and the interest expense account appear as follows:

PREPAID INTEREST   Acct. No. 117

| 1961 | | | | | 1962 | | | | |
| Dec. | 31 | Adjusting | J17 | 120 | Jan. | 1 | Reversing | J18 | 120 |

INTEREST EXPENSE   Acct. No. 911

1961					1961				
Feb.	5		CR3	50	Dec.	31	Adjusting	J17	120
May	15		CR8	144		31	Closing	J17	359
June	10		CR10	105					
Dec.	1		CR20	180					
				479					
				479					479
1962									
Jan.	1	Reversing	J18	120					

The prepaid interest of $120 is now in Interest Expense. As additional interest expense is incurred during the year, it will be debited directly to Interest Expense. Whenever it is the policy to debit prepayments of a particular expense directly to the expense account, adjustments for the prepayment should be reversed after the books are closed.

Comparison of the two methods. The two methods of recording prepaid expenses and the related entries at the end of an accounting period may be summarized as follows:

Prepaid expense recorded initially as an *asset*.

Adjusting entry: Transfer amount *used* to the appropriate *expense* account.

Closing entry: Transfer balance of expense account to the expense and revenue summary account.

Reversing entry: None needed.

Balance of prepaid expense at beginning of new period: In the *asset* account.

Prepaid expense recorded initially as an *expense*.

Adjusting entry: Transfer amount *unused* to the appropriate *asset* account.

Closing entry: Transfer balance of expense account to the expense and revenue summary account.

Reversing entry: Transfer amount *unused* back to the *expense* account.

Balance of prepaid expense at beginning of new period: In the *expense* account.

When prepaid expenses are charged to the asset account as they are incurred (first method), the balance of the prepayment is in the asset account after the work of the periodic summary is completed. When prepaid expenses are charged to the expense account as they are incurred (second method), the balance of the prepayment is in the expense account after the work of the periodic summary is completed.

The amount of expense that will be reported on the income statement will be the same regardless of which method is used. Similarly, the amount of the prepayment that will be listed as an asset on the balance sheet will be the same regardless of which method is used. Some accountants prefer the first method, others prefer the second method, and still others prefer the first method for some types of prepayments and the second for other types. The method adopted for each particular type of prepaid expense should be consistently followed from year to year.

Unearned revenue

Revenue received during a particular period may be only partly earned by the end of the period. Items of revenue that are received in advance represent a liability that may be termed *unearned revenue*. The portion of the liability that is discharged during the period through delivery of commodities or services has been earned; the remainder will be earned in the future. It is because of this deferment that unearned revenues are frequently called *deferred credits*. For example, magazine publishers ordinarily receive advance payment for subscriptions extending for periods ranging from a few months to a number of years. At the end of an accounting period, the portion of the receipts applicable to future periods has not been earned and should appear in the balance sheet as a liability.

Other examples of unearned revenue are rent received in advance on property owned, interest deducted in advance on notes receivable, premiums received in advance by an insurance company, tuition received in advance by a school, an annual retainer fee received in advance by an attorney, and amounts received in advance by an advertising firm for advertising services to be rendered in the future.

By accepting payment for the commodity or the service in advance, a business renders itself liable to furnish the commodity or the service at some future time. At the end of the accounting period, if some portion of the commodity or the service has been furnished, part of the revenue has been earned. The earned portion appears on the income statement. The unearned portion represents a liability of the business to furnish the commodity or the service in a future period and is reported in the balance sheet as a liability.

As in the case of prepaid expenses, two methods of accounting for items of unearned revenue will be described. Unearned rent will be used in illustrating both methods.

Unearned revenue recorded initially as a liability. When revenue is received in advance, it may be credited to a liability account. For example, assume that on July 1 a business rents a portion of its building for a period of two years, receiving $3,600 in payment for the entire term of the lease. The transaction was originally recorded by a debit to Cash and a credit to Unearned Rent. On December 31, the end of the fiscal year, one fourth of the amount has been earned and three fourths of the amount remains a liability. The adjusting entry to record the revenue and reduce the liability appears as follows:

| Dec. | 31 | Unearned Rent...................... | 218 | 900 | |
| | | Rent Income...................... | 812 | | 900 |

After this entry has been posted, the unearned rent account and the rent income account appear as follows:

UNEARNED RENT   Acct. No. 218

1961					1961				
Dec.	31	Adjusting	J17	900	July	1		CR8	3,600

RENT INCOME   Acct. No. 812

					1961					
					Dec.	31	Adjusting	J17	900	

After the amount earned, $900, is transferred to Rent Income, the balance of $2,700 remaining in Unearned Rent is a liability to render a service in the future and it therefore appears as a current liability in the balance sheet. Rent Income appears in the "Other Income" section of the income statement; the account is closed to the expense and revenue summary account along with other revenue accounts.

Unearned revenue recorded initially as revenue.   Instead of being credited to a liability account, unearned revenue may be credited to a revenue account. For example, assume the same facts as in the preceding illustration, except that the transaction was originally recorded on July 1 by a debit to Cash and a credit to Rent Income. On December 31, the end of the fiscal year, three fourths of the balance in Rent Income is still unearned and the remaining one fourth has been earned.   The adjusting entry to record the transfer to the liability account appears as follows:

Dec.	31	Rent Income.......................	812	2,700		
		Unearned Rent..................	218		2,700	

After this entry has been posted, the unearned rent account and the rent income appear as follows:

UNEARNED RENT   Acct. No. 218

					1961					
					Dec.	31	Adjusting	J17	2,700	

RENT INCOME   Acct. No. 812

1961					1961					
Dec.	31	Adjusting	J17	2,700	July	1		CR8	3,600	

The unearned rent of $2,700 is listed as a current liability in the balance sheet, and the rent income of $900 is listed as "Other Income" in the income statement. In the process of closing the books, the balance of the rent income account is closed to the expense and revenue summary account.

After the closing entries are posted and the accounts are ruled, the balance in Unearned Rent is transferred back to Rent Income by the following reversing entry:

Jan.	1	Unearned Rent......................	218	2,700	
		Rent Income.......................	812		2,700

After this entry has been posted, the unearned rent account and the rent income account appears as follows:

UNEARNED RENT   Acct. No. 218

1962					1961				
Jan.	1	Reversing	J18	2,700	Dec.	31	Adjusting	J17	2,700

RENT INCOME   Acct. No. 812

1961					1961				
Dec.	31	Adjusting	J17	2,700	July	1		CR8	3,600
	31	Closing	J17	900					
				3,600					3,600
					1962				
					Jan.	1	Reversing	J18	2,700

The unearned rent of $2,700 is now in the rent income account. This is consistent with the policy of crediting the receipt of unearned revenue directly to the revenue account. When this method of recording the receipt of the unearned revenue is employed, it is good practice to reverse the adjusting entry after the books have been closed.

Comparison of the two methods. The two methods of recording unearned revenue and the related entries at the end of the accounting period may be summarized as follows:

Unearned revenue recorded initially as a *liability*.
> Adjusting entry: Transfer amount *earned* to the appropriate *revenue* account.
> Closing entry: Transfer balance of revenue account to the expense and revenue summary account.
> Reversing entry: None needed.
> Balance of unearned revenue at beginning of new period: In the *liability* account.

Unearned revenue recorded initially as *revenue*.
> Adjusting entry: Transfer amount *unearned* to the appropriate *liability* account.
> Closing entry: Transfer balance of revenue account to the expense and revenue summary account.
> Reversing entry: Transfer amount *unearned* back to the *revenue* account.
> Balance of unearned revenue at beginning of new period: In the *revenue* account.

When unearned revenue is credited to a liability account as it is received (first method), the amount unearned is in the liability account after the work of the periodic summary is completed. When unearned revenue is credited to the income account as it is received (second method), the amount unearned is in the revenue account after the work of the periodic summary is completed.

As was explained in connection with prepaid expenses, the results obtained are the same under both methods. The method adopted for each particular kind of unearned revenue should be consistently followed from year to year.

Accrued liabilities

Some expenses accrue from day to day but are ordinarily recorded only when they are paid. Examples are interest expense on interest-bearing obligations, and salaries. The amounts of such items accrued but unpaid at the end of the fiscal period are both an expense and a liability. It is for this reason that the accrual may be referred to as an *accrued liability*, an *accrued payable*, or an *accrued expense*.

To illustrate the adjusting entry for an accrued liability, assume that on December 31, the end of the fiscal year, the salary expense account has a debit balance of $32,500. During the year salaries have been paid each Friday for the five-day week then ended. For this particular fiscal year, December 31 falls on Wednesday. Reference to the records of the business reveals that the salary accrued for these last three days of the year amounts to $375. The adjusting entry to record the additional expense and the liability is:

Dec.	31	Salary Expense.....................	611	375	
		Salaries Payable.................	214		375

After this entry has been posted, the salaries payable account and the salary expense account appear as follows:

SALARIES PAYABLE   Acct. No. 214

					1961				
					Dec.	31	Adjusting	J17	375

SALARY EXPENSE   Acct. No. 611

1961									
Dec.	31	Balance	√	32,500					
	31	Adjusting	J17	375					

The accrued salaries of $375 recorded in Salaries Payable will appear on the balance sheet of December 31 as a current liability. The **salary** expense of $32,875 now recorded in Salary Expense will appear in the income statement for the year ended December 31. The salary expense account will be closed to the expense and revenue summary account in the usual manner.

When the weekly salaries are paid on January 2 of the following year, part of the payment will discharge the liability of $375 and the remainder will represent salary expense of the first two days of January. In order to avoid the necessity of analyzing the payment, a reversing entry is made at the beginning of the new year. The effect of the entry is to transfer the credit balance in the salaries payable account to the credit side of the salary expense account. This entry appears as follows:

Jan.	1	Salaries Payable.....................	214	375	
		Salary Expense....................	611		375

After this entry has been posted, the salaries payable account and the salary expense account appear as follows:

SALARIES PAYABLE   Acct. No. 214

1962					1961				
Jan.	1	Reversing	J18	375	Dec.	31	Adjusting	J17	375

SALARY EXPENSE   Acct. No. 611

1961					1961				
Dec.	31	Balance	✓	32,500	Dec.	31	Closing	J18	32,875
	31	Adjusting	J17	375					
				32,875					32,875
					1961				
					Jan.	1	Reversing	J18	375

The liability for salaries on December 31 now appears as a credit in Salary Expense. Assuming that the salaries paid on Friday, January 2, amount to $550, the debit to Salary Expense will automatically record the discharge of the liability of $375 and the expense of $175 ($550 − $375).

The discussion of the treatment of accrued salary expense is illustrative of the method of handling accrued liabilities in general. If, in addition to accrued salaries, there are other accrued liabilities at the end of a fiscal period, separate liability accounts may be set up for each type. When these liability items are numerous, however, one liability account, termed Accrued Payables, may be used. All accrued liabilities may be recorded as credits to this account instead of to separate accounts.

Accrued assets

All assets belonging to the business at the end of an accounting period and all revenue earned during the period should be recorded in the ledger. But, during a fiscal period, it is the customary practice to record some types of revenue only as the cash is received; consequently, at the end of the period there may be items of revenue that have not been recorded. In such cases it is necessary to record the amount of the accrued revenue by debiting an asset account and crediting a revenue account. Because of the dual nature of such accruals, they are referred to as *accrued assets, accrued receivables,* or *accrued revenues.*

To illustrate the adjusting entry for an accrued asset, assume that on December 31, the end of the fiscal year, the interest income account has a credit balance of $384. Assume further that on the same date the business owns three short-term, interest-bearing notes accepted from customers. The three notes are for varying amounts and have varying due dates in January and February of the succeeding year. The interest accrued on each note from its date of issuance to December 31 is determined, and the three amounts total $67. The adjusting entry to record this claim against debtors and the additional revenue earned is as follows:

| Dec. | 31 | Interest Receivable.................... | 114 | 67 | |
| | | Interest Income.................. | 811 | | 67 |

After this entry has been posted, the interest receivable account and the interest income account appear as follows:

			INTEREST RECEIVABLE				Acct. No. 114	
1961								
Dec.	31	Adjusting	J17	67				

			INTEREST INCOME				Acct. No. 811	
					1961			
					Dec.	31	Balance	✓	384
						31	Adjusting	J17	67

The accrued interest of $67 recorded in Interest Receivable will appear on the balance sheet of December 31 as a current asset. The credit balance of $451 now recorded in Interest Income will appear in the "Other Income" section of the income statement for the year ended December 31. The interest income account will be closed to the expense and revenue summary account in the usual manner.

When the amount due on each of the three notes is collected in the succeeding year, part of the interest received will be applied to reduction of the interest receivable and the remainder will represent revenue for the new year. To avoid the inconvenience of analyzing each receipt of interest in the new year, a reversing entry is made immediately after the books are closed. The effect of the entry is to transfer the debit balance in the interest receivable account to the debit side of the interest income account. This entry is shown below:

Jan.	1	Interest Income......................	811	67	
		Interest Receivable................	114		67

After this entry has been posted, the interest receivable account and the interest income account appear as follows:

INTEREST RECEIVABLE   Acct. No. 114

1961					1962				
Dec.	31	Adjusting	J17	67	Jan.	1	Reversing	J18	67

INTEREST INCOME   Acct. No. 811

1961					1961				
Dec.	31	Closing	J17	451	Dec.	31	Balance	✓	384
						31	Adjusting	J17	67
				451					451
1962									
Jan.	1	Reversing	J18	67					

The interest receivable on December 31 now appears as a debit in Interest Income. When cash is received for the principal and the interest on each note, the transaction will be recorded in the usual manner; that is, the entire amount of the interest will be credited to Interest Income. The excess of the total credits over the debit balance of $67 in the Interest Income account will be the amount of interest earned on these notes in the new year.

The treatment of interest accrued on notes receivable illustrates the method of handling accrued assets in general. If, in addition to accrued interest, there are other accrued assets at the end of a fiscal period, separate accounts may be set up. Each of these accounts will be of the same nature as the account with interest receivable. When such items are numerous, one asset account, termed Accrued Receivables, may be opened. All accrued assets may be recorded as debits to this account instead of to separate accounts.

Questions

1. Why must accounts be "adjusted" at the end of a fiscal period?

2. Classify the following items as (1) prepaid expense, (2) unearned revenue, (3) accrued asset, or (4) accrued liability.
  (a) Salary owed but not yet due.
  (b) Property taxes paid in advance.
  (c) Rent received in advance on property owned.
  (d) Interest owed but not yet due.
  (e) Interest earned but not received.
  (f) Advertising literature on hand.
  (g) Interest received in advance by a bank for discounting a note.
  (h) Office supplies on hand.
  (i) Taxes accrued but payable in the following period.
  (j) Subscriptions collected in advance by a publisher.
  (k) Receipts from sale of season tickets for a series of concerts.
  (l) A fire insurance premium prepaid by a business.
  (m) Receipts from sale of meal tickets by a restaurant.
  (n) Life insurance premiums received by an insurance company.
  (o) Interest paid in advance at the time a note was discounted at the bank.

3. Each of the statements below describes one half of an adjusting entry. Indicate the type of account to be debited or credited to complete the entry.
  (a) An accrued asset account is debited.
  (b) An unearned revenue account is credited.
  (c) A prepaid expense account is debited.
  (d) An accrued liability account is credited.
  (e) A prepaid expense account is credited.
  (f) An unearned revenue account is debited.

4. Assuming that the appropriate accounts require adjustment in each of the following cases at the end of the year, indicate those that should be reversed ·
  (a) Prepayment of an expense is charged to an expense account.
  (b) Prepayment of an expense is charged to an asset account.
  (c) Revenue received in advance is credited to a liability account.
  (d) Revenue received in advance is credited to an income account.

5. The accountant for a real estate brokerage and management company adheres to the following uniform procedures in recording certain transactions:
  (a) Office supplies purchased are debited to Office Supplies Expense.
  (b) Insurance premiums are debited to Prepaid Insurance.
  (c) Management fees, which are payable one year in advance, are credited to Management Fees when received.

At the end of the fiscal year an adjusting entry is required for each of the foregoing. Which of the adjusting entries should be reversed as of the beginning of the following year?

6. Immediately after the closing and reversing entries have been posted, entries in certain accounts are as follows:
  (a) Unearned Rent, credit of $600.
  (b) Interest Income, credit of $200.
  (c) Interest Income, debit of $420.
  (d) Prepaid Insurance, debit of $750.
  (e) Interest Expense, debit of $150.
  (f) Interest Expense, credit of $300.
Identify each of the foregoing items as (1) asset or (2) liability.

7. The interest accrued on a particular note receivable at the end of the year is $20. In the following year the note is collected, including interest of $35. Give the credits for the receipt of the interest at the maturity date assuming (1) that the adjusting entry for $20 had been reversed; (2) that the adjusting entry had not been reversed.

8. Does the reversing of adjustments for accrued assets and accrued liabilities facilitate the recording of transactions? Explain.

9. (a) Is it almost a certainty that a business enterprise will always have prepaid insurance at the end of each fiscal year?

(b) Is it almost a certainty that a business enterprise that occasionally discounts short-term notes payable at its bank will always have prepaid interest at the end of each fiscal year?

(c) Would it be logical to record prepayments of type (a) as assets and prepayments of type (b) as expense? Discuss.

10. Is it possible to determine by examination of the unadjusted trial balance whether a particular type of prepaid expense has been recorded as an asset or as an expense? Explain.

11. Classify each of the following items as (1) current asset, (2) current liability, (3) operating expense, (4) other expense, and (5) other income.
    (a) Interest Receivable   (f) Prepaid Insurance
    (b) Interest Income   (g) Insurance Expense
    (c) Unearned Rent   (h) Interest Expense
    (d) Prepaid Interest   (i) Rent Expense
    (e) Office Salary Expense   (j) Interest Payable

Exercises

1. (a) Set up T accounts for Salary Expense, Expense and Revenue Summary, and Salaries Payable, and enter a balance of $45,620 in Salary Expense as of December 26.
    (b) Record the following entries directly in the T accounts:
        (1) Record accrued salaries of $500 as of December 31, the end of the fiscal year.
        (2) Close the salary expense account as of December 31.
        (3) Reverse the adjusting entry as of January 1.
        (4) Record the debit for salaries of $700 paid on January 2.
    (c) Answer the following questions:
        (1) Is the balance of the salary expense account on January 1 an asset, a liability, a revenue, or an expense?
        (2) What is the balance of the salary expense account on January 2?
        (3) Of the $700 salary payment on January 2, how much is expense of January?
        (4) If there had been no reversing entry on January 1, how would the debit for the $700 salary payment of January 2 have been recorded?

2. (a) Present entries, in general journal form, for the following:
Nov. 16. Received from Thomas Lane in provisional settlement of his account a $5,000, 60-day, 6% note dated November 16.
Dec. 31. Made an adjusting entry for accrued interest on the note of November 16.
Dec. 31. Closed the interest income account. The only entry in this account originated from the above adjustment.

Jan. 1. Made a reversing entry for accrued interest.

Jan. 15. Collected the note and interest.

(b) Set up T accounts for Interest Receivable and Interest Income and post the foregoing entries.

3. In their first year of operations the Regal Publishing Co. collected $192,000 from advertising contracts and $114,000 from magazine subscriptions, crediting the two amounts to Advertising Income and Subscription Income respectively. At the end of the year $70,000 of the receipts from advertising and $61,000 of the receipts from subscriptions were applicable to succeeding periods. (a) If no adjustments are made at the end of the year, will income for the year be overstated or understated, and by what amount? (b) Present the adjusting entries that should be made at the end of the year. (c) Present the entries to close the two revenue accounts. (d) Present the reversing entries.

4. The store supplies inventory of the Biscayne Company at the beginning of the fiscal year is $295, purchases of store supplies during the year total $674, and the inventory at the end of the year is $150.

(a) Assuming that the accountant records store supplies as an asset, set up T accounts for Store Supplies and Store Supplies Expense, and record the following directly in the two accounts, identifying each entry by number: (1) opening inventory; (2) purchases for the period; (3) adjusting entry at end of the period; (4) closing entry; (5) reversing entry, if appropriate.

(b) Assuming that the accountant records store supplies as an expense, set up T accounts for Store Supplies and Store Supplies Expense and follow the remaining instructions in (a) above.

5. Included among the accounts on an unadjusted trial balance at the end of the year are Prepaid Insurance, with a debit balance of $530, and Insurance Expense, with a debit balance of $720. The amount of insurance premiums applicable to future periods is determined to be $670.

(a) Assuming that in the future insurance is to be recorded as an expense, present journal entries for: (1) adjusting the accounts; (2) closing the appropriate account; and (3) reversing the adjustment, if appropriate.

(b) Assuming that in the future insurance is to be recorded as an asset, present journal entries for: (1) adjusting the accounts; (2) closing the appropriate account; and (3) reversing the adjustment, if appropriate.

6. The entries in the following account that are identified by letters are related to the work of the periodic summary. Describe each of these entries and give the name of the account to which the offsetting debit or credit was posted.

INTEREST EXPENSE

Jan.	1	(a)	25.00	Jan.	1	(b)	40.00
Jan.	1	Transactions		Dec.	31	(c)	130.00
to		during the	496.00		31	(e)	396.00
Dec.	31	year					
Dec.	31	(d)	45.00				
			566.00				566.00
Jan.	1	(f)	130.00	Jan.	1	(g)	45.00

Problems

10-1. The accounts listed below appear in the ledger of Quality Real Estate at December 31, the end of the current fiscal year. None of the year-end adjustments has been recorded.

113 Interest Receivable....	$ —		411 Rental Income........	$56,500
114 Supplies.............	600		511 Salary and Commissions	
115 Prepaid Insurance.....	1,100		Expense..............	16,200
116 Prepaid Advertising....	—		512 Taxes Expense........	2,800
117 Prepaid Interest.......	—		513 Advertising Expense...	3,300
213 Salaries and Commis-			514 Insurance Expense.....	—
sions Payable.........	—		515 Supplies Expense......	—
214 Taxes Payable........	—		611 Interest Income.......	450
215 Unearned Rent.......	—		711 Interest Expense.......	640
313 Expense and Revenue				
Summary.............	—			

The following information relating to adjustments at December 31 was obtained from physical inventories, supplementary records, and other sources:

    (a) Interest accrued on notes receivable at December 31, $65.

    (b) Inventory of supplies at December 31, $220.

    (c) The insurance register indicates that $450 of insurance has expired during the year.

    (d) Of a prepayment of $1,000 for advertising space in a local newspaper, 40% has been used and the remainder will be used in the following year.

    (e) A short-term non-interest-bearing note payable was discounted at a bank in December. The amount of the total discount of $180 applicable to December is $50.

    (f) Salaries and commissions accrued at December 31, $1,820.

    (g) Real estate taxes accrued at December 31, $1,650.

    (h) Rent collected in advance that will not be earned until the following year, $2,960.

Instructions: (1) Open the accounts listed and record the balances as of December 31.

    (2) Record the adjusting entries in a general journal and post to the appropriate accounts after each entry. Identify the postings by writing "Adjusting" in the items columns.

    (3) Prepare a compound journal entry to close the income accounts and another compound entry to close the expense accounts.

    (4) Post the closing entries. Identify the postings by writing "Closing" in the items columns.

    (5) Total and rule the revenue and expense accounts. (Do not rule Expense and Revenue Summary.)

    (6) Prepare the reversing journal entries that should be made on January 1 and post to the appropriate accounts after each entry. Write "Reversing" in the items columns.

    (7) Rule the additional accounts that are now in balance.

10-2. The following information was obtained from a review of the ledger and other records of Maricopa Appliances at the close of the current fiscal year ended December 31:

    (a) Store Supplies Expense has a debit balance of $470 at December 31. The inventory of supplies on hand at that date totals $140.

(b) Prepaid Advertising has a debit balance of $1,560 at December 31, which represents the advance payment on November 1 of a yearly contract for a uniform amount of space in 52 consecutive issues of a weekly publication. As of December 31, advertisements had appeared in 9 issues of the publication.

(c) Prepaid Insurance has a debit balance of $1,387 at December 31. Details of the premiums expired during the year ended are as follows:

No.	MONTHLY PREMIUM EXPIRATION	NO. OF MONTHS APPLICABLE TO PAST YEAR
3842	$10	12
4974A	15	7
946AR	16	5
89321	12	9

(d) Notes Receivable has a debit balance of $5,300 at December 31. The notes on hand, all of which were accepted at face value, are as follows:

DATE	FACE	TERM	INTEREST RATE
Nov. 16	$2,000	90 days	6%
Dec. 1	1,000	60 days	6%
Dec. 11	1,500	60 days	6%
Dec. 16	800	30 days	6%

(e) Rent Expense has a debit balance of $3,900 on December 31. This amount includes rent of $300 for January of the ensuing year, paid on December 31.

(f) Mortgage Payable has a credit balance of $20,000 at December 31. Interest at the rate of 7% is payable semiannually on July 1 and January 1. No entry has been made for the interest accrued since July 1.

(g) Unearned Rent has a credit balance of $1,430, composed of the following items: (1) January 1 balance of $350, representing rent prepaid for January through May, and (2) a credit of $1,080, representing payment for annual rent at $90 a month, beginning June 1.

Instructions: (1) Journalize the adjusting entries as of December 31 of the current fiscal year.

(2) Journalize the reversing entries that should be made as of January 1 of the succeeding fiscal year.

10-3. The account balances in the ledger of the R. B. Moore Co. as of June 30, the end of the current fiscal year, are as follows:

Cash	$ 8,460	R. B. Moore, Capital	$47,185
Notes Receivable	9,150	R. B. Moore, Drawing	6,000
Accounts Receivable	7,615	Sales	103,400
Merchandise Inventory	39,325	Sales Returns and Allow-	
Store Supplies	945	ances	1,950
Prepaid Insurance	2,640	Purchases	59,800
Store Equipment	5,380	Purchases Discount	960
Accumulated Depreciation—		Sales Salaries	12,650
Store Equipment	2,620	Advertising Expense	4,065
Office Equipment	2,955	Misc. Selling Expense	495
Accumulated Depreciation—		Office Salaries	5,250
Office Equipment	1,210	Rent Expense	3,000
Notes Payable	6,740	Misc. General Expense	580
Accounts Payable	7,925	Interest Income	635
		Interest Expense	415

Data needed for making adjusting entries are as follows:

(a) Merchandise inventory, June 30, $38,650.
(b) Store supplies inventory, June 30, $330.
(c) Insurance expired during the year: (e) Accrued salaries at June 30:
    Allocable as selling expense, $980   Sales salaries, $75
    Allocable as general expense, $310   Office salaries, $35
(d) Depreciation for the year: (f) Accrued interest at June 30:
    On store equipment, $525   On notes receivable, $60
    On office equipment, $270   On notes payable, $45
                                      (g) Prepaid interest on notes
                                        payable at June 30, $30

Instructions: (1) Prepare an eight-column work sheet for the current fiscal year ended June 30.

(2) Prepare an income statement, a balance sheet in report form, and a capital statement (there were no investments by the proprietor during the year).

10-4. Transaction and adjustment data related to a prepaid expense and an unearned income are summarized below:

(a) Balance of prepaid rent at January 1, the beginning of the fiscal year, $900 (for three months beginning on January 1).
    Additional rent paid, $4,200 (for one year beginning on April 1).
(b) Balance of unearned advertising at January 1, $14,000.
    Additional advertising collected during the year, $110,000.
    Unearned advertising at the end of the fiscal year, $18,000.

Instructions: (1) Set up T accounts for the asset and the expense in (a) and for the liability and the income in (b). Assuming that the prepaid expense is recorded initially as an asset and the unearned revenue is recorded initially as a liability, record directly in the T accounts the opening balance, the transactions for the year, the adjusting entries at December 31, the closing entries at December 31, and the reversing entries, if appropriate, as of January 1.

(2) Set up T accounts and follow the remaining instructions in instruction (1) except assume that the prepaid expense is recorded initially as expense and the unearned revenue is recorded initially as income.

10-5. Selected accounts from the ledger of Mayfield Co., with the account balances before and after adjustment, at the close of the fiscal year are:

	Unadjusted Balance	Adjusted Balance		Unadjusted Balance	Adjusted Balance
Interest Receivable..	$ —	$ 40	Rent Income.......	$ 6,500	$ 6,000
Supplies...........	1,820	680	Wages.............	16,100	16,190
Prepaid Insurance...	1,250	800	Depreciation Ex-		
Prepaid Taxes......	—	200	pense — Equipment.	—	600
Prepaid Interest....	—	50	Supplies Expense...	—	1,140
Accumulated Depre-			Taxes Expense......	600	700
ciation — Equipment	2,900	3,500	Insurance Expense..	—	450
Wages Payable.....	—	90	Interest Income.....	960	1,000
Taxes Payable......	—	300	Interest Expense....	450	400
Unearned Rent.....	—	500			

Instructions: (1) Journalize the adjusting entries that were recorded in the ledger at the close of the fiscal year.

(2) Insert the letter "R" in the date column opposite each adjusting entry that should be reversed as of the first day of the following fiscal year.

Receivables and merchandise inventory

Classification of receivables

The term *receivables* applies to all claims against individuals, firms, or other outsiders for the payment of money. They are acquired by a business enterprise in various types of transactions, the most common being the sale of goods or services on a credit basis. Accounts and notes receivable originating from sales transactions are sometimes referred to as *trade receivables*. They may be so designated on the balance sheet; but in the absence of other descriptive words or phrases, accounts receivable and notes receivable may be assumed to have originated from sales in the usual course of the business.

Other receivables of not infrequent occurrence include interest receivable, loans to officers or employees, and loans to affiliated companies. Separate accounts should be maintained in the general ledger for each type of receivable, and they should be set forth separately on the balance sheet.

All receivables that are expected to be realized in cash within a year are shown in the current asset section of the balance sheet. Those that are not currently collectible, such as long-term loans, should be listed under the caption "Investments," below the current asset section.

The importance of accounts and notes receivable to a particular enterprise varies with the volume of charge sales and the length of the credit period. For many businesses the revenue from sales on account is the largest factor in determining net income or loss. The amount of claims against customers may also represent a major component of total current assets. The business documents and accounting procedures employed in recording acquisitions, miscellaneous reductions, and collections of accounts and notes receivable were described and illustrated in Chapters 6 and 9. In this chapter consideration will be given to the accounting for uncollectible receivables, particularly those originating from sales on account.

Uncollectible accounts

When goods or services are sold on a credit basis, a portion of the accounts receivable usually proves to be uncollectible. This is true regardless of the care used in granting credit and the efficacy of the collection procedures employed. There are two generally accepted methods of accounting for the losses resulting from uncollectibility. One, which is termed the *direct write-off* method, recognizes a loss only when specific accounts are determined to be uncollectible. The other, known as the *allowance* or *reserve* method, recognizes estimated losses in the period in which the charge sales were made, regardless of when the uncollectibility of specific accounts is determined.

Either method may be used in appropriate circumstances. Both conform to acceptable accounting practice and are permissible in determining income for purposes of the federal income tax. The method adopted must, of course, be consistently followed from year to year.

Direct write-off of uncollectible accounts

When a firm's sales of goods or services are preponderantly on a cash basis, its losses from bad accounts will ordinarily be minor in amount. The amount of its accounts receivable at any time will also represent a relatively small portion of its current assets. These observations are based on the assumption that the credit period is short, which would be usual if most sales were on a cash basis, and that credit policies and collection procedures are adequate. Similarly, a firm that sells most of its output on account to a few companies, all of which are financially strong, will incur very few losses from inability to collect its accounts.

In the foregoing and similar situations, as well as in many small businesses, it is satisfactory to recognize bad debt losses in the period in which the accounts are determined to be uncollectible. The entry to write off an uncollectible account is as follows:

Apr.	15	Bad Debts Expense..................	717	37	
		Accounts Receivable — Roy Hewitt.	114/ √		37
		To write off the account.			

Bad Debts Expense may be classified as selling expense or general expense, depending upon the department responsible for controlling such losses. If credits and collections are a responsibility of the sales department, they should be treated as selling expenses; if a separate department within the administrative framework is charged with the responsibility, they should be reported among the general expenses.

Accounts that have been written off are sometimes unexpectedly recovered later. If the recovery is in the same fiscal period as the write-off, the entry that recorded the loss is reversed and the cash received is recorded in the usual manner. For example, if Roy Hewitt, whose account was written off in April, pays the amount later in the fiscal year, the following entry is made in the general journal:

Oct.	26	Accounts Receivable — Roy Hewitt... 114/ √	37	
		Bad Debts Expense.............. 717		37
		To reinstate account written off earlier in the year.		

The receipt of $37 from Hewitt is recorded in the cash receipts journal in the usual manner as a debit to Cash and a credit to Hewitt's account and the controlling account. It is evident that the reinstatement entry and the cash entry could be combined into a single entry debiting Cash and crediting Bad Debts Expense. It is preferable to reinstate the account receivable, however, so that the information will be available for credit purposes.

If an account written off in one fiscal period is recovered in a subsequent period, the account is reinstated as in the journal entry above, except that the credit is made to an account entitled "Recoveries of Accounts Written Off in Prior Periods" or some other appropriately titled account. The receipt of cash is then recorded in the usual manner. The credit balance in the recoveries account is reported on the income statement as a deduction from Bad Debts Expense.

Advance provision for uncollectible accounts

In many businesses it is customary to make advance provision for the probable losses that will result from failure to collect receivables acquired through sales of the current period. Two things are accomplished by anticipating the losses: (1) the estimated losses are charged to the period in which the related revenue was recognized, and (2) at the end of the period, accounts receivable are stated at their estimated realizable value.

The provision for uncollectible accounts is recorded as an adjusting entry at the end of the fiscal period. For purposes of illustration it will be assumed that at the end of an enterprise's first year of operations the accounts receivable account has a debit balance of $50,000. None of the individual accounts can be identified as wholly or partly worthless at this time, but it is estimated that, of the total amount, $2,000 will be uncollectible. Therefore Bad Debts Expense should be debited for $2,000 and the asset Accounts Receivable should be credited for the same amount. It would obviously be improper to credit any of the individual customers' accounts on the basis of the estimate. If the accounts receivable controlling account were to be credited for $2,000, the balance of the account would not agree with the sum of the balances in the subsidiary ledger. The customary practice, therefore, is to reduce the accounts receivable by crediting a *valuation* or *contra asset* account entitled "Allowance for Uncollectible Accounts." The adjusting entry is as follows:

Dec.	31	Bad Debts Expense..................	717	2,000	
		Allowance for Uncollectible Accounts.	114.1		2,000

In the process of closing the books as of December 31, the balance of $2,000 in Bad Debts Expense will be transferred to Expense and Revenue Summary along with all other expenses. After the adjusting and closing entries have been posted, the asset account, the valuation account, and the expense account will appear as follows:

ACCOUNTS RECEIVABLE   Acct. No. 114

1961										
Dec.	31	Balance	✓	50,000						

ALLOWANCE FOR UNCOLLECTIBLE ACCOUNTS   Acct. No. 114.1

					1961					
					Dec.	31	Adjusting	J12	2,000	

BAD DEBTS EXPENSE   Acct. No. 717

1961					1961				
Dec.	31	Adjusting	J12	2,000	Dec.	31	Closing	J13	2,000

The debit balance in Accounts Receivable is the face amount of the total claims against customers on open account. The credit balance in Allowance for Uncollectible Accounts is the amount to be deducted from accounts receivable to determine their expected realizable value. Thus, in the illustration the amount expected to be collected from the accounts receivable is $48,000 ($50,000 − $2,000).

Presentation of the allowance account in the balance sheet

When provision is made for the future uncollectibility of accounts receivable, the fact should be disclosed in the balance sheet. The accounts receivable may be listed at the net amount with a parenthetical notation as to the amount of the allowance for losses, or the details may be presented in the following manner:

Drake Company
Balance Sheet
December 31, 1961

Assets

Current assets:

Cash...		$ 32,700
Accounts receivable.....................................	$50,000	
Less allowance for uncollectible accounts...............	2,000	48,000
Merchandise inventory...................................		105,600

When the allowance includes provision for uncollectible notes as well as accounts receivable, the allowance should be deducted from the total of the two items.

Charging uncollectible accounts to the allowance account

Accounts receivable should be written off against Allowance for Uncollectible Accounts when there is strong evidence that the claim will not be collected. Bankruptcy of the debtor is one of the most positive indications of partial or complete worthlessness of an account. Other evidence includes death or disappearance of a debtor, failure of repeated attempts to collect, and the barring of collection by the statute of limitations.

The entry to write off a worthless account is as follows:

Feb.	21	Allowance for Uncollectible Accounts..	114.1	220	
		Accounts Receivable — John Parker .	114/√		220
		To write off the account.			

It should be noted that the debit is to the valuation account Allowance for Uncollectible Accounts rather than to the expense account Bad Debts Expense. The reason is that the loss had been previously provided for in the adjusting entry debiting the expense account and crediting the valuation account. The effect of the write-off is to reduce the asset account and the valuation account; it has no effect on the expected cash realizable value of accounts receivable as is apparent in the following tabulation:

	BEFORE WRITE-OFF OF $220	AFTER WRITE-OFF OF $220
Accounts Receivable balance............................	$50,000	$49,780
Allowance for Uncollectible Accounts balance.............	2,000	1,780
Expected cash realizable value........................	$48,000	$48,000

As additional accounts are determined to be worthless during the year, the amounts are written off against Allowance for Uncollectible Accounts. If a portion of an account is collected and the balance is uncollectible because of bankruptcy or other reasons, the amount collected is recorded in the cash receipts journal in the usual manner and the remainder is written off by a general journal entry similar to the one presented on page 233.

Instructions for write-offs should originate with the credit manager or other appropriate official. The authorizations, which should be written, are kept on file as objective evidence supporting the accounting entry.

The total amount written off during the year is rarely exactly equal to the amount of the allowance at the beginning of the year; consequently, when the trial balance is taken at the end of the year, the allowance account will have either a credit balance or a debit balance. The existence of a debit balance does not necessarily indicate that the allowance was inadequate. It may have resulted from write-offs of receivables acquired in the current year. Provision for current losses, as well as for those to be recognized in the future, will be made in the year-end adjusting entry. After the adjusting entry is recorded, the allowance account will of course have a credit balance.

Recoveries of accounts written off. When an account that has been charged to the allowance account is subsequently collected, the account should be reinstated by an entry that is just the reverse of the write-off entry. As was pointed out earlier, the purpose of the reinstatement is to provide information that will be useful in re-establishing the customer's credit.

Assuming that John Parker, whose account of $220 was written off on February 21, pays in full on June 10, the following entry is made in the general journal:

June	10	Accounts Receivable — John Parker ..	114/ √	220		
		Allowance for Uncollectible Accounts	114.1		220	
		To reinstate account previously written off.				

The receipt of $220 from John Parker would be recorded in the cash receipts journal in the usual manner.

Estimating losses from uncollectible accounts

The estimate of bad debts expense at the end of the fiscal period is based on past experience modified by forecasts of future business activity. When the trend of general sales volume is upward and there is relatively full employment, there is less likelihood of losses from uncollectible accounts than when the trend is in the opposite direction. Some types of businesses tend to incur greater losses than other types; the nature of the product or the service sold, differences in the clientele, length of the credit period, and other factors have a bearing upon the losses incurred.

The estimate of potential losses from uncollectible accounts is customarily based on either (1) sales for the period or (2) the amount and the age of accounts receivable on hand at the end of the fiscal period.

Estimate based on sales. Accounts receivable are acquired as a result of sales on account. The volume of such sales during the year may therefore be used as an indication of the probable amount of the accounts that will be uncollectible. For example, if it is known from past experience that about 1% of charge sales will be uncollectible and the charge sales for a particular year amount to $600,000, the adjusting entry at the end of the year is as follows:

Dec.	31	Bad Debts Expense.................... 717	6,000		
		Allowance for Uncollectible Accounts 114.1		6,000	

Instead of charge sales, total sales (including those made for cash) may be used in developing the percentage. The total sales figure is obtainable from the ledger without the necessity for the analysis that may be required to determine charge sales. If the ratio of sales on account to cash sales does not change materially from year to year, the results obtained will be equally satisfactory. For example, if in the example above the balance of the sales account at the end of the year is assumed to be $800,000, the application of ¾ of 1% to the amount would also yield an estimate of $6,000.

If it becomes apparent over a period of time that the amount of the write-offs is consistently greater or less than the amount provided by the adjusting entry, the percentage applied against sales data should be revised accordingly. A newly established business enterprise, having no record of credit experience, may obtain data on probable bad debts expense from trade association journals and other publications containing information on credit and collections.

Estimate based on analysis of accounts receivable. Instead of using sales data as a basis for determining the bad debts provision for the period, some businesses analyze their accounts receivable at the end of the period to determine probable uncollectibility. This process is known as *aging the accounts receivable.*

The balance of each account is classified according to the age of the claim. For example, the age intervals used might be as follows: not due; 0–30 days past due; 31–60 days past due; 61 days–6 months past due;

and over 6 months past due. After the amounts in each age group are totaled, a sliding scale of percentages is applied to obtain the estimated uncollectibles in each group, and the group estimates are totaled. The figure thus obtained is the desired balance of the allowance account after the year-end adjustment. The excess of this figure over the credit balance of the allowance account listed in the trial balance is the amount of the current provision to be made for bad debt losses.

To illustrate the foregoing, assume that an analysis of the customers' ledger indicates probable uncollectibility of $5,000; also assume that Allowance for Uncollectible Accounts is listed on the trial balance with a credit balance of $600. The amount of the adjustment is therefore $4,400 ($5,000 − $600) and the entry is as follows:

Dec.	31	Bad Debts Expense....................	717	4,400	
		Allowance for Uncollectible Accounts..	114.1		4,400

After the adjusting entry is posted, the balance in the allowance account will be $5,000, which is the desired amount. If the balance of the allowance account had been a *debit* of $800, the amount of the adjustment would have been $5,800 ($5,000 + $800).

Importance of inventories

The term *inventories* is used to designate goods held for sale in the normal course of business and also materials in the process of production or held for such use. The remainder of this chapter is devoted to problems arising in the determination of the inventory of merchandise purchased for resale, commonly called *merchandise inventory*. Consideration will be given to inventories of raw materials and partially processed materials in a later chapter.

Merchandise is one of the most active elements in the operation of wholesale and retail businesses, being continuously purchased and sold. The sale of merchandise at more than its cost provides the principal source of revenue for such enterprises. In determining net income the cost of goods sold is the largest deduction from sales; in fact, it is customarily larger than all other deductions combined. In addition, a substantial portion of a merchandising firm's resources is invested in inventory; it is usually the largest of the current assets.

Inventory determination plays an important role in matching costs with revenues of the period. The effect of inventories on the computation of the cost of goods sold was illustrated in Chapter 8. An error in the inventory figure will cause a misstatement of net income of equal amount, and in the balance sheet both assets and proprietorship will be incorrectly reported.

Inventory systems

There are two systems of determining quantities of goods in the inventory, *periodic* and *perpetual*. The periodic system relies upon a *physical* inventory taken at the end of the accounting period. The revenue from goods sold during the period is recorded in the sales account, but no entries are made to record the decrease in the inventory. It is therefore only by a physical count that the inventory can be determined. The perpetual inventory system uses accounting records that continuously disclose the amount of the inventory. A separate account for each type of merchandise is maintained in a subsidiary ledger. Increases in inventory items are recorded as debits to the appropriate accounts, and decreases are recorded as credits; the balances of the accounts are the *book* inventories of the items on hand. A physical inventory of each type of goods should be taken at least once a year to confirm the perpetual records and to provide for their correction.

Periodic inventory procedures are ordinarily used by retail enterprises that sell a great variety of low unit value merchandise, such as groceries, hardware, and drugs. The expense of maintaining perpetual inventory records is likely to be prohibitive in such cases. Firms selling a relatively small number of high unit value items, such as office equipment or fur garments, are more likely to employ the perpetual system. Most large manufacturing enterprises, as well as many smaller organizations, also use the perpetual system. Periodic procedures will be discussed in the remaining pages of this chapter; perpetual inventory procedures will be given further consideration in later chapters on cost accounting.

Determining quantities in the inventory

The first stage in the process of taking an inventory is the determination of the quantity of each type of merchandise owned by the enterprise. Where the periodic system is used, the counting, weighing, and measuring should be done at the end of the accounting period. In order to accomplish this, the inventory crew may work during the night or business operations may be suspended until the count is completed.

The details of the specific procedures for determining quantities and assembling the data vary considerably among companies. A common practice is to employ two-man teams; one person counts or otherwise determines quantity and the other lists the description and quantity on inventory sheets. The count of major items should be verified by a third person at some time during the inventory-taking period.

All of the merchandise owned by the business on the inventory date, and only such merchandise, should be included in the inventory. It may be necessary to examine sales and purchase invoices of the last few days of the accounting period and the first few days of the ensuing period to determine legal title to merchandise in transit on the inventory date. When goods are purchased or sold FOB shipping point, title passes to the buyer when the goods are shipped. When the terms are FOB destination, title does not pass to the buyer until the goods are delivered. For example, if goods purchased FOB shipping point are shipped on December 31, the last day of the buyer's accounting period, the merchandise will probably not be received until early in January. The purchase should be recorded as of December 31, however, and the goods should be included in the inventory count.

Goods may also be transferred to a retailer on a consignment basis, in which case the consignor retains title until the goods are sold by the retailer. Such merchandise should be included in the consignor's inventory even though he does not have physical possession. The consignee should not, of course, include consigned goods in his inventory.

Determining the cost of inventory

The cost of inventory includes all expenditures incurred in acquiring the merchandise, including purchasing costs, transportation, customs duties, insurance, and storage. Some of these costs are readily traceable to particular items in the inventory, and others may be prorated over all merchandise in an equitable manner. Minor costs that are difficult to allocate may be excluded from inventory cost and treated as operating expenses of the period.

If purchases discounts are treated as a deduction from the invoice price of goods purchased, they should also be deducted in assigning costs to goods in the inventory. If it is not feasible to determine the exact amount of discount applicable to each item in the inventory, a pro rata amount of the total discount for the period may be deducted from the inventory. For example, if net purchases and purchases discount for the period amount to $200,000 and $3,000 respectively, the discount represents $1\frac{1}{2}\%$ of purchases. If the inventory cost, before considering cash discount, is $30,000, the amount may be reduced by $1\frac{1}{2}\%$, or $450, to yield an inventory cost of $29,550.

Another matter of major significance in determining inventory cost is related to the fact that identical units of merchandise may be acquired at different cost prices during the period. The nature of the problem and its effect on income determination and inventory valuation may be introduced by means of a simple illustration.

During the year three identical units of a particular commodity are available for sale. The order of their acquisition and the cost of each is as follows:

Inventory, beginning of year.............	1 unit......	$ 9
Purchased in March.....................	1 unit......	13
Purchased in October..................	1 unit......	14
Total............................	3 units	$36

At the end of the year there is one unit of the commodity in the inventory, the other two having been sold. If the unit remaining in the inventory can be specifically identified as being the $9 unit, the $13 unit, or the $14 unit, the appropriate cost figure can be deducted from the total of $36 to obtain the cost of the units sold. If identification is not possible it is necessary to adopt a method of determining the *flow of costs*. Alternative methods of transferring the cost of merchandise to cost of goods sold are as follows: (1) in the order in which the expenditures were made, (2) in accordance with the average of the expenditures, and (3) in the reverse of the order in which the expenditures were made. The cost of goods sold and the cost of the inventory obtained by each of the methods are presented below.

ASSUMED COST FLOW	COST OF GOODS AVAILABLE		COST OF GOODS SOLD		COST OF INVENTORY
In order of expenditures................	$36	—	$22	=	$14
In accordance with average expenditures..	36	—	24	=	12
In reverse order of expenditures.........	36	—	27	=	9

The application of the three methods produces widely disparate amounts for the cost of goods sold and the inventory. These differences would continue on through the determination of gross profit on sales and net income.

In actual practice it may be possible to identify units with specific invoices if both the variety of merchandise carried in stock and the volume of sales are relatively small. Ordinarily, however, specific identification procedures are too laborious and costly to justify their use. It is customary, therefore, to employ a system based on an assumed flow of costs rather than attempting specific identification.

First-in, first-out method. The first-in, first-out (*fifo*) method of costing inventory is based on the assumption that costs should be charged against revenue in the order in which they were incurred. Hence the inventory is composed of the most recent costs. To illustrate the application of this method, assume the following data for a particular commodity:

Jan. 1	Inventory	200 units at $ 9	$ 1,800
Mar. 10	Purchase	300 units at 10	3,000
Sept. 21	Purchase	400 units at 11	4,400
Nov. 18	Purchase	100 units at 12	1,200
	Available for sale during year....1,000		$10,400

The physical count on December 31 indicates that 300 units of the commodity are on hand. In accordance with the assumption that the inventory is composed of the most recent costs, the cost of the 300 units is determined as follows:

Most recent costs, Nov. 18	100 units at $12	$1,200
Next most recent costs, Sept. 21	200 units at 11	2,200
Inventory, Dec. 31	300	$3,400

The cost of the units of the particular commodity sold during the year will be stated at $7,000 ($10,400 − $3,400).

In most businesses there is a tendency to dispose of commodities in the order of their acquisition. This would be particularly true of perishable merchandise and other goods in which style or model changes are frequent. Thus the fifo method is generally in harmony with the physical movement of merchandise in an enterprise. To the extent that this is the case, the fifo method approximates the results that would be obtained by specific identification of costs.

Last-in, first-out method. The last-in, first-out (*lifo*) method is based on the assumption that the most recent costs incurred should be charged against revenue. Hence the inventory is composed of the earliest costs. Assuming the cost data used in the preceding section, the cost of the inventory is determined in the following manner:

Earliest costs, Jan. 1	200 units at $ 9	$1,800
Next earliest costs, Mar. 10	100 units at 10	1,000
Inventory, December 31	300	$2,800

The cost of the commodity sold during the year will be stated at $7,600 ($10,400 − $2,800), which represents the latest costs incurred.

The lifo method of determining cost flow came into general use during the past two decades. It was originally confined to the relatively rare situations in which the units sold were from the latest purchases.

Weighted average method. The weighted average method is based on the assumption that costs should be charged against revenue on the basis of an average, taking into consideration the number of units acquired at each price. The same average unit cost is employed in computing the cost of the goods remaining in the inventory. The weighted average is determined by dividing the total costs of a commodity available for sale by the total number of units of that commodity available for sale. Assuming the same cost data as in the preceding illustrations, the weighted average cost of the 1,000 units and the cost of the inventory are determined as follows:

$$\text{Weighted average cost: } \frac{\$10,400}{1,000} = \$10.40 \text{ a unit}$$

Inventory, December 31: 300 units at $10.40 = $3,120

Deduction of the inventory from the goods available for sale will yield cost of goods sold of $7,280 ($10,400 − $3,120).

For businesses in which various purchases of identical units of a commodity are mingled, the weighted average method has some relationship to the physical flow of inventory.

Comparison of inventory costing methods. Each of the three alternative methods of costing inventories under the periodic system is based on a different assumption as to the flow of costs. If the cost of commodities and the prices at which they were sold remained perfectly stable, all three methods would yield the same results. Prices do not remain stable, however, and as a consequence the three methods will ordinarily yield different amounts for both the inventory and the cost of goods sold. The examples presented in the preceding sections illustrated the effect of rising prices. They may be summarized as follows:

	FIRST-IN FIRST-OUT	LAST-IN FIRST-OUT	WEIGHTED AVERAGE
Goods available for sale....................	$10,400	$10,400	$10,400
Merchandise inventory, December 31.......	3,400	2,800	3,120
Cost of goods sold........................	$ 7,000	$ 7,600	$ 7,280

In comparing and evaluating the results obtained in the illustration it should be borne in mind that both the amount reported as net income and the amount reported as inventory are affected. The method that yields the lowest figure for the cost of goods sold will yield the highest figure for gross profit and net income reported on the income statement; it will also yield the highest figure for inventory reported on the balance sheet. Conversely, the method that yields the highest figure for the cost of goods sold will yield the lowest figure for gross profit and net income and the lowest figure for inventory.

During periods of consistently rising prices the use of first-in, first-out yields the highest possible amount of net income. The reason for this effect is that business enterprises increase their selling prices in accordance with market trends, regardless of the fact that merchandise in stock was acquired before the price increase. In periods of declining prices the effect is reversed and the fifo method yields the lowest possible net income. The principal criticism of the fifo method is this tendency to accentuate the effect of inflationary and deflationary trends on reported income. On the other hand, the amount reported for inventory on the balance sheet will closely approximate its current replacement cost, which is desirable.

During periods of consistently rising prices the use of last-in, first-out yields the lowest possible amount of net income. The reason for this effect is that the cost of the most recently acquired units most nearly approximates the expenditure required to replace the units sold. In periods of declining prices the effect is reversed and the lifo method yields the highest possible net income. The principal justification for lifo is this tendency to minimize the effect of price trends on reported net income. A criticism of the general use of lifo is its complete lack of relationship to the physical flow of merchandise in most enterprises. The amount reported for inventory on the balance sheet may also be quite far removed from current replacement cost. If there is little change in the physical composition of the inventory from year to year, the inventory cost remains nearly constant, regardless of changes in price levels.

The weighted average method of inventory costing is, in a sense, a compromise between fifo and lifo. The effect of price trends is averaged, both in the determination of net income and the determination of inventory cost. For any given series of acquisitions the weighted average cost will be the same regardless of the direction of price trends. For example, a complete reversal of the sequence of acquisitions and unit costs presented in the illustration on page 240 would not affect the reported net income or inventory cost. The time required to assemble the data is greater for the weighted average method than for the other two methods. The additional expense incurred could be significant if there are numerous purchases of a wide variety of merchandise items.

All three methods of inventory costing are acceptable in determining income subject to the federal income tax.

The foregoing comparisons are indicative of the many factors that management should consider in selecting the inventory costing method. The method selected must be consistently employed from year to year. A change may be made if there are sufficient reasons but frequent changes in method are not justifiable.

Valuation at cost or market, whichever is lower

An alternative to stating the inventory at cost is to compare cost with market price and to value the inventory at the lower of the two. It should be borne in mind throughout the following discussion that in any case it is necessary first to determine the cost of the inventory. "Market," as used in the phrase *cost or market, whichever is lower*, is interpreted to mean the replacement cost of the goods on the inventory date. To the extent practicable, the market or replacement price should be based on quantities typically purchased from the usual source of supply. A decline in the market price is ordinarily accompanied by a reduction in the selling price. Recognition of the inventory decline charges the loss to the period in which it was incurred. For example, assume that the cost assigned to the inventory by one of the methods described in the preceding section is $50,000 and that because of a market decline in some of the items the inventory could be replaced for $46,000. If the inventory is valued at the lower figure, the $4,000 decline in value will be included in the cost of goods sold, and the gross profit and the net income for the period will be correspondingly less.

The lower of cost or market rule may be applied to (1) individual items in the inventory, (2) independent categories or departments, or (3) the inventory as a whole. The three methods are illustrated in the tabulation below.

	Cost	Market	COST OR MARKET WHICHEVER IS LOWER		
			EACH ITEM	EACH DEPT.	INVENTORY TOTAL
Dept. 1					
Commodity A.........	$ 5,950	$ 6,000	$ 5,950		
Commodity B.........	6,470	6,230	6,230		
	$12,420	$12,230		$12,230	
Dept. 2					
Commodity C.........	$ 4,300	$ 3,900	3,900		
Commodity D.........	5,600	6,300	5,600		
	$ 9,900	$10,200		9,900	
Total.................	$22,320	$22,430			$22,320
Inventory valuation......			$21,680	$22,130	$22,320

The lower of cost or market rule is customarily applied to each item in determining the inventory valuation. It usually yields the most conservative valuation, as in the illustration above. In any event, the total obtained by application to each item will never exceed the total obtained by either of the other two methods of applying the rule.

As with the method selected for determining the cost of the inventory, valuation at either (1) cost or (2) cost or market, whichever is lower, must be followed consistently from year to year. Both methods are acceptable for determining income for federal income tax purposes, except that when the last-in, first-out procedure is employed in determining cost, the inventory must be stated at cost. Another income tax rule that may be noted is that if cost or market, whichever is lower, is elected, the procedure must be applied to each item in the inventory.

Retail method of inventory costing

An additional method of inventory costing that is widely used by retail businesses, particularly department stores, is called the *retail inventory method*. It is employed in connection with the periodic system of inventories and is based on the relationship of the cost of merchandise available for sale to the retail price of the same merchandise. The retail prices of all merchandise acquired are accumulated in supplementary records and the inventory at retail is determined by deducting sales for the period from the retail price of the goods that were available for sale during the period. The inventory at retail is then converted to cost on the basis of the ratio of the cost of the merchandise available for sale to the selling price of the merchandise available for sale.

Determination of the inventory by the retail method is illustrated as follows:

	Cost	Retail
Merchandise inventory, January 1.......................	$19,400	$ 36,000
Purchases in January (net).............................	42,600	64,000
Merchandise available for sale..........................	$62,000	$100,000

Ratio of cost to retail price:
$$\frac{\$62,000}{\$100,000} = 62\%$$

Sales for January (net)..................................		70,000
Merchandise inventory, January 31, at retail price...........		$ 30,000
Merchandise inventory, January 31, at estimated cost price ($30,000 × 62%)		$ 18,600

There is an inherent assumption in the retail method that the composition or "mix" of the goods in the ending inventory, in terms of per cent of cost to selling price, is comparable to the entire stock of goods available for sale. For example, in the illustration above it is unlikely that the retail price of every item was composed of exactly 62% cost and 38% margin. It is assumed, however, that the weighted average of the cost percentages of the goods in the inventory ($30,000) is the same as in the goods available for sale ($100,000). Where the inventory is composed of different classes of goods with significantly different cost percentages, the percentages and the inventory should be developed by sections or departments.

The use of the retail method does not eliminate the necessity for taking the inventory at the end of the year. The dollar amounts recorded on the inventory sheets are selling prices instead of cost prices, however. Advantages of the retail method are as follows:

1. Inventories for use in preparing interim statements may be obtained without the necessity of a physical count.
2. Elimination of the necessity of determining unit costs when taking the physical inventory results in a saving of time and expense.
3. Comparison of the physical inventory at retail with the computed inventory at retail provides management with a check on inventory shortages.

Presentation of merchandise inventory on the balance sheet

Merchandise inventory is customarily presented on the balance sheet immediately below receivables. Both the method of determining the cost of the inventory (lifo, fifo, or average) and the method of valuing the inventory (cost, or lower of cost or market) should be disclosed. Both are significant to the reader. The details may be disclosed by a parenthetical notation or a footnote. The use of a parenthetical notation is illustrated by the following partial balance sheet:

Drake Company
Balance Sheet
December 31, 1961

Assets

Current assets:

Cash..		$ 32,700
Accounts receivable.....................................	$50,000	
Less allowance for uncollectible accounts................	2,000	48,000
Merchandise inventory — at lower of cost (first-in, first-out method) or market..................................		$105,600

It is not unusual for manufacturers and other large enterprises with diversified activities to use different costing and pricing methods for different segments of their inventories. The following note from the balance sheet of a merchandising chain is illustrative: "Merchandise inventories in stores are stated at the lower of cost or market, as calculated by the retail method of inventory. Merchandise in warehouses and in transit and food products inventories in restaurants are stated at cost."

Gross profit method of estimating inventories

When perpetual inventories are maintained or when the retail inventory method is used, the inventory on hand may be closely approximated at any time without the necessity of a physical count. In the absence of these devices the inventory may be estimated by the *gross profit method,* which utilizes an estimate of the gross profit realized on sales during the period.

If the rate of gross profit on sales is known, the dollar amount of sales for a period can be divided into its two components: (1) gross profit and (2) cost of goods sold. The cost of goods sold may then be deducted from the cost of goods available for sale to yield the inventory of goods on hand.

To illustrate this method, assume that the inventory on January 1 is $17,000, that net purchases during the month amount to $9,000, that net sales during the month amount to $15,000, and finally that gross profit is *estimated* to be 30% of net sales. The inventory on January 31 may be estimated as follows:

Merchandise inventory, January 1..........................		$17,000
Purchases in January (net).................................		9,000
Merchandise available for sale.............................		$26,000
Sales in January (net).....................................	$15,000	
Less estimated gross profit ($15,000 × 30%)...............	4,500	
Estimated cost of goods sold..............................		10,500
Estimated merchandise inventory, January 31..............		$15,500

The estimate of the rate of gross profit may be based on the actual rate for the preceding year, adjusted for any known changes in mark-ups during the current period. Inventories estimated in this manner are useful in preparing interim statements. The method may also be employed in establishing an estimate of the cost of merchandise destroyed by fire.

Questions

1. (a) How should a five-year loan to an employee be described on the balance sheet? (b) Should it be listed among the current assets?

2. Under what circumstances is the direct write-off method of accounting for losses from bad debts satisfactory?

3. Which method of accounting for uncollectible accounts recognizes the losses in the period (a) in which the sale is made? (b) in which the account is written off?

4. Why should an account receivable that has been written off be reinstated when it is subsequently collected?

5. Is the normal balance of Allowance for Uncollectible Accounts a debit or a credit after the account has been adjusted?

6. What effect does the write-off of an account receivable against the allowance account have on the expected realizable value of the accounts receivable, assuming that after the write-off there is a credit balance in the allowance account?

7. Near the end of the period Allowance for Uncollectible Accounts has a credit balance of $300. Uncollectible accounts totaling $900 are to be written off. To what account should the $900 be debited?

8. In taking the inventory at the end of the year, merchandise with an inventory value of $5,000 was omitted. (a) Did the error cause an overstatement or an understatement of the net income for the year? (b) Which items on the balance sheet at the end of the year were overstated or understated as a result of the error?

9. Assume that the error in Question 8 was not discovered and that the inventory at the end of the subsequent year is correctly stated. (a) Will the earlier error cause an overstatement or an understatement of the net income for the subsequent year? (b) Which items on the balance sheet at the end of the subsequent year will be overstated or understated as a result of the error?

10. (a) Differentiate between the periodic system and the perpetual system of inventory determination. (b) Which system requires the greater expenditure of time and funds?

11. In which of the following types of businesses would a perpetual inventory system be practicable: (a) variety store, (b) grocery wholesaler, (c) manufacturer of sheet steel, (d) retail druggist, (e) restaurant?

12. Under which, if any, of the following systems or methods of inventory determination is a periodic physical inventory unnecessary: (a) retail inventory method, (b) perpetual inventory system, (c) gross profit method, (d) periodic inventory system?

13. Under which method of cost flow are (a) the most recent costs assigned to inventory, (b) the earliest costs assigned to inventory, (c) average costs assigned to inventory?

14. The cost of a particular item of merchandise on hand is $60, the replacement cost is $55, and the selling price is $80. At what amount should the item be included in the inventory according to the rule of cost or market, whichever is lower?

15. What is the meaning of the term "market" in the "cost or market, whichever is lower" method?

16. The unit costs of three lots of commodity X available for sale during the year are $10, $11, and $12, respectively. If the weighted average method of costing is employed, will the unit cost of the lots on hand at the end of the period be $11?

17. Assuming a consistently rising price level, which of the three methods of inventory costing, fifo, lifo, or weighted average, will yield (a) the largest gross profit? (b) the smallest gross profit?

18. Which of the three methods of inventory costing, fifo, lifo, or weighted average, will in general yield an inventory cost most nearly approximating current replacement cost?

Exercises

1. At the end of the current year the accounts receivable account has a debit balance of $100,000 and the sales account has a credit balance of $1,000,000. Determine the amount of the adjusting entry to record the provision for uncollectible accounts under each of the following assumptions:

(a) The allowance account before adjustment has a credit balance of $1,500.
  (1) Losses are estimated at 1% of sales.
  (2) Analysis of the accounts in the customers' ledger indicates probable uncollectibility of $11,000.
(b) The allowance account before adjustment has a debit balance of $600.
  (1) Losses are estimated at ¾ of 1% of sales.
  (2) Analysis of the accounts in the customers' ledger indicates probable uncollectibility of $8,000.

2. The beginning inventory and the purchases of commodity X for the year are presented below:

COMMODITY X

Inventory	10 units at $40
Purchase	15 units at 42
Purchase	8 units at 41
Purchase	7 units at 44

Assuming that there are 11 units on hand at the end of the year, determine (a) the cost of the inventory and (b) the cost of goods sold by each of the following methods: (1) fifo, (2) lifo, and (3) weighted average.

3. From the following data determine the inventory by applying the rule of cost or market, whichever is lower, to (a) each item in the inventory and (b) the total inventory.

COMMODITY	QUANTITY	UNIT COST	UNIT MARKET
A	200	$1.10	$1.05
B	400	2.60	2.90
C	300	4.00	4.50
D	600	3.50	3.10

4. The cost of three classes of merchandise purchased during the month and the mark-up are given below. Determine the following for each class: (a) selling price, (b) amount of gross profit, (c) per cent of gross profit to selling price, (d) per cent of cost to selling price.

CLASS	COST	MARK-UP ON COST
A	$10,000	50%
B	21,000	66⅔%
C	15,000	100%

5. From the following information determine the estimated inventory cost on January 31, presenting the details of the computation.

		COST	RETAIL
Jan. 1	Merchandise Inventory..................	$76,080	$120,000
Jan. 1–31	Purchases (net)........................	50,920	80,000
Jan. 1–31	Sales (net)............................		90,000

6. The merchandise inventory of Baxter Specialty Store was destroyed by fire on March 24. The following data were obtained from the accounting records:

Jan. 1	Merchandise inventory........................	$30,000
Jan. 1–Mar. 24	Purchases.....................................	22,500
	Purchases returns and allowances...............	1,200
	Sales...	48,000
	Sales returns and allowances....................	400
	Estimated gross profit rate.....................	42%

Estimate the cost of the merchandise destroyed.

Problems

11-1. The following transactions, adjusting entries, and closing entries related to uncollectible accounts were completed during the current fiscal year ending December 31:

Mar. 10. Wrote off the account of Robert Norris as uncollectible, $125.

May 21. Received $26 from T. A. Vance in payment of his account, which was written off in the preceding year.

June 15. Received 10% of the $500 balance owed by Thomas Stanton, a bankrupt, and wrote off the remainder as uncollectible.

Aug. 26. Received $94 from E. J. Parker in partial payment of his account, which was written off as uncollectible in the preceding year.

Dec. 30. Wrote off the following accounts as uncollectible (compound entry): Roger Duffy, $42; D. M. Hughes, $384; Putnam and Reed, $61; Henry Todd, $220.

Dec. 31. On the basis of an analysis of the accounts receivable, the allowance for uncollectible accounts is to be adjusted to a balance of $1,200.

Dec. 31. Recorded the entry to close the appropriate account to Expense and Revenue Summary.

Instructions: (1) Open the following accounts, recording the credit balance indicated as of January 1:

114.1	Allowance for Uncollectible Accounts....	$1,000
313	Expense and Revenue Summary.............	—
718	Bad Debts Expense.......................	—

(2) Record in general journal form the transactions, adjusting entries, and closing entries described above, and post to the three accounts.

(3) Rule the expense account and rule and balance the contra asset account.

(4) The accounts receivable account has a debit balance of $22,640 at December 31. What is the expected realizable value of the accounts receivable at that date?

(5) Assuming that, instead of basing the provision for uncollectible accounts on an analysis of receivables, the adjusting entry on December 31 had been based on an estimated loss of 1% of net sales for the year of $152,000, determine the following:

(a) Bad debts expense for the year.

(b) Balance in Allowance for Uncollectible Accounts after the adjustment of December 31.

(c) Expected realizable value of the accounts receivable on December 31.

11-2. Details regarding the inventory at January 1, purchases during the year, and the inventory count at December 31 for TV Center are as follows:

Model	Inventory Jan. 1	1st Purchase	2nd Purchase	3rd Purchase	Inventory Count Dec. 31
142	5 at $ 74	5 at $ 80	10 at $ 81	—	4
143	3 at 90	10 at 90	6 at 93	5 at $ 96	6
486	3 at 160	4 at 170	5 at 170	3 at 180	2
487	—	10 at 250	5 at 265	3 at 267	5
695	6 at 200	4 at 210	6 at 210	5 at 222	3
712	1 at 180	3 at 188	4 at 190	—	3
900	5 at 300	6 at 300	5 at 320	4 at 330	2

Instructions: (1) Determine the cost of the inventory on December 31 by the first-in, first-out method. Present data in columnar form, using the columnar headings indicated below. If more than one unit cost is applied to the inventory of a particular model, use a separate line for each.

Model	Quantity	Unit Cost	Total Cost

(2) Determine the cost of the inventory on December 31 by the last-in, first-out method, following the same procedures prescribed in instruction (1).

(3) Determine the cost of the inventory on December 31 by the weighted average method, using the same columnar headings as in instruction (1).

11-3. Information needed to estimate the merchandise inventory by the retail method and the gross profit method is presented below.

(a) Retail method:

	Cost	Retail
Merchandise inventory, January 1	$161,500	$250,000
January transactions:		
Purchases	73,000 ⎫	
Purchases returns and allowances	1,230 ⎬	110,000
Purchases discounts	710 ⎭	
Sales		160,000
Sales returns and allowances		2,000

(b) Gross profit method:

Merchandise inventory, July 1	$174,000
July, Aug., Sept. transactions:	
Purchases	211,500
Purchases returns and allowances	2,100
Purchases discounts	3,400
Sales	293,500
Sales returns and allowances	6,200
Sales discounts	2,300
Estimated gross profit rate	38%

Instructions: (1) Determine the estimated cost of the inventory on January 31 in (a), presenting details of the computation.

(2) Determine the estimated cost of the inventory on September 30 in (b), presenting details of the computation.

11-4. The following preliminary income statement was prepared before the books were adjusted or closed at the end of the year:

J. B. Moyer Co.
Income Statement
For Year Ended June 30, 19—

Sales (net)		$220,000
Cost of goods sold:		
Merchandise inventory, July 1, 19—	$ 49,640	
Purchases (net)	152,400	
Merchandise available for sale	$202,040	
Less: Merchandise inventory, June 30, 19—	50,900	
Cost of goods sold		151,140
Gross profit on sales		$ 68,860
Operating expenses		49,316
Net income		$ 19,544

The following errors were discovered by the independent accountant retained to conduct the annual audit:

(a) A number of errors were discovered in pricing inventory items, in extending amounts, and in footing inventory sheets. The net effect of the corrections, excluding any listed below, was to add $2,700 to the amount stated as the ending inventory on the income statement.

(b) An invoice for merchandise of $1,100, dated June 28, was not received until after June 30 and had not been recorded. The goods had arrived on June 30 and were included in the ending inventory.

(c) An invoice for merchandise of $300, dated June 28, had been properly recorded but the goods were in transit on June 30 and had not been included in the ending inventory. Title had passed.

(d) A sales invoice for $900, dated June 30, had not been recorded. The goods were shipped on June 30, FOB shipping point, and their cost, $600, was included in the ending inventory.

(e) A sales order for $1,500, dated June 30, had been recorded as a sale but the goods were not shipped until July 5. The cost of the merchandise ($1,000) was excluded from the ending inventory.

(f) An item of office equipment, received on June 30, was included in the ending merchandise inventory at its cost, $400. The invoice had been recorded correctly.

Instructions: (1) Journalize any necessary entries to correct accounts in the general ledger, inserting the identifying letters in the date column. All purchases and sales were made on account. (An assistant will make the necessary corrections to the subsidiary ledgers.)

(2) Determine the correct figure for the ending inventory by recording the incorrect amount and each correction in a T account. Use the identifying letters as references.

(3) Prepare a revised income statement.

11-5. The unadjusted trial balance of Bicycle Imports, distributor of imported bicycles, as of the end of the current fiscal year, is as follows:

Bicycle Imports
Trial Balance
September 30, 19—

Cash	9,640	
Accounts Receivable	22,100	
Allowance for Uncollectible Accounts		300
Merchandise Inventory	34,600	
Notes Payable		14,000
Accounts Payable		10,650
Joseph Pitman, Capital		20,170
Joseph Pitman, Drawing	9,000	
Sales		164,000
Purchases	106,000	
Operating Expenses (control account)	27,000	
Interest Expense	780	
	209,120	209,120

Data needed for adjustments at September 30:

(a) The cost of the merchandise inventory is determined by the first-in, first-out method and the rule of the lower of cost or market is applied to each item on hand. The inventory of repair parts on September 30, determined in accordance with the foregoing, is $3,840. Details regarding the inventory of bicycles are as follows:

Description	Number	Unit Cost	Unit Market
Model A	410	$22	$21
Model X-40	320	30	32
Model X-50	190	35	36

(b) Losses from uncollectible accounts are estimated at ½ of 1% of sales.
(c) Prepaid interest on notes payable, $160.
(d) Interest accrued on notes payable, $75.

Instructions: (1) Determine the merchandise inventory at September 30.

(2) Journalize the necessary adjusting entries.

(3) Prepare (a) an income statement, (b) a balance sheet in report form, and (c) a capital statement, without the use of a conventional work sheet.

11-6. Monarch Sales Co. has just completed its fourth year of operations. The direct write-off method of recording uncollectible accounts has been employed during the entire period. The manager of the firm is considering the possibility of changing to the allowance method of recognizing bad debts. Information is requested as to the effect that an annual provision of 1% of sales would have had on bad debts expense reported for each of the past four years. It is also considered desirable to know what the balance of Allowance for Uncollectible Accounts would have been at the end of each year. The following data have been obtained from the accounts:

		Uncollectible Accounts Written Off	Year in Which Uncollectible Accounts Written Off Were Acquired			
Year	Sales		1st	2nd	3rd	4th
1st	$500,000	$ 500	$ 500			
2nd	600,000	4,700	4,000	$ 700		
3rd	700,000	6,000	400	5,000	$ 600	
4th	800,000	6,700		500	5,500	$ 700

Instructions: (1) Assemble the desired information, using the following columnar captions:

	Bad Debts Expense			Balance of
Year	Expense Actually Reported	Expense Based on 1% of Sales	Increase in Amount of Expense	Allowance Account End of Year

(2) Does it appear that the estimate of 1% of sales is reasonably close to the actual experience with uncollectible accounts? Give reasons for your answer.

Plant assets—depreciation

Nature of plant assets

Plant assets were described in Chapter 2 as tangible assets of a relatively fixed or permanent nature that are used in the operations of a business. A characteristic which may be inferred from the description is that such assets are not held for sale. Each of the characteristics essential for classification as a plant asset is briefly discussed in the paragraphs that follow.

Tangible. Equipment, furniture, building, and land are all tangible in nature. Intangible assets, such as patents, that fulfill the other requirements for plant assets are classified as a separate category and will be discussed in a later chapter.

Long lived. There is no standard criterion as to the minimum length of life required for classification as a plant asset. Assets that are consumed in the process of one use, such as letterheads, or over a relatively short period of time, such as carbon paper, are classified as supplies. An asset that is used repeatedly and has a life of several years or longer is generally classified as a plant asset.

Used in the business. The frequency of use is not a controlling factor. For example, stand-by equipment for use in the event of breakdown of regular equipment or for use during periods of greater than normal business activity is included in plant assets.

Not held for sale. Assets acquired for purposes of resale in the normal course of business are classified as current assets regardless of their durability. Land and buildings acquired as a speculation should not be classified as plant assets. Likewise, if a plant asset is removed from use and held for sale, it ceases to be a plant asset.

Because of their relative permanency, plant assets are often called *fixed assets.* Other descriptive titles frequently employed are *property, plant,* or *equipment,* used either singly or in various combinations.

Determining initial costs

The initial cost of a plant asset includes all expenditures necessary to get it in place and ready for use. Unnecessary expenditures resulting from carelessness, vandalism, or other abnormal causes should be excluded. Such items do not add to the utility of the asset and should be charged to operating expenses. For example, if a plant asset is damaged while it is being unloaded or readied for use, the expenditures required to repair the asset should be charged as an expense of the period.

Expenditures incurred for sales taxes, transportation, insurance in transit, installation, or other necessary items should be charged to the plant asset to which they relate. When a secondhand asset is purchased, the initial costs of getting it ready for use, such as expenditures for new parts, repairs, and painting, are properly chargeable to the asset account.

The cost of land includes not only the negotiated price but broker's commissions, title fees, surveying fees, and other expenditures connected with securing title. If delinquent real estate taxes are assumed by the buyer, they also are chargeable to the land account. Expenditures for streets, sewers, street lights, and similar permanent improvements are additions to the cost of the land, whether paid to contractors or to a taxing authority as a special assessment. If buildings are located on land acquired for a plant site, the cost of their razing or removal, less any salvage recovered, is properly chargeable to the land account.

The cost of constructing a building includes the fees paid to architects and engineers for plans and supervision, insurance during construction, and all other necessary expenditures applicable to the project. The cost of walks, paving, fencing, underground water systems, and similar improvements closely related to the building are charged to the building account. Interest incurred during the construction period on money borrowed to finance a building project should be treated as an expense. It is a payment for the use of funds rather than an essential cost of the building.

Nature of depreciation

All plant assets except land lose their usefulness with the passage of time. The several factors that contribute in varying degrees to this decline in utility are wear, the action of the elements, inadequacy, and obsolescence. As indicated in Chapter 5, the cost of such assets must be charged to expense in a systematic manner during their useful life. This expired cost periodically matched against revenue is called *depreciation*.

The factors contributing to decline in utility may be divided into two categories, *physical* depreciation, which includes wear and deterioration, and *functional* depreciation, which includes inadequacy and obsolescence. A plant asset is said to be inadequate if its capacity is insufficient to meet the needs of the owner. For example, if the capacity of a newspaper press is insufficient to fulfill the demands of increased circulation, it is inadequate regardless of the fact that it is still operating efficiently. A plant asset is obsolete if the product that it produces is no longer in demand or if a newer machine can produce the product at considerably less cost or can produce a product of superior quality. The continued acceleration of technological progress during this century has made obsolescence an increasingly important component of depreciation. The several factors comprising depreciation can be defined but in practice it is not feasible or necessary to consider them individually in recording depreciation expense.

The meaning of the term "depreciation," as it is used in accounting, is frequently misunderstood. The same term is also commonly used in business to connote a decline in market value, hence the confusion. Any relationship between the unexpired cost of plant assets as reported on the balance sheet and the cash realizable values of the assets is merely coincidental. Plant assets are held for use rather than for sale, and their market values are irrelevant. It is assumed that the enterprise will continue indefinitely as a going concern. Consequently the decision to dispose of any particular plant asset will be based on its utility to the enterprise rather than the amount that could be realized from its sale.

Another common misconception is that depreciation accounting provides a fund of cash for the replacement of plant assets. Expired portions of the cost of the assets are periodically transferred to expense by debits to depreciation expense accounts and credits to accumulated depreciation accounts. The cash account is not affected by the entries and, of course, would not be affected if the entries were omitted. The confusion originates from the fact that depreciation expense, unlike most expenses, does not require an equivalent outlay of cash in the period in which the expense is recorded. The recognition of depreciation in the accounts and statements is not affected by any plans concerning replacement of the asset.

Recording depreciation

It has been observed in earlier chapters that each adjusting entry for supplies, prepaid insurance, and other prepaid assets affects a balance sheet account and an income statement account. The same is true of adjustments for depreciation. The expense is recorded by a debit to an appropriately titled expense account and the reduction in the asset is recorded by a credit to a *contra asset* or *valuation* account. Titles applied to the valuation account include *Accumulated Depreciation, Allowance for Depreciation,* and *Reserve for Depreciation,* followed by the title of the asset account to which it is related. The first is preferred over the other two because it avoids erroneous connotations that may be associated with "allowance" and "reserve." An adjusting entry to record depreciation of a building at the end of the second year following the year of acquisition is illustrated below:

Dec.	31	Depreciation Expense — Building......	715	2,000	
		Accumulated Depreciation—Building.	124.1		2,000

The expense account is closed to Expense and Revenue Summary in exactly the same manner as the other expense accounts are closed.

After adjusting and closing entries have been posted, the asset account, the valuation account, and the expense account appear as follows:

BUILDING   Acct. No. 124

1961									
July	1		J10	80,000					

ACCUMULATED DEPRECIATION — BUILDING   Acct. No. 124.1

					1961				
					Dec.	31	Adjusting	J15	1,000
					1962				
					Dec.	31	Adjusting	J23	2,000

DEPRECIATION EXPENSE — BUILDING   Acct. No. 715

1962					1962				
Dec.	31	Adjusting	J23	2,000	Dec.	31	Closing	J24	2,000

In the foregoing illustration the depreciation for the entire year was recorded in an adjusting entry at the end of the year. In preparing interim statements it would be necessary to record accrued depreciation for the year to date in the adjustments column of the monthly work sheets. An alternative is to record depreciation in the accounts at the end of each month.

Theoretically, depreciation begins to accrue on the date that a plant asset is placed in service. In practice, however, it is usually considered unnecessary to recognize a period of time of less than a month. Thus, a full month's depreciation would be recorded for assets placed in service at any time during the first half of a month. Similarly, depreciation of assets placed in service during the last half of a month may be ignored for that particular month.

Depreciation methods

There are a number of accepted methods of determining depreciation, all of which employ estimates. The factors that must be considered, regardless of the method used, are:

1. Cost of the asset.
2. Estimated useful life of the asset.
3. Estimated residual value of the asset.

The various expenditures included in the initial cost of depreciable assets were discussed earlier in the chapter. The estimated life of an asset or functional group of assets is stated in units of time or production. The actual useful life of any particular type of plant asset will not necessarily be uniform for all businesses. Climate and other conditions, maintenance policies, minimum standards of usefulness, and other considerations will influence the estimate. Suggested estimates for various assets are available in trade association and other publications. Bulletin F, published by the Internal Revenue Service, contains life estimates for many kinds of assets used by a wide variety of industries. The bulletin contains estimates for specific assets as well as for some functional groups. For example, adding machines are estimated to be useful for 10 years, and safes and vaults for 50 years; the composite life estimate for office equipment taken as a whole is 15 years.

The residual value of a depreciable asset is the amount expected to be realized upon its eventual disposition. It is generally termed *scrap*, *salvage*, or *trade-in* value. The amount received from a sale or trade of used equipment may be substantial in relationship to original cost. This would be the case, for example, of salesmen's automobiles traded after two years of use or typewriters traded every four years. On the other hand, the salvage value of specialized manufacturing equipment or of a building may be insignificant. In some cases the amount realized from the sale of scrap may be nullified by dismantling and removal expenses. When residual value is expected to be nominal in amount it may be ignored in determining depreciation.

The selection of a method of depreciation is a function of management. The method selected should provide for a reasonable and systematic allocation of cost over the useful life of the asset. Different methods may be used for different classes of depreciable assets. In any case they should be applied consistently from year to year. Depreciation methods commonly used are (1) straight line, (2) units of production, (3) declining balance, and (4) sum of the years-digits.

Straight line method.　　The straight line method of determining depreciation yields equal periodic charges to expense over the estimated life of the asset. To illustrate this method, assume the cost of a depreciable asset to be $10,000, its residual value to be $500, and its estimated life to be 10 years. The annual depreciation is computed as follows:

$$\frac{\$10,000 - \$500}{10 \text{ years}} = \$950 \text{ annual depreciation}$$

The relationship of the annual depreciation to the total amount to be depreciated is sometimes stated as a per cent of the cost of the asset. Thus, in the example, the depreciation rate could be stated as 9.5% of cost ($950 ÷ $10,000). When nominal residual values are excluded from consideration in determining depreciation, the estimated life may be converted directly to a depreciation rate. For example, a life of 40 years is equivalent to a rate of $2\frac{1}{2}\%$, a life of 10 years is equivalent to a rate of 10%, and a life of 8 years is equivalent to a rate of $12\frac{1}{2}\%$.

The straight line method is widely used. In addition to its simplicity it provides a reasonable allocation of costs to periodic revenue when usage is relatively uniform from period to period.

Units of production method.　　The units of production method relates depreciation to the estimated productive capacity of the asset. Depreciation is first computed for an appropriate unit of production, such as hours, miles, or number of operations. The depreciation for each period is then determined by multiplication of the unit depreciation by the number of units used during the period. For example, assume that a machine with a cost of $21,000 and estimated residual value of $1,000 is expected to have an estimated life of 40,000 hours. The depreciation for a unit of one hour is computed as follows:

$$\frac{\$21,000 - \$1,000}{40,000 \text{ hours}} = \$.50 \text{ an hour depreciation}$$

Assuming that the machine was in operation for 2,000 hours during a particular year, the depreciation for that year would be $1,000 ($.50 × 2,000).

When the amount of usage of a plant asset varies considerably from period to period, the units of production method is preferable to the straight line method. The necessity of maintaining a record of the amount of usage is a disadvantage, however.

Declining balance method.　　The declining balance method provides a steadily declining periodic depreciation charge over the estimated life of the asset. Of several variants in technique, the one customarily used applies twice the straight line depreciation rate to the declining book value of the asset. For example, if the estimated life of an asset is 5 years, the depreciation rate is 40% (20% × 2). For the first year the rate is applied to the cost of the asset; in succeeding years it is applied to the declining book value (cost − accumulated depreciation). The method is illustrated by the following tabulation:

Year	Cost	Accumulated Depreciation at Beginning of Year	Book Value at Beginning of Year	Rate	Depreciation for Year
1	$10,000.00	—	$10,000.00	40%	$4,000.00
2	10,000.00	$4,000.00	6,000.00	40%	2,400.00
3	10,000.00	6,400.00	3,600.00	40%	1,440.00
4	10,000.00	7,840.00	2,160.00	40%	864.00
5	10,000.00	8,704.00	1,296.00	40%	518.40

It should be noted that estimated residual value is not considered in determining the depreciation rate. It is also ignored in computing periodic depreciation, except that the asset should not be depreciated below the estimated residual value. In the foregoing example it was assumed that the book value at the end of the fifth year, $777.60, approximates the estimated trade-in value. If the estimated residual value had been $1,000, the depreciation for the fifth year would have been $296.00 instead of $518.40.

The declining balance method may be applied to all types of depreciable assets. Its use is most appropriate, however, in cases in which the decline in productivity or earning power of the asset is proportionately greater in the early years of its use than in later years. Further justification for its use is based on the tendency of repairs to increase with the age of an asset. The reduced amounts of depreciation in later years are therefore offset to some extent by increased maintenance expenses.

Sum of the years-digits method. The sum of the years-digits method also provides a steadily declining periodic depreciation charge over the estimated life of the asset. This is accomplished by applying a successively smaller fraction each year to cost less residual value. The numerator of the changing fraction is the number of remaining years of life and the denominator is the sum of the digits representing the years of life. Assuming an estimated life of 5 years, the denominator of the fraction is 15 (1 + 2 + 3 + 4 + 5); for the first year the numerator is 5, for the second year 4, and so on. For a $16,000 asset with an estimated life of 5 years and residual value of $1,000, the schedule of depreciation is as follows:

YEAR	COST LESS RESIDUAL VALUE	RATE	DEPRECIATION FOR YEAR	ACCUMULATED DEPRECIATION AT END OF YEAR	BOOK VALUE AT END OF YEAR
1	$15,000	5/15	$5,000	$ 5,000	$11,000
2	15,000	4/15	4,000	9,000	7,000
3	15,000	3/15	3,000	12,000	4,000
4	15,000	2/15	2,000	14,000	2,000
5	15,000	1/15	1,000	15,000	1,000

The sum of the years-digits method may be applied to all types of depreciable assets and yields periodic charges similar to those provided by the declining balance method. The recent popularity of both methods has been due in part to the income tax advantage of rapid write-offs. The greater depreciation deductions in the earlier years of the life of a plant asset reduce the income tax for those years and correspondingly increase the amount of funds available to pay for the asset or for addition to working capital.

Capital and revenue expenditures

In addition to the initial cost of acquiring a plant asset, other costs related to its efficiency or capacity are incurred from time to time during its service life. It is often difficult to differentiate between expenditures that add to the utility of the asset for more than one accounting period and those that constitute an expense of the period in which they are incurred. Costs that are chargeable to an asset account or its related accumulated depreciation account are frequently termed *capital expenditures;* those that are chargeable to current operations are referred to as *revenue expenditures.*

Expenditures for an addition to a plant asset would clearly constitute capital expenditures. For example, the cost of installing an air conditioning unit in an automobile or of adding a wing to a building should be charged to the respective asset accounts. It is equally clear that expenditures for maintenance and repairs of a recurring nature should be classified as revenue expenditures. Thus, the cost of replacing spark plugs in an automobile or of repainting a building should be charged to expense. In less obvious situations several criteria may be considered in classifying the expenditures.

Expenditures that increase operating efficiency or capacity for the remaining useful life of an asset should be capitalized. For example, if the power unit attached to a machine is replaced by one of greater capacity, the cost and accumulated depreciation applicable to the old motor should be removed from the accounts and the cost of the new one charged to the asset account. Expenditures that increase the useful life of an asset beyond the original estimate are also capital expenditures. They should be debited to the accumulated depreciation account, however, rather than to the asset account. To illustrate, assume that a machine with an estimated life of ten years is completely overhauled at the end of its seventh year of use. It is expected that the extraordinary repairs will extend the life of the machine an additional three years over the original estimate. The expenditures restore or "make good" a portion of the depreciation recorded in prior years and it is consequently appropriate to debit them to the accumulated depreciation account.

When the cost of improvements or extraordinary repairs is substantial or there is a material change in estimated life, the depreciation charge for future periods should be computed on the basis of the book value and the estimate of the remaining useful life.

Individual expenditures that are minor in amount are usually treated as repair expense even though they may have the characteristics of capital expenditures. The consequent saving in time and accounting expenses justifies the sacrifice of a small degree of accuracy. Some businesses establish a minimum amount for classifying an item as a capital expenditure.

Disposal of plant assets

Plant assets that are no longer useful may be discarded, sold, or applied toward the purchase of other plant assets. Before recording the disposal, the depreciation expense accrued for the period to date should be recorded. The details of the entry to record the disposal will vary, but in all cases it is necessary to remove the book value of the asset from the accounts. This is accomplished by debiting the appropriate accumulated depreciation account for the total depreciation to the date of disposal and crediting the asset account for the cost of the asset.

Discarding of plant assets. When plant assets that are no longer useful cannot be sold they are discarded. For example, if fully depreciated office equipment acquired at a cost of $1,000 is discarded as worthless, the following entry is made:

Apr.	1	Accumulated Depreciation — Office Equipment	123.1	1,000	
		Office Equipment..................	123		1,000
		To write off equipment discarded.			

If the office equipment had not been fully depreciated, it would have been necessary to record a loss at the time of its disposal. To illustrate, assume that the balance in the accumulated depreciation account as of the preceding December 31, the end of the fiscal year, is $800 and that the equipment is depreciated at the rate of 10%. The entry to record the depreciation for the three months of the current year is as follows:

Apr.	1	Depreciation Expense—Office Equipment	714	25	
		Accumulated Depreciation — Office Equipment.	123.1		25
		To record 3 months' depreciation on equipment discarded.			

The equipment is then removed from the accounts and the loss is recorded by the following entry:

Apr.	1	Accumulated Depreciation — Office Equipment	123.1	825	
		Loss on Disposal of Plant Assets........	912	175	
		Office Equipment..................	123		1,000
		To write off equipment discarded.			

Losses and gains on the disposal of plant assets are nonoperating items and are reported in the "Other Expense" and "Other Income" sections, respectively, of the income statement.

It should be noted that plant assets are not necessarily removed from the general ledger immediately after they become fully depreciated. If they are continued in use the cost and accumulated depreciation should remain in the accounts.

Sale of plant assets. The entry to record the sale of a plant asset is similar to the entries illustrated in the preceding section except that the cash or other asset received must also be recorded. If the selling price is in excess of the book value of the asset the transaction results in a gain instead of a loss. To illustrate various possibilities, assume that office equipment acquired at a cost of $1,000 and depreciated at the rate of 10% is sold on October 1 of the seventh year of its use. The accumulated depreciation in the account as of the preceding December 31 is $600. The entry to record the depreciation for the nine months of the current year is as follows:

Oct.	1	Depreciation Expense—Office Equipment	714	75	
		Accumulated Depreciation—Office Equipment	123.1		75
		To record 9 months' depreciation on equipment sold.			

Three different assumptions as to the price at which the equipment is sold and the related entry, in general journal form, are presented below.

1. Selling price $325, which is exactly equal to the book value of the asset:

Oct. 1 Cash.   325
      Accumulated Depreciation — Office Equipment.   675
          Office Equipment.   1,000

2. Selling price $200, which is $125 less than the book value of the asset:

```
Oct. 1  Cash.................................................   200
            Accumulated Depreciation — Office Equipment............   675
            Loss on Disposal of Plant Assets........................   125
                Office Equipment...................................        1,000
```

3. Selling price $425, which is $100 greater than the book value of the asset:

```
Oct. 1  Cash.................................................   425
            Accumulated Depreciation — Office Equipment............   675
                Office Equipment...................................        1,000
                Gain on Sale of Plant Assets.........................         100
```

Exchange of plant assets. Old equipment is frequently traded in for new equipment having a similar use. The trade-in allowance granted by the seller is deducted from the price of the new equipment and the balance is paid in cash at the time of the exchange or in accordance with the credit agreement. If the trade-in allowance is greater than the book value of the asset, there is a gain on disposal; if it is less than the book value there is a loss. According to the Internal Revenue Code, however, gains and losses resulting from the exchange of similar types of plant assets are not recognized for income tax purposes. The non-recognition affects not only the amount of taxable income in the year of the exchange but also the cost basis of the asset acquired and the amount of deductible depreciation expense in subsequent years. As a matter of expediency many accountants record exchanges in conformity with the provisions of the Code.

As a basis for illustrating the two methods of recording the exchange, assume the following data:

Cost of old delivery equipment traded in..............................	$4,000
Accumulated depreciation on the delivery equipment as of December 31, the close of the preceding fiscal year.....................................	$2,800
Depreciation from January 1 to June 30, the date of the exchange..........	$ 400
Price of the new delivery equipment...................................	$5,000
Trade-in allowance granted on the old equipment......................	1,100
Balance paid in cash...	$3,900

Depreciation accrued for the current year is recorded as follows:

June	30	Depreciation Expense—Delivery Equip..	614	400	
		Accumulated Depreciation — Delivery Equipment....................	121.1		400
		To record 6 months' depreciation on equipment traded in.			

Gain or loss recognized. The computation of the gain realized on the old equipment and the entry in general journal form to record the exchange are presented on the following page.

Trade-in allowance on old equipment..........................		$1,100
Book value of old equipment		
Cost..	$4,000	
Accumulated depreciation.................................	3,200	800
Gain on exchange..		$ 300

June 30	Accumulated Depreciation — Delivery Equipment.........	3,200	
	Delivery Equipment....................................	5,000	
	Delivery Equipment................................		4,000
	Cash...		3,900
	Gain on Disposal of Plant Assets.....................		300

Gain or loss not recognized. If the gain or loss on an exchange transaction is not recognized in the accounts the amount recorded as the cost of the new asset is (1) the book value of the old asset plus (2) the cash paid or to be paid.

The cost basis of the new equipment, assuming the same transaction data, is determined as follows:

Book value of old equipment...	$ 800
Cash paid..	3,900
Cost of new equipment..	$4,700

The effect of the nonrecognition of the gain from the exchange on the cost basis of the new truck may also be computed as follows:

Price of new equipment......................................	$5,000
Less unrecognized gain on exchange..........................	300
Cost of new equipment (same as above).......................	$4,700

The entry to record the exchange, in general journal form, follows:

July 1	Accumulated Depreciation — Delivery Equipment..........	3,200	
	Delivery Equipment....................................	4,700	
	Delivery Equipment................................		4,000
	Cash...		3,900

If the exchange had resulted in an unrecognized loss instead of a gain, the loss would have been *added* to the price of the new equipment in the computation above.

It should be noted that the nonrecognition of the gain or loss at the time of the exchange is in reality a postponement. In the above illustration the periodic depreciation on the new equipment will be based on a cost of $4,700 instead of $5,000. By excluding the unrecognized gain of $300 from the cost basis of the asset, the total amount of depreciation expense over the life of the asset will be reduced by a corresponding amount.

Subsidiary ledgers for equipment

A general ledger account for equipment usually includes all of the equipment that is used for one function of the business. Typical accounts are Office Equipment, Store Equipment, and Delivery Equipment.

For example, the office equipment account includes such equipment as desks, chairs, filing cabinets, typewriters, and many other items used in the office. Records of cost, date of acquisition, and accumulated depreciation may be maintained for each of these items through the medium of a subsidiary ledger. The account Office Equipment and the related account Accumulated Depreciation — Office Equipment then become controlling accounts for the subsidiary ledger.

Although there are no standard account rulings for the equipment ledger, the form should provide space for recording the asset, the accumulated depreciation, and miscellaneous descriptive data. For purposes of illustration, an office equipment ledger of four accounts will be assumed. The controlling accounts in the general ledger and the four accounts in the subsidiary ledger are shown on this and the following page.

General Ledger

OFFICE EQUIPMENT   Acct. No. 123

1961						
Jan.	4	CP1	260	00		
Apr.	18	P4	205	00		
Aug.	12	P8	96	48		
			561	*48*		

ACCUMULATED DEPRECIATION — OFFICE EQUIPMENT   Acct. No. 123.1

				1961				
				Dec.	31	J4	37	35
				1962				
				Dec.	31	J15	52	04
							89	*39*

Office Equipment Ledger

EQUIPMENT RECORD

ITEM__Desk_____ GENERAL LEDGER ACCOUNT__Office Equipment__

SERIAL NO.__---_____ DESCRIPTION__Metal_____

FROM WHOM PURCHASED__Office Equipment Co._____

ESTIMATED LIFE__20 years__ ESTIMATED SCRAP OR TRADE-IN VALUE__---_____ DEPRECIATION PER YEAR__$10.00__

DATE			EXPLANATION	ASSET			ACCUMULATED DEPRECIATION			BOOK VALUE
MO.	DAY	YR.		DR.	CR.	BAL.	DR.	CR.	BAL.	
1	4	61		200 00		200 00				200 00
12	31	61						10 00	10 00	190 00
12	31	62						10 00	20 00	180 00

EQUIPMENT RECORD

ITEM __Chair__   GENERAL LEDGER ACCOUNT __Office Equipment__

SERIAL NO. __- - -__   DESCRIPTION __Metal__

FROM WHOM PURCHASED __Office Equipment Co.__

ESTIMATED LIFE __15 years__ ESTIMATED SCRAP OR TRADE-IN VALUE __- - -__   DEPRECIATION PER YEAR __$4.00__

MO.	DAY	YR.	EXPLANATION	ASSET DR.	ASSET CR.	ASSET BAL.	ACCUM. DEPR. DR.	ACCUM. DEPR. CR.	ACCUM. DEPR. BAL.	BOOK VALUE
1	4	61		60 00		60 00				60 00
12	31	61						4 00	4 00	56 00
12	31	62						4 00	8 00	52 00

EQUIPMENT RECORD

ITEM __Typewriter__   GENERAL LEDGER ACCOUNT __Office Equipment__

SERIAL NO. __38-6241__   DESCRIPTION __Standard__

FROM WHOM PURCHASED __Howe Typewriter Co.__

ESTIMATED LIFE __5 years__ ESTIMATED SCRAP OR TRADE-IN VALUE __$55.00__   DEPRECIATION PER YEAR __$30.00__

MO.	DAY	YR.	EXPLANATION	ASSET DR.	ASSET CR.	ASSET BAL.	ACCUM. DEPR. DR.	ACCUM. DEPR. CR.	ACCUM. DEPR. BAL.	BOOK VALUE
4	18	61		205 00		205 00				205 00
12	31	61						20 00	20 00	185 00
12	31	62						30 00	50 00	155 00

EQUIPMENT RECORD

ITEM __Filing Cabinet__   GENERAL LEDGER ACCOUNT __Office Equipment__

SERIAL NO. __- - -__   DESCRIPTION __Four drawer, metal__

FROM WHOM PURCHASED __Hale, Thompson & Co.__

ESTIMATED LIFE __12 years__ ESTIMATED SCRAP OR TRADE-IN VALUE __- - -__   DEPRECIATION PER YEAR __$8.04__

MO.	DAY	YR.	EXPLANATION	ASSET DR.	ASSET CR.	ASSET BAL.	ACCUM. DEPR. DR.	ACCUM. DEPR. CR.	ACCUM. DEPR. BAL.	BOOK VALUE
8	12	61		96 48		96 48				96 48
12	31	61						3 35	3 35	93 13
12	31	62						8 04	11 39	85 09

At the end of the fiscal year the amount of the periodic adjustment for depreciation is determined for each individual account in the subsidiary ledger. In each case the depreciation is recorded in the subsidiary account as a credit to Accumulated Depreciation. The sum of the individual credits is the amount needed for the adjusting entry in the general journal. For example, the following credits to accumulated depreciation are recorded in the four subsidiary accounts as of December 31, 1961:

Desk............................	$10.00
Chair...........................	4.00
Typewriter.....................	20.00
Filing cabinet.................	3.35
Total.........................	$37.35

On the basis of this information the following adjusting entry is recorded in the general journal:

Dec.	31	Depreciation Expense—Office Equip....	714	37.35		
		Accumulated Depreciation — Office				
		Equipment.....................	123.1			37.35

When an asset is disposed of, the subsidiary account is credited for its cost and debited for the accumulated depreciation, reducing both balances to zero. The account is then removed from the ledger and filed for future reference.

The sum of the balances in the subsidiary ledger should be compared periodically with the balances in the controlling account. The balances in the subsidiary ledger as of December 31, 1962 are summarized as follows:

ITEM	COST	ACCUMULATED DEPRECIATION	BOOK VALUE
Desk..........................	$200.00	$ 20.00	$180.00
Chair.........................	60.00	8.00	52.00
Typewriter....................	205.00	50.00	155.00
Filing Cabinet................	96.48	11.39	85.09
Total....................	$561.48	$ 89.39	$472.09

The totals obtained for the cost of the assets and the accumulated depreciation agree with the balances in the controlling accounts appearing on page 265.

Subsidiary ledgers for plant assets are useful to the accounting department in (1) determining the periodic depreciation expense, (2) recording the disposal of individual items, (3) preparing tax returns, and (4) preparing insurance claims in the event of insured losses. The forms may also be expanded to provide spaces for accumulating data on the operating efficiency of the asset. Such information as frequency of break-downs, length of time out of service, and cost of repairs is useful to management in comparing similar equipment produced by different manufacturers. When purchasing new equipment, the experience records aid in deciding upon the size, model, and other specifications, and the best source of supply.

All plant assets should be physically counted and inspected periodically to determine that they are still owned, still in use, and the extent of any necessary repairs. Subsidiary accounts or some type of inventory listing is essential in making such examinations. A common practice is to number serially all subsidiary accounts and attach a corresponding identification tag to the asset.

Composite depreciation rates

Because of the clerical expense involved, some firms do not maintain a subsidiary account for each individual plant asset in a functional group. If most of the individual items have a low cost and depreciation is a relatively minor portion of the total expenses, the computation of depreciation by functional groups is satisfactory. In such cases a *composite rate*, based on the average life of all items in the group, is employed. A variant is to determine a composite rate for the assets acquired in each particular year. For example, if the average life of the office equipment group is determined to be 12½ years, a straight line rate of 8% would be applied against the balance in the office equipment account to determine the annual depreciation. When a composite rate is used, depreciation on assets acquired or disposed of during the year is frequently computed at one half of the annual rate.

It should be borne in mind that the periodic amount of depreciation is based on estimates. The effect of such factors as obsolescence and inadequacy on the useful life of plant assets is particularly difficult to forecast.

A reasonable system of depreciation, consistently applied, will satisfy the standards of good accounting.

Plant assets on the balance sheet

The balance sheet presentation of plant assets and accumulated depreciation was illustrated in Chapter 2. There are many possible variations in arrangement. If the number of accounts is too great to be accommodated on the balance sheet, summary totals only may be presented with the details set forth in a supporting schedule.

The compact arrangement illustrated below is quite commonly used. It has the advantage of requiring only one line for each asset.

Clarkdale Enterprises
Balance Sheet
December 31, 1961

Assets

	Cost	Accumulated depreciation	Book value	
Total current assets..				$462,500
Plant assets:				
Office equipment..............	$ 20,000	$ 3,000	$ 17,000	
Factory equipment............	250,000	92,000	158,000	
Buildings....................	100,000	26,000	74,000	
Land.......................	10,000	—	10,000	
Total plant assets...........	$380,000	$121,000		259,000

Questions

1. Name the four characteristics of plant assets.

2. Indicate which of the following expenditures incurred in connection with the acquisition of a printing press should be charged to the asset account: (a) freight charges, (b) interest on funds borrowed to make the purchase, (c) insurance while in transit, (d) cost of special foundation, (e) fee paid to factory representative for assembling and adjusting, (f) new parts to replace those damaged in unloading.

3. In order to increase the size of its customer parking area, the Bayside Supermarket buys an adjoining lot and an old building for $10,000. The net expense incurred in razing the building and leveling the land, after deducting the amounts received from the sale of salvaged building materials, is $1,700. To what account should the $1,700 be charged?

4. (a) Discuss the nature of depreciation as the term is used in accounting. (b) Does the recognition of depreciation in the accounts provide a fund of cash for the replacement of plant assets?

5. (a) What is meant by "book value" of a plant asset? (b) Does the value at which plant assets are shown on the balance sheet closely approximate their market value?

6. Name and describe the four factors that contribute to depreciation.

7. (a) What is the nature of the account Accumulated Depreciation? (b) What is its normal balance? (c) Do credits to the account increase or decrease the balance of the account? (d) Do credits to the account have the effect of increasing or decreasing the book value of the related plant assets?

8. Convert each of the following life estimates to a depreciation rate, stated as a per cent, assuming that residual value of the plant asset is to be ignored: (a) 5 years, (b) 8 years, (c) 10 years, (d) 20 years, (e) 25 years, (f) 40 years.

9. A plant asset with a cost of $20,000 has an estimated trade-in value of $2,000 and an estimated life of 10 years. (a) What is the annual depreciation, computed by the straight line method? (b) The annual depreciation is what per cent of the cost of the asset?

10. Would you suggest that the straight line or the units of production method of depreciation be used in depreciating a building with an estimated life of 50 years? Discuss.

11. What portion of the cost of a plant asset with a life estimate of 4 years is written off in the first year by the declining balance method, using twice the straight line rate?

12. An asset with an estimated life of 4 years is to be depreciated by the sum of the years-digits method. (a) What is the denominator of the depreciation fraction? (b) What is the numerator of the fraction for the first year?

13. When should the cost and accumulated depreciation of a fully depreciated plant asset be removed from the accounts?

14. In what sections of the income statement are gains and losses from the disposal of plant assets presented?

15. A plant asset with a book value of $2,000 is traded for a similar asset with a price of $25,000. The trade-in allowance is $5,000. (a) What is the amount of cash to be paid? (b) What is the gain or loss on the disposal? (c) If the gain or loss is not recognized in the accounts, at what amount will the new asset be recorded? (d) If the gain or loss is not recognized in the accounts at the time of the exchange, how will it be recognized in the future?

16. Differentiate between capital expenditures and revenue expenditures.

17. Immediately after acquiring a used truck a new motor is installed at a cost of $400 and the tires are replaced at a cost of $250. To what account or accounts should these items be charged?

18. After a building has been in use for 20 years the roof is replaced at a cost of $5,000. The expenditure is expected to increase the estimated useful life of the asset by 5 years. To what account should the expenditure be charged?

19. If a subsidiary ledger is maintained for store equipment, what are the related controlling accounts?

Exercises

1. A building acquired on January 10 at a cost of $100,000 has an estimated life of 50 years. Assuming that it will have no residual value, determine the depreciation for each of the first two years (a) by the straight line method and (b) by the declining balance method, using twice the straight line rate.

2. A diesel generator with a cost of $46,000 and estimated salvage value of $1,000 is expected to have a useful operating life of 150,000 hours. During November the generator was operated 600 hours. Determine the depreciation for the month.

3. Details of the subsidiary truck ledger of a hauling and storage company are summarized below. (a) Determine the amount to be credited to the accumulated depreciation section of each of the subsidiary accounts for the current year. (b) Present the general journal entry to record depreciation for the year.

Truck No.	Cost	Residual Value	Useful Life in Miles	Accumulated Depreciation at Beginning of Year	Miles Operated During Year
1	$ 6,000	$ 500	100,000	$4,000	10,000
2	5,000	300	100,000	4,500	8,000
3	10,000	850	150,000	3,000	20,000
4	12,000	1,000	200,000	6,000	25,000

4. A plant asset acquired at a cost of $15,000 has an estimated trade-in value of $2,500 and an estimated useful life of 10 years. Determine (a) the annual depreciation charge by the straight line method, (b) the rate of depreciation based on cost, by the straight line method, (c) the amount of depreciation for the first year computed by the sum of the years-digits method.

5. On June 24 Tonto Department Store acquires a new accounting machine with a list price of $2,200, receiving an allowance of $400 on an old machine and giving a note for the remainder. The following information about the old equipment is obtained from the account in the office equipment ledger: cost, $1,000; accumulated depreciation on December 31, the close of the preceding fiscal year, $800; annual depreciation, $100. Present general journal entries: (a) to record depreciation accrued for the year, (b) to record the transaction on June 24, recognizing any gain or loss, (c) to record the transaction on June 24, not recognizing the gain or loss.

6. On the first day of the fiscal year a delivery truck with a list price of $5,500 is acquired in an exchange transaction in which there was a loss of $1,000. The truck is to be depreciated over four years by the straight line method, assuming a trade-in value of $500. Determine the following: (a) annual depreciation expense, assuming that loss is recognized, (b) annual depreciation expense, assuming that loss is not recognized, (c) the amount of the exchange loss included in the annual depreciation expense determined in (b).

Problems

12-1. The following expenditures and receipts are related to land and buildings, the receipts being identified by an asterisk.

(a) Cost of real estate acquired as a plant site: Land........	$ 30,000
Building.....	20,000
(b) Delinquent real estate taxes on property, assumed by purchaser.......................................	1,600
(c) Cost of dismantling and removing the building..........	1,800
(d) Fee paid to attorney for title search...................	300
(e) Cost of land fill and grading the land.................	1,200
(f) Paid to building contractors.........................	250,000
(g) Architect's fee for plans and supervision...............	18,000
(h) Premium on insurance during construction—1 year policy	1,900
(i) Cost of repairing windstorm damage during construction..	2,500
(j) Interest accrued on building loan during period of construction......................................	9,000
(k) Cost of paving parking lot for employees...............	900
(l) Real estate taxes accrued during period of construction...	1,500
(m) Special assessment for installation of street lights, paid to city	800
(n) Proceeds from sale of salvage materials from old building...	600*
(o) Proceeds from insurance company for windstorm damage.	2,000*
(p) Refund of portion of premium on insurance during construction	400*
	$336,500

Instructions: By use of a columnar form with captions for Land, Building, and Other, list the letters identifying each item and place the amounts in the appropriate columns. Total the columns.

12-2. An item of new equipment acquired at a cost of $36,000 at the beginning of a fiscal year has an estimated life of 4 years and an estimated salvage value of $3,000.

Instructions: (1) Determine for each of the four years the depreciation per year and the book value of the equipment at the end of the year by each of the following methods:

(a) Straight line.
(b) Declining balance (at twice the straight line rate).
(c) Sum of the years-digits.

Present the data in tabular form, using the following headings for each schedule:

	DEPRECIATION	BOOK VALUE
YEAR	EXPENSE	END OF YEAR

(2) On the first day of the fourth year the equipment was traded in for similar equipment priced at $40,000. The trade-in allowance on the old equipment was $10,000 and a note was given for the balance. Assuming that the sum of the years-digits method of depreciation had been used, journalize the entry to record the transaction, (a) recognizing the gain or loss on disposal and (b) not recognizing the gain or loss on disposal.

12-3. The following transactions, adjusting entries, and closing entries were completed by Home Store during a three year period. All are related to the use of delivery equipment.

1961
Apr. 8. Purchased a used delivery truck for $1,250, paying cash.
    14. Paid garage $150 for new tires and $172 for extensive repairs to the truck.
Aug. 20. Paid garage $48 for miscellaneous repairs to the motor.
Dec. 31. Recorded depreciation on the truck for the fiscal year. The estimated life of the truck is 2 years, with a trade-in value of $300. The straight line method of depreciation is used; the minimum unit of time to be considered is a month.
Dec. 31. Closed the appropriate accounts to Expense and Revenue Summary.
1962
June 25. Traded in the used truck on a new truck priced at $3,043, receiving a trade-in allowance of $500, and paying the balance in cash. (Record depreciation to date in 1962; gain or loss on exchange is not to be recognized.)
Oct. 10. Paid garage $35 for a new tire and $26 for repairs to the truck.
Dec. 31. Recorded depreciation on the truck, estimated life, 3 years; trade-in value, $800.
    31. Closed the appropriate accounts to Expense and Revenue Summary.
1963
Mar. 18. Sold the truck for $2,200, receiving cash. (Record depreciation.)
Dec. 31. Closed the appropriate accounts to Expense and Revenue Summary.

Instructions: (1) Open the following accounts in the ledger:

121 Delivery Equipment
121.1 Accumulated Depreciation — Delivery Equipment
614 Depreciation Expense—Delivery Equipment
615 Truck Repair Expense
912 Loss on Disposal of Plant Assets

(2) Record the transactions, adjusting and closing entries in general journal form, posting to the accounts after each entry. At the end of each year rule the accounts that are closed and rule and balance the other accounts containing more than one item.

12-4. The following transactions and adjustments affecting office machines were completed by Progressive Development Co. during a three year period.

1961
Apr. 2. Purchased the following office machines from Business Machines, Inc., paying $570 cash and issuing a note payable for the balance:

8-bank adding machine, No. 49764	$290
8-bank calculator, No. 63483	600
Electric typewriter, No. 962145	580

July 10. Purchased a printing calculator, No. 5461A, from Morrow Co. on account, $646.

Dec. 31. Recorded depreciation for the year.

1962
May 24. Purchased a bookkeeping machine, No. 9742, from Morrow Co. on account, $6,500.

Oct. 18. Purchased a 10-bank calculator, No. 42961, from Business Machines, Inc., paying cash, $900.

Oct. 29. Sold the 8-bank calculator for cash, $350.

Dec. 31. Recorded depreciation for the year.

1963
Mar. 28. Traded the printing calculator for a new model, No. 36942, from Morrow Co. The price of the new calculator was $700. The allowance on the old machine was $430, the balance being paid in cash. (Gain or loss is not to be recognized.)

Dec. 31. Recorded depreciation for the year.

The company uses the straight line method of computing depreciation. Additional details needed for determining depreciation are as follows:

Item	Estimated Trade-in Value	Estimated Life
8-bank adding machine.	$ 50	8 yrs.
8-bank calculator.	60	10 yrs.
Electric typewriter.	100	5 yrs.
Printing calculators.	70	8 yrs.
Bookkeeping machine.	500	10 yrs.
10-bank calculator.	60	10 yrs.

Instructions: (1) Open the following accounts in the general ledger: Office Machines, 121; Accumulated Depreciation — Office Machines, 121.1. As each item is acquired, open an account in the subsidiary ledger, using the form illustrated on pages 265 and 266.

(2) Record the entries in general journal form, posting to the two general ledger accounts and to the subsidiary ledger accounts after each entry.

(3) Balance and rule the controlling accounts in the general ledger, as of December 31, 1963.

(4) Prepare a schedule of office machines from the subsidiary ledger as of December 31, 1963, using the following columnar captions:

Item	Cost	Accumulated Depreciation	Book Value

12-5. In each of the following selected problems it is assumed that subsidiary equipment ledgers are maintained and that the fiscal year ends on December 31. Depreciation is recorded only at the end of each year, except for depreciation on items disposed of during the year.

(a) Mar. 18. Discarded a duplicating machine (office equipment), realizing no salvage. Details from the subsidiary account are as follows: cost, $190; accumulated depreciation, $190. Present the necessary journal entry.

(b) May 13. Sold 10 desks (office equipment) for cash, $200. The desks were identical and had been acquired at the same time. Details from the subsidiary ledger are as follows: total cost, $1,100; total accumulated depreciation on preceding December 31, $672; total annual depreciation, $96. Present the necessary entries in general journal form.

(c) June 28. Traded in an old delivery truck for a new one priced at $3,000, receiving a trade-in allowance of $600 and paying the balance in cash. Details from the subsidiary ledger are as follows: cost, $2,500; accumulated depreciation on preceding December 31, $1,925; annual depreciation, $660. Present the necessary entries in general journal form, recognizing the gain or loss.

(d) Aug. 5. Discarded store equipment, realizing no salvage. Details from the subsidiary ledger are as follows: cost, $300; accumulated depreciation on preceding December 31, $220; annual depreciation, $36. Present the necessary entries.

(e) Oct. 11. Traded in an old refrigerated display case (store equipment) for a new one priced at $1,500, receiving a trade-in allowance of $250 and giving a note for the balance. Details from the subsidiary ledger are as follows: cost, $1,000; accumulated depreciation on preceding December 31, $850; annual depreciation, $100. Present the necessary entries in general journal form, using the income tax method.

(f) Jan. 12. Paid $5,200 for replacing roof on building. It is estimated that the new roof will extend the life of the building from an original estimate of 30 years to a total life of 35 years. Details from the subsidiary ledger are as follows: cost, $60,000; accumulated depreciation on preceding December 31, $38,000; age of building, 19 years. (1) Present the entry, in general journal form, to record the payment. (2) What is the amount of depreciation on the building for the year in which the roof was replaced?

12-6. A number of unrelated errors in recording transactions are described below:

(a) Incoming transportation charges of $100 on an item of factory equipment were debited to Purchases.

(b) The $400 cost of a major motor overhaul expected to prolong the life of a truck beyond the original estimate was charged to Delivery Equipment. The truck was acquired new two years earlier.

(c) A payment of $3,000 to the city as a special assessment for paving streets was charged to Taxes Expense.

(d) The $1,500 cost of repainting the interior of a building that had been owned for seven years was charged to Building.

(e) The sale of a printing press for $2,000 was recorded by a $2,000 credit to Printing Press. The original cost of the press was $12,000 and the related balance in Accumulated Depreciation at the end of the year preceding the year of sale was $8,000. Depreciation of $400 accrued during the year of sale had not been recorded.

(f) The cost of a building, $6,000, plus razing costs of $1,000 was charged to Loss on Disposal of Plant Assets. The building and the land on which it was located had been acquired for a total cost of $20,000 ($14,000 debited to Land; $6,000 debited to Building), as a site for a supermarket.

(g) The $350 cost of repairing factory equipment damaged in the process of installation was charged to Factory Equipment.

Instructions: Journalize the necessary correcting entries, assuming that they are recorded in the same fiscal year in which the errors occurred. Identify each entry by letter.

Practice set 1

Part 2
Greer Wholesale Shoes

This is a continuation of Practice Set 1, Part 1 of which is presented at the end of Chapter 8. The same journals and ledgers are to be used.

Transactions for November

Instructions: (17) Record the following transactions in the appropriate journals, posting to the ledgers when instructed to do so.

Nov. 1. Received $30,000 in cash as an additional investment in the business by the proprietor, Thomas R. Greer.

1. Purchased for $60,000 facilities which have been rented by the enterprise. Of this amount $55,000 is allocated to the building and $5,000 to the land. In payment, issued check No. 722 for $35,000 and a 5-year, 6% mortgage note for $25,000. (Record this transaction in the Cash Payments Journal. Enter the credit to Mortgage Payable in the Sundry Accounts Dr. column and encircle it to indicate that it is a credit.)

1. Issued Check No. 723 for $720 for premium on three year insurance policy on the building.

2. Purchased merchandise on account from Western Manufacturing Co., $3,390.

2. Received a check for $750 for three months' rent of space in the building (credit Unearned Rent).

3. Discarded an item of office equipment, realizing no salvage. Details are as follows: cost, $150; accumulated depreciation as of November 1, $110.

3. Issued Check No. 724 for $155.55 to Merchants Supply Co. in payment of its invoice for $155.55.

3. Received checks as follows:
  A check for $1,448.44 from Town & Country, Inc. in payment of our invoice for $1,520.20 less the return of $42.20, less a 2% discount.
  A check for $2,849.84 from Parker & Son in payment of our invoice for $2,940.85, less the return of $32.85, less a 2% discount.

Nov. 3. Sold merchandise on account to Central Department Store, $2,530.62, Sale No. 1172.

   3. Issued checks as follows:
Check No. 725 for $200 for advertising in trade periodical.
Check No. 726 for $59.75 for miscellaneous selling expense.
Check No. 727 for $3,007.52 to Western Manufacturing Co. in payment of its invoice for $3,068.90 less a 2% discount.

   3. Received $2,165.40 from cash sales for November 1-3.

Instructions: (18) Post to the *subsidiary* ledgers (see instruction 5, page 189).

Nov. 6. Sold merchandise on account to Macon & Elder, $1,805.60, Sale No. 1173.

   6. Discounted at the bank a $4,000, 60-day, noninterest-bearing note payable, dated today. The bank deducted interest at the rate of 6% and credited Greer's bank account for the proceeds, $3,960.

   7. Issued Check No. 728 for $67.50 for advertising.

   7. Issued Credit Memo No. 109 for $130.62 to Central Department Store for the return of merchandise on the sale of November 3.

   8. Issued Check No. 729 for $1,244.60 to Stride-Rite Shoe Co. in payment of its invoice for $1,270 less a 2% discount.

   8. Made the following purchases on account:
Fashion Shoes, Inc., merchandise, $2,608.
Merchants Supply Co., office supplies, $10.60; store supplies, $59.50; miscellaneous selling expense, $20.

   9. Issued Check No. 730 for $37.50 for repairs to office equipment. (Charge Miscellaneous General Expense.)

   10. Received a check for $1,907.28 from Arnold Shoe Store in payment of our invoice for $1,946.20 less a 2% discount.

   10. Issued checks as follows:
Check No. 731, $3,322.20, to Western Manufacturing Co. in payment of its invoice for $3,390 less a 2% discount.
Check No. 732 for $2,800 for biweekly salaries divided as follows: sales salaries, $1,900; office salaries, $900.
Check No. 733 for $2,700 for store equipment priced at $3,000 acquired in an exchange. Details on the old equipment traded in are as follows: cost, $1,200; depreciation accumulated at November 1, $800. (Record entire transaction in cash payments journal; gain or loss is not to be recognized.)

   10. Received $2,150.85 from cash sales for November 6–10.

Instructions: (19) Post to the *subsidiary* ledgers.

Nov. 13. Issued Check No. 734 for $300 to Thomas R. Greer for personal use.

13. Purchased merchandise on account from Barton Shoe Corp., $1,987.50.

13. Made the following sales on account:
Sale No. 1174, Varsity Shop, $2,300.
Sale No. 1175, T. L. Jordan, Inc., $709.10.

14. Received a check for $2,352 from Central Department Store in payment of our invoice for $2,530.62 less the return of $130.62, less a 2% discount.

15. Received check for $1,769.49 from Macon & Elder in payment of our invoice for $1,805.60 less a 2% discount.

15. Purchased office equipment on account from Ross & Co., $326.

15. Issued Check No. 735 for $18.45 to a cash customer for merchandise returned.

16. Made the following sales on account:
Sale No. 1176, Arnold Shoe Store, $1,500.40.
Sale No. 1177, Finch Bootery, $2,182.50.

17. Received a credit memorandum for $87.50 from Barton Shoe Corp. for the return of merchandise on its invoice of November 12.

17. Issued Check No. 736 for $2,555.84 to Fashion Shoes, Inc. in payment of its invoice for $2,608 less a 2% discount.

17. Received from Finch Bootery a 60-day, 6% note for $592.30, dated November 17, in settlement for the sale of October 20.

17. Issued Credit Memo No. 110 for $19.10 to T. L. Jordan, Inc. for the return of merchandise on the sale of November 13.

17. Received $1,676.35 from cash sales for November 13–17.

Instructions: (20) Post to the *subsidiary* ledgers.

Nov. 20. Received from Varsity Shop a 60-day, 6% note for $2,768 dated November 20, in settlement for the sale of October 20.

20. Made the following purchases on account:
Western Manufacturing Co., merchandise, $3,641.20.
Merchants Supply Co., store supplies, $50; office supplies, $25.50.

20. Issued Check No. 737 for $1,862 to Barton Shoe Corp. in payment of its invoice for $1,987.50 less the return of $87.50, less a 2% discount.

21. Received a check for $30 from the sale of store equipment. Details are as follows: cost, $320; accumulated depreciation at November 1, $256; depreciation for November, $2.

Nov. 21. Made the following sales on account:
Sale No. 1178, Parker & Son, $2,850.90.
Sale No. 1179, Town & Country, Inc., $1,120.50.

23. Received checks as follows:
A check for $2,254 from Varsity Shop in payment of our invoice for $2,300, less a 2% discount.
A check for $676.20 from T. L. Jordan, Inc. in payment of our invoice for $709.10, less the return of $19.10, less a 2% discount.

23. Purchased merchandise on account from Fashion Shoes, Inc., $1,710.30.

24. Issued Credit Memo No. 111 for $25 to Town & Country, Inc. for the return of merchandise on the sale of November 21.

24. Issued Check No. 738 for $2,300 for biweekly salaries divided as follows: sales salaries, $1,700; office salaries, $600.

24. Received $2,041.40 from cash sales for November 20–24.

Instructions: (21) Post to the *subsidiary ledgers.*

Nov. 27. Discounted at the bank at 6% the Finch Bootery note for $592.30 and received credit for the proceeds, $593.23.

27. Issued Check No. 739 for $118.75 to Merchants Supply Co. in payment of its invoice for $118.75.

27. Received a check for $2,138.85 from Finch Bootery in payment of our invoice for $2,182.50 less a 2% discount.

27. Made the following sales on account:
Sale No. 1180, Central Department Store, $2,245.62.
Sale No. 1181, Macon & Elder, $894.10.

28. Purchased merchandise on account from Western Manufacturing Co., $2,100.72.

28. Issued Check No. 740 for $85 to Ross & Co. in payment of its invoice for $85.

29. Issued Check No. 741 for $3,568.38 to Western Manufacturing Co. in payment of its invoice for $3,641.20, less a 2% discount.

30. Issued checks as follows:
Check No. 742 for $126.40 for advertising.
Check No. 743 for $410.80 for freight charges on merchandise purchased.
Check No. 744 for $400 to Thomas R. Greer for personal use.
Check No. 745 for $214.65 for utilities expense. (Charge Miscellaneous General Expense.)

30. Received $1,475.65 from cash sales for November 27–30.

Instructions: (22) Post to the subsidiary ledgers.

Posting to the general ledger

Instructions: (23) Total each column of the various special journals. Prove the equality of debits and credits in each journal. Make the following computation to determine the cash balance at November 30: cash balance, November 1, plus debits to cash, minus credits to cash. The balance obtained should be $6,050.20.

(24) Post all items that need to be *individually* posted to the general ledger, beginning with the purchases journal and proceeding through the other journals in the order indicated in Instruction (5) on page 189.

(25) Rule the journals, and post to the appropriate accounts in the general ledger.

(26) Prepare a trial balance on eight-column paper, listing only the accounts with balances.

Data for adjustments

The additional data required to complete the work sheet are as follows:

Interest accrued on notes receivable on November 30.....	$ 4.61
Provision for doubtful accounts for November...........	138.00
Merchandise inventory on November 30................	28,495.50
Inventories of supplies on November 30:	
Store supplies.....................................	245.80
Office supplies....................................	155.00
Insurance expired during November...................	59.40
Prepaid interest on notes payable on November 30......	24.00
Depreciation expense for November:	
Store equipment..................................	57.60
Office Equipment.................................	22.35
Building...	160.00
Interest accrued on mortgage on November 30..........	120.83
Salaries payable on November 30:	
Sales salaries....................................	680.00
Office salaries...................................	240.00
Rent earned during November.......................	250.00

Instructions: (27) Prepare an income statement, a balance sheet, a capital statement, and schedules of accounts receivable and accounts payable, employing the exhibit and schedule designations illustrated on page 171 through 173.

(28) Complete the work of the periodic summary for the month of November, following the outline on page 163.

Systems and controls

Accounting systems

One of the areas of specialization in accounting described in Chapter 1 is the design and installation of accounting systems. In developing principles of accounting in the intervening chapters attention has been focused to a large extent on the analysis and recording of accounting data, preparation of financial statements, and uses of accounting data by management. Consideration has also been given, however, to some aspects of accounting systems, such as special journals, charts of accounts, subsidiary ledgers, and documentary evidence of transactions.

There are an infinite number of variations in the details of accounting systems. In each particular case the system must be tailored in accordance with the nature of the enterprise, the volume of transactions of various types, and the number and capacities of the personnel. Every accounting system, regardless of the size or complexity of the enterprise for which it is designed, is composed of the following interrelated components:

1. *Documentary evidence.* Written evidence of transactions must be created at the time of the transaction. Examples of business documents include deeds, contracts, invoices, checks, and cash register tapes.
2. *Procedures.* The procedures for channeling the documents into the accounting records must be carefully established and adhered to by all employees of the enterprise.
3. *Written records.* The written records include the journals, ledgers, supplementary analyses, and financial statements.
4. *Equipment and personnel.* The type of equipment used in recording, classifying, and summarizing data will affect to a considerable degree the design of the other components of the system. Equipment ranges from adding machines and cash registers to elaborate electronic data processing units.

The core of the accounting process is the coordination of the components of the system into a harmonious plan. An unsatisfactory accounting system places a handicap on the management of an enterprise and may impair its operations. A properly designed system should provide for: (1) the efficient accumulation and recording of data, (2) a basis for evaluating all phases of a firm's operations, (3) timely reports to management, (4) assignment of authority and responsibility, and (5) prevention of errors and fraud.

Internal control

In a small business it is possible for the owner-manager to instruct and supervise the employees personally. As the number of employees and the complexities of an enterprise increase, it becomes increasingly difficult for management to maintain contact with all phases of operations. It is necessary to delegate authority and to rely on reports and other forms of accounting data rather than on personal observation.

Plans and procedures designed to meet the need for controlling operations are called *internal control*. It comprises the plan of organization and the related methods and procedures adopted within a company to: (1) safeguard its assets, (2) produce accurate accounting data, (3) contribute to efficient operation, and (4) encourage adherence to management policies. In a broad sense internal control also includes such activities as motion and time study, quality control, and statistical analysis. The portion of internal control related to the accounting system is sometimes referred to as *internal check*.

Some degree of internal control is needed in all businesses. For example, the requirement that each cash sale be recorded by depressing the appropriate keys on a cash register is a fundamental part of internal control. The use of sales tickets, sales invoices, and other documentary evidences of transactions are also a part of internal control. The details of a system of internal control will of necessity vary with the nature and size of a firm. There are, however, a number of broad principles that should be considered. They are presented and briefly discussed in the paragraphs that follow.

Control over a sequence of related transactions should be divided among different persons. Complete control by one individual over a sequence of related transactions presents opportunities for inefficiency, errors, and fraud. For example, one person should not be authorized to order merchandise, verify the receipt of the goods, and pay the supplier. To do so would invite such abuses as placing orders on the basis of friendship with a supplier rather than on price, quality, and other objective factors; perfunctory verification of the quantity and quality of goods received; conversion of goods to the personal use of the employee; and carelessness in verifying the validity and accuracy of invoices.

When the responsibility for executing the related transactions is divided among different individuals, the possibilities of such occurrences are minimized. The responsibility for purchasing, receiving, and paying should be divided among three persons or departments. Documentary evidence of the work of each department, including purchase orders, receiving reports, and invoices, is routed to the accounting department for comparison and recording. It should be noted that the "checks and balances" provided by distributing authority among various departments is accomplished without duplication of effort. The work of each department, as evidenced by the business documents that it prepares, must "fit" with those prepared by the other departments.

The responsibility for maintaining the records should be separated from the responsibility for operations and custody of assets. If the employees who perform transactions also record the transactions, the control function of the accounts in the ledger is lost. For example, the person who receives remittances from customers on account should not journalize the transactions or have access to the ledgers. Separation of the two functions lessens the likelihood of errors and defalcation.

All feasible proofs and security measures should be utilized. This principle applies to a wide variety of techniques and procedures such as the use of controlling accounts and subsidiary ledgers, the use of a bank account and other safekeeping measures for cash, investments, and other valuable documents, and the use of various types of mechanical equipment. Cash registers are widely employed in making the initial record of cash sales. The conditioning of the public to observe the amount recorded as the sale or to accept a printed receipt from the sales clerk increases the machine's effectiveness as a part of internal control. Other devices with a similar feature include gasoline pumps and automatic counters in city buses.

Responsibility should be clearly established. The duties and authority of each employee should be definitely fixed. Again using the cash register as an example, each sales clerk should be assigned a separate cash drawer and register key. By such means daily proof of the handling of cash can be obtained for each clerk. Similarly, if a number of employees are assigned to posting entries to customer's accounts, each should be assigned to a particular alphabetical section so that errors can be traced to the person responsible.

Using a bank account

Checks have taken the place of currency in the more important transactions involving payments of cash. When checks are received from customers, they are recorded as debits to Cash, the assumption being that the customer has sufficient funds on deposit. Similarly, when checks are given in payment, they are recorded as credits to Cash even though the checks are not presented to the drawer's bank until some time later. The forms used by the depositor in connection with a bank account are signature card, deposit ticket, check, and bank statement.

Signature card. At the time of opening an account the bank requires that a *signature card* be signed personally by each individual authorized to sign checks. The card is used by the bank to determine the authenticity of the signature on checks presented to it for payment. Some firms require two signatures on each check as a control over the issuance of checks.

Deposit ticket. The details of a deposit are listed by the depositor on a printed form supplied by the bank. A specimen of this form, which is called a *deposit ticket*, is illustrated at the right. The bills and the coins in the deposit are shown in total in the two spaces provided, and the checks are listed individually. Each check should be identified on the deposit ticket by the name or the address of the bank on which it is drawn, or by the code numbers of the American Bankers' Association printed on the check. The deposit ticket serves as the basis for the bank's entry crediting the depositor.

Deposit tickets are frequently prepared in duplicate. The carbon copy is stamped or initialed by the teller and returned to the depositor as a receipt. Some banks immediately record the total amount of the deposit on a window posting machine which automatically issues a printed receipt form for the depositor. Deposits may be mailed to the bank or placed in a night deposit vault, in which case the bank mails the duplicate deposit ticket or receipt to the depositor.

ORIGINAL		
FOURTH NATIONAL BANK		
ALLENTOWN, PENNSYLVANIA		

ACCOUNT NUMBER

8 9 0 — 1 2 3 6 4

Mellon Company
PLEASE PRINT EXACT TITLE OF ACCOUNT

July 15, 1961

Checks and other items are received for deposit subject to the terms and conditions of this bank's collection agreement.

CURRENCY		476	00
COIN		32	97
CHECKS	60-205	475	92
2	60-127	246	50
3	13-24	55	75
4	8-21	436	20
5	60-132	208	66
6			
7			
TOTAL ——→		1,932	00
A	B	C	D

Deposit ticket

Check. A *check* is a written instrument signed by the depositor, ordering his bank to pay a specified sum of money to a designated person or to his order. There are three parties to a check: the *drawer*, the one who signs the check; the *drawee*, the bank on which the check is drawn;

and the *payee*, the one to whose order the check is drawn. Check forms may be obtained in a variety of styles. The name and address of the depositor may be printed on each check, and the checks may be serially numbered for purposes of internal control. Some banks employ automatic check-sorting and posting machines, in which case their identification number and the depositor's account number are printed on each check in magnetic ink.

Many companies use a check with a detachable remittance advice which identifies the invoice or other item for which payment is made. A carbon copy of the check may be prepared for use in recording the transaction in the cash payments journal, or the information may be entered in a *stub* such as that illustrated below. The check stub may also be used as a memorandum record of the current bank balance.

Check and stub

Bank statement

Banks maintain an original and a carbon copy of all checking accounts. The original becomes the statement of account which is mailed to the depositor, usually at the end of each month. Like any account with a customer or creditor, it begins with the opening balance, lists debits (deductions by the bank) for the period, credits (additions by the bank) for the period, and ends with the balance at the close of the period. Accompanying the bank statement are the depositor's checks received by the bank during the period, arranged in the order of payment. The *paid* or *canceled* checks are marked "paid" together with the date of payment. Bank memorandums describing the nature of miscellaneous debits and credits during the period are also enclosed with the statement. A typical bank statement is illustrated on page 285.

Bank reconciliation

The account, Cash in Bank, in the depositor's ledger is the reciprocal of the account with the depositor in the bank's ledger. The former is an

Statement of *Account*
WITH
THE FOURTH NATIONAL BANK

890-12364

Mellon Company
813 Hamilton St.
Allentown, Pa.

CHECKS AND OTHER DEBITS			DEPOSITS	DATE	BALANCE
	BALANCE BROUGHT FORWARD →			July 1	4,218.60
819.40	122.54			July 1	3,276.66
369.50	732.26	20.15		July 3	2,154.75
293.20	550.00		1,781.30	July 8	3,092.85
126.32	791.50			July 10	2,175.03
25.93	160.00		262.50	July 12	2,251.60
431.00	126.15		1,932.00	July 15	3,626.45
125.00	62.30			July 17	3,439.15
475.00	1,332.50		1,190.18	July 22	2,821.83
229.50	28.30	40.00		July 23	2,524.03
56.30	160.00	25.91	750.93	July 24	3,032.75
873.10	394.25			July 25	1,765.40
21.10	126.20	DM 3.00	CM 400.00	July 26	2,015.10
468.50			1,896.50	July 29	3,443.10
57.20	26.12			July 31	3,359.78

CM — Credit Memorandum   NSF — Not sufficient funds   PS — Payment stopped
DM — Debit Memorandum   OD — Overdraft   SC — Service charge

The reconcilement of this statement with your records is essential. Any error or exception should be reported immediately.

Bank statement

asset with a debit balance, and the latter is a liability with a credit balance. It might seem that the two balances should be equal in amount, but at any specific date it is unlikely that this will be so. The lack of agreement between the two accounts is caused by either or both of the following: (1) delay by either party in recording transactions, (2) errors by either party in recording transactions.

There is almost always a time lag of one day or more between the date a check is written and the date that it is presented to the bank for payment. If the depositor mails deposits to his bank or uses the night depository a delay by the bank in recording the deposit is also probable. On the other hand the bank may debit or credit the depositor's account for transactions about which the depositor will not be informed until later. Examples are service or collection fees charged by the bank and the proceeds of notes receivable given to the bank for collection.

In order to discover and correct any recording errors that may have been made by the bank or the depositor, it is necessary that the depositor *reconcile* the bank statement with his own records. The bank reconciliation is divided into two major sections; one section begins with the balance according to the bank statement and ends with the adjusted balance, the other section begins with the balance according to the depositor's books and ends with the adjusted balance. Both sections must yield the same amount for the adjusted balance. The form and content of the two sections is presented in tabular form below:

Balance per bank statement..		xx
Add: Additions by depositor not on bank statement...................	xx	
Bank errors..	xx	xx
		xx
Deduct: Deductions by depositor not on bank statement..............	xx	
Bank errors..	xx	xx
Adjusted balance..		xx
Balance per books...		xx
Add: Additions by bank not recorded in books......................	xx	
Book errors..	xx	xx
		xx
Deduct: Deductions by bank not recorded in books..................	xx	
Book errors..	xx	xx
Adjusted balance..		xx

The amount of the "balance per books" is the balance of the ledger account Cash in Bank. If the receipts and payments for the month have not been posted, it is necessary to compute the month-end balance. It is also possible to use the balance according to the check stubs as of the last day of the month.

To achieve a maximum of internal control, the bank reconciliation should be prepared by an employee who does not engage in or record bank transactions. Errors or irregularities discovered should be reported to the chief accountant, controller, or other supervisory official.

The following procedures are employed in locating the reconciling items and determining the adjusted balance of Cash in Bank:

1. Compare individual deposits listed on the bank statement with unrecorded deposits appearing in the preceding reconciliation and with duplicate deposit slips or other record of deposits. Deposits not recorded by the bank are added to the balance according to the bank statement.

2. Arrange paid checks returned by the bank in numerical order and compare them with outstanding checks appearing on the preceding reconciliation and with checks listed in the cash payments journal. Checks issued that have not been returned by the bank are outstanding and are deducted from the balance according to the bank statement.

3. Trace bank credit memorandums to the cash receipts journal. If there are any unrecorded additions to the bank account, the amounts are added to the balance according to the books.

4. Trace bank debit memorandums to the cash payments journal. If there are any unrecorded deductions from the bank account, the amounts are deducted from the balance according to the books.

5. Errors discovered during the process of making the foregoing comparisons are listed separately on the reconciliation. For example, if an erroneous amount is recorded in the cash payments journal, the amount of the error is added to or deducted from the balance according to the books. Similarly, errors by the bank are added to or deducted from the balance according to the bank statement.

Illustration. The bank statement appearing on page 285 will be used as the basis for illustration. After the Mellon cash receipts and cash payments journals for July were posted, the balance in the cash in bank account is $2,242.99. According to the bank statement the balance on July 31 is $3,359.78. Application of the procedures outlined above reveals the following reconciling items:

1. Deposit of July 31 not recorded on bank statement............... $ 816.20
2. Checks outstanding: No. 712, $1,061.00; No. 994, $316.40; No. 996, $167.59.. 1,544.99
3. Note collected by bank (credit memorandum) not recorded in cash receipts journal....................................... 400.00
4. Collection fee charged by bank (debit memorandum) not recorded in cash payments journal.................................... 3.00
5. Check No. 976 for $732.26 to Belden Co. on account recorded in cash payments journal as $723.26............................. 9.00

The reconciliation is completed when the two amounts obtained for the adjusted balance are in agreement.

Mellon Co.
Bank Reconciliation
July 31, 1961

Balance per bank statement..		$3,359.78
Add: Deposit of July 31, not recorded by bank......................		816.20
		$4,175.98
Deduct: Outstanding checks		
No. 712.....................................	$1,061.00	
No. 994.....................................	316.40	
No. 996.....................................	167.59	1,544.99
Adjusted balance......................................		$2,630.99
Balance per books.....................................		$2,242.99
Add: Note collected by bank............................		400.00
		$2,642.99
Deduct: Collection fee.................................	$3.00	
Error in recording check No. 976.................	9.00	12.00
Adjusted balance......................................		$2,630.99

Entries based on bank reconciliation

Unrecorded transactions evidenced by bank debit and credit memorandums must be recorded and errors revealed by the reconciliation must be corrected. The necessary entries may be recorded in the cash receipts and cash payments journals if they have not been posted for the month. If the journals have already been posted, the entries should be recorded in the general journal.

The entries for Mellon Co., based on the bank reconciliation in the preceding section, are as follows:

July	31	Cash in Bank.......................	400	
		Notes Receivable..................		400
		Note collected by bank.		
	31	Accounts Payable — Belden Co........	9	
		Miscellaneous General Expense........	3	
		Cash in Bank.....................		12
		Error in recording check No. 976 and bank collection fee.		

After the foregoing entries are posted, the cash in bank account will have a debit balance of $2,630.99, which agrees with the adjusted balance shown on the bank reconciliation. In recording the transactions and the correction as of July 31, it was assumed that financial statements were to be prepared as of July 31. If this was not the case, the entries could have been recorded in the cash receipts and cash payments journals for August. If a memorandum record of the bank balance is maintained in the check stubs, the last stub should be revised by adding the net adjustment of $388 ($400 − $12).

Internal control of cash receipts

A bank account is one of the principal devices for maintaining control over cash. To achieve maximum effectiveness all cash received must be deposited in the bank and all payments must be made by checks drawn on the bank or from special cash funds. When such a system is strictly adhered to there is a double record of cash, one maintained by the business and the other by the bank.

Department stores and other retail businesses ordinarily receive cash from two principal sources: (1) over the counter from cash customers and (2) by mail from charge customers making payments on account. At the close of the business day each sales clerk counts the cash in his cash drawer and records the amount on a memorandum form. An employee from the cashier's department removes the cash register tapes on which total receipts are recorded for each cash drawer, recounts the cash, and compares the total with the memorandum and the tape, noting any discrepancies. The cash is taken to the cashier's office, where it is combined with the mail receipts and a deposit ticket prepared. The cash register tapes and memorandum forms are forwarded to the accounting department, where they become the basis for entries in the cash receipts journal.

The employees who open the mail record the amount received from each customer on the upper portion of the statement of account that customarily accompanies the remittance. If the remittance slip is not enclosed with the remittance, the employee records the information on a similar form. The remittances, usually in the form of checks and money orders, are sent to the cashier's department, as indicated above, and the remittance advices are delivered to the accounting department where they become the basis for entries in the cash receipts journal and for posting to the customers' accounts in the subsidiary ledger.

The duplicate deposit ticket or other bank receipt form obtained by the cashier is forwarded to the chief accountant, controller, or treasurer where the amount is compared with the amount recorded by the accounting department as a debit to Cash in Bank.

Cash short and over

It frequently happens, particularly in a retail business with many cash sales, that the amount of cash actually received during a day does not agree with the cash register tally of cash receipts. Whenever there is a difference between the records and the actual cash and no error can be found in the records, it must be assumed that the mistake occurred in making change. If the actual cash is less than the amount shown by the cash records, an entry is made in the cash payments journal debiting an account entitled Cash Short and Over and crediting Cash in Bank. If the actual cash is greater than the balance in the records, an entry is made in the cash receipts journal debiting Cash in Bank and crediting Cash Short and Over.

If there is a debit balance in the cash short and over account at the end of the fiscal period, it is an expense and may be included in Miscellaneous General Expense on the income statement. If there is a credit balance, it is revenue and may be listed in the Other Income section.

Special cash funds

Retail stores and other businesses that receive cash directly from customers must maintain a fund of currency and coins in order to make change. It is also not practicable to require that all payments be made by check. Procedures for meeting such requirements may be adopted without lessening the effectiveness of the control over cash.

Cash on hand. If it is necessary to maintain a fund for making change, the fund may be established by drawing a check for the required amount, charging the account Cash on Hand and crediting Cash in Bank. No additional charges or credits to the cash on hand account are necessary unless the amount of the fund is to be increased or decreased. At the close of each business day the total receipts are deposited and the change fund is retained. The desired composition of the fund is maintained by exchanging bills or coins for bills or coins of other denominations at the bank.

Petty cash. In most businesses there is a frequent need for payments of relatively small amounts, such as to the postman for postage due, to a delivery man for transportation charges, or to an employee for the purchase of urgently needed supplies at a nearby retail store. It is readily apparent that payment by check in such cases would result in delay, annoyance, and excessive expense of maintaining the records. It is usual, therefore, to maintain a special cash fund that is designated *petty cash.*

A petty cash fund is established by drawing a check payable to Petty Cash for the total amount of the estimated payments for a specified period, such as the month. The entry to record the creation of a fund of $50 on August 1 appears in the cash payments journal on page 292. The check for $50 is cashed and the money is placed in the custody of an employee authorized to disburse the funds in accordance with stipulated restrictions as to maximum amount and purpose. Each time a disbursement is made from the fund, a petty cash voucher is prepared. The voucher contains the essential details of the transaction. It is signed or initialed by the cashier for petty cash, and the payee signs as evidence of having received the money. A petty cash voucher is shown below.

PETTY CASH VOUCHER	NO. 1
DATE Aug. 1, 1961	
PAID TO Western Union	AMOUNT
FOR Telegram	1 30
CHARGE TO Miscellaneous General Expense	
PAYMENT RECEIVED: S. O. Hall	APPROVED BY NER

Petty cash voucher

The amount of each petty cash voucher and the account to be charged may be recorded on a petty cash analysis sheet similar to that illustrated below, or at the time the fund is to be replenished the vouchers may be sorted by account titles and the amounts summarized by listing on an adding machine tape. When the amount of the fund is reduced to the minimum amount considered necessary, the petty cash analysis sheet or the adding machine tapes, together with the receipted vouchers, are forwarded to the accounting department. The vouchers are reviewed, the arithmetical summary verified, and the disbursing officer is requested to draw a check for the amount required to replenish the fund. This check is cashed and the money is placed in the fund.

PETTY CASH ANALYSIS SHEET

DATE	VCHR. NO.	DESCRIPTION	PETTY CASH		DISTRIBUTION				
							SUNDRY		
			RECEIPTS	PAYMENTS	MISC. SELL. EXPENSE	MISC. GEN. EXPENSE	ACCOUNT	AMOUNT
1961								
Aug. 1		Check No. 115	50.00					
1	1			1.30		1.30		
2	2			6.25	6.25			
5	3			1.28			Store Supplies	1.28
9	4			11.90	11.90			
12	5			1.75	1.75			
14	6			5.85		5.85		
16	7			3.72			Delivery Exp.	3.72
19	8			11.50			Office Supplies	11.50
19		Totals	50.00	43.55	19.90	7.15		16.50
19		Balance		6.45				
			50.00	50.00				

Petty cash analysis sheet

The entry to record the expenses of $43.55 reported on the petty cash analysis sheet illustrated above, and to record the replenishing check of like amount, appears in the cash payments journal on page 292. It should be noted that although the actual payments occurred during the period August 1 to August 19 the expenses were not recorded in the journal until the latter date. Furthermore, the check for $43.55 was not used to pay the expenses but to replenish the fund. This time lag in formally recording the expenses is typical. Because of this, the fund should always be replenished at the close of an accounting period. The actual amount of cash in the fund will then be equal to the balance in the petty cash account, and the expenses will be charged to the period in which they were incurred.

The initial debit to Petty Cash will continue as the balance of the account unless it is decided to increase or decrease the amount of the fund.

CASH PAYMENTS JOURNAL

DATE		ACCOUNT DEBITED	CHECK NO.	POST. REF.	SUNDRY ACCOUNTS DR.	ACCOUNTS PAYABLE DR.	PURCHASES DISCOUNT CR.	CASH IN BANK CR.
1961 Aug.	1	Petty Cash	115		50 00			50 00
	19	Misc. Selling Exp.	187		19 90			43 55
		Misc. Gen. Exp.			7 15			
		Store Supplies			1 28			
		Delivery Exp.			3 72			
		Office Supplies			11 50			

Other special funds. Other funds may be established to meet the special needs of a business. For example, money advanced to a salesman for travel expenses may be accounted for in the same manner as petty cash. A standard amount is advanced, and upon receipt of expense reports from the salesman the expenses are recorded and the fund replenished. A similar technique may be used to provide a working fund for a sales office located in another city. The amount of the fund may be deposited in a local bank and the sales representative authorized to draw checks for payment of rent, salaries, and other operating expenses. Each month the representative sends the invoices, bank statement, paid checks, bank reconciliation, and other business documents to the home office. The data are audited, the expenditures are recorded, and a reimbursing check is returned for deposit in the local bank.

NOTES RECEIVABLE

DATE RECEIVED		OUR NO.	PAYABLE BY	PAYABLE AT	DATE OF NOTE	TIME
1961 Jan.	5	111	Henry James & Co.	First National Bank of Akron	1– 3–61	60 days
	9	112	C. L. Collins	Our office	1– 7–61	30 days
	14	113	Lyle & Blosser Corp.	Union Trust Co., City	1–12–61	90 days
	24	114	K. M. Jonathan	Second National Bank, Canton	1–23–61	60 days
Feb.	3	115	John F. Freeman	Merchants Bank, City	2– 2–61	60 days
	11	116	George Winestock	Union Bank, Marion	2– 9–61	60 days

Notes receivable register, left page

Supplementary records for notes

The notes receivable and notes payable accounts in the general ledger are primarily summarizing devices. They are not designed for recording detailed information concerning the terms of each note and its disposition. If numerous notes are received from customers or issued to creditors it is customary to record the details of each note in a notes receivable register or a notes payable register. The registers are similar in design and either may be used without the other. A register for notes receivable is illustrated below.

The initial entries are recorded in the register at the time a note is received, the details as to name of the maker, place of payment, amount, term, interest rate, and due date being determined from the note. Daily reference to the due date section calls attention to which notes, if any, are to be presented for collection. When a note is sent to a bank for collection, is discounted, is paid by the maker, or is dishonored, such information is recorded in the section entitled "Disposition." The amount of any contingent liability for notes receivable discounted to be reported on the balance sheet at the end of the fiscal year is readily determined by examining the entries in the register. If notice of dishonor is not received within a few days after the due date of the note, it is presumed to have been paid.

The use of note registers in no way affects the ledger entries for recording note transactions discussed in Chapter 9.

Insurance

An important means of safeguarding a firm's investment in plant assets is through insurance against losses from fire, windstorm, and other catastrophes. Potential losses resulting from injury to customers or employees while on the business premises, from dishonesty of employees, and from business interruptions caused by fire are only a few of the

REGISTER

YEAR	J	F	M	A	M	J	J	A	S	O	N	D	FACE		INTEREST RATE	DISPOSITION
							DUE DATE									
1961			4										1,280	75	6%	Pd. 3/4
1961		6											250	00	——	Pd. 2/6
1961				12									2,500	00	6%	Discounted 1/15
1961			24										118	50	——	Dishonored 4/3
1961				3									687	50	5%	Pd. 4/3
1961				10									200	00	6%	Bank for coll. 4/8 Pd. 4/10

Notes receivable register, right page

many other risks that may need to be insured against. The responsibility for appropriate insurance coverage ordinarily rests with the treasurer, controller, or other accounting officer. It is also the responsibility of the accounting department to determine and record the amount of insurance expense applicable to each accounting period.

The contract between the insurer and the insured is called the *insurance policy*, and the amount paid for the contract is called the *insurance premium*. Insurance policies are written for a definite amount and for a definite period of time, most commonly for one, three, or five years. The amount of insurance that should be carried on a particular asset does not necessarily correspond to its original cost or book value. The reproduction cost of the asset less accumulated depreciation thereon is a better criterion of the appropriate coverage. In any event the insured may not recover more than the actual loss incurred.

A large firm may have literally hundreds of insurance policies in effect. For even a small business the number may be considerable. The review of insurance coverage and the determination of periodic insurance

INSURANCE

DATE OF POLICY		POLICY NO.	INSURER	PROPERTY OR PURPOSE	AMOUNT	TERM	EXPIRATION DATE	UNEXPIRED PREMIUM	
1956									
Mar.	5	24983	Midland Fire	Store Equip.	5,000	5	3/5/61	2	96
Oct.	18	469AC	National Fire	Building	30,000	5	10/18/61	110	00
1958									
Jan.	30	9847	U. S. Fire	Office Equip.	2,000	3	1/30/61		60
June	4	79481	Acme Fire & Cas.	Merchandise	25,000	3	6/4/61	47	75
July	20	A3971	American Fire	Building	5,000	3	7/20/61	13	37
Nov.	3	4948	National Fire	Merchandise	6,000	3	11/3/61	22	90
1959									
Feb.	10	36421	Midland Fire	Office Equip.	2,000	3	2/10/62	7	93
Sept.	26	874AD	National Fire	Store Equip.	4,000	3	9/26/62	25	41
1960									
Apr.	3	4967	Phoenix Mutual	Merchandise	10,000	5	4/3/65	168	81
May	26	1121X	Liberty Auto	Delivery Equip.		1	5/26/61	225	00
Aug.	13	11214	U. S. Fire	Building	10,000	3	8/13/63	118	42
Aug.	19	F2184	Bankers Surety	Fidelity	10,000	1	8/19/61	136	00
Oct.	1	6947	Columbia Fire & Cas.	Public Liability	100,000	1	10/1/61	94	50
1961									
Jan.	30	12496	U. S. Fire	Office Equip.	3,000	3	1/31/64	33	12
Mar.	5	37468	Midland Fire	Store Equip.	5,000	5	3/5/66	90	60
Apr.	2	2396Y	Liberty Auto	Delivery Equip.		1	4/21/62	180	00
May	26	2694Y	Liberty Auto	Delivery Equip.		1	5/26/62	542	40
June	4	96423	Acme Fire & Cas.	Merchandise	25,000	3	6/4/64	346	32

Insurance register, left page

expense are facilitated by the use of a multicolumn form termed an insurance register.

An insurance register for a small business is illustrated below. The data for the insurance policies in effect at the beginning of the year are taken from the register for the preceding year; policies acquired during the year are recorded in the order of their acquisition. At the end of each month the insurance expense for that month is determined by adding the appropriate column. For example, the June expiration column in the illustration is totaled at the end of that month and an adjusting entry debiting Insurance Expense and crediting Prepaid Insurance for $123.90 is recorded in the general journal.

At the end of the year the total expired premiums and the two unexpired premium columns are added. The total of the first unexpired premium column should agree with the total debits to Prepaid Insurance, the total of the expired premiums column should agree with the credits to the account, and the total of the last column should agree with the balance of Prepaid Insurance after all adjustments have been posted.

REGISTER — 1961

JAN.	FEB.	MAR.	APR.	MAY	JUNE	JULY	AUG.	SEPT.	OCT.	NOV.	DEC.	TOTAL	UNEXPIRED PREMIUM
1 48	1 48											2 96	—
11 00	11 00	11 00	11 00	11 00	11 00	11 00	11 00	11 00	11 00			110 00	—
60												60	—
9 55	9 55	9 55	9 55	9 55								47 75	—
1 91	1 91	1 91	1 91	1 91	1 91	1 91						13 37	—
2 29	2 29	2 29	2 29	2 29	2 29	2 29	2 29	2 29	2 29			22 90	—
61	61	61	61	61	61	61	61	61	61	61	61	7 32	61
1 21	1 21	1 21	1 21	1 21	1 21	1 21	1 21	1 21	1 21	1 21	1 21	14 52	10 89
3 31	3 31	3 31	3 31	3 31	3 31	3 31	3 31	3 31	3 31	3 31	3 31	39 72	129 09
45 00	45 00	45 00	45 00	45 00								225 00	—
3 82	3 82	3 82	3 82	3 82	3 82	3 82	3 82	3 82		3 82	3 82	45 84	72 58
17 00	17 00	17 00	17 00	17 00	17 00	17 00	17 00					136 00	—
10 50	10 50	10 50	10 50	10 50	10 50	10 50	10 50	10 50				94 50	—
	92	92	92	92	92	92	92	92	92	92	92	10 12	23 00
		1 51	1 51	1 51	1 51	1 51	1 51	1 51	1 51	1 51	1 51	15 10	75 50
			15 00	15 00	15 00	15 00	15 00	15 00	15 00	15 00	15 00	135 00	45 00
					45 20	45 20	45 20	45 20	45 20	45 20	45 20	316 40	226 00
					9 62	9 62	9 62	9 62	9 62	9 62	9 62	67 34	278 98
108 28	108 60	108 63	123 63	123 63	123 90								

Insurance register, right page

Alternative account forms

The first ledger form illustrated in the text was a formalized version of the T account, the left half being designated for debits and the right half for credits. A form with debit, credit, and balance columns has been used for the subsidiary accounts in the customers' and creditors' ledgers. The balances in customers' accounts are normally debits and those in creditors' accounts are normally credits. An opposite balance may be identified by an asterisk or other notation, or it may be recorded in red. Posting machines automatically identify such balances. The same three-column forms may be used for general ledger accounts, in which case it is advisable to identify each balance as debit or credit to avoid errors and confusion, particularly when taking a trial balance.

There are many forms of ledger accounts available. One that is widely used provides two balance columns, one identified as debit and the other as credit. This form is illustrated below. When the posting to the accounts is performed manually, it is customary to compute and record the balance in the account only at such times as the information is needed. Posting machines automatically record the balance after each posting. When an account is in balance, a line may be drawn through the balance column that is ordinarily used for that account. For example, after an expense account has been closed, a line is inserted in the debit balance column opposite the last entry.

CASH IN BANK   ACCT. No. 1111

DATE		ITEMS	POST. REF.	DEBIT	CREDIT	BALANCE DEBIT	BALANCE CREDIT
1962 Jan.	1	Balance				6,354 21	
	31		CR5	9,873 35			
	31		CP4		8,683 30	7,544 26	

ACCOUNTS PAYABLE   ACCT. No. 2113

DATE		ITEMS	POST. REF.	DEBIT	CREDIT	BALANCE DEBIT	BALANCE CREDIT
1962 Jan.	1	Balance					3,650 75
	31		P4		7,135 20		
	31		PR2	85 90			
	31		CP4	5,961 50			4,738 55

Four-column general ledger accounts

Use of accounting machines

Accounting records may be prepared manually or by the use of various machines. In small businesses all of the records, from the original documents through journalizing, posting, and the preparation of statements, may be prepared manually. Even in small businesses, however, the use of typewriters, adding machines, and cash registers is not uncommon. Preponderantly manual operations may also be aided by the use of carbons. For example, the sales invoice, journal record, and posting to the customer's account may be prepared simultaneously through the use of carbons.

As the volume and complexity of transactions performed by an enterprise increases, the recording process becomes more involved, and greater attention is given to increasing efficiency and reducing costs. Many machines include automatic devices for reducing errors and quickly detecting those that do occur; they also classify and summarize data at far greater speeds than are possible by manual operations. Timeliness in preparing accounting reports for the use of management is of the utmost importance. It is also important that weekly pay checks for a firm with thousands of employees be prepared accurately and on time.

Transactions may be recorded by means of punched holes in a card. Sorting and collating machines are then used to assemble, classify, and merge the financial data, and finally, summaries of the data are automatically printed by tabulating equipment. One of the recently devised systems employs magnetic ink in recording data. This medium was used to record the identification number of the bank and of the depositor in the check illustrated on page 284. Upon receipt of such checks by the drawee bank, the amount for which the check is drawn is typed in magnetic ink in the lower right section. The checks are then sorted and posted to depositors' accounts by machines that "read" the magnetic characters.

The use of electronic data processing equipment for record keeping has increased rapidly in recent years. Data enter into the equipment on magnetic tape, paper tape, or other media, in the form of a special system of notation called a *binary code*. The data are processed and stored in accordance with a series of instructions comprising a *program*, and the desired information emerges from high-speed printers.

Questions

1. When should the written evidence of business transactions be created?

2. Name five requisites of a properly designed accounting system.

3. (a) What is the meaning of internal control? (b) Do nearly all businesses need some degree of internal control?

4. Why should the responsibility for maintaining accounting records be separated from responsibility for custody of assets?

5. The doorman of a movie theater usually tears admission tickets in half and returns one half to the patron. In what way does this procedure operate as a part of internal control?

6. What principle of internal control is violated by assigning three sales clerks to the same cash drawer?

7. What purpose is served by preparing a duplicate deposit ticket?

8. Name and identify the three parties to a check.

9. What information is reported in a bank statement?

10. What is the purpose of preparing a bank reconciliation?

11. Identify each of the following reconciling items as: (1) an addition to the balance per bank, (2) a deduction from the balance per bank, (3) an addition to the balance per books, or (4) a deduction from the balance per books. (None of the transactions reported by bank debit and credit memorandums has been recorded by depositor.)

    (a) Deposit in transit.
    (b) Collection fees charged by bank.
    (c) Outstanding checks.
    (d) Check of a customer returned by bank to depositor because of insufficient funds.
    (e) Note collected by the bank.
    (f) Check for $10 charged by bank as $100.
    (g) Check drawn by depositor for $75 recorded in cash payments journal as $57.
    (h) Bank service charge.

12. Which of the items listed in Question 11 will require an entry in the depositor's books?

13. The procedures employed by Kent, Inc. for over the counter receipts are as follows: Each sales clerk counts the cash in his cash drawer at the close of business. He then removes the cash register tape and prepares the memorandum daily cash form, noting any discrepancies. An employee from the cashier's office recounts the cash, compares the total with the memorandum, and takes the cash to the cashier's office. (a) Indicate the weak link in internal control. (b) How can the weakness be corrected?

14. The procedures employed by Polk Company for mail receipts are as follows: The mail clerk sends all remittances and remittance advices to the cashier. The cashier deposits the cash in the bank and forwards the remittance advices and duplicate deposit slips to the accounting department. (a) Indicate the weak link in internal control. (b) How can the weakness be corrected?

15. The combined cash count of all cash registers at the close of business is $11.50 less than the cash sales indicated by the cash register tapes. What entry is made to record the discrepancy?

16. Is it possible for a firm that deposits all receipts and makes all payments by check to use a petty cash fund? Discuss.

17. The petty cash account has a debit balance of $200. At the end of the accounting period there is $50 in the petty cash fund. Should the fund be replenished as of the last day of the period? Discuss.

18. The assistant office manager, who is the custodian of the petty cash fund, is about to leave for his vacation. In his absence the authority to make disbursements from the fund is to be transferred to another employee. By what means can definite responsibility be assigned to the two employees?

19. What two purposes are served by an insurance register?

Exercises

1. After the cash receipts and cash payments journals are posted at the end of September, the cash in bank account has a balance of $6,370.84. The bank statement for September indicates a balance of $7,165.87. The reconciling items are as follows:

(a) Checks outstanding, $1,420.60.
(b) Bank debit memorandum for service charge, $5.20.
(c) Deposit in transit not recorded by bank, $638.37.
(d) A check for $79 in payment of advertising expense had been erroneously recorded in the cash payments journal as $97.

Prepare a bank reconciliation.

2. On the basis of the facts in Exercise 1 present the general journal entries that should be made by the depositor.

3. Accompanying a bank statement is a debit memorandum for $454.50, representing the principal ($450) and interest ($4.50) on a discounted note that had been dishonored by Blakely Co. The depositor had been notified by the bank at the time of the dishonor but had made no entries. Present the necessary entry by the depositor, in general journal form.

4. Present the entries, in general journal form, to record the following:

(a) A petty cash fund of $100 is established.
(b) A request for replenishment of the fund is accompanied by petty cash vouchers as follows: Miscellaneous Selling Expense, $38.40; Miscellaneous General Expense, $41.80; Supplies, $15.85. The fund is replenished.

5. The following insurance premiums were paid on policies acquired during the current fiscal year ending December 31:

POLICY	EFFECTIVE DATE	PREMIUM	TERM
(a)	January 2	$414	3 years
(b)	February 18	75	1 year
(c)	March 12	489	5 years
(d)	June 28	144	3 years

Determine the following amounts for each policy: (1) premium expired monthly, (2) premium expired during the year, (3) unexpired premium at the end of the year. A month is the minimum period of time to be considered in allocating premium expirations.

Problems

13-1. The bank statement for Century Motors indicates a balance of $7,483.90 on August 31 of the current year. Cash in Bank has a debit balance of $5,460.05 after the cash journals have been posted for August. Comparison of the statement, and the accompanying checks and memorandums, with the books reveals the following reconciling items:

(a) Checks outstanding total $2,696.55.

(b) The bank had credited Century Motors for the proceeds of a note left for collection: principal, $500.00; interest $10.00.

(c) A deposit of $1,360.20 had been made too late to appear on the bank statement.

(d) The bank charged Century Motors $2.50 as a collection fee.

(e) A check for $245.00 returned with the statement had been recorded in the books as $425.00. The check was in payment of a premium on a fire insurance policy.

Instructions: (1) Prepare a bank reconciliation.

(2) Journalize the necessary entries. Although the cash journals have already been posted, the books have not been closed.

13-2. Benson Supply Co. has just adopted the policy of depositing all cash receipts and making all payments by check. As of December 31, the close of the past year, all cash owned by the business was on deposit in a bank account. The following transactions relating to special funds were completed in January of the current year:

(a) Jan. 2. Drew Check No. 647 for $50 to Petty Cash to establish a petty cash fund.

2. Drew Check No. 648 for $400 to Cash, to establish a change fund.

(b) The following disbursements, each evidenced by a petty cash voucher, were made from the petty cash fund during the month:

Jan. 5. Postage, $12.00 (Office Supplies). Voucher No. 1.

9. Express charges on merchandise purchased, $8.35.

14. Newspapers, $1.10 (Misc. Gen. Expense).

17. Repairs to cash register $10.20 (Misc. Sell. Expense).

19. Delivery charges on merchandise sold, $5.85 (Delivery Expense).

22. Store supplies, $4.60.

25. Repairs to display case, $4.15 (Misc. Sell. Expense).

28. Newspapers, $1.10.

(c) Jan. 31. Drew Check No. 692 to replenish the petty cash fund.

31. The currency and coins in the change fund total $395.10. Memorandum records of the daily overages and shortages have been maintained but not recorded in the accounts. Drew Check No. 693 to restore the change fund to its original amount.

Instructions: (1) Open T accounts for Cash on Hand, 1112, and Petty Cash, 1113.

(2) Record the transactions of January 2 in a cash payments journal like that illustrated on page 292.

(3) Record the petty cash transactions in a petty cash analysis sheet like that illustrated on page 291.

(4) Record the transactions of January 31.

(5) Post to the two T accounts.

13-3. Mentor Specialties owns the following notes receivable on June 1. The firm has no contingent liability for notes receivable discounted on this date.

Our No.	Payable by	Payable at	Date of Note	Time	Face	Interest Rate
75	Brooks & Co.	Our office	Mar. 24	90 days	$ 295	—
76	W. S. Hatch Co.	Merchants Bank, City	Apr. 12	60 days	1,500	6%
77	John R. Dana	First National Bank, Troy	Apr. 16	90 days	850	6%
78	Central Corp.	Merchants Bank, City	Apr. 28	60 days	1,200	6%
79	Spencer Shop	First National Bank, Troy	May 8	30 days	600	6%
80	A. L. Murray	Our office	May 22	60 days	900	—

The following transactions affecting notes receivable were completed during June:

June 3. Discounted the Central Corp. note at Merchants Bank; discount rate, 6%.

4. Sent Spencer Shop's note to First National Bank for collection.

6. Received a 90-day, 6% note for $1,400 on account from Bigelow, Inc. The note is dated June 4 and is payable at Merchants Bank, City.

8. Received check from First National Bank for the principal and interest due on Spencer Shop's note, less a collection charge (Misc. General Expense) of $1.50.

9. Sent W. S. Hatch Co.'s note to Merchants Bank for collection.

12. Received notice from Merchants Bank that W. S. Hatch Co. dishonored their note. Charged the note to the maker's account.

15. Discounted the John R. Dana note at Merchants Bank; discount rate, 6%.

22. Received check from Brooks & Co. for note due today.

24. Received a 60-day, 6% note for $760 on account from Baker & Peck. The note is dated June 23 and is payable at our office.

30. Received a 30-day non-interest-bearing note for $400 from M. A. Harris on account. The note is dated June 28 and is payable at Citizens Bank, Lima.

Instructions: (1) Open a four-column account for Notes Receivable, 1115, and record the balance of $5,345 as of June 1 of the current year.

(2) Record the notes receivable listed above in a notes receivable register like the one illustrated in this chapter. Assume that the notes were received on the day that they are dated.

(3) Record the transactions in general journal form and make the necessary entries and notations in the notes receivable register.

(4) Post the journal entries to the notes receivable account in the general ledger and determine the balance at the end of the month.

(5) If a balance sheet is prepared as of June 30:

(a) At what amount will notes receivable be listed?

(b) What is the amount of the contingent liability for notes receivable discounted?

13-4. The following transactions are selected from those completed by Emerson Industries during January of the current year, the first month of operations:

Jan. 5. Issued check for $1,206 to Midland Fire Insurance Co. in payment of the premium on the following insurance policies, all dated January 3:

POLICY NO.	PROPERTY	AMOUNT	TERM	PREMIUM
4793	Building	$50,000	3 years	$630
4794	Merchandise	30,000	3 years	378
4795	Equipment	10,000	5 years	198

6. Issued three checks totaling $1,800 to sales representatives as advances on traveling expenses.

14. Issued check for $669 to Apex Casualty Insurance Co. in payment of premiums on insurance policies dated January 13. Details are as follows:

937AB	Delivery equip.		1 year	$540
8946	Public liability	$100,000	1 year	129

20. Issued check for $198 to Bankers Guaranty Insurance Co. in payment of premium on an insurance policy dated January 18. Details are as follows:

1864X	Fidelity	$10,000	1 year	$198

27. Issued check for $408 to American Fire Insurance Co. in payment of premium on an insurance policy dated January 25. Details are as follows:

15933	Merchandise	$20,000	5 years	$408

31. Received reports from the three sales representatives indicating expenditures for travel totaling $1,565. Issued three checks totaling $1,565 to the representatives.

Instructions: (1) Open the following accounts in the general ledger, using the four-column form illustrated in this chapter:

Advances to Salesmen, 1114   Travel Expense, 6117
Prepaid Insurance, 1120   Insurance Expense, 7118

(2) Record the transactions in general journal form and post to the accounts.

(3) Record the data in an insurance register like the one illustrated in this chapter. One month is the minimum length of time to be considered in allocating insurance expirations.

(4) Journalize the insurance adjustment as of January 31 and post to the accounts.

(5) Considering only the insurance policies acquired in January:

  (a) What will be the total amount of insurance expired during the year?
  (b) What will be the total amount of unexpired insurance at December 31?

13-5. All data necessary for reconciling the bank statement of Roberts College Shop as of March 31 of the current year are presented below.

Balance in the cash in bank account as of March 1 . . . . $6,424.60
Total of Cash in Bank Dr. column in cash receipts journal for
  March. 7,695.30

All receipts are deposited after banking hours twice each week and on the last day of the month. The firm's records indicate the following deposits during March.

DATE	AMOUNT	DATE	AMOUNT	DATE	AMOUNT
Mar. 4	$ 642.20	Mar. 14	$1,272.30	Mar. 25	$ 784.40
7	1,136.80	18	843.50	28	1,023.70
11	597.60	21	930.90	31	463.90

Total of Cash in Bank Cr. column in cash payments journal for
March... $6,499.50

The numbers of the checks and the amounts recorded in the cash payments
journal during March are as follows:

CHECK No.	AMOUNT	CHECK No.	AMOUNT	CHECK No.	AMOUNT
845	$150.60	853	$127.80	861	$348.10
846	42.30	854	98.70	862	65.20
847	386.20	855	243.90	863	190.80
848	3.50	856	475.80	864	200.00
849	12.70	857	723.40	865	674.30
850	568.10	858	24.50	866	542.10
851	432.20	859	100.00	867	130.80
852	292.30	860	250.00	868	416.20

The bank reconciliation for February 28 of the current year is as follows:
Balance per bank statement............................. $7,013.70
Add: Deposit of February 28, not recorded by bank........ 736.20

$7,749.90

Deduct: Outstanding checks
        No. 801 $145.60
        825   22.80
        842   560.10
        843   215.30
        844   381.50......................... 1,325.30

Adjusted balance...................................... $6,424.60

Balance per books..................................... $6,427.50
Deduct: Collection and service charges................... 2.90

Adjusted balance...................................... $6,424.60

Data selected from the bank statement for March are as follows:
Balance, March 1..................................... $7,013.70
Deposits:

DATE	AMOUNT	DATE	AMOUNT	DATE	AMOUNT
Mar. 1	$ 736.20	Mar. 12	$ 597.60	Mar. 22	$ 930.90
5	642.20	15	1,272.30	26	784.40
8	1,136.80	19	843.50	29	1,023.70

Balance, March 31.................................... $7,590.80

Bank memos and checks accompanying the bank statement are as follows,
with the checks arranged in numerical order:
Bank debit memo for service and collection fees.............. $ 4.50
Bank debit memo for check returned because of insufficient funds   120.00
Bank credit memo for note collected: principal, $200; interest, $2   202.00

CHECK No.	AMOUNT	CHECK No.	AMOUNT	CHECK No.	AMOUNT
801	$145.60	851	$432.20	859	$100.00
842	560.10	852	292.30	860	250.00
844	381.50	853	217.80	861	348.10
845	150.60	854	98.70	863	190.80
846	42.30	855	243.90	864	200.00
847	386.20	856	475.80	865	674.30
848	3.50	857	723.40	866	542.10
850	568.10	858	24.50	868	416.20

Instructions: (1) Prepare a bank reconciliation for March 31.

(2) Present in general journal form the entries to be recorded in the cash receipts and cash payments journals as of March 31. If errors in recording checks are discovered, assume that such checks were in payment of accounts payable. Assume also that the titles of subsidiary accounts will be inserted later.

13-6. The bank statement for Burton Construction Co. for June of the current year indicates a balance of $25,470.66 on June 30. The balance according to the check stubs as of the same date is $26,665.90. The balance of Cash in Bank, in the ledger as of June 1, is $26,460.50; pencil footings of the cash receipts and cash payments journals for June indicate receipts and payments for the month of $94,315.60 and $92,290.80, respectively. Comparison of the statement and the accompanying checks and memorandums reveals the following reconciling items:

(a) Checks outstanding: No. 982, $124.30; No. 1046, $12.50; No. 1053, $275.00; No. 1054, $315.10; No. 1055, $18.46; No. 1057, $450.00.

(b) A counter check for $100.00 included with the canceled checks had not been recorded in the cash payments journal or the check stubs. It was a personal withdrawal of cash by A. R. Burton, the proprietor.

(c) A deposit of $5,640.00 on June 15 had not been recorded in the check stubs. The cash received, all of which was deposited, had been properly recorded in the cash receipts journal.

(d) A returned check for $330.00 was erroneously charged on the bank statement as $380.00.

(e) A deposit of $3,820.60 on June 20 had been recorded twice in the check stubs. There was no error in the cash receipts journal.

(f) A debit memorandum indicated that the bank had deducted the principal, $4,000.00, and interest, $60.00, on a note that had been discounted at the bank by Burton Construction Co. Prior notice of the failure of Plaza Market Co. to pay the note and of the bank's charge had been received by Burton Construction Co. but no entry had been made in either the cash payments journal or the check stubs.

Instructions: (1) Prepare a reconciliation of the bank statement with the cash in bank account after giving effect to receipts and disbursements already recorded in the cash journals.

(2) Determine the net amount of the adjustment to the check stub balance as of June 30, presenting the computations.

(3) Present, in general journal form, the entries that should be made in the cash journals before they are ruled and posted.

Voucher system

Control of cash payments

The routing of all funds through a bank account is an essential part of all systems for controlling cash. It is common practice for both business enterprises and nonprofit organizations to require that every payment of cash be evidenced by a check signed by designated officials. A seeming exception to the system is made for payments from petty cash and other special funds. As was demonstrated in the preceding chapter, however, checks are employed in reimbursing such funds so that they too are kept under control.

When the owner of a business has personal knowledge of all goods and services purchased, he may sign checks with the assurance that the creditors have complied with the terms of their contracts and that he is paying the exact amount of the obligation. Such all-embracing knowledge of affairs by disbursing officials is seldom possible, however. In enterprises of even moderate size the responsibility for issuing purchase orders, inspecting commodities received, and verifying contractual and arithmetical details of invoices is divided among the employees of various departments. It is desirable, therefore, to coordinate these related activities and to link them with the ultimate issuance of checks to creditors. One of the systems employed for this purpose is known as the *voucher system.*

Basic features of the voucher system

A voucher system is composed of records, methods, and procedures employed in (1) verifying and recording liabilities and (2) paying and recording cash payments. As in all other sections of systems of accounting and internal control, there are many possible variations in detail. The discussion and the illustrations that follow are based on the assumption of a merchandising enterprise of moderate size, with separate departments for purchasing, receiving, accounting, and disbursing.

A voucher system employs (1) vouchers, (2) a voucher register, (3) a file for unpaid vouchers, (4) a check register, and (5) a file for paid vouchers. The term *voucher* is widely used in accounting. In a general sense it means any document that serves as evidence of authority to pay cash, such as an invoice approved for payment, or as evidence that cash has been paid, such as a canceled check. The term has a narrower meaning when applied to the voucher system: a voucher is a special form on which is recorded pertinent data about a liability and the particulars of its payment. The invoice and other supporting documents are often attached to the special form so that the treasurer's department has all of the evidence necessary to authenticate the amount of the indebtedness and to approve its payment.

The voucher register is a multicolumn journal in which all vouchers are recorded. It is similar to and replaces the purchases journal described in Chapter 7. It contains special columns and a sundry column for recording debits to Purchases and other accounts, and a column for recording credits to Accounts Payable. In addition, space is provided for indicating the date each voucher is paid and the number of the check issued in payment.

After a voucher is recorded in the voucher register, it is filed in an unpaid voucher file, where it remains until it is paid. The amount due on each voucher represents the credit balance of an account payable, and the voucher itself is comparable to an individual account in a subsidiary accounts payable ledger; accordingly, a separate subsidiary ledger is unnecessary.

The check register is a columnar journal in which all payments are recorded. It is similar to and replaces the cash payments journal described in Chapter 7. Each check issued is in payment of a voucher that has previously been recorded as an account payable in the voucher register. The effect of each entry in the check register is consequently a debit to Accounts Payable and a credit to Cash in Bank.

After the payment of a voucher is recorded in the check register, the voucher is placed in a paid voucher file. Thereafter the vouchers in the paid voucher file may be examined by employees or independent auditors requiring information about a specific invoice. Eventually the paid vouchers are destroyed in accordance with the firm's policies on the retention of records.

The following flow chart illustrates the routing of a voucher for a $500 purchase of merchandise, the entry in the voucher register to record the purchase, and the entry in the check register to record the payment of the liability.

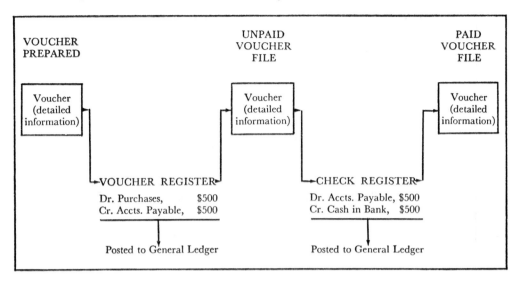

Preparation of vouchers

A voucher form is illustrated on page 308. The face of the voucher provides spaces for the name and address of the creditor, the date and number of the voucher, and pertinent details of the invoice or other supporting document, such as the vendor's invoice number and the amount and terms of the invoice. One half of the back of the voucher is devoted to the account distribution and the other half to a summary of the voucher and the details of payment. Spaces are also provided for the signature or initials of various employees.

Vouchers are customarily prepared by the accounting department on the basis of an invoice or a memorandum that serves as evidence of the expenditure. This is usually done only after the following comparisons and verifications have been completed and noted on the invoice.

1. Comparison with a copy of the purchase order to verify quantities, prices, and terms.
2. Comparison with the receiving report to determine receipt of the items billed.
3. Verification of the arithmetical accuracy of the invoice.

Spaces for indicating the accounts to be debited are provided in the account distribution section of the voucher. Titles of the accounts most frequently debited may be printed on the form; other titles are inserted as needed.

The use of the remaining sections of the back of the voucher is largely self-evident. If there should be a reduction in the voucher because of a return or an allowance, the amount is inserted in the space provided for "Adjustment." Ordinarily the details of such reductions

VOUCHER   No. **641**

D. L. MARTIN CO.

Date __November 1, 1961__

Payee _____Superior Wholesale Company_____

_____1043 N. Atlantic Avenue_____

_____New York 12, New York_____

Date	Details	Amount
October 29, 1961	Invoice. No. 4693-C F.O.B. New York, 2/10, n/30	450.00

Attach Supporting Papers

Voucher — face

ACCOUNT DISTRIBUTION			VOUCHER No. **641**

Date __11-1-1961__   Due __11-8-1961__

Debit	Amount		
Purchases	450	00	
Store Supplies •			
Advertising Exp.			
Delivery Exp.			
Misc. Selling Exp.			
Misc. General Exp.			

Payee
Superior Wholesale Company
1043 N. Atlantic Avenue.
New York 12, New York

Voucher Summary

Amount	450	00
Adjustment		
Discount	9	00
Net	441	00

Approved *R. G. Davis*   Controller

Recorded *T. N.*

Payment Summary

Date   11-8-61

Amount   441.00

Check No.   633

Approved *C. S. Reed*   Treasurer

Recorded *B. W.*   *RM*

Credit Accounts Payable	450	00

Distribution Approved *G. B. White*

Voucher — back

in the amount of the liability will become known during the process of verifying the invoice and will be given effect in determining the amount of the voucher.

After all data except details of payment have been inserted, the invoice or other supporting evidence is attached to the face of the voucher and it is then folded, with the account distribution and summaries on the outside. At the time the treasurer or other disbursing officer pays the voucher, the date, the check number, and the amount are inserted in the appropriate spaces.

An important characteristic of the voucher system is the requirement that a voucher must be prepared for each expenditure. In fact, a check may not be issued except in payment of a properly authorized voucher. As was indicated earlier in this section, the voucher for a purchase of merchandise is ordinarily not prepared until after the goods have been received and the correctness of the invoice has been determined. The same procedure would apply to expenditures for supplies, equipment, and other tangible assets. Such vouchers may be paid immediately after they are prepared or at a later date, depending upon the credit terms. Vouchers for expenditures that accrue from day to day, such as salaries and electric power, are prepared for the period for which payment is to be made. For example, a voucher for salaries would be prepared for a weekly, biweekly, or other payroll period; a voucher for electric power would be prepared on the basis of the monthly billing from the utility company.

Voucher register

After approval by the designated official, each voucher is recorded in a journal known as a *voucher register*. It is usually ruled to provide columns for the date of the entry, the voucher number, the name of the payee, the date of payment, and the number of the check issued in payment. In addition, it contains one amount column for recording credits to the accounts payable account and a variable number of amount columns for recording debits.

A typical form of a voucher register is illustrated on pages 310 and 311. The vouchers are entered in numerical sequence, each being recorded as a credit to Accounts Payable (sometimes entitled Vouchers Payable) and as a debit to the account or accounts to be charged for the expenditure. Debits to accounts for which there is no special column are recorded in the Sundry Accounts Debit section of the register.

When a voucher is paid, the date of payment and the number of the check are inserted in the appropriate columns in the voucher register. The effect of such notations is to provide a ready means of determining

VOUCHER REGISTER

	DATE	VCHR. NO	PAYEE	PAID DATE	CHK. NO.	ACCOUNTS PAYABLE CR.	PURCHASES DR.	
	1961							
1	Nov. 1	641	Superior Company	11–8	633	450 00	450 00	1
2	1	642	Adams Realty Co.	11–1	626	600 00		2
3	2	643	Foster Publications	11–2	627	52 50		3
4	3	644	Benson Express Co.	11–3	629	36 80	24 20	4
5	3	645	Office Outfitters			784 20		5
6	3	646	Moore & Co.	11–11	640	1,236 00	1,236 00	6
7	6	647	J. L. Brown Co.	11–6	631	22 50		7
8	6	648	Turner Corp.			395 30	395 30	8
43	28	683	Mason & Whitney, Inc.			235 10	235 10	43
44	28	684	Stone & Co.	11–29	670	14 30		44
45	29	685	Evans Corp.	11–29	671	1,015 00		45
46								46
47	30	686	Central Motors			112 20		47
48	30	687	Petty Cash	11–30	673	48 60		48
49	30					15,551 60	11,640 30	49
50						(2113)	(5111)	50

Voucher register — left page

at any time the amount of individual unpaid vouchers. The total amount of the outstanding liability can also be determined at any time by adding the individual amounts of the vouchers indicated by the voucher register as being unpaid.

At the end of the month all of the amount columns are totaled and the equality of debits and credits is verified. Any errors discovered are corrected before the posting is begun. The individual amounts in the Sundry Accounts Dr. column are posted as debits to the accounts indicated; the total of the column is not posted. The totals of the other amount columns are posted to the accounts indicated in the columnar headings, Accounts Payable as a credit and the others as debits. Posting references are inserted in the usual manner.

Unpaid voucher file

After a voucher is recorded in the voucher register, it is placed in the unpaid voucher file. Each voucher is comparable to a creditor's account and the entire file constitutes the subsidiary accounts payable ledger.

There are variations in systems for filing unpaid vouchers, but all systems include some provision for efficiently determining the amounts to be paid each day. The method of filing invoices by due date described

VOUCHER REGISTER

| | STORE SUPPLIES DR. | ADV. EXP. DR. | DEL. EXP. DR. | MISC. SELLING EXP. DR. | MISC. GENERAL EXP. DR. | SUNDRY ACCOUNTS DR. | | | |
						ACCOUNT	POST. REF.	AMOUNT	
1									1
2						Rent Expense	6114	600 00	2
3		52 50							3
4				12 60					4
5	34 20					Office Equipment	1313	750 00	5
6									6
7					22 50				7
8									8
43					14 30				43
44					14 30				44
45						Notes Payable	2111	1,000 00	45
46						Interest Expense	9111	15 00	46
47			112 20						47
48	4 30		16 20	19 50	8 60				48
49	59 80	176 40	286 10	48 30	64 90			3,275 80	49
50	(1119)	(6112)	(6113)	(6117)	(7123)			(√)	50

Voucher register — right page

in Chapter 7 is equally acceptable for filing vouchers. It brings to the attention of the disbursing official the vouchers that are to be paid on each day. It also provides management with a convenient means of continuously forecasting the amount of funds needed to meet maturing obligations.

Filing unpaid vouchers by due date does not provide a direct means of locating vouchers payable to a particular creditor. If this is an important consideration, the unpaid vouchers may be filed alphabetically by creditors. Classification of vouchers by due date is then maintained in a supplementary record known as a *tickler*. An alternative is to prepare all vouchers in duplicate. The originals are then filed according to due date and the carbon copies are filed by name of creditor.

When a voucher is to be paid, it is removed from the file and a check is issued in payment. The date, the number, and the amount of the check are inserted on the outside of the voucher for use in recording the payment in the check register.

Check register

The payment of a voucher is recorded in a *check register*, an example of which is illustrated on page 312. The check register is a modified form of the cash payments journal and is so called because it is a complete record of all checks. Payments are recorded by debits to Accounts Payable and credits to Cash in Bank. Any cash discounts taken are recorded in the Purchases Discount Cr. column. Check forms are usually prenumbered as an aid in establishing control. It is therefore customary to record all checks in the check register in sequential order, including occasional checks that are voided because of an error in their preparation.

In order to plan future expenditures intelligently, to take advantage of all available cash discounts, and to maintain a high credit rating, it is essential that the treasurer's department know the amount of cash available at all times. The use of check stubs in maintaining such a continuous record was illustrated in the preceding chapter. An alternative procedure is to record bank deposits and balances in memorandum columns of the check register, as is done in the illustration. It has the advantage of greater convenience and avoids the necessity of repeating details on the check stubs that are already available in the check register. It should be noted that the columns for Bank Deposits and Bank Balance

CHECK REGISTER

	DATE	CHK. NO.		PAYEE	VCHR. NO.	ACCOUNTS PAYABLE DR.	PURCHASES DISCOUNT CR.	CASH IN BANK CR.	BANK		
									DEPOSITS	BALANCE	
	1961									8,743|10	
1	Nov.	1	626	Adams Realty Co.	642	600|00		600|00	1,240|30	9,383|40	1
2		2	627	Foster Publications	643	52|50		52|50		9,330|90	2
3		2	628	Hill and Davis	636	1,420|00	14|20	1,405|80	865|70	8,790|80	3
4		3	629	Benson Exp. Co.	644	36|80		36|80	942|20	9,696|20	4
5		3	630	L. D. Scott Co.	628	1,510|60		1,510|60	752|30	8,937|90	5
6		6	631	J. L. Brown Co.	647	22|50		22|50	846|10	9,761|50	6
7		8	632	Office Outfitters	630	350|00		350|00		9,411|50	7
8		8	633	Superior Company	641	450|00	9|00	441|00	1,016|40	9,986|90	8
42		29	668	Voided							42
43		29	669	Valley Power Co.	681	39|40		39|40		9,536|10	43
44		29	670	Stone & Co.	684	14|30		14|30		9,521|80	44
45		29	671	Evans Corp.	685	1,015|00		1,015|00	765|50	9,272|30	45
46		30	672	Graham & Co.	659	830|00	16|60	813|40		8,458|90	46
47		30	673	Petty Cash	687	48|60		48|60	938|10	9,348|40	47
48		30				17,322|90	198|20	17,124|70			48
49						(2113)	(5113)	(1111)			49

Check register

are memorandum in nature; their use has no effect on the cash receipts journal nor on posting procedures.

The amount columns in the check register are totaled and debit-credit equality is proved at the end of each month in the usual manner. Only the totals of the columns are posted to the general ledger.

Paid voucher file

After payment is recorded in the check register, the voucher is forwarded to the voucher register clerk for the recording of the date and the check number in the voucher register. The voucher is then filed for future reference. The file of paid vouchers may be maintained in numerical order to permit easy review by the auditors. Cross referencing by name of creditors may be provided by an alphabetical file of carbon copies of the vouchers or by maintaining a card file of creditors on which the voucher numbers are recorded.

Comparison of controlling account with unpaid vouchers

When the voucher system is employed, the vouchers in the unpaid voucher file are comparable to a subsidiary ledger for accounts payable. At the end of each month the balance in the accounts payable account should be compared with the total of the unpaid vouchers to determine that the two records are in agreement.

After the voucher register and the check register illustrated earlier in this chapter are posted for the month, the accounts payable account in the ledger appears as follows:

ACCOUNTS PAYABLE   ACCT. No. 2113

| | | POST. | | | BALANCE | |
DATE	ITEMS	REF.	DEBIT	CREDIT	DEBIT	CREDIT
1961						
Nov. 1	Balance	√				9,388 80
30		VR26		15,551 60		
30		CP26	17,322 90			7,617 50

The list of unpaid vouchers may be prepared from the vouchers or from the voucher register. When prepared from the voucher register, it is necessary to scan the pages for the preceding month or as far back as there may be vouchers outstanding. If the amount of a voucher has been reduced by a credit memorandum, it is also necessary to refer to the voucher for the revised amount of the liability. The list supporting the balance in the accounts payable account above is as follows:

D. L. Martin Co.
Schedule of Unpaid Vouchers
November 30, 1961

NUMBER	PAYEE	AMOUNT
645	Office Outfitters	$ 784.20
648	Turner Corp................................	395.30
665	Modern Furniture Co........................	1,840.60
668	Bell Supply Co.............................	936.80
672	Landon & Norris............................	475.10
673	Caldwell Corp..............................	1,682.30
674	A. T. Stafford Co..........................	319.70
679	Taylor & Baker, Inc........................	836.20
683	Mason & Whitney, Inc.......................	235.10
686	Central Motors.............................	112.20
		$7,617.50

Special problems

Most of the transactions recorded in the voucher register illustrated earlier in this chapter were routine expenditures for goods and services. The two exceptions were Voucher No. 685 for the payment of a note and interest, and Voucher No. 687 for the reimbursement of the petty cash fund.

The significant aspect of the note transaction is its timing. The liability for the $1,000, 6%, 90-day note had been properly recorded at the time of its issuance as a credit to Notes Payable. The effect of

VOUCHER REGISTER

	DATE	VCHR. NO.	PAYEE	PAID DATE	PAID CHK. NO.	ACCOUNTS PAYABLE CR.	PURCHASES DR.	
1	1961 Dec. 1	688	Thomas & Bryan	12–8	By note	2,000 00	2,000 00	1
16	12	703	Moore & Co.		A	1,000 00	1,000 00	16
22	15	709	Apex Equipment Co.	12–16	692	500 00		22
23		710	Apex Equipment Co.			500 00		23
24		711	Apex Equipment Co.			500 00		24
33	20	720	Furniture Mart	12–28	Vchr. 731–3	2,100 00		33
41	28	731	Furniture Mart	12–28	716	700 00		41
42		732	Furniture Mart			700 00		42
43		733	Furniture Mart			700 00		43

the entry to record the voucher on November 29 was to transfer the liability from Notes Payable to Accounts Payable. Such an entry is appropriate only if it is accompanied by an entry in the check register debiting Accounts Payable and crediting Cash in Bank, which was the case in the illustration. If a balance sheet date were to intervene between the recording of the voucher and its payment, the liability would be incorrectly classified as an account payable instead of a note payable. A similar situation may arise in connection with accruals, such as the accrual of property taxes; the voucher should not be prepared and recorded until the date of payment, otherwise taxes payable may be incorrectly reported on the balance sheet as accounts payable.

The point to be noted in connection with the voucher for petty cash is that the expenditures of $48.60 recorded in the voucher register are supported by petty cash vouchers. The check for $48.60 issued in payment of the voucher is then cashed and the money is placed in the petty cash fund, restoring the fund to its original amount.

Changes in the amount of a voucher or changes in plans for payment occurring after a voucher has been recorded require special treatment. The effects of such modifications on the operation of the voucher system are discussed in the paragraphs that follow.

Issuance of notes payable. When a note is issued in settlement of a voucher, the transaction is recorded by a general journal entry similar to the one shown at the top of the following page.

VOUCHER REGISTER

| | STORE SUPPLIES DR. | ADV. EXP. DR. | DEL. EXP. DR. | MISC. SELLING EXP. DR. | MISC. GENERAL EXP. DR. | SUNDRY ACCOUNTS DR. | | AMOUNT | |
						ACCOUNT	P R.		
1									1
16									16
22						Store Equipment		1,50 00	22
23									23
24									24
33						Office Equipment		2,100 00	33
41						Accounts Payable		2,100 00	41
42									42
43									43

Dec.	8	Accounts Payable	2,000	
		Notes Payable		2,000
		Issued in settlement of Voucher		
		No. 688.		

The date of the entry and the notation "By note" are inserted in the Payment Summary section of the voucher and in the Paid column of the voucher register, as illustrated by Voucher 688 in the voucher register on page 314. The voucher is then filed in the paid voucher file.

Purchases returns and allowances. As has already been indicated, vouchers are not prepared and submitted for approval until the necessary comparisons and verifications have been completed; hence any adjustments to the invoice arising from returns, allowances, or arithmetical errors are ordinarily resolved in the process. Although it would be possible to record the voucher at the invoice amount and then to record the adjustment in a separate entry, the value of accumulating the additional information in the accounts is usually not worth the extra time and cost; consequently it is customary to prepare the voucher for the revised amount. To illustrate, assume that in the process of verifying an invoice for $1,000 of merchandise it is determined that items billed at $100 do not correspond with the purchase order and are to be returned. Both the purchase of $1,000 and the return of $100 could be recorded in the accounts, but the more practicable alternative is to record the purchase at $900. The invoice and the memorandum evidencing the return would be attached to the voucher and the voucher would be made out for $900.

An adjustment in the amount of a voucher occurring after it has been entered in the voucher register is recorded as an entry in the general journal. For example, assume that in the foregoing illustration the merchandise had appeared to be satisfactory but that after the voucher for $1,000 had been recorded a latent defect is discovered in items billed at $100. The entry to record the return appears below. It should be noted that the return is credited directly to Purchases; there would be little merit in crediting only a portion of returns and allowances to a separate account.

Dec.	10	Accounts Payable.................	100	
		Purchases......................		100
		Adjustment to Voucher No. 703		

The memorandum evidencing the return is attached to the voucher in the unpaid voucher file and the amount of the voucher is reduced by $100. These procedures are necessary to insure that the check in payment of the voucher is drawn for $900. In order to call attention to the fact that the amount entered in the voucher register no longer is the amount of the voucher, the letter "A" (for adjustment), or other appropriate notation, should be inserted in the Paid column, as illustrated by Voucher 703 on page 314. If such adjustments are frequent, an additional memorandum column for disclosing the specific amounts may be provided in the voucher register.

Installment and partial payments. Occasionally the liability incurred in the acquisition of an asset is paid in installments over a period of time. If the amounts and the dates of the installment payments are established by the original terms of the agreement, a separate voucher should be prepared for each installment. The use of a single voucher that is partially paid and partially unpaid is likely to lead to uncertainties and time-consuming errors. The method of recording a series of vouchers in the voucher register is illustrated by Vouchers 709, 710, and 711 in the illustration on page 314.

If the decision to pay an invoice in installments is made after the single voucher for the entire amount has been recorded, the original voucher is marked "Canceled" and separate vouchers are prepared for each anticipated payment. An additional entry debiting and crediting Accounts Payable is also recorded in the voucher register. This type of situation is illustrated by the entries for Vouchers 720, 731, 732, and 733 in the illustration on page 314.

Purchases discount

Purchases of merchandise are customarily recorded at the invoice price and cash discounts taken are credited to the purchases discount account at the time of payment. There are two methods of reporting such purchases discount.

The most widely accepted view is that discounts taken represent adjustments to the quoted price of the goods. Accordingly, the balance of Purchases Discount should be reported in the income statement as a deduction from Purchases. This has been the practice in this text. For example, the cost of merchandise with an invoice price of $1,000, subject to terms of 2/10, n/30, is recorded initially at $1,000. If payment is made within the discount period, the discount of $20 reduces the cost to $980. If the invoice is not paid until after the discount period, the cost of the merchandise remains at $1,000.

The foregoing treatment of discounts taken may be attacked on the grounds that the date of payment should not affect the cost of a commodity. The additional payment required beyond the discount date adds nothing to the value of the goods; it is in the nature of an expense.

An alternative method of reporting purchases discount taken is based on the view that such discounts are in the nature of interest earned on funds paid to the creditor before the due date of the obligation. According to this concept the balance of Purchases Discount should be reported in the income statement as "Other Income." In terms of the example above, the cost of the merchandise is considered to be $1,000 regardless of the time of payment. If payment is made within ten days, revenue of $20 is realized.

The objection to this alternative procedure, which is still employed to some extent, lies in its recognition of revenue from the act of purchasing a commodity. Theoretically, an enterprise might make no sales of merchandise during an accounting period yet report as revenue the amount of the cash discounts taken.

Cash discounts lost. A third view of discounts on commodities purchased considers them to be price adjustments regardless of when payment is made. When this system is employed, the amount of the discount available is deducted from the invoice at the outset and only the net amount is recorded in the accounts. Again assuming the same data as in the preceding sections, the invoice for $1,000 would be recorded as a debit to Purchases of $980 and a credit to Accounts Payable for the same amount.

Efficiently managed enterprises maintain sufficient working capital to pay within the discount period all invoices that are subject to a cash discount. It is therefore only rarely that the amount paid to a creditor will exceed the net amount recorded as the liability. When it does occur, the excess amount is debited to Discounts Lost rather than to Purchases or to the asset for which payment is being made. The balance in Discounts Lost should be reported in the income statement as an expense.

It should be noted that under this system cash discounts are strictly construed as an adjustment to a quoted price. If upon occasion the purchaser does not receive the benefit of the lower price because of late payment, the excess amount paid is considered to be an expense rather than an upward adjustment of the price of the commodity purchased.

A major advantage of this system is that all commodities and services purchased are recorded initially at their net price and, except for possible returns and allowances, no subsequent adjustments are necessary. The amount considered to be the cost of an item is not affected by the timeliness of payment. The fact that the amount of the cash discounts taken during an accounting period will not be disclosed in the accounts is of little consequence. It is more important that management be informed of the available discounts that were lost because of carelessness, poor planning, or other inefficiencies. Remedial action may then be initiated.

A criticism of the system is that the amount reported on the balance sheet as accounts payable is less than the amount that may have to be paid to discharge the liability. The deduction of the discount is based on the expectation that the accounts will be paid within the discount period. To the extent that this does not occur, the liabilities will have been understated.

The recording of vouchers at their net amount does not affect the form of the voucher register presented earlier in this chapter. It does affect the check register, however. It is necessary to replace the Purchases Discount Cr. column with a column entitled "Discounts Lost Dr." For example, if the voucher recorded at $980 is paid after the discount period has expired, the payment would be recorded as follows:

Debit: Accounts Payable............$ 980
            Discounts Lost   20
Credit: Cash in Bank 1,000

Remittance advice

Checks sent to creditors in payment of account are frequently accompanied by a notification of the particular invoice that is being paid. The purpose of such notification, sometimes called a *remittance advice*, is to assure proper credit on the books of the creditor. Misunderstandings are less likely to arise and the possible need for exchanges of correspondence is avoided.

A separate form called a *remittance slip* may be enclosed with the check, or the information may be inserted on the body of the check or on an attachment to the check. In any event the only information required is the invoice number or other appropriate identification.

A check containing remittance information is known as a *voucher check*. Its use is entirely independent of the voucher system. When the voucher system is employed, however, it is possible to design the check form and the face of the voucher form so that both may be prepared at the same time, the voucher being the carbon copy. The check then remains attached to the voucher until the time of payment, when it is signed, placed in a window envelope, and mailed. The payee of the check detaches the lower half of the check form, which is the remittance advice section, before cashing the check. Preparation of the check and the voucher in a single operation is practicable only if cash discounts are invariably taken and voucher adjustments for returns and allowances are infrequent. Where its use is feasible, it may provide a significant saving in office expenses.

Voucher system and management

The voucher system not only provides effective accounting controls but also aids management in discharging other responsibilities. For example, continuous information is readily available for use in planning for future cash requirements. This in turn enables management to make the maximum use of cash resources. Invoices on which cash discounts are allowed can be paid within the discount period. Other invoices can be paid in accordance with the credit terms, thus minimizing costs and maintaining a favorable credit standing. Seasonal borrowing for working capital purposes can also be planned more accurately, with a consequent saving in interest costs.

Questions

1. Does the requirement that all checks be signed by a responsible official provide sufficient internal control over cash payments? Discuss.

2. What is the effect of the voucher system, in general terms, on (a) liabilities and (b) cash?

3. Does the voucher system provide internal control over cash receipts?

4. What are the five basic forms and files employed in the voucher system?

5. What special journal studied earlier is supplanted by (a) the voucher register and (b) the check register?

6. What comparisons and verifications should be made prior to vouching an invoice for merchandise?

7. Do payments of currency and coins from a petty cash fund constitute an exception to a system requiring that all funds be routed through the bank? Explain.

8. In designing a voucher register for use by a particular firm, what is the criterion for determining the captions of the special debit columns?

9. From the point of view of management, which is generally of greater significance, the date that an account payable should be paid or the identity of the creditor?

10. A voucher is prepared for an invoice dated May 15, terms 2/10, n/30. (a) Under what date should the voucher be filed? (b) Assuming that there is insufficient cash to pay the voucher on the last day of the discount period, under what date should it be refiled?

11. (a) When the voucher system is employed, is the accounts payable account in the general ledger a controlling account? (b) Is there a subsidiary creditor's ledger?

12. Under what circumstances will the amount of an unpaid voucher not correspond to the amount of the voucher as recorded in the voucher register, assuming that there has been no error in preparing and recording the voucher?

13. (a) What accounts are debited and credited when a note is given in settlement of a voucher? (b) When should a new voucher authorizing payment of the note be prepared and recorded in the voucher register?

14. After an invoice for store supplies of $100 has been vouched and recorded (but not paid), items totaling $20 are returned to the creditor. (a) What accounts are debited and credited to record the return? (b) What is the amount of the voucher, as revised? (c) What is the amount of the voucher, as indicated in the voucher register?

15. Merchandise with an invoice price of $5,000 is purchased subject to 2/10, n/30 terms. What is the cost of the merchandise according to each of the following assumptions:

    (a) Discounts taken are considered to be reductions from invoice price.
        (1) The invoice is paid after the discount period has expired.
        (2) The invoice is paid within the discount period.

    (b) Discounts taken are considered to be other income.
        (1) The invoice is paid after the discount period has expired.
        (2) The invoice is paid within the discount period.

    (c) Discounts allowed are considered to be reductions from the invoice price.
        (1) The invoice is paid after the discount period has expired.
        (2) The invoice is paid within the discount period.

Exercises

1. Record the following selected transactions in a voucher register similar to the one illustrated on pages 310 and 311, omitting the Paid columns and the five special columns at the right of the Purchases Dr. column:

Date	Voucher No.	Payee	Amount	Account Distribution
Sept. 1	1	J. T. Becker, Inc.	$1,000	Purchases
1	2	Petty Cash	100	Petty Cash
2	3	Powers & Co.	500	Office Equipment
3	4	Evans Valve Co.	850	Purchases
3	5	Citizens Bank	2,020	Notes Payable, $2,000
				Interest Expense, $20
30	48	Petty Cash	74	Purchases, $10
				Office Supplies, $15
				Misc. Sell. Exp., $19
				Misc. Gen. Exp., $30

2. Record the following selected transactions in a check register similar to the one illustrated on page 312, omitting the columns for Bank Deposits and Balance:

Date	Check No.	Payee	Voucher No.	Amount
Nov. 3	1	Gates Equipment Co.	2	$500, less 2% discount
3	2	Petty Cash	3	50
4	3	A. L. Jackson Co.	1	900, less 1% discount
5	4	Morrow & Co.	5	600
16	15	Petty Cash	21	46

3. Record in general journal form the following selected transactions, indicating above each entry the name of the journal in which it should be recorded (assume the use of a voucher register as on pages 310 and 311 and a check register as on page 312).

May   2. Recorded Voucher No. 968 for $1,500, payable to M. S. Turner Co., for merchandise.

        6. Recorded a reduction of $100 in Voucher No. 968, granted by by M. S. Turner Co. because of defective merchandise.

       11. Issued Check No. 952 for balance due on Voucher No. 968, less 1% discount.

       15. Issued a note payable for $1,000 to Scott & Walker in settlement of Voucher No. 950.

4. Present entries, in general journal form, to record the following related transactions, assuming that invoices for commodities purchased are recorded at their invoice price:

     (a) Recorded Voucher No. 746 for $2,000, payable to Barrows Corp. for merchandise; terms 2/10, n/30.

     (b) Returned merchandise with an invoice price of $500 to Barrows Corp., receiving credit.

     (c) Issued Check No. 762 for Voucher No. 746, assuming:

         (1) Payment within the discount period.

         (2) Payment after the expiration of the discount period.

5. Present entries in general journal form to record the transactions listed in Exercise 4, assuming that vouchers for commodities purchased are recorded at their net price after deducting the allowable discount.

Problems

14-1. R. E. Osborn & Co. has the following unpaid vouchers outstanding as of August 31 of the current year:

436	Whitelaw Corp.	$ 500
442	G. M. Masters	1,000
443	Allen Corp.	400

The following vouchers and checks were prepared and recorded during the first week in September:

Sept.   1. Check No. 445 to Whitelaw Corp. in payment of Voucher No. 436.

        1. Voucher No. 448 to Kane Co. for merchandise, $600.

        2. Voucher No. 449 to L. M. Griffith & Co. for office equipment, $1,450.

        3. Check No. 446 to Allen Corp. in payment of Voucher No. 443, 2% discount.

Sept. 3. Voucher No. 450 to Merchants Supply Co. for store supplies, $27.
       3. Voucher No. 451 to Scottsdale Progress for advertising, $15.
       4. Check No. 447 to Merchants Supply Co. in payment of Voucher No. 450.
       4. Voucher No. 452 to R. E. Osborn for a personal withdrawal, $500.
       4. Check No. 448 to R. E. Osborn in payment of Voucher No. 452.
       4. Voucher No. 453 to Parker-Savoy for miscellaneous general expense, $21.
       5. Voucher No. 454 to Reed & Knox for merchandise, $1,800.
       5. Check No. 449 to Scottsdale Progress in payment of Voucher No. 451.
       5. Check No. 450 to G. M. Masters in payment of Voucher No. 442, 1% discount.
       5. Voucher No. 455 to reimburse petty cash, $45. Petty cash vouchers indicate the following expenditures: store supplies, $8; delivery expense, $21; miscellaneous selling expense, $6; repairs expense, $10.
       5. Check No. 451 in payment of Voucher No. 455.

Instructions: Record the transactions for September in a voucher register like that illustrated on pages 310 and 311 and a check register like that illustrated on page 312, omitting the columns for Bank Deposits and Bank Balance. Assume that appropriate notations are made in the Paid columns of the voucher register when August vouchers are paid.

14-2. The Blair Company has the following unpaid vouchers outstanding as of July 31 of the current year:

Voucher No.	Company	Date of Invoice	Amount	Terms
175	Warner, Inc.	July 14	$ 500	n/30
198	Harrison Bros.	July 28	1,300	1/10, n/30

The vouchers prepared and checks issued during the month of August are presented below:

VOUCHERS

Date	Voucher No.	Payee	Amount	Terms	Distribution
Aug. 2	201	Barton & Son	$1,500	2/10, n/30	Merchandise
3	202	Cellet, Inc.	2,400	n/30	Store equipment
5	203–5	Ray Motors, Inc.	4,600	$2,000 down, balance in 2 equal monthly payments	Delivery equipment
10	206	Danville Supply	400	cash	Store supplies
13	207	Searls Bros.	1,200	2/10, n/30	Merchandise
17	208	Conrad & Evans	250	cash	Advertising expense
19	209	C. A. Wilson	460	n/30	Merchandise
24	210	Kent Federal Bank	1,010	——	Note payable $1,000, and interest $10
27	211	Superior Supply	350	n/30	Store supplies
29	212	Daily Chronicle	125	cash	Advertising expense

CHECKS

DATE	CHECK No.	PAYEE	IN PAYMENT OF VOUCHER No.	AMOUNT
Aug. 5	209	Ray Motors, Inc.	203	$2,000
7	210	Harrison Bros.	198	1,287
10	211	Danville Supply	206	400
12	212	Barton & Son	201	1,470
14	213	Warner, Inc.	175	500
17	214	Conrad & Evans	208	250
22	215	Searls Bros.	207	1,176
24	216	Kent Federal Bank	210	1,010
29	217	Daily Chronicle	212	125
31	218	Cellet, Inc.	202	2,400

Instructions: (1) Set up an account for Accounts Payable, Acct. No. 2113, and record the balance of $1,800 as of August 1.

(2) Record the August vouchers in a voucher register with the following amount columns: Accounts Payable Cr., Purchases Dr., Store Supplies Dr., Advertising Expense Dr., and Sundry Accounts Dr.

(3) Record the August checks in a check register with the following amount columns: Accounts Payable Dr., Purchases Discount Cr., and Cash in Bank Cr.

(4) Total and rule the registers, post to the accounts payable account, and bring down the balance in this account.

(5) Prepare a schedule of unpaid vouchers.

14-3. The Brighton Company has the following unpaid vouchers outstanding as of October 31 of the current year:

749	Hughes Corp.	$	750
757	Snyder & Gray		3,400
758	Gilbert, Inc.		395

Vouchers and checks prepared and recorded, bank deposits, and related transactions during November are as follows:

Nov. 1. Check No. 754 to Gilbert, Inc. in payment of Voucher No. 758.

3. Voucher No. 759 to Brown & Thomas for merchandise, $1,600.

4. Voucher No. 760 to Valley Bank for note payable, $5,000, and interest, $50.

4. Check No. 755 to Valley Bank in payment of Voucher No. 760.

5. Check No. 756 to Hughes Corp. in payment of Voucher No. 749, 2% discount. Bank deposit, $6,310 (record check and deposit on same line).

8. Voucher No. 761 to Vance Supply Co. for store supplies, $42, and miscellaneous general expense, $29.

10. Voucher No. 762 to George Barton Corp. for merchandise, $900.

11. Check No. 757 to Brown & Thomas in payment of Voucher No. 759, 1% discount.

12. Voucher No. 763 to Display Fixtures, Inc. for store equipment, $3,000.

13. Adjustment to Voucher No. 762 for merchandise returned, $50.

13. Voucher No. 764 to Murray Express for freight charges on the following: purchases, $42; merchandise sold (delivery expense), $65; store equipment, $28.

Nov. 13. Check No. 758 to Murray Express in payment of Voucher No. 764. Bank deposit, $4,640 (record check and deposit on same line).
   16. Voucher No. 765 to Payroll for salary expense, $1,625.
   16. Voucher No. 766 to Continental Corp. for merchandise, $1,250.
   16. Check No. 759 to Payroll in payment of Voucher No. 765.
   17. Vouchers No. 767 and 768 to Display Fixtures, Inc. replacing Voucher No. 763, each for $1,500.
   17. Check No. 760 to Display Fixtures, Inc. in payment of Voucher No. 767.
   19. Voucher No. 769 to Ross Publications for advertising, $190.
   20. Check No. 761 to Vance Supply Co. in payment of Voucher No. 761. Bank deposit, $3,135 (record check and deposit on same line).
   23. Voucher No. 770 to Gilbert, Inc. for merchandise, $2,160.
   24. Check No. 762 to Ross Publications in payment of Voucher No. 769.
   25. Check No. 763 to Snyder & Gray in payment of Voucher No. 757.
   26. Check No. 764 to George Barton Corp. in payment of Voucher No. 762.
   26. Cancellation of Voucher No. 766 by issuance of a note payable.
   26. Voucher No. 771 to George Barton Corp. for merchandise, $1,845.
   27. Voucher No. 772 to Murray Express for freight charges on the following: purchases, $63; merchandise sold (delivery expense), $124.
   27. Check No. 765 to Murray Express in payment of Voucher No. 772.
   30. Voucher No. 773 to Payroll for salary expense, $1,675.
   30. Voucher No. 774 to Petty Cash to reimburse the fund for the following disbursements: store supplies, $18; delivery expense, $13; miscellaneous selling expense, $46; miscellaneous general expense, $11.
   30. Check No. 766 to Payroll in payment of Voucher No. 773.
   30. Check No. 767 to Petty Cash in payment of Voucher No. 774. Bank deposit, $4,326 (record check and deposit on same line).

The bank statement indicates a November 30 balance of $11,482. The numbers of the paid checks returned with the statement are as follows:

748	753	756	760	763
749	754	757	761	765
752	755	759	762	766

Comparison of paid checks returned with the bank statement for October reveals that No. 720 for $18 is still outstanding.

The deposits listed on the bank statement agree with the amounts listed in the check register.

Instructions: (1) Set up a T account for Accounts Payable, Acct. No. 2113, and record the balance as of November 1.

(2) Record the transactions for November, using a voucher register like the one illustrated on pages 310 and 311, a check register like the one illustrated on page 312, and a two-column general journal. Insert the amount $9,465 in the Bank Balance column of the check register before recording the transactions. Assume that appropriate notations are made in the Paid columns of the voucher register when October vouchers are paid.

(3) Total and rule the voucher register and the check register.

(4) Post from the journals to the accounts payable account and bring down the balance.

(5) Prepare a schedule of unpaid vouchers as of November 30.

(6) Prepare a bank reconciliation as of November 30.

14-4. H. L. Eaton Co. records all vouchers at the net price after deducting cash discounts. Available discounts not taken are recorded in the check register as a debit to Discounts Lost. The following are selected from among the transactions recorded in March of the current year.

Mar. 3. Recorded Voucher No. 1214; payee, Atlas Corp.; invoice total, $1,800; terms, 2/10, n/30; account distribution, Purchases.

8. Recorded Voucher No. 1226; payee, Prudential Realty Co.; amount, $3,200; account distribution, Mortgage Payable, $3,000; Interest Expense, $200.

8. Recorded Check No. 1215 in payment of Voucher No. 1226.

10. Recorded Vouchers No. 1230 and 1231; payee, Jordan Construction Co.; amount of each voucher, $3,000; account distribution, Building Repairs.

11. Recorded Check No. 1219 in payment of Voucher No. 1230.

13. Recorded Voucher No. 1240; payee, Petty Cash; amount, $50; account distribution, Petty Cash (to increase amount of fund).

13. Recorded Check No. 1225 in payment of Voucher No. 1240.

14. Recorded Voucher No. 1243; payee, Henry Reed, Inc.; invoice total, $1,500; items returned, $200; terms, 1/10, n/30; account distribution, Purchases.

16. Recorded Voucher No. 1250; payee, Corbin & Co.; invoice total, $700; terms, 1/10, n/30; account distribution, Purchases.

17. Recorded return of merchandise with an invoice price of $100 to Atlas Corp. (Voucher No. 1214).

19. Recorded Voucher No. 1261; payee, Modern Equipment Co.; invoice total, $6,500; account distribution, Office Equipment.

22. Recorded Check No. 1235 in payment of Voucher No. 1243.

24. Recorded Vouchers No. 1268 ($2,000) and No. 1269 ($4,500) to replace Voucher No. 1261.

25. Recorded Check No. 1240 in payment of Voucher No. 1268.

28. Recorded issuance of note payable in settlement of Voucher No. 1269.

30. Recorded Check No. 1253 in payment of Voucher No. 1250; discount lost, $7.

31. Recorded Check No. 1255 in payment of Voucher No. 1214; discount lost; $34.

Instructions: Record the transactions in (1) a voucher register similar to the one illustrated on pages 310 and 311 (with amount columns for Accounts Payable Cr., Purchases Dr., and Sundry Accounts Dr. only); (2) a check register similar to the one illustrated on page 312, modified to provide for discounts lost and omitting columns for Bank Deposits and Bank Balance; and (3) a two-column general journal.

15

Concepts and principles

Need for concepts and principles

The historical development of accounting principles and techniques has been closely related to the economic development of the country. In its earlier stages the primary objective of accounting was to provide financial data of an enterprise in the form of an income statement and a balance sheet. The statements were used primarily by the owners and creditors of the enterprise as a means of appraising the results of its operations and its financial position. Business enterprises were ordinarily managed by their owners, and if a substantial amount was owed to a bank or a supplier, the important creditors frequently participated in management decisions.

With the increase in the size and complexity of business enterprises, there developed a greater demarcation between "management" and "outsiders." The latter group, which is composed of owners (stockholders), creditors, government, labor unions, customers, and the general public, continues to be interested in the profitability, stability, and financial status of business enterprises. Management is interested, of course, in these same aspects of the enterprise but, in addition, relies upon accounting to provide an important element of internal control and specialized reports for use in guiding operations and planning for the future. Much of the two preceding chapters was devoted to the role of accounting in maintaining internal control. Additional aspects of this important function of accounting, as well as special accounting reports, are presented in later chapters.

As business organizations grew in size and complexity, the accompanying accounting problems became more complex and the need for a framework of concepts and generally accepted principles became more evident.

Development of concepts and principles

Financial statements and other accounting reports are significant only to those who have a clear understanding of the underlying principles upon which the reports have been based. It is equally evident that accountants must be in substantial agreement among themselves as to the meaning and importance of the guides and standards that, collectively, comprise accounting principles. Responsibility for their development has rested primarily on practicing accountants and accounting teachers, working both independently and as groups under the sponsorship of such organizations as the American Accounting Association and the American Institute of Certified Public Accountants.

Various terms are employed by accountants in referring to a particular accounting standard. In addition to *principle* and *concept*, the terms *axiom, assumption, postulate, convention, tenet,* and *doctrine* are frequently encountered in accounting literature. An examination of the similarities and differences in meaning of these terms is not essential to the understanding of the particular principles that will be discussed in this chapter; they are mentioned only for the sake of completeness.

It should be borne in mind that the word "principle" as used in this context does not have the same authoritativeness as universal principles or natural laws employed in the study of astronomy, physics, or the other physical sciences. Accounting principles have been developed by man to enhance the usefulness of accounting data in an ever-changing society. They represent the best possible guides, based on reason, observation, and experimentation, to the achievement of the desired results. The selection of the best single method, or of several equally good methods, among a number of alternatives, has come about gradually, and in some subject matter areas is still in a state of change. General acceptance among the leaders of the accounting profession is the criterion for determining an accounting principle.

The remainder of this chapter is devoted to the underlying assumptions, concepts, and principles of the greatest importance and widest applicability. As the discerning student will discover, some of them have been briefly introduced in earlier chapters.

Business entity

The *business entity* concept assumes that a business enterprise is separate and distinct from the persons who supply the assets used in the business. This is true regardless of the legal form of the business organization. The accounting equation, Assets = Equities, or Assets = Liabilities + Proprietorship, is an expression of the entity concept; it is as if the business itself owns the assets and in turn owes the various claimants. Thus, the accounting process is primarily concerned with the enterprise as a productive economic unit and is only secondarily concerned with the investor as a claimant of the assets.

It is important that the student understand the distinction between the business entity concept employed in accounting for a sole proprietorship and the legal concept of a sole proprietorship. The nonbusiness assets, liabilities, revenues and expenses of a sole proprietor are excluded from the business accounts. If a sole proprietor owns several distinct business enterprises, each may be treated as a separate entity for accounting purposes. On the other hand, a sole proprietor is personally liable for his business debts and may be required to use nonbusiness assets to satisfy the business creditors. Conversely, business assets are not immune from claims of the sole proprietor's personal creditors.

Differences between the business entity concept and the legal nature of both the partnership form and the corporate form of organization will be considered in later chapters. For accounting purposes, however, revenues and expenses of any enterprise are viewed as affecting the business assets and liabilities, not the owners' assets and liabilities.

Going concern

Only in rare instances is a business organized with the expectation of remaining in existence for only a specified period of time. In most cases there is no means of foretelling the length of life of an enterprise, and an assumption must be made. The nature of the assumption will affect the manner of recording some of the business transactions, which in turn will affect the data reported in the periodic statements and other accounting reports.

It is customary to assume that a business entity has a reasonable expection of continuing in business at a profit for an indefinite period of time. This assumption that an enterprise is a *going concern* provides much of the justification for recording plant assets at acquisition cost and depreciating them in a systematic manner without reference to their current realizable values. It is pointless to report plant assets on the balance sheet at their estimated realizable values if there is no immediate expectation of selling them. This is true regardless of whether the current market value of the plant assets is less than their book value or greater than their book value. If the firm continues to use the assets, the fluctuation in market value causes no gain or loss, nor does it enhance or diminish the usefulness of the assets. Thus, if the going concern assumption is a valid concept, the recovery of the investment in plant assets is assured even though the assets may be individually marketable only at a loss.

The going concern assumption similarly supports the treatment of prepaid expenses as assets even though they may be virtually unsalable. To illustrate, assume that on the last day of its fiscal year a wholesale firm receives from a printer a $20,000 order of catalogs. In the absence of the assumption that the firm is to continue in business, the catalogs would be merely scrap paper and the value reported for them on the balance sheet would be negligible.

A less direct effect of the going concern concept is that it helps to focus attention on earnings rather than assets. The earning power of an enterprise is more significant than the market value of its individual assets in judging the over-all worth of a business. Because of this emphasis on earnings, the accountant directs his attention to the proper allocation of revenues and expenses to the current period and needs not be concerned with determining the market value of assets that will not be sold.

Unit of measurement

All business transactions are recorded in terms of money. Other pertinent information of a nonfinancial nature may also be recorded, such as the description of assets acquired, the terms of purchase and sale contracts, and the purpose, amount, and term of insurance policies. But it is only through the record of dollar amounts that the diverse transactions and activities of a business may be measured, reported, and periodically compared. Money is both the common factor of all business transactions and the only practicable unit of measurement that can be employed to achieve homogeneity of financial data.

The use of the monetary unit as the common denominator imposes two major limitations on accounting for and reporting the activities of an enterprise: (1) it restricts the scope of accounting reports and (2) it assumes a stability of the measurement unit.

Scope of accounting reports. Many factors affecting the activities and future prospects of an enterprise cannot be expressed in monetary terms. In general, accounting does not attempt to report such factors. For example, information regarding the capabilities of the management, the state of repair of the plant assets, the effectiveness of the employee welfare program, the attitude of the labor union, and the relative strength or weakness of the firm's principal competitors, cannot be expressed in monetary terms. Although such information is important to investors and creditors, accountancy assumes no responsibility for providing it.

Stability of monetary unit. The dollar is far inferior, as a unit of measurement, to such quantitative standards as the pound, gallon, or yard, which have remained unchanged for centuries. The instability of the purchasing power of the dollar is well known. The disruptive effects of inflation on accounting reports during the past two decades are acknowledged by accountants but to date recognition has not been given in the accounts to the declining value of the unit of measurement.

To indicate the nature of the problem, assume that the plant assets acquired by an enterprise for $100,000 twenty years ago are now to be replaced with similar assets which at present price levels will cost $200,000. The original cost was charged to revenue as depreciation expense over the twenty year period, and, assuming that the enterprise has earned an income or at least broken even during the period, the initial outlay of $100,000 has been recovered. The amount recovered represents only one half of the cost of replacing the assets, however, or stated in another manner, the $100,000 recovered is worth only half as much as the sum originally invested. From either point of view, the firm has suffered a loss in purchasing power which, in a sense, is a loss of capital. If the depreciation charge had been based on the replacement cost of $200,000, sufficient funds would have been available, assuming operations were at the break-even level, to replace the assets. The foregoing illustration is somewhat oversimplified and is not representative of the intricacies of the problem. The most obvious difficulty encountered in basing depreciation on replacement cost is that replacement cost at some indeterminate future date is not ascertainable.

Accounting records and reports are based on verifiable objective evidence and the use of subjective estimates or opinions should be avoided. It is for this reason that accounting treats all dollars alike. Until such time as an acceptable method of giving effect to the fluctuating dollar is devised, accountancy is likely to continue to employ the assumption of stability.

It should be added that information regarding the effects of inflation on an enterprise is frequently presented in supplementary financial schedules.

Accounting period

A complete and accurate picture of the degree of success achieved by an enterprise cannot be obtained until it discontinues operations and converts its assets into cash. Then, and only then, is it possible to determine with finality its net income. But innumerable decisions regarding the business must be made by management and interested outsiders throughout the period of its existence, and it is therefore necessary to prepare periodic reports on operations and financial position.

Reports may be prepared on the basis of the completion of a particular job or project, but the more usual practice is to prepare them at specified time intervals. For a number of reasons, including custom and various legal requirements, the maximum interval between reports is one year. Periodic measurements are always tentative and conditional. In spite of their provisional nature, however, they are essential to management and other interested parties as a basis for decision making.

It is this element of periodicity that creates many of the problems of accountancy. For example, the necessity for adjusting entries discussed in earlier chapters is directly attributable to the division of an enterprise into arbitrary time periods. Problems of inventory costing, of recording uncollectible accounts, and of selecting depreciation methods are also directly related to the periodic measurement process. The fundamental problem is the determination of periodic net income. It should be noted that the amounts of the assets and equities presented on the balance sheet will also be affected by the methods employed in determining net income. For example, regardless of the cost flow assumption employed in determining the cost of goods sold during the period, the costs assigned to the remaining inventory will be the residual amount.

The determination of periodic net income is a two-fold problem involving (1) the revenue realized during the period and (2) the expired costs to be allocated to the period. It is thus a problem of matching costs and revenues, the residual amount being the provisional net income or loss for the particular period.

Recognition of revenue

Revenue is measured by the amount charged to customers for goods delivered or services rendered to them. The problem created by periodicity is one of timing; at what point is the revenue realized? For any particular accounting period the question is whether revenue items should be recognized and reported as such in the current period or whether their recognition should be postponed to a future period.

Various criteria are acceptable for determining when revenue is realized. In any case the criteria adopted should be reasonably in accord with the terms of the contractual arrangements with the customer and based in so far as possible on objective evidence. The criteria of greatest applicability are described in the remaining paragraphs of this section.

Point of sale. It is customary to consider revenue from the sale of commodities as being realized at the time title passes to the buyer. It is at this point that the sale price has been agreed upon, the buyer acquires the right of ownership in the commodity, and the seller has an enforceable claim against the buyer. The realization of revenue from the sale of services may be determined in a somewhat similar manner although there is frequently a time lag between the time of the initial agreement and the completion of the service. For example, assume that a contract provides that certain repair services be performed, either for a specified price or on a time and materials basis. The initial contract to sell the services does not constitute a sale until the work has been performed.

Theoretically, revenue from the production and sale of commodities and services emerges continuously as effort is expended. As a practical matter, however, it is ordinarily not possible to make an objective determination until the sales price is agreed upon and the seller has completed his portion of the contract.

Receipt of payment. The recognition of revenue may be postponed until payment is received. When this criterion is adopted, revenue is considered to be earned at the time the cash is collected, regardless of when the sale was made. The cash basis is widely used by physicians, attorneys, and other enterprises in which professional services are the source of revenue. It has little theoretical justification but has the practical advantage of avoiding the problem of estimating losses from uncollectible accounts. Its acceptability as a fair method of timing the recognition of revenue is influenced somewhat by its simplicity and the fact that it may be used in determining income subject to the federal income tax. It is not an appropriate method of measuring revenue from the sale of commodities.

Degree of contract completion. Enterprises engaged in large construction projects may devote several years to the completion of a particular contract. If the point of sale criterion is employed, the revenue from a contract is not recognized until the job is completed. For example, assume that a contractor is engaged in a project that will require three years to complete, for which he is to receive fifty million dollars. Assume also that the costs incurred on the contract during the three-year period total forty six million dollars. It would be unrealistic to assume that the net income of four million dollars was earned entirely in the year in which the contract was completed.

In such situations as the foregoing it is acceptable to view the revenue as being earned over the entire life of the contract. The amount earned in any particular period is determined on the basis of the percentage of the contract that has been completed during the period. The costs incurred during the period are then matched against the revenue recognized. There is, of course, an element of subjectivity, and hence of possible error, in the determination of the amount of revenue earned. The financial statements may be more useful, however, in spite of estimates, than would be the case if none of the revenue were recognized until the completion of the contract.

A somewhat comparable situation to long-term construction contracts arises in connection with revenue from rentals, loans, and other services that are definitely measureable on a time basis. Neither the point of sale or receipt of payment is an appropriate criterion for determining the emergence of revenue from such sources. Both the amount of total revenue to be earned and the period over which it is to be earned are readily ascertainable. For example, if a building is leased for a period of three years at a rental of $36,000, the revenue is realized at the rate of $1,000 a month. It is immaterial whether the rent is received in a lump sum at the beginning of the lease, in installments over the life of the lease, or at its termination. In accordance with the concept of the going concern, it is assumed that the owner will supply the use of the building during the term of the lease and that the lessee will fulfill his part of the contract.

A third adaptation of the criterion of contract performance is widely used in reporting revenue realized from sales on the installment plan. In the typical installment sale the purchaser makes a "down payment" and agrees to pay the remainder in specified amounts at specified intervals over a period of time. The seller may retain technical title to the goods or take other means to facilitate repossession in the event the purchaser defaults on his payments. Such sales may be treated in the same manner as any other sale on account, in which case the revenue is considered to be realized at the point of sale. The alternative is to consider each receipt of cash to be composed of (1) a partial return of cost and (2) gross profit.

As a basis for illustration, assume that in the first year of operations the installment sales of a dealer in household appliances totaled $300,000, that the cost of the goods sold on installment totaled $180,000, and that down payments and installment payments received during the year totaled $140,000. The per cent of cost of goods sold to sales was 60% (180,000 ÷ 300,000) and the per cent of gross profit to sales was 40% (120,000 ÷ 300,000). According to the installment method of reporting, the cash receipts of $140,000 are assumed to represent a return of cost in the amount of $84,000 (60% × $140,000) and gross profit of $56,000 (40% × $140,000). Collections in future periods from the year's sales would similarly be treated as a pro rata return of cost (60%) and gross profit (40%).

As in the cash basis of revenue recognition, there is little theoretical justification for the installment method of determining revenue. Although it is generally accepted as an appropriate method, many accountants are inclined to the view that installment sales and the conversion of receivables into cash are separate and distinct transactions and should be so treated.

Allocation of costs

As has been demonstrated in earlier chapters, properties and services acquired by an enterprise are generally recorded at cost. When they are sold or consumed, the costs are matched with the related revenue to determine the amount of net income or loss. The costs of properties or services acquired that are on hand at any particular time represent assets. Such costs may also be referred to as "unexpired costs." As the assets are sold or consumed they become "expired costs" or "expenses."

Theoretically, it is possible to assign all costs to each specific product sold or each service rendered. If this were done, the net income of an enterprise could be measured in terms of units of output. In practice, however, it would be difficult and costly to fragmentize cost allocations to such a degree. As stated earlier in this chapter, the matching of costs and revenues on a periodic time basis is satisfactory.

The techniques of determining and recording cost expirations have been described and illustrated in earlier chapters. In general, there are two approaches to cost allocations: (1) compute the amount of the expired cost or (2) compute the amount of the unexpired cost. For example, it is customary to determine the portion of plant assets that have expired. After recording the depreciation for the period, the balances of the plant asset accounts minus the balances of the related accumulated depreciation accounts represent the unexpired cost of the assets. The alternative approach must be employed for merchandise and supplies unless perpetual inventory records are maintained. The cost of the merchandise or supplies on hand at the close of the period is ordinarily determined by taking a physical inventory and the remaining costs in the related accounts are assumed to have expired. It might appear that the first approach emphasizes expired costs and the second emphasizes unexpired costs. This is not the case, however, as the selection of the method is based on convenience or practicability.

Many of the costs allocable to a period are treated as an expense at the time of incurrence for the reason that they will be wholly expired at the end of the period. For example, when a monthly rent is paid at the beginning of a month the cost incurred is unexpired and hence it is an asset. But it is customary to charge the rental directly to the appropriate expense account, thus avoiding the necessity of an additional entry later. The proper allocation of costs among periods is the paramount consideration; a variety of accounting techniques may be employed in any particular case.

Consistency

A number of accepted alternative principles affecting the determination of net income and asset values have been presented in earlier sections of the text. Recognizing that different methods may be used under varying circumstances, some guide or standard is needed to assure a high degree of comparability of the periodic financial statements of an enterprise. It is common practice to compare the current income statement and balance sheet with the preceding statements.

The amount and direction of change in income or financial position from period to period is highly significant to the reader and may greatly influence his decisions. Therefore, interested persons should be able to assume that the successive financial statements of an enterprise are consistently based on the same generally accepted accounting principles. If the principles are not applied consistently, the trends indicated could be the result of changes in accounting methods rather than the result of changes in business conditions or managerial effectiveness.

The concept of consistency does not completely prohibit changes in accounting methods. For example, an enterprise that initially adopted the first-in, first-out assumption of inventory flow might at some later date decide to change to the last-in, first-out flow assumption. Such a decision should be made only after a careful study of the effects and the desirability of the change. In addition, the change in method should be disclosed in the financial statements for the period in which the change was effected.

Adequate disclosure

Financial statements and their accompanying footnotes or other explanatory materials should contain all of the pertinent data believed essential to the reader's understanding. Criteria for standards of disclosure are of necessity nebulous and indefinite. They are based largely on value judgments rather than on objective facts.

The usefulness of financial statements is enhanced by the use of headings, subheadings, and the merging of items in significant categories. For example, detailed information as to the amount of cash in various special and general funds, the amount on deposit in each of several banks, and the amount invested in a variety of marketable government securities, is not needed by the reader of financial statements. Such information displayed on the balance sheet would impede rather than aid in understanding. On the other hand, if the terms of loan agreements impose restrictions on the distribution of earnings, the details should be disclosed. Some of the less obvious situations that accountants agree should be adequately disclosed on financial statements are briefly described in the following paragraphs.

Accounting methods employed. When there are several acceptable alternative methods that have a significant effect on amounts reported on the statements, the particular method adopted should be disclosed. Examples include inventory cost flow assumptions, inventory pricing methods, and criteria of revenue recognition.

Changes in accounting methods. When a significant change is made in accounting methods, such fact should be disclosed in the statements for the year in which the change is made. The usual practice is to disclose the quantitative effect on net income and on balance sheet items.

Contingent liabilities. Contingent liabilities arising from discounted notes receivable, litigation, guarantees of products, possible tax assessments, or from other causes should be disclosed.

Events subsequent to date of statements. Events occurring or becoming known after the close of the period which may have a significant effect on the financial statements should be disclosed. For example, if an enterprise should suffer a crippling loss from a fire or other catastrophe between the end of the year and the issuance of the statements, the facts should be disclosed. Similarly, such occurrences as the settlement of pending litigation, the initiation of litigation, or the sale or purchase of plant facilities after the close of the period should be made known if they materially affect the company.

Materiality

In adhering to the principle of disclosure, the accountant must consider the relative importance of any event, accounting procedure, or change in procedure that affects items on the financial statements. Absolute accuracy in accounting and full disclosure in reporting are not ends in themselves, and there is no need to exceed the limits of practicability. The determination of what is material and what is unimportant requires the exercise of judgment; precise criteria cannot be applied.

The size of an item and its nature must be considered in relationship to the size and nature of other items. The erroneous classification of a $10,000 asset on a balance sheet exhibiting total assets of ten million dollars would probably be immaterial. If the assets totaled only $100,000, however, it would certainly be material. If the $10,000 represented a loan to an officer of the enterprise, it might well be material even in the first assumption. If the amount of the loan was increased to $100,000 between the close of the period and the issuance of the statements, both the nature of the item at the balance sheet date and the subsequent increase in amount would certainly require disclosure.

The principle of materiality may be applied to procedures employed in recording transactions. As was stated in an earlier chapter, minor expenditures for plant assets may be treated as an expense of the period rather than as an asset. The saving in accounting costs is justified if the practice does not materially affect the financial statements. In establishing a dollar amount as the dividing line between a revenue charge and a capital charge, consideration would need to be given to such factors as: (1) amount of total plant assets, (2) amount of plant assets in relationship to other assets, (3) frequency of occurrence of expenditures for plant assets, (4) nature and expected life of the plant assets, and (5) probable effect on the amount of periodic net income reported.

Custom also influences criteria of materiality. Until recent years it was customary to report cents in all corporation financial statements. Of a sample of 600 corporation annual reports for 1959, 574 companies, or 96% of the group, omitted cents from their statements. This is in sharp contrast to the approximately 40% of the same companies that omitted cents in their 1946 statements.[1] A few of the companies presented the usual statements with the figures rounded to the nearest thousand dollars. The cents or sometimes amounts less than a thousand dollars reported by a large or medium-sized corporation are certainly not material amounts. In fact, they tend to imply a degree of accuracy that does not exist.

A technique known as "whole-dollar" accounting has also been developed in recent years. The elimination from accounting entries of the cents amounts wherever possible and at the earliest practicable point in the accounting sequence may effect savings in office costs and improve productivity. There are some accounts, such as those with customers and creditors, in which it is not feasible to round to the nearest dollar. In many of the asset, revenue, and expense accounts, however, the errors introduced by rounding the amounts of individual entries at the time of recording tend to be compensating in nature, and the amount of the final error is not material.

It should not be inferred from the foregoing that whole-dollar accounting encourages or condones errors. The unrecorded cents are not lost; they are merely reported in a manner that reduces bookkeeping costs without materially affecting the accuracy of accounting data.

Conservatism

Periodic statements are of necessity affected to a considerable degree by the selection of accounting procedures and other value judgments.

---

[1] *Accounting Trends and Techniques, 14th ed.*, 1960 (New York: American Institute of Certified Public Accountants), p. 17

Historically, accountants have tended to be conservative, and in selecting among alternatives they have favored the method or procedure that yielded the lesser amount of net income or asset value. This attitude of conservatism was frequently expressed in the admonition to "anticipate no profits and provide for all losses." Such an attitude of pessimism was due in part to the need for an offset to the optimism of business management. It could also be argued that potential future losses to an enterprise from poor management decisions would be lessened if net income and assets were understated.

Current accounting thought has shifted somewhat from this philosophy of conservatism. Conservatism is no longer considered to be a sanction for the understatement of net income and assets or the overstatement of liabilities. Revenue should be recognized when earned and costs should be matched against revenue in accordance with principles based on reason and logic. The element of conservatism may be considered only when other factors affecting a choice of alternatives are neutral. The concepts of consistency, disclosure, and materiality take precedence over conservatism, and the latter should be a factor only where the others do not play a significant role. The choice of methods should be grounded on the desire to report with the highest possible degree of objectivity.

Questions

1. Of what significance is acceptability in the development of accounting principles?

2. Name four other terms that may be used in referring to rules or abstract ideas of broad significance in accounting.

3. What is the basic assumption of the "business entity" concept?

4. Would a banker considering a loan to a sole proprietorship have any interest in the amount and nature of the personal assets and liabilities of the proprietor? Explain.

5. When a sole proprietor pays a personal or family expense by drawing a check on his business bank account, what is the effect on the business (a) assets, (b) expenses, (c) net income, (d) capital?

6. If a railroad were to discontinue operations and go out of business, the portion of its right-of-way located in swamp or desert land would be of little value. Why are such assets not reported on the balance sheet at their estimated market value?

7. The totals of the three principal sections of the balance sheet of an enterprise, prepared in accordance with generally accepted accounting principles, are: assets, $200,000; liabilities, $50,000; capital, $150,000. (a) Is it possible that the assets might realize only $100,000 if the business were to be discontinued and the assets sold separately? (b) Is it possible that a prospective purchaser might justifiably offer the proprietor $300,000 for the business? (c) Which is the more significant measure of the worth of the enterprise, the estimated value of its assets considered individually, or its earnings?

8. (a) Are accounting principles based on the assumption of a stable monetary unit? (b) Is it desirable that management consider the fluctuating value of the dollar in making business decisions?

9. In what respect are the dollars of the current year's depreciation on assets acquired twenty-five years ago not comparable to the dollars of salary expense for the current year?

10. Is it true that accountants are generally unaware of the instability in the value of the dollar?

11. If it were unnecessary to prepare annual financial statements during the life of a business enterprise, would there be any necessity for recording annual adjusting and closing entries?

12. Does the periodic adjusting entry for prepaid insurance affect assets only, expenses only, or both assets and expenses?

13. Differentiate between revenue and net income.

14. At which point is revenue from sales of merchandise on account more commonly recognized, time of sale or time of cash receipt?

15. The transactions described below occurred during the current year. In each case indicate whether the revenue should be recognized in the current year or in the following year:

(a) Received in the current year an order for merchandise for delivery in the following year.

(b) Sold season tickets for a series of basketball games; one fourth of the games are to be played in December of the current year and the remainder in the following year.

(c) Received a cash deposit in the current year which is to be applied in payment of goods to be manufactured and delivered in the following year.

(d) Rented a building for the last month of the current year, allowing the tenant to postpone rental payment until the following year.

16. A firm employing the installment method of accounting has $400,000 of installment sales during the current year, on which the gross profit is 40%. The down payments and installment payments received during the current year total $150,000. What is the amount of gross profit considered to be realized in the current year?

17. One accountant charges all expenditures for insurance premiums to an expense account and records an adjustment for the unexpired premium at the end of the period. Another accountant charges all such expenditures to an asset account and records an adjustment for the expired premiums at the end of the period. Are the two accountants applying different principles to the allocation of costs?

18. An enterprise changes from the direct write-off method of recognizing bad debts expense to the allowance method. The total bad debts expense of $30,000 reported in the current year is composed of $13,000 of direct write-offs and the $17,000 for which the offsetting credit was made to Allowance for Uncollectible Accounts.

   (a) Would it be accurate to state that the enterprise had taken a "double" deduction for bad debts expense in the current year?

   (b) What is the quantitative effect of the change in method on the net income of $130,000 reported in the current year?

   (c) Is the effect of the change material?

   (d) Should the effect of the change in method be disclosed in the financial statements?

19. Of the following matters, considered individually, indicate those that are material and should be disclosed either on the financial statements or in accompanying explanatory notes.

   (a) A firm is officially charged with violation of antitrust laws and may be required to sell an important subsidiary company.

   (b) A change in accounting methods of the current year increased the amount of net income that would otherwise have been reported from $2,600,000 to $2,602,000.

   (c) Between the end of its fiscal year and the date of publication of the annual report, a company receives notification from the Internal Revenue Service of an additional income tax assessment of $2,000,000 on an earlier year's income. (Annual net income, after income tax, reported in the past 5 years has ranged from $3,000,000 to $10,000,000.)

   (d) A manufacturing company employs the last-in, first-out method of determining the cost of inventory.

20. In each of the following statements of alternatives, indicate the method that is the more "conservative."

   (a) (1)First-in, first-out or (2) last-in, first-out method of costing inventory when prices are rising.

   (b) (1) Lower of cost or market or (2) cost method of valuing inventory when prices are falling.

   (c) (1) Sum of the years-digits or (2) straight line method of depreciation in year plant assets are acquired.

   (d) (1) Point of sale or (2) installment method of reporting gross profit on installment sales.

Exercises

1. Apex Specialty Co. sells most of its products on a cash basis but extends short-term credit to some of its customers. Invoices for sales on account are placed in a file and not recorded until the cash is received, at which time the sale is recorded in the same manner as a cash sale. The net income reported for the first three years of operations was $60,000, $75,000, and $120,000, respectively. The total amount of the uncollected sales invoices in the file at the end of each of the three years was $4,000, $9,000, and $16,000. In each case the entire amount was collected during the first month of the succeeding year. (a) Determine the amount by which net income was overstated or understated for each of the three years. (b) What items on the balance sheet were overstated or understated as of the end of the third year?

   2. The Atlas Construction Co. contracts to build a dam and related structures for $3,000,000 within two and one-half years from the date of the contract. The total costs to be incurred in fulfilling the contract are estimated at $2,400,000. At the close of the fiscal year in which work is begun on the contract the costs incurred total $600,000. Determine the amount of revenue and the net income to be recognized for the year, assuming that the recognition of revenue is to be spread over the life of the contract.

3. The cost of the merchandise inventory of the Edward S. Mueth Co. at the close of its first fiscal year, according to three different methods, is as follows: FIFO, $38,000; Average, $36,000; LIFO, $34,000. If the average cost method is employed, the net income reported will be $23,000. (a) What will be the amount of net income reported if the FIFO method is adopted? (b) What will be the amount of net income reported if the LIFO method is adopted? (c) Which of the three methods is the most conservative? (d) Is the selection of the method to be employed of sufficient materiality to require disclosure in the financial statements?

4. At the close of three successive years a firm failed to record accrued sales commissions expense as follows: first year, $20,000; second year, $14,000; third year, $30,000. In each case the commissions were paid during the first month of the succeeding year and charged as an expense of that year. (a) Determine the amount by which net income was overstated or understated in each of the following years: first, second, third, fourth. (b) What items on the balance sheet would have been overstated or understated as of the end of the third year as a result of the errors?

5. Data related to the installment sales of Regal Furniture Co. for the current fiscal year are as follows:

Sales (on installment plan)	$200,000
Cost of goods sold (on installment plan)	110,000
Total cash received from customers on the $200,000 of installment contracts	80,000

Determine the amount of gross profit that would be recognized according to (a) the point of sale method and (b) the installment method.

Problems

15-1. A business enterprise pays $5,400 for a three-year insurance policy, effective July 1, 1961. Their fiscal year ends on December 31. Among the many possible methods that might be employed in allocating this cost against revenue are the following:

    (a) Charge one third of the premium to expense in each of the following years: 1961, 1962, 1963.
    (b) Charge the entire premium to expense in 1961.
    (c) Charge 1961 with $1,000, one half of the cost of the premium on a one-year policy; 1962 and 1963 with $2,000 each, the cost of the premium on a one-year policy; and 1964 with the remaining balance.
    (d) Charge the entire premium to expense in 1964.
    (e) Report the unexpired premium at the cancellation value at December 31 of each year and charge the decrease to expense of the period.

The cancellation values at December 31 are as follows: 1961, $4,200; 1962, $2,540; 1963, $840.

Instructions: Determine the amount of the overstatement or understatement of net income for each of the years, 1961, 1962, 1963, and 1964, that would result from the use of each of the allocation methods listed. (Pro rata allocation of the premium over the life of the policy is the usual and acceptable method.)

15-2. During its first three years of operations, the Beckett Co. determined the cost of the merchandise inventory at the end of the period by the first-in, first-out method, depreciation expense by the straight-line method, and bad debts expense by the direct write-off method. The amounts of net income reported and the amounts of the foregoing items for each of the three years were as follows:

	First Year	Second Year	Third Year
Net income reported............	$50,000	$80,000	$ 95,000
Ending merchandise inventory...	70,000	85,000	100,000
Depreciation expense...........	10,000	10,000	12,000
Bad debts expense.............	500	3,000	4,000

The firm is considering the possibility of changing to the following methods in determining net income for the fourth and subsequent years: last-in, first-out inventory, declining balance depreciation at twice the straight line rate (on new acquisitions), and provision for bad debts through the use of an allowance account. In order to consider the probable future effect of these changes on the determination of net income, the management requests that net income of the past three years be recomputed on the basis of the proposed methods. The inventory, depreciation, and bad debts expense for the past three years, computed in accordance with the proposed methods, are as follows:

	First Year	Second Year	Third Year
Ending merchandise inventory...	$68,000	$70,000	$75,000
Depreciation expense...........	20,000	16,000	13,200
Bad debts expense.............	3,600	4,000	5,500

Instructions: Recompute the net income for each of the three years, presenting the figures in an orderly manner.

15-3. Condensed income statement data for Modern Furniture Sales for the first three years of operations are as follows:

	First Year	Second Year	Third Year
Sales........................	$180,000	$240,000	$200,000
Cost of goods sold.............	93,600	132,000	118,000
Gross profit on sales...........	$ 86,400	$108,000	$ 82,000
Operating expenses............	60,000	62,000	63,000
Net income...................	$ 26,400	$ 46,000	$ 19,000

All sales were made on the installment basis. The amounts collected from customers in each of the three years were as follows:

	First Year	Second Year	Third Year
Collected from sales of first year..	$80,000	$ 60,000	$35,000
Collected from sales of second year		100,000	80,000
Collected from sales of third year..			90,000

Instructions: Determine the amount of net income that would have been reported in each of the three years if the installment basis had been employed, ignoring the possible effects of uncollectible accounts on the computations. Present figures in good order.

15-4. The balance sheet and income statement prepared from the unadjusted accounts of Starr Sports Center at the close of the first year of operations are presented below.

Starr Sports Center
Balance Sheet
December 31, 19—

Cash....................................	$2,100
Equipment	5.000
A. J. Starr, Capital.....................	$7,100

Starr Sports Center
Income Statement
For Year Ended December 31, 19—

Sales..		$80,000
Purchases....................................		70,000
Gross profit on sales.........................		$10,000
Operating expenses		
Salary expense...............................	$11,000	
Rent expense.................................	3,900	
Utilities expense.............................	800	
Advertising expense..........................	500	
Miscellaneous expense.......................	2,700	
Total operating expenses...................		18,900
Net loss......................................		$ 8,900

You are engaged to review the accounting methods employed and, if material errors are found, to prepare revised statements. The following information is elicited during the course of the review:

(a) The business was established on January 2 by an investment of $16,000 in cash by the proprietor. The only transactions recorded have been those in which cash was received or disbursed. The books have not been closed for the year.

(b) The equipment listed on the balance sheet at $5,000 was purchased for cash on January 9. Equipment purchased July 2 for $1,000 in cash was recorded as "purchases." Equipment purchased on December 18 for $2,000, for which a 60-day non-interest-bearing note was issued, was not recorded.

(c) Depreciation on equipment has not been recorded. The equipment is estimated to have a useful life of 10 years and a salvage value of 10% of its original cost. (Use straight-line method.)

(d) Accounts receivable from customers at December 31 total $8,500.

(e) A total of $12,000 is owed to merchandise creditors on account at December 31.

(f) The merchandise inventory at December 31, as nearly as can be determined, has a cost of $28,000.

(g) Insurance premiums of $980 were charged to miscellaneous expense during the year. The unexpired portion at December 31 is $460.

(h) Rent expense includes an advance payment of $300 for the twenty-fourth month of the two-year lease.

(i) Miscellaneous expense includes $500 of transportation costs on merchandise purchased.

(j) Salaries owed but not paid on December 31 total $390.

(k) Uncollectible accounts are estimated at $600.

(l) The classification of expenses as "selling" and "general" is not considered to be sufficiently important to justify the cost of the analysis.

(m) The proprietor made no additional investments, or withdrawals, during the year.

Instructions: (1) On the basis of the preliminary statements, prepare a trial balance as of December 31 of the current year on an eight-column work sheet.

(2) Record the adjustments and corrections in the adjustments columns and complete the work sheet.

(3) Prepare an income statement, capital statement, and balance sheet.

15-5. Central Press Co. manufactures and sells printing presses. The installment method of recognizing gross profit is employed in accounting for sales on the installment plan. Details of a particular installment sale, amounts collected from the purchaser, and the repossession of the press, are presented below.

First year.

Sold for $30,000 a press having a cost of $18,000, received a down payment of $10,000 and five notes for $4,000 each, maturing at intervals of six months.

Received payment of $4,000 for the first note.

Second year.

Received payment of $8,000 for the second and third notes.

Third year.

The purchaser defaults on the fourth note and Central Press Co. repossesses the press, canceling the remaining notes. Because of hard usage and inadequate maintenance, the press is estimated to be worth only $6,000.

Instructions: (1) Determine the gross profit to be recognized in the first year.

(2) Determine the gross profit to be recognized in the second year.

(3) Determine the gain or loss to be recognized from the repossession of the press.

Payrolls—payroll taxes

Importance of payroll records

Detailed and accurate payroll data must be maintained by employers. Payroll data are essential to the determination of employee earnings and to the payment of amounts due employees at regular intervals: weekly, biweekly, semimonthly, monthly, or in accordance with some other fixed plan.

Most employers are required by federal laws to collect certain taxes levied against the earnings of their employees. They collect the taxes by withholding a portion of the employees' pay. Most employers are also subject to federal taxes levied upon the amount of their payroll. In addition, many employers are required to pay state payroll taxes, and in some states and cities they are required to collect other taxes levied upon the earnings of their employees. All of these federal, state, and city payroll taxes must be paid and detailed reports must be submitted at prescribed intervals.

Employers frequently obligate themselves to withhold specific sums from employees' earnings for the payment of union dues, insurance premiums, or charitable contributions, and for the purchase of U. S. government bonds.

Payroll records are also required by management in the control, analysis, and distribution of labor costs. At the same time, payroll records may be used in contract negotiations with labor unions and in settlements of grievances between a company and a union. This brief recital of legal requirements, customary practices, and managerial uses is evidence of the need for accurate and complete payroll records.

Types of remuneration

The term salary is usually applied to payment for managerial, administrative, or similar services. The rate of salary is ordinarily expressed

346

in terms of a month or a year. Remuneration for manual labor, both skilled and unskilled, is commonly referred to as wages and is stated on an hourly, weekly, or piecework basis. In practice, the terms salary and wages are often used interchangeably. The basic salary or wages of an employee may be supplemented by commissions, bonuses, pensions, profit sharing plans, and cost-of-living adjustments. Although remuneration is usually paid in money, payment may be in other media such as meals, lodging, securities, or other property.

Employer-employee relationship

Not all persons who perform services for a business are classified as employees. The relationship of employer and employee generally exists when the person for whom the services are performed has the right to control and direct the individual in the performance of his services. Thus, a sales clerk in a department store and a receptionist in a physician's office are clearly employees. On the other hand, a public accountant engaged to audit the accounting records of a business chooses his own means of performing his services and is not subject to the control and guidance of his client. He is an independent contractor rather than an employee. Similarly, a lawyer retained to negotiate a contract or defend a lawsuit is an independent contractor. Other examples of independent contractors are architects, physicians, and public stenographers.

Remuneration paid to independent contractors is frequently termed a fee rather than salary or wages. In any event, such payments are not subject to the various payroll taxes and should not be included in the payroll.

Computation of earnings

The earnings of each employee for each pay period are usually calculated by multiplying the time worked during the period by the agreed rate per hour, week, month, or other unit of time. In some cases, earnings are the product of the units of work completed times the rate per unit or piece. The earnings of salespeople are sometimes calculated by multiplying their sales for the period by an agreed percentage.

Timekeeping. When remuneration is based upon time, a record of the time worked by each employee is needed. Maintaining such records is called *timekeeping*. The records that are compiled may be very simple or quite elaborate, depending upon the nature of the business and the number of employees. Sometimes such records are merely notations in a small memorandum book. In other cases the employees may be required to record the time of their arrival and departure each day. Many businesses use time clocks and clock cards to record this information. Although a detailed record of time worked by each employee may not always be needed in order to calculate earnings, such information may be helpful in analyzing and distributing labor costs and in maintaining attendance records required by state and federal regulations.

Wage rates, overtime. Wages and salaries must be paid at the rate agreed upon in each case. For businesses engaged in interstate commerce, the rates must also conform to the requirements of the Federal Fair Labor Standards Act. This Act, commonly known as the Wages and Hours Law, requires employers who are covered by the statute to pay a minimum rate of 1½ times the regular rate for all hours worked in excess of 40 per week. Persons holding executive, administrative, and certain supervisory positions are not covered by this provision of the law.

In many industries the practice of paying premium rates for overtime hours has been considerably extended. Certain overtime hours may be paid for at twice the base rate. Work on Sundays and holidays may be paid for at overtime rates regardless of the total number of hours worked during the week. It is also a common practice for companies that work night shifts to pay premium rates to those who work during these generally less desirable hours.

The calculation of gross earnings is illustrated below. The computation assumes that Paul Corey is employed at the rate of $2.60 per hour for the first 40 hours and $3.90 ($2.60 + $1.30) for all hours in excess of 40. His time card for the week ended October 27 reveals that he worked 45 hours. The hours worked and the calculation of gross earnings is as follows:

DAY	HOURS WORKED	REGULAR HOURS	OVERTIME HOURS
Monday...........................	8	8	
Tuesday..........................	8	8	
Wednesday.......................	8	8	
Thursday.........................	8	8	
Friday...........................	9	8	1
Saturday.........................	4		4
Total hours......................	45	40	5

Hours worked at regular rate...................40 x $2.60 = $104.00
Hours worked at overtime rate................ 5 x $3.90 =   19.50
Total earnings............................... $123.50

Deductions from earnings

In most instances the amount actually paid to the worker is less than the amount of his earnings. The difference is due primarily to the taxes assessed against the employee that the employer is required to withhold. In addition to these, the employee may authorize various other deductions.

F.I.C.A. tax. Most employers are required by the Federal Insurance Contributions Act to withhold a portion of the earnings of each of their employees. The amount withheld is the employees' contribution to the federal program of old age and survivors' insurance. It is frequently referred to as the *F.I.C.A.* tax or the *F.O.A.B.* tax, the latter term emphasizing the benefits rather than the contributions feature of the law. Unless specifically exempted, every employer is required to withhold the tax. At the present time the rate is 3% of the first $4,800 paid to each employee in the calendar year.[1] Although Congress may change the tax rate and the maximum amount subject to the tax, such changes will not affect the accounting principles or the method of recording the transactions.

Federal income tax. Except for certain types of employment, all employers are required to deduct a portion of the earnings of their employees for federal income tax purposes. As a part of the pay-as-you-go system of paying income taxes, it is frequently referred to as the *withholding tax*. The amount to be withheld varies with the amount of earnings and the number of exemptions to which the employee is entitled. An exemption is allowed for the worker, for each person that qualifies as a dependent, such as the worker's children, and for the worker's wife, unless she is also employed and claims her own exemption. Additional exemptions are allowed to the worker and his wife for old age (65 or older) and for blindness. Every employee is required to inform his employer of his status in this respect by submitting a withholding exemption certificate.

Withholding exemption certificate

---

[1]Under present law the rates in future years are to be as follows: through 1962 — 3⅛%; 1963 to 1965 — 3⅝%; 1966 to 1967 — 4⅛%; 1968 and thereafter — 4⅝%.

The amount of the tax to be withheld from the earnings of each employee is calculated by taking into account the amount of his earnings, the length of the pay period, the number of exemptions claimed, and the tax rates currently in force. Most employers find it expedient to consult withholding tables prepared by the government. From a table for the appropriate pay period (daily, weekly, biweekly, semimonthly, monthly, etc.) the amount of tax to be withheld can be found for any amount of earnings and any number of exemptions.

Other taxes. All states have a program of unemployment compensation insurance that is financed, in part, by a tax on employers. A few states also require contributions from employees, in which case the employer is compelled to withhold the amount of the contribution from the employees' earnings and to remit this amount to the state bureau or agency that administers the program.

A number of states and a few cities levy a tax based on income. The state or the city statutes may require the employer to withhold the tax from his employees' earnings.

Other deductions. The deductions from earnings discussed above are compulsory; neither the employer nor the employee has any choice in the matter. In addition to these deductions, however, there may be other deductions authorized by employees either individually or as a group. For example, the deduction of union dues or group insurance premiums may be provided for in the contract between the employer and the union representing the workers. A partial list of other deductions that may be taken from earnings of employees follows:

(1) Deductions to accumulate funds to be used to purchase United States Savings Bonds for the employees.
(2) Deductions to pay the premiums on life, health, hospital, or accident insurance for the employees.
(3) Deductions authorized by the employees for a supplementary retirement annuity or pension.
(4) Deductions authorized to be paid to a charitable organization (Red Cross, Community Chest, etc.).
(5) Deductions authorized to repay a loan or an advance from the company or a loan from the company credit union.
(6) Deductions authorized to pay for purchases of a product or a service of the company.

Whatever the nature of the deduction, the accounting problem is essentially the same. If the employer makes these deductions, he must keep an accurate record of their amount and must dispose of the funds as authorized. Most of the deductions made from employees' earnings are current liabilities of the employer.

Calculation of net pay

The net pay of a worker is his total earnings less payroll deductions. It is the amount that the employee receives on pay day. For this reason, net pay is frequently referred to as take-home-pay. The calculation of net pay for Paul Corey that resulted from his total earnings of $123.50 shown on page 348 is illustrated below.

Prior to the week ended October 27, Corey's earnings for the year were $4,745.30. The portion of the $123.50 subject to F.I.C.A. tax is $54.70 ($4,800 maximum minus $4,745.30). The tax on $54.70 at the rate of 3% is $1.64.

The withholding exemption certificate illustrated earlier shows that Corey claims four exemptions for income tax purposes. Reference to the income tax withholding table for a weekly payroll period discloses that for earnings of $123.50, with four exemptions claimed, the amount to be withheld is $12.80.

The employer has a group insurance plan whereby part of the premium is deducted from the employees' earnings. The amount deducted from Corey's pay is 70 cents a week. Corey has also authorized the employer to withhold $3.75 each week for the purchase of United States Savings Bonds. At the end of each five-week period, a bond is purchased in his name and is delivered to him. He has also authorized a deduction of $2 each week for six weeks for the local Community Chest.

The various deductions and the amount to be paid to Corey for the week ended October 27 are summarized as follows:

Earnings (as calculated)...............................		$123.50
Deductions:		
F.I.C.A. Tax...	$ 1.64	
Federal Income Tax..................................	12.80	
Group Insurance.....................................	.70	
U. S. Savings Bond..................................	3.75	
Community Chest....................................	2.00	
Total Deductions.....................................		20.89
Net pay..		$102.61

It is customary for the employer to furnish a statement of earnings and deductions to the employee with each paycheck or pay envelope. Special payroll checks with detachable stubs are widely used. The pay period, the earnings, and the various deductions are shown on the stub. The employee removes the stub before cashing the check. The check issued to Corey for the period ended October 27 is shown on the following page.

The payroll

A *payroll* is a list of employees showing their earnings for a stated period together with other relevant information. The columnar headings

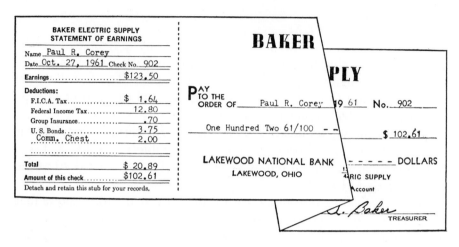

Payroll check

and the arrangement of data on payroll forms varies considerably, though all payrolls provide for essentially the same information. A typical weekly payroll form is illustrated below.

There are a number of points that should be noted in the payroll form. The exact period covered by the payroll should be clearly indicated; in this case it is the week ended October 27, 1961. This particular payroll covers all employees of the business, both sales personnel and office personnel. If there were a large number of employees divided into several departments or categories, a separate payroll sheet could be prepared for each department or category.

PAYROLL FOR WEEK ENDED

NAME	EM- PLOYEE NO.	DAILY TIME							REGU- LAR HOURS	OVER- TIME HOURS	REGU- LAR RATE	EARNINGS		
		S	M	T	W	TH	F	S				AT REGU- LAR RATE	AT OVER- TIME RATE	TOTAL
Allen, Robert..	5		8	8	8	8	8	0	40		1.80	72.00		72.00
Corey, Paul....	6		8	8	8	8	9	4	40	5	2.60	104.00	19.50	123.50
Decker, Elaine.	9		8	8	8	8	6	0	38		1.50	57.00		57.00
Engel, Lee.....	3		8	8	8	8	8	4	40	4	1.80	72.00	10.80	82.80
Gibson, Harold.	4											150.00		150.00
Hall, Mary....	1		8	8	8	8	8	2	40	2	1.60	64.00	4.80	68.80
Kane, John....	7		8	0	8	8	8	0	32		1.90	60.80		60.80
Nolan, Frank...	8		8	8	8	8	9	4	40	5	1.60	64.00	12.00	76.00
Spencer, Mark.	10		8	8	8	8	8	0	40		2.00	80.00		80.00
Vollmer, Linda.	2		8	8	7	8	8	0	39		1.50	58.50		58.50
Total........												782.30	47.10	829.40

Other Deductions: AR — Accounts Receivable

Weekly payroll record, left page

The Daily Time columns are self-explanatory. The information as to hours worked is obtained from a time-clock record or a similar record of the arrivals and departures of employees. The regular hours worked are multiplied by the regular rate to yield the regular earnings; the overtime hours are multiplied by the overtime rate to yield the overtime earnings; the two amounts are then added to determine the total earnings. It will be noted that there is no record of hours worked by Harold Gibson. He is employed in an administrative capacity and is paid at the rate of $150 per week, regardless of the number of hours spent on the job.

The two columns under the heading Taxable Earnings are for memorandum purposes only. Employers are subject to unemployment compensation taxes based upon the first $3,000 of remuneration paid to each employee during the calendar year. They are also required to pay federal insurance contribution (F.I.C.A.) taxes based upon the first $4,800 of compensation paid to each employee during the calendar year. Information regarding each employee's year-to-date earnings is obtained from the *employees' earnings record*, which is discussed later in the chapter. Paul Corey's cumulative earnings, exclusive of the current week, were $4,745.30; therefore none of the current week's earnings are subject to the unemployment compensation taxes and only $54.70 is subject to the F.I.C.A. tax. Harold Gibson has exceeded the $4,800 level prior to the current week; hence none of his remuneration for the current week is included in the Taxable Earnings columns. The earnings of Lee Engel and Mark Spencer have previously exceeded the $3,000 level but have not yet reached $4,800; therefore their weekly earnings are excluded from the Unemployment Compensation column but are included in the F.I.C.A. column.

OCTOBER 27, 1961

TAXABLE EARNINGS		DEDUCTIONS						PAID		ACCOUNTS DEBITED	
UNEM-PLOYMENT COMP.	F.I.C.A.	F.I.C.A. TAX	FEDERAL INCOME TAX	GROUP INSUR-ANCE	U. S. BONDS	OTHER	TOTAL	NET AMOUNT	CHECK NO.	SALES SALARY EXPENSE	OFFICE SALARY EXPENSE
72.00	72.00	2.16	8.50	.50	1.25	CC 1.50	13.91	58.09	901	72.00	
	54.70	1.64	12.80	.70	3.75	CC 2.00	20.89	102.61	902	123.50	
57.00	57.00	1.71	5.70	.30			7.71	49.29	903	57.00	
	82.80	2.48	8.00	.40		AR 6.00	16.88	65.92	904		82.80
			18.70	1.20	7.50	CC 4.00	31.40	118.60	905		150.00
68.80	68.80	2.06	7.80	.30	2.50	CC 1.50	14.16	54.64	906	68.80	
60.80	60.80	1.82	8.70	.40			10.92	49.88	907	60.80	
76.00	76.00	2.28	4.60	.50	6.25	CC 2.00	15.63	60.37	908		76.00
	80.00	2.40	7.70	.70	3.75		14.55	65.45	909	80.00	
58.50	58.50	1.76	5.90	.40		CC 1.00	9.06	49.44	910		58.50
393.10	610.60	18.31	88.40	5.40	25.00	CC12.00 AR 6.00	155.11	674.29		462.10	367.30

CC — Community Chest   HC — Hospital Care

Weekly payroll record, right page

The Deductions columns are self-explanatory, with the exception of the "Other" column. This column is used to list withholdings for which no special column is provided. In the illustration, the column records withholdings for Community Chest donations (marked "CC") and a deduction of $6 from the pay of Lee Engel to apply on an account receivable (marked "AR"). The individual items are sorted and classified and a separate total is shown for each class.

The difference between the total earnings and the total deductions is the net amount to be paid, which is entered in the Paid column. The check number is recorded as the checks are written.

The last two columns of the payroll illustrated are used to accumulate the total wages or salaries to be charged to the expense accounts. This process is usually termed *payroll distribution*. If there is an extensive account classification of labor expense, the charges may be analyzed on a separate payroll distribution sheet.

The columns in the payroll sheet should be added and the totals should be proved before the payroll is entered in the books of account or checks are issued to employees. The tabulation below indicates the method of verification.

Earnings:
At Regular Rate	$782.30	
At Overtime Rate	47.10	
Total		$829.40

Deductions:
F.I.C.A. Tax	$ 18.31	
Income Tax Withheld	88.40	
Group Insurance	5.40	
U. S. Bonds	25.00	
Community Chest	12.00	
Accounts Receivable	6.00	
Total		155.11
Paid — Net Amount		$674.29

Accounts Debited:
Sales Salary Expense	$462.10	
Office Salary Expense	367.30	
Total (as above)		$829.40

There are innumerable variations in the procedures that may be followed in preparing payrolls. As the number of employees becomes greater, it is customary to use specialized machines for accumulating and recording the data. A wide variety of equipment is available. It is possible to obtain the various totals needed, to write the checks, and to accumulate data in the employees' earnings records from a single machine recording of the basic data. Regardless of the mechanical aids employed, however, all payroll procedures and systems have the same purpose: to compile and record the necessary information in an expeditious manner.

Entering the payroll in the accounts

The general journal entry to record the payroll illustrated on the preceding pages is as follows:

Oct.	27	Sales Salary Expense......................	611	462 10		
		Office Salary Expense.....................	711	367 30		
		F.I.C.A. Taxes Payable.................	215.1		18 31	
		Employees Income Taxes Payable........	215.2		88 40	
		Group Insurance Payable...............	216.1		5 40	
		Bond Deductions Payable...............	216.2		25 00	
		Community Chest Donations Payable.....	216.3		12 00	
		Accounts Receivable — Lee Engel.......	114/ √		6 00	
		Salaries Payable......................	214		674 29	
		Payroll for week ended Oct. 27				

The two debits in the entry are to expense accounts. The amount and the nature of the deductions from the workers' earnings have no effect on the amount of expense incurred by the business. Of the seven credits in the entry, six represent an increase in a specific liability and one represents a decrease in the asset Accounts Receivable. The liabilities will be paid at various times. For example, payments to the insurance company for group insurance may be made annually or quarterly, bonds are purchased as the accumulation for each particular employee reaches the necessary amount, and the Community Chest donations will be paid at the conclusion of the period during which deductions are made. The payment of the liability for F.I.C.A. taxes, employees' income taxes, and salaries will be discussed later in the chapter.

An alternative to recording the payroll information in the general journal is to treat the payroll record as a special journal. If this is done, the totals of the various columns are posted directly to the appropriate ledger accounts and the posting references are written below the totals in the payroll record.

While direct posting of the payroll may be expedient, it is generally preferable to summarize the payroll in the general journal, as illustrated. Sometimes the data relating to all of the pay periods that ended during the month are combined into one monthly general journal entry. Regardless of the method used, the payroll record should be retained for a minimum period of four years, as required by federal statutes.

Paying the payroll

The procedures for recording payment of the payroll are affected by the method of payment and the accounting system employed for cash payments generally. Employees may be paid (1) by checks drawn on the regular bank account, (2) with currency, or (3) by special payroll checks drawn on a payroll bank account. In the following discussion of the three methods, the payroll of Baker Electrical Supply for the week ended October 27, shown on pages 352 and 353 will be used as the basis for the illustration.

Regular checks. As was shown earlier, the payroll is recorded in the general journal as debits to salary expense accounts and credits to liability and asset accounts, including a credit to Salaries Payable for the net amount to be paid to the employees. If the employees are paid by checks drawn on the regular bank account and the voucher system is not used, the payment is recorded directly in the cash payments journal as a debit to Salaries Payable and a credit to Cash. The entry may be recorded on a single line of the cash payments journal regardless of the number of checks written because the name of each employee, the amount paid, and the number of each check are available in the payroll record. The entry in the cash payments journal will appear as follows:

CASH PAYMENTS JOURNAL

DATE	CHECK NO.	ACCOUNT DEBITED	POST. REF.	SUNDRY ACCOUNTS DR.	ACCOUNTS PAYABLE DR.	PURCHASES DISCOUNT CR.	CASH CR.
1961 Oct. 27	901–10	Salaries Payable......	214	674 29			674 29

When cash disbursements are controlled through use of the voucher system it is necessary to prepare a voucher for the net amount to be paid the employees. The voucher is then recorded in the voucher register as a debit to Salaries Payable and a credit to Accounts Payable.

The payment of the payroll is then recorded in the check register as a debit to Accounts Payable and a credit to Cash in Bank.

Currency. Some employers pay their employees in currency rather than by check. Currency is frequently used as the medium of payment when the payroll is paid each week, or when the business location or time of payment are such that banking or check cashing facilities are not readily available to employees. In such cases one check payable to Payroll may be drawn for the entire amount to be paid. The check is then cashed at the bank and the money is inserted in individual payroll envelopes. Payment in currency may be more convenient for the employees but for the employer it involves greater risk of theft and errors. The recording routines are identical with those discussed in the preceding section, except that there would be only one check and there would be no check numbers opposite the name of each employee on the payroll record.

Payroll checks. Many employers, particularly those with a large number of employees, use a special payroll check similar to that illustrated on page 352. A single check for the entire amount to be paid the employees is drawn on the regular bank account and deposited in a special payroll account at the bank. The individual payroll checks are then drawn against the special payroll account, and the numbers of the payroll checks are inserted in the payroll record.

In order to relieve the treasurer or other executives of the task of signing hundreds or thousands of payroll checks each payday, it is customary for some other designated employee, such as the paymaster, to perform this duty. Sometimes mechanical means of signing the checks are employed. Another advantage of this system is that the task of reconciling the regular bank statement is simplified. The paid payroll checks are returned separately from regular checks and are accompanied by a statement of the special bank account. Any balance shown by the bank statement should always be equal to the sum of the outstanding payroll checks.

The entries to record the payments of the payroll under this system are similar to those previously illustrated. Assuming that Baker Electrical Supply uses payroll checks and employs the voucher system, the voucher for the amount of the payroll would be recorded in the voucher register as a debit to Salaries Payable and a credit to Accounts Payable for $674.29. This would be followed by an entry in the check register debiting Accounts Payable and crediting Cash for $674.29. It should be noted that it is unnecessary to set up an account in the ledger for the special payroll bank account. The amount deposited is equaled by the total of the payroll checks, thus reducing the balance to zero.

Employee's earnings record

In order to determine the amount of F.I.C.A. tax to be withheld from the earnings of each employee, it is necessary to know the cumulative earnings for the year to date. The amounts to be entered in the Taxable Earnings columns of the payroll record are also determined by reference to the cumulative earnings of each employee. In addition, quarterly and annual amounts of earnings and of certain deductions of each employee must be reported by the employer on various tax forms. The employee's earnings record may also be useful in determining the rights of employees to bonuses, pensions, and vacation leaves and in answering questions in connection with the Wage and Hour Law.

The form of the employee's earnings record varies, but all types show essentially the same information. A portion of the earnings record of Paul Corey is presented on the following pages.

EMPLOYEE'S

NAME   Corey, Paul R.

ADDRESS   1986 Belmont Street   PHONE   ED 1-1149

              Lakewood 12, Ohio

MALE √   MARRIED √   NUMBER OF   PAY   PER DAY ____

FEMALE ___   SINGLE ____   EXEMPTIONS 4   RATE $104.00   WEEK √

                                                        MONTH ____

OCCUPATION Salesman   EQUIVALENT HOURLY RATE $2.60

LINE NO.	PERIOD ENDED	TIME WORKED		RATE	EARNINGS			
		DAYS	HOURS		AT REGULAR RATE	AT OVERTIME RATE	TOTAL	CUMULATIVE TOTAL
39	Sept.29		42	2.60	104.00	7.80	111.80	4,425.50
THIRD QUARTER					1,352.00	126.50	1,478.50	
40	Oct. 6		40		104.00		104.00	4,529.50
41	Oct. 13		42		104.00	7.80	111.80	4,641.30
42	Oct. 20		40		104.00		104.00	4,745.30
43	Oct. 27		45		104.00	19.50	123.50	4,868.80
44	Nov. 3		42		104.00	7.80	111.80	4,980.60
45	Nov. 10		44		104.00	15.60	119.60	5,100.20
51	Dec. 22		40		104.00		104.00	5,763.20
52	Dec. 29		43		104.00	11.70	115.70	5,878.90
FOURTH QUARTER					1,352.00	101.40	1,453.40	
YEARLY TOTAL					5,408.00	470.90	5,878.90	

Employee's earnings record, left page

The upper portion of the form is used to record miscellaneous personal data about the employee, including such information as the employee's address, employee number, social security number, and number of withholding exemptions.

The record should provide a line for each payroll period in the year, a line for each of the quarterly totals, and a line for the yearly totals. Columnar headings are similar to those on the payroll record. The entries in Corey's record for the week ended October 27 should be compared with the entries opposite Corey's name in the payroll record for the same week (pages 352 and 353). Note that the amount in the Cumulative Total column for the week ended October 20 is $4,745.30. It was on the basis of this information that the amount of F.I.C.A. tax to be withheld on October 27 was based on earnings of $54.70 ($4,800 − $4,745.30).

EARNINGS RECORD

SOC. SEC. NO. _259-08-8114_   EMPLOYEE NO. _6_   YEAR _1961_

DATE EMPLOYEED _June 15, 1957_

DATE OF BIRTH _April 22, 1932_

DATE EMPLOYMENT TERMINATED _____

		DEDUCTIONS				PAID		
F.I.C.A. TAX	FEDERAL INCOME TAX	GROUP INSURANCE	U. S. BONDS	OTHER	TOTAL	NET AMOUNT	CHECK NO.	LINE NO.
3.35	11.00	.70	3.75		18.80	93.00	862	39
44.36	143.00	9.10	48.75	AR 35.00	280.21	1,198.29		
3.12	9.20	.70	3.75	CC 2.00	18.77	85.23	872	40
3.35	11.00	.70	3.75	CC 2.00	20.80	91.00	883	41
3.12	9.20	.70	3.75	CC 2.00	18.77	85.23	893	42
1.64	12.80	.70	3.75	CC 2.00	20.89	102.61	902	43
	11.00	.70	3.75	CC 2.00	17.45	94.35	912	44
	11.90	.70	3.75	CC 2.00	18.35	101.25	923	45
	9.20	.70	3.75		13.65	90.35	968	51
	11.90	.70	3.75		16.35	99.35	979	52
11.23	141.20	9.10	48.75	12.00	222.28	1,231.12		
144.00	570.20	36.40	195.00	CC 12.00 AR 35.00	992.60	4,886.30		

Employee's earnings record, right page

Withholding statement

On or before January 31 of each year most employers must furnish to each employee a statement of the total remuneration paid (before payroll deductions) and the total amount of F.I.C.A. tax and income tax withheld during the preceding calendar year. The report is made on Form W-2; the original is sent to the Director of Internal Revenue for the district, the duplicate and triplicate are given to the employee, and the quadruplicate is retained by the employer. The employee is required to submit the duplicate Form W-2 with his income tax return. The withholding tax information for Paul Corey based on his earnings record is shown on the following page.

SOCIAL SECURITY INFORMATION		INCOME TAX INFORMATION	

Baker Electrical Supply
24913 Carnegie Blvd.
Lakewood 12, Ohio   27-0118342
Type or print EMPLOYER'S identification number, name, and address above.

WITHHOLDING TAX STATEMENT 1961
Federal Taxes Withheld From Wages

Copy A—For District Director

$ 4,800.00	$ 144.00	$ 5,878.90	$ 570.20
Total F.I.C.A. Wages paid in 1961	F.I.C.A. employee tax withheld, if any	Total Wages* paid in 1961	Federal Income Tax withheld, if any

┌   259-08-8114

Paul R. Corey
1986 Belmont Street
Lakewood 12, Ohio

└

Type or print EMPLOYEE'S social security account no., name, and address above.

FORM W-2—U. S. Treasury Department, Internal Revenue Service   *Before payroll deductions or "sick pay" exclusion.

EMPLOYER: See instructions on other side.

FOR USE OF INTERNAL REVENUE SERVICE

Employee's Copy and Employer's Copy compared . . . .

Withholding statement

Employer's payroll taxes

The payroll taxes discussed thus far were those imposed upon employees. The employer is concerned with these taxes because he is obliged by law to withhold the proper amounts from the workers' pay and to remit these amounts to the appropriate governmental agency. The taxes to be discussed in the following sections are borne by the employer, that is, they are business *expenses*.

F.I.C.A. tax. Employers, as well as employees, are required to contribute to the Federal Insurance Contributions Act tax. This contribution is the same as that required of employees, namely 3% of the first $4,800 of earnings paid (before payroll deductions) to each employee during the calendar year.[2]

Federal unemployment compensation tax. Unemployment insurance is a major feature of the national social security program. It provides some relief to those who become unemployed as a result of economic forces outside of their control and it also tends to encourage full employment. To finance the administration of the program, all employers covered by the law are nominally subject to a federal tax of 3.1% on the first $3,000 paid to every covered employee during a calendar year. Since credits are given for payments to the various states for the state unemployment compensation tax, the effective federal rate is actually only .4%. No part of the federal unemployment compensation tax is levied on the employees.

The number of employers covered by this federal law is not so large as under the F.I.C.A. tax. Only employers of four or more persons are subject to the federal unemployment compensation tax. The types of employment excluded are substantially the same for both taxes.

[2]The rate of the F.I.C.A. tax on employers, like the rate on employees, may be changed by the Congress at any time. See footnote on page 349 for schedule of future rates.

State unemployment compensation tax. The amounts collected by the federal government from the tax discussed in the preceding section are paid to the various states for use in administering their unemployment compensation programs.   Money paid to unemployed persons who qualify for benefits comes from the state tax levied upon the employers, based upon the earnings of employees. A very few states require employee contributions. The various state laws differ with respect to the types of covered employment and the number of workers an employer must have before the tax is applicable. In no case is the required number of workers greater than four; in a number of states it is one.

State taxes are usually based on the first $3,000 of earnings paid to each employee during the calendar year. The tax rates, however, are not uniform among the states.   In general, the maximum rate is 2.7%, although in some states the upper limit is higher. Almost every state has a merit-rating plan under which employers who provide steady employment for their workers earn a rating that reduces the tax rate below the maximum charged in that state.

Recording employer's payroll taxes

The employer's payroll taxes may be determined and recorded at the end of each payroll period or at the end of each month.   In either case the basic data needed to compute the taxes are obtained from the payroll records. According to the payroll record of Baker Electrical Supply for the week ended October 27 (pages 352 and 353), the amount of earnings subject to the F.I.C.A. tax is $610.60, and that subject to the unemployment compensation taxes is $393.10.   Assuming that Baker Electrical Supply is currently subject to a state unemployment tax rate of 2.7%, the taxes accrued for the week are as follows:

F.I.C.A. — 3% of $610.60..	$18.32
State Unemployment Compensation — 2.7% of $393.10..............	10.61
Federal Unemployment Compensation — .4% of $393.10.............	1.57
Total...	$30.50

The general journal entry to record the expense for the week and the liability for the taxes accrued is as follows:

Oct.	27	Payroll Tax Expense......................	719	30	50		
		F.I.C.A. Taxes Payable..................	215.1			18	32
		State Unemployment Taxes Payable........	215.3			10	61
		Federal Unemployment Taxes Payable.....	215.4			1	57
		Payroll taxes accrued for the week ended October 27.					

If the employer's taxes are recorded monthly instead of weekly, the procedure is exactly the same as illustrated above except that the data for the four or five payroll periods ending within the month are combined before the several taxes are computed.

Practice differs as to the disposition of the debit for the amount of the payroll tax expense. Since the taxes have a direct relationship to remuneration paid, some accountants charge them directly to the appropriate wage and salary accounts. Others charge them to Payroll Tax Expense, as was done above, and classify the account as a general expense on the income statement.

Payment of payroll taxes

The requirements for paying the employer's payroll taxes and the amounts withheld from employees differ for the various taxes. The regulations governing the filing of returns and the payment of the liabilities are summarized in the sections that follow.

Income taxes withheld and F.I.C.A. taxes. The income taxes and the F.I.C.A. taxes withheld from employees, together with the employer's share of the F.I.C.A. taxes, are required to be paid quarterly. Both taxes are reported on a single tax form, which must be filed during the month following the close of the quarter. For example, the taxes for January, February, and March must be reported and paid by April 30.

If the sum of the income taxes withheld from employees and the total F.I.C.A. taxes (on employer and employee) exceeds $100 for the first or the second month of any quarter, the employer is required to deposit the amount due for that month in the Federal Reserve Bank in his district. The deposit, which may be accepted by authorized commercial banks, should be made by the fifteenth of the following month. For example, if during the month of January an employer withholds $87.50 of income taxes and the F.I.C.A. taxes (both employer's and employees' share) are $18, the total of $105.50 must be deposited by February 15. The employer receives as evidence of the deposit a "Federal Depositary Receipt." The receipts are then submitted with the quarterly tax report.

The amount due for the third month of the quarter, regardless of the amount, may accompany the quarterly return or may be deposited by the employer. When the amounts due for each month in the quarter are deposited by the fifteenth of the following month, the employer is allowed an additional ten days in which to file the quarterly report. For example, if the taxes for January, February, and March are deposited by February 15, March 15, and April 15 respectively, the quarterly return need not be filed until May 10; otherwise it is due on April 30.

State unemployment compensation tax. The state laws vary with respect to the type and the number of tax forms or returns that employers must file. In general, employers are required to file a tax return and to pay the tax during the month following each calendar quarter.

Federal unemployment compensation tax. The federal unemployment compensation tax is payable annually. The tax return for the calendar year, accompanied by the remittance, must be filed by January 31 of the following year.

Recording payment. Payment of the various taxes is recorded in the same manner as the payment of other liabilities, that is, by a debit to the particular liability account — Employees Income Taxes Payable, F.I.C.A. Taxes Payable, State Unemployment Taxes Payable, or Federal Unemployment Taxes Payable — and a credit to Cash. Monthly payments to a Federal Reserve Bank for federal income taxes withheld and for F.I.C.A. taxes are considered as payments of the respective liabilities.

When the voucher system is used, it is necessary to prepare a voucher immediately prior to the payment of each tax due. To illustrate, assume that Baker Electrical Supply, whose fiscal year ends on December 31, follows the procedures previously outlined in recording its liability for taxes. After the books have been adjusted and closed for December 31, 1961, the balances in the various tax liability accounts as of January 1, 1962, are as follows:

```
F.I.C.A. Taxes Payable (December)................................  $ 81.72
Employees Income Taxes Payable (December)......................    286.70
State Unemployment Taxes Payable (October-December)............     45.77
Federal Unemployment Taxes Payable (January-December)..........    113.38
```

The vouchers for the payment of these liabilities are recorded in the voucher register as follows, assuming arbitrarily that each liability is to be paid on January 30, 1962:

VOUCHER REGISTER

DATE	VCHR. NO.	PAYEE	PAID DATE	PAID CK. NO.	ACCOUNTS PAYABLE CR.	SUNDRY ACCOUNTS, DR. ACCOUNT	POST. REF.	AMOUNT
1962								
Jan. 30	908	Internal Revenue Service.......	1–30	891	368 42	F.I.C.A. Taxes Pay... Employees Income Taxes Payable....	215.1 215.2	81 72 286 70
30	909	State Treasurer..	1–30	892	45 77	State Unemployment Taxes Payable....	215.3	45 77
30	910	Internal Revenue Service.......	1–30	893	113 38	Federal Unemployment Taxes Payable	215.4	113 38

Adjustments at the end of the fiscal period

If the end of a fiscal period does not coincide with the end of a payroll period, it is necessary to record the accrued salaries for the incomplete payroll period; otherwise the expenses for the period will be understated and, as of the last day of the period, proprietorship will be overstated and liabilities will be understated. The adjusting entry results in a debit to the appropriate expense accounts and a credit to salaries payable.

After the books have been closed, the foregoing adjusting entry is reversed so as to avoid disrupting the usual payroll procedures. The entry to record the first payroll in January would be made in the usual manner.

The adjustment for the incomplete payroll period does not affect the amount of the employer's tax liability for the month in which the incomplete payroll period occurs. Payroll taxes are based on remuneration *paid* rather than on remuneration *earned*. It is for this reason that accrued taxes on accrued payroll are not deductible as an expense in computing income subject to the federal income tax. On the other hand, there is sound justification for the point of view that the period that benefits from the services of the employees should be charged with the payroll taxes related to those services. Accordingly, some accountants adjust the accounts for the accrued payroll taxes related to an incomplete payroll period. In most cases, however, the amount is relatively small, and since the effect upon the final net income of the fiscal period is usually not material, many consider it preferable to follow income tax procedures and ignore the accrual.

Completed payroll periods

In many business firms there is a lag of a variable number of days between the end of the payroll period and the payment of the payroll. Such a delay may be necessitated by the time required to complete the records and prepare the checks. For example, an employer who pays his employees on Friday may end the payroll period on Wednesday; the two-day lag between Wednesday and Friday being required to process the payroll. In order to simplify the explanations and avoid confusion over dates, the illustrations in this chapter were based on the assumption that payment was made on the last day of the payroll period.

The time lag in payment does not affect the accounting procedures for completed payroll periods throughout the year. If the payroll for the last completed period is unpaid on the last day of the year, the related employer's payroll taxes should be accrued if it is desired to relate such taxes to the period in which the wages were earned. On the other hand, if the income tax concept of tax accrual at time of wage payments is followed, the employer's payroll taxes would not be accrued.

It should also be noted that the F.I.C.A. and unemployment compensation taxes of both the employee and the employer must be determined as of the calendar year in which wages are to be paid rather than for the calendar year in which they are earned. To illustrate, assume that an employee's earnings record indicates prior cumulative earnings of $5,800 and that his salary for the payroll week ending December 30, is $120. If the payroll is paid on December 30 or 31, the $120 salary would not be subject to F.I.C.A. taxes or unemployment compensation taxes. If the payroll is paid in January, the salary would be fully taxable.

Questions

1. Identify the types of remuneration.
2. (a) What federal taxes must most employers withhold from employees?
   (b) What accounts are used to record the amounts withheld?
3. (a) What is the purpose of the Withholding Exemption Certificate?
   (b) What are exemptions?
4. (a) What is the primary use of the payroll record presented on pages 352 and 353?
   (b) Is it a special journal from which postings are made to the ledger?
5. Indicate the three ways in which employees may be paid.
6. The Roberts Restaurant pays its employees weekly by checks drawn on a payroll bank account. (a) At what times should deposits be made in the account? (b) How is the amount of the deposit determined? (c) Is it necessary to have an account entitled "Payroll Bank" in the ledger? Explain. (d) The bank statement for the payroll bank account for the month ended October 31 indicates a credit balance of $392.47. Assuming that the bank has made no errors, how do you explain this fact?
7. An employer who pays in currency draws a check for $4,722.83 for the payroll of August 24. After the money is inserted in the envelopes for the 45 employees there remains $12 in currency. Assuming that the arithmetical accuracy of the payroll record has been determined and that the details on the pay envelopes agree with the payroll record, what would you do to locate the error?
8. Indicate the principal uses of the employee's earnings record.
9. (a) Identify the payroll taxes borne by the employer. (b) When must each tax be paid?
10. What records are used in preparing Withholding Statements (Form W-2) at the end of the year?
11. When an employer who uses the voucher system pays his employees every week, a voucher is prepared for each payroll. Should a voucher also be prepared for each tax liability at the same time? Explain.
12. Under the federal income tax laws, when do the F.I.C.A. tax and unemployment compensation taxes become a liability?

Exercises

1. James Monroe is employed at the rate of $3.00 per hour, with time-and-one-half for all hours in excess of 40 worked during a week. Data to be considered in preparing the payroll record, Monroe's pay-check, and his earnings record for the current week ended September 20 are as follows: Hours worked, 46; Federal income tax withheld, $19.60; Cumulative earnings for year prior to current week, $4,720.30; F.I.C.A. tax withheld prior to current week, $141.61. Compute the following for the week ended September 20: (a) Monroe's earnings; (b) F.I.C.A. tax to be withheld (3% on maximum of $4,800); (c) Take-home pay.

2. In the following summary of columnar totals of a payroll record, some amounts have been intentionally omitted:

Earnings:			(6) U. S. Bonds.......	40.50
(1) At regular rate.....	$1,292.60		(7) Total deductions...	183.70
(2) At overtime rate....	———		(8) Net amount paid...	1,236.50
(3) Total earnings.....	———		Accounts debited:	
Deductions:			(9) Sales Salaries......	874.00
(4) F.I.C.A. tax.......	42.61		(10) Office Salaries.....	———
(5) Income tax withheld	———			

(a) Determine the totals omitted in lines (2), (3), (5), and (10). (b) Present the general journal entry to record the payroll. (c) Present, in general journal form, the entry to record the voucher for the payroll. (d) Present, in general journal form, the entry to record the payment of the payroll.

3. Total wage and salary expense of Potter Laundry for the year was $100,000, of which $12,000 was exempt from the F.I.C.A. tax and $20,000 was exempt from state and federal unemployment taxes. Determine the employer's payroll tax expense for the year, using the following rates: F.I.C.A., 3%; state unemployment, 1.9%; federal unemployment, .4%.

4. According to a summary of the payroll records of Jameson and Co. for the four weekly payrolls paid in July, the amount of earnings subject to the F.I.C.A. tax is $11,646.30 and the amount subject to the unemployment compensation taxes is $9,823.65. Assuming rates of 3%, 2.5%, and .4%, present the general journal entry to record the payroll tax expense and taxes accrued for the month.

Problems

16-1. The Modern Sales Co. has nine employees. They are paid on an hourly basis, receiving time-and-one-half pay for all hours worked in excess of 40 a week. The record of time worked for the week ended Saturday, October 28, of the current year, together with other relevant information, is summarized below:

Name	No.	M	T	W	TH	F	S	Rate per Hour	Bond Deductions	Income Tax Withheld
A	17	8	8	8	8	8	2	$1.80		$ 9.20
B	24	8	8	8	4	9	0	1.75	$2.50	7.10
C	19	8	8	8	8	8	3	2.25	1.25	11.50
D	18	8	8	0	8	8	0	2.00		4.80
E	23	6	8	6	8	8	4	1.80	3.75	6.20
F	22	8	8	8	8	8	0	2.50		9.20
G	15	8	8	8	8	8	4	3.00	5.00	16.90
H	26	8	4	8	8	8	5	1.90	1.25	11.90
I	20	8	8	8	8	8	4	2.20	2.50	13.80

Cumulative earnings paid (before deductions) prior to the current week were as follows: A, $3,700; B, $3,200; C, $4,720; D, $2,960; E, $2,840; F, $4,350; G, $5,200; H, $2,980; I, $4,770.

C, F, and I are office employees, the others are salesmen. A group insurance deduction of $.50 per week is made from each employee's earnings. The following tax rates apply: F.I.C.A., 3% on maximum of $4,800; state unemployment (employer only), 1.6%; federal unemployment, .4%.

Instructions: (1) Prepare a payroll record similar to that illustrated on pages 352 and 353 of the textbook.

(2) Journalize the entry to record the payroll for the week.

(3) The company uses a voucher system and a payroll bank account. Give the entries in *general journal form* to record the payroll voucher and the payment of the payroll. The payroll checks are issued in the order of the names on the payroll, beginning with Check No. 382.

(4) Journalize the entry to record the employer's payroll taxes for the week.

16-2. The following accounts, with the balances indicated, appear in the ledger of Electronic Products Co. on December 1 of the current year:

214	Salaries Payable......................................	——
215.1	F.I.C.A. Taxes Payable...........................	$ 233.37
215.2	Employees Income Taxes Payable.................	1,068.80
215.3	State Unemployment Taxes Payable...............	124.30
215.4	Federal Unemployment Taxes Payable.............	264.72
216.1	Bond Deductions Payable........................	380.30
216.2	Hospital Deductions Payable......................	81.00
611	Sales Salary Expense.............................	87,236.70
711	Officers Salary Expense...........................	36,300.00
712	Office Salary Expense.............................	9,260.30
719	Payroll Tax Expense..............................	4,117.54

The following transactions relating to payroll, payroll deductions, and payroll taxes occur during December:

Dec. 1. Prepared Voucher No. 746, payable to Merchants National Bank, for $131.25 to purchase U. S. Savings Bonds (2 at $37.50 and 3 at $18.75) for employees.

2. Issued Check No. 732 in payment of Voucher No. 746.

Dec. 14. Prepared Voucher No. 787, payable to Merchants National Bank, for the amount of employees' income tax and F.I.C.A. tax due on December 15.

14. Issued Check No. 765 in payment of Voucher No. 787.

15. Prepared a general journal entry to record the biweekly payroll for the period ending yesterday. A summary of the payroll record follows: Deductions:F.I.C.A. tax, $57.60; income taxes withheld $537.80; bond deductions, $71.25; hospital deductions, $81.

Salary Distribution: officers salaries, $1,650; sales salaries $3,924; office salaries, $480.

Net Amount: $5,306.35.

15. Prepared Voucher No. 792, payable to Payroll Bank Account, for the net amount of the biweekly payroll.

15. Issued Check No. 789 in payment of Voucher No. 792.

16. Prepared Voucher No. 799, payable to Memorial Hospital, for $162 for contributions withheld from employees' earnings during the past two pay periods.

17. Issued Check No. 793 in payment of Voucher No. 799.

29. Prepared a general journal entry to record the biweekly payroll for the period ending yesterday. A summary of the payroll record follows: Deductions: F.I.C.A. tax, $54.68; income taxes withheld, $526.30; bond deductions, $76.50.

Salary Distribution: officers salaries, $1,650; sales salaries, $3,813; office salaries, $480.

Net Amount: $5,285.52.

29. Prepared Voucher No. 851, payable to Payroll Bank Account, for the net amount of the biweekly payroll.

29. Issued Check No. 843 in payment of Voucher No. 851.

29. Prepared Voucher No. 854, payable to Merchants National Bank, for $75 to purchase U. S. Savings Bonds (2 at $37.50) for employees.

30. Issued Check No. 847 in payment of Voucher No. 854.

31. Prepared a general journal entry to record the employer's payroll taxes on earnings paid in December. Taxable earnings for the two payrolls, according to the payroll records, are as follows: subject to F.I.C.A. tax, $3,742.60; subject to unemployment compensation tax, $2,126. The following rates apply: F.I.C.A., 3%; state unemployment, 2.3%; federal unemployment, .4%.

Instructions: (1) Open the accounts listed and enter the balances shown under date of December 1.

(2) Record the transactions, using a voucher register like the one on pages 310 and 311, a check register like the one on page 312 but omitting the columns for Bank Deposits and Bank Balance, and a general journal. After each entry, post all items affecting the accounts opened in the ledger.

(3) Journalize the adjusting entry on December 31 to record salaries for the incomplete payroll period. Salaries accrued are as follows: officers salaries, $165; sales salaries, $380; office salaries, $48. Post to the accounts.

(4) Journalize the entry to close the salary expense and payroll tax expense accounts to Expense and Revenue Summary, post to the accounts, and extend all account balances to the appropriate balance columns.

(5) Journalize the entry on January 1 to reverse the adjustment of December 31. Post to the accounts.

(6) Assume that Vouchers Nos. 937, 938, and 939 are prepared on January 29 for the payment of the liabilities for payroll taxes shown on December 31. List the taxes, the period of time to which each applies, and the amount of each voucher using the following headings:

VOUCHER NUMBER	TAX	PERIOD COVERED	AMOUNT OF VOUCHER

16-3. George Bryson, proprietor of Ideal Office Equipment Co., employs twelve people. Two office employees and five salesmen are paid straight weekly salaries; three salesmen and two deliverymen are employed on an hourly basis with time-and-one-half for hours in excess of 40 a week. The data necessary for the preparation of the payroll for the week ended August 5 of the current year are presented in the tabulation and notations below:

NAME	EM- PLOYEE No.	M	T	W	TH	F	S	HOURLY OR WEEKLY RATE	INCOME TAX WITH- HELD	CLASSIFI- CATION
Alban, Robert.....	18	8	8	8	8	6	8	$ 2.40	$ 9.60	Sales
Baldwin, Carl......	8	8	6	8	8	8	3	2.20	5.20	Delivery
Easton, Thomas....	9							90.00	11.80	Sales
Gillis, Fred........	6							100.00	9.20	Office
Hart, Ronald......	7							120.00	15.10	Sales
Johns, David......	2							150.00	23.30	Sales
Moore, Victor.....	14	8	6	8	8	8	2	1.80	......	Delivery
Miller, Ann.......	19							65.00	11.70	Office
Price, Chester......	17	8	8	8	8	8	8	2.00	9.20	Sales
Reed, Walter......	15	8	8	6	7	8	8	2.00	12.50	Sales
Story, Roger.......	10							85.00	10.20	Sales
Tracy, Edward....	16							120.00	11.50	Sales

Prior to the present week, the compensation paid (before considering deductions) to Fred Gillis, Ronald Hart, David Johns, and Edward Tracy totaled $2,920, $3,600, $4,750, and $2,960, respectively. No other employee will exceed $3,000 during the current week. The following tax rates apply: F.I.C.A., 3% on maximum of $4,800; state unemployment, 2.7%; federal unemployment, .4%.

Instructions: (1) Prepare a payroll record similar in form to the one on pages 352 and 353 of the textbook, deleting the deduction columns not needed and adding another column for payroll distribution.

(2) Journalize the entry to record the payroll for the week.

(3) Assuming the use of a voucher system and payment by regular check (Nos. 732–743), give the entries, in *general journal form*, to record the payroll voucher and its payment.

The following transactions are selected from those completed by Ideal Office Equipment Co. during the remainder of August:

Aug. 14. Prepared a voucher, payable to First National Bank, for employees' income taxes, $464.30, and F.I.C.A. taxes $171.54, on salaries paid in July.

14. Issued a check to First National Bank in payment of the above voucher.
28. Prepared a general journal entry to record the employer's payroll taxes for the payroll periods ending August 5, 12, 19, and 26. A summary of relevant information taken from the four payroll sheets follows: taxable earnings subject to F.I.C.A. tax, $3,927.60; taxable earnings subject to unemployment compensation tax, $2,076.80.

Instructions: (4) Give the entries, in *general journal form*, to record the transactions of August 14 and 28.

(5) Journalize the adjusting entry on August 31 to record the salaries for the incomplete payroll period, August 28 to 31 (Monday through Thursday). Accrue two thirds of the weekly salary for employees on a weekly basis. All employees on an hourly basis worked 8 hours on each of the four days. There have been no changes in weekly or hourly salary rates.

16-4. The following information relative to the payroll of Spector Wholesalers for the week ended December 30 of the current year appears on the payroll record and other records:

Salaries:
    Sales Salaries............ $33,900
    Office Salaries........... 7,200
    Warehouse Salaries...... 4,100
                    $45,200

Deductions:
    Income tax withheld..... $ 4,260
    Bond deductions........ 700
    Hospital deductions..... 300
    F.I.C.A. tax withheld is assumed to total the same amount as the employer's tax.

Tax Rates:
    F.I.C.A., 3%.
    State unemployment (employer only), 1.6%.
    Federal unemployment, .4%.

Instructions: (1) Assuming that the payroll for the last week of the year is to be paid on December 31, present the following entries:
    (a) December 30, to record the payroll. Of the total payroll for the last week of the year $9,800 is subject to the F.I.C.A. tax and $4,310 is subject to unemployment compensation taxes.
    (b) December 30, to record the employer's payroll taxes on the payroll to be paid on December 31.

(2) Assuming that the payroll for the last week of the year is to be paid on January 2 of the following fiscal year, present the following entries:
    (a) December 31, to record the payroll.
    (b) January 2, to record the employer's payroll taxes on the payroll to be paid on January 2.

Property, sales, and income taxes

Taxes in general

The operations of most governmental units are supported by required contributions called *taxes*. Taxes are levied on various segments of the population, such as property owners, consumers, business enterprises, wage earners, and employers. There are many taxing agencies, including the federal and state governments and various local units, such as the county, city, township, and school district.

Taxes are frequently classified according to the relationship of the tax rate to the base against which the rate is applied. A tax rate that remains constant regardless of the size of the tax base is said to be a *proportional* tax. For example, when a real estate tax is levied at a single fixed rate per dollar of valuation, it is proportional. If the tax rate increases as the base against which it is levied increases, it is termed a *progressive* tax. As an example, income tax systems usually provide for successively higher rates against additional segments of income. The opposite of a progressive tax is a *regressive* tax, which is levied at lower rates as the tax base increases. For example, the fee for obtaining a corporation charter is frequently based upon the number of shares authorized, with a successively lower rate per share as the number of shares increases.

Relationship to accounting

Accounting and taxes are closely interrelated. The taxes incurred by a business enterprise usually amount to a substantial portion of the sales dollar, and it is necessary that these taxes be properly recorded in the accounts and reported in the financial statements. Some taxes are payable in advance; others accrue and are payable after the close of the period to which they relate. A knowledge of the various tax laws is essential in the determination of the period to which the tax applies and of the amount of the prepayment or the accrued liability at the time a balance sheet is prepared.

371

The amount of the liability for many taxes is determined from information supplied by the accounting records. Outstanding examples of this type are payroll taxes, sales taxes, and income taxes. Failure on the part of management to maintain accurate records may result in the assessment of penalties or the payment of a greater amount of tax than the law requires. The responsibility for preparing tax reports for a business usually rests with the accounting department.

There are four types of taxes that affect almost every business enterprise: (1) payroll taxes, (2) property taxes, (3) sales taxes, and (4) income taxes. Payroll taxes were discussed in the preceding chapter; this chapter will be devoted to a brief discussion of the remaining three.

Property taxes

Property taxes are a principal source of revenue for local governmental units. Counties, cities, and school districts, for example, secure most, and in some cases all, of their funds by imposing taxes upon the owners of property. In some states, the central government imposes taxes on property

Types of property. In law, all property is either real property or personal property. *Real property*, also called *realty* or *real estate*, includes land and anything permanently attached to the land. Buildings, trees, fences, water lines, sidewalks, and other improvements to land come within the definition of real property.

All property not classified as realty is termed *personal property*, or *personalty*. Such property is subdivided into two major categories, *tangible* and *intangible*. Tangible personalty includes equipment, merchandise, supplies, and other physical assets. Intangible personalty includes investments in stocks and bonds, accounts and notes receivable, prepaid insurance, bank deposits, and other assets having no physical existence.

It is not always a simple matter to distinguish between realty and tangible personalty. The boiler and other components of a steam heating system are obviously a part of a building and hence real property. A typewriter and a filing cabinet are just as obviously tangible personal property. Air-conditioning equipment may be classified as either, depending upon the type of equipment and the manner of installation. In many cases it is necessary to consult regulations issued by the taxing authority to determine the classification of property for tax purposes. Improper classification may result in the payment of more taxes than is necessary.

Tax base. The method of determining the value of property for tax purposes varies among taxing jurisdictions and for different types of property. The value assigned to real estate is frequently determined by the tax assessor without reference to cost, book value, or other evidence provided in the accounts and records of the owner. In general, the assessed value tends to be lower than the fair market value of the property. Personal property may also be appraised by an assessor, or the owner may be required to declare the value of his property. In the latter case the cost of the property is usually the starting point in determining value for tax purposes. Methods of determining the amount of depreciation to be deducted from cost in arriving at the tax base are usually prescribed by statute or administrative regulations.

Tax rates. A governmental unit determines its tax rate each year by dividing the total revenue to be raised from the tax by the total assessed value of the property within its jurisdiction. For example, if the budgeted revenue requirements of a county for the year amount to $2,000,000 and the value of all taxable property in the county is $100,000,000, the county tax rate will be set at 20 mills (2 cents) per $1 of assessed value ($2,000,000 ÷ $100,000,000). A person whose property is assessed at $30,000 will be required to pay a tax of $600 for the year (.02 x $30,000). In some cases the tax rate on tangible personal property is lower than the tax rate on real property.

Payment of taxes. The time specified for payment of property taxes varies greatly among governmental units. Real estate taxes and personal property taxes may be billed together or they may be billed separately and at different times. Frequently the law provides for payment in two installments. If taxes are not paid on time, they become *delinquent* and the property owner may be charged with an additional sum as a penalty. If the taxes and the penalties are not paid within a specified number of months or years, the property may be seized by the government and sold. Property taxes become a *lien* against the property, usually from the date of assessment until they are paid. A purchaser of property on which the taxes have not been paid acquires it subject to the lien of the government.

In many cases property is subject to property taxes levied by more than one jurisdiction. For example, the property located in a certain school district may also be within the boundaries of a town or city, and the latter, in turn, within a county. In such cases, it is not unusual for the county to bill and collect the taxes for all of the jurisdictions. The tax receipts are then distributed among the various units.

Accounting for property taxes

Taxes levied on the property of a business are an operating expense. The liability for property taxes does not accrue day by day in the manner that interest accrues. Rather, the liability relates to the ownership of property on a particular day of the year, as specified by the statutes of the taxing jurisdiction or by court decision. On the other hand, the tax expense recurs each year and should be spread over the months in the year in an equitable manner. The problem is complicated by the fact that the exact amount of the liability may not be known until an appreciable period of time after the date the liability attaches.

Various methods of accounting for property taxes are acceptable as long as the method selected is followed consistently from year to year. The method described below provides for monthly allocation over the fiscal year of the taxing authority for which the tax is levied.[1]

In the illustration that follows it is assumed that the fiscal year of both the taxing authority and the taxpayer is the calendar year. It is also assumed that property taxes are assessed on January 1 for the ensuing year, that statements are mailed in mid-April, and that taxes are payable in two equal installments, on June 15 and October 15.

The first entry on the taxpayer's books will record one twelfth of the tax liability for the year on January 31. Inasmuch as the exact amount of the tax for the year will not be known until the statement is received, it is necessary to estimate the amount. The estimate is based on the experience of the preceding year, taking into consideration any known changes in the tax or assessed value. Assuming that the estimate of property tax for the current year is $1,500, the amount allocable to January is one twelfth of this amount, or $125. The entry to record the accrual on the taxpayer's books is as follows:

Jan. 31   Property Tax Expense............................. 125.00
              Property Taxes Payable...........................   125.00

An entry for the same amount is made at the end of February and March. On April 20 the taxpayer receives a statement for $1,551, half of which is payable on June 15, and half on October 15. The correct amount of tax allocable to each month is thus one twelfth of $1,551, or $129.25. When the difference between the actual expense and the estimated expense is not material, which is usually the case, it is unnecessary to go back and correct the prior allocation. Instead, the difference is adjusted in the entry for the month in which the amount of the tax becomes known. The amount to be recorded in April is therefore determined as follows:

---

[1]Recommended by *Accounting Research Bulletin* No. 43, "Restatement and Revision of Accounting Research Bulletins," 1953 (New York: American Institute of Certified Public Accountants), pp. 81–85.

Amount of tax chargeable for Jan., Feb., Mar., 3 x $129.25	$387.75
Amount actually charged for Jan., Feb., Mar., 3 x $125.00	375.00
Deficiency in prior periods	$ 12.75
Tax expense applicable to April	129.25
Accrual for April	$142.00

On the basis of this computation, the following entry is made at the end of April:

Apr. 30 Property Tax Expense	142.00	
Property Taxes Payable		142.00

At the end of May an additional expense of $129.25 and an increase in the liability of like amount are recorded; and when the first installment is paid on June 15, the payment is recorded as follows:

June 15 Property Taxes Payable	646.25	
Property Tax Expense	129.25	
Cash		775.50

Monthly allocations of $129.25 are recorded in July, August, and September in the usual manner by debits to the expense account and credits to the liability account. When the second half of the tax bill is paid on October 15, the payment is recorded as follows:

Oct. 15 Property Taxes Payable	387.75	
Property Tax Expense	129.25	
Prepaid Property Taxes	258.50	
Cash		775.50

The effect of the debits in the foregoing entry is (1) to reduce to zero the liability for taxes accrued for July, August, and September, (2) to charge October with its pro rata share of tax expense, and (3) to set up as an asset the pro rata share of tax expense for November and December.

At the end of November, and again at the end of December, the following entry is made:

Nov. 30 Property Tax Expense	129.25	
Prepaid Property Taxes		129.25

The complete series of transactions for the year may be traced through the T accounts appearing at the top of the following page.

Delinquent taxes on property purchased

It is not unusual to purchase property that is subject to a lien for deliquent property taxes and penalty charges. These amounts constitute an additional cost of the property rather than expenses, since they are taken into account in arriving at the price the purchaser is willing to pay the vendor. To illustrate, assume that on April 4 Paul Foster purchased a building site for which he agreed to pay the vendor $5,000. Delinquent taxes, penalties, and interest accumulated on the property amounted to

Cash

		June 15	775.50
		Oct. 15	775.50
			1,551.00

Property Tax Expense

Jan. 31	125.00
Feb. 28	125.00
Mar. 31	125.00
Apr. 30	142.00
May 31	129.25
June 15	129.25
July 31	129.25
Aug. 31	129.25
Sept. 30	129.25
Oct. 15	129.25
Nov. 30	129.25
Dec. 31	129.25
	1,551.00

Property Taxes Payable

June 15	646.25	Jan. 31	125.00
Oct. 15	387.75	Feb. 28	125.00
	1,034.00	Mar. 31	125.00
		Apr. 30	142.00
		May 31	129.25
		July 31	129.25
		Aug. 31	129.25
		Sept. 30	129.25
			1,034.00

Prepaid Property Taxes

Oct. 15	258.50	Nov. 30	129.25
		Dec. 31	129.25
			258.50

$625. The total cost of the property is $5,625, and this amount should be debited to Land. Credits totaling the same amount will be made to Cash and the appropriate liability accounts in accordance with the terms agreed upon.

Special assessments

The owners of land are sometimes subject to a special tax to reimburse the local government for the cost of improvements on or adjacent to their property. Such taxes are called *special assessments*. Improvements commonly financed in this way include the installation of sewers, water mains, and street lights; the paving of streets; and the laying of curbs and sidewalks. Because the benefits received for special assessment taxes continue over a long period of time, these taxes are properly chargeable to the land account rather than to an expense account. Any subsequent expenditures for repairs to the improvements, whether by way of additional assessments or through general tax levies, constitute expense.

Sales taxes

Sales taxes are an important source of revenue for many states and cities. Such taxes may apply only to the sale of commodities or they may also apply to the sale of specified services such as dry cleaning, shoe repairs, and rentals of certain kinds of property. Such taxes are usually imposed only upon retail sales or sales to consumers. The sale of certain commodities may be exempt from tax. For example, in some jurisdictions the tax does not apply to the sale of food for consumption off the premises of the seller. Sales of gasoline, cigarettes, and other commodities subject to a special tax by the state may also be exempted from the sales tax.

Sales taxes are levied as a per cent of all sales except those specifically exempted. In some states the tax is levied directly upon the seller. In others the statutes impose the tax upon the purchaser but require the seller to collect the tax. Sales tax returns, accompanied by a remittance for the amount due, are required to be filed monthly, quarterly, or semi-annually, depending upon the law of the state or the city.

Sales taxes imposed upon the purchaser

When the law imposes a sales tax on the purchaser and requires that the merchant collect and remit to the taxing authority, the tax must be added to the amount of each taxable sale. The tax usually attaches at the time of the sale, regardless of when payment is to be received; hence, the liability for the tax should be recorded at the time of sale. For example, a cash sale of $50 subject to a sales tax of 2% should be recorded as a debit to Cash of $51, a credit to Sales of $50, and a credit to Sales Taxes Payable of $1. A sale on account would be recorded in the same manner except that the debit to Cash would be replaced by a debit to Accounts Receivable.

Modern cash registers provide for recording the amount of each sale and the amount of the tax separately. When such devices are not employed, the money received for the sale and that received for the tax may be physically separated until the close of the day. In any event, the system should provide a means of determining the exact amount of sales taxes collected each day on cash sales. Appropriate entries can then be recorded in the cash receipts journal, as illustrated below.

CASH RECEIPTS JOURNAL

DATE		ACCOUNT CREDITED	POST. REF.	SALES CR.	SALES TAXES PAYABLE CR.	CASH DR.
1962						
Feb.	1	Sales	✓	839 24	16 78	856 02
	2	R. B. Nolan	✓			216 50
	2	Sales	✓	791 86	15 84	807 70

The amount of sales tax imposed on a sale on account is reported as a separate item on the sales slip or invoice. If such original evidences are used as a sales journal, separate totals are obtained for sales and for sales taxes payable at the end of the month and the appropriate entry is recorded in the general journal. A sales journal designed to record sales subject to a sales tax is illustrated below.

SALES JOURNAL

DATE		SALE NO.	ACCOUNT DEBITED	POST. REF.	ACCOUNTS RECEIVABLE DR.		SALES TAXES PAYABLE CR.		SALES CR.	
1962										
Feb.	2	495	J. L. Parker	√	15	30		30	15	00
	2	496	Henry Baker	√	87	72	1	72	86	00
	2	497	C. T. Meyer	√	168	81	3	31	165	50

Reductions in the amount of sales taxes payable resulting from sales returns and allowances may be recorded in the Sundry Accounts Dr. column of the cash payments journal or in the general journal. If the number of such transactions is significant, the appropriate journal may be modified by the addition of a column for Sales Taxes Payable Dr.

When some of the sales of an enterprise are exempt from the sales tax, it is necessary to provide an efficient means of determining separate totals for taxable sales and nontaxable sales. In addition to the use of special cash register keys, memorandum columns for accumulating the information may be inserted in the appropriate journals.

Sales taxes imposed upon the seller

When a sales tax is imposed upon the seller, there is ordinarily no separate charge made to the customer. It is then necessary only to segregate taxable sales from exempt sales. The tax liability can be determined at the end of each month and an entry made to record the expense and the liability. For example, assume that the sales taxes for the month of March were determined to be $486.32. The following general journal entry would be necessary:

March 31 Sales Tax Expense................................. 486.32
         Sales Taxes Payable............................ 486.32
         Sales taxes for the month.

Any balance in the sales taxes payable account on a balance sheet date is reported as a current liability. The sales tax expense account is closed to Expense and Revenue Summary at the end of the fiscal period. There is not complete agreement as to where Sales Tax Expense should be shown on the income statement. Some accountants classify it as an operating expense, often under the heading of "Selling Expenses." Many accountants show the item as a deduction from gross sales. This latter treatment is preferable, as it shows the amount of revenue actually provided to the business by the sales of the period.

Federal income tax

The federal income tax system, which is codified in the Internal Revenue Code, dates from the ratification of the 16th Amendment to the Constitution in 1913. It is the largest single source of revenue for the federal government. For a recent year some fifty-nine million income tax returns were filed by individuals, of which approximately four fifths required the payment of tax.

The income tax is assessed against individuals, estates, trusts, and corporations. It is important to note that the tax is not imposed upon business units as such, but upon taxable entities. A corporation is a legal entity that has an existence entirely apart from its stockholder owners. All business corporations are required to file an annual income tax return. Even though a corporation operates several distinct and unrelated businesses, the operating results of all units are combined in a single tax return.

A sole proprietorship is usually treated as a distinct entity for accounting purposes, but the business enterprise and its owner are not separable under the income tax law. The proprietor must report the net income or the net loss of his business enterprise (or enterprises) in his personal income tax return, together with any other items of taxable income and allowable deductions.

Partnerships are ordinarily not taxable entities, but they are required to file an informational return showing the results of operations and each partner's share of the net income or the net loss. The individual partners then report their respective shares in their personal returns. It is the distributive share of the income rather than the amount actually withdrawn from the firm that must be reported in the personal tax return of each partner.

Under certain circumstances specified in the Code it is possible for some corporations to elect to be treated as partnerships for income tax purposes. Conversely, it is possible for partnerships to elect to be taxed as though they were corporations.

Accounting methods

The law recognizes the fact that no uniform method of accounting can be prescribed for all taxpayers. As a safeguard, however, the tax authorities are given discretion to prescribe a method of accounting that will clearly reflect income if the method employed by the taxpayer is faulty. Each taxpayer is required to make a return of his true income, and he must necessarily maintain such records as will enable him to do so. In general, taxpayers have the option of using either the *accrual basis* or the *cash basis* of determining income. Once adopted, however, the tax-payer may change from one method to the other only with official permission.

Accrual basis. Under the accrual basis or method of accounting, revenue is recorded in the period in which it is earned, even though it is not received during the same period, and expenses are recorded as they are incurred, even though they are not paid during the same period. This is the method of accounting that has been developed throughout the preceding chapters of this book. The effect of the various year-end adjustments discussed in earlier chapters is to assign revenue and expenses to the appropriate period, regardless of when cash is received or paid.

In determining the income from a business in which the production, purchase, or sale of merchandise is a material factor, purchases and sales of merchandise must be accounted for on the accrual basis. Thus a sale must be recorded as such in the year in which the goods are sold, regardless of when the cash is received in payment. Similarly, purchases must be recorded when title passes and a liability is incurred, regardless of when payment is made. Appropriate adjustments must be made, of course, for the inventories on hand at the beginning and the end of the year.

Entirely apart from income tax considerations, the accrual basis yields a fair determination of the annual income of business enterprises. It is the only fair method of accounting for purchases and sales of merchandise.

Cash basis. In contrast to the accrual basis, the cash basis or method of accounting recognizes revenue in the period in which it is actually received and recognizes expenses only as they are paid. Business and professional enterprises that sell services rather than commodities frequently use the cash basis of accounting. Under this system, for example, a physician maintains a memorandum record of fees charged to patients, recording them as revenue only as cash is received. No provision is made in the accounts for estimated uncollectible accounts. Charges to patients that eventually prove to be uncollectible are not recorded as bad debts expense because they have not previously been recorded as revenue. Bills for rent, electricity, and other expenses are not recorded until they are paid. It is readily apparent that the cash basis of accounting requires fewer entries and records and is less complex than the accrual basis.

Taxpayers employing the cash basis are required to recognize revenue in the year in which it is *constructively* received. Revenue is constructively received when it is available to the taxpayer without any restrictions. For example, if on December 31 a taxpayer receives a check or money order in payment of services, the amount should be reported as earned in December, even though the instrument is not "cashed" until the following January. Other examples are interest credited to a savings account and maturing interest coupons on bonds. They are constructively received on the date the money becomes available, regardless of when the taxpayer may actually receive the cash.

A taxpayer using the cash basis may not treat the entire cost of long-lived business assets as an expense in the year of purchase. As under the accrual basis, he may deduct depreciation each year. Similarly, when property or casualty insurance premiums are paid in advance for more than one year, only the pro rata amount is deductible each year.

Almost all individuals not engaged in business for themselves use the cash basis. When a taxpayer's income is composed exclusively of salary, dividends, interest, and perhaps rentals, this basis is simpler and in general yields satisfactory results. Taxpayers who do not maintain books of account are *required* to report on the cash basis.

Gross income

An income tax return must be filed by every individual under 65 years of age whose *gross income* for the taxable year is $600 or more. Individuals who are 65 years old or older must file a return if their *gross income* is $1,200 or more for the taxable year. The following excerpt from the statutory definition of gross income is indicative of the breadth of the term: "...all income from whatever source derived, including (but not limited to) the following items: (1) compensation for services, including fees, commissions, and similar items; (2) gross income derived from business; (3) gains derived from dealings in property; (4) interest; (5) rents; (6) royalties; (7) dividends; (8) alimony and separate maintenance payments;..."[2]

In spite of the inclusiveness of this general definition of gross income, a number of items are excluded either because they do not constitute income under the 16th Amendment or because they are specifically exempted by the Internal Revenue Code. A tabulation of the principal items included in gross income and the principal items excluded from gross income is given on the following page.

The lists are illustrative only and are not intended to be complete. In practice it is often necessary to refer to the law and to interpretations of the law in order to determine whether a particular item of income is taxable or exempt from tax.

---

[2]Internal Revenue Code, Sec. 61 (a).

INCLUDED IN GROSS INCOME (Must be Reported)	EXCLUDED FROM GROSS INCOME (Not Reported)
Wages, salaries, bonuses, and commissions.	Pensions and disability compensation to war veterans and their families.
Tips and gratuities for services rendered.	Federal and state social security benefits.
Interest.	Gifts, inheritances, and bequests.
Dividends in excess of $50.	Dividends up to $50.
Industrial, civil service, and other pensions, and endowments (annuities may be partially exempt).	Workmen's compensation insurance, damages, etc., for bodily injury or sickness.
Rents and royalties.	Life insurance proceeds received because of death of insured.
Income from a business or a profession.	Interest on state and municipal bonds.
Taxable gains from the sale of real estate, securities, and other property.	Interest on certain federal bonds issued before March 1, 1941.
The taxpayer's share of partnership income.	G. I. benefits and military bonuses received from federal or state governments.
The taxpayer's share of estate or trust income.	Scholarship received by college student for which no services are required.
Contest prizes.	
Gambling winnings.	

Tax base

The amount of the tax each individual is required to pay depends upon the amount of his gross income, the amount of the deductions that he may subtract from gross income, and the tax rates currently in effect. The deductions allowed by the law are divided into two principal categories: (1) deductions from *gross income* to arrive at what is termed *adjusted gross income* and (2) deductions from *adjusted gross income* to arrive at *taxable income*. Deductions in the second category are further subdivided into expenses of various types and personal exemptions. Individuals may use a so-called *standard deduction* in place of the amounts of actual expenses in the second category

The foregoing may be presented in outline fashion as follows:

Gross Income		$8,800
Deductions (generally of a business nature)		2,300
Adjusted Gross Income		$6,500
Deductions:		
Expenses (generally of a personal nature) or the Standard Deduction	$725	
Personal Exemptions	600	1,325
Taxable Income (tax rates are applied to this base)		$5,175

Deductions from gross income

As indicated in the outline above, the deductions allowable in determining adjusted gross income are generally of a business nature. The six categories of such deductions that are of general applicability are discussed in the following paragraphs.

Business expenses. Ordinary and necessary expenses incurred by the taxpayer in the operation of a trade, business, or profession (other than as an employee) are deductible from gross income of the business or profession. Salaries and wages, payroll taxes, property taxes, depreciation, utility expenses, insurance, advertising, travel, and interest on business indebtedness are examples of deductible business expenses. The tax forms provide spaces for reporting sales, cost of goods sold, gross profit from sales, business expenses, and finally, net income. This final net income figure is the *adjusted gross income* derived from the business.

Travel expenses of employee. Expenses of travel, meals, and lodging incurred by an employee while *away from home overnight* in connection with his employment are deductible from gross income. When the employee is required to travel but is not away from home overnight, the expenses of transportation only are deductible from gross income. To illustrate, assume that during the taxable year a taxpayer received a salary of $9,000. In connection with his employment he was required to make several trips away from home overnight, during which he spent $450 for transportation, meals, and lodging. His *adjusted gross income* from salary was $8,550 ($9,000 − $450). Had the travel been local and not requiring absence from home overnight, the amounts spent for transportation only would have been deductible.

Expenses of outside salesmen. An "outside salesman" is an employee engaged principally in the solicitation of business for his employer at places other than the employer's place of business. For such employees, expenses incurred for meals, split commissions paid on subcontracts, and other expenses related to their employment are deductible from gross income.

Reimbursed expenses. Expenses incurred by an employee for the benefit of the employer are deductible from gross income by the employee to the extent of any reimbursement received from the employer. The amount received by the employee as reimbursement must, of course, be included in gross income. For example, assume that a taxpayer received a salary of $8,400 and an entertainment allowance of $600 during the taxable year. During the same period he spent $550 in entertaining customers and prospective customers of his employer. The taxpayer's *adjusted gross income* from salary is $8,450 ($8,400 + $600 − $550).

Expenses attributable to rents and royalties. Expenses incurred by a taxpayer that are directly connected with earning rent or royalty income are allowable as deductions from gross income. Expenses commonly incurred in connection with rental properties include depreciation, taxes, repairs, utilities expense, wages of custodian, and interest on indebtedness on the property. For example, a taxpayer received $1,500 during the taxable year as rent for a one-family house and incurred related expenses of $840. His *adjusted gross income* from rent was $660 ($1,500 — $840).

Losses from sale or exchange of property. Deductible losses from the sale or exchange of property are deducted from gross income in arriving at adjusted gross income. In order for the loss to be deductible, the property must have been acquired or held for the production of income. For example, losses from the sale of stocks and bonds are deductible; a loss from the sale of the taxpayer's residence is not deductible.

Adjusted gross income

The amounts of the adjusted gross income of each type are added to yield the total adjusted gross income. If the taxpayer should incur a net loss from the operation of a business or from rentals, such a loss is deductible from adjusted gross income in the other categories. This point is illustrated by the following summary of adjusted gross income for a taxpayer for the current taxable year:

Source of Income	Gross Income	—	Allowable Deductions	=	Adjusted Gross Income
Salary............................	$10,600		$ 350		$10,250
Dividends (after $50 exclusion)........	510				510
Interest........................	200				200
Rentals.........................	1,200		1,440		(240)
Adjusted Gross Income..					$10,720

Deductions from adjusted gross income

After adjusted gross income is computed, certain deductions therefrom are allowed in arriving at *taxable income*, which is the base against which the tax rates are applied. Deductions in this group may be subdivided into the following categories:

(1) Personal expenses (not related to income-producing activities.)
(2) Expenses for the production of income (sometimes referred to as *nonbusiness* expenses.)
(3) Personal exemptions.

The more usual items in these three categories are discussed in the paragraphs that follow.

Contributions. Contributions by an individual to corporations, foundations, or associations created exclusively for religious, charitable, scientific, literary, or educational purposes, or for the prevention of cruelty to children or animals, are deductible provided the organization is nonprofit and does not devote a substantial part of its activities to influencing legislation. Contributions to the federal, state, or local governments, or to agencies thereof, and to organizations of war veterans are also deductible. The total amount of the deduction for contributions may not exceed 20% of adjusted gross income, except that there is an additional allowance of up to 10% of adjusted gross income for contributions to churches, hospitals, schools, and medical research organizations.

Interest. Interest may be personal, such as on indebtedness on the taxpayer's home, or nonbusiness, as on indebtedness incurred to buy securities. (Interest attributable to a business or to rents and royalties is deductible from *gross income.*)

Taxes. Many state and local taxes of a personal or nonbusiness nature are deductible from adjusted gross income. Examples of taxes that are deductible and taxes that are not deductible follow:

DEDUCTIBLE	NOT DEDUCTIBLE
Real estate taxes.	State inheritance taxes.
Personal property taxes.	Hunting and fishing licenses.
State income taxes.	Auto inspection fees.
Retail sales taxes assessed against the consumer.	Federal estate and gift taxes.
	Federal income taxes.
Auto license fees.	FICA taxes (employee's share).
State gasoline taxes.	Federal excise taxes on *personal* expenditures, such as taxes on furs, jewelry, cosmetics, admissions, transportation, and telephone.
Poll taxes.	

Losses. Losses of nonbusiness property resulting from fire, storm, automobile accident, or other casualty, or from theft, are deductible to the extent not compensated for by insurance. It should be noted that only loss or damage to the taxpayer's own property is deductible; there is no deduction for personal injuries or for damages to another's property caused by the taxpayer. The basis for determining the amount of any casualty loss of nonbusiness property is the cost less depreciation or the fair market value of the property, whichever is lower.

Medical expenses. Medical expenses paid are deductible to the extent that they exceed 3% of adjusted gross income. Medical expenses include such items as hospital expenses; fees to physicians, dentists, surgeons, etc.; and the cost of eyeglasses, hearing aids, artificial teeth, and medicines, except that medicines may be included in medical expenses only to the extent that their aggregate cost exceeds 1% of adjusted gross income. For example, if a taxpayer with an adjusted gross income of $7,000 has paid $95 for medicines and $400 for other medical expenses during the year, his medical expense deduction would be computed as follows:

Adjusted Gross Income..		$7,000
Medical Expenses:		
Medicines...	$95	
Less 1% of $7,000...	70	$ 25
Other medical expenses...		400
Total...		$ 425
Less 3% of $7,000...		210
Medical Expense Deduction...		$ 215

The maximum amount of the medical expense deduction is $2,500 for each exemption claimed on the tax return, with a maximum of $5,000 on a single return and $10,000 on a joint return of husband and wife.

If the taxpayer or his spouse is 65 years of age or older, he is not subject to the 3% restriction on medical expenses incurred for either of them. Medical expenses incurred for dependents are subject to the 3% limitation regardless of the age of the taxpayer or of the dependents.

Care-of-dependent expenses. Women and widowers who, in order to earn a living, must pay for the care of dependents, are allowed a deduction therefor. Only the actual amount spent for such care may be claimed as a deduction, and the maximum deduction is $600 per year regardless of the amount spent or the number of dependents involved. In order to be entitled to this deduction, the expenses must be incurred for a child or a stepchild under the age of 12, or a dependent, regardless of age, who is physically or mentally incapable of caring for himself.

A working wife is allowed the deduction only if she files a joint return with her husband and their combined adjusted gross income is less than $5,100. If their combined adjusted gross income is more than $4,500, the allowable deduction is reduced to the extent of the excess income. However, this limitation does not apply if the taxpayer's husband is incapable of self-support because of mental or physical defects.

No deduction may be claimed for amounts paid to a person whom the taxpayer is allowed to claim as a dependent. Thus, if a widow paid her mother $500 during the year to take care of her children while she was employed and the mother qualified as a dependent, she could not claim a deduction for the child-care expenses.

Expenses for production of income. Expenses incurred in the production or collection of income, or in the management or maintenance of income-producing property are deductible. Examples are union dues, rental of safe deposit boxes for safekeeping of securities, and fees paid to an investments counselor. Expenses incurred in connection with the determination, collection, or refund of any tax are also deductible.

Standard deduction. Instead of listing the amounts of the various deductions described above, the taxpayer may claim a standard deduction.

The amount of the standard deduction is 10% of the adjusted gross income, with a top limit of $1,000. For example, if a taxpayer's adjusted gross income is $8,000 and his itemized deductions from adjusted gross income total $520, he may claim a standard deduction of $800 (10% of $8,000). If the total of his itemized deductions was in excess of $800, it would be to his advantage to claim them rather than the standard deduction. If the adjusted gross income is $10,000 or more, the standard deduction is limited to $1,000; there is, however, no limit to the total amount of the itemized deductions. Thus a taxpayer with adjusted gross income of $17,000 and allowable itemized deductions of $1,400 may claim the entire $1,400.

Personal exemptions. As a means of adjusting the burden of taxation to the economic responsibilities of the taxpayer, the law permits a deduction for personal exemptions. In recent years the amount of each exemption has been $600, though it may be changed at any time by Congress.

Each taxpayer is entitled to one exemption for himself. If husband and a wife file a joint return (combining the income and the deductions of both spouses) they are allowed two exemptions.

An additional exemption is allowed for each dependent of the taxpayer. In general, a dependent is a person who meets all of the following requirements: (1) received over one half of his support from the taxpayer during the year, (2) had less than $600 of gross income during the year, and (3) is closely related to the taxpayer. However, a child of the taxpayer who is either under 19 years of age at the close of the calendar year or who has been a full-time student at an educational institution during each of five months of the year is not required to meet the second requirement. Thus, a son under 19, or over 19 and attending college, may earn more than $600 and still qualify as a dependent provided the parent contributes more than one half of the son's support.[3]

A taxpayer and his spouse may each claim an extra exemption for blindness, and another exemption if he or she is 65 years of age or older. Thus, if both a taxpayer and his wife are over 65 and both are blind, they may take a total of six personal exemptions. The extra exemptions for blindness and old age do not apply to dependents.

Taxable income

The base to which the tax rates are applied is adjusted gross income less the total amount of the deductions outlined above. This is called *taxable income.*

---

[3]If the son's gross income is $600 or more, he must file a tax return. He would be entitled to claim his own exemption in spite of the fact that his father is also permitted to claim him as a dependent.

Capital gains and losses

Gains and losses resulting from the sale or the exchange of certain kinds of assets are accorded special treatment for income tax purposes. Such properties are termed *capital assets*, and the gains and losses incurred upon their sale or exchange are called *capital gains* and *capital losses*. Capital assets most commonly held by taxpayers include shares of stock, bonds, personal residence, and land. Under certain conditions equipment and buildings used in business are also treated as capital assets. Details of capital gains and losses must be reported on a special schedule provided for the purpose and attached to the income tax return. The statutes and regulations regarding this subject are too voluminous and complex for inclusion in this brief discussion of the federal income tax.

Income tax rates

The income tax rates are progressive in nature. The lowest segment of taxable income is subjected to the lowest rate and each additional segment is subjected to a higher rate than the one preceding.

Taxpayers who have an adjusted gross income of less than $5,000 and who wish to use the standard deduction must determine the amount of the income tax by reference to a table prepared by the government. The table shows the tax for any amount of adjusted gross income under $5,000 for various numbers of exemptions.

Taxpayers who have an adjusted gross income of $5,000 or more or who do not wish to use the standard deduction must compute the amount of the income tax by applying the schedule of current tax rates.

A portion of the current tax rate schedule applicable to single taxpayers and married persons filing separate returns follows:

SINGLE TAXPAYERS

If the taxable income is: *The tax is:*
Not over $2,000...................20% of the taxable income

Over	But not over			*of excess over*
$ 2,000 —	$ 4,000.............	$ 400, plus 22% —	$ 2,000
4,000 —	6,000..............	840, plus 26% —	4,000
6,000 —	8,000.............	1,360, plus 30% —	6,000
8,000 —	10,000.............	1,960, plus 34% —	8,000
10,000 —	12,000.............	2,640, plus 38% —	10,000
12,000 —	14,000.............	3,400, plus 43% —	12,000
14,000 —	16,000.............	4,260, plus 47% —	14,000
16,000 —	18,000.............	5,200, plus 50% —	16,000

The income tax on a single person with taxable income of $6,750 would be computed as follows, applying the above schedule:

Tax on $6,000.	$1,360
Tax on $750 at 30%.	225
Total tax.	$1,585

The schedule of tax rates is frequently changed by Congress, but the progressive characteristic is a permanent feature of the income tax system.

Husband and wife. Husbands and wives may file separate returns and apply the tax schedule above or they may combine their income and deductions in a single *joint* return. If a joint return is made, the tax is computed as though each spouse had earned one half of their combined income. This is accomplished by the use of a rate schedule in which the segment of income in each tax bracket is exactly double the amount shown in the tax schedule applicable to single persons. A portion of the current schedule applicable to joint returns is presented below.

MARRIED TAXPAYERS — JOINT RETURN

If the taxable income is:	*The tax is:*
Not over $4,000.	20% of the taxable income

Over	*But not over*			*of excess over*
$ 4,000 —	$ 8,000.	$ 800, plus 22% —	$ 4,000
8,000 —	12,000.	1,680, plus 26% —	8,000
12,000 —	16,000.	2,720, plus 30% —	12,000
16,000 —	20,000.	3,920, plus 34% —	16,000
20,000 —	24,000.	5,280, plus 38% —	20,000
24,000 —	28,000.	6,800, plus 43% —	24,000

To illustrate the relationship between the two rate schedules, assume that the taxable income of husband and wife is $16,000. The tax on a joint return would be $3,920. If exactly half of the income and deductions were those of the husband and the other half were attributable to the wife, the tax on each separate return (taxable income of $8,000) would be $1,960, or a total of $3,920 for both returns. Thus the total tax for separate returns would be the same as for a joint return. On the other hand, if the wife had no income and the husband filed a separate return, the tax on a taxable income of $16,000 would be $5,200, an excess of $1,280 over the tax liability on a joint return.

For the two years following the year in which a husband or a wife dies, the surviving spouse may continue to use the rate schedule applicable to a joint return, provided the surviving spouse: (1) maintains as his or her home a household in which a dependent son or daughter resides and (2) does not remarry during the taxable year.

Head of household. Persons who qualify as a head of a household are subject to a special schedule of tax rates that fall between the schedule applicable to single persons and the schedule applicable to married persons filing a joint return. To qualify as the head of a household, an individual must be unmarried at the close of the taxable year and must, in general, maintain as his home a household in which one or more of the following described persons live: (a) an unmarried son or daughter or one of their dependents, or (b) any other close relative who qualifies as a dependent. The head of household status may also be claimed by a taxpayer who maintains a separate household in which his dependent mother or father lives.

Credits against the tax

There are a number of credits that may be deducted from the income tax liability to arrive at the amount owed. Some of them, such as the credit for partially tax-exempt interest on federal obligations, the credit for taxes imposed by foreign countries, and the retirement income credit, are of limited applicability and go beyond the scope of this discussion. The credit for income taxes withheld by employers from salaries and wages of employees is of widest applicability and requires no further explanation. The credit allowed individuals for dividends received from domestic corporations is explained in the following paragraph.

Dividends-received credit. The income of corporations is taxed twice, the first time to the corporation when the income is earned, and the second time to the stockholders when dividends are received. This double taxation is partially alleviated by the exclusion from income of the first $50 of dividends received during the year. In addition to this provision, individuals are allowed a credit against the tax equal to 4% of the amount of the remaining dividends. To illustrate, assume that a taxpayer received dividends aggregating $600 during the taxable year. Of this total, $50 would be excluded and the remaining $550 would be included in gross income. The dividends-received credit to be deducted from his income tax liability would be 4% of $550, or $22.

Tax returns; payment

Every individual who has a gross income for the year in excess of the minimum stated in the law must file a tax return. This is true even though he may not have to pay any tax. A taxpayer who maintains books of account may choose for his fiscal year any twelve-month period ending on the last day of a month.[4] Most individual taxpayers choose the calendar year. The period chosen cannot be changed without permission from the government. A taxpayer who does not keep books must file on a calendar year basis.

---

[4]Taxpayers who maintain their books on a 52-week basis (53 weeks every 5 or 6 years) ending on a particular day of the week may elect to file their tax return on the same basis.

An annual tax return must be filed within three and one-half months after the end of the taxpayer's taxable year, accompanied by any balance due. A taxpayer whose income has been subject to tax withholding or who has been making payments on his estimated tax may find he has no more to pay, but he must nevertheless file a final return. If his tax has been overpaid, he may either ask for a refund or apply the amount against his tax liability for the next year.

The manner in which employers withhold income tax from wages paid to their employees was discussed in the preceding chapter. An individual whose income is not subject to withholding, or only partially so, or an individual whose income is fairly large must estimate his income tax in advance and file a tax form known as a *Declaration of Estimated Income Tax*. The estimated tax for the year, after deducting the estimated amount to be withheld and any credit for overpayment from prior years, must be paid during the year. There is provision for installment payments in most cases. In general, owners of businesses, professional people, taxpayers whose estimated income from salary exceeds certain minimum amounts, and persons with anticipated income from investments are required to follow this procedure. They must, of course, also file a final return at the proper time and pay any balance due or indicate the disposition of any overpayment.

Individual income tax problem illustrated

John R. Todd owns and operates a shoe store; he also owns an apartment house. He is married and has three children, whom he has supported during the year. The oldest child, who is 20 years of age and has attended college during nine months of the year, earned $738; the second child, aged 11, earned $85; the third child had no income. Both Mr. and Mrs. Todd are under 65 years of age and are not blind.

According to their books of account and other records, Mr. and Mrs. Todd's gross income for the year and their various deductions were as follows:

Net income from business owned...	$21,000
(Sales, $115,000; cost of goods sold, $70,000; total business expenses, $24,000.)	
Net income from rent of apartment building...........................	2,300
(Rent income, $4,200; taxes, $450; insurance, $150; repairs, $400; depreciation, $900.)	
Dividends on corporation stocks:	
Mr. Todd..	250
Mrs. Todd...	450
Interest on corporation bonds..	250
Life insurance proceeds received.....................................	10,000
(Policy on life of taxpayer's mother, who died during year.)	
Contributions to Church, United Fund, Red Cross, etc..................	500

Interest payments on personal loans....................................	$ 300
Property taxes on residence...	350
State sales tax paid on items bought for family use......................	100
Fire loss on home and furnishings.....................................	600
(Damage, $3,000; received from insurance company, $2,400.)	
Family medical expenses:	
Medicines..	45
Other expenses..	450
Payments during year on Declaration of Estimated Income Tax	4,800

On the basis of the foregoing facts and the schedule of tax rates appearing on page 389, the tax liability of Mr. and Mrs. Todd on a joint return is computed as shown on the following page. In actual practice the official tax form would be used and additional supporting information would be presented.

There are several points in the illustration that should be noted. The allowable deductions from gross income are subtracted from the particular gross income to which they relate, yielding the adjusted gross income for that particular activity. In the tax form special schedules are provided for reporting details of business operations, rent income, dividends, and interest. The net gain or loss from each schedule is then carried to another section of the tax form, where all items of adjusted gross income are totaled.

The insurance proceeds of $10,000 are not taxable. The income earned by the two children is not taxable to the parents. A tax return must be filed by the oldest child, however, in which he can claim one exemption.

Contributions were well below the maximum amount allowable and were fully deductible. The total medical expenses were less than 3% of adjusted gross income; hence none of the amount was deductible. The standard deduction allowable in this case was $1,000; since the actual deductions exceeded this amount, it was advantageous to claim the actual deductions.

Income tax records

Most individuals do not find it necessary to keep formal journals and ledgers relating to their personal financial affairs. It is apparent, however, that each taxpayer should keep records that are sufficient to enable him to prepare his tax returns. It is wise to keep a copy of all returns submitted. A record of all tax withholdings and payments should also be retained. The burden of proof as to the accuracy of the tax return and the payments that have been made rests upon the taxpayer.

Since the income of a sole proprietorship, as such, is not taxed, it is not necessary to have an account for income tax in the ledger. If the proprietor pays his tax by checks drawn on the business bank account, the transactions are recorded as personal withdrawals.

MR. AND MRS. JOHN R. TODD
COMPUTATION OF FEDERAL INCOME TAX

Income:

Business:

Sales		$115,000	
Cost of goods sold		70,000	
Gross profit		$ 45,000	
Expenses		24,000	
Net income from business			$21,000

Apartment building:

Rent income		$ 4,200	
Taxes	$450		
Insurance	150		
Repairs	400		
Depreciation	900	1,900	
Net income from apartment building			2,300

Dividends on corporation stocks:

$700 less $100 exclusion		600
Interest on corporation bonds		250
Adjusted gross income		$24,150

Personal Deductions and Exemptions:

Contributions	$ 500	
Interest	300	
Property taxes	350	
State sales tax	100	
Fire loss	600	
Total	$ 1,850	
Exemptions, 5 at $600 each	3,000	4,850
Taxable income		$19,300

Tax on $19,300:

On $16,000	$ 3,920	
On $3,300 at 34%	1,122	
Total tax		$ 5,042

Credits:

Dividends received (4% of $600)	$ 24	
Payments on declaration of estimated tax	4,800	4,824
Balance due (to accompany tax return)		$ 218

Questions

1. The real estate tax rate in a certain county is $32.27 per thousand dollars of valuation. (a) Is this a progressive, proportional, or regressive tax? (b) What is the tax rate per dollar of valuation?

2. Identify the following as realty, tangible personalty, or intangible personalty: (a) shares of stock, (b) automobile, (c) accounting machine, (d) ventilating ducts installed in a building, (e) office furniture, (f) notes receivable, (g) metal fence around parking lot, (h) building, (i) accounts receivable.

3. Central Manufacturing Co. contracts to purchase land for $100,000 and pays delinquent property taxes thereon of $15,000. To what account should the $15,000 be charged?

4. Why should special assessment taxes for improvements be charged to the land account?

5. Do sales taxes imposed on the purchaser ordinarily attach at the time of sale or when payment is received?

6. What accounts should be debited and credited to record a $100 sale on account that is subject to a 2% sales tax chargeable to the customer?

7. A particular taxpayer owns three unincorporated business enterprises, maintaining a separate accounting system for each. (a) Is a separate income tax return required for each enterprise? (b) May the owner elect to file a separate return and determine the tax on each enterprise separately?

8. (a) Are partnerships ordinarily subject to the federal income tax? (b) Is it possible for some partnerships to elect to be taxed as a corporation?

9. The proprietor of an unincorporated enterprise earned a net income of $30,000 during the year, of which he withdrew $18,000. What amount must he include in his income tax return?

10. A taxpayer owns 25% of the stock of the Fielding Corporation, which earned a net income of $200,000 for the year, before federal income taxes of $104,000. The taxpayer received cash dividends of $12,000 on his stock during the year. What is the amount of income from the corporation that the taxpayer must include in his personal income tax return?

11. In which month were the following items of income constructively received by a taxpayer reporting on the cash basis?

    (a) Bonus of $2,000 for past year; check is dated and received on January 2 and deposited in the bank on January 5.

    (b) Bond interest of $100; coupons are payable on December 15 and are deposited in the bank on January 5.

    (c) Interest of $127 on savings account; savings account is credited on December 31, but amount is not withdrawn by taxpayer until two and one half years later.

12. A physician who uses the cash basis of reporting income determines at the end of the year that $1,800 of fees due from patients are uncollectible. Is it permissible to deduct the $1,800 from gross income in determining taxable income? Discuss.

13. Which of the items listed below should be included in gross income reported on the income tax return of an individual?

    (a) Interest on notes receivable.
    (b) Salary as employee of the state.
    (c) Corporation bonds received as a bequest from an estate.
    (d) Interest on the bonds received in (c) above.
    (e) Damages received from personal injuries sustained in an accident.
    (f) Profit on sale of corporation stocks.

(g) Cash received in repayment of a loan to a friend.
(h) Interest on municipal bonds.
(i) Rent received on portion of residence.

14. Identify the following items as (1) deductible from gross income in determining adjusted gross income, (2) deductible from adjusted gross income in determining taxable income, or (3) not deductible:

(a) Employer's share of F.I.C.A. taxes paid on business payroll.
(b) Contributions to a political campaign fund.
(c) Interest on personal loan.
(d) Fee paid for assistance in preparing personal income tax return.
(e) Federal excise tax on airplane fares for family vacation.
(f) Insurance on taxpayer's residence.
(g) State sales taxes on clothing purchased for family use.
(h) Travel expenses incurred by employee while away from home overnight on employer's business.
(i) State gasoline tax (car not used in business).
(j) Union dues.
(k) Property taxes on apartment building held as an investment.
(l) Windstorm damage to family residence, not covered by insurance.
(m) Personal exemption.

15. What is the amount of the standard deduction for adjusted gross income of (a) $6,500, (b) $9,000, (c) $25,000.

16. Taxpayer father contributes more than half of the cost of his son's support during the taxable year. The son was in college nine months and earned a total of $1,000. (a) Is the father entitled to an exemption for his son? (b) Is the son required to file an income tax return?

17. Is it disadvantageous for a taxpayer to increase his earnings if by so doing he reaches a higher income tax bracket? Explain.

Exercises

1. The real estate tax rate for Greenfield is $25.68 per thousand dollars of valuation. Equipment used in business is subject to tax at one half the real estate rate. On tax listing day, the total cost of all equipment recorded in the accounts of Mason Co. is $27,400; accumulated depreciation determined in accordance with the regulations of the taxing authority totals $11,100. Determine the property tax on the equipment.

2. L. D. Thomas, Inc. purchased for $36,000 vacant land on which there are delinquent taxes and penalties amounting to $1,220. Present the entries, in general journal form, to record (a) payment of $10,000 in cash and the issuance of a mortgage note to Realty Associates for $26,000 and (b) payment of the delinquent taxes and penalties to the county treasurer.

3. In recording sales in its early months of operations, Davis Home Appliances failed to differentiate between the amount of sales and the amount of a 3% sales tax charged on all sales. Credits to the sales account and debits to the sales returns and allowances account included the sales tax. Permission is granted by the state tax department to estimate the amount of tax due for the quarter. Balances in the sales account and the sales returns and allowances account are $123,202.44 and $1,342.83, respectively. (a) Determine the amount of tax due. (b) Present the entry, in general journal form, to record payment of the tax (the books have not been closed).

4. A married taxpayer has adjusted gross income of $13,500; he is entitled to 4 exemptions; his payments for medicines totaled $190 and other medical expenses amounted to $718. Determine the amount of his allowable deduction for medical expenses.

5. A married taxpayer received $700 of cash dividends during the year and his wife received $250. (a) What is the amount of dividend income to be included in gross income in a joint return? (b) What is the amount of the dividends-received credit?

6. A husband and wife filing a joint return have 4 exemptions. Other summary data related to their income tax return are as follows:

Gross income, including dividends (after the exclusion) of $500..	$15,000
Deductions from gross income.............................	2,000
Deduction from adjusted gross income (contributions, etc.)......	850
Payments on declaration of income tax......................	2,000

Determine (a) adjusted gross income, (b) taxable income, (c) total tax, and (d) balance due, presenting details. (Use rate schedule appearing in this chapter.)

Problems

17-1. The Meredith Co. prepares interim statements at the end of each month and closes its books annually on December 31. On January 31 of the current year the accountant estimates that the property tax assessment for the city's fiscal year ending December 31 will be $3,000. On April 10 a tax statement for $3,324 is received; one half is payable on May 15 and the other half on November 15.

Instructions: Present, in general journal form, the entries to record the following:

Jan. 31. Property tax allocation.
April 30. Property tax allocation (assume proper entries were made at the end of February and March).
May 15. Payment of first half of the tax bill.
June 30. Property tax allocation.
July 31. Property tax allocation.
Nov. 15. Payment of second half of the tax bill (assume proper entries were made at the end of August, September, and October).
Dec. 31. Property tax allocation.

17-2. The state statutes require that retailers collect a sales tax of 3% on all sales to consumers except on certain items, such as seeds and fertilizers, and on sales to governmental units, such as public schools, the city, and the county. In the event the amount collected is less than 3% of taxable sales, the deficiency must be borne by the retailer. Quarterly remittances are payable by the end of the month following the quarter.

The balances in certain accounts of Denton Hardware Co. as of March 31 (after adjustment for tax liability) and June 30 of the current fiscal year (which ends on December 31) are as follows:

	MARCH 31	JUNE 30
Sales Tax Payable	$ 3,129.59	$ 4,027.20
Sales	110,860.20	252,495.10
Sales Returns and Allowances	1,920.40	4,162.50
Sales Tax Expense	15.10	15.10

Supplementary records indicate that sales for the second quarter of the year included nontaxable sales of $4,842.30 and that returns and allowances on nontaxable sales for the same period amounted to $295.70.

Instructions: (1) Determine the amount of the liability for sales taxes for the second quarter of the year, presenting your figures in good order.

(2) Present the entry as of June 30 to record the additional liability for sales taxes for the second quarter.

(3) Present the entry on July 31, in general journal form, to record payment of the sales tax liability for the second quarter.

(4) On the basis of the information presented above, determine the amount of the net taxable sales for the *first* quarter of the year.

17-3. Robert G. Boyd has just completed his first full calendar year of practice as an architect. He is unmarried, under 65 years of age, and has good vision. During the calendar year he contributed more than half of the cost of supporting his brother, who is a student and resides with his parents. The brother's income for the year totaled $550.

Mr. Boyd has maintained a detailed record of cash receipts and disbursements, including those of a personal nature. A summary of his records is presented below.

RECEIPTS

Professional fees	$34,175
Borrowed from bank (professional purposes)	2,500
Inheritance from grandfather's estate	1,000
Dividends on corporation stocks	320

DISBURSEMENTS

Cost of new automobile (purchased January 6)	4,200
Office equipment (purchased March 24)	600
Salary of draftsmen and typist	10,100
Payroll taxes	476
Fees to collaborating engineers	2,750
Office rent	2,400
Telephone expense (office)	294
Electricity (office)	168
Insurance on office equipment (1-year policy)	36
Payment on loan from bank (see above)	1,500
Blueprint expense	532

Office supplies expense..	$ 65
Interest on bank loan...	105
Automobile operating expenses (gasoline, oil, etc.)...............	471
Purchase of Scott Corporation stock............................	1,620
Life insurance premiums..	650
Contributions to church, United Fund, and Red Cross............	410
Personal and living expenses....................................	5,120
Payment on Declaration of Estimated Income Tax...............	4,000

The automobile was used $\frac{1}{3}$ of the time for professional purposes. It is to be depreciated on the straight line basis assuming 4 years of life and a trade-in value of $900. Allocate $\frac{1}{3}$ of the depreciation and other automobile expenses to professional purposes.

Office equipment was acquired in the previous year at a cost of $2,600. Use a composite depreciation rate of 10%, taking depreciation for $\frac{3}{4}$ year on the equipment purchased on March 24 of the current year.

Instructions: Determine Mr. Boyd's taxable income and income tax, presenting the details in good order. Apply the appropriate table of tax rates appearing in this chapter.

17-4. The preliminary income statement of the Queen City Camera Shop appearing below was prepared as of the close of the calendar year in which the business was established. You are engaged to review the business records, revise the accounting system to the extent necessary, and prepare a corrected schedule for submission with the income tax return of the proprietor.

Sales...		$98,874
Purchases..		89,120
Gross profit on sales.....................................		$ 9,754
Operating expenses:		
Salaries...	$10,430	
Rent..	1,800	
Store equipment......................................	4,600	
Insurance...	390	
Utilities..	485	
Fuel..	310	
Advertising...	250	
Taxes..	516	
Donations..	83	
Miscellaneous...	618	19,482
Net loss...		$ 9,728

The following information was obtained during the course of your examination:

(a) The preliminary income statement is in agreement with the records of cash receipts and disbursements. Uncollected charges to customers are evidenced by duplicate sales tickets. Unpaid invoices for merchandise and other expenditures are filed in an unpaid file.

(b) Uncollected sales to customers on account at December 31 amount to $4,315.

(c) Unpaid invoices at December 31 for expenditures of the past year are summarized as follows:

Merchandise	$6,891
Utilities	46
Fuel	58

(d) The inventory of merchandise on hand at December 31 was $16,325.

(e) Withdrawals of $5,000 by the proprietor were included in the amount reported as Salaries.

(f) The store equipment was installed on March 3. It has an estimated composite life of 10 years and a residual value of $400. Depreciation is to be claimed for 10 months.

(g) A total of $215 of insurance premiums was unexpired at December 31.

(h) Payments classified as Donations were contributions to charitable, religious, and educational organizations.

Instructions: Prepare a statement of income from the business for submission with the income tax return of R. J. Duncan, the proprietor, employing the accrual method of accounting.

17-5. Henry B. Taylor is married and has two dependent children. The older child, 18 years of age, earned $750 during the year, and the younger child earned $90. Mr. Taylor also contributed more than half of the cost of supporting his mother, who received gross income of $675 during the year. Both Mr. and Mrs. Taylor are under 65 years of age and have good vision. They submit the following details of their receipts and disbursements for the year ended December 31:

RECEIPTS

Mr. Taylor:

Salary as vice president of Stewart Electronics Co.	$20,016.00
(Earnings, $24,000; income tax withheld, $3,840; FICA tax withheld, $144).	
Reimbursement from employer for travel expenses	1,450.00
Rent from property owned	3,600.00
Interest on bonds of City of Mesa	400.00

Mrs. Taylor:

Withdrawals from Barker & Co., a partnership in which she is a partner (distributive share of the net income for the year, $4,100)	2,400.00
Insurance proceeds (death of father)	10,000.00
Dividends on corporation stocks	412.50
Interest on U. S. Treasury Bonds issued in 1959	140.00

DISBURSEMENTS

Mr. Taylor:

Travel expenses on trips for Stewart Electronics Co.	1,227.00
Rental property:	
Property taxes	318.20
Insurance (one-year policies)	85.00
Painting and repairs	522.50
Mortgage payments:	
Principal	2,000.00
Interest	540.00
(Building was acquired several years ago at a cost of $25,000 and is being depreciated at the rate of 4%).	
Charitable contributions	513.00

Interest on mortgage on residence............................	$ 356.15
Automobile license fee on family cars.......................	30.00
Real estate tax on residence................................	594.35
Sales tax on items purchased for personal or family use.......	152.00
State gasoline tax..	53.00
Medical Expenses:	
Medicines...	195.00
Medical and dental fees, hospital charges................	968.00
Accident damages to family car not covered by insurance.....	100.00
Payments during year on Declaration of Estimated Income Tax	3,200.00
Mrs. Taylor:	
Charitable contributions................................	165.00

Instructions: Determine Mr. and Mrs. Taylor's taxable income and income tax, presenting the details in good order. Apply the appropriate table of tax rates appearing in this chapter.

17-6. The Knox Company, whose fiscal year is January 1–December 31, accrues its property taxes over the fiscal year of the county taxing authority, which is July 1–June 30. The company receives a 1961–62 tax statement for $1,536 on October 15, 1961, paying half of the liability on November 10, 1961, and half on May 5, 1962.

Instructions: (1) Present the entries, in general journal form, relating to month-end allocations for property taxes and tax payments for the period January 1 to June 30, 1962.

The company estimates that its property tax assessment for 1962–63 will be $1,620. The tax bill received on October 13, 1962, indicates a liability of $1,524. The first half is paid on November 10, 1962.

Instructions: (2) Present the entries, in general journal form, relating to month-end allocations for property taxes and tax payments for the period July 1 to December 31, 1962.

Partnerships — organization and operation

Definition of partnership

The Uniform Partnership Act, which has been enacted into law in many states, defines a partnership as "an association of two or more persons to carry on as co-owners a business for profit." As used in the definition, the term "business" includes all trades, occupations, and professions; therefore, the discussion that follows will apply equally to mercantile partnerships, service partnerships, and partnerships of physicians, attorneys, accountants, and other professions.

Partnerships for the conduct of business activities may be formed for a wide variety of reasons. For example, the proprietor of an established business may form a partnership with one or more of his associates, or even with a competitor, in order to obtain additional capital or new managerial talents. The sole proprietor of a business may wish to reduce the burden of his responsibilities or withdraw from active management without completely divesting himself of ownership.

Two or more persons may form a partnership to undertake a new business venture. The amount of investment required or the various skills needed to give maximum assurance of success, or both, are often important factors that influence a decision to adopt the partnership form of business unit. In many cases an alternative is to adopt the corporate form of organization, which is discussed in later chapters. The corporate form of organization may not be used, however, by certain professions because of restrictions in state statutes or in professional codes of ethics. Hence, a group of physicians, attorneys, or C.P.A.s that wishes to band together to practice a profession do so as a partnership.

Characteristics

In order to understand fully the duties and the responsibilities of the partners among themselves and to outside parties, it is necessary to look beyond the legal definition quoted above. A partnership is a distinctly personal organization, and it is from this personal quality that the characteristics described in the following paragraphs are derived.

Mutual agency. Each partner is the agent of the partnership for the purpose of the partnership business. Thus, the acts of each partner in carrying on the business in the usual way are binding upon the partnership. The partners may agree among themselves as to division of responsibility; for example, authority for purchasing may be vested in one partner and authority over credits and collections may be delegated to another partner. In spite of such arrangements, however, a partner may act without authority and bind the partnership as to third parties who have no knowledge of his lack of authority.

Limited life. Because of its personal nature, the length of life of a partnership is highly unpredictable. Dissolution of a partnership may result from a variety of causes, including the death, bankruptcy, incapacity, or withdrawal of one of the partners. A partner may sell his interest to someone outside the firm or a new partner may be added to the business, but any change in the personnel of the partners results in a dissolution of the old partnership. A new partnership may be formed, of course, to continue the operations of the business.

Unlimited liability. Each partner is individually liable to creditors for debts incurred by the partnership. Thus, if a partnership becomes insolvent, the creditors may proceed against any one of the partners regardless of the amount of the partner's interest in the partnership. Some states permit the organization of limited partnerships, in which the liability of all partners except one may be limited to the amount of their investments.

Co-ownership of property. The property invested in a partnership by a partner ceases to be his own property. It becomes the property of all the partners jointly. Upon dissolution of the partnership and distribution of its assets, the partners have no special claim to any specific asset. Each member's claim against the assets is measured by the amount of the balance in his capital account. It is, therefore, important that assets invested in the business by the partners be valued fairly. For example, if a partner contributes land with a fair value of $20,000, it should be recorded at that amount and his capital should be credited for the same amount, regardless of the fact that the land may have cost him only $12,000.

Participation in income. The co-ownership of income is an essential characteristic of partnerships. Net income and net loss are distributed among the partners in accordance with their agreement.

Accounting in general

Most of the day-to-day accounting for a partnership is exactly the same as that for any other form of business organization. With minor exceptions, the chart of accounts is no different from the chart of accounts of a similar business conducted by a sole proprietor. The special journals described in earlier chapters may be employed by a partnership without any alterations in form. It is in the areas of the formation, income distribution, dissolution, and liquidation of partnerships that transactions peculiar to partnerships arise. This chapter and the one that follows will be devoted to the special accounting problems in these areas.

Formation of a partnership

A partnership is created by a voluntary contract containing all the elements essential to any other enforceable contract. Although our interest is in accounting rather than in legal intricacies of contracts, a few general observations are in order.

It is not essential that the contract establishing the partnership be in writing, nor even that its terms be specifically expressed orally. The courts have frequently ruled that, on the basis of the acts of the individuals associated, a contract of partnership did in fact exist. The serious and far-reaching effects of a partnership contract, particularly with regard to mutual agency and unlimited liability, are such that a carefully considered written contract is highly advisable.

The contract, known as the *articles of copartnership*, should contain — in addition to such usual items as the names of the partners, the name of the partnership, the nature and the location of the business, and the period of time covered by the contract — provisions regarding the following features:

1. Investment to be made by each partner, including the description and valuation to be placed on all assets contributed.
2. Delegation of responsibilities among the partners and amount of time to be devoted to partnership affairs.
3. Time as of which books are to be closed and the manner in which net income and losses are to be divided.
4. Limitations on withdrawals of funds by the partners.
5. Method of settling disputes among the partners.
6. Provisions relating to the withdrawal, expulsion, or death of a partner.

After the partners have reached an agreement and have signed the articles of copartnership, the partners make their respective contributions of capital to the firm and the opening entries are recorded in the books.

Recording the investment

A separate entry is made for the investment of each partner in a partnership. The various assets contributed by a partner are debited to the proper asset accounts; if liabilities are assumed by the partnership, the appropriate liability accounts are credited; and the partner's capital account is credited for the net amount.

To illustrate the entries required to record the initial investment, assume that George M. Alden and James D. Barker, who are sole proprietors of competing hardware stores, agree to combine their enterprises in a partnership. Each is to contribute specified amounts of cash and other business assets. It is also agreed that the partnership is to assume the liabilities of the individual businesses. The entries to record the investments of cash are recorded in the cash receipts journal as follows:

CASH RECEIPTS JOURNAL

DATE	ACCOUNT CREDITED	POST. REF.	SUNDRY ACCOUNTS CR.	SALES CR.	ACCTS. REC. CR.	SALES DISC. DR.	CASH DR.
1961 Jan. 1	George M. Alden, Capital		7,000				7,000
	James D. Barker, Capital		10,000				10,000

The entries to record the other assets contributed and the liabilities transferred by each partner are as follows:

Jan. 1 Accounts Receivable.............................. 6,300
    Merchandise Inventory.......................... 18,600
    Store Equipment............................... 5,400
    Office Equipment.............................. 1,500
        Allowance for Uncollectible Accounts............ 1,300
        Accounts Payable.............................. 2,500
        George M. Alden, Capital..................... 28,000

Jan. 1 Accounts Receivable.............................. 2,600
    Merchandise Inventory.......................... 13,000
    Store Equipment............................... 3,000
        Allowance for Uncollectible Accounts............ 500
        Notes Payable................................ 2,000
        Accounts Payable.............................. 1,100
        James D. Barker, Capital..................... 15,000

The amounts at which the noncash assets are stated are those agreed upon by Alden and Barker, the partners. They are not necessarily in agreement with the balances appearing in the accounts of the two separate businesses before the partnership was organized. For example, the store equipment stated at $5,400 may have appeared on Alden's ledger at an original cost of $10,000 with accumulated depreciation of $6,500, or a book value of $3,500. On the other hand, the book value of the store equipment contributed by Barker may have been greater than the amount at which it was accepted for partnership purposes. Original cost of the equipment, its current condition, changes in price levels, and the bargaining ability of the partners are some of the factors that influence the values assigned to the assets invested.

The equipment contributed to the partnership could have been recorded at the amount of the original cost to the partners, with credits to accumulated depreciation accounts for the amounts necessary to bring the book value into agreement with the values assigned by the partners. For example, the store equipment invested by Alden could have been recorded at $10,000, with an offsetting credit to the accumulated depreciation account for $4,600, effecting a book value of $5,400. The preferred practice is to record only the net amount agreed upon, however, as it represents the acquisition cost to the partnership. The same reasoning cannot be applied, however, to recording the value ascribed to receivables invested by a partner. It is necessary to debit Accounts Receivable for the face value and to credit Allowance for Uncollectible Accounts for the amount estimated to be uncollectible. At the time the accounts are taken over by the partnership, it is not possible to determine which accounts in the subsidiary ledger will become partially or wholly uncollectible.

The valuation of invested assets at an amount other than the basis of the contributing partner creates some problems in the determination of taxable income. Inasmuch as the transfer of assets to the partnership is not a sale by the partner or a purchase by the partnership, the contributing partner has no gain or loss on the transaction and there is no change in the basis of the assets. To illustrate the point, assume that land acquired by an individual at a cost of $10,000 is later contributed to a partnership and that the agreed valuation for the land is $20,000. The land account would be debited for $20,000 and the contributing partner's capital account would be credited for the same amount. According to the Internal Revenue Code, however, the contributing partner realizes no taxable income from the transaction and the basis of the land to the partnership remains at $10,000. If the land should subsequently be sold by the partnership, the gain or the loss realized for income tax purposes would be the difference between the selling price and $10,000. A further complication arises with depreciable assets valued at a figure other than the basis of the contributing partner. Detailed analysis of the ramifications of this conflict between accounting and the income tax law is beyond the scope of this discussion. In the absence of any statement to the contrary, it will be assumed in all problems in this book that the depreciation of assets contributed by partners will be based on the values assigned to them by the partners.

Drawing accounts

The drawing accounts of the partners serve the same purpose as the drawing account of a sole proprietor. Ordinarily the partnership agreement provides that the partners may make withdrawals of cash or other property from time to time in anticipation of the enterprise earning a net income. At the end of the fiscal period the net income or loss in the expense and revenue summary account is transferred to the respective capital accounts in accordance with the partnership agreement. The debit balances in the drawing accounts are also transferred to the respective capital accounts in the same manner as for a sole proprietorship.

An alternative procedure is to close the expense and revenue summary account to the drawing accounts instead of to the capital accounts. The balances in the drawing accounts are then closed to the related capital accounts.

Division of income or loss

Division of the net income or loss among the partners in exact accordance with their agreement is of the utmost importance. If the agreement is silent on the matter, the law provides that all partners share equally, regardless of differences in the amounts of capital contributed or time devoted to the business. The partners may make any agreement they wish in regard to the division of income and losses. If misunderstandings are to be avoided, the agreement must be clearly stated.

As in the case of a sole proprietorship, the net income of a partnership may be said to include a return for the services of the owners, for the capital invested, and for economic or pure profit. A partner is not an employee of the partnership, nor is his capital contribution a loan. Thus, partners are entitled neither to a specified salary for their services nor to interest on their capital investments unless they make provisions for them in their agreement.

If the service and capital contributions of partners are equal, an equal sharing in partnership income is equitable. But if one partner contributes three times as much capital as the other, the distribution of income should take into account the unequal contribution of capital. Or, if the services of one partner are much more valuable to the partnership than those of the other, provision for unequal service contributions should be made.

In the discussion that follows, the division of income should not be confused with the withdrawal of income. Even though the two are related, separate entries are required for each. Division of income is recorded by appropriate entries in the expense and revenue summary account and the capital accounts. Withdrawals are recorded by debits to drawing accounts and credits to the cash account or to the accounts of other assets withdrawn.

Income division in arbitrary ratio

The simplest plan for dividing net income is to adopt an arbitrary ratio that is to continue for a specified number of years or for the duration of the partnership. The agreement may provide for an equal sharing on the grounds that the partners are to make equal contributions of capital and services. If there are to be differences in the contributions by the partners, such differences may be recognized by selecting another ratio, such as 3:2 or 2:1.

The effect of several ratios on the division of net income of $18,000 earned by Alden and Barker is illustrated below.

Income Ratio	Alden	Barker
1:1	$ 9,000	$9,000
3:2	10,800	7,200
2:1	12,000	6,000

The distribution of the income is recorded at the end of the fiscal period as one of the closing entries. Assuming that Alden and Barker had agreed on the ratio of 3:2, the distribution would be recorded as follows:

Dec. 31 Expense and Revenue Summary.................	18,000	
George M. Alden, Capital....................		10,800
James D. Barker, Capital.....................		7,200

A report of the division of income may be presented as a separate statement accompanying the balance sheet and the income statement or it may be added at the bottom of the income statement. Assuming that the latter procedure was selected, the lower part of the income statement would appear as follows:

Net income..		$18,000
Division of net income:		
George M. Alden, ⅗ of total.......................	$10,800	
James D. Barker, ⅖ of total.......................	7,200	
Net income..		$18,000

Income division recognizing investment

When partners invest widely differing amounts in the firm, they may wish to recognize this fact in their income-sharing arrangements. The degree to which investment may be taken into account can vary from division of the entire net income on the basis of investments to the allowance of a fair rate of return on capital. Regardless of the extent to which differences of investment are to be emphasized, it is quite important that the agreement specify the exact method of determining capital investment. For example, capital investment as of any of the following dates may be used: (1) the date of formation of the partnership, (2) the beginning of the fiscal year, (3) the end of the fiscal year before the division of income, (4) the average capital during the fiscal year.

The agreement should also specify the treatment to be accorded withdrawals and accumulations of income in determining capital investment. To illustrate this point, assume that A and B have agreed that partnership income is to be divided in accordance with the ratios of capital invested at the beginning of each current year. The original investments and the changes in capital accounts during the first year of operations were as follows:

		A, Capital		B, Capital
Original investment...........		$30,000		$20,000
Income for first year, 3:2 ratio..	$15,000		$10,000	
Withdrawals during first year...	20,000		5,000	
Net increase (decrease) in capital		(5,000)		5,000
Balance at end of first year.....		$25,000		$25,000

If the net changes in capital for the year are considered to be permanent adjustments to the capital accounts, the amount invested by each partner at the beginning of the second year of operations will be $25,000 and the income division ratio for the second year would change from 3:2 to 1:1. On the other hand, the $5,000 decrease in A's capital may be considered to be an advance withdrawal of anticipated income of the second year, and the $5,000 increase in B's capital account may be considered to be subject to withdrawal at B's convenience. According to the second view, there has been no change in the amounts considered to be permanent capital, and the income division ratio would remain at 3:2.

Examples of accounting for income-sharing arrangements that give specific recognition to capital investments are described in the paragraphs that follow.

Original capital. The original capital investments of Alden and Barker were $35,000 and $25,000, respectively, or a total of $60,000. Assuming that they had agreed to divide income in the ratio of their original investments, their respective shares of the net income of $18,000 would be computed in the following manner:

$$\text{Alden: } \frac{35,000}{60,000} \times \$18,000 = \$10,500$$

$$\text{Barker:} \frac{25,000}{60,000} \times \$18,000 = \$7,500$$

The entry to close the expense and revenue summary account to the respective capital accounts would be the same, except for the amounts, as the entry shown earlier for division in an arbitrary ratio. Presentation of the facts on the income statement for the year would also be similar.

Instead of using capital investment as the sole determinant of income division, the partners may agree to allow interest on the investments and to divide the remaining income in an arbitrary ratio. The particular rate of interest to be used would, of course, be a matter of agreement. Assuming that Alden and Barker had agreed to allow interest on original investments at 6% and to divide the remainder equally, the division would be detailed on the income statement as follows:

Net income..		$18,000
Division of net income:		
George M. Alden:		
Interest on original investment at 6%..............	$2,100	
½ of remaining balance........................	7,200	$ 9,300
James D. Barker:		
Interest on original investment at 6%..............	$1,500	
½ of remaining balance........................	7,200	8,700
Net income...		$18,000

The closing entry to transfer the net income from the expense and revenue summary account to the capital accounts would be:

Dec. 31 Expense and Revenue Summary.................	18,000	
George M. Alden, Capital....................		9,300
James D. Barker, Capital....................		8,700

Average capital. When there is a possibility that the capital accounts of partners may change materially from time to time, the agreement may specify that net income be divided according to the ratio of average capital for the year. Or, if investment is not to be the sole factor in the division, a specified interest rate may be applied to average capital rather than to the capital balances at a particular date.

The unit of time employed in computing the average capital of a partner is ordinarily a month or a day. A simple method of computation, using a month as the time unit, is outlined below:

1. Multiply the amount of the capital at the beginning of the year by the number of months elapsed between that date and the date of a change in capital.
2. Multiply the amount of the capital after the first change by the number of months elapsed between that date and the date of the second change in capital.

3. Continue with the same procedure to the end of the year.
4. Total the products obtained by the series of multiplications. This total is the capital in terms of month-dollars.
5. Divide the total month-dollars by 12, which yields the average capital.

The foregoing procedure is repeated for the capital of each partner. If only the ratio of the average capitals is needed, the last step may be omitted, as the ratio of the total month-dollars of capital of each partner will be identical with the ratio of their average capitals. To illustrate the computations, it will be assumed that net income is to be divided according to the ratio of average capital, that specified weekly withdrawals in anticipation of net income are not to be considered as changes in capital, and that the dates of additional investments and withdrawals are to be advanced or carried back to the nearest month end. The original investments and changes in capital revealed by the capital and drawing accounts of Alden and Barker are as follows:

	ALDEN	BARKER
Jan. 1, investment....	$35,000	$25,000
Mar. 24, withdrawal....		4,000
July 2, withdrawal....	10,000	
Nov. 11, investment....		6,000

The ratio of average capital and the division of net income are determined as follows:

	DATE	CAPITAL BALANCE	MONTHS UNCHANGED	MONTH-DOLLARS	
Alden:					
	Jan. 1	$35,000 ×	6	= $210,000	
	July 2	25,000 ×	6	= 150,000	$360,000
			12		
Barker:					
	Jan. 1	$25,000 ×	3	= $ 75,000	
	Mar. 24	21,000 ×	7	= 147,000	
	Nov. 11	27,000 ×	2	= 54,000	276,000
			12		
Total......					$636,000

DIVISION OF NET INCOME

$$\text{Alden: } \frac{360,000}{636,000} \times \$18,000 = \$10,188.68$$

$$\text{Barker: } \frac{276,000}{636,000} \times \$18,000 = \underline{7,811.32}$$

Total....................$18,000.00

The division of the net income would be presented on the income statement in the following manner:

Net income..	$18,000.00
Division of net income:	
George M. Alden, 30/53 of total..............	$10,188.68
James D. Barker, 23/53 of total...............	7,811.32
Net income.......................................	$18,000.00

Instead of using average capitals as the sole determinant of income division, the agreement may specify the allowance of interest on the average capitals, with the remaining income divided in an arbitrary ratio. If this had been the case with Alden and Barker, the average capitals would have been computed by dividing the month-dollars (determined earlier) by 12, as follows:

	MONTH-DOLLARS				AVERAGE CAPITAL
Alden:	$360,000	÷	12	=	$30,000
Barker:	$276,000	÷	12	=	$23,000

Assuming that the articles of copartnership specified an allowance of 6% interest on average capital, with the remaining balance divided equally, the income of $18,000 would be allocated as follows:

Net income...		$18,000
Division of net income:		
George M. Alden:		
Interest on average capital at 6%.................	$1,800	
½ of remaining balance.........................	7,410	$ 9,210
James D. Barker:		
Interest on average capital at 6%.................	$1,380	
½ of remaining balance.........................	7,410	8,790
Net income..		$18,000

Income division recognizing services of partners

As a means of recognizing differences in ability and in amount of time devoted to the business, articles of copartnership often provide for salaries to partners. The salary may be paid periodically in much the same manner as payments to other employees, it may be paid at irregular intervals, or there may be no payments that are specifically identified as salary. Regardless of the procedure, it must be borne in mind that the partners are not employees of the firm, and that their "salaries" are portions of net income rather than expenses of the business. As was stated earlier, a clear distinction must be made between payments to the partners, which are chargeable to their drawing accounts, and the division of net income, which is recorded by closing the expense and revenue summary account to the capital accounts.

To illustrate the division of net income where the agreement provides for salaries, assume that Alden and Barker provide for monthly salaries of $600 and $500, respectively, with the balance of the income to be divided equally. The division of the net income for the year would then be reported as follows:

Net income..		$18,000
Division of net income:		
George M. Alden:		
Salary...................................	$7,200	
½ of remaining balance.........	2,400	$9,600
James D. Barker:		
Salary...................................	$6,000	
½ of remaining balance....................	2,400	8,400
Net income..		$18,000

The foregoing report would be made and the partners' capital accounts would be credited for $9,600 and $8,400, respectively, regardless of whether they actually withdrew the amounts of their salary allowances. If they did withdraw their salaries monthly, the withdrawals should be accumulated as debits in the drawing accounts during the year. It is not uncommon, however, for periodic withdrawals of salary allowances to be charged to a partner's salary expense account. In such cases, it is preferable to transfer the balance of the salary accounts to the drawing accounts at the end of the period. The distributions of income are thus removed from the expense category and properly classified as withdrawals.

Income division recognizing services of partners and investment

Partners may agree that the most equitable plan of income-sharing is to allow salaries commensurate with the services rendered and also to allow interest on the capital investments. The remainder would then be shared in an arbitrary ratio. Combining the assumptions of the last two illustrations concerning salary, interest, and the remaining balance yields the following division of net income for Alden and Barker:

Net income..		$18,000
Division of net income:		
George M. Alden:		
Salary...................................	$7,200	
Interest on average capital at 6%..................	1,800	
½ of remaining balance..........................	810	$ 9,810
James D. Barker:		
Salary...................................	$6,000	
Interest on average capital at 6%..................	1,380	
½ of remaining balance..........................	810	8,190
Net income..		$18,000

On the basis of the information in the foregoing income statement, the entry to close the expense and revenue summary account would be recorded in the general journal as follows:

Dec. 31 Expense and Revenue Summary..................	18,000	
George M. Alden, Capital....................		9,810
James D. Barker, Capital....................		8,190

Net income less than sum of salary and interest. In all of the illustrations presented thus far, the net income has exceeded the sum of the allowances for salary and interest. It is obvious that this will not necessarily always be the case. If the net income is less than the total of the special allowances, the "remaining balance" will be a negative figure that must be divided among the partners as though it were a loss. The effect of this situation may be illustrated by assuming the same salary and interest allowances as in the preceding illustration but changing the amount of net income to $10,000. The salary and interest allowances to Alden total $9,000 and the comparable figure for Barker is $7,380. The sum of these amounts, $16,380, exceeds the net income of $10,000 by $6,380. It is therefore necessary to deduct $3,190 (½ of $6,380) from each to arrive at the net income, as shown below.

Net income..			$10,000
Distribution of net income:			
George M. Alden:			
Salary..		$7,200	
Interest on average capital, at 6%..................		1,800	
		$9,000	
Deduct: ½ of remaining balance...................		3,190	$ 5,810
James D. Barker:			
Salary..		$6,000	
Interest on average capital, at 6%..................		1,380	
		$7,380	
Deduct: ½ of remaining balance...................		3,190	4,190
Net income..			$10,000

In closing Expense and Revenue Summary at the end of the year, $5,810 would be credited to George M. Alden, Capital, and $4,190 would be credited to James D. Barker, Capital.

Statements for a partnership

Details of the division of net income should be disclosed in the financial statements prepared at the end of the fiscal period. This may be done by adding a section to the income statement, which has been illustrated a number of times in the preceding pages, or the data may be presented in a separate statement. Factors that will affect the form to be used include the length of the main body of the income statement, the number of partners, and the amount of detail to be presented.

Details of the changes in partnership capital during the period should also be presented in a capital statement. The purpose of the statement and the data included in it correspond to the capital statement of a sole proprietorship. There are a number of variations in form, one of which is illustrated below.

Alden and Barker
Capital Statement
For Year Ended December 31, 1961

	G. M. Alden	J. D. Barker	Total
Capital, January 1..............	$35,000	$25,000	$60,000
Additional investment...........		6,000	6,000
	$35,000	$31,000	$66,000
Net income for the year.........	9,810	8,190	18,000
	$44,810	$39,190	$84,000
Withdrawals..................	17,200	10,000	27,200
Capital, December 31...........	$27,610	$29,190	$56,800

The capital balances of the partners would be presented in the proprietorship section of the Alden and Barker balance sheet for December 31, 1961, in the following manner:

Proprietorship

George M. Alden, capital............................	$27,610	
James D. Barker, capital............................	29,190	
Total proprietorship...............................		$56,800

Partnerships and federal income tax

As was stated in Chapter 17, partnerships are not ordinarily taxable entities. They are nevertheless required to file an informational tax return, disclosing the details of revenue and expenses and the distributive shares of each partner. Each partner then includes his distributive share of the ordinary partnership net income and of such special items as dividends, capital gains and losses, and charitable contributions in his own income tax return.

Partnerships that meet certain specified requirements of the Internal Revenue Code may, however, elect to be taxed as corporations. Partnerships electing this optional treatment pay an income tax on partnership income, and the individual partners are not required to include their distributive shares of income in their personal returns.

Questions

1. Is it possible that a partner may lose a greater amount than the amount of his investment in the partnership enterprise?

2. In the absence of an agreement to the contrary, do partners have equal authority in conducting the affairs of the partnership?

3. A partner whose authority is limited by agreement to matters related to personnel enters into a contract for the purchase of merchandise by the partnership. Is the partnership bound by the contract? Discuss.

4. Ames, Bell, and Clark are considering the formation of a partnership in which Ames is to invest $30,000 and devote one-fourth time, Bell is to invest $15,000 and devote one-half time, and Clark is to make no investment and devote full time. (a) In the absence of a specific agreement on the matter, how should the periodic net income or net loss be divided? (b) Would Clark be correct in assuming that inasmuch as he is not contributing any assets to the firm he is risking nothing?

5. As a part of his initial investment, a partner contributes equipment that had cost him $20,000 and on which the accumulated depreciation is $12,000. The partners agree on a valuation of $5,000. How should the equipment be recorded in the accounts of the partnership?

6. It is agreed that accounts receivable of $5,000 invested by a partner will be collectible to the extent of 80%. How should the accounts receivable be recorded in the general ledger of the partnership?

7. Included among the assets invested by Martin in the partnership of Martin and Tyler is a tract of land accepted by the firm at a valuation of $15,000. Its cost to Martin had been $5,000. (a) If the land is sold by the partnership for $20,000, what is the gain according to the partnership books? (b) What is the total gain according to the federal income tax law?

8. In the absence of contractual provisions regarding the matter, how should net income or net loss be divided among partners?

9. What accounts are debited and credited to record a partner's withdrawal of his weekly salary allowance?

10. What accounts are debited and credited to record the division of net income among partners at the end of the fiscal year?

11. The balance in a partner's capital account was $20,000 on January 1, the beginning of the fiscal year. On July 1 he invested an additional $10,000 in the partnership. Assuming that there were no other changes in his capital during the year, exclusive of income and monthly drawings, what was the amount of his average capital?

12. The income-sharing agreement of Davis and Evans provides for annual salary allowances of $9,000 and $6,000 respectively to the partners, with the remainder divided equally. For the year just ended the net income of the firm is $11,000 before giving effect to the salary allowances. (a) How should the net income be divided? (b) Would the fact that the partners had withdrawn the amounts of their salary allowances (charged to drawing accounts) affect the division of net income?

13. The net income of Staley and Taylor is $40,000 for the current fiscal year. Staley's share of the income is $25,000, of which he withdrew $15,000; Taylor's share is $15,000, of which he withdrew $10,000. Assuming that the partnership has not elected to be taxed as a corporation, what are the respective amounts of partnership net income that the partners should report in their individual income tax returns?

Exercises

1. Ralph Grant plans to invest the following assets in the partnership of Grant and Harper: cash, $10,000; accounts receivable with a face value of $19,000 and an allowance for uncollectible accounts of $1,600; and equipment with a cost of $5,000 and accumulated depreciation of $3,500. The partners agree that $600 of the accounts receivable are completely worthless and are not to be accepted by the partnership, that $2,000 is a reasonable allowance for the uncollectibility of the remaining accounts, and that the equipment is to be valued at $2,500. Give the entry in general journal form, to record Grant's investment on the partnership books.

2. Baldwin and Cooper form a partnership with investments of $40,000 and $20,000 respectively. Determine their participation in net income of $27,000 for the year under each of the following assumptions: (a) no agreement concerning division of income; (b) income divided in accordance with original capital investments; (c) interest at the rate of 5% allowed on original investments and the balance divided equally; (d) allowance of salary of $5,000 and $10,000 respectively, and the balance divided equally.

3. Determine the participation of Baldwin and Cooper in a net income of $9,000 for the year according to each of the four assumptions as to income division listed in Exercise 2.

4. The capital accounts of Vinson and Warner have balances of $50,000 and $30,000 respectively at the beginning of the year. The agreement provides for the allowance of interest on beginning capital at the rate of 6%, salaries of $8,000 and $6,000 respectively, and equal division of the remaining income. Determine the distributive shares of the partners in net income of (a) $20,000, (b) $42,000, (c) $5,000.

5. The articles of copartnership of A. R. Olson and J. B. Parks provide for salary allowances to the partners of $800 and $500 a month respectively, with the remaining net income divided equally. After closing all revenue and expense accounts at the end of the year, Expense and Revenue Summary has a credit balance of $20,000. The two drawing accounts have debit balances of $9,600 and $5,500 respectively. (a) Present journal entries to close the expense and revenue summary account and the drawing accounts. (b) What is the amount of the net increase or decrease in the capital accounts resulting from the entries in (a)?

Problems

18-1. On July 1 of the current year Charles Arnold and Joseph Beck form a partnership to engage in the retail clothing business. Arnold is to invest certain business assets at valuations to be agreed upon, is to transfer business liabilities, and is to contribute sufficient cash to bring his total capital to $35,000. Details regarding the book values of the business assets and liabilities, and the agreed valuations, follow:

	ARNOLD'S LEDGER BALANCE	AGREED VALUATION
Accounts Receivable......................	$ 9,000	$ 9,000
Allowance for Uncollectible Accounts.......	1,000	2,000
Merchandise Inventory...................	22,000	19,000
Store Equipment........................	3,500⎫	
Accumulated Depreciation—Store Equipment	2,500⎭	1,400
Office Equipment.......................	2,400⎫	
Accumulated Depreciation—Office Equipment	1,800⎭	400
Accounts Payable.......................	8,000	8,000

Beck agrees to invest $30,000 in cash.

The articles of copartnership include the following provisions regarding the distribution of net income: interest on original investment at 6%, salaries of $9,000 and $6,000 respectively, and the remainder equally.

Instructions: (1) Give the entries, in general journal form, to record the investments of Arnold and Beck on the partnership books.

(2) Prepare a balance sheet as of July 1, the date of formation of the partnership.

(3) After adjustments and the closing of revenue and expense accounts at June 30, the end of the first full year of operations, the expense and revenue summary account has a credit balance of $21,500. Present the journal entry to close Expense and Revenue Summary.

18-2. Vincent Gordon and James Hall are in the process of forming a partnership. They have agreed that Gordon is to invest $60,000 and that Hall is to invest $40,000. Gordon is to devote one fourth of his time to the business and Hall is to devote full time. The following plans for the division of income are under consideration:

(a) Equal division.
(b) In the ratio of original investments.
(c) In the ratio of time devoted to the business.
(d) Interest of 5% on original investments and the remainder equally.
(e) Interest of 6% on original investments, salaries of $4,000 (Gordon) and $10,000 (Hall), and the remainder equally.
(f) Plan (e), except that Hall is also to be allowed a bonus equal to 10% of the amount by which net income exceeds the salary allowances.

Instructions: Determine the division of income under each of the following assumptions: net income of $36,000, net income of $21,000, net income of

$10,000. Present the data in tabular form, using the following columnar headings:

Plan	$36,000		$21,000		$10,000	
	Gordon	Hall	Gordon	Hall	Gordon	Hall

18-3. The income-sharing agreement between Evans and Foster provides for monthly salary allowances of $600 and $400 respectively, with the remaining net income divided in the ratio of average capital. In computing average capital, the increases and the decreases during the first half of the month are dated as of the first of the month and those during second half are dated as of the first of the following month; withdrawals equivalent to the salary allowances are not considered to be reductions in capital.

Both partners withdrew the entire amount of their salary allowances during the year. Evans also withdrew an additional $4,000 on March 18. All withdrawals were charged to the appropriate drawing accounts. Details of the capital accounts for the year are as follows:

Paul Evans, Capital			John Foster, Capital		
	19--			19--	
	Jan. 1 Bal.	20,000		Jan. 1 Bal.	26,000
	Nov. 12	6,000		May 10	4,000
				Sept. 21	2,000

The credit balance in Expense and Revenue Summary after all revenue and expense accounts have been closed is $27,460.

Instructions: (1) Determine the average capital ratio, presenting computations.

(2) Prepare the income division section of the income statement for the current year.

(3) Prepare a capital statement for the current year.

(4) Present the journal entries to close the expense and revenue summary account and the drawing accounts.

18-4. David Scott and Albert Trump, partners, engage you to review their accounts at the close of their first year of operations, with particular regard to year-end adjustments and division of income. Their fiscal year ends on June 30. During the course of your examination you determine the following facts:

(a) All income and expense accounts have been closed to Expense and Revenue Summary, which has a credit balance of $8,280.

(b) Accrued salaries of $900 at the end of the current year were not recorded.

(c) Expired insurance of $480 during the year was not recorded.

(d) The cost of an addition to the building completed in midyear, $8,000, was charged to Repair Expense.

(e) As a result of the error in (d), depreciation of buildings was understated by $200.

(f) Sales of $3,500 on account on June 30 were not recorded. (The inventory was correctly stated.)

(g) The original capital investments of the partners, dated July 1 of last year, were $28,000 and $20,000 respectively. There were no other entries in the capital accounts during the current year.

(h) Withdrawals during the year, all of which were charged to Salary Expense, were as follows: Scott, $300 a month and $4,000 on October 1; Trump, $500 a month.

(i) The agreement as to division of income is as follows:

   (1) Interest at the rate of 6% is to be allowed on capital balances at the beginning of the year, diminished by interest at the same rate per annum on withdrawals in excess of salary allowances drawn each month.

   (2) Scott, who devotes half time to the business, is to have a salary allowance of $300 a month. Trump, who devotes full time to the business, is to have a salary allowance of $500 a month. As general manager, Trump is also allowed a bonus of 10% of the excess of net income over the sum of the interest and salary allowances.

   (3) Any balance remaining is to be divided equally.

Instructions: (1) Present the necessary adjusting and correcting entries as of June 30 of the current year. Reductions and increases in net income should be charged and credited directly to Expense and Revenue Summary.

(2) Prepare the income division section of the income statement.

(3) Prepare a capital statement.

(4) Present the journal entries to close the expense and revenue summary account and the drawing accounts.

18-5. The capital accounts of J. B. Norton, A. L. Owens, and T. D. Parker, partners, have balances of $30,000, $40,000, and $20,000 respectively on April 1 of the current year. Their agreement provides that each partner be allowed 5% on his capital balance at April 1, the beginning of the fiscal year; that Norton, the managing partner, be allowed a yearly salary of $10,000; and that the remaining net income or loss be divided equally. The net income for the year was $12,250.

Instructions: (1) Prepare the income division section of the income statement for the current year.

(2) Prepare the journal entry to close the expense and revenue summary account.

(3) Determine each partner's share, assuming that the net income for the year had been $40,000.

(4) Determine each partner's share, assuming that there had been a net loss of $6,500 for the year.

18-6. The account balances in the ledger of King, Lane, and Marsh on December 31, the end of the current fiscal year, are as follows:

Cash......................	$ 10,260	Office Supplies..............	$ 520
Accounts Receivable.........	36,700	Prepaid Insurance.	1,480
Allowance for Uncollectible		Prepaid Rent..............	.....
Accounts.................	1,200	Store Equipment............	15,900
Merchandise Inventory......	58,000	Accumulated Depreciation —	
Store Supplies..............	1,180	Store Equipment..........	4,800

Office Equipment............	$ 6,400	Sales.......................	$271,000
Accumulated Depreciation —		Purchases..................	178,400
Office Equipment.........	2,100	Sales Salaries..............	20,150
Accounts Payable...........	30,600	Advertising Expense.........	3,800
Salaries Payable.............	.....	Depreciation Expense — Store	
Payroll Taxes Payable.......	240	Equipment...............	.....
Employees Income Taxes Pay-		Store Supplies Expense.......	.....
able....................	210	Miscellaneous Selling Expense.	2,950
David King, Capital.........	25,000	Rent Expense..............	9,750
David King, Drawing........	.....	Office Salaries..............	6,400
Philip Lane, Capital.........	15,500	Bad Debts Expense..........	.....
Philip Lane, Drawing........	8,400	Depreciation Expense — Office	
Willard Marsh, Capital......	17,500	Equipment...............	.....
Willard Marsh, Drawing.....	6,000	Insurance Expense...........	.....
Expense and Revenue Sum-		Office Supplies Expense......	.....
mary....................	.....	Miscellaneous General Expense	1,860

Data for adjustments on December 31 are as follows:

Merchandise Inventory, $60,300.

It is estimated that accounts receivable of $2,450 will be uncollectible.

Store equipment and office equipment are depreciated at composite annual rates of 10% and 12½% respectively. Depreciation is charged for one-half year on equipment purchased during the year. Current year's purchases included in the accounts are as follows: store equipment, $2,400; office equipment, $960. (There were no reductions in equipment during the year.)

Inventories of supplies: store supplies, $530; office supplies, $310.

Expired insurance, $350.

Rent of $750 for January of the succeeding year was paid in December of the year just ended.

Accrued sales salaries, $240; accrued office salaries, $80.

The partnership agreement contains the following provisions regarding the division of income:

(a) Interest at 6% is allowed to the partners on their capital investment at the beginning of the year. (There were no additional investments during the year.)

(b) Lane and Marsh are allowed salaries of $700 and $500 a month respectively.

(c) The remaining balance is divided equally among the partners.

Instructions: (1) Enter the accounts in an eight-column work sheet, including those which do not have balances.

(2) Complete the work sheet.

(3) Prepare an income statement, including the income division section.

(4) Prepare a capital statement.

(5) Prepare a balance sheet.

Partnerships—
dissolution and liquidation

Partnership dissolution

One of the basic characteristics of the partnership form of organization is its limited life. Any change in the personnel of the membership results in the dissolution of the partnership. Thus, the death, bankruptcy, or withdrawal of a partner causes dissolution. Similarly, the admission of a new partner effects the dissolution of the old firm.

Dissolution of the partnership is not necessarily followed by the winding up of the affairs of the business. For example, if one of three partners in a business retires, the remaining partners may continue to operate the business. Or a partnership composed of two partners may admit an additional partner. In all such cases, a new partnership is formed and new articles of copartnership should be prepared and signed by the partners.

When a partnership goes out of business, it ordinarily sells most of the assets, pays the creditors, and distributes the remaining cash or other assets to the partners in accordance with their claims. This process of winding up the affairs is frequently referred to as the liquidation of the partnership. The accounting for liquidations will be discussed in the latter part of this chapter.

Admission of a new partner

A new partner may be admitted to a partnership only with the consent of all the old partners. It does not follow, however, that a partner cannot dispose of part or all of his interest in the firm without the consent of the remaining partners. If he does so without consent, he is liable to his copartners for any damages caused by his act. The person who buys the interest acquires the selling partner's rights to share in income and to assets upon liquidation. He does not automatically become a partner, however, and has no voice in partnership affairs unless he is admitted to the firm. In the discussion that follows, the consent of all parties will always be assumed.

A new partner may be admitted to a partnership through either of two procedures:

1. Purchase of an interest from one or more of the old partners.
2. Investment in the partnership.

Under the first procedure, the capital interest of the new partner is obtained from the old partners; and neither the total assets nor the total capital of the business is affected. When the second procedure is followed, both the total assets and the total capital of the business are increased.

Admission by purchase of interest from partners

When a new partner is admitted by the purchase of an interest from the old partners, the price for the interest is paid to the old partners. The amount received is the property of the partners individually rather than of the partnership; and hence, the cash or other consideration paid is not recorded in the accounts of the partnership. The only entry required is the transfer of the appropriate amounts of capital from the capital accounts of the old partners to the capital account established for the new partner.

As an example of the foregoing, assume that partners John Abbott and Henry Beck have capital balances of $30,000 each. Each of them sells one sixth of his capital interest to Roger Carson for $5,000, for which Carson pays cash. The only entry required in the partnership accounts is as follows:

```
John Abbott, Capital.....................................   5,000
Henry Beck, Capital......................................   5,000
    Roger Carson, Capital................................         10,000
```

The effect of the transaction on the partnership accounts is presented in the following diagram:

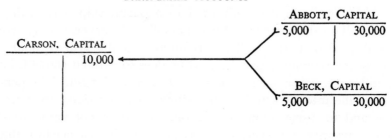

PARTNERSHIP ACCOUNTS

ABBOTT, CAPITAL
| 5,000 | 30,000 |

CARSON, CAPITAL
| | 10,000 |

BECK, CAPITAL
| 5,000 | 30,000 |

The foregoing entry is made regardless of the amount paid by Carson for the one-sixth interest. If the firm had been earning a high rate of return on the investment and Carson was very eager to obtain the one-sixth interest, he might have paid considerably more than $10,000. Had other circumstances prevailed, he might have acquired the one-sixth interest for considerably less than $10,000. In either event, the journal entry appearing above would not be affected.

After the admission of Carson, the total capital of the firm is $60,000, in which he has a one-sixth interest, or $10,000. It does not follow that he will be entitled to a similar share of the partnership net income. Division of net income or loss will be in accordance with the new partnership agreement.

Admission by contribution of assets to the partnership

Instead of buying an interest from the former partners, the new partner may make an investment in the business. In this case both the assets and the capital of the firm are increased. For example, George Logan and Thomas Macy are partners with capital accounts of $18,000 and $12,000, respectively. William Nichols invests $10,000 cash in the business, for which he is to receive a proprietary interest of $10,000. The entry to record this transaction, in general journal form, is:

```
Cash.....................................................  10,000
     William Nichols, Capital............................           10,000
```

The essential difference between the circumstances of the admission of Nichols above and of Carson in the preceding example may be observed by comparing the following diagram with the one on page 422.

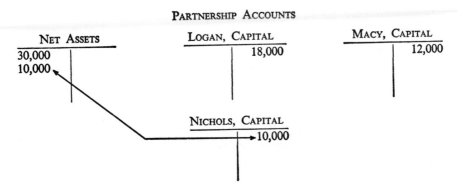

PARTNERSHIP ACCOUNTS

After the admission of Nichols, the total capital of the new partnership is $40,000, of which he has a one-fourth interest, or $10,000. The extent of his participation in partnership income will be governed by the articles of copartnership; in the absence of any agreement he will be entitled to share equally with the other partners.

In the above example it was assumed that the assets of the Logan and Macy partnership were fairly stated in terms of current values at the time of the admission of Nichols. Hence, no adjustments were made to any of the asset accounts prior to his admission. When the circumstances are otherwise, the book values should be brought into agreement with current fair values. The net amount of the revaluation is then allocated to the capital accounts of the old partners in accordance with their income-sharing agreement. For example, if the balance of the merchandise inventory account was $14,000 and the current replacement value was $17,000, the following entry should have been recorded prior to the admission of Nichols (assuming that Logan and Macy share equally in net income):

Merchandise Inventory....................................	3,000	
George Logan, Capital.................................		1,500
Thomas Macy, Capital.................................		1,500

If a number of assets are revalued, the adjustments may be debited or credited to a temporary account entitled "Asset Revaluations." After all adjustments are made, the net balance of the account is closed to the capital accounts.

Bonus or goodwill to former partners

The value of a successful going business may exceed the book value of the proprietorship, even though the asset and capital accounts have been adjusted to reflect current values. Under such conditions, the amount that a new partner will be required to invest in an existing partnership may be in excess of the proportionate interest which he receives in the new firm. The excess investment may be credited to the original partners as a *bonus*, or the capital accounts of the original partners may be increased through the recognition of an asset called *goodwill*.

Bonus. When the amount invested by the new partner is greater than the amount credited to his capital account, the excess may be divided among the capital accounts of the former partners in their income ratio. As a basis for illustration, assume that L. B. Elliott and G. H. Foster, partners, have agreed to admit B. T. Gorham to the partnership; that capital balances of Elliott and Foster are $25,000 each after adjusting asset values in preparation for the change in organization; that they share equally in net income; and that Gorham is to invest $30,000 in cash for which he is to receive a one-fourth interest.

The amount of the credit to the new partner's capital account and the amount and allocation of the bonus are determined in the following manner:

CREDIT TO NEW PARTNER'S CAPITAL ACCOUNT

Total capital of old partnership................................	$50,000
Investment by new partner (Gorham)..........................	30,000
Total capital of new partnership..............................	$80,000
Credit to capital account of new partner (Gorham) ¼ of $80,000.....	$20,000

AMOUNT AND ALLOCATION OF BONUS CONTRIBUTED BY
NEW PARTNER TO FORMER PARTNERS

Investment by new partner....................................	$30,000
Deduct: Credit to capital account of new partner..............	20,000
Bonus to former partners.....................................	$10,000
Allocation of bonus in income ratio (50%–50%):	
Credit to Elliott's capital account............................	$ 5,000
Credit to Foster's capital account............................	5,000

The entry to record the admission of Gorham, in general journal form, is as follows:

Cash..	30,000	
L. B. Elliott, Capital...............................		5,000
G. H. Foster, Capital...............................		5,000
B. T. Gorham, Capital..............................		20,000

After the foregoing entry has been posted, the capital accounts of the new partnership will have the following balances: Elliott, $30,000; Foster, $30,000; Gorham, $20,000. The credit of $20,000 to the new partner's capital account represents one fourth of the total proprietorship of $80,000.

Goodwill. Although the new partner may be quite willing to invest the amount required to obtain the fractional interest agreed upon, he may object to having his capital account credited with less than the amount he is investing. In terms of the preceding example, Gorham may be willing to invest $30,000 for a one-fourth interest, but he may have objections to receiving a capital credit of only $20,000.

An alternative method of giving effect to the agreement among the parties is to record the goodwill of the firm in the accounts. Goodwill, in the sense in which it is used in business, is an intangible asset that may attach to a business as a result of location, reputation, management, or other advantageous factors. Its existence is evidenced by a rate of return on the investment that is in excess of the normal rate for other firms in the same line of business. Goodwill may also be defined as the value attached to a business over and above the value of the physical property. There are numerous methods of estimating goodwill; but in any event, the amount to be recognized upon the admission of a partner will depend upon the agreement. It is not proper for a going concern arbitrarily to recognize goodwill in its accounts, but in this example the goodwill developed by the old partnership is recognized in setting up the new partnership.

Assuming that Gorham is to receive credit for $30,000, the entire amount of his investment, which is to represent a one-fourth interest, the goodwill and its allocation are calculated in the following manner:

Investment of new partner (Gorham)...........................		$ 30,000
Portion of total capital of new partnership represented by investment of new partner (Gorham)............................		¼
Total capital of new partnership, $30,000 ÷ ¼................		$120,000
Deduct: Capital accounts before recognition of goodwill		
Former partners — Elliott.........................	$25,000	
Foster.........................	25,000	
New partner — Gorham.........................	30,000	80,000
Goodwill to be recognized.................................		$ 40,000
Allocation of goodwill in income ratio (50%–50%):		
Former partners — Elliott.................................		$ 20,000
Foster.................................		20,000

The entries to record the goodwill and the admission of the new partner are as follows, in general journal form:

Goodwill..	40,000	
L. B. Elliott, Capital.............................		20,000
G. H. Foster, Capital.............................		20,000
Cash...	30,000	
B. T. Gorham, Capital.............................		30,000

After the foregoing entries have been posted, the capital accounts of the new partnership will have the following balances: Elliott, $45,000; Foster, $45,000; Gorham, $30,000. The $30,000 balance in Gorham's account is one fourth of the total capital of $120,000.

Goodwill is classified under *Intangible Assets*, which appears below the plant assets section of the balance sheet.

Bonus or goodwill to new partner

If the investment or services of a new partner are urgently needed, the former partners may be willing to credit the capital account of the incoming partner with an amount in excess of his investment. The additional credit to the new partner may be charged to the capital accounts of the former partners or to a goodwill account.

Bonus. The bonus to the incoming partner may be charged to the capital accounts of the former partners in accordance with their income-sharing ratio. The partnership of D. M. Jordan and S. T. Kyle, with proprietary interests of $18,000 and $24,000, respectively, agree to admit A. P. Lane to the partnership with a cash investment of $15,000, for which he is to receive a one-third interest. Jordan and Kyle share net income in the ratio of 2:3. The amount of the credit to the new partner's capital account and the amount and allocation of the bonus may be determined as follows:

CREDIT TO NEW PARTNER'S CAPITAL ACCOUNT

Total capital of old partnership...............................	$42,000
Investment of new partner (Lane).............................	15,000
Total capital of new partnership...............................	$57,000
Credit to capital account of new partner (Lane), ⅓ of $57,000.......	$19,000

AMOUNT AND ALLOCATION OF BONUS CONTRIBUTED BY
FORMER PARTNERS TO NEW PARTNER

Credit to capital account of new partner......................	$19,000
Deduct: Investment by new partner..........................	15,000
Bonus to new partner.......................................	$ 4,000
Allocation of bonus contribution in income ratio (2:3):	
Debit to Jordan's capital account...........................	$ 1,600
Debit to Kyle's capital account.............................	2,400

The entry to record the admission of Lane is as follows, in general journal form:

Cash..	15,000	
D. M. Jordan, Capital.................................	1,600	
S. T. Kyle, Capital....................................	2,400	
A. P. Lane, Capital.................................		19,000

Goodwill. The old partners may not care to have their capital accounts decreased. Inasmuch as the admission of the new partner is expected to improve the fortunes of the firm, the parties may prefer to recognize the acquisition of goodwill and credit the capital account of the new partner accordingly. To continue the illustration of the preceding section, the goodwill to be recognized in the alternative method is determined in the following manner:

Investment of former partners (Jordan & Kyle).................	$42,000
Portion of total capital of new partnership represented by investment of former partners (Jordan & Kyle).......................	⅔

Total capital of new partnership, $42,000 ÷ ⅔................. $63,000
Deduct: Capital accounts before recognition of goodwill
   Former partners — Jordan........................ $18,000
                Kyle.......................... 24,000
   New partner   — Lane......................... 15,000   57,000
Goodwill to be recognized................................... $ 6,000

The entry to record the goodwill and the admission of Lane, in general journal form, is as follows:

Cash... 15,000
Goodwill.. 6,000
   A. P. Lane, Capital............................   21,000

After the foregoing entries have been posted, the capital accounts of the new partnership will have the following balances: Jordan, $18,000; Kyle, $24,000; Lane, $21,000. The $21,000 balance in Lane's account is one third of the total capital of $63,000.

Withdrawal of a partner

When a partner retires or for some other reason withdraws from the firm, the remaining partners may continue the business as a new partnership. If one or more of the remaining partners purchase the interest of the withdrawing partner, the settlement is made between the partners individually. The only entry required on the books of the partnership is a debit to the proprietorship account of the one withdrawing and a credit to the proprietorship account of the partner or partners acquiring the interest.

If the settlement with the withdrawing partners is made by the partnership, the effect is to reduce the assets and the proprietorship of the firm. As stated earlier, any change in the membership of the firm causes its dissolution. In order to determine the proprietary interest of the withdrawing partner, the asset accounts should be adjusted to bring them into agreement with current fair values. The net amount of the adjustment should be allocated among the capital accounts of the partners in accordance with the income ratio. In the event the cash or other available assets are insufficient to make complete payment at the time of withdrawal, a liability account should be credited for the balance owed to the withdrawing partner.

The value of the going concern may be greater or less than the total proprietorship, depending on the relative profitableness of the business in the past and prospects for the future. If the withdrawing partner is to receive an amount that is greater than his proprietary interest, the excess may be treated as a bonus and charged to the capital accounts of the remaining partners. For example, assume that after asset adjustments the capital accounts of Reed, Shaw, and Taylor have balances of $30,000, $20,000, and $25,000; that their income ratio is 3:2:3; and that Taylor, the withdrawing partner, is to receive $31,000 for his interest.   The entry to record the agreement is as follows:

John Reed, Capital.	3,600	
Albert Shaw, Capital.	2,400	
Ralph Taylor, Capital.	25,000	
Payable to Ralph Taylor.		31,000

As an alternative to reducing the capital accounts of the remaining partners, the goodwill indicated by the terms of the agreement may be recorded in the accounts.   The bonus of $6,000 to the withdrawing partner is in reality his share of the goodwill developed by the firm. Inasmuch as he receives three eighths of the partnership net income, the $6,000 represents three eighths of the goodwill.   The total goodwill is thus $6,000 ÷ ⅜ or $16,000.   The entries to record the goodwill and the withdrawal of Taylor under this alternative procedure are as follows:

Goodwill	16,000	
John Reed, Capital.		6,000
Albert Shaw, Capital.		4,000
Ralph Taylor, Capital.		6,000
Ralph Taylor, Capital.	31,000	
Payable to Ralph Taylor.		31,000

A variation would be to recognize only the goodwill allocated to the withdrawing partner, in which event an entry debiting Goodwill and crediting Ralph Taylor, Capital for $6,000 would replace the first of the two entries above.   The justification for this variant is conservatism. Because of its intangible nature and the inherent difficulties of objectively determining its value, there is a general reluctance to recognize goodwill in the accounts.

The agreement between the withdrawing partner and the remaining partners may provide for settlement at an amount less than the proprietary interest of the withdrawing partner. In such cases the remainder in the withdrawing partner's capital account is allocated to the remaining partners in their income-sharing ratio.   If the facts in the preceding illustration are changed to assume that Taylor is to receive $20,000 for his interest, the entry to record the settlement would be as follows:

Ralph Taylor, Capital.	25,000	
Payable to Ralph Taylor.		20,000
John Reed, Capital.		3,000
Albert Shaw, Capital.		2,000

Death of a partner

The death of a partner effects the dissolution of the partnership. In the absence of any contrary agreement, the books should be closed as of the date of death and the net income for the fractional part of the year transferred to the capital accounts. It is not unusual for the agreement to stipulate that the books remain open to the end of the fiscal year or until the affairs are wound up, if that should occur earlier. The net income is then prorated to the periods before and after death, or the agreement may provide that the usual income ratio be employed for both.

The balance in the capital account is then transferred to a liability account with the estate. The surviving partner or partners may continue the business or the affairs may be wound up. If the former course is followed, the procedures for settling with the estate will conform to those outlined earlier for the withdrawal of a partner. Accounting for the liquidation of a partnership is discussed in the following section.

Liquidation of a partnership

A partnership may wind up its affairs and go out of business for a variety of reasons, including accomplishment of the purpose for which it was organized, termination of the period covered by the agreement, withdrawal or death of a partner, or unprofitability of the business. The winding-up process may be referred to generally as *liquidation*. Although liquidation refers specifically to the payment of liabilities, it is often used in a broader sense to include the entire winding-up process.

When the ordinary business activities are discontinued preparatory to liquidation, the books should be adjusted and closed in accordance with the customary procedures of the periodic summary. The only accounts remaining open will then be the various asset, valuation, liability, and capital accounts. The sale of the assets is referred to as *realization*. As cash is realized, it is applied first to the payment of the claims of creditors. After all liabilities have been paid, the remaining cash is distributed to the partners in accordance with their proprietary interests as indicated by their capital accounts.

If the assets are sold piece-meal, the liquidation process may extend over a considerable period of time. This creates no special problem, however, if the distribution of cash to the partners is postponed until all of the assets have been sold. As a basis for illustration, assume that Alden, Beeler, and Craig, partners, decide to liquidate their partnership. Their income and loss ratio is 5:3:2. After discontinuing the ordinary business operations and closing the books, the following summary of the ledger is prepared:

Cash...	$11,000
All other assets...................................	64,000
Total liabilities..................................	$ 9,000
J. Alden, Capital.................................	22,000
B. Beeler, Capital................................	22,000
H. Craig, Capital.................................	22,000
Total..	$75,000 $75,000

Accounting for the liquidation will be illustrated by three examples based on the foregoing statement of facts. In all cases it will be assumed that all noncash assets are disposed of in a single transaction and that all liabilities are paid at one time. This is merely for the sake of brevity. In addition, "Assets" and "Liabilities" will be used as account titles in place of the various asset, valuation, and liability accounts that in actual practice would be used in recording the transactions.

Gain on realization. Alden, Beeler, and Craig sell all noncash assets for $72,000, realizing a gain of $8,000 ($72,000 − $64,000). The gain is divided among the capital accounts in the income and loss ratio, the liabilities are paid, and the remaining cash is distributed to the partners according to the balances in their capital accounts. A tabular summary of the transactions follows:

				PROPRIETORSHIP		
	CASH	OTHER ASSETS	LIABILITIES	J. ALDEN 50%	B. BEELER 30%	H. CRAIG 20%
Balances before realization......	$11,000	$64,000	$ 9,000	$22,000	$22,000	$22,000
Sales of assets and division of gain	+72,000	−64,000		+ 4,000	+ 2,400	+ 1,600
Balances after realization.......	$83,000		$ 9,000	$26,000	$24,400	$23,600
Payment of liabilities..........	− 9,000		−9,000			
Balances...................	$74,000			$26,000	$24,400	$23,600
Distribution of cash to partners..	−74,000			−26,000	−24,400	−23,600

The entries to record the several steps in the liquidation procedure are as follows, in general journal form:

Sale of assets

Cash...	72,000	
Assets.....................................		64,000
Loss and Gain on Realization...............		8,000

Division of gain

Loss and Gain on Realization...............	8,000	
J. Alden, Capital.........................		4,000
B. Beeler, Capital........................		2,400
H. Craig, Capital.........................		1,600

Payment of liabilities

| Liabilities.. | 9,000 | |
| Cash.. | | 9,000 |

Distribution of cash to partners

J. Alden, Capital.....................................	26,000	
B. Beeler, Capital....................................	24,400	
H. Craig, Capital....................................	23,600	
Cash..		74,000

It should be noted that the gain on the sale of the assets is divided among the capital accounts in the income-sharing ratio and that the cash is distributed among the partners in accordance with their proprietary interests as indicated by the balances in their capital accounts.

Loss on realization; no capital deficiencies. Assume that in the foregoing example Alden, Beeler, and Craig dispose of the assets, except cash, for $44,000, incurring a loss of $20,000 ($64,000 − $44,000). The various steps in the liquidation are summarized as follows:

| | | | | PROPRIETORSHIP | | |
	CASH	OTHER ASSETS	LIABILITIES	J. ALDEN 50%	B. BEELER 30%	H. CRAIG 20%
Balances before realization......	$11,000	$64,000	$ 9,000	$22,000	$22,000	$ 22,000
Sale of assets and division of loss.	+44,000	−64,000		−10,000	− 6,000	− 4,000
Balances after realization.......	$55,000		$ 9,000	$12,000	$16,000	$18,000
Payment of liabilities...........	− 9,000		− 9,000			
Balances....................	$46,000			$12,000	$16,000	$18,000
Distribution of cash to partners..	−46,000			−12,000	−16,000	−18,000

The entries required to record the liquidation appear below, in general journal form:

Sale of assets

Cash.....................................	44,000	
Loss and Gain on Realization............................	20,000	
Assets.......................................		64,000

Division of loss

J. Alden, Capital.....................................	10,000	
B. Beeler, Capital....................................	6,000	
H. Craig, Capital....................................	4,000	
Loss and Gain on Realization........................		20,000

Payment of liabilities

| Liabilities.. | 9,000 | |
| Cash.. | | 9,000 |

Distribution of cash to partners

J. Alden, Capital..	12,000	
B. Beeler, Capital.......................................	16,000	
H. Craig, Capital..	18,000	
Cash..		46,000

Loss on realization; capital deficiency. In the preceding illustration the capital account of each partner was more than sufficient to absorb the loss from realization. Each partner shared in the distribution of cash to the extent of the remaining credit balance in his capital account. The share of the loss chargeable to a partner may be such that it exceeds his proprietary interest. The resulting debit balance in his capital account, which is referred to as a *deficiency*, is a claim of the partnership against the partner. Pending collection from the deficient partner, the partnership cash will not be sufficient to pay the other partners in full. In such cases the available cash should be distributed in such a manner that, if the claim against the deficient partner cannot be collected, each of the remaining capital balances will be sufficient to absorb the appropriate share of the deficiency.

Assuming that Alden, Beeler, and Craig sell the partnership assets for $10,000, the liquidation will proceed as follows:

	CASH	OTHER ASSETS	LIABIL- ITIES	J. ALDEN 50%	B. BEELER 30%	H. CRAIG 20%
					PROPRIETORSHIP	
Balances before realization......	$11,000	$64,000	$ 9,000	$22,000	$22,000	$22,000
Sale of assets and division of loss.	+10,000	−64,000		−27,000	−16,200	−10,800
Balances after realization.......	$21,000		$ 9,000	$ 5,000 (Dr.)	$ 5,800	$11,200
Payment of liabilities..........	− 9,000		− 9,000			
Balances....................	$12,000			$ 5,000 (Dr.)	$ 5,800	$11,200
Distribution of cash to partners..	−12,000				− 2,800	− 9,200
Balances....................				$ 5,000 (Dr.)	$ 3,000	$ 2,000

According to the summary above, the cash balance after payment of the liabilities is $12,000; Alden has a deficiency of $5,000; and the proprietary interests of Beeler ($5,800) and Craig ($11,200) total $17,000. The cash should be allocated between Beeler and Craig in such a manner as to allow for the possibility that the claim against Alden may be partly or wholly uncollectible. If the entire $5,000 claim should prove to be uncollectible, the loss would be divided between the two partners in the ratio of 3:2. Therefore, Beeler should be paid enough to leave a balance of ⅗ of $5,000, or $3,000, in his capital account; and Craig should have a remaining balance of ⅖ of $5,000, or $2,000, after his cash payment. Accordingly, Beeler is paid $2,800 and Craig is paid $9,200.

The entries to record the liquidation to this point, in general journal form, are as follows:

Sale of assets

Cash...	10,000	
Loss and Gain on Realization...........................	54,000	
Assets...		64,000

Division of loss

J. Alden, Capital.....................................	27,000	
B. Beeler, Capital....................................	16,200	
H. Craig, Capital....................................	10,800	
Loss and Gain on Realization.........................		54,000

Payment of liabilities

Liabilities...	9,000	
Cash...		9,000

Distribution of cash to partners

B. Beeler, Capital....................................	2,800	
H. Craig, Capital....................................	9,200	
Cash...		12,000

The affairs of the partnership are not completely wound up until the claims among the partners are settled. Payments to the firm by the deficient partner are credited to his capital account. Any uncollectible deficiency becomes a loss and is written off against the capital balances of the remaining partners. Finally, the cash received from the deficient partner is distributed to the other partners in accordance with their proprietary claims.

To continue with the illustration, the capital balances after the cash distribution of $12,000 are as follows: Alden, $5,000 debit; Beeler, $3,000 credit; Craig, $2,000 credit. The entries on the books of the partnership, under three different assumptions as to final settlement, are presented below.

Assuming that Alden pays the full amount of his deficiency, the final entries, in general journal form, will be:

Receipt of deficiency

Cash...	5,000	
J. Alden, Capital....................................		5,000

Distribution of cash to partners

B. Beeler, Capital....................................	3,000	
H. Craig, Capital....................................	2,000	
Cash...		5,000

If we assume that Alden pays $3,000 of his deficiency and the remainder is considered to be uncollectible, the final entries, in general journal form, will be as follows:

Receipt of part of deficiency

Cash...	3,000	
J. Alden, Capital......................................		3,000

Division of loss

B. Beeler, Capital..	1,200	
H. Craig, Capital...	800	
J. Alden, Capital......................................		2,000

Distribution of cash to partners

B. Beeler, Capital..	1,800	
H. Craig, Capital...	1,200	
Cash...		3,000

Finally, if it is assumed that Alden is unable to pay any part of his deficiency, the loss to the other partners will be recorded in the following entry:

Division of loss

B. Beeler, Capital..	3,000	
H. Craig, Capital...	2,000	
J. Alden, Capital......................................		5,000

The salient points in the foregoing discussion and illustrations of liquidation are: (1) losses and gains on realization are divided in accordance with the income-and-loss ratio; and (2) cash is distributed among the partners in accordance with their proprietary claims, as indicated by the credit balances in their capital accounts, after taking into consideration the possibility of a loss that may result from the inability to collect from a deficient partner.

Questions

1. With the consent of Gordon and Harris, Fisher sells to his son his entire interest in the partnership of Fisher, Gordon, and Harris. (a) What effect does the transaction have on the assets and the capital of the firm? (b) Would the effect be any different if Fisher gave his interest to his son?

2. Adams, Baker, and Carey, partners, mutually agree that upon the death of any partner he shall be succeeded by his oldest son. Does this agreement have the effect of preventing the dissolution of the partnership upon the death of one of the original partners?

3. Differentiate between "dissolution" and "liquidation" of a partnership.

4. Taylor, a partner in the firm of Roberts, Shaw, and Taylor, sells his investment (capital balance of $20,000) to Warren for $22,000. (a) Does the withdrawal of Taylor dissolve the partnership? (b) Are Roberts and Shaw required to admit Warren as a partner?

5. The credit to a newly admitted partner's capital account is to be greater than the value of the assets (excluding goodwill) that he is contributing to the firm. Do the old partners or the new partner receive the bonus?

6. Goodwill is to be recognized at the time of admission of a new partner and the credit to the new partner's capital account is to be the amount of his investment (excluding goodwill). Are the capital accounts of the old partners or of the new partner credited for the amount of the goodwill recognized?

7. X and Y are partners, sharing gains and losses equally. At the time they decide to terminate the partnership their capital balances are $30,000 and $50,000 respectively. After all assets are sold and all liabilities are paid, there is a cash balance of $60,000. (a) What is the amount of the loss on realization? (b) How should the loss be divided between X and Y? (c) How should the cash be divided between X and Y?

8. C, D, and E share net income and losses equally. After dividing the losses on realization and paying the liabilities, there is $5,000 in cash and the balances in the capital accounts are as follows: C, $5,000, cr.; D, $2,000, cr.; E, $2,000, dr. How should the $5,000 be divided?

9. A, B, and C arrange to import and sell orchid corsages for a university dance. It is agreed that the net income or loss on the venture is to be shared equally. A and B advance $20 and $10 respectively of their own funds to pay for advertising and other expenses. (a) After collecting for all sales and paying creditors they have $150 in cash. How should the money be distributed? (b) Assuming that they have only $12 instead of $150, how should the money be distributed? Does any of the three have claims against another and, if so, how much?

Exercises

1. Burton and Carter, partners, have capital balances of $20,000 and $30,000 respectively. They admit Davis, who purchases one half of Burton's interest for $8,000 and one third of Carter's interest for $8,000. Present the journal entry to record the admission of Davis.

2. The capital balances of Evans and Ford, partners, are $10,000 each. They share equally in income. They admit Grover to the partnership with an investment of $14,500 in cash, for which he is to receive a one-third interest. Present journal entries for two alternative methods of recording the admission of Grover.

3. Miller and Newman are partners with capital investments of $30,000 and $20,000 respectively. They divide income in the ratio of their capital investments. Present the journal entries necessary to admit Orton under each of the following conditions:

    (a) Orton invests $25,000 in cash, receiving a one-third interest in the firm.

    (b) Orton invests $25,000 in cash and $20,000 in merchandise inventory, receiving a one-half interest in the firm. The total capital is to be increased by $45,000.

    (c) Orton buys one half of the interest of each partner, paying Miller $12,000 and Newman $8,000.

   (d) Orton invests $28,000 in cash, receiving a one-third interest in the firm. His capital account is to be credited for the entire amount of his investment.

   (e) Orton invests $22,000 in cash, receiving a one-fourth interest in the firm. Present alternative methods of recording his investment.

4. After the adjustment of asset values at the date of Dugan's retirement from the firm, the capital balances of Dugan, Edwards, and Frost are $30,000, $25,000, and $15,000 respectively. Their income-and-loss ratio is 5:3:2. The partners agree that Dugan is to receive $40,000 for his interest. Edwards and Frost will continue to operate the business. Give the journal entries to record Dugan's withdrawal under each of the following conditions:

   (a) Edwards and Frost each purchase one half of Dugan's interest.

   (b) The goodwill of the firm, as indicated by the agreement with Dugan, is to be given recognition in the accounts, and Dugan is to withdraw $10,000 in cash and the remainder in installments.

   (c) No goodwill is to be recognized. Dugan is to withdraw $15,000 in cash from the partnership and the remainder in installments.

   (d) The goodwill attributable to Dugan's interest is to be given recognition in the accounts, and Dugan is to receive $5,000 in cash and seven $5,000 interest-bearing notes maturing at six-month intervals.

5. After closing the books preparatory to liquidating the partnership, the capital accounts of Ross, Sutton, and Taylor have credit balances of $15,000 each. They share income and losses equally. The assets are sold for cash at a loss of $15,000 and all creditors are paid. (a) What is the amount of cash remaining? (b) How should it be distributed among the partners?

6. Immediately prior to disposing of all assets and winding up partnership affairs, the capital account balances of Jackson and King are $8,000 and $4,000 respectively. They share income and losses equally. After selling the assets for cash and paying the liabilities, there is $3,000 of cash remaining. Jackson believes that the cash should be divided in the ratio of 8:4, or $2,000 for himself and $1,000 for King. King contends that the cash should be divided in the income-and-loss ratio, or $1,500 for each. How should the cash be divided?

Problems

19-1. John McNeil and Paul Nelson are partners sharing income in the ratio of 3:1. After adjustments to asset values as of April 30 of the current year, their proprietary interests in the firm are $24,000 and $16,000 respectively. Martin Owen is to be admitted to the partnership with a cash investment of $20,000.

Instructions: Record the admission of Owen to the firm, in general journal form, under each of the following assumptions (if fractional dollars are involved, round final amounts to nearest dollar):

   (1) Owen to receive credit for the amount of his investment, which is to represent a one-fourth interest.

   (2) Owen to receive credit for the amount of his investment, which is to represent a one-third interest.

   (3) Owen to receive a one-fourth interest; total capital to be increased only by the amount of his cash investment.

(4) Owen to receive a one-half interest; McNeil and Nelson to retain their present capital balances.

(5) Owen to receive a two-fifths interest; total capital to be increased only by the amount of his cash investment.

(6) Owen to receive a two-fifths interest; goodwill to be recorded.

(7) Owen to receive a one-fifth interest; no goodwill to be recorded.

19-2. Edward Allen is to retire from the partnership of Allen and Associates as of December 31 of the current year. After closing the books and giving effect to revisions in asset values as of that date, the capital balances of the partners are as follows: Edward Allen, $40,000; Harold Benson, $30,000; James Clark, $20,000. They have shared net income and losses in the ratio 4:2:1.

Instructions: Present the entries, in general journal form, to record the withdrawal of Allen under each of the following assumptions:

(1) Benson and Clark each purchase one half of Allen's interest for $25,000, in each case paying him $10,000 in cash and giving an interest-bearing note for $15,000.

(2) Allen receives $14,000 in cash from the firm and a note for $38,000, to be collected over a period of three years. The partnership goodwill indicated by the settlement is not to be recorded in the accounts of the firm.

(3) Allen receives from the firm $20,000 in cash and four $6,000, interest-bearing notes maturing at six-month intervals. The goodwill attributable to Allen's interest is to be recorded in the accounts of the firm.

(4) Allen withdraws $26,500 in cash in full settlement.

(5) Allen receives $10,000 in cash, real estate, and a note for $20,000. The real estate had been included in Allen's original contribution to the capital of the partnership. He had acquired the property for $12,000 (land $1,000, building $11,000); when contributed to the firm it had been valued at $10,000 (land $1,000, building $9,000); and its adjusted valuation at December 31 is $16,000 (land $4,000, building $12,000). The total goodwill of the firm, as indicated by the settlement with Allen, is to be recorded in the accounts.

19-3. Jacobsen, Kelly, and Little decide to discontinue business operations as of April 30 and to liquidate their enterprise. The firm's post-closing trial balance at that date appears at the top of the following page.

The partners share net income and losses in the ratio 3:2:1. The realization and liquidation transactions are summarized as follows:

(a) Collected $3,200 of accounts receivable; the remainder are worthless.

(b) Sold the merchandise for $10,000 cash.

(c) Sold the supplies for $350 cash.

(d) Sold the equipment for $1,000 cash.

(e) Sold the land and building for $22,000, purchaser paying $15,000 cash and assuming the mortgage. The mortgage holder released the partners from further liability.

(f) Paid miscellaneous expenses in connection with the sale of the assets, $500. (Charge to Loss and Gain on Realization.)

(g) Realized $550 cash from cancellation of the insurance policies.

(h) Distributed the loss on realization to the partners' capital accounts.

(i) Paid the notes payable in full.

(j) Paid the accounts payable in full.

(k) Distributed remaining cash to the partners.

Jacobsen, Kelly, and Little
Post-Closing Trial Balance
April 30, 19—

Cash...	10,000	
Accounts Receivable..............................	6,000	
Allowance for Uncollectible Accounts.................		2,000
Merchandise Inventory............................	19,400	
Prepaid Insurance................................	800	
Supplies..	700	
Equipment......................................	4,500	
Accumulated Depreciation — Equipment...............		3,800
Building..	20,000	
Accumulated Depreciation — Building.................		4,000
Land...	4,000	
Notes Payable...................................		2,000
Accounts Payable................................		3,600
Mortgage Payable................................		7,000
P. Jacobsen, Capital..............................		18,000
R. Kelly, Capital................................		15,000
J. Little, Capital................................		10,000
	65,400	65,400

Instructions: (1) Set up T accounts for all of the accounts appearing in the trial balance and for Loss and Gain on Realization.

(2) Record the April 30 balances in the T accounts.

(3) Present entries, in general journal form, to record the liquidation; post to the accounts; rule the accounts.

(4) Assuming a net loss on realization of $36,000, determine each partner's share of the cash remaining after paying the creditors (no entries required).

(5) Assuming a net loss on realization of $39,000, determine each partner's share of the cash remaining after paying the creditors (no entries required).

19-4. J. D. Baxter and L. G. Cook have operated a successful enterprise, sharing income and losses in the ratio 3:2. H. M. Ellis is to be admitted to the partnership on November 1 of the current year in accordance with the following agreement:

(a) Assets and liabilities of the old partnership are to be valued at their book values as of October 31, except for the following:

Land is to be valued at $3,000.

Buildings are to be valued at $16,000.

Equipment is to be valued at $52,400.

Supplies are to be valued at 25% less than book value.

Accounts receivable amounting to $800 are to be written off and provision is to be made for the probable uncollectibility of an additional $365.

(b) Baxter is to withdraw cash of $6,200 and Cook is to withdraw cash of $4,000.

(c) Ellis is to invest sufficient cash to acquire a one-sixth interest after crediting the initial $10,000 to the old partners as a bonus.

(d) The income-sharing ratio of Baxter, Cook, and Ellis is to be 5:3:2.

The post-closing trial balance of Baxter and Cook as of October 31 follows:

Baxter and Cook
Post-Closing Trial Balance
October 31, 19--

Cash...	14,060	
Accounts Receivable.............................	11,160	
Supplies.......................................	1,300	
Prepaid Insurance..............................	690	
Equipment.....................................	72,950	
Accumulated Depreciation — Equipment............		27,040
Buildings......................................	18,000	
Accumulated Depreciation — Buildings.............		6,000
Land..	1,500	
Accounts Payable...............................		9,940
Wages Payable.................................		770
Taxes Payable.................................		1,210
J. D. Baxter, Capital...........................		38,900
L. G. Cook, Capital............................		35,800
	119,660	119,660

Instructions: (1) Present general journal entries as of October 31 to record the revaluations, using a temporary account entitled Asset Revaluations. The balances in the accumulated depreciation accounts are to be eliminated.

(2) Present the additional entries, in general journal form, to record the remaining transactions related to the formation of the new partnership. Assume that all transactions occur on November 1.

(3) Present a balance sheet for the new partnership as of November 1.

19-5. Immediately prior to beginning the process of liquidation, the partners in the firm of Fisher, Gibson, and Hahn have capital balances of $60,000, $30,000, and $20,000 respectively. The cash balance is $40,000, the book value of other assets totals $95,000, and liabilities total $25,000. The partners share income and losses in the ratio of 2:2:1.

Instructions: Present the entries, in general journal form, to record (a) the sale of the assets, (b) the distribution of the loss or gain on realization, (c) the payment of creditors, and (d) the distribution of cash to the partners under each of the assumptions described below. Use "Assets" as the account title for the noncash assets, and "Liabilities" as the account title for creditors' claims. It is suggested that summaries similar to those illustrated in this chapter be prepared as a basis for the entries.

(1) All of the other assets are sold for $100,000 in cash.

(2) All of the other assets are sold for $45,000 in cash.

(3) All of the other assets are sold for $12,500 in cash.
    After the available cash is paid to the partners:
      (a) The partner with the debit capital balance pays the amount owed to the firm.
      (b) The additional cash is distributed.

(4) All of the other assets are sold for $8,000 in cash.
    After the available cash is paid to the partners:
      (a) The partner with the debit capital balance pays 25% of his deficiency to the firm.
      (b) The remaining partners absorb the remaining deficiency as a loss.
      (c) The additional cash is distributed.

20

Corporations— nature and formation

Definition of a corporation

Without doubt the most frequently quoted definition of a corporation is the one formulated in 1819 by Chief Justice Marshall. In the decision on the Dartmouth College case he stated that: "A corporation is an artificial being, invisible, intangible, and existing only in contemplation of the law." The concept underlying this definition has become the foundation for the prevailing legal doctrine that a corporation is an artificial person, created by law and having a distinct existence separate and apart from the natural persons who are responsible for its creation and operation.

Corporations may be classified in a number of ways. For example, the term *public corporation* may refer to a municipality or other political division, and the term *private corporation* may refer to all corporations other than incorporated governmental units. On the other hand, business corporations whose ownership is widely held may be termed *public* or *open corporations*, and those with a relatively small group of owners may be termed *private* or *close corporations*. *Nonprofit corporations* include those organized for charitable, educational, or other philanthropic purposes. Regardless of the nature or purpose of a corporation, it is created in accordance with the statutes and is a separate legal entity.

Almost without exception, all large business enterprises in the United States are organized as corporations. Mass production by assembly-line methods requires large investments in inventories, buildings, machinery, and other properties. The large sums needed are usually obtainable only through the pooling of the resources of a number of people in a corporation. The corporate form of organization is also advantageous to individuals who wish to invest savings in business enterprises without incurring responsibilities for management or risking their entire capital.

Characteristics of a corporation

As a legal entity, the corporation has certain characteristics that distinguish it from other types of business organization. The most important of these characteristics will be considered briefly in the following paragraphs.

Separate legal existence. Being a distinct legal entity, the corporation acts under its corporate name. It may obtain, hold, and dispose of property in its corporate capacity. It may borrow funds and assume other obligations. It may enter into contracts with outsiders or with its own stockholders.

Transferable units of ownership. The proprietorship of a corporation is divided into transferable units known as *shares of stock*. Each share has the same rights and privileges as every other share of the same class. One may own a single share or many thousands of shares. The owners of the corporation, known as *shareholders* or *stockholders*, may sell their stock without interfering with the activities of the corporation. The millions of transactions that occur on stock exchanges are independent transactions between buyers and sellers.

Limited liability of stockholders. Since a corporation is a separate legal entity, it is responsible for its own acts and obligations. Ordinarily the creditors of a corporation may not look beyond the assets of the corporation for satisfaction of their claims. Thus, the loss that a stockholder may suffer is limited to the amount of his investment. The phenomenal growth of the corporate form of business would have been impossible without this feature.

Continuity of existence. The maximum life of a corporation depends upon the terms of its charter; it may be perpetual or it may continue for a specified number of years. In the latter case the term may usually be extended by an application for renewal of the charter. In contrast to a partnership, the life term of the corporation is not affected by the withdrawal, death, or incapacity of one of its owners.

Additional taxes. A corporation is required to pay a fee to the state at the time of its organization and an annual tax thereafter. If it does business in states other than the one in which it is incorporated, it may also be required to pay annual taxes to such states. The earnings of a corporation are subject to the federal income tax. When the remaining earnings are distributed to stockholders as dividends, they are again taxed as income.

Under certain conditions specified in the Internal Revenue Code, corporations with no more than ten stockholders may elect to be treated as a partnership for income tax purposes. The income of corporations electing this optional treatment must be included in the taxable income of the shareholders, regardless of whether it is distributed to the stockholders, and the corporation pays no tax.

Governmental regulation. Being creatures of the state, corporations are subject to more restrictions and regulations than are sole proprietorships and partnerships. They may not exceed the scope of activities described in the charter; in some states they are restricted as to the amount of real estate that they may own, the amount of their own shares of stock that they may reacquire, and the amount of earnings that they may distribute. Although these and other restrictions do not outweigh the advantages of the corporate form for a large firm, they may represent an important consideration for a small business.

Incorporation

It is customary to obtain the services of an attorney to guide the incorporators through the various steps in organizing a corporation. The statutory requirements vary among the states but in general it is necessary to: (1) effect a tentative organization and obtain subscriptions to stock and (2) obtain a charter or articles of incorporation. The application for a charter is filed with an official of the state government, usually the Secretary of State. Upon approval of the application, the charter is issued. It may be a separate document or the approved application may become the charter.

The following excerpts from the Ohio statutes are illustrative of the information that may be required in the application and the charter:

(A) Three or more natural persons, a majority of whom are citizens of the United States, may form a corporation by subscribing and thereafter filing in the office of the Secretary of State articles of incorporation which shall set forth:

(1) The name of the corporation, which shall end with or include "Company," "Co.," "Corporation," "Corp.," "Incorporated," or "Inc.";

(2) The place in this state where the principal office of the corporation is to be located;

(3) The purpose or purposes for which the corporation is formed;

(4) The authorized number and the par value per share of shares with par value, and the authorized number of shares without par value, . . . ; the express terms, if any, of the shares; and, if the shares are classified, the designation of each class, the authorized number and par value per share, if any, of the shares of each class, and the express terms of the shares of each class;

(5) The amount of stated capital with which the corporation will begin business, which shall not be less than five hundred dollars.

The charter ordinarily contains only the more basic rules governing the corporation. Other regulations for the conduct of corporate affairs, consistent with the charter and the statutes, are usually adopted as by-laws. Among other things, the by-laws may provide for: (1) time and place of meetings of shareholders, method of notification, quorum requirements; (2) number of directors, term of office, manner of fixing remuneration; (3) special committees of board of directors, their appointment and authority; and (4) titles, qualifications, and duties of officers.

Working organization

The proprietors of a corporation are its shareholders. Unlike sole proprietors and partners, the shareholders have no direct control over the management of their business. They exercise control indirectly by electing a *board of directors*, whose responsibility it is to determine policies and to see that they are carried out by the employees of the corporation.

The board of directors selects the principal executives, to whom it in turn delegates the authority to manage the affairs of the corporation. The extent to which the directors determine policies varies among corporations. They may meet each month, each week, or oftener. A common practice among large corporations is to establish one or more standing committees of the directors, such as an executive committee and a finance committee. The special committees report periodically to the entire board, which confirms or disapproves of their acts and recommendations.

The principal executives of a corporation, consisting of a president, one or more vice-presidents, a secretary, a treasurer, and perhaps others, are responsible to the board of directors. It is not unusual for the president and others among the principal executives also to be members of the board of directors. As the chief executive officer, the president has the responsibility of directing and controlling the activities of the other principal executives.

The chart on the opposite page depicts the flow of authority from the board of directors through intermediate steps down to the rank and file employees. The flow of responsibility is in the reverse direction.

The number of individual stockholders in corporations varies widely; from a very small number, to figures in the hundreds of thousands. For a large, publicly held corporation, the number of stockholders in attendance at an annual meeting is relatively small. Stockholders not expecting to attend the meeting may transfer their voting rights to an agent. This delegation of voting rights is accomplished by the use of a form known as a *proxy*. The management of large corporations customarily mail proxy forms to all stockholders in advance of the annual meeting. The form, or an accompanying statement, discloses the slate of directors proposed by the management and an explanation of any

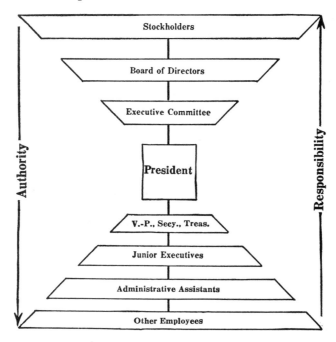

Corporate form of organization

important issues, such as a merger with another corporation, on which the stockholders are to vote.

At the stockholders' meeting the board of directors, through its chairman or the president of the corporation, presents an oral report on past operations and future plans. A printed report is also usually mailed to all stockholders soon after the end of each fiscal year. These reports may be very brief, containing only the condensed financial statements for the year, or they may include supplementary statements, charts, graphs, and explanatory text. Many corporations also issue brief quarterly reports.

Stockholders and proprietorship

The proprietorship of a corporation is commonly called *capital, net worth,* or *stockholders' equity.* As in the case of sole proprietorships and partnerships, the equity of the owners is equivalent to the excess of assets over liabilities. In a sole proprietorship the capital is reported as one item on the balance sheet; in a partnership the proprietary interest of each partner is stated separately. The amounts reported represent the investment at the balance sheet date, and no distinction is made between contributions of capital and accumulated income. In contrast, the capital section of corporation balance sheets is divided into subsections based on the source of the capital. In addition, the identity of the owners is not disclosed.

The two principal sources of capital are investments by the owners and accumulations of income. Assuming that Adams, Baker, and Cole organize a business with an investment of $20,000 each, the capital accounts would appear as follows:

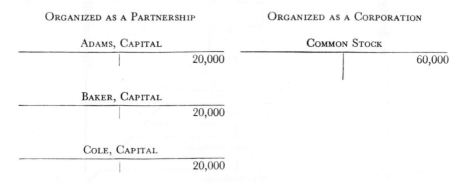

The $60,000 investment of the stockholders, sometimes referred to as the *paid-in capital*, is recorded in a stock account, properly designated as to type. This represents the legal capital of the corporation. Ordinarily it may not be returned to the stockholders except upon liquidation, and then only after the claims of creditors have been satisfied.

If the new firm earns net income of $9,000 during its first year, the capital accounts would then appear as follows, assuming no distributions of income and equal income sharing by the partners:

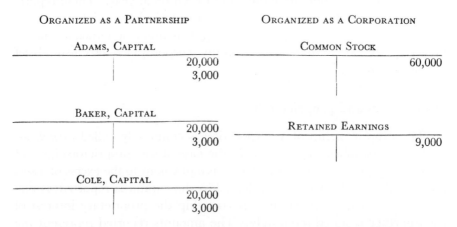

In the partnership form of organization, the net income in Expense and Revenue Summary is transferred to the respective capital accounts of the partners. In the corporate form the net income is transferred to *Retained Earnings*, thus segregating the income from paid-in capital. Net losses from operations and distributions of income are debited to the retained earnings account.

Until relatively recent years the term customarily applied to retained earnings was *earned surplus*. The meaning of the older term was often misunderstood by readers of financial statements and has to a great extent been supplanted.[1]   Other terminology frequently employed includes *accumulated earnings, earnings retained for use in the business*, and *income reinvested in the business*.

If the retained earnings account has a debit balance, this balance is termed a *deficit*. If in the foregoing illustration the new firm had incurred a net loss of $7,000 in its first year, the retained earnings account would have appeared as shown at the right, and the total capital of the corporation would have been $53,000 ($60,000 − $7,000).

RETAINED EARNINGS

7,000	

Classes of stock

The ownership of a corporation is divided into shares which may be referred to generally as the corporation's *capital stock*. The basic rights that ordinarily accompany ownership of a share of stock include (1) the right to vote, (2) the right to share in earnings, (3) the right to maintain the same fractional interest in the corporation by purchasing a proportionate number of shares of any additional issuances of stock (*pre-emptive right*), and (4) the right to share in assets upon liquidation.

If a corporation has only one class of stock, it is called *common stock* and each share has equal rights. In order to appeal to a broader investment market, a corporation may provide for one or more classes of stock with preferential rights over another class. The preference usually relates to the right to share in earnings. Such stock is called *preferred stock*. The classes of stock that a corporation may issue, together with the contractual preferences and limitations of each class, are set forth in the corporate charter or by-laws.

The authority to distribute earnings to the shareholders resides in the board of directors. Distributions of earnings are called *dividends*, and the directors are said to *declare a dividend*. A corporation can make no guarantee that its operations will be profitable, and hence it cannot

---

[1]On the financial statements of a selected group of 600 corporations, only 99 had replaced "earned surplus" with a more descriptive term by 1948; by 1959 the number replacing the older term had increased to 410. *Accounting Trends and Techniques, Fourteenth Edition*, 1960 (New York: American Institute of Certified Public Accountants), p. 13.

guarantee dividends to its shareholders. Furthermore, the directors have wide discretionary powers in determining the extent to which earnings should be retained by the corporation to provide for expansion, to offset possible future losses, or to provide for other contingencies.

A corporation with both preferred and common stock may declare dividends on the common only if it meets the requirements of the stipulated dividend on the preferred. For example, assume that the Apex Corporation has 1,000 shares of stock with a preference to a $6 dividend, and 4,000 shares of common stock outstanding. In its first three years of operation it earned $12,000, $25,000 and $60,000, respectively, and distributed 60% of the earnings each year. The distribution of the dividends among the two classes of stock is tabulated as follows:

	FIRST YEAR	SECOND YEAR	THIRD YEAR
Net income.........................	$12,000	$25,000	$60,000
Per cent to be distributed.............	60%	60%	60%
Amount of dividend distribution........	$ 7,200	$15,000	$36,000
Dividends on preferred ($6 per share)...	6,000	6,000	6,000
Balance to common (4,000 shares)......	$ 1,200	$ 9,000	$30,000
Dividends per share on common........	$ .30	$ 2.25	$ 7.50

Participating and nonparticipating preferred stock. In the foregoing illustration the holders of preferred stock received an annual dividend of $6 per share in each of the three years, in contrast to the common stockholders, whose annual per share dividends were $.30, $2.25, and $7.50. It is apparent from the example that holders of preferred stock have relatively greater assurance of receiving dividends but that holders of common stock have the potentiality of receiving larger dividends. The participation of holders of preferred stock in the earnings of a corporation is ordinarily limited to a stipulated amount. This was assumed to be the case in the example. Stock that is so limited is said to be *nonparticipating*.

If the contract provides that dividends on preferred stock may exceed the stipulated amount, such stock is known as *participating*. For example, the contract may provide that if the earnings to be distributed exceed the regular preferred dividend and a comparable dividend on common, the preferred shall share with the common in the excess earnings. To illustrate, assume that the preferred stock of the Apex Corporation, in the preceding illustration, participates equally with the common in dividends in excess of $6 per share on each class. The $36,000 dividend distribution in the third year would be allocated as follows:

	To PREFERRED	To COMMON	TOTAL
Regular dividend to preferred (1,000 × $6)...	$ 6,000		$ 6,000
Regular dividend to common (4,000 × $6)...		$24,000	24,000
Remaining $6,000 to all shares ratably.......	1,200	4,800	6,000
Total dividends......................	$ 7,200	$28,800	$36,000
Dividends per share....................	$ 7.20	$ 7.20	

Cumulative and noncumulative preferred stock. As was indicated above, most preferred stock is nonparticipating. Provision is usually made, however, to assure the accumulation of the right to the stipulated dividend if part or all of it is not paid in any particular year. This is accomplished by providing that dividends may not be paid on the common stock if any preferred dividends are in arrears. Such preferred stock is known as *cumulative.* To illustrate, assume that a corporation has outstanding 5,000 shares of cumulative preferred stock with a stipulated dividend of $5 and that dividends have been *passed* (not paid) for the preceding two years. In the current year it will be necessary to declare preferred dividends of $50,000 for the past two years and $25,000 for the current year before any dividends can be declared on the common stock. Preferred stock that does not have this cumulative right is called *noncumulative.*

Other preferential rights. Thus far the discussion of preferential rights of preferred stock has related to dividend distributions. Preferred stock may also be given a preference over common stock in its claim to assets upon liquidation of the corporation. If the assets remaining after payment of creditors are not sufficient to return the capital contributions of both classes of stock, payment would first be made to the preferred stockholders and any balance remaining would go to the common stockholders. The right may also extend to payment of arrearages in dividends on cumulative preferred stock, even though the amount of retained earnings is less than the amount required for the dividends.

Another usual difference between preferred stock and common stock is that the former may have no voting rights. Some corporations may have more than one class of preferred stock, with differences as to the amount of dividends and priority of claims. In any particular case the rights of a class of stock may be determined by reference to the articles of incorporation, the stock certificate, or some other abstract of the agreement.

Values of stock

In earlier chapters various value terms, such as cost, book value, and replacement value, were used in referring to business properties. Similarly, various value terms may be applied to a share of stock. The terms most commonly used are discussed in the remainder of this section.

Par value. As has been indicated, the ownership interest in a corporation is divided into shares of stock. A common practice is to assign an arbitrary value, known as *par value*, to shares of stock. Preferred stock is frequently, though not always, assigned a par value of $100 or $50. The par values assigned to common stock vary widely and may be even less than $1 per share. An application for a corporate charter indicating authorized common stock of $100,000 might specify 100,000 shares of $1 par value, 20,000 shares of $5 par value, 10,000 shares of $10 par value, 1,000 shares of $100 par value, or any other combination of shares and par value that would yield a total of $100,000.

Stated value. Stock may be without par value, in which case it is known as *no-par* stock. Many states provide that no-par stock must be assigned a *stated value*, which in essence is similar to a par value. The stated value assigned by the directors may be the minimum fixed by law or some higher arbitrary amount.

Book value. The total par or stated value of the outstanding stock of a corporation does not necessarily represent the total equity of the stockholders. Some of the stock may have been issued at a price different from par or stated value, and accumulations of earnings or losses are a part of capital. The stockholder equity per share of stock is termed *book value.* It is the amount that would be paid on each share of stock if the corporation were to liquidate without incurring any losses or gains on the sale of its assets. Where there is only one class of stock, the book value is determined by dividing total capital by the number of shares outstanding.

To illustrate the computation of book value when there is only one class of stock, assume that as of June 30 of the current year the Monarch Corporation has 2,000 shares of $50 par value stock outstanding. The balances in the capital accounts at the same date, and the computation of the book value are shown below:

Common Stock	$100,000
Retained Earnings (credit balance)	50,000
Total Capital	$150,000

$150,000 ÷ 2,000 shares = $75 book value.

For a corporation with both preferred and common stock, it is necessary first to allocate the total capital between the two classes. The book value of each class may then be determined by dividing the allocated capital by the number of shares outstanding. To illustrate, assume that as of December 31 of the current year the Stuart Corporation has 1,000 shares of $100 par, 6% cumulative, nonparticipating, preferred and 50,000 shares of $10 par common outstanding. Assume further that there are no preferred dividends in arrears. The balances in the capital accounts at the same date and the computation of book value are as follows:

CAPITAL

Preferred 6% stock, cumulative, $100 par (1,000 shares outstanding)	$100,000
Common stock, $10 par (50,000 shares outstanding).............	500,000
Retained earnings..	300,000
Total capital	$900,000

ALLOCATION OF TOTAL CAPITAL TO PREFERRED AND COMMON STOCK

Total capital	$900,000
Allocated to preferred stock:	
Par value...	100,000
Allocated to common stock................................	$800,000

BOOK VALUE

Preferred stock: $100,000 ÷ 1,000 shares = $100.00
Common stock: $800,000 ÷ 50,000 shares = $16.00

Assuming in the foregoing example that preferred dividends were in arrears for two years ($12 per share), retained earnings of $12,000 (1,000 × $12) would be allocated to the preferred and the computations would be as follows:

ALLOCATION OF TOTAL CAPITAL TO PREFERRED AND COMMON STOCK

Total capital...................................		$900,000
Allocated to preferred stock:		
Par value.......................................	$100,000	
Dividends in arrears...........................	12,000	112,000
Allocated to common stock................................		$788,000

BOOK VALUE

Preferred stock: $112,000 ÷ 1,000 shares = $112.00
Common stock: $788,000 ÷ 50,000 shares = $15.76

In determining book value it is evident that the various preferential rights of the particular preferred stock must be known. In addition to considering dividends in arrears, it is necessary to give effect to dividend participation rights and to preference as to assets on dissolution.

Market value. The *market value* or *market price* is the price at which a share is bought and sold at a particular moment. A stock may be "listed" on a national exchange, such as the New York Stock Exchange, a local exchange, or it may be available only in the "over-the-counter" market. Prices of stocks may fluctuate from day to day or hour to hour. Earning capacity, dividend rates, and prospects for the future affect the market price of stocks to a much greater extent than book value. For example, the common stock with a book value of $15.76 in the preceding illustration may have a market value of $7 if earnings and dividends are relatively low, or $40 if earnings and dividends are relatively high.

Redemption value. It is not uncommon for a corporation issuing pre-ferred stock to reserve the right to redeem it later under specified condi-tions. The *redemption value* is the amount per share that the corporation agrees to pay if it elects to redeem the stock; it is ordinarily somewhat in excess of par value.

Authorized, issued, and outstanding stock

The number of shares of each class of stock that a corporation is *authorized* to issue to stockholders is set forth in the charter. The exact capital needs of a corporation in its first years of operation may be difficult to determine. It is usually desirable, therefore, to provide for an authorization in excess of the number of shares expected to be issued initially. If a corporation reaches the limit of its authorization and wishes to issue additional shares, it is necessary to apply for an amendment to the charter and pay the requisite state fees.

The term *issued* needs little explanation. It is applied to the shares issued to the stockholders. A corporation may, under various circum-stances which will be discussed in a later chapter, reacquire some of the stock that it has issued. The stock remaining in the hands of the stock-holders is then referred to as the stock *outstanding*.

Presentation of capital on the balance sheet

The assets and the liabilities of a corporation are reported on the balance sheet in the same manner as the assets and the liabilities of a sole proprietorship or a partnership. The capital section is different, however. Two principal subdivisions are paid-in capital and retained or accumulated earnings. The par value of the various classes of stock issued, together with the details of dividend preferences and number of shares authorized, appears as illustrated below.

<u>Capital</u>

Paid-in capital:

Preferred 6% stock, cumulative, $50 par (5,000 shares authorized, 3,000 shares issued)...............	$150,000	
Common, $10 par (50,000 shares authorized and issued)	500,000	
Total paid-in capital...........................	$650,000	
Retained earnings..............................	200,000	
Total capital......................................		$850,000

The capital section appearing below illustrates the reporting of a deficit and some variations in terminology from the example above:

<u>Stockholders' equity</u>

Paid-in capital:

Preferred 5% stock, $25 par (5,000 shares authorized and issued)................................	$125,000	
Common, $5 par (100,000 shares authorized, 80,000 shares issued)...............................	400,000	
Total paid-in capital...........................	$525,000	
Less deficit......................................	50,000	
Total stockholders' equity.........................		$475,000

Issuing stock at par for cash or other assets

The incorporators of a corporation perform some transactions and incur obligations during the process of applying for the charter and perfecting the organization. After the charter has been granted, the corporation may begin operations. One of the early transactions may be the approval of the organization costs incurred by the incorporators and assumption of the liabilities incurred therefor.

The entries to record the investment of capital in the corporation are similar to those of other types of business organizations in that the cash and other assets received are debited and any liabilities assumed are credited. The credit to capital differs, however, in that there is only one account for each class of stock.[2] To illustrate, assume that the Peerless Corporation, organized on February 15 with an authorization of 10,000 shares of preferred stock of $50 par and 100,000 shares of common stock of $25 par, issues one half of each authorization at par for cash on

---

[2]The maintenance of records for each stockholder is discussed in Chapter 21

March 1. The entry to record the stockholders' investment and the receipt of the cash, in general journal form, is as follows:

Mar. 1	Cash......................................	1,500,000	
	Preferred Stock.........................		250,000
	Common Stock..........................		1,250,000

In the foregoing example, the capital contributions to the corporation were in the form of cash, or to state it in another manner, the corporation issued the stock for cash. Stock may be exchanged for assets other than cash, such as land, buildings, or equipment. In such cases the assets should be valued at their fair market value. The determination of the valuations is the responsibility of the board of directors. Assuming that on March 10 the Peerless Corporation acquires buildings valued at $260,000 and land valued at $40,000, giving in exchange 1,000 shares of preferred stock and 10,000 shares of common stock, the transaction would be recorded as follows:

Mar. 10	Buildings...............................	260,000	
	Land.....................................	40,000	
	Preferred Stock.........................		50,000
	Common Stock..........................		250,000

Incorporating a proprietorship or a partnership

A business enterprise operated as a sole proprietorship or as a partnership may incorporate in order more readily to acquire additional capital or to secure other advantages of the corporate form. In effecting the changes in organization it is necessary, of course, to obtain a corporate charter and to conform with the other statutory requirements of the state. The transfer of the assets and liabilities to the corporation is comparable to a sale by the proprietor or partners to the corporation.

The basic accounting procedures involved in incorporating a business are as follows:

On the books of the sole proprietorship or partnership:
   (1) Adjust and close the revenue and expense accounts of the proprietorship or the partnership.
   (2) Adjust the various asset accounts to the current fair values.
   (3) Record the transfer of the assets and the liabilities to the corporation.
   (4) Record the receipt of the stock from the corporation.
   (5) Distribute the stock (also cash or other assets not transferred) to the proprietor or the partners.

On the books of the corporation:
   (1) Record the assets and the liabilities acquired from the proprietorship or the partnership.
   (2) Record the issuance of capital stock in payment for the net assets.

To illustrate the procedures outlined above, assume that Alden and Barker, sharing equally in income and losses, dissolve their partnership and incorporate their business. The post-closing trial balance of the partnership as of May 31, the effective date of the transfer to the corporation, is as follows:

Alden and Barker
Post-Closing Trial Balance
May 31, 19–

Cash..	20,000	
Accounts Receivable...............................	60,000	
Allowance for Uncollectible Accounts		6,000
Merchandise Inventory............................	150,000	
Store Equipment..................................	12,000	
Accumulated Depreciation — Store Equipment...		4,000
Office Equipment.................................	4,000	
Accumulated Depreciation — Office Equipment..		2,000
Accounts Payable.................................		14,000
G. M. Alden, Capital.............................		120,000
J. D. Barker, Capital.............................		100,000
	246,000	246,000

All assets and liabilities are to be transferred to Alden & Barker, Inc., at their book values, except that accounts receivable are to be valued at $58,000 and merchandise inventory at $140,000. In exchange the partnership is to accept, at par, common stock with a par value of $50 per share.

The partnership books having already been adjusted and closed for the period ending May 31, the remaining entries are as follows:

Revaluation of assets

Allowance for Uncollectible Accounts.....................	4,000	
Asset Revaluations......................................	6,000	
Merchandise Inventory...............................		10,000
G. M. Alden, Capital...................................	3,000	
J. D. Barker, Capital...................................	3,000	
Asset Revaluations...................................		6,000

Transfer of assets and liabilities to the corporation

Receivable from Alden & Barker, Inc.....................	214,000	
Allowance for Uncollectible Accounts.....................	2,000	
Accumulated Depreciation — Store Equipment..............	4,000	
Accumulated Depreciation — Office Equipment.............	2,000	
Accounts Payable..	14,000	
Cash...		20,000
Accounts Receivable.................................		60,000
Merchandise Inventory...............................		140,000
Store Equipment....................................		12,000
Office Equipment...................................		4,000

Receipt of stock from the corporation

Common Stock — Alden & Barker, Inc.	214,000	
Receivable from Alden & Barker, Inc.		214,000

Distribution of stock to the partners

G. M. Alden, Capital	117,000	
J. D. Barker, Capital	97,000	
Common Stock — Alden & Barker, Inc.		214,000

The final entry recording the distribution of the stock to the partners signifies the winding up of the partnership affairs. After the foregoing entries have been posted, all accounts in the ledger will be in balance.

The entries on the books of the corporation are as follows:

Acquisition of assets and liabilities

Cash	20,000	
Accounts Receivable	60,000	
Merchandise Inventory	140,000	
Store Equipment	8,000	
Office Equipment	2,000	
Allowance for Uncollectible Accounts		2,000
Accounts Payable		14,000
Payable to Alden and Barker		214,000

Issuance of stock to the partnership

Payable to Alden and Barker	214,000	
Common Stock		214,000

It should be noted that the fixed assets are entered at their net cost to the corporation; the original cost to the partnership and the accumulated depreciation are not recorded. For accounts receivable, however, both the gross amount and the allowance for uncollectible accounts are recorded, as it is not possible to allocate the estimated loss to the accounts of specific debtors.

Organization costs

Expenditures incurred in organizing a corporation, such as legal fees, taxes and fees paid to the state, and promotional expenses, are charged to an asset account entitled *Organization Costs*. Although such costs have no realizable value upon liquidation, they are as essential as plant and equipment and have value as long as the corporation continues its operations. If the life of a corporation is limited to a definite period of time, the organization costs may well be amortized over the period by annual charges to an expense account. The length of life of most corporations is not determinable in advance, however.

The conservative practice is to write off the costs during the early years of the corporation's existence, the debit being reported as an extraordinary charge in the income statement or as a direct reduction of retained earnings. Until relatively recently, deductions for organization costs were not permitted in determining net income subject to the federal income tax, except in the year of dissolution. The Internal Revenue Code of 1954 provides that certain specified organization costs incurred after August 16, 1954 may be deducted from income ratably over a period of five years or longer.

The unamortized balance of the account is listed on the balance sheet as an intangible asset.

Questions

1. Give two possible meanings of each of the terms, "public corporation" and "private corporation."

2. What is meant by the term "close corporation"?

3. What are the basic rights of stockholders?

4. Is the relationship of stockholders to the corporation much the same as the relationship of partners to the partnership? Discuss.

5. Discuss the advantages and the disadvantages of the corporate form of organization as compared with the partnership form.

6. Might a corporation issue all preferred stock and no common stock?

7. Jones is a partner in Butler & Jones, in which his capital interest is $20,000. He also owns some stock in the Top Company acquired at a cost of $10,000. He has other assets worth $90,000. (a) If the Top Company fails, what is the maximum loss Jones might have to absorb? (b) If Butler & Jones fails, what is the maximum loss Jones might have to absorb? (c) If Jones dies, what effect would his death have on the Top Company? On the Butler & Jones partnership?

8. The par value of the common stock of the Mountain Mining Corporation is $10. The current book value and market value per share are $29.82 and $42.50, respectively. Suggest reasons for the comparatively high market value in relation to par value and to book value.

9. Harry Larkin owns 4,000 of the 10,000 shares of the Manhattan Corporation, which earned $150,000 and paid a $10 per share dividend during the current year. (a) What was Larkin's income from the company for the year? (b) Assuming that the company was organized as a partnership instead of a corporation and that Larkin is entitled to 40% of the net income, what was the amount of his income from the company for the year?

10. The Sacramento Corporation has a balance of $200,000 in Preferred Stock, representing 4,000 noncumulative, nonparticipating shares. It declares regular quarterly dividends of $2,750 on the preferred stock. (a) What is the par value of the stock? (b) What is the annual dividend rate per share: in terms of dollars; in terms of per cent of par?

11. The common stock of a particular chemical corporation has a par value of $100; that of a competitor has a par of $20. Do the par values give any indication as to which is preferable as an investment?

Exercises

1. Thomas Winters is considering purchasing some stock in Amalgamated Metals, Inc. He obtains the following information from the latest published balance sheet: current assets, $200,000; plant assets, $350,000; current liabilities, $100,000; par value common stock, $300,000; retained earnings, $150,000. There are 30,000 shares outstanding and the latest quotation on the stock exchange in $52.50. Determine the following: (a) Par value per share. (b) Total paid-in capital. (c) Total capital. (d) Book value per share. (e) Latest market value per share.

2. The capital accounts of the Roy-Ton Corporation are as follows: Preferred Stock (6%, $100 par), $500,000; Common Stock ($5 par), $10,000,000; Retained Earnings, $2,000,000. (a) What is the book value per share of each class of stock, assuming that the preferred stock is cumulative and nonparticipating, and that no dividends are in arrears? (b) Prepare the capital section of the balance sheet for the Roy-Ton Corporation.

3. The Erie Shoe Co. has stock outstanding as follows: 1,000 shares of 5%, $100 par, cumulative, nonparticipating preferred and 8,000 shares of $25 par common. During its first five years of operation the following amounts were distributed as dividends: first, None; second, $4,000; third, $15,000; fourth, $25,000; fifth, $45,000. Determine the dividends per share on each class of stock for each of the five years.

4. Pendleton, Inc. has stock outstanding as follows: 10,000 shares of 6%, $50 par, noncumulative, nonparticipating preferred and 20,000 shares of no-par common. The directors' policy is to declare a full or partial dividend on the preferred stock to the extent of current earnings, and to distribute 60% of the remainder to common stockholders. Earnings for 1958, 1959, 1960, 1961, and 1962 were $100,000, $20,000 loss, $50,000, $20,000, and $90,000, respectively. Determine the dividends per share for each year on each class of stock.

5. The outstanding stock of the Electronics Company is composed of 1,000 shares of participating preferred 5% stock with a par value of $100 and 10,000 shares of common stock with a par value of $25. The preferred stock is entitled to participate equally with the common, on a percentage basis, in dividend distributions after allowing a dividend of $1.50 per share on the common. The directors declare dividends of $30,500 for the current year. What is the dividend per share on the preferred? on the common?

Problems

20-1. The net income or loss, after income taxes, of the Raintree Corporation for a period of eight years is shown in the table below. During the entire period the corporation had outstanding 1,500 shares of cumulative 6% preferred stock, par $100, and 30,000 shares of common stock, par $10. Each year the board of directors (1) applied earnings to offset any accumulated deficit, (2) declared a partial or full dividend on the preferred stock to the extent of the available current or accumulated earnings, and (3) distributed one half of any remaining balance of current earnings as a dividend on the common stock.

| | | PREFERRED DIVIDEND | | COMMON | INCREASE OR | RETAINED |
| | NET INCOME | | TOTAL | DIVIDEND | DECREASE* IN RETAINED | EARNINGS |
YEAR	OR LOSS*	DECLARED	ARREARS	DECLARED	EARNINGS	BALANCE
1955	$ 7,000					
1956	2,000*					
1957	26,000					
1958	30,000					
1959	7,000					
1960	1,000*					
1961	19,000					
1962	32,000					

Instructions: (1) Indicate the disposition of the net income or loss for each year, using the headings shown above. Use an asterisk to denote deductions and negative items.

(2) Determine the total dividends per share declared on each class of stock.

20-2. The annual dividends declared by the Sullivan Company during a six-year period are shown in the table below. During the entire period the outstanding stock of the corporation was composed of 2,000 shares of cumulative, participating, 5% preferred stock, $50 par, and 5,000 shares of common stock, $25 par. The charter provides that the preferred participates in distributions of additional earnings after allowing a $2 dividend per share on the common stock, the additional earnings to be divided equally among all shares, common and preferred.

| | TOTAL | PREFERRED DIVIDENDS | | COMMON DIVIDENDS | |
YEAR	DIVIDENDS	TOTAL	PER SHARE	TOTAL	PER SHARE
1957	$ 2,500				
1958	10,000				
1959	22,000				
1960	4,000				
1961	19,500				
1962	24,800				

Instructions: (1) Determine the total and per share dividends declared on each class of stock for each of the six years, using the headings shown above.

(2) Determine the average annual dividend per share for each class of stock for the six-year period.

(3) Assuming that both classes of stock were sold at par at the beginning of the six-year period determine the total income earned on an investment of $1,000 (a) in preferred stock, (b) in common stock.

20-3. Selected data from the balance sheets of six corporations, identified by letter, are presented below:

A. Common stock, $100 par.............................. $1,500,000
   Retained earnings......................................   790,000
B. Total assets $1,027,300; total liabilities $353,800; common stock outstanding, 30,000 shares, $25 par.
C. Preferred 4% stock, noncumulative, nonparticipating, $50 par $ 200,000
   Common stock, $10 par................................   860,000
   Retained earnings.....................................   233,920
D. Preferred 5% stock, noncumulative, nonparticipating, $100 par $ 300,000
   Common stock, $50 par................................   1,100,000
   Deficit...   195,800
       Preferred stock has prior claim to assets upon dissolution.
E. Preferred 6% stock, cumulative, nonparticipating, $100 par.. $ 100,000
   Common stock, $50 par................................   900,000
   Retained earnings.....................................   46,980
       Dividends on preferred stock are in arrears for 4½ years.
F. Preferred 4% stock, cumulative, nonparticipating, $25 par... $ 300,000
   Common stock, $5 par.................................   1,250,000
   Retained earnings.....................................   32,500
       Dividends on preferred stock are in arrears for 5 years. Preferred stock is entitled to unpaid cumulative dividends upon dissolution, regardless of the availability of earnings.

Instructions: Determine the book value per share of each class of stock for each corporation, presenting the total capital allocated to the class and the number of shares outstanding.

20-4. The Martinville Plumbing and Heating Corporation is organized by Gates, Youngman, and Mulvany. The corporation expects to install plumbing, heating, and air conditioning systems in newly constructed buildings. The charter authorizes 50,000 shares of common stock with a par value of $5. The following transactions are completed during February of the current year, the first month of operations:

(a) Received $1,500 cash from each of the three incorporators, issuing 30-day, non-interest-bearing notes.
(b) Paid Mulvany $250 cash to reimburse him for the incorporation fees that he had remitted with the charter application.
(c) Purchased land and a building from Gates. The building has a 5%, 12-year mortgage of $20,000, and there is accrued interest of $425 on the mortgage at the time of the purchase. Delinquent property taxes of $500 are also owed at the time of the purchase. It is agreed that the land is to be valued at $8,000 and the building at $45,000, and that Gates is to accept stock at par for his equity. The corporation agrees to assume the mortgage, accrued interest, and delinquent property taxes.
(d) Purchased plumbing supplies, $18,750, from Youngman for stock at par.
(e) Paid delinquent property taxes on the land and building.
(f) Sold 5,000 shares of stock at par to Youngman for cash.
(g) Sold 1,000 shares of stock at par to Gates for cash.
(h) Paid Mulvany, who is an attorney, $250 cash and 300 shares of stock for legal fees and promotional services connected with organizing the corporation.
(i) Purchased plumbing supplies for $7,500 cash.

(j) Paid contractor $5,000 cash for an addition to the building to be used as a storage room.

(k) Purchased plumbing supplies for $2,600 on account.

(l) Sold 2,000 shares of stock at par to Mulvany for cash.

(m) Paid advertising expenses of $700.

(n) Paid the semiannual interest on the mortgage.

(o) Issued stock at par to the three incorporators to redeem the 30-day notes.

Instructions: (1) Record the corporation's transactions in general journal form.

(2) Assuming that there were no additional transactions and no accruals, prepare a balance sheet for the corporation as of February 28. Omit subcaptions for current assets, current liabilities, etc.

20-5. Benton and Ames, partners, and Marston, a sole proprietor, decide to combine their businesses as a corporation under the name of the Leader Merchandising Co. They submit their application and receive a charter with an authorization of 1,000 shares of cumulative 6% preferred stock with a par value of $100 and 15,000 shares of common stock with a par value of $50.

The post-closing trial balances of the two enterprises as of July 31, the effective date of the transfer to the corporation, are as follows:

	BENTON & AMES		MARSTON	
Cash..........................	31,000		11,200	
Notes Receivable...............	——		6,000	
Accounts Receivable.............	52,700		18,400	
Allowance for Uncollectible Accounts		2,000		800
Merchandise Inventory...........	148,000		65,000	
Prepaid Insurance...............	700		600	
Equipment.....................	17,000		8,000	
Accumulated Depreciation —				
Equipment...................		6,000		2,000
Building.......................	58,000		——	
Accumulated Depreciation —				
Building.....................		38,000		——
Land.........................	7,000		——	
Notes Payable..................		5,000		——
Accounts Payable...............		25,400		9,400
Mortgage Payable...............		5,000		——
James Benton, Capital...........		128,000		——
Martin Ames, Capital...........		105,000		——
Will Marston, Capital...........		——		97,000
	314,400	314,400	109,200	109,200

The terms as to revaluation, assets and liabilities to be transferred to the corporation, etc. are as follows:

Benton and Ames: (a) Mortgage to be paid with partnership funds; (b) accounts receivable in the amount of $5,000 to be written off as uncollectible, remainder to be valued at $44,700; (c) inventory to be valued at $130,000;

(d) building to be valued on basis of $100,000 replacement cost new, one-half depreciated; (e) all other assets and liabilities to be transferred at book value as of July 31; (f) preferred stock to be issued for the land and building, common stock for the remaining net assets.

Marston: (a) Cash in the amount of $1,200 and all notes receivable to be retained by Marston; (b) accounts receivable to be valued at $16,800; (c) merchandise inventory to be valued at $60,000; (d) equipment to be valued at $7,000; (e) all other assets and liabilities to be transferred at book value as of July 31; (f) goodwill of $20,000 to be recognized; (g) common stock to be issued for net assets.

Instructions: (1) Prepare general journal entries on the partnership books to:
- (a) Record the revaluation of the assets (income and losses are shared equally).
- (b) Record the payment of the mortgage.
- (c) Record the transfer of the assets and liabilities to the corporation.
- (d) Record receipt of the stock.
- (e) Record distribution of the stock (preferred stock is divided equally).

(2) Prepare general journal entries on Marston's books to:
- (a) Record the revaluation of the assets, including recognition of the goodwill.
- (b) Record the withdrawal of the cash and notes.
- (c) Record the transfer of the assets and liabilities to the corporation.
- (d) Record receipt of the stock.
- (e) Record transfer of stock to Marston.

(3) Prepare general journal entries on the books of Leader Merchandising Co. to:
- (a) Record the assets and liabilities acquired from Benton & Ames.
- (b) Record the assets and liabilities acquired from Marston.
- (c) Record the issuance of the stock to Benton & Ames.
- (d) Record the issuance of the stock to Marston.

(4) Prepare a balance sheet in report form for the corporation as of July 31.

Corporations—
capital stock

Premium and discount on capital stock

In the preceding chapter all issuances of capital stock were assumed to be at par value. In practice, however, stock may be issued by a corporation at a price above or below par. When it is issued above par, the excess of the contract price over par is termed a *premium*. When it is issued at a price that is less than par, the excess of par over the contract price is called a *discount*. Thus, if stock with a par value of $50 is issued at $60, the amount of the premium is $10; if the same stock is issued at $45, the amount of the discount is $5.

Theoretically, there is no reason for a newly organized corporation to issue stock at a price other than par. As has been demonstrated, the particular par value assigned to the stock is arbitrary; it is merely a part of the plan of dividing capital into a number of units of ownership. Hence, a group of persons investing their funds in a new corporation might all be expected to pay par value for the shares. The fortunes of an enterprise do not remain static, however, even when it is still in the process of organizing. The changing prospects for its future success may affect the price per share at which the incorporators can secure additional investors.

After a corporation has become established, a need for additional capital may arise. For example, losses during the early period may have depleted working capital, or the operations may have been so successful as to warrant a substantial expansion of plant and equipment. If the funds are to be obtained by the issuance of additional stock, it is apparent that the current price at which the original stock is selling in the market will affect the price that can be obtained for the new shares.

Generally speaking, the price at which stock can be sold by a corporation is influenced by (1) the financial condition of the corporation, (2) its potential earning power, (3) the availability of money for investment purposes, and (4) general business and economic conditions and prospects.

Some states do not permit the issuance of stock at a discount; in others, it may be done under specified conditions. When stock is issued at less than its par value, it is considered to be fully paid as between the corporation and the stockholder. In some states, however, the stockholders are contingently liable to creditors for the amount of the discount. That is, if the corporation is liquidated and the assets are insufficient to pay creditors in full, the stockholders may be assessed for an additional contribution up to the amount of the discount on their stock.

When capital stock is issued at a premium, the cash or other assets received are debited for the full amount, the stock account is credited for par, and the premium is credited to a premium account. For example, if the Monroe Corporation issues 1,000 shares of $100 par preferred stock at $104, the entry to record the transaction would be as follows, in general journal form:

```
Cash............................................... 104,000
    Preferred Stock...................................         100,000
    Premium on Preferred Stock........................           4,000
```

The premium of $4,000 is a part of the investment of the stockholders and is therefore a part of paid-in capital. It is distinguished from the capital stock account because it is not a part of legal capital. In many states the premium may be used as a basis for dividends to stockholders. If the premium is returned to stockholders later as a dividend, it should be made quite clear that it is not a distribution of earnings but a return of paid-in capital.

When capital stock is issued at a discount, cash or other assets are debited for the amount received, the discount account is debited for the amount of the discount, and the capital stock account is credited for par. For example, if the Monroe Corporation issues 30,000 shares of $20 par common stock at $19, the entry to record the transaction would be as follows, in general journal form:

```
Cash............................................... 570,000
Discount on Common Stock...........................  30,000
    Common Stock......................................         600,000
```

The discount of $30,000 is a negative paid-in capital account and must be offset against Common Stock to arrive at the amount actually invested by the holders of common stock.

The corporation may at some future date close out the discount account by a transfer from Retained Earnings. This is unnecessary and has the objection of obscuring the facts concerning the amount originally invested. In no case would it be proper to list the discount on the balance sheet as an asset or to amortize it against revenue as though it were an expense.

The capital section of the balance sheet of the Monroe Corporation, which appears below, is illustrative of the manner in which discount and premium may be presented on the balance sheet.

Capital

Paid-in capital:		
Preferred 5% stock, cumulative, $100 par (1,000 shares authorized and issued)................	$100,000	
Premium on preferred stock....................	4,000	$104,000
Common stock, $20 par (50,000 shares authorized, 30,000 shares issued)........................	$600,000	
Deduct discount on common stock..............	30,000	570,000
Total capital.....................................		$674,000

When assets other than cash are accepted as payment for capital stock, the assets should be recorded at their fair market value rather than at the total par value of the stock issued. For example, assume that 10,000 shares of common stock with a par value of $10 are issued in exchange for a building and land. It does not necessarily follow that the property has a value of $100,000 (10,000 × $10 par). If the fair market value of the property is actually $90,000, the stock is being issued at a discount of $10,000 and the transaction should be so recorded. The responsibility for valuation of the assets in such cases rests with the board of directors, and it is not always possible to make an objective determination of value. If shares of stock are also being issued for cash at about the same time, the price of the stock may provide a good basis for valuation of the property. Assuming in the example above that the stock is currently being issued for cash at $9 a share, a valuation of $90,000 for the property (10,000 × $9 per share) would be indicated.

No-par stock

The issuance of stock without par value was first permitted by New York in 1912. At the present time the statutes of all states authorize the issuance of such stock. The proponents of the idea of no-par stock expected its use to be beneficial in three major respects: (1) that the "bargain sale" technique of selling stock below par value would not be available and investors would make a more careful investigation before buying; (2) that stock could be issued at various prices without the difficulty of incurring a contingent liability for discounts; and (3) that the use of fair valuations on assets accepted in payment for stock would be encouraged.

The extent to which the expected benefits have materialized is difficult to determine. Over the years questionable practices sometimes followed in the issuance of securities have been eliminated to a considerable degree. Today the rules imposed by organized stock exchanges, federal and state laws, and regulation by governmental agencies combine to protect the investor from misrepresentations that in earlier days were not uncommon.

Corporations may issue both preferred and common stock without par value. Preferred stock is ordinarily assigned a par value, however. When no-par stock is issued, the entire proceeds may be credited to the capital stock account. For example, if the Wheeler Corporation issues 1,000 shares of no-par common stock on February 1 at $19 per share and an additional 1,000 shares on February 20 at $18 per share, the entries would be as follows:

Feb. 1 Cash...	19,000	
Common Stock...............................		19,000
20 Cash...	18,000	
Common Stock...............................		18,000

The laws of some states require that the entire proceeds from the issuance of no-par stock be regarded as legal capital. The entries above are in conformity with this principle, which also conforms to the original concept of no-par stock. In other states no-par stock may be assigned a *stated value* per share and the excess of the proceeds over the stated value may be credited to Paid-in Capital in Excess of Stated Value. Assuming that in the example above the stated value is $5 and the board of directors wishes to credit the common stock for stated value, the transaction would be recorded as follows:

Feb. 1 Cash...	19,000	
Common Stock...............................		5,000
Paid-in Capital in Excess of Stated Value.........		14,000
20 Cash...	18,000	
Common Stock...............................		5,000
Paid-in Capital in Excess of Stated Value.........		13,000

It is readily apparent that the accounting for no-par stock with a stated value may follow the same pattern as the accounting for stock with par value.

Subscriptions to capital stock

In the examples thus far it has been assumed that the corporation issued stock directly in exchange for cash or other assets. Ordinarily, investors first enter into an agreement to purchase, or *subscribe* to shares at a specified price per share. The terms may provide for payment in full at some future date or for installment payments over a period of time.

The amount of the subscriptions represents an asset to the corporation, and as they are received they are debited to a *stock subscriptions receivable* account. The record of the transaction is completed by a credit to a *stock subscribed* account. Legally, persons subscribing for stock become stockholders at once, but they ordinarily do not acquire all of the rights of stockholders until they have made complete payment. The written evidence of the ownership of shares, known as a *stock certificate*, is usually not issued until the entire amount of the subscription has been collected. Otherwise the corporation would run the risk of subscribers selling the stock to other persons before the subscribers had completed their payments. Withholding the stock certificate thus operates as security for the amount owed by the subscribers.

If there is more than one class of stock, a subscriptions receivable account and a stock subscribed account should be maintained for each class.

When stock is subscribed for at a price above or below par value, the stock subscriptions receivable account is debited for the subscription price rather than par. The stock subscribed account is credited at par and the difference between the subscription price and par is debited to a discount account or credited to a premium account, as the case may be.

The stock subscriptions receivable account is a controlling account. The individual accounts with each subscriber are maintained in a subsidiary ledger known as a *subscribers ledger*, which is described in more detail later in this chapter. It is used in much the same manner as the accounts receivable ledger.

Issuance of stock certificates

After a subscriber completes his agreed payments, his stock subscriptions receivable account will be in balance and it is at this time that the corporation issues the stock certificate. The stock subscribed account is then debited for the total par of the shares issued, and the capital stock account is credited for the same amount.

The capital stock accounts (Preferred Stock, Common Stock) are controlling accounts. It is necessary to maintain records of the name and address of each stockholder and the number of shares held in order to issue dividend checks, proxy forms, and financial reports. The accounts with individual stockholders are kept in a subsidiary ledger known as the *stockholders ledger*. It is described later in this chapter.

Subscriptions and stock issuance illustrated

As the basis for illustrating the entries for transactions discussed in the two preceding sections, it will be assumed that the newly organized

Marathon Corporation receives subscriptions, collects cash, and issues stock certificates in accordance with the transactions described below. The required entries, in general journal form, appear after the statement of the transaction.

(1) Received subscriptions to 5,000 shares of $20 par common stock from various subscribers at $21 per share, with a down payment of 50% of the subscription price.

April 1 Common Stock Subscriptions Receivable	105,000	
Common Stock Subscribed		100,000
Premium on Common Stock		5,000
1 Cash	52,500	
Common Stock Subscriptions Receivable		52,500

(2) Received 25% of subscription price from all subscribers.

May 1 Cash	26,250	
Common Stock Subscriptions Receivable		26,250

(3) Received final 25% of subscription price from all subscribers and issued the stock certificates.

June 1 Cash	26,250	
Common Stock Subscriptions Receivable		26,250
1 Common Stock Subscribed	100,000	
Common Stock		100,000

The effect of the foregoing transactions may also be observed in the following T accounts:

CASH		COMMON STOCK SUBSCRIPTIONS RECEIVABLE		COMMON STOCK
(1) 52,500	Bal. 105,000	(1) 105,000	(1) 52,500	(3) 100,000
(2) 26,250			(2) 26,250	
(3) 26,250			(3) 26,250	
105,000	105,000	105,000	105,000	
Bal. 105,000				

COMMON STOCK SUBSCRIBED		PREMIUM ON COMMON STOCK
(3) 100,000	(1) 100,000	(1) 5,000

After all collections are made, the subscriptions receivable account is in balance; and after the certificates are issued, the stock subscribed account is in balance. Neither account would be used again unless additional subscriptions were received. It should be noted that the ultimate effect of the series of transactions is a debit to Cash of $105,000 and credits to Common Stock of $100,000 and to Premium on Common Stock of $5,000.

If a balance sheet had been prepared after the transactions of April 1, the subscriptions receivable would appear as a current asset and the stock subscribed and premium would appear as paid-in capital. While it is true that the entire amount has not been "paid-in" in cash, the claim against the subscribers is an asset of equivalent value. The presentation of the items is illustrated in the balance sheet of the Marathon Corporation as of April 1, which appears below.

Marathon Corporation
Balance Sheet
April 1, 19--

Assets		Capital	
Current assets:		Paid-in capital:	
Cash....................	$ 52,500	Common stock subscribed..	$100,000
Common stock subscriptions		Premium on common stock.	5,000
receivable..............	52,500		
Total assets................	$105,000	Total capital..............	$105,000

Treasury stock

A corporation may reacquire some of its own outstanding stock by purchase or by donation from its stockholders. It may also accept shares of its own stock in payment of a debt owed by a stockholder, which in essence is much the same as acquisition by purchase. The term *treasury stock* may be applied only to: (1) stock of the issuing corporation, (2) that has been issued as fully paid, (3) that has been subsequently reacquired by the corporation, and (4) that has not been canceled or reissued.

Treasury stock is not an asset. A corporation can not own a part of itself. Treasury stock has no voting rights; it does not have the pre-emptive right to participate in additional issuances of stock; nor is it entitled to dividends. When a corporation purchases its own stock, it is returning capital to the stockholders from whom the purchase was made. If stockholders donate stock to the corporation, the total capital of the corporation is not affected; only the number of shares outstanding is reduced.

Corporations sometimes list treasury stock on the balance sheet as a current asset if they expect to sell it in the near future. The justification advanced for such treatment is that the stock is a readily available source of cash and is no different from a temporary investment in stock of another corporation. The same argument might well be extended to authorized but unissued stock, which is obviously indefensible. It is generally agreed among accountants that treasury stock should not be reported as an asset.

Purchased treasury stock

Although there are some legal restrictions on the practice, corporations may in general purchase shares of their own stock from stockholders. There are various reasons why a corporation may buy its own stock. For example, it may be to provide shares for resale to employees, for reissuance to employees as a bonus, or to support the market price of the stock. There are several methods of accounting for the purchase and resale of treasury stock. A commonly used method, known as the cost basis, is illustrated in the following paragraphs.

When the stock is purchased, the account Treasury Stock is debited for its cost. The par value and the price at which the stock was originally issued are ignored. When the stock is resold, Treasury Stock is credited at the price paid for it and the difference between the price paid and the selling price is debited or credited to an account entitled Paid-in Capital from Sale of Treasury Stock.

As a basis for illustration, assume that the paid-in capital of the Linden Corporation is composed of:

Common Stock, $50 par (10,000 shares authorized and issued)	$500,000
Premium on Common Stock	50,000

The assumed transactions involving treasury stock and the required entries are as follows:

(1) Purchased 800 shares of treasury stock at $65; total $52,000.

Treasury Stock	52,000	
Cash		52,000

(2) Sold 200 shares of treasury stock at $75; total $15,000.

Cash	15,000	
Treasury Stock		13,000
Paid-in Capital from Sale of Treasury Stock		2,000

(3) Sold 200 shares of treasury stock at $63; total $12,600.

Cash	12,600	
Paid-in Capital from Sale of Treasury Stock	400	
Treasury Stock		13,000

The additional capital obtained through the sale of treasury stock is reported in the paid-in capital section of the balance sheet, and the cost of the treasury stock on hand is deducted from the total of the capital accounts. After the three foregoing transactions were completed, the capital section of the balance sheet would appear as shown on the following page.

According to the capital section of the balance sheet, 10,000 shares of stock were issued, of which 400 are held as treasury stock. The number of shares outstanding is therefore 9,600. If dividends were declared at this time, the declaration would apply to 9,600 shares. Simi-

Capital

Paid-in capital:

Common stock, $50 par (10,000 shares authorized and issued).................	$500,000	
Premium on common stock..............	50,000	$550,000
From sale of treasury stock.......................		1,600
Total paid-in capital.........................		$551,600
Retained earnings...............................		100,000
Total..		$651,600
Deduct treasury stock (400 shares at cost)		26,000
Total capital.....................................		$625,600

larly, 9,600 shares could be voted at a stockholders' meeting. The computation of book value per share would also be based on the 9,600 shares outstanding.

If treasury stock transactions result in a shrinkage of capital, the net decrease would be reported as a reduction in paid-in capital, or it could be charged to Retained Earnings.

Donated treasury stock

Corporations that issue large blocks of stock in exchange for plant and equipment, an invention, mineral rights, or other noncash assets may encounter difficulty in finding subscribers willing to invest cash equal to the par value of the stock. This may be because of the highly speculative nature of the enterprise, or because the assets are overvalued, or a combination of both. As a means of avoiding the difficulty of selling new stock at a discount, the original stockholders may donate a portion of their stock to the corporation and the corporation may then resell it at any price without the purchaser incurring a contingent liability to creditors. The donating stockholders may actually incur little financial sacrifice by their action.

One of the acceptable methods of accounting for donated stock requires no entry at the time of the donation, except for a memorandum of the number of shares. As the treasury stock is sold, the proceeds are credited to a paid-in capital account entitled Donated Capital.

As a basis for illustration, assume that the Bronson Corporation originally issued 100,000 shares of $10 par common stock at par for oil properties. The stockholders then donate 20,000 shares to the corporation, which the corporation resells for cash. The entries required, in general journal form, and the capital section of the balance sheet after each entry are as follows:

(1) Issued 100,000 shares of $10 par common stock for oil properties.

Oil Properties...................................	1,000,000	
Common Stock...............................		1,000,000

Paid-in capital:

Common stock, $10 par (200,000 shares authorized, 100,000 shares issued)......................	$1,000,000

(2) Received 20,000 shares of stock from stockholders.

(Memo) Received 20,000 shares of stock as a donation.

Paid-in capital:

Common stock, $10 par (200,000 shares authorized, 100,000 shares issued less 20,000 shares of treasury stock acquired by donation).................	$1,000,000

(3) Sold treasury stock at $6 per share for cash.

Cash...	120,000	
Donated Capital.............................		120,000

Paid-in capital:

Common stock, $10 par (200,000 shares authorized, 100,000 shares issued)......................	$1,000,000	
Donated capital.............................	120,000	
Total paid-in capital.......................		$1,120,000

Redemption of preferred stock

Corporations issuing preferred stock frequently retain the right to redeem the stock. The amount to be paid per share in the event of redemption may be par or a price above par. When stock is redeemed, there is a return of capital to the stockholders, and the accounts related to the stockholders must be eliminated from the ledger. If the amount paid to the stockholders is greater than the amount received when the stock was originally issued, the excess is a distribution of earnings and should be debited to Retained Earnings. On the other hand, if the amount paid is less than the amount originally received, the difference is a retention of capital and should be credited to a paid-in capital account.

To illustrate the entries required upon redemption of stock, assume that the Ferris Corporation issued 1,000 shares of $100 par redeemable preferred stock at $103 per share. The entry to record the sale is:

Cash...	103,000	
Preferred Stock....................................		100,000
Premium on Preferred Stock.......................		3,000

After a number of years of operations, during which the corporation accumulates a substantial amount of income, it is decided to call the stock. Assuming a redemption price of $105 per share, the entry would be:

Preferred Stock......................................	100,000	
Premium on Preferred Stock..........................	3,000	
Retained Earnings...................................	2,000	
Cash...		105,000

The additional $2,000 over the issuance price paid at redemption is not an expense or a loss. Rather, it is a distribution of earnings to the preferred stockholders and is properly chargeable to Retained Earnings.

If a redemption price of $102 per share is assumed, the proper entry would be:

Preferred Stock......................................	100,000	
Premium on Preferred Stock..........................	3,000	
Paid-in Capital from Preferred Stock Redemption......		1,000
Cash...		102,000

The $1,000 of the original issuance price not returned to the stockholders is not income; it remains a part of paid-in capital and should be credited to an appropriate capital account.

Stock that does not have a redemption provision may be purchased on the open market by the issuing corporation and then retired. Stock that has been retired may ordinarily not be reissued. The redemption or retirement of stock reduces the legal capital of the corporation and hence could have an adverse effect on the creditors and on the remaining stockholders. For this reason, the states have laws and regulations that prescribe the procedures for reducing legal capital.

Records required by a corporation

For the most part, the accounts in the ledger of a corporation are comparable with those of any other type of business organization. As has been indicated in this and the preceding chapter, the *capital* accounts are different. Several other accounts that are required to record transactions peculiar to corporations will be introduced in later chapters.

The transactions involving purchases, sales, cash receipts, cash payments, and other routine operations are the same for a corporation as for other types of business organizations. The journals illustrated in earlier chapters are equally appropriate for use by a corporation. In designing special journals it is the different types of transactions and their frequency that must be considered rather than the type of legal organization.

The only distinctive records required by a corporation are those used to record the activities peculiar to the corporate form. Those in most common use are described in the paragraphs that follow.

Minute book. The secretary of the corporation records the proceedings of all meetings of the stockholders and the board of directors in the *minute book.* A copy of the charter and bylaws, with amendments thereto, are often inserted in the minute book so as to bring together in one place a complete and permanent legal record. The decisions and authorizations recorded in the minute book cover a wide range of subjects, such as results of elections of the board of directors, appointments of officers and their salaries, declarations of dividends, and borrowing of funds. The principal accounting officer and other officers refer to the minute book for authorizations and instructions.

Subscription book. The agreement between the corporation and a purchaser of the corporation's stock is recorded in a subscription contract. The contract specifies the class and number of shares, the price, and details as to payment. Each contract is signed by both parties. These contracts are assembled to form the *subscription book*. They are summarized periodically to provide the basis for the entry debiting the stock subscriptions receivable account, crediting the stock subscribed account, and debiting the discount account or crediting the premium account. Each contract also serves as the basis for posting a debit to the appropriate subscriber's account in the subscribers ledger.

Subscribers ledger. An account in the *subscribers ledger* is opened for each person who agrees to purchase stock. The subscribers ledger is a subsidiary ledger controlled by the stock subscriptions receivable account in the general ledger. As indicated above, the debits to the subsidiary accounts are posted from the contracts in the subscription book. Cash received from subscribers is recorded in the cash receipts journal, to which there may be added a special column for credits to stock subscriptions receivable. The individual items in this column are posted periodically to the accounts in the subscribers ledger, and the total is posted monthly to the controlling account. There is a separate controlling account and subsidiary ledger for each class of stock.

Stock certificate book. The evidence of ownership issued to a stockholder is called a stock certificate. On it are recorded the name of the corporation, the name and address of the stockholder, the class and special terms of the stock, the number of shares represented by the certificate, the date of issue, and the certificate number. Blank certificates may be obtained in book form similar to check books. At the time a certificate is prepared, the essential details must also be recorded on the stub or on a blank carbon copy of the certificate. The stub or carbon copy is retained by the corporation as its basic record.

An endorsement form is provided on the back of the certificate; it is filled out and signed by the stockholder when he sells the stock. The purchaser or his broker then submits the certificate to the issuing corporation, which cancels the certificate and issues a new one.

Stock certificate

Stockholders ledger. An account for each stockholder is maintained in a subsidiary ledger called a *stockholders ledger*. There is a ledger for each class of stock and each ledger is controlled by its related stock issued account in the general ledger. The stockholders ledger differs from other ledgers that have been described in that all entries are in terms of number of shares instead of dollars. To illustrate, assume that the Bell Corporation has 10,000 shares of $20 par common stock issued and outstanding. The account Common Stock would have a credit balance of $200,000 and the sum of the balances in the stockholders ledger would be 10,000 shares.

STOCKHOLDER	John L. Mason
ADDRESS	1432 Erie Ave., South Bend, Ind.

DATE			TRANSFERRED FROM OR TO	CERTIFICATE NO.		RECORD OF SHARES		
MO.	DAY	YR.		SURREN'D	ISSUED	SURREN'D	ISSUED	BALANCE
May	4	61	Original issue		393		50	50
Aug.	16	61	R. B. Dalton		561		75	125
June	18	62	Henry E. Thomas	393		50		75

Account in stockholders ledger

Postings to the accounts in the stockholders ledger may be made directly from the stock certificate stub or carbon copy of the certificate.

It should be noted that transfers of shares from one stockholder to another do not affect the controlling account, as the number of shares outstanding remains unchanged.

Questions

1. Two newly organized corporations are soliciting subscriptions to common stock at par value. The par value of the stock of one corporation is $50 and of the other is $20. Do the shares of one company represent a sounder investment than the shares of the other, and if so, which shares?

2. A corporation issues common stock at a discount and also borrows money from a bank by discounting a non-interest-bearing note payable. (a) Differentiate between the two kinds of discount. (b) Classify each discount as asset, liability, or capital.

3. When a corporation issues stock at a premium, should the amount of the premium be credited to a revenue account, a paid-in capital account, or the retained earnings account?

4. A corporation purchases 500 shares of its own $10 par common stock for $3,000, recording it at cost. (a) What effect does this transaction have on revenue or expense of the period? (b) What effect does it have on capital?

5. The treasury stock in Question 4 is resold for $5,000. (a) What is the effect on revenue of the period? (b) What is the effect on capital?

6. The liability and capital section of the balance sheet of the Parker Corporation lists liabilities, $150,000; 50,000 shares of no-par common stock outstanding, $500,000; and retained earnings, $100,000. The corporation proposes to purchase 20,000 shares from the largest stockholder at $20 a share and to retire the stock. Creditors and other stockholders object to the proposal. Give possible reasons for their objections.

7. Suggest reasons as to why a corporation might (a) redeem a preferred stock issue, (b) purchase treasury stock.

8. Discuss the following statement: "Treasury stock is properly carried as a current asset, because it can be readily converted into cash."

9. (a) What is the normal balance of each of the accounts listed below?
(b) Classify each account as asset, liability, capital, revenue, or expense.

(1) Preferred Stock Subscriptions Receivable	(6) Premium on Preferred Stock
(2) Preferred Stock Subscribed	(7) Donated Capital
(3) Common Stock	(8) Paid-in Capital from Preferred Stock Redemption
(4) Retained Earnings	(9) Discount on Common Stock
(5) Organization Costs	(10) Treasury Stock

Exercises

1. On August 1, the Blaylock Co. received subscriptions to 5,000 shares of $10 par common stock at $12, and on August 10 it received full payment from all subscribers. (a) Give the journal entries for August 1 and August 10. (b) Name two controlling accounts used in the above transactions and the related subsidiary ledger.

2. A corporation issues 10,000 shares of common stock to its principal incorporator in exchange for physical assets that are to be valued at $100,000. Give the entries in the capital accounts under each of the following assumptions: (a) the stock is $10 par, (b) the stock is $25 par, (c) the stock is no-par without a stated value, (d) the stock is $5 par.

3. The capital accounts of a corporation are: Common Stock, $10 par (10,000 shares issued and outstanding), $100,000; Premium on Common Stock, $10,000; Retained Earnings, $200,000. (a) Determine the book value per share of stock. (b) Assuming that the corporation purchases 1,000 shares of its own stock for a total of $49,000, determine the book value per share after the purchase.

4. Iceway, Inc. redeems all 5,000 shares of its $50 par preferred stock that had originally been issued at $54. Give the entry to record the redemption, assuming that the redemption price is (a) $55, (b) $52.

5. The Uranium Mining Co. issued 100,000 shares of $5 par common stock at par. It has a deficit of $100,000. All stockholders donate 20% of their stock to the company, and the stock is resold at $2. Determine the following:

    (a) Total capital before the donation.
    (b) Book value per share before the donation.
    (c) Total book value of 1,000 shares held by a particular stockholder before the donation.
    (d) Total paid-in capital after the donated stock is sold.
    (e) Total capital after the donated stock is sold.
    (f) Book value per share after the donated stock is sold.
    (g) Total book value of the 800 shares now held by the stockholder in (c).

Problems

21-1. The Northport Trailer Co. was organized on March 1 of the current year with an authorization of 2,000 shares of $100 par, 5% cumulative preferred stock and 20,000 shares of $25 par common stock. Transactions completed during March and April are summarized as follows:

Mar. 1. Received subscriptions to 10,000 shares of common stock at $26.
     1. Received cash for 40% of the subscription price from all common stock subscribers.
     2. Received subscriptions for 600 shares of preferred stock at $98.
     2. Received cash for 50% of the subscription price from all preferred stock subscribers.
     3. Paid organization costs of $1,500 and issued 200 shares of common stock to the promoters at $26 in payment for their services.
     8. Issued 800 shares of preferred stock for land valued at $12,400 and a building valued at $66,000.
   20. Purchased equipment for cash, $72,000.

Apr. 1. Received cash for 60% of the subscription price from March 1 subscribers to 5,000 shares of common stock and issued the certificates.
     1. Received cash for 40% of the subscription price from March 1 subscribers to 5,000 shares of common stock.
   15. Received balance due from preferred stock subscribers and issued the certificates.
   19. Received subscriptions to 5,000 shares of common stock at $27.

21. Received cash for 50% of the subscription price from all April 19 subscribers to common stock.
30. Received the balance due from the March 1 subscribers to 5,000 shares of common stock and issued the certificates.

Instructions: (1) Record the transactions in general journal form and post to the general ledger accounts. The accounts required are:

111 Cash	131 Organization Costs
113 Preferred Stock Subscriptions Receivable	311 Preferred Stock
	312 Preferred Stock Subscribed
114 Common Stock Subscriptions Receivable	313 Discount on Preferred Stock
	314 Common Stock
123 Equipment	315 Common Stock Subscribed
125 Buildings	316 Premium on Common Stock
126 Land	

(2) Assuming that no other transactions occurred during the period, prepare a balance sheet in report form as of April 30.

21-2. The following accounts and their balances appear in the ledger of the Brody Corporation on April 1 of the current year:

Common Stock Subscriptions Receivable..................	——
Preferred 7% Stock, par $50 (20,000 shares authorized, 12,000 shares issued).....................................	$ 600,000
Premium on Preferred Stock............................	24,000
Common Stock, no par (250,000 shares authorized, 140,000 shares issued).....................................	1,400,000
Common Stock Subscribed.............................	——
Retained Earnings....................................	862,000

Acting upon a plan to redeem its preferred stock with funds to be acquired by the issuance of additional common stock, the corporation completed the following transactions during the remainder of the fiscal year:

April 1. Holders of the common stock were issued rights to subscribe to additional shares at $15 a share, at the rate of ½ share for each share held. (No entry.)
May 1. Three fourths of the stock rights were exercised and subscriptions were received for that number of shares at $15, together with a down payment of 50% of the subscription price.
June 1. Collected the remainder due from all subscribers to common stock and issued the stock certificates.
   10. In accordance with contract provisions of the preferred stock, the 12,000 shares were redeemed at $54 and retired.
   15. Issued 17,500 shares of common stock at $18, receiving cash.
   30. After closing all revenue and expense accounts for the year and recording income taxes payable, Expense and Revenue Summary has a credit balance of $206,000. Close Expense and Revenue Summary.

Instructions: (1) Open the accounts listed and record the balances.

(2) Record the foregoing transactions in general journal form and post to the selected accounts in the ledger.

(3) Prepare the capital section of the balance sheet as of June 30.

(4) Determine the book value of the common stock as of June 30.

21-3. The following accounts and their balances appear in the ledger of the Cabrillo Corporation on July 1 of the current year:

Common Stock, par $10 (40,000 shares authorized and issued) $400,000
Premium on Common Stock.............................. 225,000
Retained Earnings (debit balance)....................... 75,000

As a means of obtaining badly needed funds to continue operations, the stockholders agree to donate one fourth of their shares to the corporation, which in turn is to reissue them at the best possible price. Transactions relating to the plan are as follows:

July 10. Received 10,000 shares of stock from stockholders.
    25. Sold 6,500 shares of treasury stock at $8
    31. Sold 3,500 shares of treasury stock at $8.50.

Instructions: Assuming for the purposes of the problem that no other transactions occurred during July:

(1) Journalize the entries to record the foregoing transactions, recording receipt of the treasury stock by a memorandum entry.
(2) Prepare the capital section of the balance sheet as of July 10.
(3) Determine the book value of the stock as of July 10.
(4) Prepare the capital section of the balance sheet as of July 31.
(5) Determine the book value of the stock as of July 31.

21-4. The capital accounts appearing in the ledger of Lamont Corp. on January 1 of the current year, together with other accounts that will be needed in the problem, are listed below:

Preferred 6% Stock, par $25 (50,000 shares authorized and
    issued)... $1,250,000
Premium on Preferred 6% Stock......................... 50,000
Preferred 4% Stock, par $25 (50,000 shares authorized)..... ——
Premium on Preferred 4% Stock......................... ——
Common Stock, par $5 (1,000,000 shares authorized; 800,000
    shares issued)... 4,000,000
Preferred 4% Stock Subscribed......................... ——
Treasury Stock.. ——
Premium on Common Stock............................. 800,000
Paid-in Capital from Sale of Treasury Stock.............. ——
Retained Earnings....................................... 2,880,000

During the year the corporation completed a number of transactions affecting the capital structure. They are summarized below.

(a) Purchased 10,000 shares of treasury common stock for $80,000 cash.
(b) Called the 6% preferred stock for redemption and retirement, paying the redemption price of $28.
(c) Sold 3,000 shares of treasury stock for $28,000 cash.
(d) Issued 25,000 shares of 4% preferred stock at $26, receiving cash.
(e) Received subscriptions to 25,000 shares of 4% preferred stock at $26, collecting 50% of the subscription price.
(f) Sold 5,000 shares of treasury stock for $50,000 cash.
(g) Received balance due from subscribers to 24,500 shares of 4% preferred stock, and issued the stock certificates.
(h) Received balance due from subscribers to the remaining 500 shares of 4% preferred stock and issued the stock certificates.

Instructions: (1) Present the entries, in general journal form, to record the transactions. (Use of T accounts is suggested for accumulating balances needed to record particular transactions and for use in remainder of problem.)

(2) Prepare the capital section of the balance sheet as of December 31. Net income for the year, after deducting income taxes, amounted to $1,021,400. Dividends charged to Retained Earnings during the year totaled $450,400.

21-5. The Stanton Company, a close corporation, was organized on March 5 of the current year and prepared its first financial statements as of October 31, the date that had been adopted as the end of the fiscal year. The balance sheet prepared by the bookkeeper as of October 31 is presented below. You are retained by the board of directors to audit the accounts and to prepare a revised balance sheet.

Stanton Company
Balance Sheet
March 5 to October 31, 19– –

Cash..................	$121,300	Accounts Payable.......	$ 75,400
Treasury stock..........	10,000	Preferred Stock	48,000
Accounts receivable.......	72,000	Common Stock	400,000
Merchandise inventory....	160,300	Retained Earnings	80,200
Equipment	80,000		
Building...............	150,000		
Land..................	10,000		
	$603,600		$603,600

The relevant facts developed during the course of your engagement are:
 (a) Stock authorized: 2,000 shares of $50 par 5% noncumulative preferred and 50,000 shares of $10 par common.
 (b) Stock issued: 1,000 shares of fully paid preferred at $48 and 30,000 shares of fully paid common at $12. The preferred was recorded at the net price and the premium on the common was credited to Retained Earnings.
 (c) Stock subscribed but not issued: 10,000 shares of common at $11, on which all subscribers have paid 50% (total of $55,000). No entry has been made for the premium. Unpaid subscriptions of $45,000 are included in accounts receivable.
 (d) The company reacquired 1,000 shares of the issued common stock for $8,000. The difference between par and the price paid was credited to Retained Earnings. (It is decided that the treasury stock is to be recorded at cost.)
 (e) No depreciation has been recognized. The equipment and the building are to be depreciated for one-half year by the declining balance method, using double the straight-line rate. Estimated life is 10 years on the equipment and 25 years on the building.
 (f) Organization costs of $5,000 were charged to advertising expense. (None of the organization costs is to be amortized.)
 (g) All insurance premiums have been charged to expense. The amount prepaid at October 31 is $1,600.
 (h) No dividends have been declared or paid.

Instructions: (1) Open T accounts for each item in the balance sheet and record the balances.

(2) Record the necessary corrections in the T accounts, setting up additional accounts as required. Corrections of net income may be entered in the retained earnings account.

(3) Prepare a balance sheet in report form as of the close of the fiscal period.

Corporations—capital, earnings, and dividends

Corporation capital

The importance of classifying the various elements of corporate capital according to source has been emphasized in preceding chapters. There are two principal subdivisions of capital, namely paid-in capital and retained earnings. The capital sections of corporate balance sheets of earlier days were frequently not very informative. The preferred and common stock accounts were reported at par, which was clear enough, but the remaining capital was often described merely as "Surplus." In such cases it was not possible for the reader to determine the sources of capital and, in the absence of such information, to form an intelligent opinion about this section of the balance sheet. For example, a "surplus" of $1,000,000 could represent retained earnings of $1,000,000, or it could be the excess of stock premiums (paid-in capital) of $1,200,000 over an accumulated deficit (losses) of $200,000.

The term "capital surplus" has also been employed in the past to describe paid-in capital in excess of par or stated value of the capital stock. The term "surplus" either alone or with such words as "capital," "paid-in," or "earned," as a descriptive caption in financial statements is no longer widely used. It is still encountered, however, particularly in accounting literature and should be understood by students of business.

Paid-in capital

The principal credits to paid-in capital accounts result from the issuance of stock. If par stock is issued at a price above or below par, the difference is recorded in a separate premium or discount account. It is also not uncommon to employ two accounts in recording the issuance of no-par stock, one for the stated value and the other for the excess over stated value. Other accounts for paid-in capital discussed in the preceding chapter were Paid-in Capital from Sale of Treasury Stock and Donated Capital.

There are numerous variations in the arrangement of the paid-in capital section of the balance sheet and also in the terminology employed. A corporation with a large amount of premium on issuance of stock and minor amounts of paid-in capital from miscellaneous sources may combine a number of accounts and report them as a single item in the balance sheet. Some of the variations in arrangement and terminology are illustrated by the three examples that follow.

Capital

Paid-in capital:

Common stock, $20 par (50,000 shares authorized, 40,000 shares issued)......................	$800,000	
Premium on common stock.....................	128,000	$928,000
From stock redemption.........................		30,000
From sale of treasury stock.....................		10,000
Total paid-in capital........................		$968,000

Stockholders' investment

Paid-in capital:

Common stock, $20 par (50,000 shares authorized, 40,000 shares issued)......................	$800,000	
Excess of issuance price of stock over par value....	$128,000	
From retirement of preferred stock..............	30,000	
From transactions in own stock................	10,000	168,000
Total paid-in capital...		$968,000

Shareholders' equity

Contributed capital:

Common stock, $20 par (50,000 shares authorized, 40,000 shares issued).........................	$800,000	
Additional paid-in capital.....................	168,000	
Total contributed capital.		$968,000

Another source of paid-in capital is from property acquired by gift. Although of comparatively rare occurrence, a corporation may be given land or land and buildings by a civic organization as an inducement to locate in a particular community. The property so acquired should be recorded in the accounts at its estimated value, there being no initial cost to the corporation. The entry is completed by a credit to an appropriate account, such as Paid-in Capital — Donation of Land and Buildings, or Donated Capital.

Paid-in capital in excess of par or stated value is ordinarily not a part of legal capital and may in many states be distributed to stockholders as dividends. The statutes of some states require that stockholders be informed of the source of such distributions. Regardless of legal requirements, a corporation using paid-in capital as a basis for dividends should make full disclosure to the stockholders.

Revaluation of assets

After a continuing period of increasing prices, the value of plant assets may be substantially higher than their original cost less accumulated depreciation. At times in the past, particularly during the period 1920–29, many corporations increased the valuation of plant assets to bring them up to their appraised values. Many of these write-ups were followed by write-downs in the following decade.

The offsetting credit resulting from an upward revision of asset values may be described on the balance sheet as "Appraisal capital," "Revaluation capital," "Capital from write-up of plant assets," or by various other descriptive phrases. The recognition of appreciation in value in the accounts is now relatively rare. Accountants generally agree with the following statement of policy: "Accounting for fixed assets should normally be based on cost, and any attempt to make property accounts in general reflect current values is both impracticable and inexpedient. Appreciation normally should not be reflected on the books of account of corporations."[1]

Corporation earnings

The determination of net income or loss for a corporation is comparable, in most respects, to that of other forms of business organization. The particular revenue and expense accounts needed depend upon the nature and volume of the business operations. Because of its separate legal existence, an individual may be both a stockholder and an employee of a corporation. Payments to such stockholder-employees for services rendered constitute expenses of the corporation. This is in contrast to sole proprietorships, in which all payments to owners are classified as withdrawals rather than expenses.

Corporation income taxes

Sole proprietorships are not entities subject to the federal income tax. The net income of such enterprises is reported by the proprietors in their individual tax returns. Corporations are distinct legal entities and, in general, are subject to the federal income tax. They may also be subject to an income tax levied by a state or city.

Corporations expecting to have a federal income tax of not more than $100,000 for the year are required to pay one half of the tax within $2\frac{1}{2}$ months after the close of the fiscal year and the remaining half three months later. Corporations with expectations of a tax in excess

---

[1] *Accounting Research Bulletin*, No. 5 "Depreciation on Appreciation," April, 1940 (New York: American Institute of Certified Public Accountants), p. 37.

of $100,000 must pay 50 per cent of the excess during the latter half of the fiscal year in which the income is earned; the remainder is due at the times indicated for corporations with a tax liability of $100,000 or less.

The amount of income tax liability determined by a corporation is subject to review and adjustment by the taxing authority. For this reason the liability for income taxes is commonly described in the current liability section of the balance sheet as "Estimated income tax payable" or "Provision for income tax." The entry to record the charge against net income, and the credit to the liability account may be made monthly if interim statements are prepared or if advance payments of the estimated tax are required. To illustrate the recording of income taxes, assume that a corporation's net income for the year ended December 31, before income tax, is $180,000, on which the federal income tax is expected to be $88,100. The entry is as follows:

| Dec. 31 | Estimated Income Tax...................................... | 88,100 | |
| | Estimated Income Tax Payable..................... | | 88,100 |

The income tax account is closed to Expense and Revenue Summary and the liability account is reduced as payments are made. Because of its nature as a charge against *net income* it is customary to report the tax in the income statement in the following manner:

Flagg Corporation
Income Statement
For Year Ended December 31, 19--

Sales...	$920,600
Net income before income tax..	$180,000
Estimated income tax...	88,100
Net income after income tax...	$ 91,900

Retained earnings

At the close of each fiscal period the balance in the expense and revenue summary account is closed to Retained Earnings. Net income increases the balance of the account; net losses and distributions of earnings to stockholders decrease the balance of the account. In the absence of changes in the capital structure or adjustments of an unusual nature, the balance of the retained earnings account at any time represents the total earnings from the date of incorporation less the total losses and dividends.

Increases or decreases in capital resulting from issuance of stock at a price other than par or stated value are not income or loss and should not be carried to the retained earnings account. Similarly, transactions in treasury stock and donations of stock or property do not result in income or loss. The changes in capital effected by such occurrences should be reported as a part of paid-in capital.

A corporation may incur losses and have little prospect of improving its operating results because of high depreciation or other fixed charges against income. In such cases the corporation may reduce the values of its assets and reduce its legal capital. In the process of shrinking assets and capital down to a more reasonable basis, the retained earnings or deficit is eliminated. The restatement of the accounts under these circumstances is called a *corporate readjustment* or *quasi-reorganization*. A new retained earnings account is opened and thereafter, for a period up to ten years, the beginning date of the account should be disclosed on the balance sheet.[2] Readers are informed in this manner that the balance has accumulated from a specific date subsequent to the date the corporation was organized.

A portion of retained earnings may be transferred to the capital stock account, thus becoming a part of permanent capital. This is done through the medium of stock dividends which are discussed later in this chapter.

It is not unusual for corporations to accumulate a substantial amount of earnings in relation to paid-in capital. The board of directors may earmark or appropriate part of the accumulation for a particular purpose, such as expansion of the physical plant. The amount so appropriated is thereafter not available for cash dividends to stockholders until the directors rescind their action. An appropriation is accomplished by transferring the desired amount from Retained Earnings to a special account designating its purpose, such as Retained Earnings Appropriated for Plant Expansion.

The amount transferred to the special account, which is called an *appropriation* or a *reserve*, remains a part of retained earnings and should be so classified on the balance sheet.

Appropriation of retained earnings

Appropriations of earnings may be required by law or contract, or they may be made at the discretion of the directors. The laws of many

---

[2]*Accounting Research Bulletin No. 43*, "Restatement and Revision of Accounting Research Bulletins," 1953, p. 47, and *Accounting Research Bulletin No. 46*, "Discontinuance of Dating Earned Surplus," 1956 (New York: American Institute of Certified Public Accountants), p. 11.

states require that a corporation retain earnings equal to the amount paid for treasury stock. For example, if a corporation with accumulated earnings of $100,000 purchases shares of its own issued stock for $40,000, the corporation would not be permitted to pay more than $60,000 in dividends. The restriction is equal to the $40,000 paid for the treasury stock and assures that legal capital will not be impaired. The entry to record the appropriation would be:

```
Retained Earnings.......................................  40,000
    Retained Earnings Appropriated for Treasury Stock Purchased        40,000
```

After the corporation sells the treasury stock, the appropriation is no longer needed and it is therefore transferred back to the retained earnings account by the following entry:

```
Retained Earnings Appropriated for Treasury Stock Purchased...  40,000
    Retained Earnings.......................................        40,000
```

When a corporation borrows a substantial amount through issuance of bonds or long-term notes, the agreement may provide for restrictions on dividends until the debt is paid. The contract may stipulate that earnings equal to the amount borrowed be restricted during the entire period of the loan, or it may require that the appropriation be built up by annual appropriations. For example, assume that a corporation borrows $500,000 on ten-year bonds. If the agreement requires that retained earnings be immediately restricted, the entry would be:

```
Retained Earnings.......................................  500,000
    Retained Earnings Appropriated for Bonded Indebtedness....        500,000
```

If equal annual appropriations were to be made over the life of the bonds, there would be a series of ten entries similar to the one above, each for the amount of $50,000. If the bond agreement did not require the restriction on retained earnings, the directors might nevertheless deem it advisable to establish the reserve. In that case it would be a *discretionary* rather than a *contractual* reserve. The entries would be exactly the same in either case.

Upon the payment of the bonded indebtedness, the restriction expires and the amount of the appropriation may be returned to the retained earnings account by the following entry:

```
Retained Earnings Appropriated for Bonded Indebtedness......  500,000
    Retained Earnings.......................................        500,000
```

It must be clearly understood that the appropriation account is not directly related to any particular group of asset accounts. Its existence does not imply that there is an equivalent amount of cash or other assets set aside in a special fund. The appropriation serves the purpose of restricting dividends but it does not assure that the cash that might otherwise be distributed as dividends will not be invested in additional inventories, equipment, or other assets, or used to reduce current liabilities.

A segregation of cash and securities may accompany appropriations of earnings, in which case the appropriation or reserve is said to be *funded*. Accumulation of special funds is discussed in the next chapter.

There are other purposes for which the directors may consider appropriations desirable. Expansion of plant facilities was mentioned earlier. Some companies with properties widely scattered geographically may assume their own risk of losses from fire, windstorm, and other casualties rather than obtain protection from insurance companies. The entry to establish a reserve for such a contingency would be:

Retained Earnings....................................	100,000	
Retained Earnings Appropriated for Self-Insurance......		100,000

An appropriation of this nature is likely to be permanent although its amount may vary as the total value of properties, the extent of fire protection, etc. fluctuates. If a fire loss occurs, it should be charged to a loss account rather than to the appropriation account, as it is a loss of the particular period and should be so reported. A company may also earmark earnings for other specific contingencies, such as inventory price declines or an adverse decision on a pending law suit. A common practice is to establish an appropriation for contingencies to provide for any eventuality.

The manner in which retained earnings are presented on the balance sheet is illustrated below. The item designated "Unappropriated" is the balance of the retained earnings account.

Retained earnings:			
Appropriated:			
For plant expansion....................	$50,000		
For contingencies......................	10,000	$60,000	
Unappropriated........................		80,000	
Total retained earnings.................			$140,000

An alternative to formalizing restrictions on retained earnings by entries in the accounts is to describe the amount and nature of the restrictions in notes to the balance sheet. For example, in the foregoing illustration the retained earnings could be presented as a single item of $140,000 with a reference to a footnote in which the restrictions of $60,000 are described.

Nature of dividends

A dividend is a distribution by a corporation to its shareholders. It must be on a pro rata basis for all shares of a particular class. The prospect of receiving dividends represents a major incentive for investment in corporation stocks. In almost all cases dividends represent distributions of earnings of the corporation. As has been noted earlier, premium on stock and other items of paid-in capital may be distributed to stockholders, but such dividends are rare. When a corporation is in the process of liquidating, the distributions to stockholders are termed *liquidating dividends*. They may represent either a distribution of paid-in capital, a distribution of earnings, or a combination of both. The discussion that follows will be concerned with dividends based on accumulated earnings.

Dividends may be paid in cash, in stock of the paying company, in scrip, or in other property. The discussion in this chapter will be mainly concerned with the two most common types of dividends — *cash dividends*, and stock of the paying company or *stock dividends*.

Ordinarily there are three prerequisites to paying a cash dividend: (1) sufficient unappropriated earnings, (2) sufficient cash, and (3) formal action by the board of directors. A substantial amount of accumulated earnings does not necessarily indicate that a corporation is able to pay dividends; there must also be sufficient cash over and above working capital needs. The amount of retained earnings is not directly related to cash; the former represents income of past periods retained in the business, but the cash provided by the income may have been used to purchase plant assets, reduce liabilities, or for other purposes. The directors of a corporation are not compelled by law to declare dividends even when both retained earnings and cash appear to be sufficient. They have broad discretionary powers in the matter. When a dividend has been declared, however, it becomes a liability of the corporation.

Seasoned corporations with a wide distribution of stock usually try to maintain a stable dividend record. They may retain a substantial portion of earnings in good years in order to be able to continue dividend payments in lean years. Dividends may be paid once a year or on a semiannual or quarterly basis. The tendency is to pay quarterly dividends on both common and preferred stock. In particularly good years the directors may declare an "extra" dividend on common stock. It may be paid at one of the usual dividend dates or at some other date. The designation "extra" indicates that the board of directors does not anticipate an increase in the amount of the "regular" dividend.

There are three different dates involved in a dividend declaration: (1) the date of declaration, (2) the date of record, and (3) the date of payment. The first is the date the directors take formal action declaring the dividend, the second is the date as of which ownership of shares is to be determined, and the third is the date payment is to be made. For example, on October 11 the board of directors declares a quarterly dividend to stockholders of record as of the close of business on October 21, payable on November 15. Notices of dividend declarations are usually reported in financial publications and newspapers.

The liability for the dividend is recorded on the declaration date, as it is incurred when the formal action is taken by the directors. No entry is required on the date of record; it merely fixes the date for determining the identity of the stockholders entitled to receive the dividend. The period between the record date and the payment date is provided to permit time to complete the postings to the stockholders' ledger and prepare the dividend checks. The liability of the corporation is paid by the mailing of the checks.

Dividends on cumulative preferred stock do not become a liability until they are declared. Dividends in arrears at a balance sheet date should be disclosed by a footnote, a parenthetical notation, or a segregation of retained earnings similar to the following:

Retained earnings:

Required to meet dividends in arrears on preferred stock..	$30,000	
Remainder....................................	16,000	
Total retained earnings........................		$46,000

Cash dividends

Dividends payable in cash are by far the most usual form of dividend. Cash dividends are usually stated in terms of dollars and cents rather than as a percentage of par. In the case of preferred stock, however, the preferential dividend rate may be based on par. For example, the annual dividend rate on 5% preferred stock of $100 par would be $5; the amount of a quarterly dividend would be $1.25 per share.

Corporations ordinarily follow a fixed pattern of dividend payment dates, such as Jan. 15, Apr. 15, July 15, and Oct. 15 or Mar. 30, June 30, Sept. 30, and Dec. 30. Assuming a sufficient balance in retained earnings, including estimated net income of the current year, the directors ordinarily consider the following factors in determining whether to pass a dividend or declare a particular amount:

(1) The company's working capital position.
(2) Resources needed for planned expansion or replacement of facilities.
(3) Maturity dates of large liabilities.
(4) Future business prospects of the company and the general outlook for the industry and the economy generally.

To illustrate the entries required in the declaration and payment of cash dividends, assume that on December 1 the board of directors of the

Peerless Corporation declares the regular quarterly dividend of $1 on the 5,000 shares of $100 par, 4% preferred stock outstanding ($5,000), and a quarterly dividend of 25¢ on the 100,000 shares of $10 par common stock outstanding ($25,000). Both dividends are to stockholders of record on December 10 and payment checks are to be issued on January 2. Entries to record the declaration and payment of the dividends are:

Dec. 1	Retained Earnings.............................	30,000	
	Cash Dividends Payable.......................		30,000
Jan. 2	Cash Dividends Payable........................	30,000	
	Cash...		30,000

Assuming that the corporation's fiscal year ends on December 31, the cash dividends payable account would be listed among the current liabilities on the balance sheet of that date.

Stock dividends

A pro rata distribution of shares of stock to stockholders, accompanied by a transfer of retained earnings to paid-in capital accounts, is called a *stock dividend*. Such distributions are usually in common stock and are issued to holders of common stock. It is possible to issue common stock to preferred stockholders or preferred stock to common stockholders, but such stock dividends are unusual and will not be discussed.

Stock dividends are quite unlike cash dividends in that there is no distribution of cash or other corporate assets to the stockholders. They are ordinarily issued by corporations that "plow back" or retain earnings for use in acquiring new facilities or otherwise expanding their operations.

The effect of a stock dividend on the capital structure of the issuing corporation is to transfer accumulated earnings to paid-in capital. To illustrate, assume that the balances of the capital accounts of Prescott Corporation on November 30 are as follows:

Common Stock, $10 par (10,000 shares issued)...................	$100,000
Premium on Common Stock.....................................	20,000
Retained Earnings...	150,000

The directors declare a 20% stock dividend (2,000 shares) on December 15, to be issued on January 10. The fair market value of the stock to be issued is estimated at $22 per share. According to the recommendation of the Committee on Accounting Procedure of the American Institute of Certified Public Accountants, retained earnings equal to the market value of the shares to be issued should be transferred to paid-in capital accounts.[3] The entries to record the declaration of the stock dividend and the issuance of the shares follow:

Dec. 15	Retained Earnings.............................	44,000	
	Stock Dividend Distributable..................		20,000
	Premium on Common Stock...................		24,000
Jan. 10	Stock Dividend Distributable....................	20,000	
	Common Stock.............................		20,000

The effect of the stock dividend is to transfer $44,000 from the retained earnings account to paid-in capital accounts, and to increase by 2,000 the number of shares outstanding. There is no change in the assets, liabilities, or capital of the corporation.

A stock dividend does not constitute income to the recipient. It does not alter the book value of his total holdings nor his fractional interest in the corporation. The following analysis of the capital accounts of the Prescott Corporation and of the holdings of a hypothetical stockholder demonstrates this point. It is assumed that there are no other changes in the capital accounts.

	Before Stock Dividend	After Stock Dividend
Corporation accounts		
Common stock...........................	$100,000	$120,000
Premium on common stock................	20,000	44,000
Retained earnings........................	150,000	106,000
Total capital.........................	$270,000	$270,000
Number of shares outstanding..............	10,000	12,000
Book value per share.....................	$27.00	$22.50
A stockholder's investment		
Shares owned............................	100	120
Total book value of holdings...............	$2,700	$2,700
Portion of corporation owned..............	1%	1%

The stock dividend distributable account on the books of a corporation is not a true liability. If a balance sheet is prepared between the date of declaration and the date of issuance, the amount should be presented as a separate item under the common stock heading.

Stock split-up

Corporations sometimes reduce the par, or stated, value of their common stock and issue a proportionate number of additional shares.

---

[3] *Accounting Research Bulletin No. 43*, "Restatement and Revision of Accounting Research Bulletins," 1953 (New York: American Institute of Certified Public Accountants), p. 51.

Such a procedure is called a *stock split-up*. For example, a corporation with 10,000 shares of $50 par value stock outstanding may reduce the par value to $25 and increase the number of shares to 20,000. A stockholder who owned 100 shares before the split-up would own 200 shares after the split-up. There are no changes in the balances of any of the corporation's accounts, hence no entry is required.

The primary purpose of a stock split-up is to reduce the selling price of stock when the shares are selling at exceedingly high levels. Such an action will permit more investors to enter the market for this particular security. A stock split-up is seldom employed by small corporations or by corporations whose stock is not listed on the organized stock exchanges.

Corrections and unusual charges and credits

Regardless of the safeguards that may be employed, it is inevitable that errors will occur in recording transactions. When the error is discovered during the same accounting period in which it occurred, a correction may be made and the financial statements will not be affected by the error. The analysis of the effect of an error and the formulation of the correction is facilitated by observing the following procedures: (1) determine the entry that was incorrectly made, (2) formulate the entry that should have been made, and (3) formulate the correcting entry. To illustrate, assume that new equipment purchased by Douglas Corporation on January 10 at a cost of $20,000 was erroneously charged to repairs expense; and that the error is discovered after adjusting entries have been made as of December 31 but before the books have been closed. Assume further that the equipment has an estimated life of ten years and that the company uses the straight-line method of depreciation. The correcting entry to be recorded as of December 31 may be determined as follows:

Entry Made	Entries That Should Have Been Made		Correcting Entries	
Repairs 20,000 Accounts Pay. 20,000	Equipment........ 20,000 Accounts Payable.	20,000	Equipment........ 20,000 Repairs.........	20,000
	Depr. Exp. — Equip. 2,000 Accum. Depr. — Equipment.....	2,000	Depr. Exp. — Equip. 2,000 Accum. Depr. — Equipment.....	2,000

In the foregoing illustration the error was corrected before the financial statements were prepared and the books were closed for the year. Had the error not been discovered and corrected, the effect on the income statement for the year and the balance sheet at December 31 would have been as follows:

(1) Income Statement — Overstatement of repairs expense, $20,000; understatement of depreciation expense, $2,000; net understatement of income, $18,000.

(2) Balance Sheet — Understatement of equipment, $20,000; understatement of accumulated depreciation, $2,000; net understatement of assets, $18,000; net understatement of retained earnings, $18,000.

When errors in revenues and expenses are not discovered until a later period, there is the problem of how they should be corrected and reported in the financial statements. There are two opposing points of view as to the reporting of income corrections of past years and of extraordinary items of revenue and expense. The latter category includes such items as gains or losses from lawsuits and losses resulting from floods, earthquakes, or other catastrophes of a nonrecurring nature not covered by insurance. In the following brief discussion of the two views it should be borne in mind that the concern is only with *material* items. Corrections and extraordinary charges or credits that are relatively insignificant in amount may be treated as current revenue or expense.

Current operating performance statement.   An income statement in which the items reported are limited to those of a normally recurring nature may be referred to as a *current operating performance* statement. The principal argument for excluding the nonrecurring items is that the income statement should present what the corporation was able to earn under normal conditions for the year. It is only in this way that comparisons can be made with other years and with the income statements of other corporations. When this view is adopted the nonrecurring items are carried directly to the retained earnings account.

Applying the foregoing to the correction of income of the earlier year for the Douglas Corporation, the entries would be:

Equipment...	20,000	
Retained Earnings.................................		20,000
Retained Earnings.....................................	2,000	
Accumulated Depreciation — Equipment...............		2,000

The entries of $20,000 and $2,000 in Retained Earnings would be reported on the statement of retained earnings as a correction of income of past years and the income statement for the second year would report net income without distortion. The manner in which the correction is reported on the retained earnings statement is illustrated on page 496.

All-inclusive statement. An income statement that includes all revenue and expense items, regardless of their source, is referred to as an *all-inclusive* statement. The basic argument is that the income statement should report the full story of operating results; the complete series of annual income statements will then include the entire income from the date of organization. Significant items of a nonrecurring nature should be set forth separately in the statement. The reader is then able to determine what the net income would otherwise have been.

Applying this view to the correction for the Douglas Corporation, the entry would be:

Equipment..	20,000	
Accumulated Depreciation — Equipment................		2,000
Correction of Income of Earlier Period.................		18,000

The credit of $18,000 would be reported on the income statement as an extraordinary credit.

It is important to note that both methods provide for disclosure of extraordinary items that should not be "buried" in other accounts. The difference between the two methods lies in the manner in which this is accomplished.

Amortization and write-off of intangibles

According to the usages of accounting, the term *intangible asset* is applied to certain long-lived legal rights and competitive advantages belonging to a business enterprise. Included are organization costs, goodwill, patents, copyrights, secret processes, leases, and similar items. A requisite to the recognition of an intangible asset in the accounts is that it be purchased. For example, if the total price paid for a going concern exceeds the fair value of the identifiable net assets, the excess is payment for goodwill and it should be recorded as such in the accounts of the purchaser. On the other hand, a firm that builds up goodwill through successful operations would not be justified in recording goodwill on its books.

Some intangible assets have a limited term of existence. For example, the exclusive right to an invention granted by a patent runs for seventeen years. Copyrights and leases also expire within a definite number of years. Other intangibles, such as organization costs, goodwill, and secret processes, ordinarily have no limitations on their term of existence; at least the length of life cannot be ascertained at the time the asset is acquired.

Intangibles that have a limited life should be amortized by periodic pro rata charges to expense. If a change in circumstances indicates a shorter or longer life than originally estimated, the amount of the periodic charge should be altered accordingly. If it should become evident that the intangible asset is worthless, it should be written off the books. If the amount of the write-off is material, it may be treated as an extraordinary item and charged directly to Retained Earnings or set forth separately in the income statement.

Intangible assets with an unlimited life should be carried on the books during the entire life of the enterprise, except that if altered circumstances result in their worthlessness they should be written off. Here, too, the manner in which the write-off is reported may follow either the current operating performance statement theory or the all-inclusive statement theory.

Despite the lack of theoretical justification, intangible assets are sometimes amortized gradually or written-off completely without regard to loss in value. As was indicated in Chapter 20, organization costs are frequently written off during the early years of a corporation's life.

Retained earnings statement

The retained earnings statement is a formal summary of the debits and the credits to the retained earnings accounts during a fiscal period. It is one of the principal statements included in published financial reports of corporations.

The retained earnings statement is divided into two major sections: (1) appropriated and (2) unappropriated. The first section is composed of an analysis of all appropriation or reserve accounts, beginning with the opening balance, listing the additions or deductions during the period, and ending with the closing balance. The second section is composed of an analysis of the retained earnings account and is similar in form to the first section. The final figure on the statement is the total retained earnings as of the last day of the period; it corresponds to the amount reported on the balance sheet.

To illustrate the form of the statement and the sources from which the information is obtained, the pertinent accounts of the Douglas Corporation and the statement are given on page 496.

Retained earnings statements are frequently shorter and simpler than the one illustrated. When a corporation has no appropriation accounts and no corrections applicable to past periods, the only changes to be reported in the statement may well be net income and dividend declarations. There are many possible variations in the form of the

Retained Earnings Appropriated for Plant Expansion

Date			PR	Dr.	Cr.	Bal.
1961						
Jan	1	Balance				30,000
Dec	31	Transfer from retained earnings			20,000	50,000

Retained Earnings

Date			PR	Dr.	Cr.	Bal.
1961						
Jan	1	Balance				95,300
Mar	10	Equipment			20,000	
	10	Accumulated depreciation — equip.		2,000		
	20	Dividends		9,875		
June	19	Dividends		9,875		
Sept	18	Dividends		9,875		
Dec	18	Dividends		17,875		
	31	Organization costs		4,000		
	31	Net income after income tax			100,000	
	31	Appropriation for plant expansion		20,000		141,800

Douglas Corporation
Retained Earnings Statement
For Year Ended December 31, 1961

Appropriated:			
Appropriated for plant expansion, balance January 1, 1961		$30,000	
Add appropriation in 1961 (see below)		20,000	
Retained earnings appropriated, December 31, 1961			$ 50,000
Unappropriated:			
Balance, January 1, 1961	$ 95,300		
Add: Net income for year after income tax	100,000		
Overstatement of repair expenses in 1960	20,000	$215,300	
Deduct: Cash dividends declared	$ 47,500		
Organization costs written off	4,000		
Understatement of depreciation expense in 1960	2,000		
Transfer to appropriation for plant expansion (see above)	20,000	73,500	
Retained earnings unappropriated, December 31, 1961			141,800
Total retained earnings, December 31, 1961			$191,800

Retained earnings statement

statement. It may also be appended to the income statement to form a combined statement of income and retained earnings, which is illustrated in Chapter 29. When there are changes in paid-in capital during the period they should be presented in a separate statement.

Questions

1. What is the more modern term for "Earned Surplus"?

2. When a corporation issues stock at a premium, does the premium constitute income?

3. When a corporation purchases some of its own stock from stockholders at a price above par, is the excess over par an expense or loss to the corporation?

4. A corporation owns iron ore deposits acquired twenty years ago at a cost of two million dollars. They are currently appraised at twice their cost. Would it be proper to add the increment in value to the asset account and credit a capital account?

5. The Suffolk Corporation records its estimated federal income tax at the close of each month. (a) Give the entry to record an estimated tax of $50,000 for January, the first month of the fiscal year. (b) Give the entry to record the payment of $200,000 of estimated income tax on September 15.

6. To what account is Estimated Income Tax closed at the end of the fiscal year?

7. What is the customary manner of presenting the provision for income tax on the income statement?

8. Does the credit balance in the retained earnings account represent cash?

9. The board of directors of a corporation votes to appropriate $100,000 of retained earnings for the possible loss of properties located in a foreign country. What is the effect of their action on (a) cash, (b) retained earnings, (c) possible dividend declarations?

10. The dates in connection with the declaration of a cash dividend are June 10, June 16, and June 30. Identify each date.

11. Name three prerequisites to the declaration of a cash dividend.

12. What is the effect of the following on assets, liabilities, and capital? (a) Declaration of a cash dividend, (b) payment of a cash dividend, (c) declaration and issuance of a stock dividend, (d) stock split-up.

13. The owner of 100 shares of Phoenix Corporation common stock receives a stock dividend of 50 shares. (a) What is the effect of the stock dividend on the book value of the stock per share? (b) Is the total book value of the 150 shares greater than, less than, or the same as, the total book value of the 100 shares immediately before the dividend?

14. Contrast "current operating performance" and "all-inclusive" as terms applied to the income statement.

Exercises

1. The Flintlock Corporation purchases 2,000 shares of its own common stock at $62. The par value is $50 and the book value before the purchase was $71. (a) Present the journal entry to provide for the appropriation of retained earnings. (b) One half of the treasury stock is sold at $68. Present the journal entry to reduce the appropriation.

2. At the end of the year the board of directors of the Atlas Company authorizes an appropriation of retained earnings for a possible inventory loss of $200,000. During the following year the company loses an estimated $220,000 through price declines of items in the inventory; no further declines are anticipated. Present the entry to dispose of the appropriation.

3. The dates in connection with a cash dividend of $50,000 on company stock are March 10, March 18, and April 1. Present the entries, in general journal form, required on each date.

4. The board of directors of the A. C. Morton Corporation declares a 10% common stock dividend on 50,000 shares of $10 par common stock. The fair market value of the stock to be issued is $21 a share. Present the entries to record (a) the declaration of the dividend, (b) the issuance of the stock.

5. Give the entry to correct each of the following errors, assuming that the corrections are made in the year in which the errors occurred.

    (a) In recording a sale of $1,000 for which a note receivable was accepted, Accounts Receivable was debited.

    (b) The cash sale for $2,000 of an item of equipment that had cost $10,000 was recorded as a $2,000 debit to Cash and credit to Sales. Depreciation accumulated on the equipment at the time of sale was $6,000.

    (c) A purchase of $400 of advertising supplies on account was debited to Purchases.

6. The errors described below occurred during or at the end of the fiscal year ending December 31. They are discovered in April of the following year. Present the correcting entries, charging or crediting corrections of income directly to Retained Earnings.

    (a) Accrued salaries of $3,000 were not recognized at December 31.

    (b) The $540 premium on a three-year insurance policy acquired on September 1 was charged to Insurance Expense. No adjustment was made on December 31.

    (c) A machine acquired on January 6 at a cost of $8,000 was debited to Purchases. No depreciation was recorded on December 31. Use 4-year life, salvage value of $500, sum of the years-digits method of depreciation.

    (d) Merchandise Inventory at December 31 was understated by $6,200.

Problems

22-1. The capital accounts of the A. M. Scott Corporation on February 1 of the current fiscal year are as follows:

Common Stock, par $10 (100,000 shares authorized, 75,000 shares issued).....................................	$750,000
Premium on Common Stock................................	150,000
Retained Earnings Appropriated for Contingencies............	100,000
Retained Earnings.......................................	350,000

The following transactions occurred during the year:

Feb.   2. Issued 10,000 shares of common stock for $200,000 cash.

Apr. 19. Discovered that equipment purchased for $25,000 on February 5 of the preceding year was charged to repairs expense. The equipment has an estimated life of 10 years, no salvage value, and is to be depreciated on a straight-line basis. Correct through retained earnings.

July 10. Declared cash dividend of 70¢ a share on common stock.

Aug.   2. Paid the dividend.

Jan. 10. Declared cash dividend of 90¢ per share on common stock, payable February 4.

       30. Patents with an unamortized cost of $50,000 are considered to be worthless as a result of patents on an improved product obtained by a competing firm. The board of directors authorizes their write-off and directs that the loss be charged to the retained earnings account.

       30. The board directs that the appropriation for contingencies is to be increased by $100,000.

       31. After closing revenue and expense accounts, including the income tax account, Expense and Revenue Summary has a credit balance of $300,000. Close the expense and revenue summary account.

Instructions: (1) Set up T accounts for the four capital accounts and enter the balances as of February 1, the beginning of the fiscal year.

(2) Journalize the transactions listed above, posting to the capital accounts.

(3) Prepare the capital section of the balance sheet as of January 31, the end of the fiscal year.

(4) Prepare a retained earnings statement for the fiscal year ended January 31.

22-2. Selected transactions completed by the Penrod Corporation during the current fiscal year are as follows:

Jan.   2. Received final payment from subscribers to 5,000 shares of preferred 5% stock, $50 par, and issued the stock certificates. The cash received was $49,000, which represented the final installment of 20% of the contract price. Earlier transactions related to the stock had been recorded correctly.

Feb. 21. Purchased 2,000 shares of own common stock at $14, recording the stock at cost. (Prior to the purchase there were 200,000 shares of $5 par common stock outstanding.)

Apr. 25. Sold 500 shares of treasury stock at $16, receiving cash.

May   5. Declared a semiannual dividend of $1.25 on the 5,000 shares of preferred stock, and a 25¢ dividend on the common stock, to stockholders of record on May 20, payable on June 5.

June   5. Paid the dividends.

Sept. 18. Discovered that building maintenance expense of $20,000 incurred in the preceding fiscal year had been charged to the buildings account and that depreciation of $500 had been taken thereon. Correct through Retained Earnings.

Nov. 5. Declared semiannual dividends of $1.25 on the preferred stock and 25¢ on the common stock. In addition, a 10% common stock dividend was declared on the common stock. The fair market value of the common stock to be issued is estimated at $15.

Dec. 5. Paid the cash dividends and issued the certificates for the common stock dividend.

31. The board of directors authorized the appropriation necessitated by the holdings of treasury stock.

Instructions: Record the above transactions in general journal form.

22-3. The retained earnings accounts of University Products, Inc. for the current fiscal year ended December 31 are presented below.

Retained Earnings Appropriated for Plant Expansion

Jan	1	Balance.....................			90,000
Dec	31	Transfer from retained earnings		60,000	150,000

Retained Earnings Appropriated for Treasury Stock Purchased

Jan	1	Balance.....................			45,000
Dec	31	Transfer to retained earnings...	20,000		25,000

Retained Earnings

Jan	1	Balance...................			292,000
Mar	10	Overstatement of depreciation charges of preceding year....		16,000	
	12	Understatement of income tax of preceding year..........	7,000		
Aug	18	Gain on sale of land........		45,000	
Nov	15	Cash dividend..............	50,000		
	15	Stock dividend.............	100,000		
Dec	31	Organization costs written off..	3,000		
	31	Net income after income tax....		185,000	
	31	Transfer to appropriation for plant expansion..........	60,000		
	31	Transfer from appropriation for treasury stock purchased....		20,000	338,000

Instructions: Prepare a retained earnings statement for the fiscal year ended December 31.

22-4. The capital accounts of the Bluefield Corporation on January 1 of the current year were as follows:

Preferred 4% Stock, $50 par (6,000 shares authorized and issued)...	$ 300,000
Common Stock, $10 par (500,000 shares authorized, 200,000 shares issued).......................................	2,000,000
Discount on Preferred Stock.............................	12,000
Premium on Common Stock.............................	200,000
Retained Earnings Appropriated for Treasury Stock Purchased.	135,000
Retained Earnings.............................	625,000
Treasury Stock (common, 15,000 shares at cost)............	135,000

Transactions related to capital accounts during the year are summarized below:

(a) On January 5 paid 50¢ quarterly dividend on the preferred stock and $2 annual dividend on the common stock. Both dividends had been properly recorded when declared in December of the past year. The treasury stock had been purchased prior to this declaration.

(b) Called in the preferred stock for retirement at $53, paying in addition accrued dividends of 30¢ a share.

(c) Sold 9,000 shares of treasury stock at $13.

(d) Discovered that a sales invoice for $8,000, dated the preceding December 31, was recorded as a sale on account in January. Payment was received in February. The merchandise had been excluded from the inventory at December 31.

(e) Sold 5,000 shares of treasury stock at $9.

(f) Declared annual dividends on the common stock of $1.50, payable in January of next year.

(g) Adjusted the appropriation for treasury stock purchased to the amount required.

(h) Appropriated $100,000 of retained earnings for plant expansion.

(i) Expense and Revenue Summary has a credit balance of $221,000 after closing all expense and revenue accounts, including Income Tax. Close the expense and revenue summary account.

Instructions: (1) Set up T accounts for all capital accounts listed above and enter the balances as of January 1.

(2) Journalize the transactions for the year, posting to the capital accounts. Set up additional capital accounts as needed.

(3) Prepare the stockholders' equity section of the balance sheet at December 31 of the current year.

(4) Prepare a retained earnings statement for the year.

(5) Determine the book value of the common stock at December 31.

22-5. The capital section of the balance sheet of the Bedford Corporation as of December 31, 1961, is given on the following page.

Included in the current asset section of the balance sheet were 1,000 shares of treasury stock at cost, $60,000.

Selected transactions occurring in 1962, together with related information, are given below the capital section.

Capital

Paid-in Capital:
Common stock, $50 par (20,000
  shares authorized, 16,000 shares
  issued)...................... $800,000
Premium on common stock........   64,000
    Total paid-in capital........... $864,000
Retained earnings:
  Appropriated:
    For contingencies.............. $50,000
    For treasury stock purchased.... 60,000 $110,000
  Unappropriated................   260,000
    Total retained earnings.........   370,000
Total capital..................... $1,234,000

Feb. 15. Discovered the following errors and made necessary corrections
         through the retained earnings account:

         (a) New machinery with an estimated life of 10 years was purchased
             on January 4, 1961. The cost of freight and installation, amount-
             ing to $4,000, was charged to repairs expense. (Depreciation
             method used is declining balance at twice the straight-line rate.)
         (b) Invoices for merchandise totaling $10,000, dated December 31,
             1961, were not recorded until January. The merchandise was
             not included in the inventory at December 31, 1961.
         (c) The 1961 charge for income tax was understated by $12,000.
             The additional tax has not been paid.

Mar. 15. Sold 300 shares of treasury stock at $70, receiving cash.
June 12. Received land for a plant site valued at $15,000 from the Evendale
         Industrial Development Council as a donation.
Nov. 30. Declared a cash dividend of $3 per share to stockholders of record
         on December 12, payable on December 21.
Dec. 15. Issued 400 shares of treasury stock to employees as a bonus. Market
         price of the stock, $75.
Dec. 18. Declared a 5% stock dividend to stockholders of record on Decem-
         ber 29, to be issued on January 15. The market value of the stock
         to be issued is $75.
Dec. 21. Paid the cash dividend.
Dec. 31. After closing all revenue and expense accounts, Expense and Revenue
         Summary has a credit balance of $130,000. Closed the expense and
         revenue summary account.
Dec. 31. Reduced the treasury stock restriction on retained earnings to the
         appropriate amount.

Instructions: (1) Set up T accounts for the accounts appearing in the capital
section of the balance sheet and enter the balances as of January 1, 1962.
   (2) Prepare general journal entries to record the transactions and other
information, posting to the capital accounts. Set up additional capital accounts
as needed.
   (3) Prepare the capital section of the balance sheet as of December 31, 1962.
   (4) Prepare a retained earnings statement for the year.

Corporations—long-term obligations and investments

Financing corporations

Thus far in the discussion of corporations it has been assumed that the funds required for the enterprise were obtained by issuing stock. Those purchasing stock acquire an ownership equity and expect to receive income on their investment in the form of dividends. It has been shown that the amount of dividends distributed depends upon earnings of the corporation and the dividend policies of the board of directors. The holders of preferred stock have a prior but limited claim on earnings, and the holders of common stock have a residual but unlimited claim on earnings.

Because of the ease of transferring stock and the availability of earnings through dividends, corporations have generally found investors ready to exchange their money for shares of stock. Some corporations have acquired the property of competitors in exchange for shares of their own stock. The great business of investment banking and the huge volume of trading on the stock exchanges give evidence of the present-day interest in corporate stocks.

Corporations may obtain part of the funds needed for a long period of time by borrowing. When funds are borrowed through the issuance of bonds, there is a definite commitment to pay interest and to repay the principal at some future date. Those buying the bonds are creditors, and their claims for interest and for repayment of principal rank ahead of the stockholders. Many financial institutions and nonprofit foundations are restricted by law or charter as to the proportion of their funds that may be invested in stocks. In addition, many individuals prefer to have greater certainty as to income (even though a lesser amount) and greater safety of principal than are afforded by stocks.

There are many factors that influence the incorporators or the board of directors in deciding upon the best means of obtaining funds. The subject will be limited here to a brief examination of the effect of different financing methods on the income of the corporation and its common stockholders. To illustrate, assume that three different plans for financing a $4,000,000 corporation are under consideration by its organizers. The three plans are as follows, assuming in each case that the securities will be issued at par or face value:

Plan 1.	Common stock — total par value.....................	$4,000,000
Plan 2.	5% preferred stock — total par value..................	$2,000,000
	Common stock — total par value.....................	$2,000,000
Plan 3.	4% bonds — total face value.........................	$2,000,000
	5% preferred stock — total par value..................	$1,000,000
	Common stock — total par value.....................	$1,000,000

The incorporators estimate that the enterprise will earn $600,000 annually, before considering interest on the bonds or income taxes, which are estimated at 50% of net income. The tabulation below indicates the amount of earnings that would be available to common stockholders under each of the three plans.

	PLAN 1	PLAN 2	PLAN 3
4% bonds................................			$2,000,000
5% preferred stock, $100 par................		$2,000,000	1,000,000
Common stock, $100 par....................	$4,000,000	2,000,000	1,000,000
Total.....................................	$4,000,000	$4,000,000	$4,000,000
Earnings before interest or income taxes........	$ 600,000	$ 600,000	$ 600,000
Deduct: Interest on bonds....................			80,000
Balance...................................	$ 600,000	$ 600,000	$ 520,000
Deduct: Income taxes.......................	300,000	300,000	260,000
Net income...............................	$ 300,000	$ 300,000	$ 260,000
Dividends on preferred stock.................		100,000	50,000
Available for dividends on common stock........	$ 300,000	$ 200,000	$ 210,000
Earnings per share on common stock..........	$ 7.50	$ 10.00	$ 21.00

According to the first plan, the earnings per share on the common stock would be $7.50 per share. Under the second plan, the effect of issuing 5% preferred stock for half of the capitalization results in $10 earnings per common share. The issuance of 4% bonds in plan three, with the remaining capitalization split between preferred and common, results in a return of $21 per share on common stock. Obviously, under this set of conditions the third plan is the most attractive for common stockholders. As the total of assumed earnings increases beyond $600,000, the spread between the yield to common stockholders under plan 1 and plan 3 would become even greater.

In the example the estimate of the earning capacity of the corporation is perhaps optimistic. As successively smaller amounts of earnings are assumed, the comparative attractiveness of the second and third plans decreases. This is illustrated by the tabulation below, in which earnings, before deducting interest and income taxes, are assumed to be $200,000.

	PLAN 1	PLAN 2	PLAN 3
4% bonds.....................................			$2,000,000
5% preferred stock, $100 par.................		$2,000,000	1,000,000
Common stock, $100 par.....................	$4,000,000	2,000,000	1,000,000
Total......................................	$4,000,000	$4,000,000	$4,000,000
Earnings before interest or income taxes........	$ 200,000	$ 200,000	$ 200,000
Deduct: Interest on bonds....................			80,000
Balance....................................	$ 200,000	$ 200,000	$ 120,000
Deduct: Income taxes.......................	100,000	100,000	60,000
Net income................................	$ 100,000	$ 100,000	$ 60,000
Dividends on preferred stock.................		100,000	50,000
Available for dividends on common stock......	$ 100,000	—	$ 10,000
Earnings per share on common stock..........	$ 2.50	—	$ 1.00

Bonds payable

When corporations borrow a large amount for a comparatively long period of time, they may issue bonds rather than promissory notes. The total amount of a bond issue is divided into units, which may be of varying denominations. Ordinarily the standard denomination, called the *face value* or the *maturity value*, is $1,000. The contract between the corporation and the bondholder is termed the *bond indenture*. The interest on bonds may be payable at annual, semiannual, or quarterly intervals. Most bonds provide for payment on a semiannual basis.

Bonds are classified in various ways. As to the method of transfer and payment of interest, they may be *registered bonds* or *bearer bonds*. Registered bonds may be transferred from one owner to another only by proper endorsement on the certificate, and the issuing corporation maintains a record of the name and address of each bondholder. Interest payments are made by check to the owner of record. Title to bearer bonds, which are also referred to as *coupon bonds*, is transferred by delivery. Interest coupons for the entire term of the bonds are attached to the bond certificate. The coupons are in the form of checks or drafts payable to bearer, and at each interest date the holder detaches the appropriate coupon and presents it at his bank in much the same manner as an ordinary check.

When all bonds of an issue mature at the same time, they may be called *term bonds*. If the maturities vary they are called *serial bonds*. For example, one tenth of an issue of $1,000,000, or $100,000, may mature eleven years from the issuance date, another $100,000 may mature twelve years from the issuance date, and so on until the final $100,000 matures at the end of the twentieth year. Bonds that may be exchanged for other securities under specified conditions are called *convertible bonds*. If the issuing corporation reserves the right to pay off the bonds before maturity, they are referred to as *callable bonds*.

A *secured bond* is one that gives the bondholder a claim on particular assets in the event of nonpayment. The properties mortgaged or pledged as security may be specific buildings and equipment, the entire plant, or stocks and bonds of other companies owned by the debtor corporation. Bonds issued on the basis of the general credit of the corporation are called *debenture bonds*.

The liability incurred by the issuance of bonds is recorded in the account Bonds Payable. If there is more than one bond issue, a separate account should be maintained for each issue. Bonds Payable are reported on the balance sheet as long-term or fixed liabilities. As the maturity date comes within one year of the balance sheet date, they should be transferred to the current liability classification if they are to be paid out of current assets. If they are to be paid with segregated funds or if they are to be replaced with another bond issue, they should remain in the noncurrent category and their disposition disclosed by an explanatory note. The listing in the balance sheet should include data as to security, interest rate, and due date.

All bonds of a particular issue are given the same date and the interest begins to accrue thereafter. If the bonds are issued at face value on this date, the transaction is recorded by a debit to Cash and a credit to Bonds Payable. Frequently a part or all of the bonds are sold some time after the interest has begun to accrue. In such cases the purchaser is required to pay the accrued interest. To illustrate, assume that $4\frac{1}{2}\%$ bonds in the face amount of $100,000, dated January 1, are sold on March 1 at 100 plus accrued interest. Prices of bonds are stated in terms of percentage of face value, hence the price "100" indicates that the bonds are sold at face value. The entry to record the issuance of the bonds is:

Mar. 1 Cash......................................	100,750	
Bonds Payable.............................		100,000
Interest Expense...........................		750

The credit of $750 to the interest expense account is in reality interest payable. It is simpler, however, to credit the expense account so that when the interest is paid the entire amount of the payment may be debited to the expense account. The entry to record the semiannual interest payment on June 30 is:

| June 30 | Interest Expense..................................... | 2,250 | |
| | Cash.. | | 2,250 |

The debit balance of $1,500 ($2,250 − $750) in the interest expense account at June 30 represents the interest expense for the four months that the bonds have been outstanding.

Bonds sold at a premium

Bonds may be sold at a price above or below face value, depending upon the rate of interest offered and the general credit standing of the corporation. If a corporation has unusually high credit or offers a rate of interest that is higher than the market rate, investors may be willing to pay a premium for the bonds. For example, assume that on January 1 a corporation issues $100,000 of 5%, 10-year bonds at 106, with interest payable annually on January 1. The transaction is recorded as follows:

Jan. 1	Cash..	106,000	
	Bonds Payable............................		100,000
	Premium on Bonds Payable.................		6,000

The investors paid the premium because they were willing to lend money to the corporation at less than the contract rate of 5%. The premium represents an advance payment by the investors for the privilege of receiving interest in excess of the prevailing market rate.

The issuing corporation has incurred two liabilities: (1) to repay $100,000, the face amount of the bonds in 10 years, and (2) to pay annual interest of $5,000 for 10 years. The $6,000 premium is not income to the corporation; rather it is interest collected from the bondholders that will be repaid to them over the life of the bonds. This may be demonstrated by determining the movement of cash related to the bond issue. As shown by the following tabulation, the excess of the cash paid during the 10-year period over the cash received from the sale of the bonds is $44,000. This represents the total interest expense for the 10-year period.

Cash to be paid:			
Face of the bonds.......................................		$100,000	
Interest — 10 payments of $5,000 each (5% of $100,000)		50,000	$150,000
Cash received:			
Face of the bonds.......................................		$100,000	
Premium on the bonds..................................		6,000	106,000
Total interest expense for 10 years.....................			$ 44,000
Interest expense per year...............................			$ 4,400

The total interest expense for the life of the bonds is spread ratably over the ten years by amortizing $1/10$ of the premium against interest expense each year. The entry to record the payment of interest is:

Dec. 31	Interest Expense..............................	5,000	
	Cash.......................................		5,000

Premium on the bonds is amortized by the following entry:

Dec. 31	Premium on Bonds Payable.....................	600	
	Interest Expense.............................		600

The debit of $5,000 to the expense account in the first entry is partially offset by the $600 credit to the expense account in the second entry, leaving a net interest expense of $4,400 for the year. At the time the bonds mature, the premium account will be completely written off.

Bonds sold at a discount

When the contract rate of interest on a bond issue is less than the prevailing market rate for comparable bonds, the bonds can be sold only at a discount. For example, assume that on January 1 a corporation issues 4%, 10-year bonds with a face value of $100,000. The going rate of interest on similar securities being somewhat in excess of 4%, the bonds are sold at 96. The entry for the transaction is:

Jan. 1	Cash..	96,000	
	Discount on Bonds Payable....................	4,000	
	Bonds Payable..............................		100,000

The bond discount is not an immediate loss or expense to the corporation. Rather, it represents a deferred charge to interest expense. The corporation has contracted to repay at maturity an amount greater than it received in cash. In return, however, it will pay interest at a lower rate than the prevailing one. The discount may be considered analogous to interest deducted in advance when a note is discounted.

The corporation contracts to pay: (1) $100,000, the face amount of the bonds, in 10 years, and (2) annual interest of $4,000 for 10 years. The total interest cost for the ten years, as indicated in the tabulation below, will be $44,000, or $4,400 per year on a straight line basis.

Cash to be paid:		
Face of the bonds..................................	$100,000	
Interest — 10 payments of $4,000 each (4% of $100,000)....	40,000	$140,000
Cash received:		
Face of the bonds..................................	$100,000	
Less discount on the bonds.........................	4,000	96,000
Total interest expense for 10 years......................		$ 44,000
Interest expense per year..............................		$ 4,400

The entry for the payment of the annual interest and the entry to amortize the discount are:

```
Dec. 31   Interest Expense...............................   4,000
              Cash........................................              4,000

      31   Interest Expense...............................    400
              Discount on Bonds Payable...................               400
```

Over the life of the bonds the charges to the interest expense account will total $44,000, and the bond discount account will be in balance when the bonds fall due.

Another method of amortizing bond premium and discount emphasizes a uniform *rate* of interest over the years rather than an equal amortization each year. The accounting principles, however, are the same.

Extended illustration of accounting for bond premium

The two preceding illustrations were intentionally simplified in order to emphasize the basic principles. In both illustrations it was assumed that: (1) the bonds were sold on the issuance date, (2) the interest was payable annually, and (3) the interest payment date coincided with the last day of the fiscal year. In actual practice there is often interest accrued on the bonds at the time of sale, the interest is usually payable semiannually, and neither of the interest payment dates may coincide with the end of the fiscal year. To illustrate the effect of these factors, assume that on April 1, 10-year, 6% bonds dated March 1, with a face value of $100,000, are sold to an insurance company for $105,950, plus accrued interest. The interest is payable on March 1 and September 1, and the corporation fiscal year ends on December 31. All entries related to the bonds during the fiscal year in which they are issued are presented below, together with supporting data:

Sale of bonds

Premium on the bonds, $5,950. Interest accrued on $100,000 at 6% for one month (March 1 — April 1), $500.

```
Apr. 1   Cash.......................................   106,450
              Bonds Payable............................              100,000
              Premium on Bonds Payable.................                5,950
              Interest Expense.........................                  500
```

Payment of semiannual interest

Interest for the six-month period March 1 to September 1, $3,000.

```
Sept. 1   Interest Expense............................    3,000
               Cash.....................................               3,000
```

Adjusting entry for interest accrued at end of fiscal year

Interest accrued for the four-month period September 1 to December 31 is $2,000.

Dec. 31   Interest Expense........................   2,000
               Interest Payable........................   2,000

Amortization of bond premium

The bonds run 10 years or 120 months from March 1. They were not sold until April 1, however, so the corporation has the use of the borrowed funds for 119 months. Time elapsed from April 1 to December 31, 9 months. Therefore the amount of premium to be amortized is 9/119 × $5,950, or $450.

Dec. 31   Premium on Bonds Payable................   450
               Interest Expense........................   450

After the books are closed as of December 31 the entry accruing the bond interest should be reversed. The interest expense account for the year in which the bonds were issued and for the following fiscal year appears below. The entries for the remaining years will follow the pattern of the second year, except for the year in which the bonds are paid. It may be noted that the interest expense for the 9-month period, April 1 to December 31, is $4,050, which is three fourths of $5,400, the interest expense for the succeeding 12-month period.

INTEREST EXPENSE

Sept. 1	Semiannual payment	3,000	Apr. 1	Accrual at time of sale	500
Dec. 31	Adjustment	2,000	Dec. 31	Premium amortization	450
			31	Exp. & Rev. Summary	4,050
		5,000			5,000
Mar. 1	Semiannual payment	3,000	Jan. 1	Reversal	2,000
Sept. 1	Semiannual payment	3,000	Dec. 31	Premium amortization	600
Dec. 31	Adjustment	2,000	31	Exp. & Rev. Summary	5,400
		8,000			8,000
			Jan. 1	Reversal	2,000

Bond discount and bond premium on the balance sheet

The balance of the bond discount account is viewed as deferred interest that will be gradually added to interest expense over the life of the bonds. It is ordinarily reported on the balance sheet under the caption "Deferred expense" or "Deferred charges," which is usually the last subheading of the asset section.

Premium on bonds is considered to be an advance of interest that is returned to bondholders as a part of the periodic interest payments. It is ordinarily reported on the balance sheet under the caption "Deferred credits," which is usually the last subheading of the liability section.

There is good theoretical justification for treating bond discount or premium as contra accounts related to the bonds payable account. For example, a $100,000 bond issue sold at 95 is reported, according to this view, as bonds payable of $100,000 less discount of $5,000, or a net liability of $95,000. As the discount is amortized, the net amount of the liability gradually increases until it reaches the face value of $100,000 at maturity. An objection to this approach is that the agreement requires the payment of face value, and it is that amount for which the corporation is liable.

Bond sinking fund

The indenture may provide that funds for the payment of bonds at maturity be accumulated over the life of the issue. The amounts set aside are kept separate from other assets in a special fund called a *sinking fund*. Cash deposited in the fund is ordinarily invested in income-producing securities. The periodic deposits plus the earnings on the securities should approximately equal the face amount of the bonds at maturity. Control over the fund may be exercised by the corporation or it may be in the hands of a *trustee*, which is usually a bank or trust company.

When cash is transferred to the sinking fund, an account called Sinking Fund Cash is debited and Cash is credited. The purchase of securities is recorded by a debit to Sinking Fund Securities and a credit to Sinking Fund Cash. As interest or dividends on the investments are received, the cash is debited to Sinking Fund Cash and Sinking Fund Income is credited. To illustrate the accounting for a bond sinking fund, assume that the Arrow Corporation issues $100,000 of 10-year bonds dated January 1, with the provision that equal annual deposits be made in the bond sinking fund at the end of each of the ten years. It is estimated that the fund securities will yield approximately 3% per year. Reference to compound interest tables indicates that an annual deposit of approximately $8,725 is sufficient to provide a fund of $100,000 at the end of ten years. The pattern of entries for the fund transactions is as follows:

Deposit of cash in the fund

A deposit is made at the end of each of the ten years.

Dec. 31 Sinking Fund Cash.............................	8,725	
Cash.......................................		8,725

Purchase of securities

The time of purchase and the amount invested at one time vary, depending upon market conditions and unit price of securities purchased.

Jan. 6 Sinking Fund Securities.........................	8,700	
Sinking Fund Cash...........................		8,700

Receipt of income from securities

Interest and dividends are received at different times during the year. The amount earned per year increases as the fund increases. The entry below summarizes the receipt of income for the year on the securities purchased with the first deposit.

Dec. 31 Sinking Fund Cash............................. 260
         Sinking Fund Income.........................   260

Sale of securities

Securities may be sold from time to time and the proceeds reinvested. Prior to maturity all securities are converted into cash. The entry below records the sale of securities at the end of the tenth year.

Dec. 31 Sinking Fund Cash........................... 88,900
         Sinking Fund Securities.....................   88,700
         Gain on Sale of Securities..................   200

Payment of bonds

The cash available in the fund at the end of the tenth year is made up of:

Proceeds from sales of securities..............	$ 88,900
Income earned in tenth year.................	2,700
Last annual deposit........................	8,725
Total...................................	$100,325

Dec. 31 Bonds Payable........................... 100,000
         Cash....................................   325
         Sinking Fund Cash......................   100,325

In the above illustration the fund exceeded the amount required by $325. This was transferred to the regular cash account. If the fund had amounted to $99,500 the regular cash account would have been drawn upon for the $500 deficiency.

Sinking Fund Income represents earnings of the corporation and is reported on the income statement as "Other Income." The cash and securities comprising the sinking fund are classified on the balance sheet as *Investments*. The investments section ordinarily appears immediately below the current assets section.

Restriction of dividends

In order to safeguard the maintenance of working capital during the period that the bonds are outstanding, the bond indenture may provide that earnings of a specific amount be unavailable for dividends. Assuming that the Arrow Corporation, in the example above, is required by the indenture to appropriate $10,000 each year for the ten-year life of the bonds, the following entry would be made annually:

Dec. 31 Retained Earnings......................... 10,000
         Retained Earnings Appropriated for Bonded
            Indebtedness...........................   10,000

As was indicated in the preceding chapter, an appropriation has no direct relationship to a sinking fund; each is independent of the other. When there is both a fund and an appropriation for the same purpose, the appropriation may be said to be *funded*.

Redemption

Many bond contracts provide that the corporation may redeem the bonds within a stated period of time at a stipulated price, usually at a premium. Such bonds are known as *callable bonds*. A corporation may also retire all or a portion of its bonds before maturity by purchasing them on the open market. Such action is advisable when the bonds are selling at less than their book value and the corporation has available cash. The book value of the bonds is the face value plus the unamortized premium or minus the unamortized discount.

When a corporation retires bonds at a price below their book value, the corporation realizes a gain; if the price is in excess of book value, a loss is incurred. To illustrate redemption and retirement, assume that on June 30 the Barton Corporation has a bond issue of $100,000 outstanding, on which there is an unamortized premium of $4,000. The corporation has the option of calling the bonds at 105, which it exercises on this date. The entry to record the redemption is:

June 30 Bonds Payable...........................	100,000	
Premium on Bonds Payable................	4,000	
Loss on Redemption of Bonds..............	1,000	
Cash..................................		105,000

If the bonds were not callable, the corporation might purchase a portion on the open market and retire them. Assuming that the corporation does buy $25,000 of bonds at 96 on June 30, the entry to record the retirement would be:

June 30 Bonds Payable...........................	25,000	
Premium on Bonds Payable................	1,000	
Cash..................................		24,000
Gain on Retirement of Bonds.............		2,000

It should be noted that only the portion of the premium relating to the bonds retired is written off the books. The difference between the book value of the liability, $26,000, and the cash paid, $24,000, is recognized as a gain. The company is better off by $2,000 because it was able to liquidate a liability for less than the amount payable.

Long-term notes

Corporations may issue notes in place of bonds. The notes may run for a period of 2 to 5 years, anticipating a bond issue when the bond market is more favorable. Or they may be for longer periods, up to 25 years, to avoid the expense of a bond issue, when funds are available from financial institutions such as life insurance companies. For example, if funds are obtained from three or four large life insurance companies, the transaction is less involved than is dealing with thousands of bond-holders.

These corporation notes may have many features similar to bond issues. They may provide for a note sinking fund. They commonly have other safeguards to insure payment at maturity. They differ from bond issues in that they are ordinarily placed privately with a few lenders and in that they do not commonly involve premiums or discounts.

The account maintained with an issue of long-term notes is similar to that maintained with an issue of bonds. The title of the account should indicate the nature of the issue. The balance is reported as a long-term liability on the balance sheet.

Investments in stocks and bonds

The issuance of stocks and bonds, the declaration and the payment of dividends, and other related transactions have thus far been discussed from the standpoint of the issuing corporation. Whenever a corporation records a transaction between itself and the owners of its stock or bonds, there is a reciprocal entry on the books of the investor. Investments in corporate securities may be made by individuals, partnerships, industrial corporations, financial corporations such as banks and life insurance companies, and other types of organizations. In this and the following sections of the chapter, attention will be given to some of the principles underlying the accounting for investments in stocks and bonds on the books of investors.

Corporate securities may be purchased directly from the issuing corporation or from other investors. Stocks and bonds may be *listed* on an organized exchange, or they may be *unlisted*, in which case they are said to be bought and sold *over the counter*. The services of a broker are usually employed in buying and selling both listed and unlisted securities. The record of transactions on stock exchanges is reported daily in the financial pages of newspapers. This record usually includes data on the volume of sales and the high, low, and closing prices for each security traded during the day. Prices for stocks are quoted in terms of fractional dollars, $1/8$ of a dollar being the usual minimum fraction. Some low-priced stocks are sold in lower fractions of a dollar, such as $1/16$ or $1/32$. A price of $40^3/_8$ per share means \$40.375; a price of $40^1/_2$ means \$40.50; and so on. As indicated earlier, prices for bonds are quoted as a percentage of face value; thus the price of a \$1,000 bond quoted at $104^1/_2$ would be \$1,045.

The cost of securities purchased includes not only the price paid but also other costs incident to the purchase, such as broker's commission and postage charges for delivery. When bonds are purchased between interest dates, the purchaser pays the seller the interest accrued from the last interest payment date to the date of purchase. The amount of the interest paid should be debited to Interest Income, as it is an offset against the amount that will be received at the next interest date. To illustrate, assume that a \$1,000 bond is purchased at 102 plus brokerage fees of \$5.30 and accrued interest of \$10.20. The entry to record the transaction, in general journal form, is as follows:

April 2	Investment in Taylor Co. Bonds..............	1,025.30	
	Interest Income...........................	10.20	
	Cash....................................		1,035.50

When stocks are purchased between dividend dates, there is no separate charge for the pro rata amount of the dividend. Dividends do not accrue from day to day, since they become an obligation of the issuing corporation only as they are declared by the directors. The price of stocks may be affected by the anticipated dividend as the usual declaration date approaches, but this anticipated dividend is only one of many factors that influence stock prices. Commissions and delivery charges paid to brokers are, of course, added to the price paid in arriving at the total cost of stocks purchased.

Temporary investments

A corporation may have on hand an amount of cash considerably in excess of its immediate requirements, but it may believe that this cash will be needed in operating the business, possibly within the coming year. Rather than allow this excess cash to lie idle until it is actually needed, the corporation may invest all or a portion of it in income-yielding securities. Such securities are known as *temporary investments*. These investments may actually be held by the corporation for several years, but they are still considered to be temporary if they can be turned into cash readily at any time that the business needs additional cash in its normal operations. Because of their ready marketability and comparative price stability, bonds, notes, and other evidences of indebtedness issued by the federal government are particularly suitable for this purpose.

Securities representing a temporary investment are classified on the balance sheet as current assets and are shown immediately below cash. They are usually valued at cost or at the lower of cost or market. If their market value declines substantially below cost and there is evidence that the fluctuation is not temporary, the securities should be stated at market value. The reduction in value is treated as a loss of the period. If the same securities are still owned at a subsequent balance sheet date and their market price has increased, the current market value should be disclosed parenthetically on the balance sheet.

Minor declines in the market value of temporary investments need not be given recognition in the accounts. The market value at the balance sheet date may be disclosed by a footnote or a parenthetical statement such as that illustrated on page 520.

Declines in the market value of securities are not recognized as losses for income tax purposes regardless of whether they are recorded in the accounts. When the securities are sold, the gain or the loss to be recognized for tax purposes is determined by comparing the proceeds from the sale with the original cost.

Long-term investments

Investments that are not a ready source of cash in the normal operations of the business are known as *long-term investments*. A business may make long-term investments simply because it has cash that it cannot use in its normal operations; but a corporation is more likely to make long-term investments for other reasons.

It is not unusual for a corporation to purchase stocks or bonds as a means of establishing or maintaining business relations with the issuing company. Such investments are ordinarily held for an indefinitely long period and are not sold so long as the relationship remains satisfactory. Corporations may also acquire all or a substantial portion of the voting stock of another corporation in order to control its activities. Similarly, a corporation may organize a new corporation for the purpose of marketing a new product, or for some other business reason, receiving stock in exchange for the assets transferred to the new corporation. Cash and securities in bond sinking funds are also considered long-term investments, as they are accumulated for the purpose of paying the bond liability.

Investments in long-term securities are recorded in the accounts at cost and are so shown on the balance sheet. Fluctuations in price subsequent to acquisition are ordinarily ignored except when there has been a material decline, in which case the value may be reduced or the facts may be disclosed by a parenthetical notation on the balance sheet.

Long-term investments are listed on the balance sheet under the caption "Investments," which ordinarily follows current assets.

Income from investments in stocks

Cash dividends declared on stock owned either as temporary investments or as long-term investments may be recorded by a debit to Dividends Receivable and a credit to Dividend Income. The receivable account is then credited when the cash is received. For federal income tax purposes dividends are not considered to be income until they are available to the stockholder. For this reason a common practice is to record dividends only as they are received. Although this is a deviation from accrual accounting, the practice ordinarily causes no material distortion of income when followed consistently.

A dividend in the form of additional shares of stock is ordinarily not income and hence no entry is necessary beyond a notation as to the additional number of shares now owned. The receipt of such a stock dividend does, however, affect the cost basis of each share of stock. For example, if a 25-share common stock dividend is received on 100 shares of common stock originally purchased for $4,500 ($45 per share), the unit cost basis of the 125 shares becomes $4,500 ÷ 125, or $36 per share.

Income from investments in bonds

Interest on bonds held as temporary investments is recorded in the same manner as interest on notes receivable. Interest received during a fiscal period is recorded as a debit to Cash and a credit to Interest Income. At the end of a fiscal period an adjusting entry debiting Interest Receivable and crediting Interest Income is made for interest accrued. After the books are closed, the entry is reversed in order that all receipts of bond interest during the year may be credited to the income account.

When interest is recorded on temporary bond investments, the fact that these investments may have been purchased for more or less than their face value is ignored. But when the cost of bonds purchased for long-term investments is greater or less than the par value, the amount of the premium or the discount may be written off over the remaining life of the bonds in much the same manner in which the debtor corporation accounts for a premium or a discount on the original issuance of the bonds. To illustrate, assume that twenty $1,000, 5% bonds of the Standard Corporation are purchased on July 1, 1961, at 105½ plus a brokerage fee of $55. Interest on the bonds is payable semiannually

on April 1 and October 1 and the bonds are due 8¾ years from the date
of purchase. Entries on the books of the purchaser at the time of purchase and for the remainder of the year would be as follows:

Transaction	Entry
JULY 1, 1961: Purchase of bonds: $20,000 par value at 105½..... $21,100 Brokerage................... 55 Total cost.................. $21,155 Accrued interest, $20,000 at 5% for 3 months, or $250.	Investment in Standard Corp. Bonds.......... 21,155 Interest Income....... 250 Cash..................... 21,405
OCTOBER 1, 1961: Receipt of semiannual interest; $20,000 at 5% for 6 months, or $500.	Cash............... 500 Interest Income..... 500

DECEMBER 31, 1961:
(a) Interest accrued: $20,000 at 5% for
    3 months, or $250.
 	
(b) Amortization of premium: $1,155 for
    8¾ years, or $66 for 6 months.
	Interest Receivable.... 250
	   Interest Income..... 250
	
	Interest Income....... 66
	   Investment in Stand-
	   ard Corp. Bonds..... 66

The net effect of the four entries in the interest income account is a
credit of $434, which represents interest at 5% for 6 months ($500) less
amortization of premium for 6 months ($66). By following the foregoing
procedures, the premium of $1,155 will be amortized against interest
income over the life of the bonds, and the investment account will be
reduced to $20,000 at the maturity date.

A similar procedure may be applied to bonds purchased at a price
below face value. The amount of the discount is accumulated by
periodic entries debiting the investment account and crediting Interest
Income. It may be noted that when speculative bonds are purchased
at a substantial discount, it would be imprudent to accumulate the
discount because of the uncertainty of payment at maturity.

Sale of investments

When shares of stock that have been held as either temporary or
long-term investments are sold, the cash account is debited for the
proceeds (selling price less commission and other costs) and the investment account is credited for the cost of the shares sold. If there is a gain,

it is credited to an account entitled Gain on Sale of Investments; if there is a loss, it is debited to an account entitled Loss on Sale of Investments.

A sale of bonds held as temporary investments is recorded in the same manner as a sale of stocks. A sale of bonds held as a long-term investment is also recorded in the same manner except when a premium or a discount has been amortized. If a premium or a discount has been amortized, the investment account is credited for the book value of the investment and not its original cost. The gain or the loss is then the difference between the book value and the amount received. For example, assume that the bonds of the Standard Corporation in the previous example are sold at 98 plus accrued interest on December 31, 1963. At that time the following entries are made:

Amortization of premium for year

Dec. 31	Interest Income............................	132	
	Investment in Standard Corp. Bonds.......		132

Sale of bonds and collection of accrued interest

Dec. 31	Cash....................................	19,850	
	Loss on Sale of Investments...............	1,225	
	Interest Income........................		250
	Investment in Standard Corp. Bonds.......		20,825

In the foregoing entry the investment account was credited for the book value of the bonds sold, which was determined as follows:

Cost of bonds, July 1, 1961.........................		$21,155
Deduct premium amortization: 1961................. $	66	
1962.................	132	
1963.................	132	330
Book value, December 31, 1963.....................		$20,825

Corporation balance sheet

Several examples of the capital section of corporation balance sheets have been presented in preceding chapters. An example of a complete balance sheet, illustrating other items peculiar to corporations, is presented on page 520.

It should be borne in mind that there are innumerable variations in the form of corporation financial statements, as well as many alternatives in the terminology employed. A selection of statements taken from the annual reports of a number of corporations is presented in Appendix B.

FIELDCREST CORPORATION
Balance Sheet
December 31, 1961

Assets

Current assets:
Cash..		$111,379
Marketable securities, at cost (market value, $68,000)............		70,000
Accounts and notes receivable........................	$112,000	
Less allowance for uncollectible accounts............	2,000	110,000
Inventories, at lower of cost or market.......................		172,880
Prepaid expenses..		12,000
Total current assets.....................................		$ 476,259

Investments:
Bond sinking fund..		$ 53,962
Investment in affiliated company...........................		140,000
Total investments.......................................		193,962

	Cost	Accumulated Depreciation	Book Value
Plant assets:			
Machinery and equipment.................	$600,000	$ 66,200	$533,800
Buildings...............................	220,000	79,955	140,045
Land....................................	50,000	—	50,000
Total plant assets......................	$870,000	$146,155	723,845

Intangible assets:
Goodwill..	$100,000	
Organization costs..	18,000	
Total intangible assets..................................		118,000
Total assets..		$1,512,066

Liabilities

Current liabilities:
Accounts payable..		$ 58,710
Estimated income tax payable...............................		90,500
Dividends payable..		18,000
Accrued liabilities..		7,400
Total current liabilities....................................		$ 174,610

Long-term liabilities:
Debenture 5% bonds payable, due December 31, 1969...........	200,000

Deferred credit:
Premium on bonds payable.................................	5,600
Total liabilities...	$ 380,210

Stockholders' equity

Paid-in capital:
Common stock, $20 par (50,000 shares authorized, 20,000 shares issued)........................	$400,000	
Premium on common stock........................	320,000	
Total paid-in capital.................................		$720,000

Retained earnings:
Appropriated:			
For bonded indebtedness................	$ 60,000		
For plant expansion...................	150,000	$210,000	
Unappropriated................................		201,856	
Total retained earnings....................			411,856
Total stockholders' equity..................................			1,131,856
Total liabilities and stockholders' equity..........................			$1,512,066

Questions

1. Contrast the status of interest on bonds payable and cash dividends on stock in determining the income tax of corporations making such payments.

2. Identify the following terms: (a) bond indenture, (b) debenture bond, (c) coupon bond, (d) registered bond.

3. If a corporation issues 5% bonds at a time when the market rate of interest on securities of this type is lower than 5%, is it likely that the bonds will be sold at face value, at a discount, or at a premium?

4. Under what caption is discount on bonds payable reported on the balance sheet?

5. What is the purpose of a bond sinking fund?

6. To whom does the income earned on sinking fund securities belong: the corporation, the trustee, or the bondholders?

7. What is the purpose of establishing an appropriation of retained earnings for bonded indebtedness?

8. Bonds Payable has a balance of $100,000 and Discount on Bonds Payable has a balance of $2,000. If the issuing corporation purchases its bonds at 96, what is the amount of gain or loss on redemption?

9. To what account should brokerage commission on the purchase of securities be charged?

10. What is the cost of the following securities, exclusive of commissions, etc.: (a) bonds with a face value of $10,000 purchased at $97\frac{1}{2}$; (b) 100 shares of stock purchased at $45\frac{3}{4}$.

11. Is the interest accrued on bonds included in the quoted price?

12. Are brokerage commissions on the sale of securities owned considered to be an expense of the period or a reduction in the sales proceeds?

13. A stockholder owning 100 shares of Hercules Co. common stock acquired at a total cost of $4,500 receives a common stock dividend of 50 shares. (a) What is the unit cost basis of the 150 shares? (b) If the stockholder later sells 100 shares at 50, what is the gain or loss?

Exercises

1. Two companies are financed as follows:

	Company A	Company B
4% Bonds Payable, (issued at face value)....	$ 200,000	$500,000
5% Preferred Stock, $50 par..............	300,000	500,000
Common Stock, $10 par.................	1,000,000	500,000

Income taxes are estimated at 50% of net income. Determine the earnings per share of common stock if the net income before bond interest and income taxes for both companies is (a) $300,000, (b) $100,000, (c) $70,000.

2. The Fremont Corporation issues $100,000 of 10-year, 4% bonds at 98 on the first day of the fiscal year.

(a) Which is higher, the market rate of interest or the contract rate of interest?
(b) Give the entry to record the issuance of the bonds.
(c) Give the entry to amortize the discount at the end of the year.
(d) What is the amount of the bond interest expense each year?

3. The Waldorf Corporation issues $5,000,000 of 20-year bonds on the first day of the fiscal year. The bond indenture provides that a sinking fund be accumulated by twenty annual deposits, beginning at the end of the first year. The corporation expects to earn 4% on the fund and accordingly deposits $168,000 annually.

(a) Give the entry to record the first deposit.
(b) Give the entry to record the investment of the entire first deposit in securities.
(c) Assuming that the fund earns exactly 4%, give the summary entry to record receipt of the income for the year following the first deposit.

4. The bond indenture for the Waldorf Corporation bonds (Exercise 3) also provides that dividends be restricted by equal annual appropriations of retained earnings which are to total the face value of the bonds at maturity. Give the entry to record the appropriation at the end of the first year.

5. The Feldspar Corporation issued $1,500,000 of 10-year, 4% bonds dated April 1, 1961. Interest is payable semiannually on April 1 and October 1. (a) Give all entries related to the bonds in 1961, assuming that the issue was sold on July 1 for $1,429,800 plus accrued interest. (b) What reversing entry should be made on January 1, 1962?

6. Assuming that on April 1, 1963 the Feldspar Corporation (Exercise 5) purchases $100,000 of its outstanding bonds at 94 and retires them, give the entries to record the transaction.

7. Charles Reeder purchased 100 shares of Consolidated Steel Co. common stock several years ago at 64 plus brokerage fees of $25. During the current year he received a common stock dividend of 25 shares. (a) What is his cost basis per share after he received the stock dividend? (b) If he sells the 25 shares at 68, and pays brokerage fees of $10, what will be the amount of his gain or loss?

8. The Badger Corporation purchases $100,000 of 5% bonds of the Everest Corporation at 106. The bonds are due ten years from the date of purchase. (a) Assuming that they are classified as temporary investments, (1) determine the amount of the annual income, (2) determine the gain or loss when the bonds are sold at 104½ exactly three years from the date purchased (no interest accrued), (3) determine the total income from the bonds for the entire period held, including gain or loss on sale. (b) Assuming that the bonds are classified as long-term investments and the premium is amortized, make the three determinations required in (a).

Problems

23-1. The following transactions were completed by the Banner Corporation.

1961

Mar. 31. Issued $1,500,000 of 20-year, 4½% bonds at 104. Interest is payable semiannually on March 31 and September 30.

Sept. 30. Paid the semiannual interest on the bonds.

Dec. 31. Recorded the adjusting entry for interest payable.

31. Recorded amortization of premium on bonds.

1962

Jan. 1. Reversed the adjusting entry for interest payable.

Mar. 31. Paid the semiannual interest on the bonds.

Sept. 30. Paid the semiannual interest on the bonds.

Dec. 31. Recorded the adjusting entry for interest payable.

31. Recorded amortization of premium on bonds.

Instructions: (1) Record the foregoing transactions in general journal form.

(2) State the amount of the interest expense in (a) 1961 and (b) 1962.

23-2. During 1961 and 1962 Monarch Machines, Inc. completed the following transactions relating to its $2,000,000 issue of 25-year, 5% bonds dated April 30. Interest is payable on April 30 and October 31. The corporation's fiscal year is the calendar year.

1961

July 15. Sold the entire bond issue, receiving $1,934,550 plus accrued interest.

Oct. 31. Paid the semiannual interest on the bonds.

Dec. 31. Deposited $19,250 in a bond sinking fund.

31. Appropriated $36,700 of retained earnings for bonded indebtedness.

31. Recorded the adjusting entry for interest payable.

31. Recorded amortization of bond discount.

31. Closed the interest expense account.

1962

Jan. 1. Reversed the adjustment for interest payable.

10. Purchased various securities with sinking fund cash at a cost of $18,850.

Apr. 30. Paid the semiannual interest on the bonds.

Oct. 31. Paid the semiannual interest on the bonds.

Dec. 31. Recorded the receipt of $960 of income on sinking fund securities, depositing the cash in the sinking fund.

31. Deposited $40,000 cash in the sinking fund.

31. Appropriated $80,000 of retained earnings for bonded indebtedness.

31. Recorded the adjusting entry for interest payable.

31. Recorded amortization of bond discount.

31. Closed the interest expense account.

Instructions: (1) Record the transactions in general journal form. (Carry computations to the nearest dollar.)

(2) Prepare a columnar table, using the headings shown below, and present the information for each of the two years:

				Account Balances at End of Year		
	Bond Interest			Sinking Fund		
	Expense for	Bonds	Discount			Appropriation
Year	Year	Payable	on Bonds	Cash	Securities	for B.I.

23-3. The following transactions relate to certain investments of the Sacramento Corporation:

1961

Apr. **1.** Purchased $200,000 of Acme Corporation's 10-year, 6% coupon bonds, dated March 1, 1961, directly from the issuing company for $192,860 plus accrued interest. Acme is an important customer of the Sacramento Corporation and it is expected that the bonds will be held until maturity.

May **10.** Purchased as a long-term investment 1,200 common shares of Bell, Inc. at 61½ plus commission and other costs of $420.

July **15.** Received a semiannual dividend of $1.75 per share on the Bell, Inc. stock.

Sept. **1.** Deposited the coupons for semiannual interest on the Acme Corporation bonds.

Dec. **31.** Recorded the adjustment for interest receivable on the Acme Corporation Bonds.

     31. Recorded the amortization of discount on the Acme Corporation bonds.

1962

Jan. **1.** Reversed the adjustment for interest receivable.

Jan. **15.** Received a semiannual dividend of $1.75 per share and a 10% stock dividend on the Bell Inc. stock.

Mar. **1.** Deposited coupons for semiannual interest on the Acme Corporation bonds.

July **1.** Sold the Acme Corporation bonds at 98½ plus accrued interest. The broker deducted $450 for commission and taxes, remitting the balance.

July **15.** Received the semiannual dividend of $1.75 per share on the Bell, Inc. stock.

Oct. **1.** Sold 300 shares of Bell, Inc. stock at 65. The broker deducted commission and other costs of $85, remitting the balance.

Instructions: Record the foregoing transactions in general journal form.

23-4. The rough draft of the balance sheet for the Fletcher Equipment Company as of June 30 of the current year, appearing on page 525, is presented to you for review.

During the course of your review and examination of the accounts and records, you assemble the following pertinent data:

(a) Marketable securities are stated at cost; the market value is $99,000.

(b) Treasury stock is composed of 800 shares purchased at $60 a share.

(c) Accounts receivable, machinery, buildings, land, and goodwill are stated at cost. Losses from uncollectible accounts and depreciation expenses have been recorded correctly in the usual manner.

(d) Inventories are valued at the lower of cost or market.

Assets

Current assets:

Cash...................................		$156,000
Marketable securities....................		102,000
Treasury stock..........................	$ 48,000	
Deduct reserve for treasury stock purchased	48,000	
Accounts receivable		135,000
Inventories.............................	$505,000	
Deduct reserve for possible price declines..	100,000	405,000
Discount on bonds payable...............		5,000
Prepaid expenses........................		6,000
Total current assets....................		$ 809,000

Plant assets:

Machinery.............................	$520,000	
Buildings..............................	220,000	
Land..................................	40,000	
Goodwill..............................	50,000	
Total plant assets.....................		830,000
Total assets............................		$1,639,000

Liabilities

Accounts payable........................		$ 98,000
Dividends payable.......................		48,000
Accrued liabilities......................		18,000
Bonds payable..........................	$350,000	
Deduct bond sinking fund...............	45,000	305,000
Total liabilities.....................		$ 469,000

Stockholders' equity

Paid-in capital:

Common stock..........................		$400,000

Earnings and reserves:

Premium on common stock..............	$ 85,000	
Reserve for uncollectible accounts........	15,000	
Reserve for depreciation — machinery.....	190,000	
Reserve for depreciation — building.......	85,000	
Reserve for income taxes................	75,000	
Retained earnings.......................	320,000	770,000
Total stockholders' equity.............		1,170,000
Total liabilities and stockholders' equity......		$1,639,000

(e) Bonds payable (20-year) are due 15 years from the balance sheet date. They are secured by a first mortgage and bear 5% interest.

(f) The common stock is $20 par; 50,000 shares are authorized, 20,000 shares have been issued.

(g) The reserve for income taxes is the estimated liability for taxes on income of the current fiscal year ended June 30.

Instructions: Present a revised balance sheet in good form. Titles of items may be changed where appropriate. Arrange the balance sheet in the account form, with assets on one sheet and liabilities and capital on another sheet.

23-5. The Western Corporation issued $2,000,000 of 6% debenture bonds on April 1, 1961 at 97½. Interest is payable on April 1 and October 1. The bonds mature on April 1, 1971, but may be called at 102 on any interest date after 4 years from the date of issue. The company's fiscal year ends on December 31. The following transactions and adjustments were selected from those relating to the bonds over the ten-year period.

1961

Apr.   1. Issued the bonds for cash.
Oct.   1. Paid semiannual interest.
Dec. 31. Recorded accrual of the interest.
       31. Recorded amortization of the discount.
       31. Closed the interest expense account.

1962

Jan.   1. Reversed the adjusting entry for accrued interest.
Apr.   1. Paid semiannual interest.
July   1. Recorded amortization of discount related to interest on bonds purchased. (See next transaction.)
       1. Purchased $200,000 of bonds on the open market at 99 plus accrued interest, and retired them.
Oct.   1. Paid semiannual interest.
Dec. 31. Recorded accrual of the interest.
       31. Recorded amortization of the discount.
       31. Closed the interest expense account.

(Assume that all intervening transactions and adjustments have been recorded properly, and that the number of bonds outstanding has not changed during this period.)

1966

Jan.   1. Reversed the December 31, 1965 adjusting entry for accrued interest.
Apr.   1. Paid semiannual interest.
       1. Recorded amortization of discount related to interest on bonds called. (See next transaction.)
       1. Called and retired $1,500,000 of the bonds.
Oct.   1. Paid semiannual interest.
Dec. 31. Recorded accrual of the interest.
       31. Recorded amortization of the discount.
       31. Closed the interest expense account.

(Assume that all intervening transactions and adjustments have been recorded properly, and that the number of bonds outstanding has not changed during this period.)

1971

Jan.   1. Reversed the December 31, 1970 adjusting entry for accrued interest.
Apr.   1. Paid semiannual interest.
       1. Recorded amortization of the discount.
       1. Paid the bonds at maturity.
Dec. 31. Closed the interest expense account.

Instructions: Record the foregoing transactions in general journal form. (It is suggested that memorandum T accounts for Interest Expense, Discount on Bonds Payable, and Bonds Payable be maintained.)

Departments and branches

Departmentalization

Enterprises selling two or more distinct classes of services or commodities may departmentalize their accounting system. Departmental accounting yields information concerning the relative profitability of the various services rendered or types of products sold. When management is so informed, plans for increasing income can be formulated more intelligently. The effect of new policies can also be determined more accurately.

Departmental accounting is more likely to be used by a large business than by a small one. Some degree of departmentalization may be employed by a small enterprise, however. For example, the owner of a one-man real estate and property insurance agency could easily account separately for real estate commissions and insurance commissions. He would then know the amount of gross profit derived from each source and could observe the trend from period to period. Analysis of the division of his time between the two activities and of his operating expenses may indicate the desirability of devoting more time to one department and less to the other.

Departmental accounting for a large enterprise is likely to be both feasible and desirable. In a modern city department store, for example, there are a number of distinct departments each under the control of a departmental manager. Each salesclerk is restricted to a particular department, and each sale, whether for cash or on account, can easily be identified departmentally. Some of the expenses of a department, such as the salaries of the salesclerks and of the manager, are directly chargeable to the department. Others, such as light, heat, and other occupancy expenses, may be distributed among the departments on the basis of usage. When net income is determined by departments, the relative operating effectiveness may be evaluated.

527

Gross profit by departments

The degree to which departmental accounting may be adopted for a merchandising enterprise varies. Analysis of operations by departments may end with the determination of gross profit on sales, or it may be continued through selling and general expenses to net income from operations. The accounting procedures required for the determination of gross profit on sales will be discussed first.

In order to determine gross profit on sales by departments, it is necessary to determine by departments each element entering into gross profit. There are two basic methods of doing this: (1) setting up departmental accounts and identifying each item by department at the time of the transaction, or (2) maintaining only one account for the element and then allocating it among the departments at the time the income statement is prepared. Ordinarily, the first method is used unless the time required in analyzing each transaction is too great. Allocation among departments at the end of a period is likely to yield less accurate results than the first method, but some degree of accuracy may be sacrificed if by doing so there is a commensurate saving of time and expense.

The elements that must be departmentalized in order to determine gross profit by departments are as follows:

Sales	Purchases
Sales Returns and Allowances	Purchases Returns and Allowances
Sales Discount	Purchases Discount
Merchandise Inventory	

Departmental accounts may be established for each of the foregoing elements, and the charges and the credits to the accounts may be determined at the time the transactions are recorded.

In journalizing transactions relating to gross profit, additional columns are provided for each department in the special journals. For example, in a furniture store which sells furniture and floor coverings, the sales journal may have a credit column for Furniture Sales and a credit column for Rug Sales. To facilitate the journalizing of departmental transactions, the supporting documents such as sales invoices, vouchers, and cash register readings must identify the department affected by each transaction. Postings to departmental accounts from the special journals follow the procedures described in earlier chapters.

Net operating income by departments

Departmentalization may be carried beyond gross profit on sales. There are various intermediate points to which it may be extended, such as gross profit less selling expenses (gross selling profit), gross profit less all operating expenses (net operating income), net income before income tax, or net income after income tax. The underlying principle is the same for all degrees of departmentalization, namely, to assign to each department the portion of expense incurred for its benefit.

Some expenses may be easily identified with the department benefited. For example, if each salesperson is restricted to a particular sales department, the sales salaries may be assigned to the appropriate departmental salary accounts each time the payroll is prepared. On the other hand, the salaries of company officers, executives, and office personnel are not identifiable with a specific sales department and must be allocated to the various departments on some equitable basis.

Many accountants prefer to apportion all expenses to departments only at the end of the accounting period. When this is done, there is no need for departmental expense accounts in the general ledger and there is an accompanying saving in the number of postings. The apportionments may be made on the work sheet, which serves as the basis for preparing the departmental income statement.

Apportionment of operating expenses

As was indicated in the preceding section, some operating expenses are directly identifiable with particular departments and some are not. Expenses should be apportioned to the respective departments in accordance with the cost of the service rendered. Determining the amount of an expense chargeable to each department is not always a simple matter. In the first place, it requires the exercise of judgment; and accountants of equal ability may well differ in their opinions as to the proper basis for apportionment. Secondly, the cost of collecting data for use in making an apportionment must be kept within reasonable bounds; consequently information that is readily available may be used even though it is not entirely satisfactory.

To illustrate the apportionment of operating expenses, assume that the Nelson Company, with two sales departments, extends its departmentalization through net income from operations. The company's operating expenses for the calendar year and the methods used in apportioning them are presented in the paragraphs that follow.

Sales Salaries is apportioned to the two departments in accordance with the distributions shown in the payroll records. Of the $42,000 total in the account, $27,000 is chargeable to Department A and $15,000 is chargeable to Department B.

Advertising is apportioned according to the amount of advertising expense incurred for each department. The Nelson Company employs newspaper advertising, billboards, and handbills. Analysis of the newspaper space indicates approximately an even split between the two departments. The billboard advertising emphasizes the name and the location of the company, and the total cost of handbills is minor. The total expense of $6,000 is therefore apportioned evenly, $3,000 to Department A and $3,000 to Department B.

Depreciation of Store Equipment is apportioned in accordance with the average cost of the equipment in each of the two departments. The computations are as follows:

	TOTAL	DEPARTMENT A	DEPARTMENT B
Cost of store equipment:			
January 1.................	$13,600	$ 8,800	$ 4,800
December 31...............	14,400	8,000	6,400
Total....................	$28,000	$16,800	$11,200
Average....................	$14,000	$ 8,400	$ 5,600
Per cent.............	100%	60%	40%
Depreciation expense..........	$ 1,650	$ 990	$ 660

Officers Salaries is apportioned on the basis of the relative amount of time devoted to each department by the officers. Obviously, this can be only an approximation. The number of employees in each department may have some bearing on the matter, as may the number of sales, special promotional campaigns, and other factors that vary from period to period. Of the total officers salaries of $26,000, it is estimated that 60%, or $15,600, is chargeable to Department A and 40%, or $10,400, is chargeable to Department B.

Rent Expense is usually apportioned on the basis of the floor space devoted to each department. For a multistory building, recognition may be given to differences in the value of the various floors and locations. For example, the space near the main entrance of a department store is more valuable than the same amount of floor space located far from the elevator on the sixth floor. The salesrooms and the office of the Nelson Company are located on one floor with total floor space of 200,000 square feet. Department A occupies 88,000 square feet, Department B occupies 72,000 square feet, and the remaining space is devoted to show windows and the office. The rent expense is apportioned as follows:

	TOTAL	DEPARTMENT A	DEPARTMENT B
Floor space, square feet..........	160,000	88,000	72,000
Per cent......................	100%	55%	45%
Rent expense.................	$ 7,200	$ 3,960	$ 3,240

Property Taxes and Insurance Expense are related primarily to the value of the merchandise inventory and the store equipment. Although there are differences between assessed value for tax purposes, value for insurance purposes, and book value, the latter is most readily available and is considered to be satisfactory as a basis for apportioning these expenses. The computation of the apportionment follows:

	TOTAL	DEPARTMENT A	DEPARTMENT B
Merchandise Inventory:			
January 1..................	$138,300	$ 74,800	$ 63,500
December 31...............	143,700	85,100	58,600
Total..................	$282,000	$159,900	$122,100
Average........	$141,000	$ 79,950	$ 61,050
Average cost of store equipment (computed previously)........	14,000	8,400	5,600
Total......................	$155,000	$ 88,350	$ 66,650
Per cent....................	100%	57%	43%
Property taxes...............	$ 3,300	$ 1,881	$ 1,419
Insurance expense............	1,900	1,083	817

Heating and Lighting Expense, when combined in one account, may be apportioned on the basis of floor space. This assumes that the number of lights, their candlepower, and the extent of usage is uniform throughout the sales departments. If there are major variations and the total lighting expense is material, further analysis and separate apportionment may be advisable. Based on the relative per cent of floor space computed earlier, the heating and lighting expense is apportioned as follows:

	TOTAL	DEPARTMENT A	DEPARTMENT B
Floor space, square feet..	160,000	88,000	72,000
Per cent....................	100%	55%	45%
Heating and lighting expense.....	$ 2,400	$ 1,320	$ 1,080

Delivery Expense, Office Salaries, Bad Debts Expense, Miscellaneous Selling Expense, and *Miscellaneous General Expense* are examples of expenses that may be difficult to apportion equitably. For lack of a better basis, the Nelson Company apportions the foregoing expenses on the basis of sales.

	TOTAL	DEPARTMENT A	DEPARTMENT B
Sales...........	$400,000	$280,000	$120,000
Per cent.....	100%	70%	30%
Delivery Expense....	$ 4,100	$ 2,870	$ 1,230
Bad Debts Expense............	2,000	1,400	600
Miscellaneous Selling Expense....	1,800	1,260	540
Office Salaries...............	9,000	6,300	2,700
Miscellaneous Expense.........	1,100	770	330

Work sheet

The form of the work sheet for a departmentalized business corresponds to the form presented in Chapter 8 except for the income state-

	Account Titles	Trial Balance		Adjustments		
		Dr.	Cr.	Dr.	Cr.	
1	Cash	19,500				1
2	Accounts Receivable	35,600				2
3	Allowance for Uncollectible Accounts		500		(c) 2,000	3
4	Merchandise Inventory — A	74,800		(b) 85,100	(a) 74,800	4
5	Merchandise Inventory — B	63,500		(b) 58,600	(a) 63,500	5
6	Prepaid Insurance	4,700			(d) 1,900	6
7	Investments	18,000				7
8	Store Equipment	14,400				8
9	Accumulated Depr.—Store Equip...		6,200		(e) 1,650	9
10	Notes Payable		15,000			10
11	Accounts Payable		29,300			11
12	Common Stock		100,000			12
13	Retained Earnings		35,100			13
14	Sales — A		280,000			14
15	Sales — B		120,000			15
16	Sales Returns and Allowances—A...	2,500				16
17	Sales Returns and Allowances—B...	900				17
18	Purchases—A	182,300				18
19	Purchases—B	77,600				19
20	Sales Salaries	40,000		(f) 2,000		20
21	Advertising Expense	6,000				21
22	Delivery Expense	4,100				22
23	Miscellaneous Selling Expense	1,800				23
24	Officers Salaries	24,600		(f) 1,400		24
25	Office Salaries	8,600		(f) 400		25
26	Rent Expense	7,200				26
27	Property Taxes	3,300				27
28	Heating and Lighting	2,400				28
29	Miscellaneous General Expense	1,100				29
30	Interest Income		500			30
31	Dividend Income		1,100			31
32	Gain on Sale of Investments		6,000			32
33	Interest Expense	800		(g) 150		33
34		593,700	593,700			34
35	Expense and Revenue Summary....			(a) 74,800	(b) 85,100	35
36	Expense and Revenue Summary....			(a) 63,500	(b) 58,600	36
37	Bad Debts Expense			(c) 2,000		37
38	Insurance Expense			(d) 1,900		38
39	Depreciation Exp.—Store Equip.....			(e) 1,650		39
40	Salaries Payable				(f) 3,800	40
41	Interest Payable				(g) 150	41
42	Estimated Income Tax			(h) 13,316		42
43	Estimated Income Tax Payable.....				(h) 13,316	43
44				304,816	304,816	44
45	Net Operating Income—Loss					45
46						46
47	Net Income after Income Tax					47
48						48

Work sheet of a

| | Income Statement | | | | | | Balance Sheet | | |
| | Dept. A | | Dept. B | | Nondepartmental | | | | |
	Dr.	Cr.	Dr.	Cr.	Dr.	Cr.	Dr.	Cr.	
1							19,500		1
2							35,600		2
3								2,500	3
4							85,100		4
5							58,600		5
6							2,800		6
7							18,000		7
8							14,400		8
9								7,850	9
10								15,000	10
11								29,300	11
12								100,000	12
13								35,100	13
14		280,000							14
15				120,000					15
16	2,500								16
17			900						17
18	182,300								18
19			77,600						19
20	27,000		15,000						20
21	3,000		3,000						21
22	2,870		1,230						22
23	1,260		540						23
24	15,600		10,400						24
25	6,300		2,700						25
26	3,960		3,240						26
27	1,881		1,419						27
28	1,320		1,080						28
29	770		330						29
30						500			30
31						1,100			31
32						6,000			32
33					950				33
34									34
35	74,800	85,100							35
36			63,500	58,600					36
37	1,400		600						37
38	1,083		817						38
39	990		660						39
40								3,800	40
41								150	41
42					13,316				42
43								13,316	43
44	327,034	365,100	183,016	178,600					44
45	38,066			4,416	4,416	38,066			45
46	365,100	365,100	183,016	183,016	18,682	45,666	234,000	207,016	46
47					26,984			26,984	47
48					45,666	45,666	234,000	234,000	48

departmentalized business

ment columns. In order to facilitate the preparation of departmental income statements, the work sheet is expanded to include one set of columns for each department and one set of columns for income and expense items not allocated to departments. A work sheet for Nelson Company illustrating the use of the income statement columns appears on pages 532 and 533. The merchandise inventory adjustments are recorded in the usual manner except that two lines are used for Expense and Revenue Summary. This facilitates transferring the departmental inventories to the proper income statement columns. Sales and other departmental accounts are extended to the departmental columns.

Interest income, interest expense, income tax, and any other nondepartmental items are transferred to the nondepartmental column. After all items have been extended, the columns are totaled in the usual manner, the net operating income for each department being transferred to the nondepartmental column.

Income statements

Departmental income statements do not differ in form from the all-inclusive income statement for the enterprise, except that the departmental statements may conclude with net income from operations. For example, the income statement for Department A, prepared from the work sheet illustrated on pages 532 and 533, would conclude with a net operating income of $38,066; the final amount on the Department B statement would be a net operating loss of $4,416. All departmental income statements for a period may be spread over a single sheet, with the totals for all departments presented at the extreme left or right of the page, or separate departmental statements and an all-inclusive statement may be prepared on separate sheets. The final figure on the all-inclusive statement for Nelson Company would be net income of $26,984, after income tax. The departmental statements are ordinarily of concern only to management and are not issued to stockholders or other outsiders.

Effect of discontinuing a department

A series of departmental income statements, based upon sound methods of expense apportionment, may indicate that one or more departments are barely breaking even or are incurring losses. Careful analysis of the operations of the less successful departments may lead to an infinite variety of conclusions as to what should be done. It may be that certain expenses can be reduced without loss in sales; perhaps expenditures for advertising should be increased; a change in pricing policies or in merchandise lines may be indicated; or the remedial measures decided upon may involve several changes in policy.

The most drastic solution to the problem of an unprofitable department is, of course, to discontinue it. A careful analysis should be made before arriving at such a decision, however. It is quite possible that the discontinuance of a loss department may result in a reduction rather than an increase in the net operating income of the enterprise as a whole.

For example, departmental income statements prepared from the work sheet on pages 532 and 533 would indicate that Department B realized gross profit of $36,600 on sales and was charged with expenses of $41,016, which yielded a net loss of $4,416. If the entire $41,016 of expenses could have been saved by the elimination of Department B, the enterprise would have earned additional net operating income of $4,416. A review of the individual expense items reveals, however, that such would not have been the case. Some of the individual expenses could have been saved in their entirety, others would have been reduced to a varying extent, and others would have been the same regardless of whether or not Department B was in operation. For example, if the Department B sales force had been dismissed, the expenditure of $15,000 for sales salaries would not have been necessary. There would presumably have been a reduction in heating and lighting expense, but not by as much as $1,080. The $10,400 of officers salaries and the $3,240 of rent expense charged to Department B would have been incurred even though Department B had not been in operation.

It is evident that it would not be advisable to discontinue Department B unless the sales of Department A could be increased sufficiently. There are likely to be other factors that have an important bearing on the situation. It may be that customers attracted by Department B make substantial purchases in Department A. Discontinuance of Department B might consequently result in a reduction in sales by Department A.

The foregoing discussion has suggested ways in which data may be useful to management in making important policy decisions. It should be kept in mind that the particular basis used in apportioning expenses to departments will affect the outcome reported. Acceptance of the data, which depends on estimates, must be tempered with judgment.

Branch operations

Just as a firm may add a new department in an effort to increase its sales and income, it also may open new stores in different locations with the same objective in mind. Among the types of retail businesses in which branch operations were first successfully developed on a major scale were variety, grocery, and drug stores. There are a number of large corporations with hundreds or thousands of retail stores (branches) distributed over a large area. In addition to the national chain store organizations, there are many of a regional or local nature. The growth of suburban shopping centers in recent years has added materially to the number of firms, especially department stores, that have expanded through the opening of branches.

Although commonly associated with retailing, branch operations are carried on by banking institutions, service organizations, and many types of manufacturing enterprises. Regardless of the nature of the business, each branch ordinarily has a branch manager. Within the framework of general policies set by top management, the branch manager may be given wide latitude in conducting the business of the branch. Data concerning the volume of business handled and the profitability of operations at each location are essential as a basis for decisions by the principal executives. It is also necessary to maintain a record of the various assets at the branch locations and of liabilities incurred by each branch.

In the remainder of this chapter we shall deal with a central office and one branch. We shall also consider branch accounting applicable to a merchandising business. The fundamental considerations are not materially affected, however, by a multiplicity of branches or by the particular type of business.

Systems for branch accounting

There are various systems of accounting for branch operations. The system may be highly centralized, in which case the accounting for the branch is done at the home office. Or the system may be almost completely decentralized, in which event the branch is responsible for the detailed accounting and the home office carries only summary accounts for the branch. Or there may be some variation between these two extremes. Although there are many possible variations, two typical methods of branch accounting will be described.

Centralized system. The branch may prepare only the basic record of its transactions, such as sales invoices, time tickets for employees, and vouchers for liabilities incurred. Copies of all such memorandums are forwarded to the home office, where they are recorded in appropriate journals in the usual manner. When this system is used, the branch has no journals or ledgers. If the operating results of the branch are to be determined separately, which is normally the case, separate branch accounts for sales, costs, and expenses must be maintained in the home office ledger. It is apparent that the principles of department accounting will apply in such cases, the branch being treated as a department or as a number of subdepartments.

One important result of centralizing the bookkeeping activities at one location may be substantial savings in office expense. There is also greater assurance of uniformity in accounting methods employed. On the other hand, there is some likelihood of delays and inaccuracies in submitting data to the home office, with the result that periodic reports on the operations of a branch are not available at the proper times.

Decentralized system. When the accounting for branches is decentralized, each branch maintains its own accounting system, with journals and ledgers. The account classification for assets, liabilities, income, and expenses in the branch books conforms with the classification employed by the home office. The accounting processes are comparable to those of an independent business, except that the branch does not have capital accounts. A special account entitled Home Office takes the place of the capital accounts. The process of preparing financial statements and adjusting and closing the books is substantially the same as for an independent enterprise. It is this system of branch accounting to which the remainder of the chapter will be devoted.

Reciprocal accounts in branch accounting

When the branch has a ledger with a full complement of accounts, except capital accounts, it is apparent that there must be some tie-in between the branch ledger and the general ledger at the home office. The properties at the branch are a part of the assets of the entire enterprise, and liabilities incurred at the branch are similarly liabilities of the enterprise as a whole. Although the accounting system at the branch is much like that of an independent company, the fact remains that it is not a separate entity.

The tie-in between the home office and the branch is accomplished by the control-account-subsidiary-ledger technique, with an added modification that makes the branch ledger a self-contained unit. The basic features of the system are shown in the chart below. In the home office ledger, the account Branch #1 has a debit balance of $100,000. This balance represents the sum of the assets minus the sum of the liabilities recorded on the ledger at the branch. The various asset and liability accounts in the branch ledger are represented in the chart by one account for all assets ($120,000) and one account for all liabilities ($20,000). In order to make the branch ledger self-balancing, an account entitled Home Office is added. It has a credit balance of $100,000. The two accounts, Branch #1 in the home office books and Home Office in the branch books, have equal but opposite balances and are known as *reciprocal accounts*. The home office account in the branch ledger replaces the capital accounts that would be used if the branch were a separate entity. Actually, the account does represent the branch's portion of the entire capital of the home office.

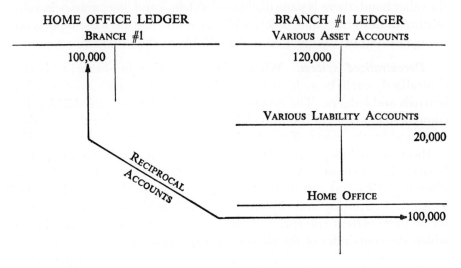

HOME OFFICE LEDGER — BRANCH #1: 100,000

BRANCH #1 LEDGER — VARIOUS ASSET ACCOUNTS: 120,000

VARIOUS LIABILITY ACCOUNTS: 20,000

HOME OFFICE: 100,000

RECIPROCAL ACCOUNTS

When the home office sends assets to the branch, it debits Branch #1 for the totals and credits the appropriate asset accounts. Upon receiving the assets, the branch debits the appropriate accounts and credits Home Office. To illustrate, assume that branch operations are begun by sending $10,000 in cash to the newly appointed branch manager. The entries in the two ledgers are presented in T accounts as follows:

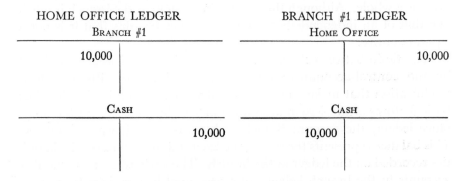

HOME OFFICE LEDGER — BRANCH #1: 10,000

BRANCH #1 LEDGER — HOME OFFICE: 10,000

CASH: 10,000

CASH: 10,000

When the branch disburses the cash, it will record the transactions as though it were an independent entity. For example, if the branch purchases office equipment for $4,000, paying cash, the transaction will be recorded in the branch books by a debit to Office Equipment and a credit to Cash. No entry is required in the home office books because there is no change in the amount of the investment at the branch.

As the branch incurs expenses and earns revenue, the transactions are recorded in its books in the usual manner. Such transactions do affect the amount of the total investment of the home office at the branch, but recognition of the change is postponed until the books are closed at the end of the accounting period. At that time the expense and revenue summary account in the branch books is closed to Home Office. If operations have resulted in a net income, the account Home Office will be credited. In the home office books a net income at the branch is recorded by a debit to Branch #1 and a credit to Branch Net Income. For a net loss the entry would be just the reverse.

In a merchandising enterprise all or a substantial part of the stock in trade of the branch is usually supplied by the home office. A shipment of merchandise from the home office is recorded by a debit to Branch #1 and a credit to Shipments to Branch #1. The branch records the transaction in its books by a debit to Shipments from Home Office and a credit to Home Office. It is evident from the T accounts below that the two shipments accounts are also reciprocal accounts.

HOME OFFICE LEDGER		BRANCH #1 LEDGER	
BRANCH #1		HOME OFFICE	
20,000			20,000

SHIPMENTS TO BRANCH #1		SHIPMENTS FROM HOME OFFICE	
	20,000	20,000	

From the point of view of the home office, the account Shipments to Branch #1 is an unallocated reduction of its merchandise inventory and purchases accounts. From the standpoint of the branch, the account Shipments from Home Office is comparable to a purchases account. The final disposition of these accounts is described later in the chapter.

Illustration of decentralized branch accounting

Having described the underlying principles applicable to branch accounting on a decentralized basis, a series of illustrative entries will now be presented. We will begin with the opening of a branch and carry its operations through a complete accounting period. Typical transactions between the home office and the branch, and between the branch and outsiders, will be considered. Transactions between the home office and outsiders will be ignored unless they affect the branch. A summary of transactions, together with the entries on the home office books and the branch books, is presented below in general journal form.

Transactions	Home Office Books	Branch Books

(1) The home office established Branch #1, sending $10,000 in cash and $30,000 in merchandise to begin operations	Branch #1........40,000
	  Cash.......... 10,000
	  Shipments to
	    Branch #1...... 30,000
		Cash............10,000
		Shipments from
		Home Office......30,000
		  Home Office.... 40,000

(2) The branch purchased on account merchandise costing $10,000.		Purchases........10,000 Accounts Pay... 10,000
(3) The branch sold merchandise for $16,000 in cash and for $8,000 on account.		Cash............16,000 Accounts Rec...... 8,000 Sales.......... 24,000
(4) The branch paid operating expenses amounting to $3,500.		Operating Exp.... 3,500 Cash.......... 3,500
(5) The branch collected $6,000 on accounts receivable.		Cash............ 6,000 Accounts Rec... 6,000
(6) The branch paid $1,000 on accounts payable.		Accounts Pay...... 1,000 Cash.......... 1,000

(7) The branch sent $20,000 in cash to the home office.	Cash............20,000
	  Branch #1...... 20,000
		Home Office......20,000
		  Cash.......... 20,000

The entries to adjust and close the books of the branch at the end of the accounting period, together with the entries on the books of the home office to record the net income of the branch, are as follows:

Adjusting & Closing	Home Office Books	Branch Books
(a) To record the ending merchandise inventory of the branch		Mdse. Inventory...22,000 Expense and Revenue Summary.. 22,000
(b) To close the sales account of the branch.		Sales............24,000 Expense and Revenue Summary.. 24,000

Adjusting & Closing	Home Office Books	Branch Books

(c) To close the cost and expense accounts of the branch.		Expense and Revenue Summary.....43,500
		  Shipments from
		  Home Office.... 30,000
		  Purchases....... 10,000
		  Operating Exp.. 3,500

(d) To close the expense and revenue summary account on the books of the branch and to record the net income of the branch on the books of the home office.	Branch #1........ 2,500
	  Branch Net Income.......... 2,500
		Expense and Revenue Summary..... 2,500
		  Home Office.... 2,500

Entry (d), shown in both the branch journal and the home office journal, records the net income of the branch. Whenever a net income or loss is recorded by a branch, the home office must record the change in its investment at the branch and the corresponding effect on the net income of the company.

After the foregoing entries have been posted, the home office accounts affected and the branch ledger accounts appear as follows:

HOME OFFICE LEDGER		BRANCH LEDGER	
CASH		**CASH**	

(7) 20,000	(1) 10,000	(1) 10,000
		(3) 16,000
		(5) 6,000
		
		  32,000
		Balance 7,500
			(4) 3,500
			(6) 1,000
			(7) 20,000
			Balance 7,500
			  32,000

Other cash transactions of the home office would also be recorded in the account above.

ACCOUNTS RECEIVABLE	

(3) 8,000
 	
  8,000
Balance 2,000
	(5) 6,000
	Balance 2,000
	  8,000

HOME OFFICE LEDGER	BRANCH LEDGER

MERCHANDISE INVENTORY

(a)	22,000		

ACCOUNTS PAYABLE

(6)	1,000	(2)	10,000
Balance	9,000		
	10,000		10,000
		Balance	9,000

BRANCH #1				HOME OFFICE			
(1)	40,000	(7)	20,000	(7)	20,000	(1)	40,000
(d)	2,500	Balance	22,500	Balance	22,500	(d)	2,500
	42,500		42,500		42,500		42,500
Balance	22,500					Balance	22,500

BRANCH NET INCOME				EXPENSE AND REVENUE SUMMARY			
		(d)	2,500	(c)	43,500	(a)	22,000
				(d)	2,500	(b)	24,000
					46,000		46,000

Branch Net Income will be closed to the home office expense and revenue summary account.

SALES

(b)	24,000	(3)	24,000

SHIPMENTS TO BRANCH #1				SHIPMENTS FROM HOME OFFICE			
		(1)	30,000	(1)	30,000	(c)	30,000

Shipments to Branch #1 is a deduction from purchases. It will be closed to the home office expense and revenue summary account.

HOME OFFICE LEDGER			BRANCH LEDGER		
			PURCHASES		
		(2)	10,000	(c)	10,000
			OPERATING EXPENSES		
		(4)	3,500	(c)	3,500

Branch financial statements

Branch financial statements differ from those of a complete enterprise in two minor respects. On the income statement the shipments from the home office appear in the cost of goods sold section following purchases. On the balance sheet the account Home Office takes the place of the capital accounts. Actually it is not capital in the usual sense, but merely the balancing account. Statements for the branches are used only by management and are not published.

Combined statements for home office and branch

An income statement prepared on the basis of the home office ledger will present details of sales, costs, and expenses of the home office only. The net income of each of the branches may then be added near the end of the statement. The balance sheet prepared from the home office ledger will contain the controlling accounts for the various branches. The nature and the amounts of the various assets and liabilities at the branch locations will not be disclosed. Such statements may serve a useful purpose for management, but they are obviously unsuitable for presentation to stockholders and creditors.

Accordingly, it is necessary to combine the data on the income statements of the home office and the branches to form one over-all income statement. The data on the balance sheets of the home office and of the various branches are also combined to form one balance sheet for the enterprise. The preparation of the combined statements is facilitated by the use of work sheets. The work sheets are similar in that each has a column for the home office account balances, a column for the account balances of each branch, a set of columns headed "Eliminations," and a final column to which the combined figures are extended.

The work sheet for the combined income statement of Taylor Corporation is presented on page 544, followed by the combined income statement. The account Shipments from Home Office is canceled by a credit in the Eliminations column, and the account Shipments to Branch #1 is canceled by a debit in the Eliminations column.

Taylor Corporation
Work Sheet for Combined Income Statement
For Month Ended March 31, 1962

	Home Office	Branch #1	Eliminations Dr.	Eliminations Cr.	Combined Income Statement
Sales.........................	47,000	24,000			71,000
Cost of Goods Sold:					
Mdse. Inv., March 1.............	41,000				41,000
Purchases.....................	52,000	10,000			62,000
	93,000				
Shipments from Home Office......		30,000		30,000	
Less Shipments to Branch #1......	30,000		30,000		
Mdse. Available for Sale.........	63,000	40,000			103,000
Less Mdse. Inv., March 31.......	35,000	22,000			57,000
Cost of Goods Sold..............	28,000	18,000			46,000
Gross Profit on Sales.............	19,000	6,000			25,000
Operating Expenses...............	10,500	3,500			14,000
Net Income.....................	8,500	2,500	30,000	30,000	11,000

Taylor Corporation
Income Statement
For Month Ended March 31, 1962

Sales...		$71,000
Cost of goods sold:		
Merchandise inventory, March 1, 1962..............	$ 41,000	
Purchases..	62,000	
Merchandise available for sale.....................	$103,000	
Less mdse. inventory, March 31, 1962................	57,000	
Cost of goods sold.............................		46,000
Gross profit on sales................................		$25,000
Operating expenses................................		14,000
Net income from operations.........................		$11,000

The work sheet for the combined balance sheet of Taylor Corporation appears on page 545. The data in the first two columns were taken from the individual balance sheets of the home office and the branch. The reciprocal account Branch #1 is canceled by a credit elimination, and the reciprocal account Home Office is canceled by a debit elimination. The total of each balance sheet item is then extended to the Combined Balance Sheet column and the work is completed by footing the two sections of the column. It should be noted that the entries in the

Eliminations columns of the work sheets are needed only in the preparation of the combined statements; they are not recorded on either set of books.

Taylor Corporation
Work Sheet for Combined Balance Sheet
March 31, 1962

	Home Office	Branch #1	Eliminations Dr.	Eliminations Cr.	Combined Balance Sheet
Debit balances:					
Cash..........................	53,000	7,500			60,500
Accounts Receivable.............	46,000	2,000			48,000
Merchandise Inventory...........	35,000	22,000			57,000
Prepaid Insurance...............	250				250
Branch #1......................	22,500			22,500	
Equipment.....................	15,000				15,000
Total.......................	171,750	31,500			180,750
Credit balances:					
Accumulated Depreciation........	3,000				3,000
Accounts Payable...............	28,000	9,000			37,000
Home Office....................		22,500	22,500		
Common Stock..................	100,000				100,000
Retained Earnings...............	40,750				40,750
Total.......................	171,750	31,500	22,500	22,500	180,750

The balance sheet prepared from the data in the Combined Balance Sheet column of the work sheet is as follows:

Taylor Corporation
Balance Sheet
March 31, 1962

Assets			Liabilities and Capital	
Cash........................		$ 60,500	Accounts payable.............	$ 37,000
Accounts receivable...........		48,000	Common stock...............	100,000
Merchandise inventory........		57,000	Retained earnings............	40,750
Prepaid insurance............		250		
Equipment......... $15,000				
Less accumulated				
depreciation....... 3,000		12,000		
Total assets.................		$177,750	Total liab. and capital........	$177,750

Shipments billed at selling price

In the foregoing discussion and illustrations, the billing for merchandise shipped to the branch has been assumed to be at cost price. When all or most of the merchandise handled by the branch is supplied by the home office, it is not unusual for billings to be made at selling price. An advantage of this procedure is that it provides a convenient control over inventories at the branch. The branch merchandise inventory at the beginning of a period (at selling price), plus shipments during the period (at selling price), less sales for the period yields the ending inventory (at selling price). Comparison of the physical inventory taken at billed prices with the book amount discloses any discrepancies. If they are material in amount, remedial action by the management is needed.

When shipments to the branch are billed at selling prices, no gross profit on sales will be reported on the branch income statement. The merchandise inventory on the branch balance sheet will also be overstated by the amount of the mark-up included in the billed prices of the goods on hand. In combining the branch and home office statements it is necesssary to convert the data back to cost by eliminating the mark-up from both the shipments accounts and the inventory accounts.

Analyses of operations

With the ever-increasing size of business units, the need for analysis of operations is likewise growing. It is necessary to account separately for the various parts of which these large units are made up. This accounting involves first an analysis of the accounts, by departments or by branches, followed by a consolidation to show the unit as a whole.

In the large five-and-ten-cent store chains, for example, there is first a breakdown by commodities sold and second a breakdown by branches selling these commodities. For efficient administration of large mercantile establishments, it is necessary to have both departmental analysis and branch analysis. More and more attention is being directed to accounting for small units under a central administration.

Questions

1. A business enterprise with four well-defined departments plans to departmentalize its accounts to the point of determination of gross profit on sales. What accounts should be departmentalized?

2. How does the availability of departmental income statements aid the principal executives of an enterprise in assigning responsibilities and measuring performance?

3. If an enterprise has four departments, is it necessary to establish a separate advertising expense account for each department in order to determine net operating income by departments?

4. For each of the following types of expenses, select the allocation basis listed that is most appropriate:

Expense:	Basis of allocation:
(a) Advertising	(a) Physical space occupied
(b) Rent	(b) Departmental sales
(c) Insurance	(c) Value of inventory and equip-
(d) Officers salaries	ment used
(e) Miscellaneous selling expense	(d) Actual usage
	(e) Time devoted to department

5. Are departmental income statements ordinarily included in the published annual reports of department stores?

6. The Department X income statement for the year just ended indicates gross profit on sales of $70,000, operating expenses of $95,000, and net operating loss of $25,000. The net operating income for all other departments of the enterprise for the same year was $125,000. It is estimated that the discontinuance of Department X would not have affected the gross profit of the other departments and that its discontinuance would have resulted in a reduction of $35,000 in total operating expenses. Assuming the accuracy of these estimates, what would the net operating income of the enterprise have been if Department X had been discontinued?

7. Where are the branch accounting records maintained in a decentralized system?

8. Differentiate between a customer's ledger and a branch ledger with regard to (a) the type of accounts in the ledger and (b) the preparation of a trial balance of the ledger.

9. After the books are closed, the asset accounts at a branch total $70,000, the allowance for uncollectible accounts and accumulated depreciation accounts total $10,000; there are no liabilities to outsiders. (a) What is the title of the remaining account in the branch ledger and what is its balance? (b) What is the title of the related account on the books of the parent organization and what is its balance? (c) Do these accounts appear on the combined balance sheet?

10. At the close of each accounting period the Midway Co. charges each of its branches with interest on the net investment in the branch. At the end of the current year the home office debits the branch accounts for various amounts and credits Interest Income for a total of $26,000. The branches make comparable entries, debiting Interest Expense and crediting Home Office. How should the interest income and interest expense be handled on the work sheet for the combined income statement?

11. During the first year of operations of a branch, the home office shipped merchandise that had cost $120,000 to the branch. The branch was billed at $200,000, which was the selling price of the merchandise. Branch net sales for the period totaled $100,000 (all sales were at the billed prices). (a) What should be the amount of the branch ending physical inventory at billed prices? (b) Assuming that there are no inventory shortages at the branch, what is the cost of the closing inventory? (c) Which of the two amounts should be added to the home office inventory for presentation on the combined balance sheet?

Exercises

1. The Werner Department Store maintains a record of the number of column inches of newspaper advertising devoted to each department. Space occupied by the name of the store, sale dates, etc., is prorated over the departments in proportion to the space used by each department. For the month of March it used 4,400 column inches of space at a cost of $1.50 per column inch. The column inches used by each department were as follows: A. 1,300; B. 200; C. 300; D. 960; E. 800; F. 440. Determine the amount of advertising expense to be apportioned to each department.

2. Monarch Furniture Inc. conducts a retail furniture business in a three-story building. The departments and the floor space occupied by each are as follows:

Receiving and Storage — Basement	—	10,000 sq. ft.
Department A —	First Floor	— 10,000 sq. ft.
Department B —	Second Floor	— 6,000 sq. ft.
Department C —	Second Floor	— 4,000 sq. ft.
Department D —	Third Floor	— 5,000 sq. ft.
Department E —	Third Floor	— 3,000 sq. ft.
General Office —	Third Floor	— 2,000 sq. ft.

The building is leased at an annual rent of $50,000, allocated to the floors as follows: basement, 10%; first floor, 50%: second floor, 25%; third floor, 15%. Determine the amount of rent to be apportioned to each department.

3. Department A earned net operating income of $25,000 which represented 10% of its net sales; Department B earned net operating income of $16,000, which represented 16% of its net sales; Departments A, B, and C earned combined net operating income of $62,000, which represented 12.4% of combined net sales. Determine the items indicated by X in the following tabulation:

	A	B	C	Total
Net sales	$ X	$ X	$ X	$ X
Net operating income	25,000	16,000	X	62,000
Per cent of net sales	10%	16%	X%	12.4%

4. Peerless Products Co. maintains sales offices in a number of cities. The home office supplies the sales manager at each office with a working fund of $10,000 with which to meet payrolls and pay other office expenses. Give the entries on the home office books to record the following:

(a) Established a $10,000 fund for branch #25.
(b) Received a report from Branch #25 indicating the following payments: sales salaries, $6,000; office salaries, $1,200; rent, $1,000; advertising, $800. Sent check to replenish the fund.

5. Give the journal entries to record the following transactions on the books of the branch. (This is not a complete list of transactions for the period).

Mar. 1. The branch receives from the home office: cash, $3,000; furniture and fixtures, $900; merchandise at cost, $4,800.
   5. The branch purchases merchandise on account from an outside firm, $2,800.
   7. The branch sells merchandise on account for $5,000, for cash $2,300.
   18. The branch pays general operating expenses of $1,200.
   22. The branch sends the home office cash of $1,000.
   26. The branch receives merchandise at cost from the home office, $2,200.
   30. The branch reports a net income of $1,600.

6. The Burbank Co. maintains accounts entitled Encino Branch and Sherman Oaks Branch. Each branch maintains an account entitled Home Office. The Sherman Oaks Branch received instructions from the home office to ship to the Encino Branch merchandise costing $1,000 that had been received from the home office. Give the journal entry to record the transfer of the merchandise on the books of (a) the home office, (b) the Sherman Oaks Branch, and (c) the Encino Branch.

Problems

24-1. The Mercantile Mart operates two sales departments: Department A, composed of hardware and small appliances; and Department B, composed of paints, wallpaper, and related supplies. The trial balance at June 30, the end of the current fiscal year, is presented on page 550.

Data for end-of-year adjustments are:

Merchandise Inventories, June 30:

Department A......................................	$59,840
Department B......................................	16,160
Supplies used during the year:	
Store supplies (charge to Store Supplies Expense)......	840
Office supplies (charge to Miscellaneous General Expense)	400
Insurance expired....................................	3,800
Depreciation of equipment...........................	3,000
Estimated income tax...............................	21,510

The bases to be used in apportioning expenses, together with other essential information are as follows:

Sales salaries — Payroll records: Department A, $24,000; Department B, $12,400.

Advertising — Usage: Department A, $2,600; Department B, $1,600.

Depreciation of equipment — Book value of equipment at beginning of year: Department A, $12,040; Department B, $5,160.

Store supplies — Requisitions: Department A, $600; Department B, $240.

Administrative and office salaries — Department A, 75%; Department B, 25%.

Rent, heating, and lighting — Floor space: Department A, 5,200 sq. ft.; Department B, 2,800 sq. ft.

Insurance and property tax — Average merchandise inventory.

Miscellaneous selling expense, miscellaneous general expense — Volume of gross sales.

Instructions: Prepare a twelve-column work sheet.

Mercantile Mart
Trial Balance
June 30, 19—

Cash....................................	46,940	
Accounts Receivable.....................	36,200	
Merchandise Inventory, Department A........	57,200	
Merchandise Inventory, Department B........	18,800	
Prepaid Insurance.........................	7,800	
Supplies..................................	2,470	
Equipment................................	30,000	
Accumulated Depreciation — Equipment.......		12,800
Accounts Payable.........................		19,200
Common Stock............................		100,000
Retained Earnings.........................		6,750
Sales, Department A.......................		254,200
Sales, Department B.......................		155,800
Sales Returns and Allowances, Department A...	2,900	
Sales Returns and Allowances, Department B...	1,720	
Purchases, Department A....................	158,568	
Purchases, Department B....................	111,832	
Purchases Discount, Department A............		2,660
Purchases Discount, Department B............		1,520
Sales Salaries.............................	36,400	
Advertising Expense.......................	4,200	
Miscellaneous Selling Expense...............	3,200	
Administrative and Office Salaries............	20,000	
Rent Expense.............................	8,000	
Heating and Lighting......................	2,800	
Property Tax Expense......................	1,500	
Miscellaneous General Expense..............	2,400	
	552,930	552,930

24-2. Modern Products, Inc., of New York, opened a branch office in Cleveland on June 1 of the current year. Transactions and adjustments reflecting branch operations for the current year ended December 31, are summarized below:

(a) Received cash advance from home office, $25,000.

(b) Purchased office equipment for cash, $5,000.

(c) Shipments of merchandise received from the home office totaled $180,000, billed at cost.

(d) Purchased merchandise on account, $20,000.

(e) Sales on account, $150,000; cash sales, $35,000.

(f) Paid creditors on account, $12,500.

(g) Received cash from customers on account, $115,000.

(h) Paid operating expenses, $25,000 (all expenses are charged to Operating Expenses, a controlling account).

(i) Sent $100,000 cash to home office.

(j) Recorded accumulated depreciation, $450, and allowance for uncollectible accounts, $550.

(k) Merchandise inventory at December 31, $57,500.

Instructions: (1) Present the entries on the branch books, in general journal form, to record the foregoing transactions, adjustments, and year-end closing. Post to the following T accounts: Cash, Accounts Receivable, Allowance for Uncollectible Accounts, Merchandise Inventory, Office Equipment, Accumulated Depreciation, Accounts Payable, Home Office, Expense and Revenue Summary, Sales, Shipments from Home Office, Purchases, and Operating Expenses.

(2) Prepare an income statement for the period and a balance sheet as of December 31 for the branch.

(3) Present the entries required on the home office books, in general journal form. Post to a T account entitled Cleveland Branch.

24-3. The adjusted trial balances of the home office of Bell, Incorporated and of its Dallas branch, as of October 31, the close of the current fiscal year, are as follows:

	Home Office Dr.	Home Office Cr.	Dallas Branch Dr.	Dallas Branch Cr.
Cash..........................	73,000		21,500	
Accounts Receivable.............	102,000		33,000	
Allowance for Uncollectible Accounts.....		975		850
Merchandise Inventory...........	278,000		70,000	
Prepaid Expenses................	700		200	
Dallas Branch...................	113,050			
Equipment......................	31,000		10,000	
Accumulated Depreciation........		24,000		1,500
Notes Payable..................		19,000		
Accounts Payable...............		61,000		3,800
Home Office....................				113,050
Common Stock..................		300,000		
Retained Earnings..............		72,775		
Expense and Revenue Summary......	305,000	278,000	95,000	70,000
Sales..........................		843,000		300,000
Shipments to Branch............		130,000		
Purchases......................	670,000		45,000	
Shipments from Home Office......			130,000	
Operating Expenses.............	156,000		84,500	
	1,728,750	1,728,750	489,200	489,200

Instructions: (1) Prepare an income statement and a balance sheet for the branch.

(2) Prepare an income statement for the home office.

(3) Prepare the journal entry to record branch income on the home office books.

(4) Prepare a balance sheet for the home office, giving effect to the journal entry in (3).

(5) Prepare a work sheet for a combined income statement and a work sheet for a combined balance sheet.

(6) Prepare a combined income statement and a combined balance sheet.

24-4. The Mason Store apportions depreciation of equipment on the basis of average cost of the equipment and apportions personal property taxes on the basis of the combined total of average cost of the equipment and average value of the merchandise inventories. Depreciation of equipment amounted to $10,000 and personal property taxes amounted to $8,000 for the year. Data on equipment and inventories are as follows:

	Average Cost	
Departments	Equipment	Inventories
Service		
1	$ 10,000	
2	15,000	
Sales		
A	25,000	$120,000
B	30,000	80,000
C	20,000	200,000
Total	$100,000	$400,000

Instructions: Determine the apportionment of the depreciation and the property taxes.

24-5. The work sheet for a combined income statement is presented below. Shipments were billed at cost.

Harris & Co.

Work Sheet for Combined Income Statement

For Month Ended January 31, 19--

	Home Office	Branch #1	Combined Income Statement
Sales...........................	300,000	100,000	
Shipments to Branch..............	100,000		
Total........................	400,000	100,000	500,000
Cost of Goods Sold:			
Mdse. Inventory, Jan. 1.........	200,000	5,000	205,000
Shipments from Home Office.....		100,000	
Purchases....................	400,000		500,000
Mdse. Available for Sale.........	600,000	105,000	705,000
Less Mdse. Inventory, Jan. 31.....	300,000	30,000	330,000
Cost of Goods Sold.............	300,000	75,000	375,000
Gross Profit on Sales..............	100,000	25,000	125,000
Operating Expenses...............	40,000	10,000	50,000
Net Income from Operations.......	60,000	15,000	75,000

Instructions: (1) Determine the rate of gross profit to sales, and net income to sales, computed on the basis of the amounts listed in the combined income statement column of the work sheet.

(2) Prepare a correct combined income statement.

(3) Determine the correct rate of gross profit to sales and net income to sales for the company.

Manufacturing

Manufacturing operations

Manufacturers employ labor and use machinery in converting raw materials into finished goods. In thus changing the form of the commodities, their activities differ from those of merchandisers. The commodities purchased by a manufacturer are his raw materials, but they were finished goods to the manufacturer from whom he bought them. Flour is raw material to the baker but finished goods to the miller. Steel plate is raw material to the automobile manufacturer but finished goods to the steel producer. The designation *raw materials* or *finished goods* has significance only in connection with a specific manufacturer and his relation to the commodity.

The extent of business activity in manufacturing is apparent to anyone who contemplates the vast variety of changes in form that take place in producing the commodities and the services used by society. Manufacturing provides work for a large percentage of the employed and uses a large share of the capital equipment of the country.

In order to record transactions identified with manufacturing operations, it is necessary to expand the ledger. For example, one or more accounts is required for accumulating the salaries and wages paid to factory personnel. The cost of depreciation, electric power, insurance, maintenance, and of other goods and services used in a factory must also be recorded in the accounts. New subsidiary ledgers may be needed to permit a division of labor and to establish internal controls. Periodic reports to management must include data that will be useful in measuring the efficiency of manufacturing operations and in planning for future periods.

Asset and liability accounts

Many of the asset and liability accounts employed by a manufacturing enterprise are identical with those found in the ledger of a merchandising business. But there are some accounts that are either peculiar to manufacturing or are likely to be of greater significance in manufacturing than in merchandising operations. A brief discussion of some of these accounts is presented in the sections that follow.

Current assets. The merchandise inventory account appearing in the ledger of a merchandising business is displaced by three inventory accounts representing (1) goods in the state in which they were acquired, (2) goods in the process of manufacture, and (3) goods in the state in which they are to be sold. These inventories are called respectively *raw materials, work in process,* and *finished goods.* The costs of operating the factory, including labor and the various manufacturing expenses, are added to the cost of the raw materials in determining the cost of work in process and finished goods. The balances in these inventory accounts may be presented on the balance sheet in the following manner:

Inventories:

Finished goods	$300,000	
Work in process	55,000	
Raw materials	123,000	$478,000

Other current assets of significant amount are factory supplies on hand for use in maintaining and servicing machinery, prepaid insurance of various kinds, largely related to the use of machinery, and various other prepayments for factory services.

Plant assets. Because of the extensive use of machinery in manufacturing, the portion of total capital invested in plant assets by a manufacturing business tends to be larger than that of a trading concern. The buildings housing the machinery must be designed or adapted to fit the special needs of the manufacturing operations and hence are likely to be owned or leased on a long-term basis. The number of items of machinery and equipment is usually sufficient to warrant the use of subsidiary plant ledgers such as those illustrated in Chapter 12.

The cost of tools and other portable equipment of small unit value is usually charged to a tools account rather than to machinery or a similarly titled account reserved for major items. Because of breakage, pilferage, and relatively short life it is usually impracticable to apply the usual depreciation methods to small tools. One of the methods commonly employed to determine the cost expiration is to take a periodic inventory of the tools on hand, estimate their fair value based on original cost, and charge the remaining amount to Tools Expense. The same method may be used in accounting for dies, molds, patterns, and spare parts.

Returnable containers may also be accounted for on an inventory basis, employing estimates of the number in the hands of customers that are likely to be returned. Other problems of estimation arise if a container deposit is required, particularly if the deposit is greater than the cost of the container.

Enterprises engaged in extracting natural resources, such as metal ores or other minerals, will also have appropriate accounts for recording the cost of the property and the allocation of such costs against periodic revenues. The portion of the cost of natural resources charged to expense is termed *depletion*. The amount of the periodic charge is based on the amount of the deposit removed in relation to the cost of the entire deposit. For example, if it is estimated that a mineral deposit contains 1,000,000 tons of ore of uniform grade and that the cost of the mineral rights is $400,000, the depletion is 40 cents per ton. Assuming that 70,000 tons were mined during a particular fiscal year, the depletion of $28,000 would be recorded by the following entry:

```
Depletion Expense....................................  28,000
    Accumulated Depletion..............................           28,000
```

The accumulated depletion account is a contra asset account; it is presented on the balance sheet as a deduction from the cost of the mineral deposit. In determining income subject to the federal income tax, the amount of depletion allowed as a deduction from revenue is usually greater than the amount based on cost. The Internal Revenue Code provides for a depletion deduction equal to a specified per cent of revenues, the per cent varying with the type of mineral. "Percentage depletion" is mentioned here only because references to it are frequently encountered in the financial press.

Intangible assets. Manufacturers may acquire exclusive rights to manufacture and sell products of a specified type or design. Such rights, called *patents*, are issued by the federal government to the inventor and continue in effect for 17 years. A manufacturing firm may develop new products in its own research department and obtain patents on them, or it may buy patent rights from others. When patents are purchased, the cost should be charged to a patents account and written off, or amortized, over the expected years of usefulness. This may, of course, be less than the remaining legal life of the patent. The unamortized balance is reported on the balance sheet as an intangible asset.

The cost of obtaining patents from the government is usually nominal. The cost of the experimental work leading to the development of a new product may be substantial and in theory should be treated as an asset in the same manner as patent rights purchased from others. In practice, however, many research projects may be under way at the same time, costs may be incurred over a period of years, and the ultimate success or failure of the effort may be in doubt. Accordingly, some businesses treat their research and development costs as a part of current operating expense. To the extent that the amount of research costs incurred do not fluctuate greatly from year to year, the use of this method may not materially affect the amount of reported net income.

Exclusive rights to publish and sell literary, artistic, and musical compositions are called *copyrights*. They also are issued by the federal government and extend for 28 years with the privilege of renewal for a like term. The costs assigned to a copyright include all costs of creating the work plus the cost of obtaining the copyright. A copyright purchased from another should be recorded at its cost. Because of the uncertainty regarding the useful life of a copyright, it is usually amortized over a short period of time.

Deferred charges. Prepayments that are expected to benefit the operations of a number of years should be classified on the balance sheet as *deferred charges*. Examples are bonus payments to secure a long-term lease, discount on bonds payable, costs of rearrangement of factory layout or removal to a new location, and unusual development costs.

Long-term liabilities. Manufacturing enterprises often issue bonds or long-term notes to finance large investments in expanded facilities. The amount due currently, if any, should be reported on the balance sheet as a current liability, described somewhat as follows: "Payments on long-term debt due within one year."

Businesses that issue a long-term warranty on their products may record the estimated amount of the liability that will have to be paid thereon in the future. Such items are frequently described as a "provision" or "reserve," but it is preferable to use the designation "Estimated Liability for Product Warranties." If the warranty is for a short period of time, the estimated liability may be presented as a current liability. Both the amount that may have to be paid and the timing of the payment can only be estimated, and for this reason it is not customary to divide the liability between the current and long-term liability section of the balance sheet.

Cost and expense accounts

The accounts maintained for the cost of goods sold, selling expenses, and general expenses do not differ from those employed by a trading concern. The additional cost and expense accounts required are related to the manufacturing activities and should provide for the recording of: (1) the cost of raw materials put into production; (2) the cost of labor used directly in converting the raw materials into finished goods; and (3) the various expenses incurred in the manufacturing operations.

These three distinct categories are referred to as *direct materials, direct labor*, and *manufacturing expense* or *factory overhead*.

Direct materials represent the delivered cost of the raw materials that enter directly into the finished product. Direct labor represents the wages of the workmen who devote their time to converting the raw materials into finished goods. Factory overhead includes all of the remaining expenses of operating the factory. Examples are taxes, insurance, depreciation, and maintenance related to all factory plant and equipment, supplies used in the factory but not entering directly into the finished product, and wages for factory supervision.

The overhead items represent perhaps the most important group in present-day manufacturing. With increasing use of machinery, more and more of the factory payroll is related to the care and upkeep of the machinery rather than being applied directly to raw materials.

Controlling accounts and subsidiary ledgers

A characteristic feature of accounting systems for manufacturing enterprises is the use of subsidiary ledgers. For purposes of analysis and control, an extensive classification of such accounts as Materials and Factory Overhead is essential. These requirements, together with the multiplicity of repetitive transactions usually found in factory operations, necessitate a division of duties among personnel of the accounting staff that can be best accomplished through the technique of controlling accounts and subsidiary ledgers.

Each subsidiary ledger, which should be designed to fulfill specific needs, may have little resemblance to the customary general ledger account forms. The partial columnar form illustrated below is designed for accumulating the amounts of each type of factory overhead. Postings to the columns are made directly from vouchers, from the general journal, and from other original memoranda. The entries are preponderantly debits so there is no need for both debit and credit columns. The occasional credit to an expense resulting from an error or cancellation of a charge may be designated as a negative item by the use of

INDIRECT LABOR		REPAIRS		POWER		PROPERTY TAXES		INSURANCE	
P. R.	AMOUNT	P. R.	AMOUNT	P. R.	AMOUNT	P. R.	AMOUNT	P. R.	AMOUNT
V 2412	1,416	V 2316	165	V 2670	752	J 121	473	J 122	515
V 2517	1,625	V 2425	218						

Subsidiary ledger for Factory Overhead

parentheses, asterisks, or other devices. At the end of each month the columns are footed and the total compared with the net amount charged to Factory Overhead in the general ledger during the month.

Statement of cost of goods manufactured

Inasmuch as manufacturing activities differ materially from selling and general management activities, it is customary to segregate the two groups of accounts in the summarizing process at the end of the accounting period. The manufacturing group is usually reported in a separate statement in order to avoid a lengthy and complicated income statement. The data reported in the separate statement are those needed to determine the cost of the goods manufactured during the period. It is therefore comparable to that section of the income statement of a trading concern that shows the net cost of goods purchased. The relationship between the statement of cost of goods manufactured and the income statement is illustrated below:

Baxter Manufacturing Company
Income Statement
For Year Ended June 30, 1962

Sales..		$415,100
Cost of goods sold:		
Finished goods inventory, July 1, 1961.....................	$ 38,500	
Cost of goods manufactured.............................	294,675 ←	
Total cost of finished goods available for sale..............	$333,175	
Less finished goods inventory, June 30, 1962...............	51,000	
Cost of goods sold....................................		282,175

Baxter Manufacturing Company
Statement of Cost of Goods Manufactured
For Year Ended June 30, 1962

Work in process, July 1, 1961.............................		$ 20,000
Direct materials..	$124,075	
Direct labor...	98,750	
Factory overhead.......................................	77,850	
Total manufacturing costs................................		300,675
Total work in process during year.........................		$320,675
Less work in process, June 30, 1962.......................		26,000
Cost of goods manufactured...............................		$294,675

Many details were omitted from the foregoing partial statements in order to emphasize their relationship. Complete statements are illustrated later in the chapter.

Adjusting and closing manufacturing accounts

The process of adjusting the accounts of a manufacturing business is similar to that for a mercantile firm. Accounts for supplies, prepaid insurance, and other prepaid expenses must be adjusted to agree with the inventories on hand at the end of the period, and the amounts consumed must be transferred to appropriate expense accounts. Accrued wages and other accrued liabilities and assets are also recorded in the usual manner. The adjustments to the beginning and ending merchandise inventory accounts in a trading concern are replaced by adjustments for the three inventory accounts, raw materials, work in process, and finished goods. The first two accounts are adjusted through an account entitled *Manufacturing Summary* and the third is adjusted through Expense and Revenue Summary.

In closing the books at the end of the accounting period, the temporary accounts that appear in the statement of cost of goods manufactured are closed to Manufacturing Summary. The final balance of this account, which represents the cost of goods manufactured during the period, is then closed to Expense and Revenue Summary. The remaining temporary accounts (sales, expenses, etc.) are then closed to Expense and Revenue Summary in the usual manner.

The relationship of the manufacturing summary account to the expense and revenue summary account is illustrated below:

Manufacturing Summary

1962			1962	
June 30 Work in Process Inventory (beginning).....	20,000		June 30 Work in Process Inventory (ending).......	26,000
30 Raw Materials Inventory (beginning).........	32,000		30 Raw Materials Inventory (ending).......	28,725
30 Raw Materials Purchases..............	120,800		30 To Expense and Revenue Summary......	294,675>
30 Direct Labor..........	98,750			
30 Factory Overhead.....	77,850			
	349,400			349,400

Expense and Revenue Summary

1962			1962	
June 30 Finished Goods Inventory (beginning)....	38,500		June 30 Finished Goods Inventory (ending).......	51,000
30 From Manufacturing Summary..........	294,675	◄		

Work sheet of a manufacturing enterprise

The eight-column work sheet illustrated in Chapter 8 is expanded by the addition of a pair of columns for the statement of cost of goods manufactured. All items that enter into the determination of the cost of goods manufactured are extended to the Manufacturing Statement columns. The difference between the totals of the Manufacturing Statement columns, which represents the cost of goods manufactured, is transferred to the Income Statement Dr. Column.

The illustration and the discussion of the work sheet is based on data taken from the accounts and records of Baxter Manufacturing Company. The trial balance at the end of the fiscal year is recorded in the first two columns of the work sheet presented on pages 562 and 563. Examination of the accounts and the supporting records reveals the following data for recording the adjustments:

(1)	Inventories: Finished goods	$51,000
	Work in process	26,000
	Raw materials	28,725
	Factory supplies	4,000
(2)	Accounts receivable estimated to be uncollectible	2,500
(3)	Insurance expired	2,600
(4)	Depreciation and amortization: Office equipment	1,800
	Factory equipment	17,600
	Buildings	3,000
	Patents	2,500
(5)	Accrued salaries and wages: Direct labor	890
	Indirect labor	300
	Sales salaries and commissions	775
(6)	Accrued interest on notes payable	1,250
(7)	Estimated income tax	15,100

The adjusting entries are recorded on the work sheet in the manner illustrated in earlier chapters, except for the inventories of raw materials, work in process, and finished goods. As explained earlier, the raw materials and the work in process inventory accounts are adjusted through Manufacturing Summary.

The raw materials inventory at the beginning of the fiscal period has become a part of the cost of goods manufactured. Raw Materials Inventory is therefore credited for the value of the beginning inventory, $32,000, and Manufacturing Summary is debited for the same amount. The raw materials inventory at the end of the period must be deducted from the costs charged to the manufacturing summary account and recorded as an asset. Raw Materials Inventory is therefore debited for $28,725 and Manufacturing Summary is credited for the same amount.

In a like manner, the inventory of work in process at the beginning of the period must be transferred to the manufacturing summary account, and the work in process at the end of the period must be deducted from the cost of work in process and recorded as an asset. The first transfer is accomplished by crediting Work in Process Inventory and by debiting Manufacturing Summary for $20,000. The second transfer is accomplished by debiting Work in Process Inventory and by crediting Manufacturing Summary for $26,000.

The finished goods inventory account is adjusted through the expense and revenue summary account in the same manner as the merchandise inventory of a mercantile business. The beginning finished goods inventory is transferred to the expense and revenue summary account by crediting Finished Goods Inventory and debiting Expense and Revenue Summary for $38,500. The ending finished goods inventory is recorded by debiting Finished Goods Inventory and crediting Expense and Revenue Summary for $51,000.

The remaining adjustments are recorded on the work sheet in the usual manner, and the Adjustments columns are totaled to prove the equality of debits and credits. Each account balance, as adjusted, is then extended to the appropriate column, except for the beginning and ending inventory amounts appearing opposite Manufacturing Summary and Expense and Revenue Summary. They are extended individually rather than at the net figure as both amounts will be used in preparing the statements. In the illustration all property tax, insurance, and building expenses were charged to manufacturing. If a portion of these and other expense items were to be allocated to selling and general expenses, the appropriate amounts would be extended to the Income Statement Dr. column. In closing the books, part of the balance of such accounts would be closed to Manufacturing Summary and part to Expense and Revenue Summary.

After all of the amounts have been extended to the appropriate columns, the work sheet is completed in the following manner:

(1) The Manufacturing Statement columns are totaled. In the illustration the total of the Dr. column is $349,400 and the total of the Cr. column is $54,725.

(2) The amount of the difference between the two Manufacturing Statement columns is determined and entered in the Manufacturing Statement Cr. column and the Income Statement Dr. column. This amount ($294,675 in the illustration) is the cost of goods manufactured.

(3) The totals of the last six columns are entered and the Manufacturing Statement columns, which are now in balance, are ruled.

(4) The amount of the final balance of net income is determined and is recorded in the Income Statement Dr. column and in the Balance Sheet Cr. column.

(5) The totals of the last four columns are entered. The columns, which are now in balance, are ruled.

BAXTER MANU
WORK
FOR YEAR ENDED

	Trial Balance		Adjustments		
Account Titles	Dr.	Cr.	Dr.	Cr.	
1 Cash.................................	22,240	....	....	....	1
2 Accounts Receivable...................	41,500	....	....	....	2
3 Allowance for Uncollectible Accounts........		450	(b) 51,000	(h) 2,050	3
4 Finished Goods Inventory..................	38,500	....	(b) 51,000	(a) 38,500	4
5 Work in Process Inventory................	20,000	....	(d) 26,000	(c) 20,000	5
6 Raw Materials Inventory..................	32,000	....	(f) 28,725	(e) 32,000	6
7 Factory Supplies........................	10,000	....		(g) 6,000	7
8 Prepaid Insurance.......................	5,500	....		(i) 2,600	8
9 Office Equipment.......................	18,000	....			9
10 Accum. Depr.—Office Equipment...........	....	6,300	....	(j) 1,800	10
11 Factory Equipment......................	276,000				11
12 Accum. Depr.—Factory Equipment.	....	145,900	....	(k) 17,600	12
13 Buildings.............................	125,000				13
14 Accum. Depr.—Buildings.................	....	17,000	....	(l) 3,000	14
15 Land.................................	35,000				15
16 Patents...............................	30,000	....		(m) 2,500	16
17 Accounts Payable.......................	....	38,600			17
18 First-Mortgage 5% Notes Payable..........	....	100,000			18
19 Common Stock.........................	....	150,000			19
20 Retained Earnings......................	....	132,400			20
21 Sales.................................	....	415,100	....		21
22 Raw Materials Purchases.................	120,800				22
23 Direct Labor...........................	97,860	....	(n) 890		23
24 Indirect Labor..........................	19,000	....	(n) 300		24
25 Factory Maintenance....................	8,000				25
26 Heat, Light, and Power..................	11,800				26
27 Property Taxes.........................	5,000				27
28 Miscellaneous Factory Expense............	2,050				28
29 Sales Salaries and Commissions............	27,800	....	(n) 775		29
30 Advertising Expense.....................	19,300				30
31 Miscellaneous Selling Expense.............	2,500	....			31
32 Officers Salaries........................	23,060	....			32
33 Office Salaries.........................	8,300	....			33
34 Miscellaneous General Expense............	2,790	....			34
35 Interest Expense........................	3,750	....	(o) 1,250		35
36	1,005,750	1,005,750	....		36
37 Expense and Revenue Summary.............	....	....	(a) 38,500	(b) 51,000	37
38 Manufacturing Summary..................	....	....	(c) 20,000	(d) 26,000	38
39 Manufacturing Summary..................	....	....	(e) 32,000	(f) 28,725	39
40 Factory Supplies Expense.................	....	....	(g) 6,000	....	40
41 Bad Debts Expense......................	....	....	(h) 2,050	....	41
42 Insurance Expense......................	....	....	(i) 2,600	....	42
43 Depreciation—Office Equipment...........	....	....	(j) 1,800	....	43
44 Depreciation—Factory Equipment..........	....	....	(k) 17,600	....	44
45 Depreciation—Buildings.................	....	....	(l) 3,000	....	45
46 Amortization of Patents..................	....	....	(m) 2,500	....	46
47 Salaries and Wages Payable...............	....	....	....	(n) 1,965	47
48 Interest Payable........................	....	....	....	(o) 1,250	48
49 Estimated Income Tax...................	....	....	(p) 15,100	....	49
50 Estimated Income Tax Payable............	....	....	....	(p) 15,100	50
51			250,090	250,090	51
52 Cost of Goods Manufactured...............	....	....	....	....	52
53					53
54 Net Income after Income Tax...............	....	....	....	....	54
55					55

Work sheet of a

FACTURING COMPANY
SHEET
JUNE 30, 1962

	Manufacturing Statement		Income Statement		Balance Sheet		
	Dr.	Cr.	Dr.	Cr.	Dr.	Cr.	
1					22,240		1
2					41,500		2
3						2,500	3
4					51,000		4
5					26,000		5
6					28,725		6
7					4,000		7
8					2,900		8
9					18,000		9
10						8,100	10
11					276,000		11
12						163,500	12
13					125,000		13
14						20,000	14
15					35,000		15
16					27,500		16
17						38,600	17
18						100,000	18
19						150,000	19
20						132,400	20
21				415,100			21
22	120,800						22
23	98,750						23
24	19,300						24
25	8,000						25
26	11,800						26
27	5,000						27
28	2,050						28
29			28,575				29
30			19,300				30
31			2,500				31
32			23,060				32
33			8,300				33
34			2,790				34
35			5,000				35
36							36
37			38,500	51,000			37
38	20,000	26,000					38
39	32,000	28,725					39
40	6,000						40
41			2,050				41
42	2,600						42
43			1,800				43
44	17,600						44
45	3,000						45
46	2,500						46
47						1,965	47
48						1,250	48
49			15,100				49
50						15,100	50
51	349,400	54,725					51
52		294,675	294,675				52
53	349,400	349,400	441,650	466,100	657,865	633,415	53
54			24,450			24,450	54
55			466,100	466,100	657,865	657,865	55

manufacturing enterprise

Statements

The work sheet serves as the source of information in preparing the income statement, which appears on this page; the balance sheet, page 565; and the statement of costs of goods manufactured, page 566. Data for the preparation of the retained earnings statement are obtained from the retained earnings account in the ledger and from the work sheet. In the illustration on page 566, the amount of the beginning balance and of the dividends declared was obtained from the ledger; the net income figure was obtained from the work sheet.

Baxter Manufacturing Company
Income Statement
For Year Ended June 30, 1962

Sales...			$415,100
Cost of goods sold:			
Finished goods inventory, July 1, 1961		$ 38,500	
Cost of goods manufactured......................		294,675	
Total cost of finished goods available for sale.......		$333,175	
Less finished goods inventory, June 30, 1962.......		51,000	
Cost of goods sold............................			$282,175
Gross profit on sales..............................			$132,925
Operating expenses:			
Selling expenses:			
Sales salaries and commissions..................	$28,575		
Advertising expense............................	19,300		
Miscellaneous selling expense...................	2,500		
Total selling expenses.......................		$50,375	
General expenses:			
Officers' salaries..............................	$23,060		
Office salaries................................	8,300		
Depreciation — office equipment	1,800		
Bad debts expense............................	2,050		
Miscellaneous office expense...................	2,790		
Total general expenses......................		38,000	
Total operating expenses........................			88,375
Net income from operations.......................			$ 44,550
Other expense:			
Interest expense...............................			5,000
Net income before estimated income tax.............			$ 39,550
Estimated income tax.............................			15,100
Net income after income tax.......................			$ 24,450

Income statement of a manufacturing enterprise

Baxter Manufacturing Company
Balance Sheet
June 30, 1962

Assets

Current assets:

Cash...............................		$ 22,240	
Accounts receivable...................	$ 41,500		
Less allowance for uncollectible accounts.	2,500	39,000	
Inventories (at lower of cost or market)			
Finished goods	$ 51,000		
Work in process....................	26,000		
Raw materials......................	28,725	105,725	
Factory supplies......................		4,000	
Prepaid insurance....................		2,900	
Total current assets.................			$173,865

Plant assets:	Cost	Accumulated Depreciation	Book Value	
Office equipment......................	$ 18,000	$ 8,100	$ 9,900	
Factory equipment....................	276,000	163,500	112,500	
Buildings............................	125,000	20,000	105,000	
Land................................	35,000	—	35,000	
Total plant assets...................	$454,000	$191,600		262,400

Intangible assets:		
Patents...............................		27,500
Total assets............................		$463,765

Liabilities

Current liabilities:			
Accounts payable.....................	$38,600		
Estimated income tax payable..........	15,100		
Salaries and wages payable.............	1,965		
Interest payable......................	1,250		
Total current liabilities...............		$ 56,915	
Long-term liabilities:			
First mortgage 5% notes payable (due 1970)		100,000	
Total liabilities...........................			$156,915

Stockholders' Equity

Common stock, no-par (30,000 shares authorized and issued).................	$150,000	
Retained earnings.......................	156,850	
Total stockholders' equity................		306,850
Total liabilities and stockholders' equity......		$463,765

Balance sheet of a manufacturing enterprise

Baxter Manufacturing Company
Statement of Cost of Goods Manufactured
For Year Ended June 30, 1962

Work in process inventory, July 1, 1961.............			$ 20,000
Raw materials:			
Inventory, July 1, 1961.........................		$ 32,000	
Purchases.....................................		120,800	
Cost of materials available for use...............		$152,800	
Less inventory, June 30, 1962...................		28,725	
Cost of materials placed in production..........		$124,075	
Direct labor....................................		98,750	
Factory overhead:			
Indirect labor................................	$19,300		
Factory maintenance..........................	8,000		
Heat, light, and power........................	11,800		
Property taxes...............................	5,000		
Depreciation of factory equipment...............	17,600		
Depreciation of buildings.......................	3,000		
Amortization of patents........................	2,500		
Factory supplies expense.......................	6,000		
Insurance expense.............................	2,600		
Miscellaneous factory expense...................	2,050		
Total factory overhead........................		77,850	
Total manufacturing costs........................			300,675
Total work in process during period................			$320,675
Less work in process inventory, June 30, 1962........			26,000
Cost of goods manufactured.......................			$294,675

Statement of cost of goods manufactured

Baxter Manufacturing Company
Retained Earnings Statement
For Year Ended June 30, 1962

Balance, July 1, 1961......................................		$144,400
Net income for year after income tax.......................	$24,450	
Less cash dividends.......................................	12,000	
Increase in retained earnings..............................		12,450
Balance, June 30, 1962....................................		$156,850

Statement of Cost of Goods Manufactured. All of the amounts appearing in the Manufacturing Statement columns of the work sheet are reported in a more formalized manner in the statement of cost of goods manufactured. The work in process inventory at the beginning of the period is the first item on the statement. It is composed of the cost of the raw materials, the direct labor, and the factory overhead determined to be applicable to the inventory of partially processed products at the end of the preceding period.

The cost of the materials placed in production is composed of the beginning inventory and net cost of the materials purchased during the period, less the ending inventory. Direct labor is presented as a single item. The factory overhead items are listed separately and totaled. The sum of the materials used, the direct labor, and the factory overhead represents the total manufacturing costs incurred during the period. Addition of this amount to the beginning inventory of work in process yields the total work in process during the period. From it is deducted the ending inventory of work in process to yield the cost of goods manufactured.

Adjusting and closing entries

After the financial reports have been prepared, the adjusting entries and the closing entries are recorded in the general journal. The Adjustments columns of the work sheet are used as the basis for the adjusting entries. Since all manufacturing costs are to be summarized in the manufacturing summary account, the adjustments for the raw materials inventory and the work in process inventory are made to this account. The adjustments for the finished goods inventory are made to the expense and revenue summary account.

The Manufacturing Statement and Income Statement columns of the work sheet provide the necessary information for the closing entries. All manufacturing items are transferred to the manufacturing summary account. The debit balance of the manufacturing summary account, which represents the cost of goods manufactured, is then transferred to the expense and revenue summary account. All remaining revenue and expense items are closed into the same account. The balance of the expense and revenue summary account then represents the net income or loss for the period and is closed to Retained Earnings.

Inventory determination

The procedures for determining the quantities and prices of raw materials in the inventory at the end of the accounting period correspond to those described in Chapter 11. The cost of the inventory of finished goods and of work in process is obtained by combining the amounts of raw materials, direct labor, and factory overhead represented in the physical quantities. These latter computations are based on estimates.

The cost of the raw materials included in the work in process and finished goods inventories is more readily determinable than the other cost elements. The quantities of the various materials are measurable with a fair degree of accuracy. Although changes in the form of the materials as a result of the application of labor are evident, the number of hours of labor and the varying costs per hour must be estimated.

Records of direct labor used may be compiled for test periods during the year, and the information thus obtained may be used in estimating the cost of direct labor in the inventories.

Factory overhead includes all of the remaining factory expenses. They are referred to as "indirect cost" because they have no direct relationship to particular commodities produced. They do have a relationship to direct labor, however, because time is an element in both. Wages are related to time spent, and most manufacturing expenses accrue with the passage of time. An *overhead rate* can be established by dividing total factory overhead for a period by direct labor costs for the same period. In the illustration of the Baxter Manufacturing Company the overhead costs total $77,850 and direct labor costs total $98,750; the overhead rate is therefore 77,850 ÷ 98,750, or approximately 78.8%. The cost of the ending inventories of finished goods and work in process were computed as follows:

Finished Goods Inventory

Cost elements	Product A	Product B	Total
Raw materials............................	$17,567	$ 5,272	$22,839
Direct labor..............................	9,750	6,000	15,750
Factory overhead (78.8%).................	7,683	4,728	12,411
Total inventory cost....................	$35,000	$16,000	$51,000

Goods in Process Inventory

Cost elements	Product A	Product B	Total
Raw materials...........................	$ 7,977	$ 8,189	$16,166
Direct labor.............................	2,250	3,250	5,500
Factory overhead (78.8%).................	1,773	2,561	4,334
Total inventory cost....................	$12,000	$14,000	$26,000

Perpetual inventories and cost accounting

The accounting procedures described in this chapter require the taking of physical inventories of raw materials, work in process, and finished goods whenever financial statements are prepared. To determine the inventories monthly would require a great deal of time and labor and would interfere with manufacturing operations. It is also apparent that the procedures used in pricing the inventories of finished goods and work in process are inexact. As the number of types of products manufactured increases, the reliability of the data decreases.

In a highly competitive free enterprise economy, it is essential that management be supplied with current information on the cost of producing each type of product manufactured. In order to increase efficiency and to reduce costs, it is essential to know the facts of the current situation. The management of a manufacturing enterprise is constantly faced with the problem of improving its products, developing new products, or discontinuing those that are unprofitable. Choices must be made as to the type and the cost of raw materials to be used, the quality of and the price to be paid for labor, and many other factors.

A specialized field of accounting called *cost accounting* has been developed to meet the needs of industry. One of the basic elements of a cost accounting system is the use of perpetual inventories; another is the determination of unit costs of products manufactured. Both of these elements are incorporated in the accounts. The next two chapters are devoted to an introduction to the basic principles of cost accounting.

Questions

1. Name the three inventory accounts of a manufacturing enterprise that replace the merchandise inventory account of a merchandising enterprise.

2. Why is it not practicable to maintain a subsidiary ledger for small tools?

3. If the balance in Patterns before adjustment at the end of the accounting period is $35,000 and the estimated worth of the usable patterns on hand, based on cost, is $22,000, what is the amount of patterns expense for the period?

4. What is the term applied to the periodic charge for the removal of timber from a forest tract?

5. (a) For what period of time are (1) patents and (2) copyrights granted? (b) Why are patents and copyrights frequently amortized over a shorter period than the maximum life?

6. What are the three major classifications of manufacturing costs?

7. Certain commodities and the type of business owning them are listed below. Identify the commodities as raw materials or finished goods.

Commodity:		Owned by:	
(a) Sugar	(1) Bakery	(2) Sugar refinery	
(b) Lumber	(1) Lumber mill	(2) Furniture manufacturer	
(c) Sheet steel	(1) Steel mill	(2) Refrigerator manufacturer	
(d) Paint	(1) Toy manufacturer	(2) Paint manufacturer	

8. Is the salary of the vice president in charge of manufacturing operations a direct labor cost, factory overhead, or general expense?

9. Is factory overhead more closely related to direct materials or to direct labor? Discuss.

10. Immediately prior to closing the manufacturing summary account it has a debit balance of $520,000. (a) What does this account represent? (b) To what account is Manufacturing Summary closed?

Exercises

1. The following items appear on a statement of cost of goods manufactured: materials consumed, $200,000; direct labor, $300,000; factory overhead, $400,000; ending inventory of work in process, $145,000. (a) What is the rate of overhead based on direct labor cost? (b) If the direct labor cost included in the inventory of work in process is $45,000, what is the cost of the direct materials included in the inventory?

2. On the basis of the following information, prepare a statement of cost of goods manufactured for Mohawk Corporation for May of the current year:

Selling expense (control)	$18,000
Raw materials purchases	90,000
Direct labor	95,000
Finished goods inventory, May 1	55,000
Raw materials inventory, May 1	30,000
Work in process inventory, May 1	18,000
General expense (control)	22,000
Factory overhead (control)	60,000
Finished goods inventory, May 31	90,000
Work in process inventory, May 31	21,000
Raw materials inventory, May 31	36,700

3. On the basis of the information in Exercise 2, present the journal entries as of May 31 to: (a) Adjust the three inventory accounts. (b) Close the appropriate accounts to Manufacturing Summary. (c) Close Manufacturing Summary.

Problems

25-1. The statement of cost of goods manufactured for the Ballard Company is presented below:

Ballard Company
Statement of Cost of Goods Manufactured
For Year Ended December 31, 1961

Work in process inventory, January 1, 1961		$ 85,000
Raw materials:		
Inventory, January 1, 1961	$170,000	
Purchases	300,000	
Total cost of materials available for use	$470,000	
Less inventory, December 31, 1961	165,000	
Cost of materials placed in production	$305,000	
Direct labor	247,000	
Factory overhead	203,000	
Total manufacturing costs		755,000
Total work in process during period		$840,000
Less work in process inventory, December 31, 1961		105,000
Cost of goods manufactured		$735,000

Instructions: (1) Prepare journal entries to adjust the work in process inventory and raw materials accounts on December 31, the end of the fiscal year.

(2) Prepare the journal entry to close the raw materials purchases account, the direct labor account, and the factory overhead control account to the manufacturing summary account.

(3) Prepare the journal entry to close the manufacturing summary account.

25-2. The work sheet for the Van Horn Manufacturing Company, with the adjustments columns omitted, is presented on page 571.

Van Horn Manufacturing Company
Work Sheet
For Year Ended December 31, 1962

Account Titles	Trial Balance Dr.	Trial Balance Cr.	Manufacturing Statement Dr.	Manufacturing Statement Cr.	Income Statement Dr.	Income Statement Cr.	Balance Sheet Dr.	Balance Sheet Cr.
Cash in Bank	30,000						30,000	
Finished Goods Inventory	35,000						26,000	
Work in Process Inventory	52,000						60,000	
Raw Materials Inventory	10,000		10,000	8,000			8,000	
Factory Supplies	12,000						4,000	
Machinery and Equipment	300,000						300,000	
Accum. Depr. — Mach. and Equipment		120,000						140,000
Buildings	160,000						160,000	
Accum. Depr. — Buildings		48,000						54,000
Land	90,000						90,000	
Patents	16,000						12,000	
Bonds Payable		100,000						100,000
Discount on Bonds Payable	4,000						3,800	
Common Stock		200,000						200,000
Retained Earnings		103,000						103,000
Sales		725,000				725,000		
Raw Materials Purchases	125,000		125,000					
Direct Labor	190,000		190,000					
Indirect Labor	50,000		50,000					
Miscellaneous Factory Expense	87,000		87,000					
Operating Expense (control)	135,000				135,000			
	1,296,000	1,296,000						
Expense and Revenue Summary					35,000	26,000		
Manufacturing Summary			52,000	60,000				
Depr. Exp. — Machinery and Equipment			20,000					
Depr. Exp. — Buildings			6,000					
Amortization of Patents			4,000					
Factory Supplies Expense			8,000					
Interest Expense					2,200			
Interest Payable								2,000
Estimated Income Tax					43,600			
Estimated Income Tax Payable								43,600
Cost of Goods Manufactured				484,000	484,000			
			552,000	552,000	699,800	751,000	693,800	642,600
Net Income After Income Tax					51,200			51,200
					751,000	751,000	693,800	693,800

Instructions: (1) Journalize the entries to record the adjustments for inventories, depreciation, amortization of patents, bond interest and discount, and income tax.

(2) Journalize the entries to close the manufacturing accounts and the manufacturing summary account.

(3) Journalize the entries to close the revenue and expense accounts and the expense and revenue summary account.

(4) Prepare a statement of cost of goods manufactured.

(5) Prepare an income statement.

25-3. The account titles and the amounts listed below were abstracted from the incomplete work sheet of Plainfield Products, Inc. for the current fiscal year ended September 30. All of the accounts relate to the manufacturing activities and the amounts stated are after year-end adjustments.

Work in Process Inventory, beginning of year.	$ 46,000
Raw Materials Inventory, beginning of year.	65,500
Raw Materials Inventory, end of year.	48,075
Raw Materials Purchases.	621,875
Direct Labor.	425,000
Superintendence.	100,000
Indirect Labor.	37,500
Maintenance and Repairs.	15,000
Heat, Light, and Power.	21,500
Property Taxes.	9,250
Factory Supplies Expense.	10,750
Depreciation Expense — Machinery and Equipment.	37,250
Depreciation Expense — Buildings.	10,000
Insurance Expense.	6,000
Amortization of Patents.	8,000
Miscellaneous Factory Expense.	4,000

The costs of raw materials and of direct labor allocable to the inventory of work in process at the end of the year are estimated to be $25,250 and $15,000, respectively.

Instructions: (1) Compute the overhead rate based on direct labor cost.

(2) Determine the cost of the inventory of work in process at the end of the year, using the overhead rate computed in (1).

(3) Prepare a statement of cost of goods manufactured.

25-4. The trial balance of the Stallings Manufacturing Company at December 31, the end of the current fiscal year, is shown on the opposite page.

Data needed for year-end adjustments are presented below:

(1) Of the accounts receivable at December 31, it is expected that $5,400 will prove to be uncollectible.

(2) Insurance expired, $5,400, allocable as follows: Factory Overhead, $4,400; General Operating Expenses, $1,000.

Stallings Manufacturing Company
Trial Balance
December 31, 19--

Cash..	174,200	
Accounts Receivable.........................	102,300	
Allowance for Uncollectible Accounts...........		800
Finished Goods Inventory.....................	58,400	
Work in Process Inventory....................	31,500	
Raw Materials Inventory.....................	43,000	
Factory Supplies.............................	11,000	
Office Supplies..............................	3,600	
Prepaid Insurance...........................	9,800	
Office Equipment............................	30,000	
Accumulated Depreciation—Office Equipment...		13,000
Factory Equipment..........................	520,000	
Accumulated Depreciation—Factory Equipment.		150,000
Buildings...................................	250,000	
Accumulated Depreciation — Buildings.........		45,000
Land.......................................	70,000	
Patents....................................	30,000	
Accounts Payable...........................		108,000
Bonds Payable..............................		200,000
Premium on Bonds Payable...................		8,600
Common Stock (no par, 50,000 shares).........		300,000
Retained Earnings..........................		194,460
Sales......................................		2,126,000
Raw Materials Purchases.....................	699,000	
Direct Labor................................	560,000	
Factory Overhead (control)..................	394,280	
General Operating Expenses (control)..........	151,280	
Interest Expense............................	7,500	
	3,145,860	3,145,860

(3) Depreciation and patent amortization:
 (a) Office equipment, $4,000.
 (b) Factory equipment, $50,000.
 (c) Buildings, $9,000, allocable as follows: Factory Overhead, $8,200; General Operating Expenses, $800.
 (d) Patent amortization, $10,000.
(4) Salaries and wages accrued, $9,200, allocable as follows: Direct Labor, $7,000; Factory Overhead, $800; General Operating Expenses, $1,400.
(5) The interest rate on the bonds is 5%, payable on April 1 and October 1. The bonds mature in 10 and ¾ years from January 1 of the year just ended. Accrue the interest for October-December, and amortize the premium for the year.
(6) An annual dividend of $1.00 per share was declared by the Board of Directors in December, payable on January 3 of the following year.
(7) Inventories at December 31:
 (a) Factory supplies, $2,400.
 (b) Office supplies, $600.
 (c) Raw materials, $36,500.

(d) Work in process is estimated to include raw materials of $10,000, direct labor of $5,000 and factory overhead based on the ratio of total factory overhead to total direct labor cost.

(e) Finished goods is estimated to include raw materials of $23,600, direct labor of $21,000 and factory overhead based on the ratio of total factory overhead to total direct labor cost.

(8) Income taxes are estimated at $94,220.

Instructions: (1) Prepare a work sheet, observing the following special instructions:

(a) In listing the accounts and the amounts in the trial balance, leave 5 blank lines between Factory Overhead and General Operating Expenses and 5 blank lines between General Operating Expenses and Interest Expense.

(b) After recording the adjustments through item (7)(c) of the adjustments data, determine the per cent of total factory overhead to total direct labor cost and complete the computation of the inventories of work in process and finished goods.

(c) Record the remaining adjustments and complete the work sheet in the usual manner.

(2) Prepare a statement of cost of goods manufactured.

(3) Prepare an income statement.

(4) Prepare a retained earnings statement (the balance of the account remained unchanged during the year).

(5) Prepare a balance sheet.

(6) Present journal entries to close the books (assume that all adjusting entries have been recorded).

Cost accounting— job order system

Cost accounting systems

Cost accounting is the specialized branch of accounting concerned with the determination of "costs". It does not take the place of, but rather extends beyond the usual limits of, general accounting. The manufacturing processes of American industry are intricate and varied. Management needs accurate and timely information about the costs of operating each manufacturing department, the cost incurred in each process, and the cost of each type of product. Data developed through cost accounting systems are used in controlling current operations and planning future operations.

Principles and techniques in cost accounting systems have evolved gradually over the years. The two principal types of cost accounting systems are *job order cost accounting* and *process cost accounting*. Either of these systems may be used with or without standard costs. This chapter will be devoted primarily to job order (or job lot) cost accounting; the following chapter will deal with process cost accounting and, to a lesser extent, with the use of standard costs.

General accounting and job order cost accounting

General accounting contains references to costs. For example, in the beginning chapters of this book, accounts were assembled on the income statement to determine *cost of goods sold*. In dividing the life of a mercantile enterprise into periods of a year or a month, only *expired costs* or *expenses* applicable to such periods were reported on the income statement. In Chapter 25, the balances of certain accounts were assembled in a periodic statement to determine *cost of goods manufactured*. In these instances the costs were determined for a particular period of time, no attempt being made to determine the cost of manufacturing a particular item or group of items.

Manufacturing enterprises in which a job order cost system may be used advantageously are those that manufacture a variety of products on a job order basis. The job orders may specify the manufacture of products to fill special orders or of items carried as a usual part of the stock in trade. The accounting system provides for recording the costs of each job, so that as a job is completed the total cost incurred may be divided by the number of units manufactured to yield the cost of each unit of finished product.

Manufacturing costs may be classified as direct material, direct labor, and manufacturing expense or factory overhead. Accounts are provided for accumulating the cost of all direct materials and direct labor used on each job, to which there is added a portion of the factory overhead. An illustrative summary of the costs incurred in completing a job is given at the right.

JOB ORDER No. 478
1,000 UNITS OF PRODUCT A

Direct Materials Used........	$169
Direct Labor Used...........	296
Factory Overhead Applied.....	198
Total Cost................	$663
Unit Cost ($663 ÷ 1,000)......	66.3¢

Flow of costs in perpetual inventory accounts

Perpetual inventory accounts for materials and supplies, work in process, and finished goods are necessary requisites of a cost accounting system. Each of these accounts is debited currently for all additions and credited for all deductions. The balance of each account thus represents the inventory on hand.

All expenditures incident to manufacturing move through the work in process account and into the finished goods account. The flow of costs through the perpetual inventory accounts is shown in the following diagram:

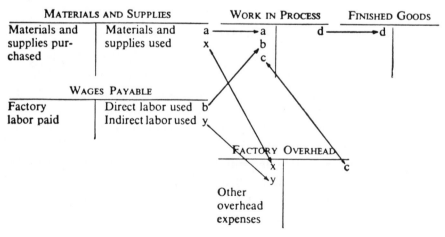

Materials and supplies used and factory labor used are classified as direct and indirect. In the diagram the direct costs are transferred to Work in Process (a and b) and the indirect costs are transferred to Factory Overhead (x and y). The factory overhead costs, which include factory supplies used and indirect labor as well as depreciation, insurance, and other indirect manufacturing expenses, are also tranferred to Work in Process (c). As a job is completed, the costs are transferred from Work in Process to Finished Goods (d).

In the diagram the materials and the supplies are combined in a single perpetual inventory account. An alternative would be to maintain one account for materials, which might be entitled "Raw Materials" or "Direct Materials," and another account for supplies, which might be entitled "Factory Supplies."

Materials and supplies

When direct materials and supplies are purchased, their cost, including transportation, is debited to Materials and Supplies. When they are withdrawn from the storeroom for use in manufacturing, the account is credited. Direct materials identified with the finished product are debited to Work in Process. Indirect materials, such as lubricants and abrasives, that are used in the manufacturing process but are not identified with the finished product are debited to Factory Overhead.

The materials and supplies account is a controlling account. The related subsidiary ledger, which is called the *stores ledger*, contains a separate account for each type of material and supply. An account in the stores ledger is illustrated below:

Material No. *23*								Unit	*Pound*
Received				Issued				Balances	
Rec. Report No.	Quan- tity	Unit Cost	Amount	Requi- sition No.	Quan- tity	Unit Cost	Amount	Quan- tity	Amount
Bal.	1,200	.50	600					1,200	600
				692	500	.50	250	700	350
196	3,000	.54	1,620					3,700	1,970
				704	{700 {100	.50 .54	350 54	2,900	1,566

Stores ledger account

Information concerning the quantity, unit cost, and total value of stores received is obtained from the *receiving report*. Stores are issued to the manufacturing departments on the basis of *requisitions* issued by the scheduling department or the various manufacturing departments. Upon presentation of a requisition the *stores clerk* issues the materials or supplies, posts to the proper stores ledger account, and records their cost on the requisition.

The cost of the materials and supplies issued may be determined by the *first-in, first-out* method, the *last-in, first-out* method, or the *weighted average cost* method. The fifo method was used in the illustration on page 577. Of the 800 pounds of Material No. 23 issued in response to Requisition No. 704, 700 pounds were priced at 50¢, and 100 pounds were priced at 54¢.

The perpetual inventory system for materials and supplies has two important advantages: (1) it provides for the charging of materials to jobs and of supplies to factory overhead accurately and without delay, and (2) it avoids the necessity of a complete physical inventory of stores at one time, with the attendant interruption of production. Comparisons between a physical count of an item and the related stores ledger can be made at any time, so that inventory taking can be a continuous process, spread throughout the year.

Charges to the materials and supplies controlling account are posted monthly from the voucher register or purchases journal in the usual manner. The credits to the account are determined from a summary of the requisitions issued during the month. This flow of stores into production is recorded by the following entry:

Work in Process...	6,500	
Factory Overhead...	420	
Materials and Supplies...................................		6,920

Factory labor

Factory labor is not acquired and stored in advance of its use; hence there is no perpetual inventory account for labor. In order to charge each job order with the cost of the direct labor incurred on the job and to charge factory overhead with the indirect labor cost, it is necessary to record labor costs on *time tickets*. Each time ticket provides space for recording the time that the particular employee began work on a job, the time he ceased work on that job, the total time worked, the rate of pay, and the total cost. If a particular employee works on three different job orders during a day, the data will be recorded on three different time tickets. A similar report must be made for employees whose services are classified as indirect labor.

The time tickets are summarized at the end of each month or other time period and Work in Process and Factory Overhead are charged for the appropriate amounts of the total labor costs incurred. The entry is completed by a credit to Wages Payable for the liability. The entry is illustrated as follows:

Work in Process..	5,000	
Factory Overhead...	1,100	
Wages Payable...		6,100

When the payroll is paid, which may be weekly, biweekly, or at some other regular interval, it is recorded in the usual manner. If the voucher system is employed, a voucher is prepared and recorded in the voucher register as a debit to Wages Payable and a credit to Accounts Payable.[1] Payment of the payroll is then recorded in the check register. If the voucher system is not used, the intermediate step is omitted and payment is recorded in the cash payments journal as a debit to Wages Payable and a credit to Cash. In either event, the credit balance in Wages Payable at the end of an accounting period represents the liability for accrued wages.

Factory overhead

Factory overhead includes all manufacturing costs except materials and labor that are charged directly to the individual job orders. Examples of factory overhead costs are supplies, indirect labor, depreciation, electricity, fuel, insurance, and property taxes. It is customary to have a controlling account in the general ledger for factory overhead. Details of the various types of expense are accumulated in a subsidiary ledger or on overhead analysis sheets. Debits to Factory Overhead come from various sources. For example, the charge for supplies is obtained from the summary of the requisitions, the charge for indirect labor is obtained from the summary of the time tickets, charges for electricity and water may be posted from the voucher register, and charges for depreciation and expired insurance are recorded as adjustments at the end of the accounting period.

Although factory overhead cannot be specifically identified with particular jobs, it is as much a part of manufacturing costs as direct materials and labor. As the use of machines and automation increase, factory overhead represents an ever larger portion of total costs. There are numerous methods of applying overhead to job orders. In general,

---

[1]The provisions to be made for income taxes and F.I.C.A. taxes withheld, and for other withholdings, were outlined in Chapter 16. They are ignored in this discussion in order to concentrate attention on cost accounting techniques.

factory overhead is related to the passage of time, and one of the common methods is to apply it to jobs in proportion to the amount of direct labor incurred.

It is obvious that the relationship between total factory overhead and total direct labor cannot be determined precisely until the end of an accounting period, and that the relationship will vary from period to period. If the cost system is to be of maximum usefulness, it is equally obvious that cost data must be available as each job is completed. Some degree of accuracy may be readily sacrificed in return for timeliness. Therefore, in order that job costs may be available currently, factory overhead is applied by the use of a *predetermined overhead rate*.

The rate is based on estimates of the total amount of factory overhead and of the total amount of direct labor for the year ahead. For example, if it is estimated that the total factory overhead costs for the year will be $48,000 and that the total direct labor cost will be $60,000 an overhead rate of 80% (48,000 ÷ 60,000) may be applied to the direct labor cost of the jobs in process during the year.

As indicated above, the actual overhead costs incurred are debited to Factory Overhead. The amount of overhead costs applied to jobs is credited to Factory Overhead and debited to Work in Process. Assuming that the actual cost of direct labor during a month is $5,000 and that the predetermined overhead rate is 80%, the entry to apply factory overhead to production would be as follows:

Work in Process....................................	4,000	
Factory Overhead.................................		4,000

It is inevitable that the overhead costs applied and the overhead costs incurred during a particular period will differ in amount. If the amount applied exceeds the actual costs, Factory Overhead will have a credit balance and the overhead is said to be *overabsorbed;* if the amount applied is less than the actual costs, Factory Overhead will have a debit balance and the overhead is said to be *underabsorbed*. Both situations are illustrated in the account presented below.

Factory Overhead

Date		Items	P.R.	Debit	Credit	Balance Debit	Balance Credit
May	1	Balance					300
	31	Costs incurred		4,510			
	31	Costs applied			4,000	210	

The $300 credit balance at the beginning of the month is an over-absorbed balance. During the month actual costs incurred amounted to $4,510 and overhead applied to jobs (Work in Process) amounted to $4,000. The balance at the end of the month is a debit or underabsorbed balance of $210.

The balance of the factory overhead account is carried forward from month to month until the end of the year. If the balance fluctuates from debit to credit or is relatively small in amount, there is evidence that the predetermined rate is satisfactory. If a debit balance accumulates month after month until a considerable amount is involved, it indicates that the rate is too low. If a credit balance accumulates, the rate is too high. In either case the predetermined overhead rate should be increased or decreased to prevent the accumulation of a large balance.

Work in process

Costs incurred for the various jobs are debited to Work in Process. The charges to the account that were illustrated in the three preceding sections may be summarized as follows:

Direct Material, $6,500 — Work in Process debited and Materials and Supplies credited; data obtained from summary of requisitions.

Direct Labor, $5,000 — Work in Process debited and Wages Payable credited; data obtained from summary of time tickets.

Factory Overhead, $4,000 — Work in Process debited and Factory Overhead credited; data obtained by applying overhead rate to direct labor cost (80% of $5,000).

There are ordinarily a number of jobs in various stages of production at all times. The work in process account is a controlling account that contains summary information only. The details concerning the costs incurred on each job order are accumulated in a subsidiary ledger known as the *cost ledger*. Each account in the cost ledger, called a *job cost sheet*, has spaces for recording all direct materials and direct labor chargeable to the job, and for the application of factory overhead at the predetermined rate. Postings to the job cost sheets are made from materials requisitions and time tickets, or from summaries.

Upon completion of a job the data on the related job cost sheet are summarized, the unit cost of the finished product is computed and the sheet is removed from the cost ledger. A summary of the job cost sheets completed during the month provides the basis for an entry debiting Finished Goods and crediting Work in Process.

An illustrative work in process account and a summary of the four cost sheets in the related subsidiary ledger are presented on the following page.

Work in Process

Date		Items	P.R.	Debit	Credit	Balance Debit	Credit
May	1	Balance				1,500	
	31	Direct materials		6,500			
	31	Direct labor		5,000			
	31	Factory overhead		4,000			
	31	Jobs completed			15,960	1,040	

Cost Ledger

Job No. 71 (Summary)

Balance......................	1,500
Direct Materials..............	1,000
Direct Labor..................	1,200
Factory Overhead............	960
	4,660

Job No. 73 (Summary)

Direct Materials..............	3,000
Direct Labor..................	2,000
Factory Overhead............	1,600
	6,600

Job No. 72 (Summary)

Direct Materials..............	2,000
Direct Labor..................	1,500
Factory Overhead............	1,200
	4,700

Job No. 74 (Summary)

Direct Materials..............	500
Direct Labor..................	300
Factory Overhead............	240
	1,040

The relationship between the work in process controlling account and the subsidiary cost ledger may be observed in the following tabulation of the data from the accounts illustrated above.

Work in Process (Controlling)		Cost Ledger (Subsidiary)		
Opening balance.............	$ 1,500	Opening balance of Job No. 71 .		$ 1,500
Direct materials..............	6,500	Direct materials		
		Job No. 71.......	$ 1,000	
		Job No. 72.......	2,000	
		Job No. 73.......	3,000	
		Job No. 74.......	500	
				6,500
Direct labor......	5,000	Direct labor		
		Job No. 71.......	$ 1,200	
		Job No. 72.......	1,500	
		Job No. 73.......	2,000	
		Job No. 74.......	300	
				5,000

Factory overhead............	4,000	Factory overhead		
		Job No. 71.......	$ 960	
		Job No. 72.......	1,200	
		Job No. 73.......	1,600	
		Job No. 74.......	240	
				4,000
Jobs completed...	15,960	Jobs completed		
		Job No. 71.......	$ 4,660	
		Job No. 72.......	4,700	
		Job No. 73.......	6,600	
				15,960
Closing balance.............	1,040	Closing balance of Job No. 74		1,040

The data in the foregoing cost ledger were presented in summary fashion for illustrative purposes. A form of cost sheet providing for the current accumulation of cost elements entering into a job order and for a summary at the time the job is completed, is shown below for Job No. 72.

Job No. __72__   Date __May 7, 1962__

For __5,000 Type C Containers__   to be completed on __May 23, 1962__

_____   For__Stock__

Direct Materials		Direct Labor				Summary	
Req. No.	Amount	Time Summary No.	Amount	Time Summary No.	Amount	Items	Amount
434	400.00	2202	83.60	Bt. fwd.	1,158.00		
438	500.00	204	108.40	2234	45.20	Materials	2,000.00
441	700.00	205	67.00	237	70.00	Labor	1,500.00
464	400.00	210	129.00	242	61.60	Overhead	
		211	98.30	248	22.50	(80%)	1,200.00
	2,000.00	213	107.20	250	87.30		
	======	216	110.00	253	55.40	Total Cost	4,700.00
		222	77.60				
		224	217.40	Total	1,500.00	No. of units	
		225	106.30		======	finished	5,000
		231	53.20			Cost per unit	.94
		Fwd.	1,158.00				

Job cost sheet

When Job No. 72 is completed, the direct materials costs and the direct labor costs are totaled and entered in the summary column. Factory overhead is added at the predetermined rate of 80% of the direct labor cost, and the total cost of the job is determined. The total cost of the job, $4,700, divided by the number of units produced, 5,000, yields a unit cost of 94 cents for the Type C Containers produced.

Upon the completion of Job No. 72 the job cost sheet is removed from the cost ledger and filed for future reference. At the end of the accounting period the sum of the total costs on all cost sheets completed during the period is determined and the following entry is made:

Finished Goods...	15,960	
Work in Process		15,960

The remaining balance in the work in process account then represents the total costs charged to the uncompleted job cost sheets.

Finished goods and cost of goods sold

Finished Goods is debited for the cost of all goods transferred from the factory to the stockroom and is credited for the cost of all goods shipped.

The finished goods account is also a controlling account. The related subsidiary ledger, which has an account for each kind of commodity produced, is called the *finished goods ledger* or *stock ledger*. On the debit side of each account in the subsidiary finished goods ledger there are columns for the quantity manufactured, the unit cost, and the total cost of the lot. On the credit side there are columns for the number of units shipped, the unit cost, and the total cost of the units shipped. A finished goods account and an account in the finished goods ledger are illustrated on this and the following page.

Finished Goods

Date		Items	P.R.	Debit	Credit	Balance	
						Debit	Credit
May	1	Balance				7,190	
	31	Job Nos. 71, 72, 73		15,960			
	31	Shipping Order Nos. 641-46			15,084	8,066	

Type C Containers

Manufactured				Sold				Balance	
Job Order No.	Quan- tity	Unit Cost	Amount	Ship. Order No.	Quan- tity	Unit Cost	Amount	Quan- tity	Amount
Bal.	2,000	.98	1,960					2,000	1,960
				643	2,000	.98	1,960	—	—
72	5,000	.94	4,700					5,000	4,700
				646	2,000	.94	1,880	3,000	2,820

Finished goods ledger account

As in pricing raw materials entering into production, there are various methods of determining the cost of the finished goods sold. In the illustration the first-in, first-out method is used. The credits to the finished goods ledger for the quantities sold are posted from the shipping order or similar memorandum. The finished goods ledger clerk then records the total cost of the commodity sold on the shipping order. A summary of the cost data on the shipping orders becomes the basis for the following entry.

Cost of Goods Sold.....................................	15,084	
Finished Goods.....................................		15,084

As its title indicates, the balance of the cost of goods sold account is the total cost price of the finished goods that have been sold during the accounting period. If goods are returned by a buyer and put back in stock, it is necessary, of course, to debit Finished Goods and credit Cost of Goods Sold for the cost. On the income statement the balance of the cost of goods sold account is deducted from net sales to yield gross profit on sales.

Sales

Sales of finished goods are recorded on the books of a manufacturer employing cost accounting in the same manner in which they are re- corded on the books of a mercantile establishment. The sales invoices are entered in a sales journal, or the invoices themselves are used as a sales journal. Assuming that the sales for the month, all of which were on account, totaled $24,930, the summary entry is as follows:

| Accounts Receivable.................................. | 24,930 | |
| Sales... | | 24,930 |

It should be noted that for each sale of finished goods it is necessary to maintain a record of both the cost price and the selling price of the goods sold. As indicated above, the cost data may be recorded on the shipping orders. The sales journal may be expanded by the addition of a column for recording the total cost of the goods billed, the total of the column being posted at the end of the month as a debit to Cost of Goods Sold and a credit to Finished Goods.

Summary illustration of job order cost accounting

To illustrate further the procedures described, the following facts are assumed: The Oxford Manufacturing Co. employs a job order cost accounting system. The trial balance of the general ledger appears as follows on January 1, 1962, the first day of the fiscal year:

Oxford Manufacturing Co.
Trial Balance
January 1, 1962

Cash...	85,000	
Accounts Receivable.................................	73,000	
Finished Goods......................................	40,000	
Work in Process.....................................	20,000	
Materials and Supplies..............................	30,000	
Prepaid Expenses....................................	2,000	
Plant Assets..	850,000	
Accumulated Depreciation — Plant Assets..............		473,000
Accounts Payable....................................		70,000
Wages Payable.......................................		15,000
Common Stock.......................................		500,000
Retained Earnings...................................		42,000
	1,100,000	1,100,000

In order to reduce the illustrative entries to a manageable number and to avoid repetition, the transactions for the month of January are stated as summaries. In practice the transactions would be recorded from day to day in various journals. The descriptions of the transactions, followed in each case by the entry in general journal form, are presented below.

(a) Materials and supplies purchased on account, $62,000.
    Entry: Materials and Supplies....................... 62,000
                Accounts Payable......................... 62,000

(b) Prepaid expenses incurred on account, $1,000.

Entry: Prepaid Expenses.............................. 1,000
    Accounts Payable..........................   1,000

(c) Expenses incurred on account: Factory Overhead, $56,000
                          Selling Expenses, $25,000
                          General Expenses, $10,000

Entry: Factory Overhead.......................... 56,000
    Selling Expenses.............................. 25,000
    General Expenses............................. 10,000
    Accounts Payable..........................   91,000

(d) Materials used: Direct Materials, $60,000
                Supplies, $3,000

Summary of requisitions:

By Use

Job No. 1001..................... $12,000
Job No. 1002..................... 26,000
Job No. 1003..................... 22,000 $ 60,000
Factory Overhead.................   3,000
Total........................... $ 63,000

By Types

Material A....................... $ 16,000
Material B....................... 18,000
Material C....................... 15,000
Material D....................... 14,000
Total........................... $ 63,000

Entry: Work in Process.............................. 60,000
    Factory Overhead........................... 3,000
    Materials and Supplies.....................   63,000

(e) Factory labor used: Direct Labor, $100,000
                 Indirect Labor, $20,000

Summary of time tickets:
Job No. 1001..................... $60,000
Job No. 1002..................... 30,000
Job No. 1003..................... 10,000 $100,000
Factory Overhead.................   20,000
Total........................... $120,000

Entry: Work in Process.............................. 100,000
    Factory Overhead........................... 20,000
    Wages Payable.............................   120,000

(f) Factory overhead applied to jobs at the rate of 90% of direct labor cost, $90,000.
Summary of factory overhead applied:
Job No. 1001 (90% of $60,000)............... $ 54,000
Job No. 1002 (90% of $30,000)............... 27,000
Job No. 1003 (90% of $10,000)...............   9,000
Total....................................... $ 90,000

Entry: Work in Process.............................. 90,000
    Factory Overhead..........................   90,000

(g) Jobs completed, $229,000.
Summary of completed cost sheets:
Job No. 1001...................... $146,000
Job No. 1002...................... 83,000
Total......................... $229,000

Entry: Finished Goods.............................. 229,000
Work in Process............................. 229,000

(h) Sales on account, $290,000; cost of goods sold, $220,000.
Summary of sales invoices and shipping orders:
Product X....................... $ 19,600 $ 15,000
Product Y....................... 165,100   125,000
Product Z. 105,300   80,000
Total......................... $290,000 $220,000

Entry: Accounts Receivable........................... 290,000
Sales...................................... 290,000

Entry: Cost of Goods Sold............................ 220,000
Finished Goods............................. 220,000

(i) Cash received on accounts receivable, $300,000.

Entry: Cash.. 300,000
Accounts Receivable......................... 300,000

(j) Cash paid on accounts payable, $190,000.

Entry: Accounts Payable............................. 190,000
Cash...................................... 190,000

(k) Factory payrolls paid, $125,000.

Entry: Wages Payable................................ 125,000
Cash...................................... 125,000

(l) Depreciation expense: Factory Overhead, $7,000; Selling Expenses, $200; General Expenses, $100.

Entry: Factory Overhead............................. 7,000
Selling Expenses.............................. 200
General Expenses............................. 100
Accumulated Depreciation — Plant Assets...... 7,300

(m) Expiration of prepaid expenses: Factory Overhead, $1,000; Selling Expenses, $100; General Expenses $100.

Entry: Factory Overhead............................. 1,000
Selling Expenses............................. 100
General Expenses............................. 100
Prepaid Expenses............................ 1,200

The flow of costs through the manufacturing accounts, together with summary details of the subsidiary ledgers, is illustrated on page 589. Entries in the accounts are identified by letters to facilitate comparisons with the summary journal entries presented above.

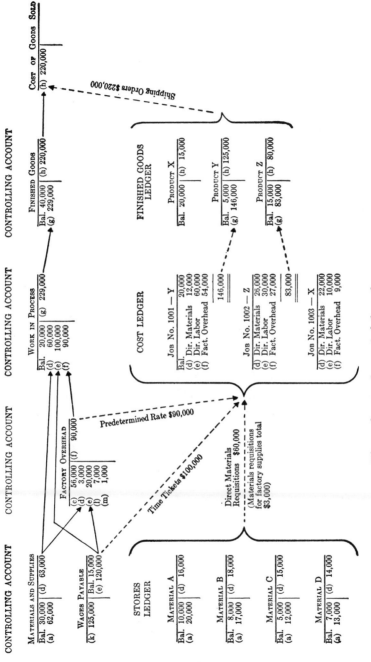

Flow of costs through job order cost accounts

The trial balance taken from the general ledger of the Oxford Manufacturing Co. on January 31 is as follows:

Oxford Manufacturing Co.
Trial Balance
January 31, 1962

Cash.	70,000	
Accounts Receivable.	63,000	
Finished Goods.	49,000	
Work in Process.	41,000	
Materials and Supplies.	29,000	
Prepaid Expenses.	1,800	
Plant Assets.	850,000	
Accumulated Depreciation — Plant Assets.		480,300
Accounts Payable.		34,000
Wages Payable.		10,000
Common Stock.		500,000
Retained Earnings.		42,000
Sales.		290,000
Cost of Goods Sold.	220,000	
Factory Overhead.		3,000
Selling Expenses.	25,300	
General Expenses.	10,200	
	1,359,300	1,359,300

The balances of the three inventory accounts, Materials and Supplies, Work in Process, and Finished Goods, represent the respective inventories on January 31. Each account controls a subsidiary ledger. A comparision of the balance of each controlling account, taken from the trial balance, with its subsidiary ledger, reveals the following:

Controlling Accounts		*Subsidiary Ledgers*		
Account	Balance	Account	Balance	
Materials and Supplies.	$29,000	Material A.	$14,000	
		Material B.	7,000	
		Material C.	2,000	
		Material D.	6,000	$29,000
Work in Process.	$41,000	Job No. 1003.		$41,000
Finished Goods.	$49,000	Product X.	$ 5,000	
		Product Y.	26,000	
		Product Z.	18,000	$49,000

The balance in the account Cost of Goods Sold represents the cost price of the goods sold during the period. It is deducted from the net sales on the income statement. Factory Overhead appears on the trial balance with a credit balance of $3,000, indicating that the overhead applied has exceeded the overhead incurred by that amount; hence the term *overabsorbed* or *overapplied* overhead. The balance of the factory overhead account is shown on interim balance sheets during the year as a deferred charge (underabsorbed) or a deferred credit (overabsorbed). Any balance in the account at the end of the year is usually closed into the cost of goods sold account, the justification being that most of the goods manufactured during the year have been sold. If the balance of the factory overhead account is material in amount or if many of the goods manufactured are still on hand, the balance may be allocated to Work in Process, Finished Goods, and Cost of Goods Sold on the basis of the total amounts of applied overhead included in those balances at the end of the year.

In the foregoing illustration all factory overhead costs were charged to one account and one predetermined rate was used in applying the overhead to production. In practice, it is customary to set up a separate account for each department or *cost center* in the factory.

Questions

1. What form is used to authorize the store room to issue materials to a manufacturing department?

2. (a) Compare the periodic system of inventories with the perpetual system. (b) Which system is superior from the standpoint of internal control?

3. How does the use of perpetual inventories for materials and finished goods simplify the taking of a physical inventory?

4. What forms are used to record the time spent by workmen on each job?

5. Name the form from which debits are posted to (a) the stores ledger, (b) the direct materials section of the cost ledger, (c) the direct labor section of the cost ledger.

6. What accounts are debited when Wages Payable is credited for the labor costs incurred during the month?

7. Is it necessary to adjust Wages Payable for the factory wages accrued at the end of an accounting period? Explain.

8. Name four controlling accounts used in job order cost accounting and the subsidiary ledger controlled by each.

9. What is the reason for using a predetermined factory overhead rate in job order cost accounting?

10. Direct labor cost and factory overhead for the year are estimated to total $1,000,000 and $2,000,000, respectively. What is the predetermined overhead rate?

11. What is the term applied to (a) a debit balance in Factory Overhead, (b) a credit balance in Factory Overhead?

12. Factory employees of the Ajax Manufacturing Co. are paid widely varying wage rates. In such circumstances would direct labor hours be a sounder basis than direct labor cost for applying factory overhead to jobs? Explain.

Exercises

1. The stores ledger account for material A indicates a purchase of 1,000 units at $2, followed by the purchase of 500 units at $1.90. After 800 units have been issued an additional 400 units are requisitioned for Job Order No. 276. Determine the cost of the 400 units, using the first-in, first-out method.

2. Present in general journal form the entry to record the issuance of $75,000 of direct materials and $2,000 of supplies to manufacturing departments.

3. After all postings are completed at the end of the accounting period, the work in process account has a debit balance of $6,235. The direct materials recorded on the two uncompleted cost sheets total $989 and $857, respectively; direct labor totals $1,122 and $968, respectively. Determine the rate of factory overhead, based on direct labor cost.

4. Present in general journal form the entries required to record the following sale of finished goods on account: sales price, $18,000, cost price, $12,700.

5. The following account appears in the ledger after postings have been completed for the month:

Work in Process

Direct Materials..........	32,000	Finished Goods...........	97,900
Direct Labor.............	40,000		
Factory Overhead........	36,000		

Direct materials charged to the uncompleted jobs total $2,500. Determine the amount of direct labor and factory overhead charged to the uncompleted jobs, assuming that the overhead rate is based on direct labor cost.

6. The following accounts appear on the trial balance of Mercer Industries, Inc. at the end of the fiscal year:

Work in Process......................	$ 150,000
Finished Goods......................	550,000
Cost of Goods Sold..................	20,000,000
Factory Overhead...................	5,000 (cr.)

Present the journal entry to close the factory overhead account.

Problems

26-1. Selected transactions completed by the Thorson Manufacturing Company during the month of February are summarized below:

(a) Materials and supplies purchased on account.........	$260,000
(b) Materials and supplies requisitioned:	
For production orders..........................	180,000
For general factory use.......................	23,000
(c) Labor used:	
Direct..	265,000
Indirect......................................	37,000
(d) Factory overhead is applied at the rate of 100% of direct labor cost.	
(e) Repairs and maintenance to factory incurred on account	32,000
(f) Factory building rental paid......................	11,000
(g) Products finished and transferred to stock...........	340,000
(h) Goods sold on account: cost, $315,000; selling price...	410,000
(i) Factory wages paid...............................	257,000

Instructions: Prepare entries in general journal form to record the foregoing summarized transactions.

26-2. On September 30, the end of the fifth month of the current fiscal year, the following balances appear in the general ledger of Danfield Manufacturing Company:

Cash......................................	$110,000	
Accounts Receivable.......................	97,500	
Finished Goods............................	60,000	
Work in Process...........................	12,000	
Materials and Supplies.....................	22,500	
Plant Assets..............................	165,000	
Accumulated Depreciation — Plant Assets......		$ 85,000
Accounts Payable..........................		60,000
Wages Payable.............................		3,300
Capital Stock.............................		150,000
Retained Earnings.........................		50,350
Sales.....................................		525,000
Cost of Goods Sold........................	345,000	
Factory Overhead..........................	1,650	
Selling and General Expenses...............	60,000	

As of the same date, balances in the accounts of selected subsidiary ledgers are as follows:

Stores Ledger
   Material X, $18,000; Material Z, $4,500
Cost Ledger
   Job #501, $7,500; Job #502, $4,500
Finished Goods Ledger
   Commodity R, 1,000 units, $30,000; Commodity S, 800 units, $12,000;
   Commodity T, 2,400 units, $18,000

The transactions completed during October are summarized as follows:

(a) Materials and supplies were purchased on account as follows:

Material X	$24,000
Material Y	25,500
Material Z	3,000

(b) Materials and supplies were requisitioned from the stores clerk as follows:

Job No. 501, Mat. X, $6,000	$ 6,000
Job No. 502, Mat. X, $7,500; Mat Y, $6,000	13,500
Job No. 503, Mat. X, $10,500; Mat. Y, $7,500	18,000
For general factory use; Mat.Z	2,250

(c) Time tickets for the month were chargeable as follows:

Job No. 501	$15,000
Job No. 502	18,000
Job No. 503	13,500
Indirect labor	4,800

(d) Factory pay checks for $52,500 were issued.

(e) Cash of $105,000 was received on accounts receivable.

(f) Various factory overhead charges of $25,500 were incurred on account.

(g) Depreciation on factory equipment was recorded, $1,500.

(h) Factory overhead was applied to jobs at the rate of 80% of direct labor cost.

(i) Selling and general expenses incurred on account, $9,000.

(j) Payments on account were $87,000.

(k) Job orders completed during the month: Job Order No. 501 produced 1,500 units of Commodity R; Job Order No. 502 produced 3,200 units of Commodity S.

(l) Total sales on account were $99,000. The goods sold were as follows (use FIFO):

1,100 units of Commodity R
2,000 units of Commodity S
1,000 units of Commodity T

Instructions: (1) Prepare T accounts for the general ledger, the raw materials ledger, the cost ledger, and the finished goods ledger. Record directly in these accounts the balances listed above, identifying them as "Bal."

(2) Prepare journal entries to record the October transactions.

(3) Post to the T accounts, using the identifying letters as dates. When posting to the finished goods ledger record quantities as well as amounts.

(4) Take a trial balance.

(5) Prove the subsidiary ledgers with the controlling accounts in the general ledger.

(6) Prepare an income statement for the six months ended October 31.

26-3. The account balances in the general ledger of the Stanton Manufacturing Corporation at May 31 of the current year are presented below. The fiscal year ends on June 30.

Cash..	$ 97,600	
Accounts Receivable............................	67,200	
Allowance for Uncollectible Accounts.............		$ 2,400
Finished Goods................................	86,400	
Work in Process................................	24,000	
Materials and Supplies..........................	36,000	
Prepaid Insurance..............................	3,360	
Factory Equipment.............................	280,000	
Accumulated Depreciation — Factory Equipment....		88,000
Office Equipment..............................	19,200	
Accumulated Depreciation — Office Equipment......		4,000
Accounts Payable..............................		60,000
Estimated Income Tax Payable...................		27,500
Cash Dividends Payable.........................		—
Wages Payable................................		2,800
Common Stock ($50 par)........................		250,000
Retained Earnings..............................		142,720
Expense and Revenue Summary...................		—
Sales..		480,000
Cost of Goods Sold.............................	352,000	
Factory Overhead..............................		1,440
Operating Expenses............................	65,600	
Estimated Income Tax..........................	27,500	

Transactions completed during June and adjustments required on June 30 are summarized as follows:

(a) Purchased materials and supplies on account........ $24,000

(b) Incurred following costs, on account:
    Factory overhead...........................$10,400
    Operating expenses......................... 4,960 15,360

(c) Factory labor costs incurred:
    Direct.....................................$12,800
    Indirect.................................... 2,400 15,200

(d) Materials and supplies requisitioned for factory use:
    Direct.....................................$ 9,600
    Indirect.................................... 400 10,000

(e) Predetermined factory overhead rate:
    100% of direct labor cost

(f) Cash disbursements:
    Wages.....................................$16,160
    Accounts payable........................... 48,000 64,160

(g) Total cost of completed job orders.................   36,800

(h) Sales, all on account:
    Selling price..............................   60,000
    Cost price................................   46,400

(i) Cash received on account....................... $62,400

(j) Declared quarterly cash dividend of $1 per share

(k) Depreciation:
      Factory equipment........................... 1,600
      Office equipment............................ 240

(l) Insurance expired:
      Chargeable to factory....................... $240
      Chargeable to operating expenses............. 80   320

(m) Uncollectible accounts receivable written off........ 640

(n) Added to allowance for uncollectible accounts....... 960

(o) Closed balance in Factory Overhead to Cost of Goods Sold

(p) Recorded additional income tax.................. 2,860

Instructions: (1) Prepare T accounts and record the initial balances indicated in the May 31 trial balance on page 595, identifying each as "Bal."

(2) Record the transactions and adjustments directly in the accounts, using the identifying letters in place of dates.

(3) Record the necessary year-end closing entries directly in the accounts, using a capital "C" to designate these entries.

(4) Prepare an income statement for the year ended June 30.

(5) Prepare a balance sheet as of June 30, in report form.

Cost accounting—process system; standard costs

Process costs systems

In job order cost systems, described in the preceding chapter, direct material, direct labor, and factory overhead are applied to each job order, but in many industries job orders are not suitable for scheduling production and accumulating the manufacturing costs. Companies manufacturing cement or flour, for example, do so on a continuous basis. The principal product is a homogeneous mass rather than a collection of distinct units. No useful purpose would be served by maintaining job orders for particular quantities of a product as the material passes through the several stages of production. Instead, the manufacturing costs incurred are accumulated for each manufacturing department or process. The cost elements are identified first with the separate processes and then with the product of those processes. For example, the cost of producing a ton of cement is the sum of the costs incurred in each of the processes divided by the number of tons produced. Other industries for which *process cost accounting* is used include the manufacture of ink, paint, soap, and paper. A manufacturer may employ a job order system for some of its products or operations and a process system for others.

The costs charged to the process accounts are similar to those charged to the work in process account under the job system. They include the three elements: direct materials, direct labor, and factory overhead. A simple work in process account is illustrated below:

WORK IN PROCESS — DEPARTMENT 1

Direct materials...............	4,000	To Dept. 2, 10,000 units.......	12,000
Direct labor.................	5,000	Cost per unit $\dfrac{\$12,000}{10,000} = \$1.20$	
Factory overhead	3,000		
	12,000		12,000

When the manufacturing procedure takes place in a sequence of different processes, the output of Process 1 becomes the raw materials of Process 2, the output of Process 2 becomes the raw materials of Process 3, and so on until the finished product emerges.

Job order and process costs distinguished

In job order cost accounting the three elements of cost are charged directly to job orders. All production consists of job orders, and all costs ultimately are identified with some specific job. In process cost accounting the elements of cost are charged to processing departments, and the cost of a unit produced in a department in a given period is obtained by dividing the cost incurred by the number of units produced. Since all goods produced in a department are identical units, it is no longer useful to classify production into job orders.

If there were but one processing department in a factory, the cost accounting procedures would be very simple. The manufacturing cost elements would be charged to the single work in process account, and the unit cost would be determined by dividing the total cost by the number of units produced. In the work in process account illustrated on page 597, the total cost of $12,000 is divided by the output, 10,000 units, to obtain a unit cost of $1.20.

Ordinarily there is more than one process in a factory. It is therefore necessary to account for each process separately, just as it is necessary to account for each job separately in a job order system. If the number of processes is small, the various process cost accounts may be maintained in the general ledger. Otherwise, the individual accounts may be segregated in a subsidiary ledger and controlled by a single work in process account in the general ledger.

As manufacturing becomes more and more standardized and the units of output tend to be alike, the use of job order costs decreases and greater emphasis is placed on the costs of the different processes. Such processes characterize not only manufacturing operations but selling operations as well. Retailing and wholesaling consist of a series of processes that result in sales. The cost of almost any activity may be divided by the units of output, and a process cost per unit may be obtained. Process cost accounting is therefore more universally applicable than job order cost accounting.

Service departments and process costs

In a factory with a number of processes, there may be one or more *service* departments that do not process the raw materials directly. They assist the processing departments in producing finished goods, however, and the costs that they incur must be charged to the processing departments. Service departments include such departments as the factory office, the building department, the power plant, and the maintenance and repair shop.

The services rendered by a service department give rise to internal transactions between that department and the processes that receive the benefit of the services. In these internal transactions the amount involved is the cost of the service rendered. For example, if the power department produced 300,000 kilowatt-hours during the month at a total cost of $6,000, the cost per kilowatt-hour is 2¢ ($6,000 ÷ 300,000). The departments that used the power would accordingly be charged for it at the 2¢ rate. Assuming that during the month Department 1 used 100,000 kwh and Department 2 used 200,000 kwh, the accounts affected by the interdepartmental transfer of cost would appear as follows:

POWER DEPARTMENT

Fuel............................	2,400	To Dept. 1 (100,000 kw.).......	2,000
Wages.........................	1,700	To Dept. 2 (200,000 kw.).......	4,000
Depreciation....................	600		
Maintenance....................	500		
Taxes..........................	300		
Insurance......................	400		
Miscellaneous..................	100		
	6,000		6,000

WORK IN PROCESS — DEPT. 1	WORK IN PROCESS — DEPT. 2
Power Dept. 2,000	Power Dept. 4,000

The costs incurred by the service departments are charged to the work in process accounts periodically. The period usually chosen is a month, although a shorter or longer period of time may be used. It is not unusual for some service departments to render services to other service departments. For example, the power department may supply electric current to light the factory office and operate various accounting and office machines. At the same time the factory office provides general supervision for the power department, maintains its payroll records, buys its fuel, and so on. In such cases the costs of the department rendering the greatest service may be distributed first, ignoring the fact that it receives benefits from other service departments.

Processing departments

An account is maintained for each processing department. All costs incurred directly by each processing department are charged to the related process account. The process account is also charged for its portion of the costs of the service departments and for the accumulated costs of partially processed materials transferred to it from another processing department. As in the case of the service departments, the costs incurred by each processing department are summarized periodically, usually monthly. The costs applicable to the output of the department during the month are then transferred to the next processing department or to the finished goods account, as the case may be. This flow of costs through the process accounts is illustrated by the following account:

WORK IN PROCESS — DEPARTMENT 2

10,000 units at $1.20 from Dept. 1	12,000	To Dept. 3, 10, 000 units......	20,000
Direct labor............ 4,600		Cost per unit $\dfrac{\$20,000}{10,000} = \$2.00$	
Factory overhead....... 2,300			
Power Dept....... 1,100	8,000		
	20,000		20,000

The debits to the above account may be grouped into two distinct categories: (1) direct material costs, which in this case are composed of 10,000 units received from Department 1 at a total cost of $12,000, and (2) direct labor, factory overhead incurred and service department costs applicable to the process, which in this case totaled $8,000. This second group of costs is called the *processing cost*. In the illustration all of the 10,000 units were completed in Department 2 and passed on to Department 3. The unit cost of the product transferred to Department 3 is $2.00, which is composed of material cost of $1.20 ($12,000 ÷ 10,000 units) and processing cost of $.80 ($8,000 ÷ 10,000 units). This cost of $2.00 per unit, the finished output of Department 2, is treated as raw materials in Department 3.

Inventories of partially processed materials

In the preceding illustration it was assumed that all materials entering Department 2 were completely processed at the end of the accounting period. In such cases the determination of unit costs is quite simple. Frequently, however, there are some materials in various stages of production in the department at the close of the period. When this is the case the processing costs must be allocated between the units that have been completed and transferred to the next process, and those that are only partially completed and remain within the department.

Materials may be placed in production at different stages of the manufacturing process. The stage at which materials are placed in production depends upon the nature of the product being manufactured. For some products it is necessary to have all the raw materials on hand before any work commences. For other products the materials may be added to production in relatively the same proportion as processing costs are incurred. In still other situations materials enter the process at relatively few points, which may or may not be evenly spaced throughout the process.

In order to allocate the processing costs between the output completed and transferred to another process and the inventory of goods within the process it is necessary to determine (1) the number of *equivalent units* of production during the period and (2) the *processing cost per equivalent unit* for the same period. The equivalent units of production are the number of units that would have been produced if there had been no inventories within the process either at the beginning or the end of the period. For example, assume that there is no inventory of goods in a particular processing department at the beginning of the period, that 1,000 units of materials enter into the process during the period, and that at the end of the period all of the units are 75% completed. The equivalent production in the processing department for the period would be 750 units (75% of 1,000). Assuming further that the processing costs incurred during the period totaled $15,000 the processing cost per equivalent unit would be $20 ($15,000 ÷ 750).

Ordinarily there is an inventory of partially processed units in the department at the beginning of the period, some units are completed during the period and transferred to the next department, and other units are partially processed and remain in the inventory at the end of the period. To illustrate the computation of equivalent units under such circumstances the following data are assumed for Department 5 for the month of March:

Inventory within Department 5 on March 1:	600 units, ⅓ completed.
Completed in Department 5 and transferred to finished goods during March:	4,000 units, completed.
Inventory within Department 5 on March 31:	1,000 units, ⅖ completed.

The equivalent units of production in Department 5 for March may be determined as follows:

To process units in inventory on March 1: 600 units × ⅔...............	400
To process units started and completed in March: 4,000 units — 600 units	3,400
To process units in inventory on March 31: 1,000 units × ⅖............	400
Equivalent units of production in March.............................	4,200

Continuing with the illustration, the next step is to allocate the costs incurred in Department 5 between the units completed during March and those remaining in process at the end of the month. If materials and processing costs were incurred uniformly throughout the month, the total costs of the process would be divided by 4,200 units to obtain the unit cost. On the other hand, if all materials were introduced at the beginning of the period, the full material cost per unit must be assigned to the uncompleted units. The processing costs would then be allocated to the finished and the uncompleted units on the basis of equivalent units of production. The T account below is based on the latter assumption:

WORK IN PROCESS — DEPARTMENT 5

Process inventory, March 1			Goods finished during March	
600 units, ⅓ completed......		1,160	4,000 units..................	14,060
From Department 4			Process inventory, March 31	
4,400 units at $1.00.........		4,400	1,000 units, ⅖ completed....	2,000
Direct labor...........	6,000			
Factory overhead.......	2,500			
Service departments.....	2,000	10,500		
		16,060		16,060
Process inventory, April 1				
1,000 units, ⅖ completed.....		2,000		

The processing costs incurred in Department 5 during March total $10,500. The equivalent units of production for March, determined on page 601, is 4,200. The processing cost per equivalent unit is therefore $2.50 ($10,500 ÷ 4,200). Of the charges to Department 5 totaling $16,060, $14,060 was transferred to Finished Goods and $2,000 remained in the account as work in process inventory. The allocations were determined as follows:

GOODS FINISHED DURING MARCH

600 units:	Inventory on March 1, ⅓ completed...............	$1,160	
	Processing cost in March		
	600 × ⅔, or 400 units at $2.50..................	1,000	
	Total..		$ 2,160
	(Unit Cost: $2,160 ÷ 600 = $3.60)		
3,400 units:	Materials cost in March, at $1 per unit.............	$3,400	
	Processing cost in March		
	3,400 at $2.50 per unit.........................	8,500	
	Total..		11,900
	(Unit Cost: $11,900 ÷ 3,400 = $3.50)		
4,000 units:	Goods finished during March..........................		$14,060

PROCESS 5 INVENTORY ON MARCH 31

1,000 units:	Materials cost in March, at $1 per unit.............	$1,000	
	Processing cost in March		
	1,000 × ⅖, or 400 at $2.50......................	1,000	
1,000 units:	Department 5 Inventory on March 31.....................		$ 2,000

By-products

If one of the products resulting from a process has little value in relation to the principal product, it is known as a *by-product*. The emergence of a by-product is only incidental to the manufacture of the principal product. The costs incurred are therefore assigned wholly to the principal product and the value of the by-product is treated as a deduction from the total cost of a main product. The value is considered to be the sales value of the by-product reduced by any additional costs necessary to complete and sell it.

For example, if a by-product with an estimated value of $200 emerges in Department 4 during a cost period, that amount would be credited to Work in Process — Department 4 and debited to an inventory account. The accounting for the sale of the by-product is comparable to that for the sale of the principal product. By-products may be left-over materials, such as sawdust and scraps of wood in a lumber mill; or they may be separated from the raw material at the beginning of production, as in the case of cotton seed from raw cotton.

Joint products

The manufacturing activities of a process or series of processes may result in two or more principal products instead of a single main product. In such cases it is necessary to allocate the manufacturing costs among the various joint products produced. One of the most common examples of joint products is the meat packing industry, where the raw material and processing costs must be allocated to a wide variety of end products. Another example is petroleum refining, with gasoline, naphtha, kerosene and other products emerging from the processing of crude oil.

There are several different methods of allocating costs to joint products. The one that will be described here is referred to as the market value method. Its essential feature is the assignment of costs to the various products in accordance with their relative sales values. To illustrate, it will be assumed that 10,000 units of product X and 50,000 units of product Y were produced at a total cost of $63,000. The market values of the two products and the allocation of the joint cost is presented below:

JOINT PRODUCT	UNITS PRODUCED	TOTAL COST	SALES VALUE PER UNIT	TOTAL SALES VALUE
X	10,000 ⎱	$63,000	$3.00	$30,000
Y	50,000 ⎰		1.20	60,000
	Total			$90,000

Allocation of Cost:

X $\dfrac{30,000}{90,000} \times \$63,000$ $21,000

Y $\dfrac{60,000}{90,000} \times \$63,000$ 42,000

Total $63,000

Unit Cost:

X $21,000 ÷ 10,000 units. $2.10

Y $42,000 ÷ 50,000 units. 84

Inasmuch as joint products result from the same process, one cannot be manufactured without the other. The assignment of cost, then, cannot be based on actual expenditures because it is impossible to determine how much of the cost effort was directed to the manufacture of each product. By apportioning costs based on relative sales values, it is assumed that the cost of producing an item is proportional to its sales value.

Illustration of process cost accounting

To illustrate further the procedures described, the following facts are assumed: The Howell Company manufactures one principal product, designated Product A. The manufacturing activity begins in Department 1, where all raw materials enter into production. The materials remain in Department 1 for a relatively short time and there is ordinarily no inventory of work in process at the end of the accounting period. A by-product, designated Product B, is also produced in Department 1. From Department 1 the materials comprising the principal product are transferred to Department 2. The processing in Department 2 is of longer duration and there are usually inventories within the department at the end of the accounting period. There are two service departments, Maintenance and Power.

The trial balance of the general ledger on January 1, 1962 is shown at the top of the next page.

A summary of the transactions and adjustments for the month of January, followed by the related entries, in general journal form, are presented below. In actual practice the transactions would be recorded from day to day in various journals.

(a) Materials and supplies purchased on account, $33,500.

Entry: Materials and Supplies. 33,500

Accounts Payable.   33,500

(b) Prepaid expenses incurred on account, $1,100.

Entry: Prepaid expenses. 1,100

Accounts Payable.   1,100

Howell Company
Post-Closing Trial Balance
January 1, 1962

Cash	18,500	
Accounts Receivable	15,000	
Product A (1,000 units at $11.50)	11,500	
Product B (600 pounds at $.50)	300	
Work in Process — Department 2 (800 units, ½ completed)	7,800	
Materials and Supplies	12,000	
Prepaid Expenses	2,150	
Plant Assets	310,000	
Accumulated Depreciation — Plant Assets		95,000
Accounts Payable		21,180
Wages Payable		1,400
Common Stock		200,000
Retained Earnings		59,670
	377,250	377,250

(c) Costs and expenses incurred on account: Maintenance Department, $200; Power Department, $300; Department 1, $600; Department 2, $400; Selling Expenses, $5,000; General Expenses, $4,500.

Entry:			
	Maintenance Department	200	
	Power Department	300	
	Work in Process — Department 1	600	
	Work in Process — Department 2	400	
	Selling Expenses	5,000	
	General Expenses	4,500	
	Accounts Payable		11,000

(d) Materials and supplies requisitioned: Maintenance Department, $400; Power Department, $2,000; Department 1, $24,600.

Entry:			
	Maintenance Department	400	
	Power Department	2,000	
	Work in Process — Department 1	24,600	
	Materials and Supplies		27,000

(e) Factory labor used: Maintenance Department, $1,200; Power Department, $1,500; Department 1, $5,890; Department 2, $13,350.

Entry:			
	Maintenance Department	1,200	
	Power Department	1,500	
	Work in Process — Department 1	5,890	
	Work in Process — Department 2	13,350	
	Wages Payable		21,940

(f) Expiration of prepaid expenses: Maintenance Department, $100; Power Department, $250; Department 1, $450; Department 2, $550; Selling Expense, $300; General Expense, $200.

Entry:			
	Maintenance Department	100	
	Power Department	250	
	Work in Process — Department 1	450	
	Work in Process — Department 2	550	
	Selling Expense	300	
	General Expense	200	
	Prepaid Expenses		1,850

(g) Depreciation charges: Maintenance Department, $100; Power Department, $350; Department 1, $600; Department 2, $900; Selling Expense, $200; General Expense, $100.

Entry:		
Maintenance Department......................	100	
Power Department............................	350	
Work in Process — Department 1................	600	
Work in Process — Department 2................	900	
Selling Expense..............................	200	
General Expense.............................	100	
Accumulated Depreciation — Plant Assets......		2,250

(h) Allocation of Maintenance Department Costs, totaling $2,000; Power Department, 5%; Department 1, 45%; Department 2, 50%.

Entry:		
Power Department............................	100	
Work in Process — Department 1................	900	
Work in Process — Department 2................	1,000	
Maintenance Department...................		2,000

(i) Allocation of Power Department Costs, totaling $4,500: Department 1, 40%; Department 2, 60%.

Entry:		
Work in Process — Department 1................	1,800	
Work in Process — Department 2................	2,700	
Power Department.........................		4,500

(j) Production in Department 1: During January 4,100 units of materials were fully processed in Department 1 and transferred to Process 2; 800 pounds of by-product B, valued at 50¢ per pound were also produced. There is no work in process on January 31.

Allocation of total costs of $34,840 charged to Department 1:

Product B, 800 × $.50...........................	$ 400
Transferred to Department 2.....................	34,440
Total Costs.....................................	$34,840

Unit Cost of product transferred to Department 2:

$34,440 ÷ 4,100................................	$ 8.40

Entry:		
Product B.....................................	400	
Work in Process — Department 2................	34,440	
Work in Process — Department 1..............		34,840

(k) Production in Department 2: During January, 4,000 units of Product A were completed and transferred to stock. The remaining 900 partially processed units were ⅔ completed on January 31.

Equivalent units of production:

To process units in inventory on January 1	
800 × ½.......................................	400
To process units started and completed in January	
4,000 − 800...................................	3,200
To process units in inventory on January 31	
900 × ⅔.......................................	600
Equivalent units of production...................	4,200

Processing costs:

Expenses incurred on account (c).................	$ 400
Labor (e).......................................	13,350
Expiration of prepaid expenses (f)................	550
Depreciation (g)................................	900
Maintenance (h)................................	1,000
Power (i)......................................	2,700
	$18,900

Unit processing costs:

$18,900 ÷ 4,200................................	$4.50

Allocation of costs of Department 2:

Units started in December, completed in January

Inventory on January 1, 800 units ½ completed...	$ 7,800	
Processing costs in January, 400 at $4.50.........	1,800	
Total ($9,600 ÷ 800 = $12.00 unit cost)........		$ 9,600

Units started and completed in January

From Department 1, 3,200 units at $8.40.........	$26,880	
Processing costs, 3,200 at $4.50.................	14,400	
Total ($41,280 ÷ 3,200 = $12.90 unit cost)......		41,280
Total transferred to Product A...............		$50,880

Units started in January, ⅔ completed

From Department 1, 900 units at $8.40...........	$ 7,560	
Processing costs, 600 at $4.50...................	2,700	
Total work in process — Department 2........		10,260
Total costs charged to Department 2..............		$61,140

Entry: Product A....................................	50,880	
Work in Process — Department 2.............		50,880

(l) Sales on account: Product A, $70,300; Product B, $800.

Entry: Accounts Receivable..........................	71,100	
Sales......................................		71,100

(m) Cost of goods sold: Product A, $46,900; Product B, $500.

Analysis of cost of goods sold:

Product A

1,000 units at $11.50....................	$11,500
800 units at $12.00....................	9,600
2,000 units at $12.90....................	25,800
	$46,900

Product B

1,000 pounds at $.50....................	$ 500

Entry: Cost of Goods Sold...........................	47,400	
Product A....................................		46,900
Product B....................................		500

(n) Cash received on account, $70,000.

Entry: Cash...	70,000	
Accounts Receivable........................		70,000

(o) Cash payments: on account, $50,000; wages, $22,000.

Entry: Accounts Payable............................	50,000	
Wages Payable..............................	22,000	
Cash.....................................		72,000

After recording and posting the foregoing entries the trial balance of the ledger is as follows:

Howell Company

Trial Balance

January 31, 1962

Cash...	16,500	
Accounts Receivable................................	16,100	
Product A..	15,480	
Product B..	200	
Work in Process — Dept. 2..........................	10,260	
Materials and Supplies..............................	18,500	
Prepaid Expenses...................................	1,400	
Plant Assets.......................................	310,000	
Accumulated Depreciation — Plant Assets.............		97,250
Accounts Payable...................................		16,780
Wages Payable.....................................		1,340
Common Stock.....................................		200,000
Retained Earnings..................................		59,670
Sales..		71,100
Cost of Goods Sold.................................	47,400	
Selling Expense....................................	5,500	
General Expense...................................	4,800	
	446,140	446,140

A chart of the flow of costs from the service and processing department accounts into the finished goods account and thence to the cost of goods sold account, is presented on the opposite page.

Process costs and business operations

In the foregoing discussion and illustrations the entire attention was necessarily directed to fundamental principles of cost determination. It should be noted that the determination of costs is not an end in itself but rather the basis for controlling operations. The cost data obtained should be supplemented by additional analyses in the never ending effort to reduce costs and improve the product.

Cost accounting goes beyond the incurrence of each cost item. The cost of producing heat or power, for example, is a composite of many individual costs. The price paid for coal and the amount of coal used are only a part of the factors influencing the total heating cost. It is not only the original outlay that is important but the use that is made of it. Cost studies go beyond the data accumulated in the accounts. In choosing between various methods of production, products to be manufactured,

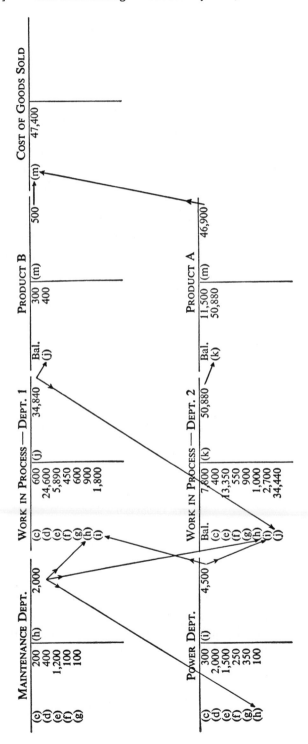

Flow of costs through process cost accounts

grades of raw materials to be purchased, and other alternatives, management needs information regarding the immediate past and estimates as to the future.

Fixed and variable costs

The nature of indirect manufacturing costs has great significance to the cost accountant and to management. Many factory overhead expenses tend to be independent of the volume of output. For example, depreciation, property taxes, property insurance, and salaries of production executives remain relatively constant in total regardless of fluctuations in the level of output. Such costs are called *fixed costs*.

Other costs, such as direct labor and direct materials, tend to vary directly with the volume of production. Such costs are referred to as *variable costs*. If output is doubled, variable costs will tend to double; if output is halved, variable costs will tend to be halved.

A third category of costs is referred to as *semivariable*. They vary with volume of production but not in direct proportion. For example, one foreman is able to supervise the workers in his department up to a certain level of production. If additional workers are added to his department, the point is eventually reached where it is necessary to hire another foreman. It is usually desirable to break down semivariable costs into fixed and variable elements.

In budgeting and planning for future operations it is necessary to consider the fixed or variable nature of the various manufacturing costs. To illustrate, assume that the current monthly production of a manufacturing plant is 1,000 units and that the total manufacturing cost is $45,000. Analysis of the costs reveals the following:

Costs		Units Produced	Unit Cost	
Fixed	$20,000			$20
Variable	25,000	1,000		25
Total	$45,000			$45

Assuming that the manufacturing facilities are adequate to permit doubling production, that the fixed costs would remain unchanged, and that variable costs would vary directly with production, the increased production would result in the following unit cost.

Costs		Units Produced	Unit Cost	
Fixed	$20,000			$10
Variable	50,000	2,000		25
Total	$70,000			$35

Assuming further that the units can be sold at $65, the gross profit realized on the 1,000 units produced at a unit cost of $45 would be $20,000 (1,000 × $20); on the 2,000 units produced at a unit cost of $35 the gross profit would be $60,000 (2,000 × $30).

The relationship of fixed costs and variable costs is also important in determining pricing policies. The difference between the total cost at one level of production and at a higher or lower level of production is sometimes called *differential* cost. To illustrate this concept, assume that a particular manufacturer normally produces 10,000 units of product in a month, for which he receives $10 per unit. He has an opportunity to sell an additional 5,000 units to an exporter at $6 per unit without interfering with his normal production or domestic pricing policies. An analysis of costs and profit margins reveals the following:

	10,000 Units		15,000 Units	
Sales — 10,000 units at $10		$100,000		$100,000
5,000 units at $ 6				30,000
Total		$100,000		$130,000
Fixed Costs	$25,000		$25,000	
Variable Costs — 10,000 units at $4	40,000		40,000	
5,000 units at $4			20,000	
Total		$ 65,000		$ 85,000
Gross Profit Margin		$ 35,000		$ 45,000

It is obvious that it would be advantageous to contract for the manufacture and sale of the additional 5,000 units at $6.00 as it would result in an additional gross profit of $10,000. Although the sale of the additional 5,000 units would bring in only $30,000, the differential costs incurred in their manufacture would total only $20,000.

Standard costs

The process and job order cost systems, described in this and the preceding chapter, are based on "historical costs" or "actual costs." The aim of both systems is to determine as accurately as possible the actual cost incurred in manufacturing the various commodities produced. The one deviation from actual cost was the use of an estimated or predetermined factory overhead rate in job order costs. The principal reason for this departure from historical cost was to permit the calculation of job costs upon the completion of each order.

Many industries and individual companies have extended the use of estimates to all manufacturing costs. Cost systems that employ estimates for direct materials, direct labor, and factory overhead are sometimes referred to as *standard cost systems*. Standard costs may be used in either the job order type of production or the process type of production. In many cases standard costs may be used for a part of the factory and actual costs for another part. Standard costs serve as a measuring stick for the determination of efficiency. If the standard cost of a product is $5.00 per unit and it is being currently produced at a cost of $5.50 the factors responsible for the excess cost should be found and remedial steps taken.

The establishment of standards requires an exhaustive study involving departmental estimates of costs at normal productive capacity and at various levels above and below normal. Motion and time studies are made of each operation and the work force is trained to use the most efficient methods. Raw materials and productive equipment are subjected to detailed study and tests in an effort to achieve maximum productivity at minimum cost. A wide variety of management skills are needed in setting standards. It requires the joint effort of accounting, engineering, personnel administration, and other managerial areas.

Variances. Regardless of the care used in establishing and revising cost standards, the actual costs incurred in any particular month or on any particular job are likely to deviate from standard. These differences are referred to as *variances*. If the actual cost incurred on a job is less than the standard cost, the variance is favorable; if actual exceeds standard, the variance is unfavorable. The total variance for a particular month or on a particular job is likely to be a complex of a number of variances. There may be variances in direct materials cost, direct labor cost, or factory overhead cost.

Material variance. Two principal factors enter into the determination of standards for direct materials cost: (1) the quantity (usage) standard and (2) the price standard. Consequently, the actual cost of materials may differ from standard because of quantity variance, price variance, or both. To illustrate, assume that the standard materials cost of producing 10,000 units of product X and the material costs actually incurred were as follows:

Standard: 20,000 units at $.50..................................... $10,000
Actual: 20,600 units at $.52..................................... 10,712

It is readily apparent that the unfavorable variance of $712 resulted in part from an excess usage of 600 units of materials and in part from an excess unit cost of $.02. The analysis of the variance is as follows:

QUANTITY VARIANCE

Quantity	Price	Amount	Variance
Actual — 20,600 × Standard — $.50		$10,300	
Standard — 20,000 × Standard — $.50		10,000	
Quantity variance — unfavorable			$300

PRICE VARIANCE

Actual — 20,600 × Actual — $.52		$10,712	
Actual — 20,600 × Standard — $.50		10,300	
Price variance — unfavorable			412
Materials variance — unfavorable			$712

Labor. As in the case of materials, labor cost standards are divided into parts: (1) the time (usage or efficiency) standard, and (2) the wage (rate or cost) standard. If the actual labor hours spent on a job differ from the standard hours there is a time variance, and if the wage rate paid differs from the standard rate there is a wage variance. The standard and actual cost of labor in the production of 10,000 units of product X are assumed to be as follows:

Standard: 8,000 hours at $2.00............................... $16,000
Actual: 7,900 hours at   2.10...............................   16,590

The unfavorable labor variance of $590 is a composite of a favorable time variance and an unfavorable wage variance, as indicated below:

TIME VARIANCE

Time	Rate	Amount	Variance
Standard — 8,000 × Standard — $2.00		$16,000	
Actual — 7,900 × Standard — $2.00		15,800	
Time variance — favorable			$200

WAGE VARIANCE

Actual — 7,900 × Actual — $2.10		$16,590	
Actual — 7,900 × Standard — $2.00		15,800	
Wage variance — unfavorable			790
Labor variance — unfavorable			$590

Factory overhead variance. When standard costs are employed, manufacturing expenses are applied to the commodities produced by use of a predetermined overhead rate, in much the same manner as was presented in Chapter 26. The procedure for establishing a standard rate is more scientific and requires a greater amount of investigation and planning. The principal objective of the system is to control or keep the expenses within the limits determined to be reasonable. An essential part of control is to assign responsibility to specific individuals, such as foremen, supervisors, and the plant superintendent.

The starting point in establishing standard overhead rates is the preparation of a detailed expense budget for each department. The expenses are grouped into two major classifications, fixed and variable. As was pointed out earlier in the chapter, the volume of variable expenses fluctuates with changes in the level of production. It is therefore necessary to prepare the budgets for varying levels of production. The yardstick for measuring the performance of each departmental foreman is the detailed budget of departmental expenses. If production is at 80% of capacity, the budget for this level of activity will be used as the standard in making comparisons with the expenses actually incurred.

The causes of differences between amounts budgeted and actual expenses may be analyzed as the controllable variance, which is the difference between the actual expenses incurred and the budget allowance; and the volume variance, which is the difference between the budget allowance and the standard expenses. Further consideration will be given to budgeting in Chapter 28.

Questions

1. (a) Differentiate between job order and process cost accounting. (b) Would you recommend a job order or a process cost system for (1) a print shop? (2) a flour mill? (3) an oil refinery? (4) an iron foundry?

2. (a) What is meant by the term *equivalent units*? (b) When is it necessary to compute equivalent units of work completed within a processing department?

3. On March 1, Work in Process — Department 1 has a balance of $3,500. What elements of cost are included in this balance?

4. Department 4 produces two products. How should the costs be allocated (a) if the products are joint products? (b) if one of the products is treated as a by-product?

5. Distinguish between (a) a physical inventory and a perpetual inventory; (b) direct labor and indirect labor; (c) by-product and joint product; (d) service department and processing department; (e) historical cost and standard cost.

6. Which of the following costs incurred by a manufacturing enterprise tend to be fixed and which tend to be variable: (a) depreciation of factory building; (b) property taxes on machinery; (c) direct labor; (d) electric power (purchased) to operate manufacturing machinery; (e) salary of factory superintendent; (f) cost of sheet steel entering into the final product; (g) cost of heating the factory; (h) payroll taxes on direct labor costs.

7. If the standard cost of a job exceeds actual cost, is the variance favorable or unfavorable?

8. What are the two types of variances between standard cost and actual cost (a) for direct materials? (b) for direct labor?

9. The standard price of a raw material used for a particular product is $1.50 a pound, the price actually paid is $1.60. If 1,000 pounds of the material are used, what is the amount of the variance?

10. May cost standards be used in (a) a process cost system? (b) a job order cost system?

Exercises

1. The charges to Work in Process — Department 1 for a cost period, together with information concerning production, are presented below. All materials are placed in process at the beginning of production.

WORK IN PROCESS — DEPARTMENT 1

1,500 units 2/3 completed	3,800	Product X, 4,000 units	16,800
Direct materials, 2,500 at $1	2,500		
Direct labor	4,500		
Factory overhead	6,000		
	16,800		16,800

Determine the following, presenting your computations: (a) equivalent units of production, (b) processing cost per equivalent unit, (c) total and unit cost of Product X started in prior period and completed in the current period, (d) total and unit cost of Product X started and completed in the current period.

2. The charges to Work in Process — Department 3 for a cost period, together with information concerning production, are presented below. No direct materials are added in Department 3. The units completed include the 1,200 in process at the beginning of the period.

WORK IN PROCESS — DEPARTMENT 3

1,200 units ¾ completed	3,240	Product A, 4,200 units	
From Dept. 2, 4,000 units	4,400	1,000 units ½ completed	
Direct labor	3,200		
Service departments	600		
Factory overhead	3,800		
	15,240		15,240

Determine the following, presenting your computations: (a) equivalent units of production, (b) processing cost per equivalent unit, (c) total and unit cost of Product A started in prior period and completed in the current period, (d) total and unit cost of Product A started and completed in the current period, (e) total cost of work in process inventory at the end of the current period.

3. The charges to Work in Process — Department 3, together with units of product completed during the cost period, are shown in the following account:

WORK IN PROCESS — DEPARTMENT 3

From Department 1	8,100	By-product X, 2,000 units	
Direct labor	5,200	Joint product A, 4,000 units	
Factory overhead	2,600	Joint product B, 900 units	

The value of X is $.45 a unit; A sells at $3.20 a unit and B sells at $8 a unit. There is no inventory of goods in process at either the beginning or the end of the cost period. Allocate the costs to the three products, and determine the unit cost of each. Present your computations.

4. During the past year the Dover Corporation produced and sold 100,000 units of product at a unit cost of $4. Selling and general expenses totaled

$100,000 and income taxes amounted to 50% of net income. The product was sold uniformly at $7 a unit. A study reveals that if the selling price were reduced to $6.50 a unit, total unit sales could probably be increased by 50%. It is estimated that total manufacturing costs would increase 25% and selling and administrative expenses would increase 15%; the income tax rate would remain the same. Determine the net income based on 100,000 units and the expected net income based on 150,000 units. Present your solution in an orderly manner.

5. The standard and actual materials and labor costs incurred on a job order were as follows:

Materials	Labor
Standard — 20,000 units at $1.00	Standard — 30,000 hours at $1.75
Actual — 21,000 units at $1.05	Actual — 29,000 hours at $1.85

Determine (1) the quantity variance, price variance, and total material variance, and (2) the time variance, wage variance, and total labor variance.

Problems

27-1. Product A is manufactured by a series of three processes, all raw materials being introduced in Department 1. From Department 1 the materials pass sequentially through Departments 2 and 3, emerging as finished product A. Inventories are priced at cost by the first-in, first-out method.

The balances in the Department 3 work in process and the finished goods inventory account were as follows on June 1:

Work in process, Department 3
  Balance — 900 units, ⅙ completed..................... $2,919
Finished goods
  Balance — 500 units at $7 a unit...................... $3,500

During the month of June, 8,900 units of A were completed in Department 3. The following costs were charged to Work in Process, Department 3, during the month:

Materials transferred from Department 2—9,000 units at $2.65	$23,850
Direct labor...	25,800
Factory overhead....................................	13,150

Inventories on June 30 were as follows:
Work in process, Department 3 — 1,000 units, ¾ completed.
Finished goods — 1,100 units.

Instructions: (1) Determine the following, presenting the computations in good order: (a) equivalent units of production, (b) unit processing cost, (c) cost of goods finished (determine unit cost of goods started in prior period and unit cost of goods started in June), (d) work in process inventory, June 30, (e) cost of goods sold (indicate number of units and unit costs), (f) finished goods inventory, June 30.

(2) Set up T accounts for Work in Process, Department 3, and for Finished Goods. Record the balances at June 1, the transactions for June in summary form, and bring down the balances at June 30. Record the number of units and degree of completion, where appropriate, in the items sections of the accounts

27-2. The Stamford Chemical Co. manufactures two products, designated X and Y. Raw material A enters Department 1 where it is ground and partially refined. The output of Department 1 is transferred to Department 2, where raw material B is added and further refining occurs. The output of Department 2 is Product X. Product Y is produced by additional processing of Product X in Department 3. There is some shrinkage in weight in each process; unit costs of the output of each department are therefore determined by dividing the accumulated costs by the number of pounds produced. There are no inventories of work in process at either the beginning or the end of the month.

The accounts in the general ledger and their balances on May 1 of the current year are as follows:

Cash.	35,000	
Accounts Receivable	28,000	
Product X (4,000 pounds at $1.65)	6,600	
Product Y (3,000 pounds at $3.00)	9,000	
Work in Process — Dept. 1	——	
Work in Process — Dept. 2	——	
Work in Process — Dept. 3	——	
Maintenance Department	——	
Raw Material A (7,000 pounds at $.50)	3,500	
Raw Material B (3,000 pounds at $.80)	2,400	
Prepaid Expenses	2,900	
Plant Assets	400,000	
Accumulated Depreciation — Plant Assets		115,000
Accounts Payable		24,000
Wages Payable		1,200
Common Stock		200,000
Retained Earnings		147,200
Sales.		——
Cost of Goods Sold	——	
General Operating Expenses	——	
	487,400	487,400

The operations for May are summarized as follows:

(a) Raw materials purchased on account: A, 40,000 pounds, $20,800; B, 18,000 pounds, $15,300.

(b) Prepaid expenses incurred on account, $1,900.

(c) Miscellaneous costs and expenses incurred on account: Department 1, $650; Department 2, $780; Department 3, $400; Maintenance Department, $1,500; General Operating Expenses, $12,610.

(d) Material A placed in Department 1 for processing, 39,000 pounds (use FIFO method).

(e) Materials B placed in Department 2 for processing, 18,000 pounds (use FIFO method).

(f) Factory labor used: Department 1, $10,000; Department 2, $9,780; Department 3, $4,320; Maintenance Department, $2,000.

(g) Expiration of various prepaid expenses: Department 1, $500; Department 2, $900; Department 3, $400; Maintenance Department, $300; General Operating Expenses, $250.

(h) Depreciation charges: Department 1, $450; Department 2, $850; Department 3, $300; Maintenance Department, $200; General Operating Expenses, $500.

(i) Allocation of Maintenance Department Costs: Department 1, 30%; Department 2, 50%; Department 3, 20%.

(j) Output of Department 1 was 31,000 pounds, which was transferred to Department 2. There is no work in process remaining in the department.

(k) Output of Department 2 was 39,000 pounds, which was transferred to Product X. There is no work in process remaining in the department.

(l) Product X in the amount of 10,000 pounds was transferred to Department 3 (use FIFO method).

(m) Output of Department 3 was 7,600 pounds, which was transferred to Product Y. There is no work in process remaining in the department.

(n) Sales on account: 30,000 pounds of Product X at $2.50, 8,000 pounds of Product Y at $4.00 (use FIFO method in crediting finished goods accounts).

(o) Cash received on account, $90,000.

(p) Cash payments: on account, $55,000; wages, $25,100.

Instructions: (1) Set up a T account for each account listed and record the balances as of May 1. Omit dates, writing "Bal." in the space normally allotted to dates.

(2) Record the entries directly in the accounts, using the identifying letters in place of dates. Use the items space for memorandums on pounds, cost per pound, and similar data. Credits to raw materials and finished goods are to be priced in accordance with the first-in, first-out method.

(3) Balance and rule the accounts and take a trial balance as of May 31.

27-3. The Winstead Co. manufactures joint products A and B. Raw Materials are introduced in Department 1 and, after processing, the output of the department is transferred to Department 2. After completion of the processing in Department 2, the two products emerge. There are two service departments, Factory Office and Repair Shop. The costs incurred by the Factory Office are allocated to the Repair Shop and the two processing departments on the basis of labor cost. The costs incurred by the Repair Shop are allocated to the two processing departments on the basis of the shop time devoted to the departments.

Transactions and other relevant data for the month of May are as follows:

(a) Materials and supplies used: Factory Office, $150; Repair Shop, $50; Department 1, $2,200.

(b) Labor costs incurred: Factory Office, $630; Repair Shop, $1,200; Department 1, $4,100; Department 2, $4,200.

(c) Miscellaneous expenses incurred on account: Factory Office, $140; Repair Shop, $380; Department 1, $760; Department 2, $1,010.

(d) Depreciation expense: Factory Office, $30; Repair Shop, $50; Department 1, $300; Department 2, $600.

(e) Allocation of Factory Office costs.

(f) Allocation of Repair Shop costs: 160 man-hours devoted to Department 1, 240 man-hours devoted to Department 2.

(g) Entire output of Department 1, 5,000 units, was transferred to Department 2, with no work in process inventory remaining in the department.

(h) Entire output of Department 2, 1,000 units of Product A and 5,000 units of Product B, was transferred to stock, with no work in process inventory remaining in the department. The unit selling prices of Products A and B are $6.00 and $3.60 respectively.

Instructions: (1) Set up T accounts for Product A, Product B, Factory Office, Repair Shop, Work in Process — Department 1, and Work in Process — Department 2. The inventories of finished products at the beginning of the month are ignored for the purposes of the problem. There are no partially processed materials in either processing department at the beginning of the month.

(2) Record the entries for the month in the T accounts, using the identifying letters in place of dates.

(3) Present the computations required to allocate total costs to the two products in entry (h).

27-4. The manufacturing operations of S. L. Barnett Co. are divided into four departments, through which the materials pass in sequential order from Department 1 through Department 4. The beginning inventory in Work in Process — Department 4 on March 1, and charges to the account during the month, were as follows:

Balance, 3,000 units, $\frac{4}{5}$ completed.......................	$6,690
From Dept. 3, 6,000 units...............................	8,400
Direct labor...	4,575
Factory overhead.....................................	2,745

During March the 3,000 units in process on March 1 were completed and of the 6,000 units entering the department, all were completed except 1,500 units, which were $\frac{2}{3}$ completed.

Charges to Work in Process — Department 4, for the month of April were as follows:

From Dept. 3, 11,000 units............................	$17,050
Direct labor...	7,600
Factory overhead.....................................	3,325

During April the units in process at the beginning of the month were completed and of the 11,000 units entering the department, all were completed, except 5,000 units, which were $\frac{3}{5}$ completed.

Instructions: (1) Set up an account for Work in Process — Dept. 4, record the balance as of March 1, and the charges and credits to the account in March. Present computations for determination of (a) equivalent units of production, (b) unit processing cost, (c) cost of goods finished, differentiating between units started in the prior period and units started and finished in March, and (d) work in process inventory.

(2) Bring down the balance of the account as of April 1 and record the transactions for April. Present computations listed in instruction (1).

(3) Determine the difference in unit cost between the product started and completed in March and the product started and completed in April. Determine also the amount of the difference attributable collectively to operations in Departments 1, 2, and 3, and the amount attributable to operations in Department 4.

Budgeting and internal reports

Accounting aids to management

The basic functions of management are planning, coordinating, and controlling. *Planning* is directed toward the establishment of desirable future objectives and the formation of an organizational structure to be followed in their achievement. *Coordination* consists of integrating individual and group effort with the over-all objectives. *Controlling* results from the evaluation of individual and group effort in terms of the predetermined goals.

The effective discharge of these functions is essential to sound business management and successful operations. In a small sole proprietorship wherein the owner personally supervises every phase of operations, the basic functions of management may be performed with little recourse to accounting data. In most companies, however, direct personal supervision by one individual is seldom possible and it is necessary to establish a chain of command from top management to division managers and department foremen. Under such circumstances, accounting becomes an indispensable tool of management. Accounting not only provides each level of management with relevant financial and operating data, but it also furnishes the basic facts required in planning, coordinating, and controlling.

Earlier chapters of this text have described a number of accounting aids to management such as internal control, financial statements, and standard costs. It is the purpose of this chapter to discuss and illustrate budgets and internal reports. Each of these accounting tools provides valuable data to the management of a business regardless of its size, form of organization, or nature of its operations, but they are especially useful in medium-sized and large companies.

Nature of budgeting

Budgeting consists of establishing specific future goals and periodically measuring actual results against the planned objectives. In this chapter, the business applications of budgeting will be stressed but it is important to recognize that budgeting has wide applicability in other areas. Budgeting, for example, plays an important role in operating a governmental agency whether it be a small rural school district or the federal government. Budgeting is also an integral part of the operations of churches and charitable institutions and is often used by families and by individuals.

A budget is a formal written statement of management's plans for the future, expressed in financial terms. A budget charts the course of future action. Thus, it serves management in the same manner that the architect's blueprints assist the builder and the navigator's flight plan aids the pilot. A budget, like a blueprint and a flight plan, should contain sound, attainable objectives rather than mere wishful thinking.

In a business enterprise, budgeting embraces both accounting and management functions. It is a management function because it is an expression of management's plans. It is an accounting function because the plans are translated into financial terms by the accounting department, and subsequent comparisons of actual performance with the plans (budget) are made from accounting reports.

Budgeting and management

Probably no other instrument contributes more directly to effective management than a budget. Each of management's primary functions is directly served by budgeting. Planning is encouraged because careful study, investigations, and research must be given to expected future operations if the budget is to contain sound, attainable goals. Advanced planning, in turn, increases the reliance of management on fact finding in making decisions and lessens the role of hunches and intuition in managing a business enterprise.

Coordination is facilitated as each level of management participates in the preparation of the budget. In addition, a budget enables top management to explain its objectives to each stratum of management and to keep these goals before the entire organization. As a result, employees within a department are motivated to work as a team and the activities of each department are integrated with those of related departments. For example, production schedules are developed in accordance with sales expectations, raw material purchases can be integrated with production and inventory requirements, and manpower requirements can be correlated with anticipated production and sales.

While managerial planning and coordination are important, they must be accompanied by control. Budgeting contributes to effective management control through the preparation of frequent budget reports in which actual performance and budget objectives are compared and variations are revealed. The disclosure of variations enables management to focus attention on the areas which require immediate corrective action. Budget objectives also serve to encourage efficiency and cost savings and act as a deterrent against waste.

Budgeting procedures

Effective budgeting is dependent upon an organizational structure in which authority and responsibility are clearly defined. The establishment of definite responsibility is an essential requirement in budgeting, for without responsibility there can be no reliable basis of accountability. In order to obtain the maximum benefits of budgeting, accountability must parallel responsibility. This means that the chart of accounts should be designed in accordance with the division of responsibilities provided in the organizational structure of a company. For example, if primary responsibility for total sales is vested in three division managers, there should be separate sales accounts for each division. Similarly, if operations are departmentalized, there should be separate cost and revenue accounts for each department.

The preparation of budgets is ordinarily assigned to a budget committee composed of the chief accounting officer or controller, the treasurer, the sales manager, the production manager, and perhaps others who have major functional responsibilities. The committee initially requests each supervisor or foreman to submit estimates for his area of operations. Requests for budget estimates should be extended to even the lowest level in the chain of command in order to enlist the cooperation of all strata of management and to avoid the resentment that may result from "know-it-all" planning by top management.

After the estimates have been received by the committee, they are reviewed and incorporated into a master plan. This process usually necessitates a revision of some of the estimates, and each supervisor is given an opportunity to defend his estimates and requests. The various budgets are then agreed upon and approved by the committee. Finally, they are distributed and explained to each supervisor in the chain of command.

Periodically, budget reports are prepared to indicate the progress being made toward the planned objectives and to inform management of favorable and unfavorable results. Such reports may be prepared weekly, monthly, or annually depending upon the type of budget and the wishes of management. When monthly reports are used, cumulative data for the year to date are often included.

Sales budget

The sales budget represents the foundation of the entire planning program and the essential starting point in budgeting. Each of the other budgets is either directly or indirectly related to the sales budget.

The sales budget may be expressed in terms of products, territories, or departments. Data for the sales budget are obtained from (1) an analysis of past sales performance, (2) a forecast of expected business conditions, and (3) market research. To illustrate the preparation of a sales budget, it is assumed that in 1961 the Bern Company sold 120,000 units of X at $6.00 each and 70,000 units of Y at $10.00 each. The forecast of general business conditions and market research indicates a 10% increase in the sales volume of X, no volume increase in Y, and an expected 10% price increase for each product in 1962. Based upon these expectations, the sales budget is as follows:

Bern Company
Sales Budget
For Year Ending December 31, 1962

Product	Sales Volume	Selling Price	Total Sales
X	132,000	$ 6.60	$ 871,200
Y	70,000	11.00	770,000
			$1,641,200

Production budget

The production budget reveals the estimated cost of manufacturing the number of units that will be needed to meet expected sales and inventory requirements. The expected volume of production is determined by subtracting the number of units on hand at the beginning of the period from the sum of the units expected to be sold and the number of units desired in the inventory at the end of the period. In the Bern Company there are 22,000 units of X and 12,000 units of Y on hand at the beginning of the year and desired ending inventories are 20,000 units of X and 15,000 units of Y. It will therefore be necessary to produce 130,000 units of X and 73,000 units of Y, as shown by the following tabulation:

	Product X	Product Y
Expected sales (per sales budget).............	132,000	70,000
Desired ending inventory.....................	20,000	15,000
Total units required........................	152,000	85,000
Beginning inventory........................	22,000	12,000
Required production........................	130,000	73,000

After volume requirements have been determined, the expected production costs are obtained by applying the expected direct materials, direct labor, and factory overhead costs per unit to the number of units that will be produced. The per unit costs are frequently derived from detailed budgets for each of the three basic elements of manufacturing costs. The production cost budget of the Bern Company shown below is based on the following estimates:

Cost elements	Product X	Product Y
Direct materials..........................	$1.00	$2.00
Direct labor.............................	2.00	3.00
Factory overhead........................	1.50	2.25
	$4.50	$7.25

Bern Company
Production Cost Budget
For Year Ending December 31, 1962

Product	Quantity	Direct Materials	Direct Labor	Factory Overhead	Total Costs
X	130,000	$130,000	$260,000	$195,000	$ 585,000
Y	73,000	146,000	219,000	164,250	529,250
		$276,000	$479,000	$359,250	$1,114,250

In a merchandising business, a purchases budget would be used in place of a production cost budget.

Operating expense budget

The operating expense budget is an estimate of the expected selling and general expenses. In the preparation of this budget, the distinction between fixed and variable expenses must be observed. Fixed expenses such as property taxes, insurance, and depreciation will not vary with the level of operating activity. In contrast, variable expenses such as salesmen's commissions, advertising, and supplies must be based on the expected volume of sales and production. Some expenses, such as depreciation on buildings and insurance, may require allocation between the selling and general expense classifications.

Estimated income statement

The estimated income statement indicates whether management's proposed operating program will yield a satisfactory net income. Much of the data required in the preparation of the estimated income statement are obtained from the sales, production cost, and operating expense budgets. The estimated income statement for the Bern Company for 1962, and the actual results for the year are given on page 625.

Bern Company
Budget Report
Income Statement
For Year Ended December 31, 1962

	Budget	Actual	Over Under*
Sales....................................	$1,641,200	$1,740,000	$ 98,800
Cost of goods sold:			
Finished goods inv., Jan. 1, 1962............	$ 172,000	$ 172,000	$ ——
Cost of goods finished.....................	1,114,250	1,250,750	136,500
Cost of goods available for sale.............	$1,286,250	$1,422,750	$136,500
Finished goods inv., Dec. 31, 1962..........	198,750	206,250	7,500
Cost of goods sold.......................	$1,087,500	$1,216,500	$129,000
Gross profit..............................	$ 553,700	$ 523,500	$ 30,200*
Operating expenses:			
Selling expenses:			
Sales salaries and commissions............	$ 92,000	$ 95,200	$ 3,200
Advertising expense.....................	64,500	69,500	5,000
Shipping expense.......................	42,400	45,900	3,500
Traveling expense......................	24,700	23,750	950*
Miscellaneous selling expense............	4,200	3,400	800*
Total selling expenses..................	$ 227,800	$ 237,750	$ 9,950
General expenses:			
Administrative and office salaries..........	$ 75,000	$ 73,000	$ 2,000*
Office supplies.........................	14,500	12,500	2,000*
Depreciation — office equipment..........	12,000	12,500	500
Bad debts expense......................	8,200	9,400	1,200
Miscellaneous general expenses...........	6,700	7,450	750
Total general expenses.................	$ 116,400	$ 114,850	$ 1,550*
Total operating expenses.................	$ 344,200	$ 352,600	$ 8,400
Net income before income tax	$ 209,500	$ 170,900	$ 38,600*
Income tax	102,000	82,000	20,000*
Net income after income tax	$ 107,500	$ 88,900	$ 18,600*

A review of the variations between the budget and the actual amounts reveals a favorable sales performance, but the actual cost of goods sold has exceeded budget estimates to such an extent that gross profit is $30,200 below planned objectives. An analysis should be made to determine the causes of the higher costs and to find means of possible corrective action. Further study of the variations indicates that actual operating expenses exceeded budget expectations. Investigation into the causes of this unfavorable variation should be directed primarily at the expenses which deviated materially from budgeted amounts.

In the foregoing example an estimated income statement for an entire year was employed. Similar budget reports are ordinarily prepared each month so that trends may be observed, estimates revised, and corrective measures taken.

Cash budget

An adequate amount of cash is essential to successful operations and to the fulfillment of management's future plans. A cash budget presents the cash balance at the beginning of a period, the estimated amount of receipts and disbursements for the period, and the expected cash balance at the end of the period. The period of time covered by a cash budget varies with the type of business and the company's cash position. When the supply of cash is critically short, a weekly or even a daily cash budget may be necessary. Ordinarily, however, twelve separate monthly budgets are prepared for the year.

In estimating cash receipts and disbursements, other budgets such as those for sales, production costs, and operating expenses must be carefully studied. Appropriate consideration should also be given to dividend declarations, plant acquisitions, issuance of additional shares of capital stock, and other future plans of management which will affect cash. After cash receipts and disbursements have been estimated, a minimum cash balance is established that will be adequate to meet cash requirements. Separate monthly cash budgets for the first three months of a year are illustrated below. Cash budgets are usually accompanied by detailed schedules of the major items summarized in the budgets.

Bern Company
Cash Budget
For Three Months Ending March 31, 1962

	January	February	March
Estimated cash receipts:			
Cash sales....................................	$ 48,000	$ 50,000	$ 53,000
Collections on accounts receivable..............	74,000	76,000	79,200
Other receipts (sale of securities, etc.)...........	5,200	4,400	3,700
Total cash receipts.........................	$127,200	$130,400	$135,900
Estimated cash disbursements:			
Raw material payments......................	$ 24,000	$ 27,500	$ 28,000
Expense payments (wages, advertising, etc.)......	93,500	98,600	99,700
Other payments (dividends, notes, etc.)..........	5,000	8,500	12,000
Total cash disbursements....................	$122,500	$134,600	$139,700
Cash increase or decrease*......................	$ 4,700	$ 4,200*	$ 3,800*
Cash balance beginning of month................	25,800	30,500	26,300
Cash balance end of month.....................	$ 30,500	$ 26,300	$ 22,500
Minimum cash balance.........................	25,000	25,000	25,000
Excess or deficiency*...........................	$ 5,500	$ 1,300	$ 2,500*

A cash budget contributes to more effective cash planning. Through a cash budget management can anticipate the need for short term borrowing and perhaps obtain more favorable borrowing terms by advance planning. Conversely, when the budget indicates periods of excess cash, such funds may be invested in readily marketable securities that will yield revenue. In the example above, borrowing would be necessary to meet cash requirements in March.

Flexible budgets

In the preceding sections of this chapter, fixed or static budgets were assumed. Under this type of budgeting all estimates are based on one level of sales or production. Fixed budgets provide a satisfactory basis for evaluating performance when actual activity coincides with antici-pated activity. Business is dynamic rather than static, however, and it is extremely difficult to estimate actual sales or production with pinpoint accuracy. Consequently, many companies use flexible budgets in meas-uring efficiency.

Flexible budgets consist of a series of separate budgets at different rates of activity. For example, production costs may be estimated at several possible levels of output and operating expenses may be budgeted at various amounts of sales. In preparing the budgets, careful considera-tion must be given to the effect of changes in volume on each item that is being budgeted. A flexible budget for selling expenses is illustrated below. The first expense is variable, the next three are semivariable, and the last two are assumed to be fixed.

Flexible Selling Expense Budget

	Budget Allowances at Various Levels of Sales			
Expense Item	$700,000	$800,000	$900,000	$1,000,000
Salesmen's salaries and commissions....	$ 35,000	$ 40,000	$ 45,000	$ 50,000
Advertising.........................	21,000	21,500	22,000	22,500
Traveling...........................	10,500	10,500	11,000	11,000
Miscellaneous......................	3,500	4,000	4,000	4,500
Depreciation — sales equipment.......	4,000	4,000	4,000	4,000
Insurance on sales equipment..........	2,000	2,000	2,000	2,000
Total selling expenses...............	$ 76,000	$ 82,000	$ 88,000	$ 94,000

In evaluating performance, actual results are compared with budget amounts which correspond to the level of activity actually achieved. If actual sales are $700,000, the actual selling expenses would be compared with budget allowances in the first column, and if actual sales are $900,000, the budget data in the third column would be used as the basis of comparison. Such comparisons provide a reliable basis for managerial control because variations between actual costs and the budget at the volume of operations actually experienced are usually the responsibility of the individual whose efficiency is being measured. The flexible budget is also a significant motivating instrument as the individual who is being judged by the budget will know in advance the budget allowances at any given level of operations. Flexible budget reports are often prepared monthly to permit frequent review of operating performance.

Nature of internal reports

Internal reports consist of schedules, statements, summaries, and exhibits that are prepared by the accounting department for management. They are designed to implement management action and to facilitate the more effective discharge of management's primary functions. Internal reports provide detailed information concerning various phases of operations. The preparation and distribution of internal reports is an important and integral part of accounting.

Some internal reports such as efficiency reports and trend reports are prepared entirely from the accounting records and they are distributed to management on a regular recurring basis. Other internal reports such as those directed toward alternative courses of action may require investigation and research beyond the accounting records, and these reports may be prepared only once.

Essentials of effective internal reports

If internal reports are to be useful to management, the following principles should be observed in their preparation.

1. The reports should fit the organization chart and be directed to those responsible for the material contained in the reports.
2. Only facts that are essential and pertinent to the intended recipient should be included.
3. The reports should be written in a language which is familiar to the recipient rather than in technical accounting terms.
4. Data should be accurate and should be presented in a clear and concise manner.
5. Recurring reports should be issued promptly in accordance with a definite time schedule.
6. The reports should reveal significant trends and relationships.

The importance of making internal reports fit the organization chart merits special comment. The organization chart of a company will reveal the various strata of management such as principal executives, division managers, and department heads or foremen. Rarely will one internal report be suitable for all levels of management because each stratum has different duties and responsibilities. The executive officers, for example, establish over-all operating plans and procedures. In contrast, department heads direct and supervise the employees under their jurisdiction and provide the day-to-day control over operations. Consequently, reports to foremen must be more frequent and more detailed than reports to either division managers or principal executives. Conversely, the scope of internal reports will be greater for executive officers than for either division managers or department heads.

Efficiency reports

Efficiency reports reveal variations between actual performance and predetermined standards or budgets. The frequency of efficiency reports depends upon the nature of the item, the need for control, and the level at which control is to be effected. For example, department foremen and line supervisors may receive daily or weekly cost reports as they represent the focal point of control over manufacturing costs. Efficiency reports frequently result in management action. Accordingly, they should be received by management as soon as possible so that waste and inefficiency can quickly be eliminated. Efficiency reports include daily or weekly reports on material usage, direct labor, idle machine hours, and inventory shortages as well as monthly comparisons of actual performance with budget expectations.

The weekly scrap report presented below is illustrative of an efficiency report prepared for a department foreman. Because scrap is unavoidable in many operations a column for normal scrap loss is frequently provided in a scrap report. A report on material usage often accompanies a scrap report as the two are closely related.

R. B. Morgan Corporation
Plating Department
Scrap Report
Week Ended March 20, 1962

| Job | Units Spoiled | | Dollar Loss | | | |
No.	Actual	Normal	Actual	Normal	Abnormal	Remarks
1446	185	180	$ 18.50	$ 18.00	$ .50	
1727	320	160	64.00	32.00	32.00	Inexperienced employee
1938	540	400	162.00	120.00	42.00	Substandard materials
2046	135	100	27.00	20.00	7.00	Machine breakdown
			$271.50	$190.00	$81.50	

Scrap reports are discussed at weekly meetings in an effort to find ways of achieving better performance. In the Morgan Corporation, the scrap losses on Jobs 1727, 1938, and 2046 are excessive and the foreman should take corrective action to prevent their recurrence.

Trend reports

Trend reports that contain data for more than one period or point of time are useful to management in planning. From the data contained in the reports, significant trends and relationships can be observed. Such knowledge is helpful to management in continuing developments that are favorable and in correcting those that are unsatisfactory. A trend report of quarterly sales by territories prepared for the sales manager is shown below.

R. B. Morgan Corporation
Sales Report
First Quarter, 1962–1961

Territory	1962	1961	Increase Decrease*
A	$225,000	$160,000	$ 65,000
B	310,000	335,000	25,000*
C	365,000	305,000	60,000
	$900,000	$800,000	$100,000

This report which reveals that quarterly sales have increased in territories A and C and have decreased in territory B would require investigation by management. The report could also have revealed each territory's contribution to total quarterly sales through the use of percentages. For example, in 1961 territory A sales accounted for 20% of total sales whereas in 1962, they represented 25% of total quarterly sales.

Break-even analysis

Break-even analysis indicates the amount of sales that will exactly equal total expenses. At this level of sales, the company will neither realize net income nor suffer a net loss. Break-even analysis is used by management in planning future operations and in considering the advisability of plant expansion.

The break-even point may be expressed mathematically or by means of a chart. In either case it is necessary to know (1) the expected fixed manufacturing, selling, and administrative expenses, and (2) the anticipated relationship of variable expenses in each of these categories to sales. The formula for computing the break-even point is:

Sales (S) = Fixed Expenses (FE) + Variable Expenses (VE)

Fixed expenses are stated in dollars, and variable expenses are expressed as a percentage of sales. Assuming fixed costs of $120,000 and variable expenses equal to forty percent of sales, the break-even point is $200,000 computed as follows:

$$S = \$120,000 + 40\%S$$
$$S - 40\%S = \$120,000$$
$$60\%S = \$120,000$$
$$S = \$200,000$$

The correctness of the result can be proved by substituting the amount of sales for S in the initial equation. In this case the equation will balance at $200,000 since variable expenses will be $80,000.

Break-even analysis may also be used to determine the amount of sales required to realize a certain amount of net income. When this information is desired by management the formula becomes:

Sales (S) = Fixed Expenses (FE) + Variable Expenses (VE) + Net Income (I)

Based on the foregoing data, sales of $300,000 would be required to earn net income of $60,000 as shown in the following calculation:

$$S = \$120,000 + 40\%S + \$60,000$$
$$S - 40\%S = \$120,000 + \$60,000$$
$$60\%S = \$180,000$$
$$S = \$300,000$$

A break-even analysis in graphic form is illustrated below.

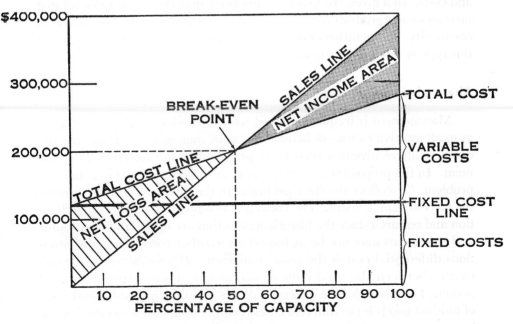

Break-even chart

The chart is based on the foregoing data and is constructed as follows:

1. Productive capacity is plotted along the horizontal axis and dollars are plotted along the vertical axis. The outside limits of the chart represent full capacity and the maximum sales potential at this level of production.
2. The sales line is drawn to indicate sales at each level of capacity. At full capacity sales will be $400,000.
3. A horizontal line is drawn at $120,000 representing fixed costs.
4. A total cost line is drawn from the point where the fixed cost line meets the vertical axis to the point of total costs, at full capacity, $280,000.
5. The intersection of the total cost line with the sales line represents the break-even point of $200,000, and dotted lines are inserted to indicate the percentage of capacity, total costs, and sales at this level of operations.
6. The areas of net income, net loss, fixed costs, and variable costs are identified.

From the chart, management can determine the approximate net income or loss at any level of production. In the foregoing illustration, for example, net income of $120,000 can be expected at full capacity as total sales will be $400,000 and total costs will be $280,000. At plant capacity of 80% net income would be $72,000 (sales $320,000 less total costs $248,000).

Break-even analysis depends on a strict set of assumptions as to sales and costs. In a given company, selling price may change as sales volume increases and variable costs may not be completely variable at each level of capacity. Recognition of these limitations is essential to effective use of this type of analysis in management planning.

Alternative cost reports

Management is frequently faced with the task of making a decision as to alternative courses of action. To assist management in making the decision, alternative cost reports are prepared by the accounting department. In the preparation of such reports, it is necessary to (1) define the problem, (2) collect the data pertinent to the decision, and (3) present the facts to management. The collection of data often requires investigation and research since the historical costs that are shown in the accounts and statements may not be as important as other costs. In many situations differential cost is the most significant. *Differential cost* is the difference between the total costs of two proposed alternative courses of action. For example, the differential cost of producing additional units of finished goods is the difference between the total cost of producing the larger output and the total cost of producing the smaller quantity.

Normally, differential costs are the variable costs because fixed costs generally remain constant.   Three applications of differential cost to specific management decisions are described in the following pages.

Acceptance of business at a special price

In considering the advisability of accepting business at a special price, management may consider the total cost of filling the order or it may consider just the variable or differential costs that are required. Total costs would be appropriate if the company were operating at full capacity, because under such conditions the additional production would increase both fixed and variable costs. But if the normal production of the company is below full capacity, additional business may be undertaken without increasing fixed costs. In such case, only the variable or differential cost of the additional production is pertinent in making a decision to accept or reject the order.

To illustrate, assume that a manufacturer normally produces 10,000 units a month for which he receives $10.00 per unit. At this level of operations, which is below full capacity, variable costs are $4.00 per unit and fixed costs are $2.50 per unit. The manufacturer has an opportunity to sell an additional 5,000 units to an exporter at $6.00 per unit without interfering with his normal production or domestic pricing policies. If the selling price of $6.00 is compared with the total per unit cost of $6.50, the additional business would clearly be rejected. However, the decision should not be based on total costs because fixed costs will not increase if the special order is accepted. The pertinent costs are the differential costs, which in this case, are the variable costs of $4.00 per unit. On this basis, a decision to accept the additional business would be indicated as selling price exceeds the differential costs by $2.00 per unit ($6.00 − $4.00) and as shown below, a gross profit of $10,000 would result.

	Present Business	Additional Business	Total Business
Sales 10,000 at $10..........................	$100,000		$100,000
5,000 at $ 6..........................		$30,000	30,000
Total sales.............................	$100,000	$30,000	$130,000
Variable costs 10,000 at $4................	40,000		40,000
5,000 at $4................		20,000	20,000
Marginal income..........................	$ 60,000	$10,000	$ 70,000
Fixed costs..............................	25,000		25,000
Gross profit.............................	$ 35,000	$10,000	$ 45,000

The excess of sales over variable costs is sometimes designated as *marginal income*. It represents the amount available to cover fixed costs after subtracting variable costs from sales. In this case the profit realized from the additional business will be equal to the marginal income of $10,000 as all fixed costs are chargeable to current business operations.

In deciding whether to accept business at a special price, consideration should also be given to the effect of the decision on regular customers and principal market areas. In the above illustration, this consideration was removed by the assumption that the goods were for foreign consumption. The problem is more complicated when only domestic markets are involved. Clearly it would be inadvisable to accept orders at a lower price in one territory which might jeopardize sales in other areas. At the same time, a manufacturer must exercise care so that there will not be a violation of the Robinson-Patman Act which prohibits price discrimination within the United States unless the difference in price can be justified by a difference in the cost of serving different customers.

Elimination of an unprofitable endeavor

In some cases a department, branch, territory, or product will be operating at a loss and management may have to decide if the unprofitable endeavor should be eliminated. It is often assumed that the net operating income of the enterprise as a whole will be increased by discontinuing the unsuccessful activity. A decision to discontinue the losing venture will eliminate the variable costs of the activity, but such fixed costs as depreciation, property taxes, and insurance will continue if the operation is terminated. Thus, as was explained in Chapter 24, it is entirely possible for the total net operating income of a company to be reduced rather than increased by eliminating an unprofitable endeavor.

The costs which are most significant in making the decision are the differential costs. To illustrate, the following data regarding the operations of a department are assumed.

Sales..	$250,000
Cost of goods sold..	200,000
Gross profit..	$ 50,000
Operating expenses...	70,000
Net operating loss...	$ 20,000

If the department is discontinued, it is believed that 100% of the cost of goods sold and 50% of the operating expenses can be eliminated. An alternative cost report based on differential cost analysis shows:

	Operations Continued	Operations Discontinued
Sales..	$250,000	—0—
Variable costs		
Cost of goods sold (100%).....................	$200,000	—0—
Operating expenses (50%).....................	35,000	—0—
Marginal income..............................	$ 15,000	—0—
Fixed costs		
Operating expenses (50%).....................	35,000	$35,000
Net operating loss............................	$ 20,000	$35,000

The differential costs are the variable costs of $235,000. If the department is continued, marginal income will be $15,000 and the net operating loss will be $20,000. In contrast, if the department is discontinued, the net operating loss will be equal to the fixed costs of $35,000. Consequently, the net operating income of the company as a whole would be reduced by closing the department.

Management should also consider the effect of the decision on employees and customers. If the department, branch, territory, or product is discontinued, the services of some employees may have to be terminated and others may have to be relocated and retrained. Equally important is the possible loss in customer relations that may not be recovered without intensive advertising and promotional effort.

Make or buy

In producing a finished product, the manufacturer often uses assembled or finished parts in addition to raw materials. The assembled or finished parts may either be made by the manufacturer or they may be purchased from suppliers. For example, an automobile manufacturer may either make or buy the engines, batteries, and chrome bumpers used in its cars. Similarly, the speakers in stereophonic record players, the picture tubes for television sets, and the metal shelves in refrigerators may either be made or purchased by the electrical appliance manufacturer. Make or buy decisions generally arise when a manufacturer has unused capacity which results in idle equipment, unused space, and idle labor.

To illustrate the collection of pertinent costs, assume that a manufacturer can purchase a small finished part for $4.25 per unit. The manufacturer is operating at 80% of plant capacity and overhead is charged to production at the rate of 100% of direct labor cost. The direct labor and direct material costs per unit to make a comparable part are expected to be $2.00 and $1.00 respectively. If overhead is charged at the current rate of 100%, the overhead cost would be $2.00 per unit and an estimated total unit cost of $5.00 would result. At this cost, it would clearly be cheaper to buy the part at $4.25 per unit. However, since unused capacity would be used in manufacturing the part there might be no increase in fixed factory overhead costs. Under these conditions overhead should not be charged to the part at the regular rate because this rate includes both fixed and variable factory overhead. Instead, only the variable overhead cost should be charged. In this case, it is anticipated that variable overhead costs such as power, lubricants, and maintenance will approximate 50% of the direct labor cost. Therefore, the estimated cost of making the part is $4.00 per unit computed as follows:

Direct labor.....................................	$2.00
Direct materials................................	1.00
Variable factory overhead (50% of direct labor)......	1.00
Total cost per unit............................	$4.00

A comparison of this cost per unit, which represents the differential cost of making the part, with the cost of buying the part, $4.25, indicates that it would be cheaper for the manufacturer to make the part.

In addition to a comparison of appropriate costs there are other factors that management should consider in arriving at a decision to make or buy. For example, if normal production of the principal product is expected to reach 100% of plant capacity in the future, it may be physically impossible to manufacture the part without increasing plant capacity. The effect of the alternative courses of action on employees and on future business relations with the supplier, who may be providing other parts or raw materials that are essential to the production of the principal product, should also be studied.

Equipment replacement

During the useful life of equipment, management may wish to investigate the alternative costs of retaining the existing asset or purchasing new equipment. In making the cost study, the accountant should consider only alternative future costs. The unexpired cost of the existing equipment is not relevant to the decision as such costs are sunk and cannot be reinvested except to the extent of the trade-in allowance or cash value obtained from disposal.

The costs which are significant to the decision are out-of-pocket costs, opportunity cost, and depreciation. *Out-of-pocket costs* are expenses directly chargeable to a job, process, or operation, which will be paid in cash. In operating equipment such costs include labor, supplies, lubricants, repairs, and power. *Opportunity cost* represents the value of an item in an alternative use. This cost is included in a replacement cost study in order to measure the income given up by foregoing an alternative use of cash such as investing the money in readily marketable securities. Opportunity cost is generally based on the average cash investment over the remaining useful life of the equipment. Depreciation should be computed on both the old and the new asset. The depreciation on the old equipment is determined by dividing the present cash value by remaining useful life. The annual depreciation previously used on the old asset is not relevant to the decision because only the current value is applicable and recoverable in the future. Thus, in a replacement cost study, future depreciation should not exceed the cash proceeds that could be realized by disposing of the asset.

To illustrate the determination of pertinent costs, the following data are assumed. The existing factory machine cost $20,000; it has been depreciated for seven years at the rate of $2,000 per year and it will have a useful life of three more years. Last year, the per unit out-of-pocket costs of operating the machine at full capacity of 10,000 units were labor, $1.50; power, $.24; supplies and lubricants, $.15; and repairs, $.06; and these costs are expected to be the same in the future. The purchase price of the new machine is $39,000 but a trade-in allowance of $3,000, which is equal to estimated cash value, will be granted. The new machine will have a useful life of 10 years with no scrap value. Capacity of the new asset will be 17,500 units but average annual output is expected to be 15,000 units. At this volume, the out-of-pocket costs per unit are expected to be labor, $1.20; power, $.20; supplies and lubricants, $.12; and repairs, $.06. The relevant costs under the two alternatives at the expected annual operating capacity of each machine are as follows:

	Retain Old Equipment 10,000 Units	Buy New Equipment 15,000 Units
Out-of-pocket costs		
Labor......................................	$15,000	$18,000
Power.....................................	2,400	3,000
Supplies and lubricants......................	1,500	1,800
Repairs....................................	600	900
Total out-of-pocket costs....................	$19,500	$23,700
Depreciation (1).............................	1,000	3,900
Opportunity cost (assuming a 5% interest rate) (2)..	75	975
Total future costs..........................	$20,575	$28,575
Total unit costs............................	$2.06	$1.91

(1) Computation of Annual Depreciation	(2) Computation of Opportunity Cost
Old machine $ 3,000 ÷ 3 = $1,000	Old machine $\dfrac{5\% \times \$3,000}{2} = \$75$
New machine $39,000 ÷ 10 = $3,900	New machine $\dfrac{5\% \times \$39,000}{2} = \$975$

On the basis of the cost comparisons, a decision to purchase the new machine seems advisable.

For certain types of equipment such as trucks, automobiles, and data processing units, management may have an opportunity to lease new equipment. Under a lease arrangement, the user (lessee) pays the owner (lessor) a monthly rental for the use of the equipment. The terms of the lease may require the lessee to pay all out-of-pocket costs or some of these costs may be assumed by the lessor. Depreciation, however, is not a cost to the lessee, because ownership of the equipment rests with the lessor. When the lease agreement is terminated, the equipment is returned to the lessor. A cost study similar to the one illustrated above may be used in deciding whether to lease new equipment.

Questions

1. What are the basic functions of management?

2. Budgeting embraces both accounting and management functions. Explain.

3. How does a budget aid management in the discharge of its basic functions?

4. Identify the individuals who normally are included in a budget committee.

5. Why should requests for budget estimates be extended to even the lowest level in the chain of command?

6. What data are needed in the preparation of a sales budget?

7. How is the expected volume of production determined in the preparation of a production cost budget?

8. What purpose is served by an estimated income statement?

9. What information is shown in a cash budget?

10. (a) Distinguish between fixed and flexible budgets. (b) Which type of budget is more effective in controlling expenses?

11. The Bell Corporation uses flexible budgets. For each of the following variable operating expenses, indicate whether there has been economical or excessive expenditures assuming actual sales were (a) $400,000, (b) $500,000.

Expense Item	Actual Amount	Budget Allowance based on Sales
Advertising expense	$18,000	4.0%
Store supplies expense	5,500	1.5%
Shipping expense	11,200	3.0%
Bad debts expense	2,200	0.5%

12. Why should internal reports fit the organization chart?

13. Distinguish between efficiency and trend reports.

14. (a) Compute the break-even point under each of the following assumptions.

	Fixed Expenses	Variable Expenses
(1)	$600,000	60% of sales
(2)	420,000	65% " "
(3)	330,000	45% " "

(b) What sales are required to realize net income of $100,000 when fixed expenses are $170,000 and variable expenses are 55% of sales?

15. Define (a) differential cost, (b) out-of-pocket cost, (c) opportunity cost.

16. What costs are pertinent in making an equipment replacement study?

Exercises

1. In the Hable Company, the following production data are accumulated for the month of May in the current year.

	Finished Goods	
	AA	BB
Units on hand, 5/1..................	2,000	3,000
Desired ending inventory, 5/31........	2,200	2,800
Units expected to be sold............	10,000	12,000
Unit costs:		
Direct materials.................	$3.00	$3.50
Direct labor.....................	4.00	5.00
Factory overhead.................	3.20	4.00

On the basis of the foregoing information (a) tabulate the volume requirements for each product and (b) prepare a production cost budget.

2. The following budget was established for the Harrison Company in April of the current year.

Sales.....................................		$200,000
Cost of goods sold........................		135,000
Gross profit..............................		$ 65,000
Operating expenses:		
Selling expenses.........................	$25,000	
General expenses........................	20,000	
Total operating expenses................		45,000
Net income......		$ 20,000

The actual operations for April produced the following results: sales, 10% over budget; cost of goods sold, 16% over budget; selling expenses, 20% over budget; general expenses, 5% over budget. Prepare a budget report showing the progress of the Harrison Company during the month of April.

3. During the week ending May 15 of the current year, work was performed by the Shantz Company on three jobs as follows:

Job Number	Good Units Produced	Units Spoiled	Average Unit Cost
57	12,000	148	$3.00
58	8,000	102	4.00
59	6,000	73	5.00

Spoilage on Job 57 was attributable to substandard material and spoilage on Job 59 was due to an inexperienced employee. Prepare a weekly scrap report assuming the normal scrap loss on each job is 1% of the good units produced.

4. In Brandel Bros. Inc. fixed expenses are expected to be $140,000 and variable expenses are expected to be 30% of sales.

(a) Compute the break-even point.
(b) Compute the sales required to realize net income of $70,000.
(c) Construct a break-even chart assuming sales of $500,000 at full capacity.
(d) Determine the probable net income if sales total $225,000.

5. The Melrose Manufacturing Company has a plant capacity of 300,000 units but normal production currently is 200,000 units. Fixed costs are $350,000 and variable costs are $5.00 per unit. The present selling price is $9.00 per unit. The company has an opportunity to sell 50,000 additional units at $6.00 per unit to a purchaser who plans to market the units under his own brand name. The additional business is not expected to increase fixed costs and will not affect the regular selling price. (a) Prepare a schedule showing whether the additional business should be accepted. (b) What is the minimum price which would produce marginal income?

6. The income statement for an unprofitable department of Allen Manufacturing Inc. shows sales $320,000, cost of goods sold $275,000, operating expenses $80,000, and net loss $35,000. It is estimated that 20% of cost of goods sold represents fixed factory overhead expenses and that 60% of the operating expenses are fixed. (a) Prepare a statement of departmental costs and revenue in terms of differential cost analysis if (1) operations are continued and (2) operations are discontinued. (b) What is the dollar amount of differential cost?

7. Hartford Inc. has been purchasing chrome door handles for its refrigerators at a delivered cost of $320.00 per hundred. Currently Hartford Inc. is operating at 70% of capacity and overhead is charged to production at the rate of 125% of direct labor cost. The direct material and direct labor costs per unit to produce comparable door handles are expected to be $1.50 and $1.00 respectively. If the handles are made, fixed overhead costs will not increase and variable costs associated with the manufacture of the handles are expected to be 60% of direct labor costs. (a) What is the differential cost of making the door handles? (b) On the basis of differential costs would it be advisable to make or to continue buying the door handles?

8. The management of the McVay Company is considering the replacement of factory machinery. The new machine costs $80,000 but a trade-in allowance equal to the cash value of $5,000 will be granted on the old machine which has a net book value of $20,000. Useful life of the new asset is ten years with no scrap value. The old machine is expected to operate at full capacity of 20,000 units during its remaining useful life of 4 years. Capacity of the new machine is 28,000 units but average annual output is expected to be 25,000 units. Comparative per unit out-of-pocket costs at expected annual capacity are:

	Old Machine	New Machine
Labor.........................	$2.00	$1.80
Power.........................	.25	.20
Supplies and lubricants...........	.18	.15
Repairs.......................	.05	.05

The McVay Company expects to earn an annual return of 6% on its investments. Prepare an alternative cost report showing the advisability of buying the new machine.

Problems

28-1. Department heads of the Bryan Manufacturing Co. were asked to submit estimates of fixed and variable expenses for the coming year, assuming that inventories at the end of the year will be the same as at the beginning of the year. The total of all direct and indirect manufacturing expenses for the year are therefore assumed to be equal to the cost of goods sold. The following report was submitted:

	Estimated Fixed Expense	Estimated Variable Expense (per unit sold)
Cost of goods sold:		
Direct materials.....................	$ 0	$1.50
Direct labor	0	2.75
Factory overhead....................	125,000	1.50
Selling expenses:		
Sales salaries.......................	22,000	.25
Advertising.........................	0	.30
Miscellaneous selling expenses..........	12,000	.35
General expenses:		
Management and office salaries	75,000	.20
Supplies............................	1,000	.05
Miscellaneous general expenses	15,000	.10

Selling price of the product is $12 a unit, and capacity output is 70,000 units per year. It is expected that 60,000 units will be sold in the coming year.

Instructions: (1) Prepare an estimated income statement for the coming year. (2) Construct a break-even chart, indicating the break-even point.

28-2. The estimated income statement included in the 1962 annual budget of A. C. Rohr, Inc. is given below. The actual income statement for the month of January, 1962 is given on the opposite page.

A. C. Rohr, Inc.

Estimated Income Statement

For Year Ending December 31, 1962

Sales..		$960,000
Cost of goods sold:		
Merchandise inventory, January 1, 1962............	$ 60,000	
Purchases......................................	696,000	
Merchandise available for sale....................	$756,000	
Less merchandise inventory, December 31, 1962.....	84,000	
Cost of goods sold.............................		672,000
Gross profit on sales..............................		$288,000
Operating expenses:		
Selling expenses:		
Sales salaries.........................	$ 57,600	
Sales commissions.....................	24,000	
Advertising expense...................	19,200	
Depreciation — store equipment........	7,200	
Store supplies expense................	6,600	
Total selling expense..........	$114,600	
General expenses:		
Office salaries........................	$28,800	
Rent expense..........................	21,600	
Bad debts expense.....................	9,600	
Depreciation — office equipment.......	3,600	
Office supplies expense...............	2,880	
Miscellaneous general expense.........	4,320	
Total general expenses.........	70,800	
Total operating expenses.........................		185,400
Net income before income tax.......................		$102,600
Income tax (40%).................................		41,040
Net income after income tax.......................		$ 61,560

In order to compare the actual results for January with the budgeted figures for the same month, it will be necessary to consider the following variations in the monthly breakdown of the annual budget estimates.

(a) Sales for January were estimated at 10% of annual sales. Expenses that were expected to vary proportionately with sales were: sales commissions, advertising expense, store supplies expense, and bad debts expense.

(b) The beginning inventory in the January budget was estimated at $60,000; the ending inventory at $48,000. The cost of goods sold and the gross profit on sales were computed at the same percentage of sales as in the annual budget, and purchases were budgeted at $55,200 for the month.

(c) Fixed expenses that were not expected to vary with sales were: sales and office salaries, rent expense, depreciation of store and office equipment, office supplies expense, and miscellaneous general expense.

A. C. Rohr, Inc.
Income Statement
For Month Ended January 31, 1962

Sales...		$86,400
Cost of goods sold:		
Merchandise inventory, January 1, 1962.............	$ 66,000	
Purchases..	48,480	
Merchandise available for sale.....................	$114,480	
Less merchandise inventory, January 31, 1962........	54,000	
Cost of goods sold................................		60,480
Gross profit on sales..............................		$25,920
Operating expenses:		
Selling expenses:		
Sales salaries...........................	$4,500	
Sales commissions.......................	2,060	
Advertising expense......................	1,728	
Depreciation — store equipment.........	600	
Store supplies expense...................	694	
Total selling expenses......................	$ 9,582	
General expenses:		
Office salaries..........................	$2,400	
Rent expense............................	1,800	
Bad debts expense.......................	864	
Depreciation — office equipment.........	300	
Office supplies expense..................	250	
Miscellaneous general expense............	390	
Total general expenses......................	6,004	
Total operating expenses.......................		15,586
Net income before income tax.....................		$10,334
Estimated income tax		4,134
Net income after income tax......................		$ 6,200

Instructions: Prepare a budget report, like the one on page 625, for January, 1962.

28-3. Condensed budget data for the R. A. Court Company are as follows:

	January	February	March
Sales............................	$150,000	$180,000	$200,000
Production costs..................	100,000	112,000	120,000
Operating expenses...............	35,000	38,000	40,000

Of the total monthly sales, 60% are expected to be for cash. All sales on account are expected to be collected in full in the month following the sale. Depreciation, insurance, and property taxes represent $3,000 of the estimated monthly production costs and $2,000 of the probable monthly operating expenses. The remaining expenses in each budget are out-of-pocket costs. Of these costs, 70% are expected to be paid in the month in which they are incurred and the balance will be paid in the next month.

At the beginning of the current year, assets include cash, $27,500, accounts receivable resulting from December charge sales, $42,000, and investments in long-term securities, $75,000. Liabilities, on January 1, consist of notes payable, $20,000, accounts payable, $31,000, and accrued expenses payable, $10,400. The note is non-interest bearing and is scheduled for payment in February. The other liabilities represent unpaid December production costs and operating expenses, respectively.

Management's future plans include a cash purchase of equipment for $10,000 in February, and the declaration and payment of a $35,000 cash dividend in March. It is expected that $1,000 of interest will be received in January and the receipt of dividend checks totaling $2,200 is anticipated in February. Management desires to maintain a minimum cash balance of $27,000.

Instructions: Prepare a monthly cash budget for the first three months.

28-4. At 100% of plant capacity the yearly income statement of the Reid Company is expected to be as follows:

Sales.....	$600,000
Cost of goods sold.....	400,000
Gross profit.....	$200,000
Operating expenses:	
Selling expenses..... $60,000	
General expenses..... 50,000	
Total operating expenses.....	110,000
Net income.....	$ 90,000

An analysis of costs and expenses reveals the following division of costs between fixed and variable:

	Fixed	Variable
Cost of goods sold	25%	75%
Selling expenses	50%	50%
General expenses	64%	36%

The management of the Reid Company is considering a plant expansion program that will permit an increase of $300,000 in yearly sales. The new facilities are expected to increase yearly fixed expenses by $63,000; the per cent of variable expenses to sales is expected to decrease by 3 percentage points.

Instructions: (1) Compute the total fixed and total variable expenses at present capacity.

(2) Determine the percentage of total variable expenses to sales at present capacity.

(3) Compute the break-even point under the proposed program.

(4) Determine the amount of sales under the proposed program that would be necessary in order to realize the $90,000 of net income which is expected to be earned under existing capacity.

(5) What is the amount of estimated net income that would result from the expansion, assuming sales of $900,000?

28-5. Virdon Inc. accumulates data on the amount of idle time of production workers, classified as to jobs and factory departments, and prepares weekly reports for the departmental foremen and the plant superintendent. Idle time data for the week ending March 17 of the current year are as follows:

	Department A			Department B			Department C	
Job No.	Productive Hours	Idle Time Hours	Job No.	Productive Hours	Idle Time Hours	Job No.	Productive Hours	Idle Time Hours
147	800	10	201	750	18	314	400	20
148	600	12	202	550	20	315	300	16
149	400	4	203	250	6	316	200	7
	1800	26		1550	44		900	43

Normal idle time loss is 1% of productive hours in Department A, 2% in Department B, and 3% in Department C. Hourly wage rates are $2.50 in Department A, $2.70 in Department B, and $3.00 in Department C. There was no overtime work. Idle time associated with Jobs 148 and 315 was attributable to a shortage of raw materials, and idle time on Jobs 202 and 314 was due to a machine breakdown.

Instructions: (1) Prepare an idle time report for the week ending March 17 for each department, classified by jobs. Use the following columnar headings for each of the three reports:

	Idle Time		Direct Labor Cost			
Job No.	Actual Hours	Normal Hours	Actual	Normal	Abnormal	Remarks

(2) Prepare an idle time report for the week ending March 17 for the plant superintendent, classified by departments. Use the following columnar headings for the report:

	Idle Time		Direct Labor Cost		
Dept.	Actual Hours	Normal Hours	Actual	Normal	Abnormal

28-6. Wayne & Warren Inc. have three sales divisions: (1) New York, (2) Pennsylvania, and (3) Ohio. Both monthly and quarterly sales reports are prepared. The monthly reports compare actual sales against budget objectives. The quarterly reports reveal significant trends and relationships. Separate quarterly reports are prepared for each of the three division managers showing the following information for each salesman in the division: (a) monthly sales in the quarter, (b) total sales in the quarter, (c) total quarterly sales last year, (d) dollar increase or decrease in quarterly sales, and (e) percentage change in quarterly sales. A quarterly sales report is also prepared for the vice-president in charge of sales showing the above information by divisions. Wayne & Warren

Inc. sell a stable product which is unaffected by seasonal fluctuations and there has been no change in selling price during the fifteen months ending March 31, 1962. Applicable sales data are presented below:

| Salesmen | Division | 1962 Sales | | | Total 1961 |
		January	February	March	Quarterly Sales
Adams	N. Y.	$23,300	$24,300	$25,200	$70,000
Baer	Pa.	19,800	21,500	23,700	62,500
Carle	Pa.	21,200	22,300	23,400	65,000
Davis	N. Y.	25,300	29,200	32,700	80,000
Hogan	Ohio	19,600	18,300	17,300	57,500
Lyons	Pa.	21,800	19,700	17,900	60,000
Stark	Ohio	18,400	18,600	19,100	55,000
Waters	N. Y.	28,100	30,300	33,400	85,000
Young	Ohio	16,300	16,500	16,700	50,000

Instructions: (1) Prepare the quarterly sales report for each division manager. (Percentages may be rounded to the nearest full percentage.)

(2) Prepare the quarterly sales report for the vice-president in charge of sales.

(3) Which salesman showed the most favorable trend in each division? Which showed the least favorable trend?

(4) Which division showed the most favorable trend? Which showed the least favorable trend?

Funds statement and other statements

Principal financial statements

The balance sheet and the income statement are the two statements most commonly included in published annual corporation reports. The former depicts the financial condition at the close of the fiscal year and the latter summarizes the factors entering into the determination of net income or loss for the latest fiscal year. Both statements are essential in appraising the efficiency of management, the soundness of the enterprise, and the prospects for the future. The statement of retained earnings or earned surplus is next in frequency of presentation.

Comparative statements

The usefulness of financial statements is greatly increased by expanding them to include comparative figures for earlier dates or periods. The trend revealed by a comparison of the current period with the preceding period may be of more significance than the facts of a particular period viewed alone. The number of published annual reports containing comparative statements has been steadily increasing. One study reveals that in a group of 600 corporation annual reports issued in 1946, 36% contained comparative balance sheets. By 1959, 84% of the same group of corporations presented comparative balance sheets. In 1946, 27% of the 600 companies presented all of their financial reports in comparative form while in 1959, 72% did so.[1]

Customary practice is to present comparative data for only one year preceding the current year, the comparative data being listed at the right of the figures for the latest date or period. In some cases a third column for reporting increases and decreases is added; in others comparative data are presented for three or more years. Further attention is given to comparative statements in Chapter 30.

---

[1] *Accounting Trends and Techniques, 14th ed.*, 1960 (New York: American Institute of Certified Public Accountants), p. 16.

Funds statement

An additional statement frequently included in published annual reports is known variously as a "funds statement," "statement of application of funds," and "source and application of funds." It presents a summary of the changes in all asset, liability, and proprietorship items for a particular period of time, usually for one year. The statement provides information that is not readily apparent from a study of comparative balance sheets.

The term "funds" has a number of different meanings in accounting usage. As employed in Chapter 23 it referred to a segregation of cash or securities for a special purpose, such as "bond sinking fund." As used in the present discussion "funds" refers to the excess of total current assets over total current liabilities, or working capital. The funds statement summarizes the flow of working capital through the business during a particular period of time. Changes in working capital during a period are significant in the analysis of operating results and of the current financial condition.

Net changes in financial condition during a year or other period of time can be determined from comparative balance sheets. Although a study of the net increases and decreases in the various balance sheet accounts yields significant information, it does not disclose the amount of working capital made available to the business and how it has been employed. For example, assume that working capital has been increased during the year as a result of earnings. This fact will not necessarily be disclosed by the net change in the retained earnings account because that account may also have been affected by dividend declarations, appropriations, write-offs of organization costs, and perhaps corrections of errors of past periods. Or assume that new equipment was purchased during the year. A comparison of the balance in the equipment account at the beginning of the year with the balance at the end of the year will not necessarily reveal the amount expended; other items of equipment may have been discarded, sold, or traded during the year.

The funds statement answers such questions as: "What happened to the company's net income?" "How much was invested in noncurrent assets during the year?" "What became of the money provided by the sale of additional stock?" It has been aptly described as the *where-got, where-gone statement*.

Preparation of the funds statement

The funds statement is prepared from data obtained from (1) comparative balance sheets at the beginning and end of the period and

(2) analyses of the changes in noncurrent accounts during the period. In order to illustrate the form of the statement and the manner in which it is prepared, certain facts regarding the Stuart Corporation will be assumed. Since its organization several years ago, the company has carried on operations in a leased plant. In 1961 land for a plant site was acquired and during 1962 a building was constructed and equipment was purchased. The comparative balance sheets of the company on December 31, 1961 and 1962, are as follows:

Assets	Dec. 31, 1961	Dec. 31, 1962	Liabilities and Capital	Dec. 31, 1961	Dec. 31, 1962
Cash..............	$ 80,000	$ 60,000	Notes payable.......	$ 10,000	$ 40,000
Accounts receivable..	120,000	160,000	Accounts payable....	150,000	130,000
Inventories.........	190,000	240,000	Bonds payable......		100,000
Equipment.........		170,000	Common stock......	200,000	350,000
Building...........		100,000	Retained earnings...	50,000	130,000
Land..............	20,000	20,000			
			Total liabilities and		
Total assets.........	$410,000	$750,000	capital..........	$410,000	$750,000

It is possible to prepare the funds statement directly from the comparative balance sheets and the details obtained from the noncurrent accounts. It is preferable, however, first to compile the needed data in working papers. The working papers for the Stuart Corporation are presented on pages 650 and 651.

After the title and the captions are inserted at the top of the various columns, prepare the working papers in the following manner:

(1) List the account titles and the amounts appearing on the comparative balance sheets, using the first amount column for the earlier date and the second for the later date.

(2) Determine the net change in each account balance and extend the amount to the appropriate column of the Net Changes section, as follows:

                                                    Extend To:

(a) Increases in asset accounts
    Decreases in liability and capital accounts } Net Changes Dr.

(b) Decreases in asset accounts
    Increases in liability and capital accounts } Net Changes Cr.

(3) Add the Net Changes columns and insert the totals, which must be equal in amount.

Accounts	Balances		
	Dec. 31, 1961	Dec. 31, 1962	
Cash...	80,000	60,000	1
Accounts receivable.............................	120,000	160,000	2
Inventories....................................	190,000	240,000	3
Equipment....................................		170,000	4
Building......................................		100,000	5
Land...	20,000	20,000	6
	410,000	750,000	7
Notes payable.................................	10,000	40,000	8
Accounts payable..............................	150,000	130,000	9
Bonds payable.................................		100,000	10
Common stock.................................	200,000	350,000	11
Retained earnings.............................	50,000	130,000	12
	410,000	750,000	13
Increase in Working Capital..			14

Working papers for

(4) Extend each amount in the Net Changes columns to one of the four remaining columns as indicated below:

Extend To:

(a) Net Changes Dr. in current asset and current liability accounts — Working Capital Increase

(b) Net Changes Cr. in current asset and current liability accounts — Working Capital Decrease

(c) Net Changes Dr. in all noncurrent accounts — Funds Applied

(d) Net Changes Cr. in all noncurrent accounts — Funds Provided

(5) Add the last four columns and insert the totals, record the increase or decrease in working capital, as illustrated, and insert the final totals.

In the illustrative working papers, the increases in working capital items are composed of an increase of $40,000 in Accounts Receivable, an increase of $50,000 in Inventories, and a reduction of $20,000 in Accounts Payable, making a total of $110,000. Decreases in working capital

Corporation
Funds Statement
December 31, 1962

	Net Changes		Funds		Working Capital	
	Dr.	Cr.	Applied	Provided	Increase	Decrease
1		20,000				20,000
2	40,000				40,000	
3	50,000				50,000	
4	170,000		170,000			
5	100,000		100,000			
6						
7						
8		30,000				30,000
9	20,000				20,000	
10		100,000		100,000		
11		150,000		150,000		
12		80,000		80,000		
13	380,000	380,000	270,000	330,000	110,000	50,000
14	. . . .	. . . .	60,000			60,000
			330,000	330,000	110,000	110,000

funds statement

items are composed of a reduction of $20,000 in Cash and an increase of
$30,000 in Notes Payable, making a total of $50,000. The net effect of the
increases and decreases is an increase in working capital of $60,000.

Net changes in noncurrent accounts are extended into the Funds
Applied or Provided columns. Net debit changes in noncurrent asset
accounts indicate that funds have been used in acquiring these assets
and therefore they represent funds applied. Net debit changes in noncurrent liability accounts indicate that funds have been used in paying
these liabilities and therefore they also represent funds applied. Similarly,
net credit changes in all noncurrent accounts represent funds provided.

As indicated earlier, it is necessary to analyze the noncurrent accounts
to determine whether the changes in the account balances resulted from
one or a series of similar transactions or from a number of dissimilar
transactions. Reference to the ledger of the Stuart Corporation reveals
that the equipment account was debited during the year for various items

purchased at a total cost of $170,000; there were no credit entries in the account. The funds applied to the purchase of equipment were therefore $170,000, and this amount is extended into the Funds Applied column. Examination of the building account reveals debits of $100,000 during the year and no credits; hence the $100,000 is also extended into the Funds Applied column. The remaining noncurrent accounts, Bonds Payable, Common Stock, and Retained Earnings, are examined to determine the details of entries during the year. Bonds Payable increased by $100,000, the amount of bonds issued at face value; Common Stock increased by $150,000 as the result of the issuance of stock at par value; and the sole entry in Retained Earnings was a credit transferring net income of $80,000 from the expense and revenue summary account. The effect of each of these items was to increase funds, and the respective amounts are extended into the Funds Provided column.

After each of the net changes has been extended to the appropriate column, each of the four columns is totaled. In the illustration on pages 650 and 651 the total of funds provided ($330,000) exceeds the total of funds applied ($270,000) by $60,000, and the increases in working capital ($110,000) exceed the decreases in working capital ($50,000) by $60,000. Thus, of the total funds provided, $60,000 has been retained as an increase in working capital. The last four columns are brought into balance by summarizing the net effect of operations on working capital. If the funds applied had exceeded the funds provided, there would have been an accompanying decrease in working capital.

Upon the basis of the foregoing analysis and the working papers, the statement on the opposite page is prepared.

Although there is considerable variation in the form of the funds statement, it is frequently composed of two distinct sections. The first section summarizes the individual sources and uses of working capital; the second presents the details from which the amount of the net increase or decrease in working capital has been determined.

Sources of Funds

There are many possible sources of funds. In the example presented in the preceding section, funds were provided by profitable operations, by the issuance of bonds, and by the issuance of common stock. Some of the frequent sources of funds are discussed briefly in the paragraphs that follow.

Decreases in noncurrent assets. The sale of investments, equipment, buildings, land, and other noncurrent assets provides funds. But the amount provided is not necessarily the same as the amount of reduction

Stuart Corporation
Funds Statement
For Year Ended December 31, 1962

Funds were provided by:

Profitable operations....................................	$ 80,000	
Issuance of bonds..	100,000	
Issuance of common stock..............................	150,000	$330,000

Funds were applied to:

Purchase of equipment................................	$170,000	
Purchase of building....................................	100,000	270,000
Increase in working capital..............................		$ 60,000

The increase in working capital is accounted for as follows:

			Working Capital	
	Dec. 31, 1961	Dec. 31, 1962	Increase	Decrease
Cash............................	$ 80,000	$ 60,000		$ 20,000
Accounts receivable.................	120,000	160,000	$ 40,000	
Inventories......................	190,000	240,000	50,000	
Notes payable.....................	10,000	40,000		30,000
Accounts payable..................	150,000	130,000	20,000	
			$110,000	$ 50,000
Increase in working capital..........				60,000
			$110,000	$110,000

Funds statement

in the account. For example, if land recorded in the account at $10,000 at the beginning of the year was sold for $15,000 during the year, the comparative balance sheet would reveal a decrease of $10,000 in land. The funds provided by the sale amounted to $15,000, however. Similarly, if investments carried at $100,000 at the beginning of the year were sold for $80,000, the net change indicated on the working papers would be $100,000, but the funds provided were in reality $80,000.

Increases in noncurrent liabilities. The amount of funds provided by the issuance of bonds or long-term notes is not necessarily measured by the amount of the net increase in the liability account. If bonds with a face value of $100,000 were issued at 90, the bonds payable account would increase by $100,000, but only $90,000 in funds would be provided by the transaction. On the other hand, if bonds were issued at a premium, the amount of the funds actually provided would be greater than the amount of the increase in the bonds payable account.

Increases in capital accounts. Perhaps the most frequently recurring source of funds is net income. The costs and the expenses that are deducted from gross profit in arriving at net income usually include depreciation of plant assets; but depreciation has not used up any current assets. It has been recorded as an expense, but it has not decreased working capital. Accordingly, the amount of working capital provided by the reported net income is understated by the amount of the depreciation expense. For this reason it is necessary to add depreciation expense to net income to obtain the amount of funds provided by normal operations.

If capital stock is issued during the period, the funds so provided will be equal to the total proceeds, which may be either greater or less than the par or stated value of the stock.

Applications of funds

Applications of working capital are indicated by net debit changes in noncurrent assets, noncurrent liabilities, and capital accounts. Some of the more usual applications are described in the paragraphs that follow.

Increases in noncurrent assets. Funds may be applied to the purchase of equipment, buildings, land, permanent investments, and patents or other intangibles. But the net increase in the noncurrent asset during the period may not be the measure of the funds applied. For example, if equipment has been purchased at a cost of $50,000 and other equipment with a cost of $10,000 has been discarded, the net increase in the account will be $40,000. These facts can be determined only by an examination of the equipment account.

Decreases in noncurrent liabilities. The liquidation of bonds payable or long-term notes represents an application of funds. In determining the amount of the funds used for such purposes, consideration must be given to bond premium or bond discount accounts and to redemption gains or losses. To illustrate, assume that bonds payable in the principal amount of $20,000, for which there is an unamortized premium of $500, are purchased by the issuing company for $20,500. The amount of working capital used to retire the bonds is $20,500.

Decreases in capital accounts. Probably the most frequent application of funds in reduction of capital results from the declaration of *cash* dividends. The issuance of *stock* dividends requires no funds and hence is not reported on the statement of application of funds. The same is true of increases or decreases in appropriations of retained earnings, as they are also transfers from one capital account to another capital account. Funds may be applied to the purchase of the company's own outstanding stock. Analysis of the accounts will reveal the actual amount of funds expended for such purposes.

Extended illustration of funds statement

In preparing the working papers for the funds statement it is advisable to provide some means of giving effect to the various analyses suggested in the foregoing discussion. This may be done by inserting a pair of Adjustment columns between the Net Changes columns and the Funds columns, as shown in the illustration on pages 656 and 657.

The basic information needed for the illustrative working papers was obtained from the comparative balance sheets of the Carson Corporation and from an examination of the noncurrent accounts in the ledger. As in the first illustration, the balance sheet items are listed in the first pair of columns on the working papers. For convenience, the accumulated depreciation account is entered as a credit along with liability and capital accounts. The net increases and decreases in the accounts between balance sheet dates are then determined and extended to the Net Changes columns.

The adjustments, which are next recorded on the working papers, are discussed below:

(a) An examination of the retained earnings account reveals a credit of $32,000 for net income for the year. This credit to the account is transferred to a line below the balance sheet totals by the following entry:

Retained earnings..............................	32,000	
Funds provided by net income....................		32,000

(b) The accumulated depreciation account indicates that depreciation expense charged to operations for the year amounted to $12,000. This expense represents a reduction in a noncurrent asset rather than a reduction in working capital. Therefore, it is added back to reported net income to correct the understatement of the amount of funds provided by profitable operations. The entry is as follows:

Accumulated depreciation — equipment.............	12,000	
Depreciation expense charged to operations (funds provided).....................................		12,000

(c) From the retained earnings account it is found that charges for cash dividends declared during the year amounted to $9,000. This represents an application of funds because the related credit was to the dividends payable account. It is immaterial whether the dividends are paid in the same year or in the following year, since it is the declaration rather than the payment that affects working capital. The adjustment to transfer the amount of the dividends to the lower portion of the working papers is as follows:

Funds applied to declaration of dividends.............	9,000	
Retained earnings.............................		9,000

Carson
Working Papers for
For Year Ended

Accounts	Balances		Net Changes		
	Dec. 31, 1961	Dec. 31, 1962	Dr.	Cr.	
Cash....................	92,000	98,000	6,000		1
Notes receivable..........	20,000	18,000		2,000	2
Accounts receivable (net)..	45,000	50,000	5,000		3
Merchandise inventory....	120,000	100,000		20,000	4
Prepaid expenses.........	3,000	2,000		1,000	5
Equipment..............	158,000	177,000	19,000		6
	438,000	445,000			7
Accumulated depreciation —equipment..........	60,000	61,000		1,000	8
Accounts payable.........	31,000	31,500		500	9
Dividends payable........	2,000	4,500		2,500	10
Bonds payable...........	100,000	80,000	20,000		11
Common stock...........	200,000	200,000			12
Retained earnings........	45,000	68,000		23,000	13
	438,000	445,000	50,000	50,000	14

Funds provided by net income.. 15
    Add: Depreciation expense charged to operations......................... 16
Funds applied to declaration of dividends.................................... 17
Funds applied to purchase of equipment..................................... 18
Funds applied to retirement of bonds.. 19

                                                                  20

Decrease in working capital... 21

                                                                   22

Explanation of Adjustments:
    (a) To record funds provided by net income, $32,000.
    (b) To add depreciation expense to net income, $12,000.
    (c) To record funds applied to declaration of cash dividends, $9,000.

Working papers for funds statement

    (d) Fully depreciated equipment with an original cost of $11,000 was scrapped during the year, no cash being realized. This action had no effect either on working capital or on net plant assets. Therefore, in order to dispose of the net changes in the two accounts as shown on the working papers, the following reversing entry is made:

Corporation
Funds Statement
December 31, 1962

	Adjustments		Funds		Working Capital	
	Dr.	Cr.	Applied	Provided	Increase	Decrease
1					6,000	
2						2,000
3					5,000	
4						20,000
5						1,000
6	(d) 11,000	(e) 30,000				
7						
8	(b) 12,000	(d) 11,000				
9						500
10						2,500
11		(f) 20,000				
12						
13	(a) 32,000	(c) 9,000				
14						
15		(a) 32,000		44,000		
16		(b) 12,000				
17	(c) 9,000		9,000			
18	(e) 30,000		30,000			
19	(f) 20,000		20,000			
20	114,000	114,000	59,000	44,000	11,000	26,000
21				15,000	15,000	
22			59,000	59,000	26,000	26,000

(d) To reverse original entry recording scrapping of fully depreciated equipment,
$11,000.

(e) To record funds applied to purchase of equipment, $30,000.

(f) To record funds applied to retirement of bonds, $20,000.

containing adjustments columns

Equipment....................................... 11,000
        Accumulated depreciation—equipment............   11,000

(e) Equipment was purchased during the year at a total cost of
$30,000. This represents an application of funds, and the follow-
ing adjusting entry is made to transfer the item to the lower section of the working papers:

Funds applied to purchase of equipment...............	30,000	
Equipment.......................................		30,000

(f) Bonds payable in the face amount of $20,000 were purchased and retired during the year, the amount paid being face value. This is also an application of funds and the adjusting entry on the working papers is as follows:

Funds applied to retirement of bonds....	20,000	
Bonds payable.................................		20,000

After the foregoing adjustments are recorded on the working papers, all of the net changes in noncurrent accounts are balanced out by amounts in the Adjustments columns. The net changes in current accounts are extended into the Working Capital columns, and the adjustments appearing below the balance sheet accounts are extended into the Funds Applied and Provided columns. After these four columns are totaled, the net increase or decrease in working capital is determined and the four columns are again totaled.

The funds statement for the Carson Corporation prepared from the working papers appears below.

Carson Corporation
Funds Statement
For Year Ended December 31, 1962

Funds were provided by:		
Operations:		
Net income per income statement........................	$32,000	
Add: Depreciation expense charged to operations...........	12,000	$44,000
Funds were applied to:		
Declaration of dividends.................................	$ 9,000	
Purchase of equipment..................................	30,000	
Retirement of bonds....................................	20,000	59,000
Decrease in working capital.................................		$15,000

The decrease in working capital is accounted for as follows:

	Dec. 31, 1961	Dec. 31, 1962	Working Capital Increase	Working Capital Decrease
Cash.................................	$ 92,000	$ 98,000	$ 6,000	
Notes receivable.....................	20,000	18,000		$ 2,000
Accounts receivable (net).............	45,000	50,000	5,000	
Merchandise inventory................	120,000	100,000		20,000
Prepaid expenses.....................	3,000	2,000		1,000
Accounts payable....................	31,000	31,500		500
Dividends payable......	2,000	4,500		2,500
			$11,000	$26,000
Decrease in working capital...........			15,000	
			$26,000	$26,000

Consolidated statements

Many corporations own a substantial portion of the outstanding stock of one or more other corporations. The corporation owning all or a majority of the voting stock of another corporation is known as the *parent* company and the corporation that is controlled is known as the *subsidiary* company. Although both corporations maintain their separate legal identities, they may be viewed as a single economic unit. The relationship between the parent and subsidiary is somewhat like that of a home office and a branch office.

The stock owned by the parent company appears on its balance sheet under the caption investments, and the income transferred by the subsidiary to the parent appears on the income statement of the parent as revenue from dividends. Transactions between the two companies may have a substantial effect on the financial statements of the parent. For example, it may borrow from or lend money to the subsidiary, or it may purchase from or sell commodities and services to the subsidiary. While the financial statements of the parent company are perfectly proper from a legal point of view, they may be inadequate from a practical point of view. Consequently, statements are frequently prepared that present the financial condition and operations of the parent and its subsidiaries as a single unit. Such statements are referred to as *consolidated statements;* specifically, *consolidated balance sheet, consolidated income statement,* and *consolidated statement of retained earnings.*

A detailed discussion of the techniques of combining parent and subsidiary statements to form consolidated statements is beyond the scope of the discussion here. In general, the working papers used are comparable to those used in combining the statements of a home office and its branches. The investment account on the balance sheet of the parent company has a reciprocal relationship to the capital stock and retained earnings accounts on the balance sheet of the subsidiary; they are eliminated in the process of consolidating the statements. If the parent company does not own all of the stock of the subsidiary, the amount in the hands of outsiders is listed in the liability or capital section of the consolidated balance sheet as *minority interest.* There are a number of other factors which may cause the related accounts to be only partially reciprocal. Similarly, in consolidating the income statements, the intercompany sales, purchases and other intercompany transactions must be eliminated and proper recognition given to intercompany profits in the inventories.

The published annual reports of corporations owning subsidiaries sometimes include both consolidated statements and parent company statements; frequently only the consolidated statements are presented.

Alternative forms of financial statements[2]

Conventional forms of the principal financial statements have been described and illustrated in earlier chapters. There are many variations in the extent to which items may be combined, the terminology that may be employed, and the general format of such statements. Little would be accomplished by a detailed discussion of all of the acceptable variations and their relative merits. However, several innovations of recent years are of sufficient importance to warrant illustration and a brief discussion.

Financial position form of balance sheet. The *financial position* form of the balance sheet emphasizes the working capital position of the enterprise by deducting current liabilities from current assets. The illustration of this form appearing below was severely condensed to focus attention on its principal features. Such condensation is not a characteristic of the form.

A. C. Webb, Inc.

Balance Sheet

December 31, 1962

Current assets...	$420,600
Deduct: current liabilities.....................................	180,400
Working capital..........	$240,200
Add:	
Investments...	150,000
Plant assets (net)...	520,500
Total assets less current liabilities............................	$910,700
Deduct:	
Long-term liabilities..	200,000
Net assets..	$710,700
Stockholders' equity	
Common stock..	$400,000
Retained earnings...	310,700
Total stockholders' equity.....................................	$710,700

Financial position form of balance sheet

In addition to the specific disclosure of the amount of working capital, the financial position form presents the amount of the excess of total assets over current liabilities and the amount of the excess of total assets over total liabilities (described as "net assets"). The "balancing" totals for the statement are thus the net assets and the total stockholders' equity. The form is not widely used but it appears to be gaining in popularity. The study to which reference was made earlier in the chapter indicates that of the 600 selected corporations, about 3% employed the financial

---

[2] A selection of corporation financial statements, including examples of the alternative forms described in this section, is presented in Appendix B.

position form or a variant in 1946, and that the proportion had increased to approximately 13% by 1959.[3]

The principal advantage claimed for the financial position form is its emphasis on working capital, which is a significant factor in judging financial stability. A major criticism is its failure to present the total of the assets and the total of the liabilities. Readers are also likely to find it less familiar than the conventional form.

Single-step form of income statement. The *single-step* form of income statement gets its name from the fact that the total of all expired costs and expenses is deducted from the total of all revenues. This is in contrast to the conventional, or multiple-step form, which contains a series of deductions and intermediate profit and income figures before arriving at net income after income tax. A single-step form, highly condensed, is illustrated below.

A. C. Webb, Inc.

Income Statement

For Year Ended December 31, 1962

Revenue		
Sales.........		$940,000
Interest income.....................		27,500
Total revenue......................		$967,500
Costs and expenses		
Cost of goods sold...................	$530,000	
Selling expenses....................	146,800	
General expenses....................	120,400	
Interest expense....................	10,500	
Income taxes	62,000	
Total costs and expenses............		869,700
Net income.........................		$ 97,800

Single-step form of income statement

The single-step form has the advantage of simplicity and also emphasizes the two major determinants of net income. All expired costs and income taxes rank equally as deductions from revenue in arriving at the net income of the enterprise. In a frequently used variant, however, income taxes and other nonrecurring items are presented in a separate last section. The objection to the single-step form is that the relationship of gross profit to sales and operating income to sales is not readily discernible. The single-step form was used by 21% of the 600 corporations in 1946; the proportion had increased to 53% by 1959.[4]

---

[3] *Accounting Trends and Techniques, 14th ed.,* 1960 (New York: American Institute of Certified Public Accountants), p. 9.

[4] *Ibid.,* p. 7.

Combined income and retained earnings statement. It is not unusual to add the analysis of retained earnings at the bottom of the income statement to form a *combined* statement of income and retained earnings. The income statement portion of the combined statement may be presented in either multiple-step form or in single-step form, as in the illustration below.

A. C. Webb, Inc.
Income and Retained Earnings Statement
For Year Ended December 31, 1962

Revenue		
Sales......		$940,000
Interest income.......		27,500
Total revenue........		$967,500
Costs and expenses		
Cost of goods sold......	$530,000	
Selling expenses.......	146,800	
General expenses.......	120,400	
Interest expense.......	10,500	
Income taxes.......	62,000	
Total costs and expenses........		869,700
Net income........		$ 97,800
Retained earnings, January 1, 1962........		262,900
		$360,700
Less dividends		50,000
Retained earnings, December 31, 1962........		$310,700

Combined income and retained earnings statement

The combined statement form emphasizes net income as the connecting link between the income statement and the retained earnings portion of the stockholders' equity, and thus facilitates understanding by the reader. A possible criticism of the combined statement is the fact that net income, a very significant figure, is "buried" in the body of the statement. If a portion of retained earnings is appropriated for various purposes, or if there have been other increases or decreases of an unusual nature, separate statements may be preferable. Again referring to the 600 corporations, the proportion employing the combined statement increased from 28% in 1946 to 44% in 1959.[5]

Rounding amounts

In preparing principal financial statements for publication a common practice is to round all amounts to the nearest dollar. The omission of

---
[5]*Ibid.*, p. 3.

the decimal point and the two digits for cents provides more space and improves the appearance and readability of the statements. The reduction in accuracy is so slight as to be meaningless. For many corporations a further rounding to thousands of dollars would have no material effect on accuracy and some corporations have recently adopted the practice.

Fiscal years

Corporations select a fiscal year at the time of organization. They may, however, subsequently elect to change to another period. Fiscal years of twelve months end on the last day of a month; those based on a 52–53 week year end on variable dates near the beginning or end of a month. Although the year most commonly elected in the past has been the calendar year, December 31 is not necessarily the most appropriate date for ending the annual accounting period. For enterprises with distinct seasonal fluctuations the most logical annual period is one that ends at the lowest point of business activity. A fiscal year selected on this basis is called a *natural business year*.

At the close of a natural business year the inventories are relatively low, and the number of incompleted transactions is likely to be smaller than during a time of greater business activity. The company benefits from a reduction in the cost of taking the inventory and determining the accounting adjustments. The time required for the audit by independent accountants is also lessened, with a consequent saving to the corporation. Financial statements prepared at the close of the natural business year are likely to give a fairer picture of financial condition and the results of the year's operations.

A compilation of suggested closing dates for 200 industry classifications has been published by the Natural Business Year Committee of the American Institute of Certified Public Accountants.

Questions

1. (a) Name the three principal financial statements usually presented in annual reports of corporations. (b) Name the two statements that are frequently combined to form one statement.

2. Are comparative financial statements more useful than those presenting data for only one date or one fiscal period? Discuss.

3. What is meant by "funds" as used in the funds statement?

4. What is the effect on working capital of borrowing $100,000 on a short-term note?

5. A corporation issues $1,000,000 of ten-year bonds at 101. Were funds applied or provided by this transaction, and what is the amount?

6. (a) Does the declaration of a cash dividend in the current year, payable in the following year, represent a fund applied or a fund provided in the current year? (b) What is the effect of the declaration on working capital? (c) Does the payment of the dividend in the following year affect working capital, and, if so, how?

7. (a) What is the effect of the declaration and issuance of a stock dividend on working capital? (b) Does it represent a fund applied or a fund provided?

8. The Regal Corporation operated at the break-even point during the past year. There were no changes during the year in noncurrent liabilities or stockholders' equity, and the only change in noncurrent assets was a decrease in plant assets resulting from a depreciation charge of $30,000. (a) What was the amount of funds provided by operations? (b) By what amount did working capital increase or decrease?

9. Why are depreciation charges for the year added to reported net income in arriving at the amount of funds provided by operations?

10. The Simpson Corporation organizes the Macon Corporation. The parent company transfers assets with a book value of $1,000,000, receiving in exchange 100,000 shares of no-par common stock of the subsidiary. The assets are recorded at $1,000,000 on the books of the subsidiary, Common Stock is credited for $800,000, and Premium on Common Stock is credited for $200,000. Name the accounts that would be eliminated in preparing a consolidated balance sheet immediately after the issuance of the Macon Corporation stock.

11. (a) Is the financial position form of balance sheet patterned after the equation: Assets = Equities? (b) What relationships between assets and liabilities are emphasized in this form?

12. In general terms, what is the difference between the single-step form of income statement and the multiple-step form?

13. Does the use of the combined statement of income and retained earnings appear to be increasing or decreasing?

14. (a) Why is it preferable to omit cents in preparing financial statements for most corporations? (b) Would the rounding of all figures to the nearest thousand dollars in statements of large corporations result in material inaccuracies?

15. For each of the following enterprises, select from the alternatives the preferable date for the close of the fiscal year.

Enterprise:	Closing date:
(a) Department store	December 31, January 31
(b) Private college	December 31, August 31
(c) Automobile sales	October 31, January 31
(d) Resort hotel (operates June 1 — Labor Day)	September 30, June 30

Exercises

1. On the basis of the following information taken from the comparative balance sheet of Caleb Corporation, prepare the section of the funds statement devoted to changes in working capital.

| | December 31 | |
	1961	1962
Cash..............................	25,000	20,000
Accounts receivable (net).........	44,000	47,000
Inventories.......................	143,000	128,000
Prepaid expenses..................	2,100	1,500
Notes payable.....................	14,000	16,000
Accounts payable..................	33,900	30,500
Estimated income tax payable......	46,600	43,200

2. The net income reported on the income statement of Henderson and Company for the current year was $72,500. Included among the year-end adjustments affecting net income were the following:

(a) Depreciation, $21,000
(b) Bad debts, $1,300
(c) Amortization of patents, $2,200
(d) Amortization of premium on bonds payable, $400
(e) Accrued interest on bonds payable, $3,500

Determine the amount of funds provided by operations.

3. On the working papers for the funds statement of Inslow Inc., the difference of $11,000 in retained earnings is extended to the net changes credit column. The charges and credits to the account during the year are shown below:

RETAINED EARNINGS

Cash dividends declared....	12,000	Balance, Jan. 1..........	80,000
Common stock dividend		Net income for year......	52,000
issued................	25,000		
Organization costs written off	4,000		
Balance, Dec. 31..........	91,000		
	132,000		132,000

Present in general journal form the adjustments that should be entered on the working papers.

4. On the basis of the following data, prepare a funds statement, including details of changes in working capital. Assume that no items of equipment were disposed of during the year and that the only entries in the retained earnings account were for net income of $32,000 and cash dividends of $17,000.

| | June 30 | |
	1961	1962
Cash..............................	$ 15,000	$ 20,000
Inventories.......................	70,000	42,000
Equipment.........................	100,000	110,000
Land..............................	50,000	60,000
	$235,000	$232,000

Accumulated depreciation..................	$ 10,000	$ 22,000
Accounts payable.........................	90,000	30,000
Common stock, $10 par...................	100,000	125,000
Premium on common stock................	——	5,000
Retained earnings........................	35,000	50,000
	$235,000	$232,000

5. Summary financial data for the Howell Corporation at December 31 of the current year are as follows: common stock, $280,000; current assets, $320,000; current liabilities, $125,000; investments, $70,000; long-term liabilities, $100,000; plant assets (net) $250,000; and retained earnings, $135,000. Prepare a financial position form of balance sheet.

6. Summary operating data for the A. P. Jordon Company during the current year ending December 31 are as follows: cost of goods sold, $350,000; general expenses, $80,000; income taxes, $30,000; interest expense, $5,000; rent income, $16,000; sales, $600,000; and selling expenses, $110,000. Prepare a single-step income statement.

Problems

29-1. The comparative balance sheets of the Conner Corporation at December 31, 1961 and 1962, appear below in condensed form:

	December 31	
Debits	1961	1962
Cash......................................	$ 50,400	$ 71,400
Accounts receivable (net).................	53,200	61,600
Merchandise inventory....................	84,000	79,100
Prepaid expenses.........................	1,960	2,800
Plant assets..............................	140,000	196,000
	$329,560	$410,900

Credits		
Accumulated depreciation — plant assets.....	$ 14,000	$ 24,080
Accounts payable.........................	42,280	46,900
Mortgage payable.........................	35,000	——
Common stock, $10 par...................	140,000	210,000
Premium on common stock................	——	14,000
Retained earnings........................	98,280	115,920
	$329,560	$410,900

Additional data obtained from examination of the accounts are as follows:

Net income for the year, $30,240.
Cash dividends declared during the year, $12,600.
The mortgage payable was due on July 1, 1964.
An addition to the plant was constructed during the year at a cost of $56,000.
During the year 7,000 shares of common stock were issued at $12 per share.

Instructions: (1) Prepare working papers for the funds statement.
(2) Prepare a funds statement including an analysis of the changes in working capital.

29-2. The comparative balance sheets of Lockwell, Inc. at June 30, 1961 and 1962, appear below in condensed form:

	June 30	
Debits	1961	1962
Cash...	$ 76,950	$ 63,150
Accounts receivable (net).....................	108,150	101,100
Inventories..................................	225,000	241,500
Prepaid expenses.............................	5,850	6,750
Equipment...................................	375,000	540,900
Buildings....................................	240,750	348,600
Land..	45,000	30,000
Goodwill....................................	12,000	——
	$1,088,700	$1,332,000
Credits		
Accumulated depreciation — equipment...........	$ 72,000	$ 96,000
Accumulated depreciation — buildings............	22,500	30,150
Accounts payable.............................	79,500	112,500
Estimated income tax payable...................	75,600	63,600
Bonds payable................................	——	150,000
Premium on bonds payable.....................	——	5,850
Common stock...............................	600,000	630,000
Premium on common stock.....................	15,000	18,000
Retained earnings............................	224,100	225,900
	$1,088,700	$1,332,000

Three accounts and additional data obtained from other accounts are presented below:

RETAINED EARNINGS

1962			1961		
June 1	Cash dividend......	24,000	July 1	Balance.........	224,100
1	Stock dividend.....	33,000	1962		
30	Goodwill written off	12,000	June 30	Net income......	70,800

EQUIPMENT

1961			1961		
July 1	Balance...........	375,000	Dec. 10	Discarded........	11,100
1962					
(Several)	Additions.......	177,000			

ACCUMULATED DEPRECIATION — EQUIPMENT

1961			1961		
Dec. 10	Equipment discarded	11,100	July 1	Balance..........	72,000
			1962		
			June 30	Depreciation expense	35,100

The equipment discarded had been fully depreciated. There was no salvage value.

The increase in the balance of the building account resulted from the construction of a new building.

Land carried in the account at $15,000 was sold during the year for $25,500. The gain was reported in the income statement. (Report entire amount of funds provided as one item.)

Bonds payable were issued at 104; premium amortization for the year amounted to $150.

The increase in the common stock and premium on common stock accounts resulted from the issuance of a 5% stock dividend.

Instructions: (1) Prepare working papers for the funds statement. (Allow three lines for retained earnings and four lines for funds provided by net income.)

(2) Prepare a funds statement, including an analysis of the changes in working capital.

29-3. The balances in the accounts of Deford, Inc., after adjustment at December 31, the close of the current year, are as follows:

Accounts Payable.....................................		57,300
Accounts Receivable................................	52,400 '	
Accumulated Depreciation — Buildings..............		27,500
Accumulated Depreciation — Equipment.............		6,700
Allowance for Uncollectible Accounts...............		1,800
Bonds Payable (due 1970).........................		70,000
Buildings...	125,000	
Bond Sinking Fund................................	40,000	
Cash in Bank.....................................	47,500	
Common Stock, $10 par...........................		150,000
Cost of Goods Sold...............................	234,600	
Dividends Payable................................		5,000
Estimated Income Tax Payable....................		24,000
Equipment.......................................	38,000	
General Expenses................................	32,960	
Estimated Income Tax...........................	24,000	
Interest Income..................................		6,200
Interest Expense.................................	4,300	
Land..	55,000	
Merchandise Inventory...........................	62,200	
Prepaid Insurance...............................	3,900	
Retained Earnings...............................		37,760
Sales...		364,800
Selling Expenses.................................	39,700	
Wages Payable...................................		8,500
	759,560	759,560

Dividends charged to Retained Earnings during the year totaled $20,000; there were no other charges and no credits to the account during the year.

Instructions: (1) Prepare a combined income and retained earnings statement using the single-step form.

(2) Prepare a detailed financial position form of balance sheet.

Statement analysis

Need for analysis

The financial condition and the results of operations of business enterprises are of interest to various groups, including the owners, managers, creditors, governmental agencies, employees, and prospective owners and creditors. The principal statements, together with supplementary statements and schedules, present much of the basic information needed to form opinions and make decisions regarding the business.

Most of the items appearing in the statements are of limited significance when considered individually. By developing relationships and comparisons with other items a much clearer picture can be obtained. The selection and preparation of analytical aids is a part of the work of the accountant.

It will be readily recognized that particular aspects of financial condition or of operations are of greater significance to some interested groups than to others. In general, the varying interests of all groups fall in three principal categories: (1) solvency, (2) profitability, and (3) stability.

Basic analytical procedures

The analytical measures obtained from statements are usually expressed as ratios or percentages. For example, the relationship of $150,000 to $100,000 ($150,000/$100,000 or $150,000:$100,000) may be expressed as 1.5, 1.5:1, or 150%.

Analytical procedures may be used to compare the amount of specific items on a current statement with the corresponding amounts on earlier statements. For example, in comparing cash of $150,000 on the current balance sheet with cash of $100,000 on the balance sheet of a year earlier the current amount may be expressed as 1.5 or 150% of the earlier amount. The relationship may also be expressed in terms of change, that is, the increase of $50,000 may be stated as a 50% increase.

Analytical procedures are also widely used to show relationships of individual items to each other and of individual items to totals on a single statement. To illustrate, assume that included in the total of $1,000,000 of assets on a balance sheet, cash appears at $50,000 and inventories at $250,000. In relative terms the cash balance is 5% of total assets and inventories represent 25% of total assets. Individual items in the current asset group could also be related to total current assets. Assuming that the total of current assets in the example is $500,000, cash represents 10% of the total and inventories represent 50% of the total.

There is no standard rule governing the rounding of computed ratios and percentages. Ordinarily, however, there is no need to carry calculations beyond one decimal point; the ratio 2.46:1, for example, may well be stated as 2.5:1 and 14.33% may be stated as 14.3%.

It should be noted that increases or decreases in items may be expressed in percentage terms only when the base figure is positive. If the base figure is zero or a negative value, the amount of change cannot be expressed as a percentage. For example, if comparative balance sheets indicate no liability for notes payable on the first, or base date, and a liability of $10,000 on the later date, the increase of $10,000 cannot be stated as a per cent of zero. Similarly, if a net loss of $10,000 in a particular year is followed by a net income of $5,000 in the succeeding year, the increase of $15,000 ($5,000 income − $10,000 loss) cannot be stated as a per cent of the loss of the base year.

In the discussion and illustrations of analytical procedures that follow the emphasis will be upon the basic significance of the various measures. It should be borne in mind that the ratios and percentages developed are not ends in themselves; they are only guides to the evaluation of financial and operating data. Many other factors, such as trends in the particular industry, changes in price levels, and general economic conditions and prospects may also need consideration in arriving at sound conclusions.

Horizontal analysis

The percentage analysis of increases and decreases in corresponding items in comparative statements is sometimes referred to as *horizontal analysis*. It may be used in all the principal accounting statements and their supporting schedules. The amount of each item on the most recent statement is compared with the corresponding item on one or more earlier statements. The increase or decrease in the amount of the item is then listed, together with the per cent of increase or decrease. When the comparison is made between two statements, the earlier statement is used as the base. If the analysis includes three or more statements, there are two alternatives in the selection of the base. The earliest date or period may be used as the basis for comparing all subsequent dates or periods, or each statement may be compared with the immediately preceding statement. The two alternatives are illustrated on page 671.

Base: Earliest Year

				Increase or Decrease*			
				1960–61		1960–62	
Item	1960	1961	1962	Amount	Per Cent	Amount	Per Cent
A	$100,000	$150,000	$200,000	$ 50,000	50%	$100,000	100%
B	100,000	200,000	150,000	100,000	100%	50,000	50%

Base: Preceding Year

				Increase or Decrease*			
				1960–61		1961–62	
Item	1960	1961	1962	Amount	Per Cent	Amount	Per Cent
A	$100,000	$150,000	$200,000	$ 50,000	50%	$ 50,000	33%
B	100,000	200,000	150,000	100,000	100%	50,000*	25%*

Comparison of the amounts in the last two columns of the first analysis with the amounts in the corresponding columns of the second analysis reveals the effect of the base year on the direction of change and the amount and per cent of change.

A condensed comparative balance sheet for two years, with horizontal percentage analysis, is presented below:

Dawson Company
Comparative Balance Sheet
December 31, 1962 and 1961

	1962	1961	Increase or Decrease*	
			Amount	Per Cent
Assets				
Current assets...............	$ 550,000	$ 533,000	$ 17,000	3.2%
Long-term investments........	95,000	177,500	82,500*	46.5%*
Plant assets (net)............	444,500	470,000	25,500*	5.4%*
Intangible assets.............	50,000	50,000	——	
Total assets.................	$1,139,500	$1,230,500	$ 91,000*	7.4%*
Liabilities				
Current liabilities............	$ 210,000	$ 243,000	$ 33,000*	13.6%*
Long-term liabilities..........	100,000	200,000	100,000*	50.0%*
Total liabilities..............	$ 310,000	$ 443,000	$133,000*	30.0%*
Capital				
Preferred 6% stock, $100 par. .	$ 150,000	$ 150,000	——	——
Common stock, $10 par.......	500,000	500,000	——	——
Retained earnings............	179,500	137,500	$ 42,000	30.5%
Total capital.................	$ 829,500	$ 787,500	$ 42,000	5.3%
Total liabilities and capital.....	$1,139,500	$1,230,500	$ 91,000*	7.4%*

The foregoing statement may be expanded to show the details of the various categories of assets and liabilities, or separate schedules may be prepared. Opinions differ as to which method presents the clearer picture. The form of supporting schedules is illustrated by the schedule of current assets appearing below. The significance of the various increases and decreases cannot be fully determined without additional information. Although total assets at the end of 1962 were $91,000 or 7.4% less than at the beginning of the year, liabilities were reduced by $133,000, or 30% and capital increased $42,000, or 5.3%. It would appear that the reduction of $100,000 in long-term liabilities was accomplished, for the most part, through the sale of long-term investments. A funds statement would, of course, provide more definite information about the changes in the composition of the balance sheet items.

A comparative schedule of current assets for two years with horizontal percentage analysis is illustrated below.

Dawson Company
Comparative Schedule of Current Assets
December 31, 1962 and 1961

	1962	1961	Increase or Decrease* Amount	Increase or Decrease* Per Cent
Cash......................	$ 90,500	$ 51,000	$ 39,500	77.5%
Marketable securities..........	75,000	75,000	—	—
Accounts receivable (net)......	115,000	120,000	5,000*	4.2%*
Merchandise inventory........	264,000	283,000	19,000*	6.7%*
Prepaid expenses.............	5,500	4,000	1,500	37.5%
Total current assets..........	$550,000	$533,000	$ 17,000	3.2%

The changes in the composition of the current assets would appear to be favorable, particularly in view of the increase in sales shown on the income statement (page 673). The reduction in accounts receivable may have come about through changes in credit terms or improved collection policies. Similarly, a reduction in the merchandise inventory during a period of increased sales indicates an improvement in management.

The comparative retained earnings statement and comparative income statement for Dawson Company, with horizontal percentage analysis, appear on page 673. Examination of the latter statement reveals an increase of 24.8% in net sales. An increase in sales, considered alone, is not necessarily favorable. The increase in sales was accompanied by a somewhat greater percentage increase in the cost of goods sold, which indicates a narrowing of the gross profit margin. Selling expenses increased markedly and general expenses increased slightly, making an over-all increase in operating expenses of 20.5% as contrasted with a 19.7% increase in gross profit.

Dawson Company
Comparative Retained Earnings Statement
For Years Ended December 31, 1962 and 1961

			Increase or Decrease*	
	1962	1961	Amount	Per Cent
Retained earnings, Jan. 1......	$ 137,500	$ 100,000	$ 37,500	37.5%
Net income for year..........	91,000	76,500	14,500	19.0%
Total.....................	$ 228,500	$ 176,500	$ 52,000	29.5%
Dividends:				
On preferred stock..	$ 9,000	$ 9,000	——	——
On common stock.........	40,000	30,000	$ 10,000	33.3%
Total....................	$ 49,000	$ 39,000	$ 10,000	25.6%
Retained earnings, Dec. 31.....	$ 179,500	$ 137,500	$ 42,000	30.5%

Dawson Company
Comparative Income Statement
For Years Ended December 31, 1962 and 1961

			Increase or Decrease*	
	1962	1961	Amount	Per Cent
Sales.......................	$ 1,530,500	$ 1,234,000	$296,500	24.0%
Sales returns and allowances....	32,500	34,000	1,500*	4.4%*
Net sales...................	$ 1,498,000	$ 1,200,000	$298,000	24.8%
Cost of goods sold............	1,043,000	820,000	223,000	27.2%
Gross profit on sales..........	$ 455,000	$ 380,000	$ 75,000	19.7%
Selling expense..............	$ 191,000	$ 147,000	$ 44,000	29.9%
General expense.............	88,500	85,000	3,500	4.1%
Total operating expense.......	$ 279,500	$ 232,000	$ 47,500	20.5%
Net operating income.........	$ 175,500	$ 148,000	$ 27,500	18.6%
Other income...............	8,500	12,000	3,500*	29.2%*
	$ 184,000	$ 160,000	$ 24,000	15.0%
Other expense...............	6,000	13,000	7,000*	53.8%*
Net income before income tax..	$ 178,000	$ 147,000	$ 31,000	21.1%
Estimated income tax.........	87,000	70,500	16,500	23.4%
Net income after income tax....	$ 91,000	$ 76,500	$ 14,500	19.0%

Obviously, the increase in net operating income and in the final net income figure is favorable. It would be erroneous for the management to conclude, however, that its operations were at maximum efficiency. A study of fixed and variable expenses and additional analysis and comparisons of individual expense accounts should be made.

The income statement illustrated is in condensed form. If desired, the statement may be expanded to include details of the cost of goods sold, selling expenses, general expenses, other income, and other expense. In general, the condensed statements ordinarily provide sufficient information for all interested groups except management. The comparative statement of cost of goods sold presented below is illustrative.

Dawson Company
Comparative Statement of Cost of Goods Sold
For Years Ended December 31, 1962 and 1961

	1962	1961	Increase or Decrease* Amount	Per Cent
Merchandise inventory, Jan. 1..	$ 283,000	$ 311,000	$ 28,000*	9.0%*
Purchases..................	1,024,000	792,000	232,000	29.3%
Merchandise available for sale..	$1,307,000	$1,103,000	$204,000	18.5%
Merchandise inventory, Dec. 31.	264,000	283,000	19,000*	6.7%*
Cost of goods sold..........	$1,043,000	$ 820,000	$223,000	27.2%

Vertical analysis

Percentage analysis may also be used to show the relationship of the component parts to the total in a single statement. This type of analysis is sometimes called *vertical analysis*. As in horizontal analysis, the statements may be prepared in either detailed or condensed form. In the latter case additional details may be presented in supporting schedules. Although the analysis is confined within each individual statement, the significance of both the amounts and per cents is increased by preparing comparative statements. The condensed comparative balance sheet of Dawson Company, with vertical analysis, is presented on page 675.

Each asset category is stated as a per cent of total assets and the liability and capital items are stated as a per cent of total liabilities and capital. The major relative changes in assets were in the current asset and long-term investment groups. In the lower half of the balance sheet, long-term liabilities and retained earnings showed the greatest relative change. Stockholders' equity increased from 64.0% at the close of 1961 to 72.8% at the close of 1962, with a corresponding decrease in the claims of creditors.

Dawson Company
Comparative Balance Sheet
December 31, 1962 and 1961

	1962		1961	
	Amount	Per Cent	Amount	Per Cent
Assets				
Current assets...............	$ 550,000	48.3%	$ 533,000	43.3%
Long-term investments........	95,000	8.3	177,500	14.4
Plant assets (net).............	444,500	39.0	470,000	38.2
Intangible assets.............	50,000	4.4	50,000	4.1
Total assets.................	$ 1,139,500	100.0%	$ 1,230,500	100.0%
Liabilities				
Current liabilities............	$ 210,000	18.4%	$ 243,000	19.7%
Long-term liabilities..........	100,000	8.8	200,000	16.3
Total liabilities..............	$ 310,000	27.2%	$ 443,000	36.0%
Capital				
Preferred 6% stock...........	$ 150,000	13.2%	$ 150,000	12.2%
Common stock...............	500,000	43.9	500,000	40.6
Retained earnings............	179,500	15.7	137,500	11.2
Total capital................	$ 829,500	72.8%	$ 787,500	64.0%
Total liabilities and capital.....	$1,139,500	100.0%	$ 1,230,500	100.0%

If supporting schedules are prepared for current assets and other groups, the percentage analysis may be based on either the total of the schedule or the balance sheet total.

In vertical analysis of the income statement, each item is stated as a per cent of net sales. The condensed comparative income statement of Dawson Company, with vertical analysis, appears on page 676. Care must be used in judging the significance of differences between percentages for the two years. For example, the decline in the gross profit rate from 31.7% in 1961 to 30.4% in 1962 is only 1.3%. In terms of dollars of potential gross profit, however, it represents a decline of approximately $19,000 (1.3% × $1,498,000). The slight increase in the per cent of selling expense to net sales also indicates the desirability of additional analysis.

Both horizontal and vertical analyses are helpful in disclosing relationships and trends in financial condition and operations of individual enterprises. Vertical analysis is also useful in comparing one company with another or with industry averages. In comparing the financial condition of Dawson Company with the financial condition of a larger firm, for example, a comparison of the percentage composition of the balance sheets would be more significant than a comparison of the dollar

Dawson Company
Comparative Income Statement
For Years Ended December 31, 1962 and 1961

	1962		1961	
	Amount	Per Cent	Amount	Per Cent
Sales......................	$ 1,530,500	102.2%	$ 1,234,000	102.8%
Sales returns and allowances....	32,500	2.2	34,000	2.8
Net sales....................	$ 1,498,000	100.0%	$ 1,200,000	100.0%
Cost of goods sold.............	1,043,000	69.6	820,000	68.3
Gross profit on sales...........	$ 455,000	30.4%	$ 380,000	31.7%
Selling expense...............	$ 191,000	12.8%	$ 147,000	12.3%
General expense..............	88,500	5.9	85,000	7.1
Total operating expense.......	$ 279,500	18 7%	$ 232,000	19.4%
Net operating income.........	$ 175,500	11.7%	$ 148,000	12.3%
Other income................	8,500	.6	12,000	1.0
	$ 184,000	12.3%	$ 160,000	13.3%
Other expense...............	6,000	.4	13,000	1.1
Net income before income tax...	$ 178,000	11.9%	$ 147,000	12.2%
Estimated income tax.........	87,000	5.8	70,500	5.9
Net income after income tax....	$ 91,000	6.1%	$ 76,500	6.3%

amounts. Trade associations and financial information services also publish summary financial and operating data by industry classifications. Comparison of these percentage analyses with those of individual companies yields information that would be difficult to obtain from consideration of the dollar amounts.

Other analytical measures

In addition to the percentage analyses discussed above there are a number of additional relationships that may be expressed in ratios and percentages. The items used in the measures are taken from the accounting statements of the current period and hence are a further development of vertical analysis. They may be compared with the corresponding measures of earlier periods, which constitutes an extension of horizontal analysis.

Some of the most significant and commonly used ratios will be discussed in the sections that follow. The examples will be based on the statements of Dawson Company that appear earlier in the chapter. In a few instances items are also taken from the company's statements for 1960.

Current ratio

The relationship between current assets and current liabilities is called the *current ratio*. It may also be referred to as the *working capital ratio* or *bankers' ratio*. The ratio is computed by dividing the total of current assets by the total of current liabilities. Marketable securities, receivables, and inventories may decline in value and there is no assurance as to when they will be converted into cash. On the other hand, current liabilities must be paid at their face value and at specific dates. It is desirable, therefore, that current assets always be materially in excess of current liabilities.

The excess of current assets over current liabilities is also frequently used as an index of current financial condition. It is referred to as *working capital* or *net working capital*. The working capital and working capital ratio of Dawson Company at December 31, 1962 and 1961 are shown below, together with the underlying data:

	1962	1961
Current assets..	$550,000	$533,000
Current liabilities....................................	210,000	243,000
Working capital......................................	$340,000	$290,000
Current ratio..	2.6:1	2.2:1

The current ratio is a more dependable indication of solvency than working capital. To illustrate, assume that Scott Corporation lists current assets of $2,000,000 and current liabilities of $1,540,000 on its balance sheet for December 31, 1962. The working capital of the corporation is $460,000 and the current ratio is 1.3:1. In comparison with the Dawson Company, Scott Corporation has a larger amount of working capital ($460,000 compared to $340,000) but a lower current ratio (1.3:1 compared to 2.6:1). Considering these facts alone a bank is more likely to grant short term loans to the Dawson Company than to Scott Corporation.

Acid-test ratio

Inventories of raw materials, work in process, and finished goods (or merchandise) often represent a large portion of total current assets. A considerable amount of time may be required to convert inventories into cash in the normal operating processes. There is also the possibility of declines in market prices and a reduction in demand, both of which will adversely affect the ability to pay current liabilities. The *acid-test* ratio gives recognition to these factors. It is the ratio of the sum of cash, receivables, and marketable securities, which are sometimes called *quick assets*, to current liabilities.

The computation of the acid-test ratio of Dawson Company is shown below.

	1962	1961
Quick assets		
Cash..	$ 90,500	$ 51,000
Marketable securities.............................	75,000	75,000
Receivables (net).................................	115,000	120,000
Total...	$280,500	$246,000
Current liabilities..................................	$210,000	$243,000
Acid-test ratio......................................	1.3:1	1.0:1

Ratio of owners' equity to liabilities

Claims against the total assets of an enterprise are divided into two basic groups, those of the creditors and those of the owners. The relationship between the total claims of the two groups provides an indication of the margin of safety of the creditors and the ability of the enterprise to withstand adverse business conditions. If the claims of creditors are large in proportion to the equity of the owners, there are likely to be substantial charges for interest payments. If earnings decline to the point of inability to meet interest payments, control of the business may pass to the creditors.

The relationship between stockholder and creditor equity is shown in the vertical analysis of the balance sheet. For example, the balance sheet of Dawson Company presented on page 675 indicates that on December 31, 1962 capital represented 72.8% and liabilities represented 27.2% of the sum of liabilities and capital (100.0%). Instead of expressing each item as a per cent of the total, the relationship may be expressed as a ratio of one to the other, as illustrated below:

	1962	1961
Total capital......................................	$829,500	$787,500
Total liabilities....................................	310,000	443,000
Ratio of owners' equity to liabilities.................	2.7:1	1.8:1

By reference to the balance sheet of Dawson Company it may be seen that the principal factor affecting the change in the ratio was the $100,000 reduction in long-term liabilities during 1962. The ratio at both dates indicates a substantial margin of safety for the creditors. As was illustrated in Chapter 23, it may be preferable to secure needed funds by borrowing rather than by issuing additional stock. If the rate of earnings on the assets thus acquired exceeds the rate of interest on the borrowed funds, the excess is income for the benefit of stockholders. The use of borrowed funds is sometimes called *trading on the equity*. The ratio of owners' equity to liabilities provides a measure of the extent of trading on the equity.

Ratio of plant assets to long-term liabilities

Long-term notes and bonds are frequently secured by mortgages on plant assets. The ratio of total plant assets to long-term liabilities provides a measure of the margin of safety of the note holders or bond holders. It also gives an indication of the potential ability of the enterprise to borrow additional funds on a long-term basis.

The ratio of plant assets to long-term liabilities of Dawson Company is computed as follows:

	1962	1961
Plant assets (net).....................................	$444,500	$470,000
Long-term liabilities.................................	100,000	200,000
Ratio of plant assets to long-term liabilities............	4.4:1	2.4:1

Accounts receivable turnover

The composition of accounts receivable changes continually during business operations. Sales on account increase the total and collections reduce the total. Firms that grant long credit terms will tend to have relatively greater amounts tied up in accounts receivable than those granting short terms. Increases or decreases in the volume of sales will also affect the amount of outstanding accounts.

Accounts receivable yield no revenue, hence it is desirable to keep the amount invested in them at a minimum. The cash made available by prompt collection of receivables may be employed to reduce the amount of bank loans and thus yield a saving of interest, it may be used to purchase merchandise in larger quantities at a lower price, it may be used to pay dividends, or for other purposes. Prompt collection also reduces the amount of loss from bad debts.

The relationship between sales volume and accounts receivable may be stated as the *accounts receivable turnover*. It is calculated by dividing net sales by the average accounts receivable. The average of the monthly balances of accounts receivable should be used in the computation, as it gives recognition to seasonal fluctuations. When such data are not available it is necessary to use the average of the balances at the beginning and end of the year. If there are trade notes receivable as well as accounts, the two should be combined.

The accounts receivable turnover of Dawson Company is computed at the top of page 680.

	1962	1961
Net sales...............................	$1,498,000	$1,200,000
Accounts receivable (net):		
Beginning of year................	$ 120,000	$ 140,000
End of year......................	115,000	120,000
Total............................	$ 235,000	$ 260,000
Average..........................	$ 117,500	$ 130,000
Accounts receivable turnover.....	12.7	9.2

Merchandise inventory turnover

Most of the observations about accounts receivable in the first two paragraphs of the preceding section are also applicable to merchandise inventory. Inventories in excess of the needs of the business tie up funds that could be used in other ways to better advantage and may increase the amount of insurance, property taxes, storage, and other expenses. There is also added risk of loss through price declines and deterioration or obsolescence of the merchandise.

The *merchandise inventory turnover* is computed by dividing the cost of goods sold by the average inventory. If monthly data are not available, it is necessary to use the average of the inventories at the beginning and end of the year. Given monthly figures for purchases and sales the interim monthly inventories can be estimated by the gross profit method described in Chapter 11.

The calculation of the merchandise inventory turnover for Dawson Company is presented below:

	1962	1961
Cost of goods sold...............	$1,043,000	$820,000
Merchandise inventory:		
Beginning of year................	$ 283,000	$311,000
End of year......................	264,000	283,000
Total............................	$ 547,000	$594,000
Average..........................	$ 273,500	$297,000
Merchandise inventory turnover...	3.8	2.8

The improvement in the turnover resulted from an increase in the cost of goods sold, combined with a decrease in average inventory. The variation in types of merchandise is too great to permit any generalizations as to what constitutes a satisfactory turnover. For example, a firm selling food should have a higher turnover than one selling furniture or jewelry, and the perishable foods department of a supermarket should have a higher turnover than the soaps and cleaners department.

Ratio of sales to assets

The ratio of sales to assets is a measure of the effectiveness of the utilization of assets. Assume that two competing enterprises have equal amounts of assets but that the sales of one are double the amount of the sales of the other. Obviously, the former is making better use of its assets. In computing the ratio, any long-term investments should be excluded from total assets as they make no contribution to sales. The units of product sold may also be used in place of the dollar amount of sales, if sales can be stated in a common unit.

Assets used in determining the ratio may be the total at the end of the year, the average at the beginning and end of the year, or the average of the monthly totals. The computation for Dawson Company is as follows:

	1962	1961
Net sales.....................................	$1,498,000	$1,200,000
Total assets (excluding long-term investments):		
Beginning of year............................	$1,053,000	$1,010,000
End of year..................................	1,044,500	1,053,000
Total......................................	$2,097,500	$2,063,000
Average.....................................	$1,048,750	$1,031,500
Ratio of sales to assets......................	1.4:1	1.2:1

Rate earned on total assets

The amount of the net income of an enterprise is always an important figure in appraising operations. The increase or decrease in net income of the current period in comparison with an earlier period is shown in horizontal analysis. The relationship of net income to net sales of a period is shown in vertical analysis.

Another relative measure frequently applied to net income is the rate earned on total assets. It is a measure of the productivity of the assets, without regard to the equity of the creditors and stockholders in the assets. The rate is therefore not affected by differences in methods of financing an enterprise. As in other operating measures based on assets, an average of the assets by months is preferable. When such data are not available the assets at the beginning or end of the year, or the average of the two amounts, may be used. The computation of the rate earned by Dawson Company on total assets appears below:

	1962	1961
Net income after income tax.....................	$ 91,000	$ 76,500
Total assets:		
Beginning of year............................	$1,230,500	$1,187,500
End of year..................................	1,139,500	1,230,500
Total......................................	$2,370,000	$2,418,000
Average.....................................	$1,185,000	$1,209,000
Rate earned on total assets.................	7.7%	6.3%

It is sometimes considered preferable to determine the rate of net operating income or of net income before income tax, to total assets. If nonoperating income is excluded from consideration, the investments yielding such income should be excluded from the assets. The use of net income before income tax eliminates the effect of changes in the tax structure on the rate of earnings. When considering published data on rates earned on assets it is obviously important that the reader take note of the exact nature of the measure.

Rate earned on stockholders' equity

Another relative measure of earnings is obtained by dividing net income by the total stockholders' equity. In contrast to the rate earned on total assets, this measure emphasizes the income yield in relationship to the amount invested by the stockholders, including both initial investment and retained earnings. The amount of the total stockholders' equity varies throughout the year; additional stock may be issued, a class of stock may be retired, dividends may be paid, and net income accrues gradually.

If monthly figures are not available, the average of the stockholders' equity at the beginning and end of the year are used. The computation for Dawson Company follows:

	1962	1961
Net income after income tax......................	$ 91,000	$ 76,500
Stockholders' equity:		
Beginning of year.............................	$ 787,500	$ 750,000
End of year...................................	829,500	787,500
Total.......................................	$1,617,000	$1,537,500
Average.....................................	$ 808,500	$ 768,750
Rate earned on stockholders' equity...............	11.3%	10.0%

Rate earned on common stockholders' equity

When a corporation has both preferred and common stock outstanding the holders of the common stock have the residual claim on earnings. The net income for the period, reduced by the preferred dividend requirements, may be stated as a per cent of the common stockholders' equity. The comments in the preceding section regarding the averaging of capital apply equally here.

Dawson Company has $150,000 of preferred 6% nonparticipating stock outstanding at both balance sheet dates, hence annual preferred dividends amount to $9,000. The common stockholders' equity is the total capital reduced by the par value of the preferred stock ($150,000). The computation is as follows:

	1962	1961
Net income after income tax	$ 91,000	$ 76,500
Preferred dividends	9,000	9,000
Remainder — identified with common stock	$ 82,000	$ 67,500
Common stockholders' equity:		
Beginning of year	$ 637,500	$ 600,000
End of year	679,500	637,500
Total	$1,317,000	$1,237,500
Average	$ 658,500	$ 618,750
Rate earned on common stockholders' equity	12.5%	10.9%

Earnings per share on common stock

One of the financial measures commonly determined is earnings per share on common stock. If there is only one class of stock, the earnings per share are determined by dividing net income by the number of shares outstanding at the end of the year. If there is both preferred and common stock outstanding, the net income must be reduced first by the amount necessary to meet the preferred dividend requirements.

Any unusual changes in the number of shares outstanding during the year, such as stock dividends or stock splits, should be disclosed in quoting dividends per share. Also, if net income includes material amounts of income or losses of a nonrecurring nature, the facts should be disclosed.

The computation of the earnings per share of common stock of Dawson Company is as follows:

	1962	1961
Net income after income tax	$91,000	$76,500
Preferred dividends	9,000	9,000
Remainder — identified with common stock	$82,000	$67,500
Shares of common stock outstanding	50,000	50,000
Earnings per share on common stock	$1.64	$1.35

Other measurements

The ratios, rates, and turnovers discussed and illustrated in the foregoing sections are representative of the many that can be developed. In analyzing the financial statements of a particular firm some of them might well be omitted; others might be stated in a different manner; and additional measures not mentioned above might be developed. Only those that assist in interpreting the statements and relationships should be prepared. It should be borne in mind that there is no magic in ratios; they are only an analytical tool.

Questions

1. For the current year ended November 30, Company X and Company Y reported net income after income tax of $600,000 and $100,000, respectively. Is Company X a more profitable company than Company Y? Discuss.

2. Illustrate (a) horizontal analysis and (b) vertical analysis, using the following data taken from a comparative income statement:

	CURRENT YEAR	PRECEDING YEAR
Net sales..........................	$1,500,000	$1,000,000
Net income after income tax...........	90,000	50,000

3. What is the advantage of comparative statements over statements for a single date or period?

4. In general, which would have the higher per cent of plant assets to total assets, a railroad or a retail clothing store?

5. As of December 31 of the current year Company A has working capital of $2,000,000 and Company B has working capital of $500,000. Is Company A in better financial condition than Company B? Discuss.

6. A company that grants terms of n/30 on all sales has an accounts receivable turnover for the year, based on monthly averages, of 4. Is this a satisfactory turnover? Discuss.

7. Why is it advantageous to have a high turnover of accounts receivable?

8. In general, which would have the higher inventory turnover, a grocery supermarket or a retail hardware store?

9. The annual sales of a chain of hardware stores increased from $3,000,000 to $6,000,000 over a five-year period. Is this conclusive evidence of the excellence of managerial policies? Discuss.

10. In comparing two dissimilar enterprises, such as a meat processing company and a manufacturer of electronic components, which measure is more appropriate as a basis for comparison, the rate of net income to sales or the rate of net income to stockholders' equity?

11. The net income, after income tax, of Walden, Inc. was $2.50 per common share in the latest year and $4 per common share for the preceding year. At the beginning of the latest year the number of shares outstanding was doubled by a stock split. There were no other changes in the amount of stock outstanding. What were the earnings per share in the preceding year, adjusted to place them on a comparable basis with the latest year?

Exercises

1. What is the amount and per cent of the increase or decrease in net income in the second year as compared with the first year, in each of the following examples:

	NET INCOME OR LOSS*	
EXAMPLE	FIRST YEAR	SECOND YEAR
1.	$125,000	$150,000
2.	50,000	25,000
3.	50,000	50,000*
4.	10,000*	60,000
5.	20,000*	40,000*
6.	30,000*	10,000*

2. On the basis of the following information determine (a) working capital, (b) current ratio, (c) acid-test ratio. (Present figures used in your computations.)

Cash..	$110,000
Marketable securities.....................................	130,000
Accounts and notes receivable (net).......................	80,000
Merchandise inventory.....................................	310,000
Prepaid expenses..	10,000
Accounts and notes payable................................	170,000
Accrued liabilities.......................................	30,000

3. The following data were abstracted from an income statement:

Sales...	$520,000
Sales returns and allowances..............................	20,000
Merchandise inventory, beginning of year..................	58,000
Merchandise inventory, end of year........................	62,000
Purchases (net)...	314,000
Operating expenses..	90,000
Estimated income tax......................................	45,000

Determine the following, presenting figures used in your computations: (a) Rate of gross profit on sales, (b) rate of net income after income tax, on sales, (c) merchandise inventory turnover.

4. The data presented below were taken from the financial statements of M. J. Fisher, Inc. for the current fiscal year. Determine the following, presenting figures used in your computations: (a) ratio of owners' equity to liabilities, (b) ratio of plant assets to long-term liabilities, (c) rate earned on stockholders' equity, (d) rate earned on common stockholders' equity, (e) earnings per share of common stock.

Plant assets (net)..		$460,000
Current liabilities.......................................	$150,000	
Long-term liabilities.....................................	200,000	
Total liabilities...		350,000

Stockholders' equity:
    Preferred 5% stock, $50 par, cumulative, nonpartici-
        pating (no change during year)................. $100,000
    Common stock, $10 par (no change during year)...   400,000
    Retained earnings

Balance, beginning of year...	$168,000		
Net income.............	57,000	$225,000	
Preferred dividends.........	$ 5,000		
Common dividends.........	20,000	25,000	
Balance, end of year........................		200,000	
Total capital.....................................			$700,000

5. The reported net income, before income tax, of Turner Machinery Co. for the past year and the preceding year was $3,000,000 and $5,000,000, respectively. There were 1,000,000 shares of common stock (no preferred) outstanding during both years. The income statement for the latest year contained a charge of $1,000,000 for loss from a patent infringement suit and the statement for the preceding year contained a credit of $1,500,000 for gain on the sale of a subsidiary company. (a) What were the earnings per share for each year, as reported, and (b) after adjustment for nonrecurring charges and credits?

Problems

30-1. Comparative statements of Knox Company are presented below and on pages 687 and 688.

Knox Company
Comparative Balance Sheet
December 31, 1962 and 1961

	1962	1961
Assets		
Current assets.....................................	$1,080,000	$ 940,000
Long-term investments..........................	200,000	300,000
Plant assets (net)...............................	1,200,000	980,000
Total assets.....................................	$2,480,000	$2,220,000
Liabilities		
Current liabilities...............................	$ 370,000	$ 280,000
Long-term liabilities............................	300,000	200,000
Total liabilities.................................	$ 670,000	$ 480,000
Stockholders' equity		
Preferred 6% stock, cumulative, nonparticipating, $50 par..	$ 500,000	$ 500,000
Common stock, no par (200,000 shares)...........	1,000,000	1,000,000
Retained earnings................................	310,000	240,000
Total stockholders' equity........................	$1,810,000	$1,740,000
Total liabilities and stockholders' equity...........	$2,480,000	$2,220,000

Knox Company
Comparative Schedule of Current Assets
December 31, 1962 and 1961

	1962	1961
Cash..	$ 180,000	$ 220,000
Marketable securities...........................	60,000	100,000
Accounts receivable (net).......................	220,000	180,000
Merchandise inventory..........................	600,000	425,000
Prepaid expenses...............................	20,000	15,000
Total current assets............................	$1,080,000	$ 940,000

Knox Company
Comparative Statement of Retained Earnings
For Year Ended December 31, 1962 and 1961

	1962	1961
Retained earnings, Jan. 1.......................	$ 240,000	$ 215,000
Net income for year............................	160,000	105,000
Total...	$ 400,000	$ 320,000
Dividends:		
On preferred stock............................	$ 30,000	$ 30,000
On common stock.............................	60,000	50,000
Total...	$ 90,000	$ 80,000
Retained earnings, Dec. 31......................	$ 310,000	$ 240,000

Knox Company
Comparative Income Statement
For Year Ended December 31, 1962 and 1961

	1962	1961
Sales...	$3,200,000	$2,560,000
Sales returns and allowances....................	100,000	60,000
Net sales......................................	$3,100,000	$2,500,000
Cost of goods sold.............................	2,060,000	1,630,000
Gross profit on sales...........................	$1,040,000	$ 870,000
Selling expense................................	$ 520,000	$ 475,000
General expense................................	200,000	185,000
Total operating expense.........................	$ 720,000	$ 660,000
Net operating income...........................	$ 320,000	$ 210,000
Other income..................................	15,000	18,000
	$ 335,000	$ 228,000
Other expense.................................	20,000	15,000
Net income before income tax....................	$ 315,000	$ 213,000
Estimated income tax...........................	155,000	108,000
Net income after income tax.....................	$ 160,000	$ 105,000

Knox Company
Comparative Statement of Cost of Goods Sold
For Year Ended December 31, 1962 and 1961

	1962	1961
Merchandise inventory, Jan. 1..................	$ 425,000	$ 355,000
Purchases (net)...............................	2,235,000	1,700,000
Merchandise available for sale..................	$2,660,000	$2,055,000
Merchandise inventory, Dec. 31.................	600,000	425,000
Cost of goods sold	$2,060.000	$1,630,000

Instructions: Prepare comparative statements and schedules for the two-year period, presenting the dollar and percentage changes for 1962 as compared with 1961.

30-2. The comparative statements presented in Problem 30-1 are the principal data for this problem. Other necessary data, taken from the statements of Knox Company for 1960, are as follows:

Accounts receivable (net).....................................	$ 200,000
Long-term investments.....................................	300,000
Total assets..	2,000,000
Total stockholders' equity (preferred and common stock outstanding same as in 1961)....................................	1,650,000

Instructions: Determine for each of the two years the following ratios, turnovers, and other measures listed below, presenting the figures used in your computations:

(1) Working capital.
(2) Current ratio.
(3) Acid-test ratio.
(4) Ratio of stockholders' equity to liabilities.
(5) Ratio of plant assets to long-term liabilities.
(6) Accounts receivable turnover.
(7) Merchandise inventory turnover.
(8) Ratio of net sales to assets.
(9) Rate earned on total assets.
(10) Rate earned on stockholders' equity.
(11) Rate earned on common stockholders' equity.
(12) Earnings per share on common stock.

30-3. The comparative balance sheet and income statement presented in Problem 30-1 are the basic data for this problem.

Instructions: (1) Prepare a comparative balance sheet for the two-year period, presenting a percentage analysis of each item to the total, for each of the years.

(2) Prepare a comparative income statement for the two-year period, presenting a percentage analysis of each item in relationship to net sales, for each of the years.

Appendix A

Alternative method of recording merchandise inventories

There are several alternatives to the method of recording merchandise inventories illustrated in Chapter 8. The alternative presented here classifies the entries for the beginning and ending merchandise inventories as *closing* entries instead of *adjusting* entries. The difference in viewpoint has a minor effect on the work sheet, the sequence of entries in the journal, and the expense and revenue summary account in the ledger. It does not affect the over-all results, nor does it alter the financial statements in any way.

Work sheet

The merchandise inventory at the beginning of the period is extended directly from the trial balance debit column to the income statement debit column, without the intermediate step of adjusting entry (a) illustrated on pages 168 and 169. The inventory at the end of the period is then inserted in the income statement credit column and the balance sheet debit column on the same line in which the beginning inventory appears, without the intermediate step of adjusting entry (b) illustrated on pages 168 and 169. This alternative procedure is illustrated by the work sheet on page 690.

Adjusting entries

The adjusting entries are exactly the same as those illustrated on page 174 except that the two inventory adjustments are excluded. The alternative procedure is illustrated on page 691.

689

BENNETT ELECTRICAL SUPPLIES

Work Sheet

For Year Ended December 31, 1961

Acct. No.	Account Titles	Trial Balance		Adjustments		Income Statement		Balance Sheet	
		DR.	CR.	DR.	CR.	DR.	CR.	DR.	CR.
111	Cash	9,675						9,675	
113	Accounts Receivable	8,900						8,900	
114	Merchandise Inventory	16,600				16,600	18,200	18,200	
115	Store Supplies	1,270			(a) 580			690	
116	Office Supplies	580			(b) 240			340	
117	Prepaid Insurance	1,520			(c) 716			804	
121	Store Equipment	12,000						12,000	
122	Accumulated Depr. — Store Equip		4,700		(d) 1,000				5,700
123	Office Equipment	3,400						3,400	
124	Accumulated Depr. — Office Equip		680		(e) 340				1,020
125	Building	28,000						28,000	
126	Accumulated Depr. — Building		3,500		(f) 700				4,200
127	Land	3,000						3,000	
211	Accounts Payable		9,270						9,270
221	Mortgage Payable		8,000						8,000
311	John Bennett, Capital		43,751						43,751
312	John Bennett, Drawing	12,000						12,000	
411	Sales		164,574				164,574		
412	Sales Returns and Allowances	3,150				3,150			
413	Sales Discount	1,314				1,314			
511	Purchases	103,920				103,920			
512	Purchases Returns and Allowances		2,640				2,640		
513	Purchases Discount		1,857				1,857		
611	Sales Salaries	14,510		(g) 152		14,662			
612	Sales Commissions	6,867		(h) 564		7,431			
613	Advertising Expense	2,580				2,580			
615	Delivery Expense	963				963			
618	Miscellaneous Selling Expense	724				724			
711	Office Salaries	5,064		(g) 60		5,124			
712	Taxes Expense	1,762				1,762			
717	Miscellaneous General Expense	693				693			
911	Interest Expense	480				480			
		238,972	238,972						
616	Store Supplies Expense			(a) 580		580			
715	Office Supplies Expense			(b) 240		240			
617	Insurance Expense — Selling			(c) 420		420			
716	Insurance Expense — General			(c) 296		296			
614	Depreciation Expense — Store Equip			(d) 1,000		1,000			
713	Depreciation Expense — Office Equip			(e) 340		340			
714	Depreciation Expense — Building			(f) 700		700			
213	Salaries Payable				(g) 212				212
212	Commissions Payable				(h) 564				564
				4,352	4,352	162,979	187,271	97,009	72,717
	Net Income					24,292			24,292
						187,271	187,271	97,009	97,009

Work sheet

GENERAL JOURNAL   Page 28

Date		Name of Account	Post. Ref.	Debit	Credit
		Adjusting Entries			
	31	Store Supplies Expense...................	616	580	
		Store Supplies........................	115		580
	31	Office Supplies Expense..................	715	240	
		Office Supplies.......................	116		240
	31	Insurance Expense — Selling..............	617	420	
		Insurance Expense — General............	716	296	
		Prepaid Insurance....................	117		716
	31	Depreciation Expense — Store Equip.......	614	1,000	
		Accumulated Depreciation — Store Equip.	122		1,000
	31	Depreciation Expense — Office Equip.......	713	340	
		Accumulated Depreciation — Office Equip.	124		340
	31	Depreciation Expense — Building..........	714	700	
		Accumulated Depreciation — Building....	126		700
	31	Sales Salaries...........................	611	152	
	.	Office Salaries...........................	711	60	
		Salaries Payable.......................	213		212
	31	Sales Commissions.......................	612	564	
		Commissions Payable..................	212		564

Adjusting entries

Closing entries

The debit to Merchandise Inventory for the ending inventory is added to the first compound closing entry illustrated on page 175 and the credit to Merchandise Inventory for the beginning inventory is added to the second compound closing entry, illustrated on the same page. The closing entries prepared according to the alternative procedure are illustrated on page 692.

Expense and revenue summary account

The first two debit postings in the expense and revenue summary account illustrated on page 176 are combined into one debit posting by the alternative procedure. Similarly, the two credit postings illustrated on page 176 are combined into one credit posting. The amount of net income transferred to the capital account is, of course, not affected. The postings to the expense and revenue summary account in accordance with the alternative method is illustrated on page 692.

GENERAL JOURNAL   Page 29

Date		Name of Account	Post. Ref.	Debit	Credit
		Closing Entries			
1961 Dec.	31	Sales..............................	411	164,574	
		Merchandise Inventory..................	114	18,200	
		Purchases Returns and Allowances.........	512	2,640	
		Purchases Discount.....................	513	1,857	
		Expense and Revenue Summary.........	313		187,271
	31	Expense and Revenue Summary...........	313	162,979	
		Merchandise Inventory..................	114		16,600
		Sales Returns and Allowances...........	412		3,150
		Sales Discount........................	413		1,314
		Purchases............................	511		103,920
		Sales Salaries	611		14,664
		Sales Commissions.....................	612		7,431
		Advertising Expense....................	613		2,580
		Delivery Expense......................	615		963
		Miscellaneous Selling Expense...........	618		724
		Office Salaries........................	711		5,124
		Taxes Expense.......................	712		1,762
		Miscellaneous General Expense..........	717		693
		Interest Expense......................	911		480
		Store Supplies Expense.................	616		580
		Office Supplies Expense................	715		240
		Insurance Expense — Selling............	617		420
		Insurance Expense — General...........	716		296
		Depreciation Expense — Store Equip.....	614		1,000
		Depreciation Expense — Office Equip.....	713		340
		Depreciation Expense — Building........	714		700
	31	Expense and Revenue Summary...........	313	24,292	
		John Bennett, Capital..................	311		24,292
	31	John Bennett, Capital...................	311	12,000	
		John Bennett, Drawing.................	312		12,000

Closing entries

EXPENSE AND REVENUE SUMMARY   Account No. 313

Date		Items	Post. Ref.	Debit	Date		Items	Post. Ref.	Credit
1961 Dec.	31		J29	162,979	1961 Dec.	31		J29	187,271
	31		J29	24,292					
				187,271					187,271

Expense and revenue summary account

Appendix B
Specimen corporation statements

Specimen statements taken from the annual reports of various corporations are presented on this and the following pages. They are illustrative of the many variations in form of statement, terminology employed, and type of data presented to stockholders. The explanatory notes and other supporting data to which references are made in the statements are not reproduced in this appendix.

CONSOLIDATED INCOME AND EARNED SURPLUS

THE AMERICAN SUGAR REFINING COMPANY and wholly-owned subsidiaries

YEAR ENDED DECEMBER 31	1960	1959
NET SALES AND OPERATING REVENUES	$338,179,391	$335,768,447
COSTS AND EXPENSES	319,997,736	315,953,550
INCOME FROM OPERATIONS	$ 18,181,655	$ 19,814,897
OTHER INCOME (EXPENSES)		
Dividends from Spreckels Sugar Company and		
Spreckels Companies	925,338	382,808
Interest on borrowings	(1,667,126)	(1,033,809)
Miscellaneous, net	119,447	132,285
INCOME BEFORE PROVISION FOR TAXES ON INCOME	$ 17,559,314	$ 19,296,181
PROVISION FOR UNITED STATES TAXES ON INCOME		
(INCLUDES CUBAN TAXES IN 1959)	8,171,163	9,240,754
NET INCOME FOR YEAR	$ 9,388,151	$ 10,055,427
EARNED SURPLUS JANUARY 1	54,405,304	51,424,845
	$ 63,793,455	$ 61,480,272
DEDUCT		
Dividends declared		
Preferred stock (excluding $35,000 on stock held in pension fund)		
—$1.75 a share each year	$ 3,115,000	$ 3,114,986
Common stock—$1.90 a share in 1960, $2.20 a share in 1959 . .	$ 3,420,000	$ 3,959,982
	$ 6,535,000	$ 7,074,968
Write-off of net assets in Cuba, less estimated income tax reductions	14,875,000	—
	$ 21,410,000	$ 7,074,968
EARNED SURPLUS DECEMBER 31	$ 42,383,455	$ 54,405,304

SEE NOTES TO CONSOLIDATED FINANCIAL STATEMENTS

Balance Sheet

LIBBEY-OWENS-FORD GLASS COMPANY

December 31, 1960

Assets

Current Assets

Cash..		$ 22,705,949.43
U. S. Government and other short-term securities, at cost		
and accrued interest (quoted market $27,958,400.00).................		27,852,878.41
Trade receivables, less reserve of $1,250,000.00.........................		14,339,515.99
Inventories, at the lower of cost or market:		
Raw materials....................................	$ 4,948,211.74	
In-process and finished products......................	17,164,009.28	
Manufacturing supplies, and materials		
and supplies in transit..........................	13,315,792.83	35,428,013.85
TOTAL CURRENT ASSETS		$100,326,357.68

Investment in Marketable Securities

Common stock of Johns-Manville Corporation—		
at cost (quoted market $31,706,480.00)..............................		11,847,359.38

Plant Improvement and Replacement Fund

Cash..$	455,345.74	
U. S. Government securities, at cost and accrued		
interest (quoted market $48,336,700.00)	47,586,512.74	
Other marketable securities, at cost and accrued		
interest (quoted market $2,528,800.00).................	2,595,844.68	50,637,703.16

Plants and Properties—on the basis of cost

Land, land improvements, buildings,		
machinery, and equipment...........................$220,640,819.23		
Less accumulated depreciation, amortization,		
and obsolescence..................................	162,007,580.51	58,633,238.72

Other Assets

Gas properties—equity at cost and		
accumulated net earnings...........................$	2,656,856.14	
Miscellaneous securities, receivables,		
deposits, and advances..............................	1,501,795.90	4,158,652.04

Patents and Licenses..		1.00
Prepaid Expenses..		760,533.33
		$226,363,845.31

Balance Sheet

LIBBEY-OWENS-FORD GLASS COMPANY

December 31, 1960

Liabilities and Shareholders' Equity

Current Liabilities

Trade accounts payable and accrued expenses.............................		$ 5,618,303.77
Employes' compensation and amounts withheld		
therefrom for taxes, bond purchases, etc.............................		11,054,852.90
Taxes—other than federal taxes on income.............................		2,698,145.57
Estimated federal taxes on income........................	$ 30,100,000.00	
Less U. S. Government tax notes........................	24,760,000.00	5,340,000.00
TOTAL CURRENT LIABILITIES		$ 24,711,302.24

Reserve for Rebuilding Furnaces.. 4,647,563.47

Shareholders' Equity

Common Stock—par value $5.00 a share—Note A:		
Authorized—20,000,000		
Outstanding—10,469,359 (after deducting		
37,500 shares in treasury)........................	$ 52,346,795.00	
Additional paid-in capital................................	5,970,338.75	
Retained earnings employed in the business................	138,687,845.85	197,004,979.60

See notes to financial statements.

$226,363,845.31

Consolidated

Balance

for the years ended December 31,

Sheet

	1960	1959

ASSETS

CURRENT ASSETS

	1960	1959
Cash....................................	$ 5,580,267	$ 6,632,427
Accounts Receivable......................	12,384,631	12,784,813
Inventories (lower of cost or market)		
Materials and Supplies...................	12,018,376	13,798,454
Finished and In Process, less Progress Billings		
of $1,592,255 ($3,305,624 in 1959).......	4,978,381	7,927,473
Prepaid Expenses.........................	1,172,151	1,551,756
Total Current Assets.................	$ 36,133,806	$ 42,694,923

PROPERTY, AT COST

	1960	1959
Tank Cars..............................	$275,343,625	$268,252,935
Land, Buildings and Equipment..............	55,164,713	50,289,979
Less Accumulated Depreciation..............	145,043,652	135,540,860
	$185,464,686	$183,002,054

OTHER ASSETS

	1960	1959
Investments..............................	$ 4,011,064	$ 937,728
Unamortized Debt Discount and Expense......	290,958	332,550
	$ 4,302,022	$ 1,270,278
	$225,900,514	$226,967,255

UNION TANK CAR COMPANY and subsidiaries

for the years ended December 31,

	1960	1959

LIABILITIES AND STOCKHOLDERS' EQUITY

CURRENT LIABILITIES

Debt Due Within One Year	$ 5,000,000	$ —
Accounts Payable and Accrued Expenses	7,825,525	9,252,798
Provision for Income Taxes	2,575,232	1,354,866
Provision for Other Taxes	921,694	832,913
Total Current Liabilities	$ 16,322,451	$ 11,440,577

LONG TERM DEBT

4¼% Notes Payable	$ 40,000,000	$ 50,000,000
4¼% Sinking Fund Debentures	17,000,000	18,500,000
3¾% Sinking Fund Debentures	25,000,000	25,000,000
	$ 82,000,000	$ 93,500,000

DEFERRED INCOME TAXES . . . . | $ 30,862,000 | $ 28,190,000 |

STOCKHOLDERS' EQUITY

Capital Stock, No Par Value

Authorized—6,000,000 shares

Issued—3,582,786 shares	$ 53,741,790	$ 53,741,790
Capital Surplus	10,603,662	10,179,378
Earned Surplus	32,764,997	30,596,612
Less 32,600 Shares of Reacquired Stock, at cost . (56,300 shares in 1959)	394,386	681,102
	$ 96,716,063	$ 93,836,678
	$225,900,514	$226,967,255

United States Steel Corporation

Consolidated Statement of

Financial Position

Current assets	Dec. 31, 1960	Dec. 31, 1959
Cash	$ 276,501,195	$ 258,430,638
United States Government securities, at cost (approximates market) . .	175,218,208	257,015,168
Receivables, less estimated bad debts	218,523,857	311,985,387
Inventories *(details on page 36)*	725,599,116	596,341,886
Total	1.395,842,376	1,423,773,079

Less

Current liabilities		
Accounts payable	373,065,094	452,895,240
Accrued taxes, less United States Government securities of $154,000,000 at December 31, 1960 and $153,300,000 at December 31, 1959	336,194,106	275,756,872
Dividends payable . . . . :	46,835,794	46,793,037
Long-term debt due within one year	31,652,777	32,789,544
Total	787,747,771	808,234,693
Working capital	608,094,605	615,538,386
Miscellaneous investments, less estimated losses	43,036,483	41,402,425
United States Government securities set aside for property additions and replacements	300,000,000	495,000,000
Plant and equipment, less depreciation *(details on page 35)*	2,787,553,310	2,511,840,798
Operating parts and supplies	48,898,855	49,924,902
Costs applicable to future periods	51,518,319	37,196,216
Total assets less current liabilities	3,839,101,572	3,750,902,727

Deduct

Long-term debt *(details on page 36)*	422,778,670	454,447,447
Reserves for insurance, contingencies and accident and hospital expenses *(details on page 35)*	114,455,398	112,727,898
Excess of assets over liabilities and reserves	$3,301,867,504	$3,183,727,382

Ownership evidenced by

Preferred stock, 7% cumulative, par value $100 (authorized 4,000,000 shares; outstanding 3,602,811 shares)	$ 360,281,100	$ 360,281,100
Common stock (authorized 90,000,000 shares; outstanding 54,033,307 shares at December 31, 1960 and 53,961,007 shares at December 31, 1959)	2,941,586,404	2,823,446,282
Par value $16⅔ per share. . . . . $ 900,555,117		
Income reinvested in business *(see page 31 for addition of $116,935,122 in 1960)* 2,041,031,287		
Total	$3,301,867,504	$3,183,727,382

Shell Oil Company and Subsidiary Companies

SOURCE AND DISPOSITION OF FUNDS

	Year 1960 Thousands of Dollars	Year 1959 Thousands of Dollars
SOURCE OF FUNDS		
Net income	$144,588	$147,418
Depreciation, depletion, amortization, etc. charged against income	201,020	195,390
Net increase in long term debt	66,524	—
TOTAL	$412,132	$342,808
DISPOSITION OF FUNDS		
Capital expenditures:		
Drilling and production	$197,639	$200,337
Oil refineries	29,140	31,524
Chemical plants	18,014	21,267
Pipe lines and other transportation facilities	6,589	5,347
Marketing and miscellaneous facilities	32,659	21,598
	284,041	280,073
Dividends paid	66,631	62,088
Net decrease in long term debt	—	9,864
Advances to Shell Oil Company of Canada, Limited	43,450	12,000
Other items	4,400	(6,085)
Working capital increase or (decrease)	13,610	(15,132)
TOTAL	$412,132	$342,808

MONSANTO CHEMICAL COMPANY

STATEMENT OF CONSOLIDATED INCOME

	1960	1959	Increase Decrease
Income:		*(In Thousands)*	
Net sales..	$890,114	$875,012	$15,102
Other	10,411	10,220	191
	900,525	885,232	15,293
Deductions:			
Cost of goods sold............................	636,371	614,439	21,932
Selling, administrative and research expenses.........	122,689	110,065	12,624
Interest	12,362	12,049	313
Minority interests.............................	1,569	1,550	19
Other	934	2,320	*1,386*
	773,925	740,423	33,502
Income Before Income Taxes.....................	126,600	144,809	*18,209*
Provision for Income Taxes:			
Current	58,207	66,443	*8,236*
Deferred	586	3,601	*3,015*
	58,793	70,044	*11,251*
Net Income.......................................	$ 67,807	$ 74,765	*$ 6,958*

AND SUBSIDIARIES

STATEMENT OF CONSOLIDATED PAID-IN SURPLUS AND RETAINED EARNINGS

PAID-IN SURPLUS

	1960	1959
	(In Thousands)	
Balance at Beginning of Year...........................	$230,517	$195,063
Additions:		
Excess of approximate market value of common capital stock distributed as a stock dividend over the par value thereof..................	16,175	21,178
Excess of amounts received over the par value of common capital stock issued under stock option plans.....................	970	13,006
Excess of approximate market value over the par value of common capital stock issued for all of the outstanding stock of Nitro Industrial Corporation.......................................		1,270
Adjustment resulting from an increase in the stated value of common stock of The Chemstrand Corporation (see retained earnings below)..	39,000	
Other	4	
Balance at End of Year....................................	$286,666	$230,517

RETAINED EARNINGS

	1960	1959
Balance at Beginning of Year............................	$272,861	$245,094
Addition—Net Income for the Year	67,807	74,765
	340,668	319,859
Deductions:		
Dividends on capital stock of parent company:		
Cash—at the rate of $1 a share.........................	23,159	22,414
Stock—2%	17,102	22,084
	40,261	44,498
Cash dividend on capital stock of The Chemstrand Corporation........	2,500	2,500
	42,761	46,998
Transfer to common capital stock account by The Chemstrand Corporation resulting from an increase in the stated value of its common stock (see paid-in surplus above)...............................	39,000	
	81,761	46,998
Balance at End of Year.......................................	$258,907	$272,861

R. H. Macy & Co., Inc.

CONSOLIDATED STATEMENT

ASSETS

	July 30, 1960	August 1, 1959
CURRENT ASSETS:		
Cash	$ 16,985,674	$ 13,043,385
Marketable securities, at amortized cost (approximate market)	2,047,883	5,344,422
Customers' accounts receivable, per accompanying statement	30,273,212	26,333,523
Macy's Bank — current account	3,309,358	245,832
Other receivables	4,920,095	3,413,791
Merchandise inventories — at Lifo cost determined by the retail inventory method, which is less than market (Note 1)	60,153,517	55,552,162
Supplies and prepaid expenses	4,953,822	4,685,441
Total current assets	$122,643,561	$108,618,556
OTHER ASSETS:		
Overpayment of Federal income taxes claimed for the five years ended January, 1947, based on the Lifo inventory method, including $2,102,699 interest accrued to 1953 (Note 1)	9,018,699	9,018,699
Miscellaneous, including investments in and advances to affiliated shopping centers at cost	8,439,941	8,465,689
PROPERTY AND EQUIPMENT, per accompanying statement	82,943,605	81,196,929
GOODWILL AND OTHER INTANGIBLE ASSETS — at cost, less accumulated amortization of $1,419,577 and $1,332,334	1,335,981	1,423,224
	$224,381,787	$208,723,097

AND CONSOLIDATED SUBSIDIARIES

OF FINANCIAL CONDITION

LIABILITIES

	July 30, 1960	August 1, 1959
CURRENT LIABILITIES:		
Accounts payable and accrued liabilities	$ 42,120,848	$ 39,926,335
Federal income taxes, less U. S. Government obligations of $9,835,491 and $8,428,903 (Note 1)	4,431,038	—
Long-term debt due within one year	1,280,803	1,186,211
Total current liabilities	$ 47,832,689	$ 41,112,546
LONG-TERM DEBT, per accompanying statement	$ 60,318,166	$ 59,005,762
DEFERRED FEDERAL INCOME TAXES, resulting from use of accelerated depreciation for tax purposes	$ 2,295,000	$ 1,760,000
INVESTMENT OF STOCKHOLDERS, represented by:		
Cumulative preferred stock, 500,000 shares authorized; par value $100 each —		
4¼% Series A — 165,600 shares issued; 5,990 in treasury; 159,610 outstanding, callable at $107.50 each	$ 15,961,000	$ 15,961,000
4% Series B — 100,000 shares issued and outstanding (Note 2)	10,000,000	10,000,000
Common stock, without par value, stated value $15 per share —		
2,500,000 shares authorized (increase to 4,000,000 approved by stockholders); 1,882,307 and 1,783,711 issued; 3,939 in treasury; 1,878,368 and 1,779,772 outstanding (Notes 3 and 4)	28,175,520	26,696,580
Additional paid-in capital; 1960 increase comprises $60,437 received over stated value of common stock issued under options and $1,606,372 credit from conversions of 5% debentures into common stock	13,094,125	11,427,316
Earnings reinvested in the business, per accompanying statement; $32,020,447 is not distributable to common stockholders under terms of long-term debt agreements	46,705,287	42,759,893
Total investment of stockholders	$113,935,932	$106,844,789
	$224,381,787	$208,723,097

Appendix B

UNITED AIRCRAFT CORPORATION

CONSOLIDATED STATEMENTS OF INCOME AND OF EARNINGS EMPLOYED IN THE BUSINESS (EARNED SURPLUS)

Years Ended December 31, 1960 and 1959

	Year 1960	Year 1959
Income:		
Sales of aeronautical products, parts and services	$987,879,119	$1,080,980,782
Royalties and other income from licensees	1,373,000	1,168,614
Dividends from affiliated companies	188,119	132,491
Other income (discount on purchases, etc.)	2,552,475	2,614,629
	$991,992,713	$1,084,896,516
Costs and Expenses:		
Cost of goods and services sold	$753,737,704	$ 831,439,978
Depreciation and amortization (see page 15)	30,024,478	28,455,543
Engineering, development, selling and administrative expenses	175,082,895	160,417,734
Interest expense and other deductions	5,163,543	2,894,850
Federal taxes on income	14,115,097	33,050,058
	$978,123,717	$1,056,258,163
Net Income for the Year	$ 13,868,996	$ 28,638,353
Earnings Employed in the Business (Earned Surplus) at beginning of the year	129,185,925	117,915,232
	$143,054,921	$ 146,553,585
Dividends on Capital Stock:		
Preference Stock—$5.00 and $4.00 per share, respectively (including in 1960 the dividend declared December 27, 1960, paid February 1, 1961)	$ 1,717,868	$ 1,391,431
Common Stock—$2.00 and $2.50 per share, respectively	12,792,920	15,976,229
	$ 14,510,788	$ 17,367,660
Earnings Employed in the Business (Earned Surplus) at end of the year	$128,544,133	$ 129,185,925

Summary of Source and Application of Funds

THE GLIDDEN COMPANY AND CANADIAN SUBSIDIARY

Years ended August 31, 1960, and August 31, 1959

source of funds	1960	1959
From operations:		
Net income	$ 6,690,356	$ 7,633,531
Provision for depreciation and amortization, which did not involve current expenditures	6,959,971	6,579,313
TOTAL FROM OPERATIONS	$ 13,650,327	$ 14,212,844
Sale of debentures	$ -0-	$ 30,000,000
Less payments of bank loans	-0-	26,000,000
	$ -0-	$ 4,000,000
Sale of Common Stock under option plan (1960 — 2,740 shares; 1959 — 9,680 shares) .	98,479	351,033
Other changes	1,109,487	(671,111)
	$ 14,858,293	$ 17,892,766

application of funds		
Dividends declared	$ 4,620,700	$ 4,609,795
Expenditures for property, plant and equipment	8,764,000	7,607,001
Increase in working capital	1,473,593	5,675,970
	$ 14,858,293	$ 17,892,766

Accountants' Report

Shareholders and Board of Directors
The Glidden Company
Cleveland, Ohio

We have examined the consolidated financial statements of The Glidden Company and its Canadian subsidiary for the year ended August 31, 1960. Our examination was made in accordance with generally accepted auditing standards, and accordingly included such tests of the accounting records and such other auditing procedures as we considered necessary in the circumstances. We made a similar examination of the financial statements of the preceding year.

In our opinion, the accompanying balance sheet, statements of income and earnings retained for use in the business, and summary of source and application of funds present fairly the consolidated financial position of The Glidden Company and Canadian subsidiary at August 31, 1960, and the consolidated results of their operations for the year then ended, in conformity with generally accepted accounting principles applied on a basis consistent with that of the preceding year.

Ernst & Ernst

Certified Public Accountants

Cleveland, Ohio
October 14, 1960

STEWART-WARNER CORPORATION

CONSOLIDATED STATEMENT OF INCOME
For the Year Ended December 31, 1960

NET SALES		$107,348,373
COST OF SALES		83,033,727
GROSS INCOME FROM SALES		$ 24,314,646
SELLING AND ADMINISTRATIVE EXPENSES:		
Advertising	$1,742,574	
Sales and service	7,306,499	
Administrative and general	3,539,552	12,588,625
INCOME FROM OPERATIONS		$ 11,726,021
Miscellaneous income		1,214,273
INCOME BEFORE TAXES		$ 12,940,294
Provision for Federal and other income taxes		6,760,000
NET INCOME FOR THE YEAR		$ 6,180,294

The accompanying notes to the financial statements are an integral part of this statement.

Notes to the consolidated financial statements:

(1) Under the Corporation's Stock Option Plan, 121,890 shares of the Corporation's authorized capital stock were reserved for options to officers and other key employees at not less than 95% of market price at date of grant, exercisable over a ten-year period; options for 48,168 of such shares were outstanding at December 31, 1960. During 1960 options were granted for 12,400 shares, options were exercised for 32,358 shares, and options were terminated for 6,512 shares.

(2) The total provision for depreciation of buildings, machinery and equipment for the year included as deductions in the statement of income amounted to $1,535,806.

and Subsidiary Companies

CONSOLIDATED STATEMENTS OF CAPITAL AND RETAINED EARNINGS
For the Year Ended December 31, 1960

CAPITAL:

Balance at December 31, 1959	$21,834,160
Add:	
Proceeds from sale to officers and key employees of 2,200 shares of treasury stock and 32,358 shares of unissued stock under the Stock Option Plan	397,380
	$22,231,540
Deduct: Cost of 7,665 shares of capital stock acquired during the year	208,497
BALANCE AT DECEMBER 31, 1960	$22,023,043

RETAINED EARNINGS:

Appropriated for increased replacement cost of plant and equipment and other contingencies (no change during the year)	$ 5,000,000
Unappropriated:	
Balance at December 31, 1959	$29,170,251
Add: Net income for the year	6,180,294
	$35,350,545
Deduct: Cash dividends ($1.35 per share)	4,449,791
Balance at December 31, 1960	$30,900,754
TOTAL RETAINED EARNINGS	$35,900,754

AUDITORS' CERTIFICATE

To the Shareholders and the Board of Directors of Stewart-Warner Corporation:

We have examined the consolidated statement of financial position of STEWART-WARNER CORPORATION (a Virginia Corporation) AND SUBSIDIARY COMPANIES as of December 31, 1960, and the related statements of income, and capital and retained earnings for the year then ended. Our examination was made in accordance with generally accepted auditing standards, and accordingly included such tests of the accounting records and such other auditing procedures as we considered necessary in the circumstances. We were unable to obtain confirmation of receivables from Government agencies but satisfied ourselves as to such balances by means of alternative auditing procedures.

In our opinion, the accompanying consolidated statement of financial position and statements of income, and capital and retained earnings present fairly the financial position of Stewart-Warner Corporation and Subsidiary Companies as of December 31, 1960, and the results of their operations for the year then ended, and were prepared in conformity with generally accepted accounting principles applied on a basis consistent with that of the preceding year.

ARTHUR ANDERSEN & CO.

Chicago, Illinois,
February 17, 1961.

COMMERCIAL

CONSOLIDATED FINANCIAL POSITION

	December 31,	
	1960	**1959**
CURRENT ASSETS		
Cash	$ 3,212,852	$ 2,895,774
U. S. Government and other marketable securities, at cost	15,107,959	8,690,456
Accounts and notes receivable (less allowance for doubtful accounts, 1960—$396,831; 1959—$448,017)	11,887,888	13,578,904
Inventories, at the lower of average cost or market		
Finished products and materials in process	6,851,038	9,404,041
Raw materials and supplies	3,601,457	4,093,143
Total Current Assets	40,661,194	38,662,318
LESS CURRENT LIABILITIES		
Accounts payable	2,594,331	3,804,543
Accrued Federal income taxes	3,635,277	3,676,168
Other accrued liabilities	2,932,591	2,258,763
Installment on long-term debt due within one year	1,560,000	1,560,000
Total Current Liabilities	10,722,199	11,299,474
WORKING CAPITAL	29,938,995	27,362,844
INVESTMENTS AND OTHER ASSETS		
Investments (see notes)	2,222,368	955,638
Non-current accounts and notes receivable	2,557,500	1,387,500
Total Investments and Other Assets	4,779,868	2,343,138
PROPERTY, PLANT AND EQUIPMENT		
Land, buildings, equipment, etc., at cost	80,425,024	78,338,029
Less accumulated depreciation, depletion and amortization	47,464,550	43,987,464
Net Property, Plant and Equipment	32,960,474	34,350,565
GOODWILL AND PATENTS	1	1
DEFERRED CHARGES	1,164,020	1,032,220
TOTAL ASSETS LESS CURRENT LIABILITIES	68,843,358	65,088,768
LESS LONG-TERM DEBT AND DEFERRED ITEMS		
3¾% Notes payable	17,200,000	18,760,000
Deferred Federal income taxes	5,004,500	4,881,600
Deferred income (see notes)	1,750,000	—
SHAREHOLDERS' EQUITY	$44,888,858	$41,447,168
SOURCE OF SHAREHOLDERS' EQUITY (see notes)		
Common stock—$1.00 par value		
Authorized—6,000,000 shares		
Issued—2,852,175 shares in 1960; 2,796,250 shares in 1959	$ 6,808,749	$ 6,752,824
Additional paid-in capital	5,964,952	4,876,092
Earnings retained in business	32,115,157	29,818,252
	$44,888,858	$41,447,168

SEE ACCOMPANYING NOTES TO FINANCIAL STATEMENTS

SOLVENTS CORPORATION

CONSOLIDATED EARNINGS AND SUMMARY OF EARNINGS RETAINED IN BUSINESS

	Year Ended December 31,	
	1960	1959
INCOME		
Net Sales	$62,337,053	$70,381,175
Other income (net)	2,056,465	1,098,470
	64,393,518	71,479,645
COSTS AND EXPENSES		
Cost of sales	41,183,675	50,014,038
Selling, research and administrative expenses (including provision for doubtful accounts, 1960—$131,888; 1959—$556,856)	8,490,741	9,170,365
Depreciation, depletion and amortization	3,648,899	3,680,229
Interest on borrowings	742,500	801,000
	54,065,815	63,665,632
EARNINGS BEFORE FEDERAL INCOME TAXES AND SPECIAL CHARGE .	10,327,703	7,814,013
FEDERAL INCOME TAXES	5,222,000	4,130,100
EARNINGS BEFORE SPECIAL CHARGE	5,105,703	3,683,913
SPECIAL CHARGE		
Additional provision for agreed Price Redetermination refunds on prior years' sales to the U. S. Government	265,888	—
Adjustment of carrying value of investments	—	833,173
NET EARNINGS FOR YEAR (per share $1.70 in 1960; $1.00 in 1959) . .	4,839,815	2,850,740
EARNINGS RETAINED IN BUSINESS AT BEGINNING OF YEAR	29,818,252	28,452,260
	34,658,067	31,303,000
DIVIDENDS PAID TO SHAREHOLDERS		
In cash ($.50 per share in 1960; $.25 in 1959)	1,398,125	685,356
In stock (2%—55,925 shares at market value of $20.47 per share in 1960; 54,828 shares at market value of $14.58 per share in 1959) . . .	1,144,785	799,392
	2,542,910	1,484,748
EARNINGS RETAINED IN BUSINESS AT END OF YEAR	$32,115,157	$29,818,252

SEE ACCOMPANYING NOTES TO FINANCIAL STATEMENTS

The B.F.Goodrich Company AND CONSOLIDATED SUBSIDIARIES

Statement of Financial Position

ASSETS	December 31, 1960	December 31, 1959
CURRENT ASSETS		
Cash	$ 17,705,757	$ 18,862,300
Marketable securities, at cost (approximate market) . . .	49,190,149	5,460,261
Accounts and notes receivable, less allowance for doubtful accounts	131,181,015	140,632,515
Inventories at lower of cost (partly last-in, first-out) or market		
Finished products	115,273,664	124,657,132
In process	13,974,616	16,048,075
Raw materials and supplies	31,216,458	36,986,539
	$160,464,738	$177,691,746
Total Current Assets	$358,541,659	$342,646,822
INVESTMENTS		
Shares of Unconsolidated Subsidiary and Associate Companies, at cost—Note A	22,386,640	19,788,647
Other investments and advances	32,481,822	28,919,287
	$ 54,868,462	$ 48,707,934
PROPERTY		
Land, buildings, machinery, equipment and leasehold improvements, at cost	378,408,024	357,269,935
Accumulated allowances for depreciation and amortization	202,891,535	192,097,959
	$175,516,489	$165,171,976
MARKETABLE SECURITIES HELD FOR PLANT EXPANSION, AT COST	20,000,000	—
DEFERRED CHARGES	4,136,097	2,937,261
	$613,062,707	$559,463,993

LIABILITIES	December 31, 1960	December 31, 1959
CURRENT LIABILITIES		
Bank loans—foreign	$ 3,355,780	$ 3,046,325
Accounts payable	28,853,691	36,171,439
Accrued expenses	25,236,057	26,934,207
Federal and foreign income taxes	19,955,948	24,224,239
Long-term debt payable within one year, less bonds purchased for sinking fund	573,000	573,000
Total Current Liabilities	$ 77,974,476	$ 90,949,210
LONG-TERM DEBT PAYABLE AFTER ONE YEAR		
Debentures—4⅝% maturing 1966 to 1985	60,000,000	—
First Mortgage Bonds—2¾% maturing in 1965, less bonds in treasury	18,861,000	21,471,000
Notes—3¼% maturing 1966 to 1977	19,000,000	19,000,000
Note of a foreign subsidiary company—3½% maturing in 1963	660,000	840,000
	$ 98,521,000	$ 41,311,000
RESERVES		
For purchase contracts, foreign losses, sales adjustments and other purposes	15,612,374	16,715,933
SHAREHOLDERS' EQUITY		
Common Stock—$10 par value:		
Authorized 10,000,000 shares, issued 9,008,704 shares —Note C	90,087,040	90,003,140
Capital in excess of par value of shares	39,192,320	39,012,460
Income retained in the business—Note B:		
Appropriated for increased replacement cost of facilities	33,000,000	33,000,000
Unappropriated	258,675,497	248,472,250
	$291,675,497	$281,472,250
Total Shareholders' Equity	$420,954,857	$410,487,850
	$613,062,707	$559,463,993

See notes to financial statements

Campbell Soup Company

CONSOLIDATED BALANCE SHEET (000 OMITTED)

	July 31, 1960	August 2, 1959
CURRENT ASSETS		
Cash	$ 7,549	$ 7,270
Marketable securities, at cost, approximates market	32,515	3,422
Accounts receivable	57,030	58,245
Inventories — *note 2*	106,309	125,616
Prepaid insurance, taxes, etc.	2,915	2,672
	$206,318	$197,225
OTHER ASSETS — *note 3*	$ 32,756	$ 17,838
PLANT ASSETS, *less depreciation* — *note 4*	$114,542	$110,701
	$353,616	$325,764
CURRENT LIABILITIES		
Payable to suppliers and others	$ 20,246	$ 17,161
Accrued payrolls, taxes, etc.	5,762	5,036
Accrued income taxes	27,008	24,765
	$ 53,016	$ 46,962
DEFERRED INCENTIVE COMPENSATION — *note 5*	$ 365	$ 164
CAPITAL AND INCOME RETAINED IN THE BUSINESS		
Capital stock — *note 6*	$ 19,357	$ 19,310
Capital surplus — *note 6*	27,215	26,179
Income retained in the business	253,663	233,149
	$300,235	$278,638
	$353,616	$325,764

Appendix C

Alternate problems

The numbers assigned to the alternate problems in the appendix correspond to the numbers of the comparable problems presented at the end of the chapters, with the addition of the letter *A*. For example, Problem 1-2A in the appendix is the alternate for Problem 1-2 appearing at the end of Chapter 1. The working papers that are available for use with the text may be used either for the problems at the end of the chapters or for the alternate problems.

Chapter 1

1-2A. On September 1 of the current year, Ruth Ward established a women's clothing store called Holiday House. Transactions completed during the month were as follows:
  (a) Deposited $10,000 in cash in a bank account for Holiday House.
  (b) Purchased equipment for cash, $3,500.
  (c) Purchased merchandise on account, $3,000.
  (d) Sold merchandise on account, $1,700.
  (e) Paid salaries and other expenses, $500.
  (f) Paid creditors on account, $1,600.
  (g) Purchased merchandise for cash, $1,000.
  (h) Purchased equipment on account, $1,000.
  (i) Sold merchandise for cash, $1,900.
  (j) Paid salaries and other expenses, $400.
  (k) Received cash from customers on account, $900.
  (l) Returned defective equipment purchased on account, $150.
  (m) Withdrew cash for personal use, $250.
  (n) Determined by taking an inventory that the cost of the goods sold during the month was $2,100.

Instructions: (1) Record the transactions in tabular form, using the following headings:

Assets				=	Liabilities	Proprietorship
Cash + Accounts + Merchandise + Equipment				=	Accounts +	Ruth Ward,
Receivable					Payable	Capital

Identify changes in proprietorship by placing the abbreviation R (revenue), CGS (cost of goods sold), E (expense), or D (drawing) at the right of each amount of increase or decrease in capital subsequent to the initial investment.

(2) Prepare a balance sheet, an income statement, and a capital statement.

(3) Which of the statements present data for the specific date, September 30, and which for the entire month of September?

1-3A. Carl Wynn operates a business known as Speedy Cleaners. The actual work of dry cleaning is done by another company at wholesale rates. The assets and the liabilities of the business on March 1 of the current year are as follows: Cash, $1,200; Accounts Receivable, $500; Supplies, $50; Delivery Equipment, $2,500; Furniture and Fixtures, $1,100; Accounts Payable, $740. His business transactions during March are summarized below:

(a) Paid rent for March, $150.
(b) Purchased supplies on account, $75.
(c) Paid creditors on account, $440.
(d) Received $850 from cash customers.
(e) Charged customers for dry cleaning services sold on account, $500.
(f) Received $600 from customers on account.
(g) Received bill from cleaning company for $750.
(h) Reimbursed a customer $20 for a garment lost by the cleaning company, which agreed to deduct the amount from the invoice received in transaction (g).
(i) Purchased an item of furniture on account, $75.
(j) Paid miscellaneous expenses, $150.
(k) Paid personal expenses by checks drawn on the business $300, and withdrew $50 in cash for personal use.
(l) Determined by taking an inventory that $60 of supplies had been used during the month.

Instructions: (1) State the assets, liabilities, and proprietorship as of March 1 in equation form similar to that shown in this chapter.

(2) Record the transactions in tabular form, determining the new balances after each transaction. Identify changes in proprietorship by placing the abbreviation R (revenue), CSS (cost of services sold), E (expense), or D (drawing) at the right of each amount of increase or decrease in capital.

(3) Prepare a balance sheet, an income statement, and a capital statement.

Chapter 2

2-2A. At the beginning of the current fiscal year Mason Home Store had a merchandise inventory of $42,300 and capital of $44,580. The physical inventory taken on June 30, the last day of the fiscal year, amounted to $33,600. The accounting records for the fiscal year reveal the following information:

Advertising expense...	$ 3,750
Depreciation expense — office equipment..................	530
Depreciation expense — store equipment..................	800
Insurance expense..	1,180
Interest expense..	370
Interest income..	720
Miscellaneous general expense.............................	1,360
Miscellaneous selling expense..............................	900
Office salary expense..	7,630
Office supplies expense.......................................	1,800
Purchases...	193,800
Rent expense...	6,400
Sales...	270,000
Sales salary expense...	19,100
Store supplies expense..	2,450
Withdrawals by the proprietor...............................	17,500

Instructions: (1) Prepare an income statement for the current fiscal year.

(2) Determine the percentage of the following items to sales: (a) cost of goods sold, (b) gross profit on sales, (c) total selling expenses, (d) total general expenses, (e) total operating expenses, (f) net income from operations.

(3) Prepare a capital statement for the current fiscal year (no additional investments were made during the year).

2-3A. Frank Hale, owner of Hale's Market, had a capital balance of $28,410 on January 1 of the current year. His merchandise inventory at the same date was $26,930. On April 1 he invested an additional $6,000 in the business. During the year he made withdrawals of $1,250 each month. The following asset and liability balances are as of December 31 of the current year; the revenue and expense amounts are for the current year ended on that date.

Accounts payable....................................	$ 12,750
Accounts receivable.................................	6,400
Advertising expense.................................	2,740
Cash...	10,980
Depreciation expense — office equipment.............	450
Depreciation expense — store equipment..............	900
Insurance expense...................................	1,760
Interest expense....................................	450
Merchandise inventory...............................	30,500
Miscellaneous general expense.......................	800
Miscellaneous selling expense.......................	790
Notes payable.......................................	6,600
Office equipment....................................	4,800
Accumulated depreciation — office equipment..........	1,300
Office salary expense................................	6,420
Office supplies......................................	320
Office supplies expense..............................	420
Prepaid insurance...................................	2,510
Purchases...	134,290
Rent expense..	7,800
Sales...	214,540
Salaries payable.....................................	720
Sales salary expense.................................	30,370
Store equipment.....................................	13,000
Accumulated depreciation — store equipment..........	3,600
Store supplies.......................................	550
Store supplies expense...............................	3,920
Taxes expense.......................................	1,100
Taxes payable.......................................	680
Utilities expense....................................	1,900

Instructions: (1) Prepare an income statement for the current fiscal year.

(2) Prepare a balance sheet in report form as of December 31 of the current fiscal year.

(3) Prepare a capital statement for the current fiscal year.

2-4A. On April 1 of the current year F. S. Walsh established a business enterprise. His transactions for the three months ending on June 30 are summarized below.

(a) Deposited cash in a business bank account........ $12,000

(b) Purchased a going business known as Ace Parcel Delivery.
    Assets acquired:

Accounts receivable........................	$2,500	
Automotive supplies.......................	600	
Office supplies............................	200	
Trucks...................................	9,000	12,300

    Liabilities assumed:

Accounts payable.........................	900

    Terms of payment:

Cash paid....	$6,400	
Note payable issued, due in four equal quarterly installments, with interest.................	5,000	11,400

(c) Delivery service revenue charged to customers on account.............................. 9,500

(d) Purchases on account:

Automotive supplies.........................	$1,400	
Office supplies............................	100	1,500

(e) Receipts of cash from customers on account....... 10,200

(f) Payments of cash for the following purposes:

Creditors on account.......................	$1,800	
Installment on note payable..................	1,250	
Interest expense...........................	75	
Prepaid insurance..........................	1,500	
Prepaid taxes.............................	450	
Automotive supplies........................	175	
Drivers' salary expense......................	4,000	
Rent expense..............................	400	
Utilities expense...........................	150	
Repairs expense...........................	250	
Withdrawals by proprietor...................	1,000	11,050

(g) Automotive supplies used....................... 1,600
(h) Depreciation of trucks........................ 900
(i) Insurance expired............................ 450
(j) Taxes expired.............................. 100
(k) Office supplies used........................ 125

Instructions: (1) List the following captions in equation form, placing the first group across the top of the sheet and the second group across the middle of the sheet.

Cash + Accounts Receivable + Automotive Supplies + Office Supplies + Prepaid Insurance + Prepaid Taxes + Trucks

− Accumulated Depreciation, Trucks = Notes Payable + Accounts Payable + F. S. Walsh, Capital   Capital Notations

(2) Record Walsh's original investment and the remaining transactions in the appropriate columns, identifying each by letter. Indicate increases by $+$ and decreases by $-$. *Do not determine the new balances of the items after each transaction.* Indicate the nature of all changes in *capital* by notations at the right of each increase or decrease. The increase in accounts payable in (d) and the decrease in cash in (f) may be shown in one amount.

(3) Insert the final balances in each column and determine that Assets $=$ Liabilities $+$ Proprietorship at June 30, the end of the period.

(4) Prepare the following statements: (a) income statement (classify expenses as "operating expenses" and "other expenses"), (b) balance sheet in report form, (c) capital statement. (The name of the business was not changed.)

Chapter 3

3-2A. The accounts in the ledger of Robert W. Holmes, physician and surgeon, are listed below, together with their balances as of January 1 of the current year: Cash, $4,500; Accounts Receivable, $6,450; Supplies, $300; Prepaid Insurance, $330; Equipment, $14,000; Accounts Payable, $1,250; Robert W. Holmes, Capital, $24,330; Robert W. Holmes, Drawing; Professional Fees, Salary Expense; Rent Expense; Laboratory Expense; Gas, Electricity, and Water Expense; Telephone Expense; Miscellaneous Expense.

Transactions completed during January were as follows:

(a) Paid office rent for January, $720.
(b) Purchased equipment on account, $2,000.
(c) Received cash from debtors on account, $3,725.
(d) Returned part of equipment purchased in (b), $200.
(e) Paid cash for renewal of insurance policy, $140.
(f) Purchased supplies on account, $80.
(g) Paid laboratory expense, $150.
(h) Paid salaries of receptionist and nurses, $1,300.
(i) Sold supplies to another doctor at cost, as an accommodation, receiving cash, $40.
(j) Received cash in payment of professional services rendered during January, $3,000.
(k) Paid cash to creditors on account, $1,600.
(l) Paid gas and electricity expense, $125.
(m) Paid telephone expense, $56.
(n) Paid miscellaneous expense, $84.
(o) Recorded fees charged to customers on account for services rendered in January, $2,300.
(p) Paid water expense, $22.
(q) Discovered that a fee of $35 was erroneously charged to a patient in (o).
(r) Paid cash from business bank account for personal expenses, $925.

Instructions: (1) Set up a ledger of T accounts and record the balances as of January 1. Identify the balances by writing "Bal." to the left of the amount.

(2) Record the transactions for January. Identify each debit and each credit by the letter designating the transaction.

(3) Prepare a trial balance as of January 31 of the current year.

(4) If there were no other expired costs for January, such as depreciation and supplies expense, what would be the amount of net income for the month?

(5) What is the tentative amount of capital as of January 31, ignoring the effect of unrecorded expirations of cost?

3-3A. The following trial balance for Bowers Company as of November 30 of the current year does not balance because of a number of errors.

Cash	2,855	
Accounts Receivable	1,265	
Supplies	375	
Prepaid Insurance	250	
Equipment	4,970	
Notes Payable		1,500
Accounts Payable		1,383
T. J. Bowers, Capital		4,544
T. J. Bowers, Drawing	100	
Sales		7,450
Salary Expense	1,150	
Rent Expense	375	
Advertising Expense	250	
Utilities Expense	820	
	12,410	14,877

In the process of comparing the amounts in the trial balance with the ledger, recomputing the balances of the accounts, and comparing the entries with the original evidences of the transactions, the following errors are discovered:

(a) The pencil footing of the credits to Cash is $5,100; the correct total is $4,900.

(b) A cash receipt of $430 was recorded as a debit to Cash of $340.

(c) A debit of $225 to Accounts Receivable was not recorded.

(d) An insurance policy acquired at a cost of $90 was recorded as a credit to Prepaid Insurance.

(e) The pencil footings of $3,779 credit and $2,496 debit in Accounts Payable are correct but the balance was computed incorrectly.

(f) A debit of $500 for a withdrawal by the proprietor was recorded as a credit to the capital account.

(g) Sales was overfooted by $1,200.

(h) The balance of $82 in Utilities Expense was entered as $820 in the trial balance.

(i) Miscellaneous Expense was omitted from the trial balance. The account has a balance of $210.

Instructions: Prepare a corrected trial balance as of November 30 of the current year.

3-4A. The following transactions were completed by Arthur Reeder during May of the current year:

(a) Deposited cash in a bank account for use in acquiring and operating Rodeo Drive-In, an outdoor theatre, $18,000.

(b) Purchased the Rodeo Drive-In for $20,000, allocated as follows: equipment, $5,000; buildings, $9,000; land, $6,000. Made a down payment of $10,000 and gave a mortgage for the balance.

(c) Paid premiums for property and casualty insurance policies, $1,200.

(d) Purchased supplies, $300, and equipment, $600, on account.

(e) Paid for newspaper advertising, $250.

(f) Cash receipts from admissions for the week, $2,100.

(g) Paid miscellaneous expenses, $60.

(h) Cash receipts from admissions for the week, $2,325.

(i) Paid semimonthly wages, $1,800.

(j) Paid miscellaneous expenses, $45.

(k) Granted concession for operation of a refreshment stand at a rental of 10% of sales, but not less than $400 a month, payable in advance on the first of the month. Received $200 cash as advance payment for the second half of May.

(l) Cash receipts from admissions for the week, $1,680.

(m) Paid semimonthly wages, $1,750.

(n) Paid cash to creditors on account, $520.

(o) Purchased supplies for cash, $34.

(p) Paid for advertising, $175.

(q) Cash receipts from admissions for remainder of the month, $2,600.

(r) Paid utilities expenses, $310.

(s) Paid creditors on account, $220.

(t) Concessionaire reported sales of $2,800 for the second half of May. Received check for balance due.

(u) Paid film rental for the month, $2,400.

(v) Paid installment, $600, and interest, $48, due on mortgage.

(w) Withdrew cash for personal use, $450.

The accounts to be used in the ledger are as follows, arranged in alphabetical order: Accounts Payable; Admissions Income; Advertising Expense; Buildings; Cash; Concession Income; Equipment; Film Rental Expense; Interest Expense; Land; Miscellaneous Expense; Mortgage Payable; Prepaid Insurance; Arthur Reeder, Capital; Arthur Reeder, Drawing; Supplies; Utilities Expense; Wages Expense.

Instructions: (1) Set up T accounts for all of the accounts listed above, arranging them in appropriate sequence.

(2) Record the transactions for May. Identify each debit and each credit by the letter designating the transaction.

(3) Prepare a trial balance as of May 31 of the current year.

Chapter 4

4-2A. The ledger of Reliable Shoe Repairs includes the accounts listed at the top of page 720. The amounts shown for the asset, liability, and capital accounts are the balances as of March 1 of the current year.

Acct. No.	Account Title	Balance	Acct. No.	Account Title	Balance
11	Cash...................	$1,863.20	22	Accounts Payable........	$ 634.70
12	Supplies	586.90	31	Charles Burton, Capital...	7,533.80
13	Prepaid Insurance.......	65.00	32	Charles Burton, Drawing..	——
14	Prepaid Rent...........	——	41	Service Sales............	——
16	Equipment..............	8,184.40	51	Wages Expense..........	——
17	Accumulated Depr.......	2,531.00	52	Utilities Expense.........	——
21	Notes Payable..........	——	53	Advertising Expense......	——
			58	Miscellaneous Expense....	——

The transactions completed by the business during March were as follows:

Mar. 2. Paid cash for advertising, $30.
 3. Paid rent for three months, $270.
 4. Purchased supplies on account, $142.70.
 5. Purchased repair equipment for $1,400, paying $400 cash and giving a note payable for the balance.
 6. Recorded cash sales for the week, $426.70.
 8. Paid premium on property insurance, $45.
 9. Paid creditors on account, $575.
 12. Paid biweekly wages, $390.
 13. Recorded cash sales for the week, $412.20.
 15. Paid cash for repairs to equipment, $79.60.
 18. Proprietor withdrew cash for personal use, $150.
 19. Purchased supplies on account, $175.
 20. Recorded cash sales for the week, $453.90.
 22. Returned supplies purchased on the 19th for credit, $19.40.
 23. Paid miscellaneous expenses, $16.50.
 26. Recorded cash sales for the week, $307.80.
 27. Paid biweekly wages, $405.
 29. Proprietor withdrew cash for personal use, $150.
 30. Paid utilities expenses for the month, $46.70.
 31. Recorded cash sales for the remainder of the month, $243.30.

Instructions: (1) Open an account in the ledger for each item listed above.

(2) Record the balances in the accounts under the date of Mar. 1, write "Balance" in the Items column, and place a check mark in the posting reference column.

(3) Record the transactions for March in a four-column general journal similar to that illustrated on page 81.

(4) Total and rule the journal. Prove the equality of debits and credits.

(5) Post to the ledger.

(6) Take a trial balance of the ledger.

(7) How many additional postings would have been required if a two-column journal had been used instead of a four-column journal?

4-3A. The selected transactions and errors described below relate to the accounts of Inland Empire Co., Ronald G. Bowen, proprietor, during the current fiscal year:

Mar. 5. Proprietor invested cash of $5,000 and office equipment of $1,000 on which there was a balance owed of $300. The account payable is to be recorded on the books of the firm.

Apr. 12. Received $612 as payment on a note receivable ($600) and interest ($12).

May 16. Discovered that cash of $400, received from a customer on account, had been journalized and posted as a debit to Cash and a credit to Commissions Revenue.

July 2. Discovered that a withdrawal of $400 by the proprietor had been charged to Salesmen's Commission Expense.

Aug. 22. Acquired land and a building to be used as an office at a total cost of $15,000, of which $2,500 was allocated to the land. The property was encumbered by a mortgage of $9,000. Paid $6,000 cash and agreed to assume the responsibility for paying the mortgage.

Sept. 22. Paid the installment due on the mortgage, $450, and interest, $45.

Nov. 9. Discovered that a cash payment of $150 for advertising had been journalized and posted as a debit to Miscellaneous Expense of $15 and a credit to Cash of $15.

Dec. 20. Discovered that $75 of office equipment returned to the supplier for credit had been journalized and posted as a debit to Accounts Receivable and a credit to Office Supplies.

Instructions: Journalize the transactions and the corrections in a two-column journal. When there are more than two items in an entry, present the entry in compound form.

4-4A. Henry Wheeler owns and manages the Gem Realty Co. which acts as an agent in buying, selling, renting, and managing real estate. The trial balance of the ledger on May 31 of the current year is shown below.

Gem Realty Co.
Trial Balance
May 31, 19—

11	Cash	2,314	
12	Accounts Receivable	3,410	
13	Office Supplies	115	
14	Prepaid Insurance	249	
16	Automobile	4,600	
17	Accumulated Depreciation — Automobile		2,100
18	Office Equipment	2,530	
19	Accumulated Depreciation — Office Equipment		990
21	Accounts Payable		186
31	Henry Wheeler, Capital		5,780
32	Henry Wheeler, Drawing	5,000	
41	Revenue from Fees		23,873
51	Salary and Commission Expense	12,400	
52	Rent Expense	1,250	
53	Advertising Expense	645	
54	Automobile Expense	218	
59	Miscellaneous Expense	198	
		32,929	32,929

The following transactions were completed by Gem Realty Co. during the month of June:

June 1. Paid rent for month, $250.

2. Purchased office equipment on account, $300.

3. Purchased office supplies on account, $53.
7. Paid premium on automobile insurance, $210.
9. Received cash from clients on account, $2,632.
14. Paid salaries and commissions, $1,466.
15. Recorded revenue earned and billed to clients during first half of month, $2,180.
15. Returned for credit an item of office equipment purchased on June 2, $35.
17. Paid advertising expense, $143.
19. Received cash from clients on account, $2,048.
22. Paid creditors on account, $494.
25. Discovered that the amount stated for the transaction of June 3 was a transposition.
27. Paid automobile expenses, $71.
28. Paid miscellaneous expenses, $55.
29. Proprietor withdrew cash for personal use, $1,000.
30. Recorded revenue earned and billed to clients during second half of month, $1,968.
30. Paid salaries and commissions, $1,321.

Instructions: (1) Open an account in the ledger for each item listed in the trial balance of May 31.

(2) Record the balance in each account under the date of June 1, write the word "Balance" in the Items column, and place a check mark in the posting reference column.

(3) Record the transactions for June in a two-column journal.

(4) Post to the ledger.

(5) An error is discovered in billing the fees for the second half of the month. The amount is $1,986 instead of $1,968. Journalize the correcting entry and post.

(6) Take a trial balance of the ledger.

(7) What is the nature of the balance in Accounts Payable?

Chapter 5

5-1A. The trial balance of Blue & White Laundromat at December 31, the end of the current fiscal year, appears at the top of the opposite page. Data needed for year-end adjustments are presented below.

Adjustment data:

(a) Laundry supplies on hand at December 31.................. $ 270
(b) Depreciation for the year................................. 1,125
(c) Insurance expired during the year........................ 190
(d) Wages accrued at December 31........................... 45

Instructions: (1) Record the trial balance on a ten-column work sheet.

(2) Complete the work sheet.

(3) Prepare an income statement, a capital statement (no additional investments were made during the year), and a balance sheet in report form.

(4) Record the adjusting entries in a two-column journal.

(5) Record the closing entries in a two-column journal.

Blue & White Laundromat
Trial Balance
December 31, 19—

Cash.	2,880	
Laundry Supplies.	1,740	
Prepaid Insurance.	372	
Laundry Equipment.	11,500	
Accumulated Depreciation.		3,900
Accounts Payable.		375
Marlene Anderson, Capital.		8,019
Marlene Anderson, Drawing.	6,000	
Sales.		15,190
Wages Expense.	2,937	
Rent Expense.	1,140	
Utilities Expense.	605	
Miscellaneous Expense.	310	
	27,484	27,484

(6) Compute the following:

(a) Per cent of net income to sales.

(b) Per cent of net income to the capital balance at the beginning of the year.

If the working papers correlating with this textbook are not used, omit Problem 5-2A.

5-2A. The ledger of Suburban Fixit Service, as of September 30 of the current year, is presented in the working papers. The books had been closed on August 31.

Instructions: (1) Prepare a trial balance of the ledger, listing only the accounts with balances, on a ten-column work sheet.

(2) Complete the ten-column work sheet. Data for the adjustments are as follows:

Supplies on hand at September 30.	$720.00
Insurance expired during the month.	42.34
Depreciation on trucks for the month.	133.00
Depreciation on equipment for the month.	85.00
Salaries accrued at September 30.	168.00

(3) Prepare an income statement, a capital statement, and a balance sheet in report form.

(4) Record the adjusting entries in a two-column journal and post.

(5) Record the closing entries in a two-column journal and post.

(6) Rule the temporary accounts. Balance and rule the remaining accounts that contain more than one entry.

(7) Take a post-closing trial balance.

5-3A. At the end of each month Bowl-Mor Lanes prepares a cumulative income statement for the year to date, an income statement for the month, and a balance sheet as of the close of the month. The books are closed annually on December 31. The trial balance at March 31 of the current year, the adjustment data needed at March 31, and the income statement for the two months ended February 28 of the current year are presented on page 724.

Bowl-Mor Lanes
Trial Balance
March 31, 19—

Cash..	4,560	
Prepaid Insurance...............................	2,284	
Bowling Supplies................................	1,540	
Equipment......................................	42,000	
Accumulated Depreciation — Equipment.............		12,600
Building.......................................	96,000	
Accumulated Depreciation — Building..............		7,200
Land...	11,500	
Accounts Payable...............................		5,794
Mortgage Payable (due 1980).....................		88,000
Frank Morgan, Capital..........................		37,305
Frank Morgan, Drawing..........................	1,200	
Bowling Fees...................................		13,260
Salaries Expense...............................	2,050	
Utilities Expense...............................	1,120	
Repairs Expense................................	880	
Advertising Expense............................	780	
Miscellaneous Expense..........................	245	
	164,159	164,159

Adjustment data at March 31 are:

(a) Inventory of bowling supplies........................... $ 500
(b) Insurance expired for the period January 1–March 31........ 597
(c) Depreciation on equipment for the period January 1–March 31 1,200
(d) Depreciation on building for the period January 1–March 31   639
(e) Accrued salaries....................................... 146

The income statement for the two months ended February 28, 19—, is as follows:

Bowl-Mor Lanes
Income Statement
For Two Months Ended February 28, 19—

Bowling fees......................................		$8,590
Operating expenses:		
Salaries expense.................................	$1,415	
Depreciation expense — equipment.................	800	
Utilities expense.................................	760	
Bowling supplies expense........................	655	
Repairs expense	595	
Advertising expense.............................	530	
Insurance expense...............................	398	
Depreciation expense — building.................	426	
Miscellaneous expense...........................	168	
Total operating expenses.....................		5,747
Net income.......................................		$2,843

Instructions: (1) Record the trial balance on a ten-column work sheet.

(2) Complete the work sheet.

(3) Prepare an interim income statement for the three months ending March 31 and a balance sheet at March 31.

(4) Prepare an income statement for March.

(5) Compute the per cent of net income to revenue for:
   (a) The two-month period ended February 28.
   (b) The three-month period ended March 31.
   (c) The month of March.

Chapter 6

6-1A. Specialty Sales Co. was established early in April of the current year. During the remainder of the month its sales of merchandise on account and related returns and allowances were as listed below. All sales were subject to terms of n/30, FOB shipping point.

Apr. 13. Sold merchandise on account to A. D. Collins, Sale No. 1, $420.

    14. Sold merchandise on account to Warner Corporation, Sale No. 2, $380.

    15. Sold merchandise on account to Miller & Co., Sale No. 3, $840.

    18. Issued credit memorandum No. 1 for $35 to A. D. Collins for merchandise returned.

    19. Sold merchandise on account to Hill & Matthews, Sale No. 4, $710.

    20. Sold merchandise on account to Miller & Co., Sale No. 5, $360.

    21. Sold merchandise on account to J. R. Altman Co., Sale No. 6, $590.

    25. Issued credit memorandum No. 2 for $90 to Warner Corporation for merchandise returned.

    26. Sold merchandise on account to Superior Distributors, Inc., Sale No. 7, $680.

    28. Sold merchandise on account to A. D. Collins, Sale No. 8, $250.

    29. Issued credit memorandum No. 3 for $20 to J. R. Altman Co. for damages to merchandise caused by faulty packing.

    30. Sold merchandise on account to Hill & Matthews, Sale No. 9, $130.

Instructions: (1) Record the above transactions, using a sales journal similar to the one illustrated on page 122 and a two-column general journal.

(2) Open the following accounts in the general ledger, using the account numbers indicated: Accounts Receivable, 113; Sales, 411; Sales Returns and Allowances, 412.

(3) Open the following accounts in the accounts receivable ledger: J. R. Altman Co., A. D. Collins, Hill & Matthews, Miller & Co., Superior Distributors, Inc., Warner Corporation.

(4) Post the journals to the accounts receivable ledger and the accounts in the general ledger.

(5) (a) What is the sum of the balances of the subsidiary accounts? (b) What is the balance of the controlling account?

6-2A. Transactions related to sales and cash receipts completed by R. Van Scotter Co. during June of the current year are described below. The terms of all sales on account are 2/10, n/30, FOB destination.

June 4. Sold merchandise on account to Morley & Larson, Inc., Invoice No. 512, $770.

5. Sold merchandise on account to Thomas & Co., Invoice No. 513, $1,860.
7. R. Van Scotter invested additional cash in the business, $2,500.
10. Issued to Morley & Larson, Inc. a credit memorandum for merchandise returned, $70.
13. Received cash for store supplies returned to the manufacturer, $30.
14. Sold merchandise on account to J. D. Baker Co., Invoice No. 514, $2,350.
14. Received cash from Morley & Larson, Inc. for the $700 due on Invoice No. 512, less discount.
16. Sold merchandise on account to Morley & Larson, Inc., Invoice No. 515, $1,400.
17. Cash sales for June 1 to 15, $10,695.
19. Sold merchandise on account to J. D. Baker Co., Invoice No. 516, $2,040.
21. Received cash from J. D. Baker Co. for Invoice No. 514, less discount.
23. Received cash from Morley & Larson, Inc. for Invoice No. 515, less discount.
28. Sold merchandise on account to Morley & Larson, Inc., Invoice 517, $2,482.
29. Received cash for a note receivable due today, $400.
30. Received cash from Thomas & Co. for Invoice No. 513.
30. Cash sales for June 16 to 30, $9,785.

Instructions: (1) Open the following accounts in the general ledger:

111 Cash	311 R. Van Scotter, Capital
112 Notes Receivable	411 Sales
113 Accounts Receivable	412 Sales Returns and Allowances
116 Store Supplies	413 Sales Discount

(2) Open the following accounts in the accounts receivable ledger: J. D. Baker Co., Morley & Larson, Inc., Thomas & Co.

(3) Record the transactions for the month in a sales journal similar to the one illustrated on page 122, a cash receipts journal similar to the one illustrated on page 129, and a two-column general journal. Immediately after recording a transaction affecting a customer's account, post to the *subsidiary ledger*.

(4) Add the columns of the special journals and post all three journals to the general ledger.

(5) Prepare a schedule of accounts receivable.

(6) What is the balance of the accounts receivable account?

6-3A. Transactions related to sales and cash receipts completed by Bancroft Distributors during November of the current year are described below. The terms of all sales on account are 2/10, n/30, FOB shipping point. All delivery charges are prepaid and charged to the customer.

Nov. 3. Issued Invoice No. 642 to Walsh & Taylor, $800; delivery, $20; total, $820.
5. Received cash from Robert R. Marsh for the balance due on his account, less discount.
6. Received cash from Adamson Co. for the balance due on their account, less discount.
7. Issued Invoice No. 643 to Robert R. Marsh, $445; delivery, $30; total, $475.
10. Issued Credit Memo No. 39 to Robert R. Marsh, $45.

Post all journals to the accounts receivable ledger.

11. Issued Invoice No. 644 to Walsh & Taylor, $2,600; delivery, $62; total, $2,662.
12. Issued Invoice No. 645 to M. L. Scott, Inc., $350; delivery, $15; total, $365.
12. Received cash from Walsh & Taylor for invoice No. 642, less discount.
13. Received cash from Adamson Co. in payment of a note receivable, $1,900.
15. Received cash from Robert R. Marsh for balance due on Invoice No. 643, less discount.

Post all journals to the accounts receivable ledger.

16. Recorded cash sales for first half of the month, $3,590.
18. Received cash from M. L. Scott, Inc. for the balance on November 1; no discount.
19. Issued Invoice No. 646 to Adamson Co., $1,972; delivery, $67; total, $2,039.
20. Received cash from Walsh & Taylor for Invoice No. 644, less discount.
21. Issued Credit Memo No. 40 to Adamson Co., $72.

Post all journals to the accounts receivable ledger.

24. Issued Invoice No. 647 to Walsh & Taylor, $1,636; delivery, $42; total $1,678.
25. Received cash refund for a premium overcharge on property insurance, $50.
26. Received cash from Adamson Co. for the balance due on Invoice No. 646, less discount.
27. Issued Invoice No. 648 to Robert R. Marsh, $1,273; delivery, $74; total, $1,347.
30. Recorded cash sales for the second half of the month, $4,330.
30. Issued Credit Memo No. 41 to Robert R. Marsh, $70.

Post all journals to the accounts receivable ledger.

Instructions: (1) Open the following accounts in the general ledger, inserting the balance as of November 1 in the accounts receivable account:

111 Cash	411 Sales
112 Notes Receivable	412 Sales Returns and Allowances
113 Accounts Receivable, $2,780	413 Sales Discount
117 Prepaid Insurance	615 Delivery Expense

(2) Open the following accounts in the accounts receivable ledger, inserting the balances indicated, as of November 1: Adamson Co., $825, including a delivery charge of $25; Robert R. Marsh, $1,285, including a delivery charge of $35; M. L. Scott, Inc., $670, including a delivery charge of $20; Walsh & Taylor.

(3) Record the transactions for the month in a sales journal similar to the one illustrated on page 135, a sales returns and allowances journal similar to the one illustrated on page 126, and a cash receipts journal similar to the one illustrated on page 129. Post to the accounts receivable ledger at the points indicated in the narrative of transactions.

(4) Add the columns of the journals and post to the general ledger accounts.

(5) (a) What is the sum of the balances of the accounts in the subsidiary ledger? (b) What is the balance of the controlling account?

Chapter 7

7-2A. Campus Clothing was established in March of the current year. Transactions related to purchases, returns and allowances, and cash payments during the remainder of the month are described below.

Mar. 14. Purchased store equipment on account from Glendale Merchants Supply, $5,000.
14. Purchased merchandise on account from Rochester Clothing, Inc., $2,700.
15. Issued check No. 1 in payment of office supplies, $27, and store supplies, $43.
16. Issued check No. 2 in payment of rent for March, $375.
17. Purchased merchandise on account from Adams & Co., $1,900.
18. Purchased merchandise on account from Walsh Brothers, $700.
18. Received a credit memorandum from Adams & Co. for returned merchandise, $150.

Post the journals to the accounts payable ledger

21. Issued check No. 3 to Rochester Clothing, Inc., in payment of invoice of $2,700, less 2% discount.
22. Received a credit memorandum from Walsh Brothers for defective merchandise, $25.
23. Issued check No. 4 to Glendale Merchants Supply in payment of invoice of $5,000.
24. Issued check No. 5 to a cash customer for merchandise returned, $31.
24. Issued check No. 6 to Adams & Co. in payment of the balance owed, less 2% discount.
25. Purchased merchandise on account from Walsh Brothers, $1,720.

Post the journals to the accounts payable ledger

28. Purchased the following from Glendale Merchants Supply on account: store supplies, $23; office supplies, $32; office equipment, $900.
29. Issued check No. 7 to Walsh Brothers in payment of the invoice of $700 less the credit of $25.
30. Issued check No. 8 in payment of transportation charges on merchandise purchased, $168.
31. Purchased merchandise on account from Rochester Clothing, Inc., $1,280.
31. Issued check No. 9 in payment of sales salaries, $540.

Post the journals to the accounts payable ledger.

Instructions: (1) Open the following accounts in the general ledger, using the account numbers indicated:

111 Cash	412 Sales Returns and Allowances
116 Store Supplies	511 Purchases
117 Office Supplies	512 Purchases Returns and Allowances
121 Store Equipment	513 Purchases Discount
122 Office Equipment	611 Sales Salaries
211 Accounts Payable	712 Rent Expense

(2) Open the following accounts in the accounts payable ledger: Adams & Co.; Glendale Merchants Supply; Rochester Clothing, Inc.; Walsh Brothers.

(3) Record the transactions for March, using a purchases journal similar to the one illustrated on pages 144 and 145, a purchases returns and allowances journal similar to the one illustrated on page 149, and a cash payments journal similar to the one illustrated on page 151. Post to the accounts payable ledger at the points indicated in the narrative of transactions.

(4) Post to the general ledger.

(5) Prepare a schedule of accounts payable.

If the working papers correlating with the textbook are not used, omit Problem 7-3A.

7-3A. Fieldcrest Supply Co. uses carbon copies of its sales invoices as a sales journal, posting to the accounts receivable ledger directly from the invoices. At the end of the month the invoices are totaled and the appropriate entry is recorded in the general journal. Purchases on account are handled in a similar manner, the invoices being used as a purchases journal. Sales and purchases on account during January of the current year were as follows:

Sales

Jan.	5. No. 681 Edward Allen Corp.	$2,300
	6. No. 682 Nelson and Co.	1,824
	10. No. 683 Fred Collins	1,350
	16. No. 684 Tucker and Walsh	500
	17. No. 685 Fred Collins	2,912
	22. No. 686 Nelson and Co.	620

Purchases

Jan.	2. Walker Corp.: store supplies, $122; office supplies, $32	$ 154
	3. Lewis Manufacturing Co., merchandise	2,475
	11. James Bell, Inc., merchandise	2,100
	18. Stewart-Barnes Co., store equipment	1,325
	19. Johnson & Co., merchandise	962
	29. Walker Corp., store supplies	23
	31. James Bell, Inc., merchandise	1,050

Other transactions completed during the month were recorded in a 4-column general journal, a cash receipts journal, and a cash payments journal, all of which are presented in the working papers. The subsidiary ledgers and the general ledger accounts affected by transactions of the month are also presented in the working papers.

Instructions: (1) Summarize the sales invoices and the purchases invoices listed above and record the appropriate entries in the 4-column general journal.

(2) Post all items affecting the *subsidiary* ledger, in the following order: sales invoices, purchases invoices, general journal, cash receipts journal, cash payments journal. When postings are made daily, which is the usual practice, the entries in customers' and creditors' accounts will appear in chronological order. The fact that in this problem postings to some of the accounts will not be in perfect date sequence is immaterial.

(3) Post all items recorded in the Sundry Accounts Dr. and Sundry Accounts Cr. columns of the journals, in the following order: general journal, cash receipts journal, cash payments journal.

(4) Foot and rule the general journal; post the columnar totals of the journals, following the same sequence as in instruction (3).

(5) Prepare a trial balance.

(6) What is the sum of the balances in the
   (a) Accounts receivable ledger?
   (b) Accounts payable ledger?

Chapter 8

8-1A. The account balances in the ledger of the Giford Company on December 31 of the current year are as follows:

Cash....................	$ 8,500	Sales....................	$129,500
Accounts Receivable.........	14,800	Sales Returns and Allowances..	3,500
Merchandise Inventory........	21,200	Purchases....................	97,000
Supplies....................	1,000	Purchases Returns and Allow...	2,500
Prepaid Insurance...........	2,200	Sales Salaries...............	16,000
Store Equipment.............	9,000	Rent Expense................	5,400
Accumulated Depreciation.....	3,000	Advertising Expense...........	1,500
Accounts Payable.............	14,500	Delivery Expense.............	1,600
Paul Giford, Capital.........	37,400	Miscellaneous Expense........	5,200

The data needed for year-end adjustments on December 31 are as follows:

Merchandise inventory on December 31........................	$18,500
Supplies inventory on December 31............................	650
Insurance expired during the year.............................	1,200
Depreciation for current year.................................	900
Accrued salaries on December 31..............................	600

Instructions: (1) Prepare an eight-column work sheet for the fiscal year ended December 31.

(2) Record the adjusting entries in a general journal.

(3) Record the closing entries in a general journal.

If the working papers correlated with this textbook are not used, omit Problem 8-3A.

8-3A. C. B. Henshaw owns and operates the Plaza Variety Shop. The general ledger balances at the beginning of the twelfth month and the journals for the twelfth month of the current year are presented in the working papers.

Instructions: (1) Post the journals to the general ledger accounts. An assistant has made all postings to the accounts in the subsidiary ledgers.

(2) Take a trial balance at December 31, on an eight column work sheet, listing only the accounts with balances.

(3) Complete the work sheet. Adjustment data are:

Merchandise inventory at December 31....................	$8,500
Insurance expired during the year........................	290
Supplies on hand at December 31........................	225
Accrued taxes at December 31............................	250
Depreciation for the current year on	
Store equipment.......................................	675
Office equipment......................................	125

(4) Prepare an income statement, a balance sheet in report form, and a capital statement. There were no additional investments of capital by the owner during the year.

(5) Record the adjusting entries in the general journal and post to the ledger.

(6) Record the closing entries and post to the ledger.

(7) Rule and balance the accounts that have two or more postings.

(8) Prepare a post-closing trial balance.

(9) Record the reversing entry or entries on January 2, post to the ledger and rule the additional account or accounts that are now in balance.

8-5A. On February 15 of the current fiscal year the following errors were discovered in the books of the Westvale Garden Center, Paul Ryan, proprietor:
(1) The adjusting entry for insurance at the end of the preceding year transferred $350 to the expense account. The amount should have been $530.
(2) Merchandise inventory at the end of the preceding year was overstated $2,500.
(3) A home freezer costing $540, purchased by Ryan on December 31 for his wife, was debited to office equipment.
(4) Three purchases returns and allowances totaling $750 were erroneously recorded as credits to purchases in December of the preceding year.
(5) Additional land costing $12,500 was purchased for the construction of a new building. The building account was debited in error; and, in addition, $500 of depreciation was incorrectly recorded on this acquisition during the preceding year.
(6) No provision was made at the end of the preceding year for accrued office salaries payable, $160.

Instructions: (1) Record the journal entries required by the foregoing errors.
(2) Open the capital account. Enter the beginning balance, $30,000 as of January 1 of the current year. Post the corrections that affect the capital account.
(3) On December 31 of the current year journalize the entries to close the expense and revenue summary account (credit balance, $10,500) and the drawing account (debit balance, $7,000).
(4) Post the closing entries to the capital account.
(5) Prepare a capital statement for the current year.
(6) Rule and balance the capital account.

Chapter 9

9-3A. The following were selected from among the transactions completed by Strome Co. during the current fiscal year:

July 5. Purchased merchandise on account from Julia Crane Co., $720.
11. Sold merchandise on account to Alm & Co., Invoice No. 576, $450.
17. Discounted a 30-day non-interest-bearing note payable for $6,000 to First National Bank; discount rate, 6%.
20. Received cash from Alm & Co. for the invoice of July 11, less 2% discount.
22. Sold merchandise on account to R. T. Miles, Invoice No. 603, $850.
23. Sold merchandise on account to W. T. Scott Co., Invoice No. 612, $1,100.
Aug. 5. Issued a 60-day, 7% note for $720 to Julia Crane Co. on account.
8. Purchased merchandise on account from Whitney & Co., $700.
15. Issued check No. 805 to Whitney & Co. for the amount due on the purchase of August 8, less 2% discount.
16. Issued check No. 822 to First National Bank for the amount due on the note dated July 17.
22. Received from R. T. Miles on account a 60-day, 6% note for $850, dated Aug. 21.
25. Sold merchandise on account to Carlton Co., Invoice No. 793, $650.
29. Received from W. T. Scott Co. on account a 1-month, 6% note for $1,100 dated August 29.

Sept.   1. Received from Carlton Co. on account a 30-day, 6% note for $650, dated September 1.
        14. Discounted R. T. Miles' $850 note, dated August 21, at Security National Bank, discount rate 6%.
        29. Received cash from W. T. Scott Co. for the amount owed on note dated August 29.
Oct.   1. Carlton Co. dishonored its note dated September 1. The dishonored note is charged to their account.
        1. Issued check No. 908 to Julia Crane Co. in payment of the note dated August 5.
        21. Received notice from Security National Bank that R. T. Miles had dishonored his note dated August 21. Issued check No. 920 in payment of the amount due; no protest fee.
        30. Received cash from R. T. Miles for the principal and interest on his dishonored note, plus additional interest at 7% on the total amount from October 20.

Instructions: Record the transactions, using the following journals: sales journal (as illustrated on page 122); purchases journal (with only one money column, headed Purchases Dr. and Accts. Pay. Cr.); cash receipts journal (as illustrated on page 199); cash payments journal (as illustrated on page 205); two-column general journal.

9-4A. The following transactions were completed by Dunbar & Co. during the current fiscal year:
Feb.   5. Received from H. H. Beckett a 90-day, non-interest-bearing note for $5,000, dated February 4, on account.
        21. Issued to T. L. Morton Co. a 2-month, 4½% note for $4,000, on account.
Mar.   12. Discounted at the Union Trust Co. at 6% the note received from H. H. Beckett dated February 4.
Apr.   21. Issued check No. 623 to T. L. Morton Co. in payment of the note issued on February 21.
        30. Discounted a 60-day, non-interest-bearing note payable for $12,000 at the Union Trust Co.; discount rate, 6%.
May   15. Received from R. G. Harris a 90-day, 4% note for $1,000, dated May 14, on account.
        31. Purchased land for a building site from Progressive Development Co. for $25,000, issuing check No. 704 for $5,000 and 5% mortgage note for the balance. The contract provides for payments of $2,000 of principal plus accrued interest at intervals of six months.
June   29. Issued check No. 751 to Union Trust Co. for the amount due on the note payable issued on April 30.
July   11. Discounted at the Union Trust Co. at 6% the note received from R. G. Harris, dated May 14.
Aug.   13. Received notice from the Union Trust Co. that R. G. Harris had dishonored the note due on August 12. Issued check No. 798 to the bank for the amount due on the note, plus a protest fee of $4.
Sept.   8. Received from Home Store a 90-day, 7% note for $800, dated September 7, on account.
Oct.   6. Received from R. G. Harris the amount due on the note dishonored on August 12, including interest at 5% from August 12 to October 5 on the maturity value of the note plus protest fee.
Nov.   30. Issued check No. 912 for installment due on mortgage note, together with interest on $20,000 for six months.

Dec. 6. Home Store dishonored its note dated September 7. Charged the dishonored note to their account.

Instructions: Record the transactions, using the following journals: cash receipts journal (as illustrated on page 201); cash payments journal (as illustrated on page 201, except for an additional column for Sundry Accounts Cr.); two-column general journal.

9-5A. The Clayton Machinery Co. received the notes described below during the three-month period, June 1 to August 31. Notes (a), (b), (c), and (d) were discounted at Williams State Bank on the dates indicated; discount rate 6%.

	Date	Face Amount	Term	Interest Rate	Date Discounted
(a)	June 7	$ 810	60 days	7%	July 3
(b)	June 21	3,000	3 months	5%	July 8
(c)	July 12	4,000	30 days	5½%	Aug. 1
(d)	July 23	720	90 days	—	Aug. 11
(e)	Aug. 18	1,400	6 months	6%	—

Instructions: (1) Determine for each note (a) the due date and (b) the amount of interest due at maturity, identifying each note by letter.

(2) Determine for each of the first four notes (a) the maturity value, (b) the discount period, (c) the discount, (d) the proceeds, and (e) the interest income or interest expense, identifying each note by letter.

(3) Present, in general journal form, the entries to record the discounting of note (a) and note (d).

Chapter 10

10-1A. The accounts listed below appear in the ledger of Pomona Realty at December 31, the end of the current fiscal year. None of the year-end adjustments has been recorded.

113	Interest Receivable.......	$ —	411	Rental Income..........	$58,400
114	Supplies.................	500	511	Salary and Com. Exp......	17,900
115	Prepaid Insurance........	1,200	512	Taxes Expense...........	3,000
116	Prepaid Advertising.......	—	513	Advertising Expense......	3,600
117	Prepaid Interest..........	—	514	Insurance Expense........	—
213	Salaries and Com. Payable.	—	515	Supplies Expense........	—
214	Taxes Payable...........	—	611	Interest Income..........	550
215	Unearned Rent..........	—	711	Interest Expense.........	680
313	Expense and Revenue Sum.	—			

The following information relating to adjustments at December 31 was obtained from physical inventories, supplementary records, and other sources:

(a) Interest accrued on notes receivable at December 31, $80.

(b) Inventory of supplies at December 31, $240.

(c) The insurance register indicates that $485 of insurance has expired during the year.

(d) Of a prepayment of $1,200 for advertising space in a local newspaper, ⅔ has been used and the remainder will be used in the following year.

(e) A short-term non-interest-bearing note payable was discounted at a bank in December. The amount of the total discount of $200 applicable to December is $75.

(f) Salaries and commissions accrued at December 31, $1,750.

(g) Real estate taxes accrued at December 31, $1,830.

(h) Rent collected in advance that will not be earned until the following year, $3,440.

Instructions: (1) Open the accounts listed and record the balances as of December 31.

(2) Record the adjusting entries in a general journal and post to the appropriate accounts after each entry. Identify the postings by writing "Adjusting" in the items columns.

(3) Prepare a compound journal entry to close the income accounts and another compound entry to close the expense accounts.

(4) Post the closing entries. Identify the postings by writing "Closing" in the items columns.

(5) Total and rule the revenue and expense accounts. (Do not rule Expense and Revenue Summary.)

(6) Prepare the reversing journal entries that should be made on January 1 and post to the appropriate accounts after each entry. Write "Reversing" in the items columns.

(7) Rule the additional accounts that are now in balance.

10-2A. The following information was obtained from a review of the ledger and other records of Butler Appliances at the close of the current fiscal year ended December 31:

(a) Store Supplies Expense has a debit balance of $530 at December 31. The inventory of supplies on hand at that date totals $210.

(b) Prepaid Advertising has a debit balance of $1,456 at December 31, which represents the advance payment on October 13 of a yearly contract for a uniform amount of space in 52 consecutive issues of a weekly publication. As of December 31, advertisements had appeared in 12 issues of the publication.

(c) Prepaid Insurance has a debit balance of $1,498 at December 31. Details of the premiums expired during the year ended are as follows:

No.	Monthly Premium Expiration	No. of Months Applicable to Past Year
2936	$12	11
1897T	17	8
8643B	14	6
7316	10	5

(d) Notes Receivable has a debit balance of $7,500 at December 31. The notes on hand, all of which were accepted at face value, are as follows:

Date	Face	Term	Interest Rate
Nov. 18	$3,000	90 days	6%
Dec. 4	1,500	60 days	6%
Dec. 15	1,800	30 days	6%
Dec. 20	1,200	30 days	6%

(e) Rent Expense has a debit balance of $5,200 on December 31. This amount includes rent of $400 for January of the ensuing year, paid on December 31.

(f) Mortgage Payable has a credit balance of $25,000 at December 31. Interest at the rate of 5% is payable semiannually on July 1 and January 1. No entry has been made for the interest accrued since July 1.

(g) Unearned Rent has a credit balance of $1,395, composed of the following items:

   (1) January balance of $375, representing rent prepaid for January through May and
   (2) a debit of $1,020, representing payment for annual rent at $85 a month, beginning June 1.

Instructions: (1) Journalize the adjusting entries as of December 31 of the current fiscal year.

(2) Journalize the reversing entries that should be made as of January 1 of the succeeding fiscal year.

10-3A. The account balances in the ledger of the R. B. Moore Co. as of July 31, the end of the current fiscal year, are as follows:

Cash....................	$ 8,460	R. B. Moore, Capital.........	$ 47,185
Notes Receivable...........	9,150	R. B. Moore, Drawing........	6,000
Accounts Receivable.........	7,615	Sales.......................	103,400
Merchandise Inventory.......	39,325	Sales Returns and Allowances..	1,950
Store Supplies..............	945	Purchases...................	59,800
Prepaid Insurance...........	2,640	Purchases Discount...........	960
Store Equipment............	5,380	Sales Salaries...............	12,650
Accumulated Depreciation —		Advertising Expense.........	4,065
Store Equipment..........	2,620	Misc. Selling Expense........	495
Office Equipment...........	2,955	Office Salaries..............	5,250
Accumulated Depreciation —		Rent Expense...............	3,000
Office Equipment..........	1,210	Misc. General Expense.......	580
Notes Payable..............	6,740	Interest Income.............	635
Accounts Payable...........	7,925	Interest Expense............	415

Data needed for making adjusting entries are as follows:

(a) Merchandise inventory, July 31, $40,130.
(b) Store supplies inventory, July 31, $350.
(c) Insurance expired during the year:
   Allocable as selling expense, $970.
   Allocable as general expense, $330.
(d) Depreciation for the year:
   On store equipment, $540.
   On office equipment, $285.
(e) Accrued salaries at July 31:
   Sales salaries, $85.
   Office salaries, $40.
(f) Accrued interest at July 31:
   On notes receivable, $80.
   On notes payable, $60.
(g) Unearned interest on notes receivable at July 31, $30.

Instructions: (1) Prepare an eight-column work sheet for the current fiscal year ended July 31.

(2) Prepare an income statement, a balance sheet in report form, and a capital statement (there were no additional investments by the proprietor during the year).

10-5A. Selected accounts from the ledger of Larson Co. are listed below, with the account balances before adjustment and after adjustment, at the close of the fiscal year:

	Unadjusted Balance	Adjusted Balance
Interest Receivable..........................	$ —	$ 70
Supplies.....................................	1,960	720
Prepaid Insurance...........................	1,350	775
Prepaid Taxes...............................	—	300
Prepaid Interest.............................	—	40
Accumulated Depreciation — Equipment........	3,300	4,100
Interest Payable.............................	—	30
Wages Payable..............................	—	180
Taxes Payable...............................	—	200
Unearned Rent..............................	—	600
Rent Income................................	7,200	6,600
Wages......................................	15,900	16,080
Depreciation Expense — Equipment...........	—	800
Supplies Expense............................	—	1,240
Taxes Expense..............................	700	600
Insurance Expense..........................	—	575
Interest Income.............................	950	1,020
Interest Expense............................	435	425

Instructions: (1) Journalize the adjusting entries that were recorded in the ledger at the close of the fiscal year.

(2) Insert the letter "R" in the date column opposite each adjusting entry that should be reversed as of the first day of the following fiscal year.

Chapter 11

11-1A. The following transactions, adjusting and closing entries related to uncollectible accounts were completed during the current fiscal year ending December 31:

Feb. 14. Wrote off the account of James Sanders as uncollectible, $125.

Mar. 18. Received $42 from C. R. Evans in payment of his account, which was written off in the preceding year.

May 21. Received 10% of the $800 balance owed by Robert Martin, a bankrupt, and wrote off the remainder as uncollectible.

July 29. Received $104 from S. E. Roberts in partial payment of his account, which was written off as uncollectible in the preceding year.

Nov. 27. Wrote off the following accounts as uncollectible (compound entry): David Curtis, $38; R. G. Filson, $397; Nixon and Marshall, $73; Thomas Saxton, $210.

Dec. 31. On the basis of an analysis of the accounts receivable, the allowance for uncollectible accounts is to be adjusted to a balance of $1,400.

Dec. 31. Recorded the entry to close the appropriate account to Expense and Revenue Summary.

Instructions: (1) Open the following accounts, recording the credit balance indicated as of January 1:

114.1	Allowance for Uncollectible Accounts...................	$950
313	Expense and Revenue Summary........................	—
718	Bad Debts Expense...................................	—

(2) Record in general journal form the transactions, adjusting and closing entries described above, and post to the three accounts.

(3) Rule the expense account and rule and balance the contra asset account.

(4) The accounts receivable account has a debit balance of $24,956 at December 31. What is the expected realizable value of the accounts receivable at that date?

(5) Assuming that instead of basing the provision for uncollectible accounts on an analysis of receivables, the adjusting entry on December 31 had been based on an estimated loss of ½% of net sales for the year of $306,000, determine the following:

(a) Bad debts expense for the year.

(b) Balance in Allowance for Uncollectible Accounts after the adjustment of December 31.

(c) Expected realizable value of the accounts receivable on December 31.

11-2A. Details regarding the inventory at January 1, purchases during the year, and the inventory count at December 31 for Carver TV Sales are as follows:

Model	Inventory Jan. 1	1st Purchase	2nd Purchase	3rd Purchase	Inventory Count Dec. 31
158	7 at $ 72	6 at $ 81	8 at $ 81	—	3
159	2 at 91	11 at 92	5 at 90	6 at $ 94	5
368	4 at 162	3 at 174	4 at 177	5 at 178	3
369	—	11 at 263	5 at 255	4 at 248	4
595	5 at 199	3 at 206	5 at 203	6 at 208	2
621	2 at 171	4 at 174	3 at 179	—	2
800	4 at 378	7 at 381	8 at 383	5 at 385	7

Instructions: (1) Determine the cost of the inventory on December 31 by the first-in, first-out method. Present data in columnar form, using the columnar headings indicated below. If more than one unit cost is applied to the inventory of a particular model, use a separate line for each.

Model	Quantity	Unit Cost	Total Cost

(2) Determine the cost of the inventory on December 31 by the last-in, first-out method, following the same procedures prescribed in instruction (1).

(3) Determine the cost of the inventory on December 31 by the weighted average method, using the same columnar headings as in instruction (1).

11-3A. Information needed to estimate the merchandise inventory by the retail method and the gross profit method is presented below:

	Cost	Retail
(a) Retail method:		
Merchandise inventory, January 1.........	$173,400	$261,000
January transactions:		
Purchases......................	102,738⎫	
Purchases returns and allowances.........	1,837⎬	135,000
Purchases discounts....................	1,457⎭	
Sales...........................		185,500
Sales returns and allowances............		4,500
(b) Gross profit method:		
Merchandise inventory, April 1.............		$168,000
April, May, June transactions:		
Purchases......................		213,700
Purchases returns and allowances........		3,200
Purchases discounts...................		2,700
Sales...........................		287,600
Sales returns and allowances............		6,100
Sales discounts.......................		2,400
Estimated gross profit rate.............		41%

Instructions: (1) Determine the estimated cost of the inventory on January 31 in (a), presenting details of the computation.

(2) Determine the estimated cost of the inventory on June 30 in (b), presenting details of the computation.

11-4A. The preliminary income statement was prepared before the books were adjusted or closed at the end of the year:

C. E. Collins Co.
Income Statement
For Year Ended August 31, 19—

Sales (net)........................		$240,000
Cost of goods sold:		
Merchandise inventory, September 1, 19—.......	$ 50,482	
Purchases (net)............................	163,700	
Merchandise available for sale..................	$214,182	
Less: Merchandise inventory, August 31, 19—....	51,300	
Cost of goods sold........................		162,882
Gross profit on sales........................		$ 77,118
Operating expenses..........................		53,437
Net income................................		$ 23,681

The following errors were discovered by the independent accountant retained to conduct the annual audit:

(a) A number of errors were discovered in pricing inventory items, in extending amounts, and in footing inventory sheets. The net effect of the corrections, excluding any listed below, was a reduction of $1,450 from the amount stated as the ending inventory on the income statement.

(b) An invoice for the purchase of merchandise for $225, dated August 27, had been properly recorded but the goods were in transit on August 31, and had not been included in the ending inventory. Title had passed.

(c) An invoice for merchandise of $1,240, dated August 29, was not received until after August 31 and had not been recorded. The goods had arrived on August 31 and were included in the ending inventory.

(d) A sales invoice for $1,300, dated August 31, had been recorded. The goods were shipped on September 1, FOB destination, and their cost, $800, was excluded from the ending inventory.

(e) A sales order for $1,600, dated August 30, had been recorded as a sale but the goods were not shipped until September 4. The cost of the merchandise ($1,100) was included in the ending inventory. Title passed on August 30.

(f) An item of office equipment, received on August 31, was included in the ending inventory at its cost, $500. The invoice had been recorded as a purchase of merchandise.

Instructions: (1) Journalize any necessary entries to correct accounts in the general ledger, inserting the identifying letters in the date column. All purchases and sales were made on account. (An assistant will make the necessary corrections to the subsidiary ledgers.)

(2) Determine the correct figure for the ending inventory by recording the incorrect amount and each correction in a T account. Use the identifying letters as references.

(3) Prepare a revised income statement.

Chapter 12

12-1A. The following expenditures and receipts are related to land and buildings, the receipts being identified by an asterisk.

(a)	Cost of real estate acquired as a plant site: Land........	$ 25,000
	Building.....	28,000
(b)	Fee paid to attorney for title search...................	2,200
(c)	Broker's commission paid...........................	1,000
(d)	Cost of dismantling and removing the building.........	1,500
(e)	Architect's fee for plans and supervision...............	15,000
(f)	Delinquent real estate taxes on property, assumed by purchaser.......................................	1,300
(g)	Cost of land fill, grading, and landscaping.............	1,800
(h)	Paid to building contractor.........................	225,000
(i)	Real estate taxes paid during construction period........	2,300
(j)	Premium paid for insurance policy covering the construction project.......................................	1,700
(k)	Cost of paving parking lot for employees...............	800
(l)	Special assessment for paving an adjacent street, paid to city	1,340
(m)	Proceeds from sale of salvage material from old building..	800*
(n)	Cost of repairing damage resulting from windstorm during construction..	3,000
(o)	Refund of portion of premium on construction insurance policy.......................................	300*
(p)	Proceeds from insurance company for windstorm damage ..	2,700*
		$306,140

Instructions: By use of a columnar form with captions for Land, Building, and Other, list the letters identifying each item and place the amounts in the appropriate columns. Total the columns.

12-3A. The following transactions, adjusting entries, and closing entries were completed by Edward S. Mueth, Florist, during a three-year period. All are related to the use of delivery equipment.

1962
May 12. Purchased a used delivery truck for $1,365, paying cash.
13. Paid garage $182 for new tires and $165 for extensive repairs to the truck.
Sept. 24. Paid garage $35 for miscellaneous repairs to the motor.
Dec. 31. Recorded depreciation on the truck for the fiscal year. The estimated life of the truck is 3 years, with a trade-in value of $200. The straight line method of depreciation is used; the minimum unit of time to be considered is a month.
Dec. 31. Closed the appropriate accounts to Expense and Revenue Summary.
1963
July 27. Traded in the used truck on a new truck priced at $4,306, receiving a trade-in allowance of $900, and paying the balance in cash. (Record depreciation to date in 1963; gain or loss on exchange is not to be recognized.)
Nov. 8. Paid garage $38 for a new tire and $29 for repairs to the truck.
Dec. 31. Recorded depreciation on the truck, estimated life, 4 years; trade-in value, $600.
31. Closed the appropriate accounts to Expense and Revenue Summary.
1964
June 25. Sold the truck for $2,900, receiving cash. (Record depreciation.)
Dec. 31. Closed the appropriate accounts to Expense and Revenue Summary.

Instructions: (1) Open the following accounts in the ledger:

121	Delivery Equipment	614	Depreciation Expense — Delivery Equipment
121.1	Accumulated Depreciation — Delivery Equipment	615	Truck Repair Expense
		912	Loss on Disposal of Plant Assets

(2) Record the transactions, adjusting and closing entries in general journal form, posting to the accounts after each entry. At the end of each year rule the accounts that are closed, and rule and balance the other accounts containing more than one item.

12-4A. The following transactions and adjustments affecting office machines were completed by Miller Construction Co. during a three-year period.

1962
May 3. Purchased the following office machines from Business Machines, Inc., paying $640 cash and issuing a note payable for the balance:

10-key adding machine, No. 52847...................	$266
8-bank adding machine, No. 66835...................	302
Copying machine, No. 85412........................	772

Aug. 28. Purchased an 8-bank calculator, No. 5816B, from Morrow Co. on account, $650.
Dec. 31. Recorded depreciation for the year.
1963
May 7. Purchased a bookkeeping machine, No. 8429, from Morrow Co. on account, $7,200.

Oct. 25. Purchased a printing calculator, No. 43647 from Business Machines, Inc., paying cash, $651.
Nov. 5. Sold the 8-bank adding machine for cash, $185.
Dec. 31. Recorded depreciation for the year.
1964
Sept. 4. Traded the 8-bank calculator for a new model, No. 39264, from Morrow Co. The price of the new calculator was $750. The allowance on the old machine was $426, the balance being paid in cash. (Gain or loss is not to be recognized.)
Dec. 31. Recorded depreciation for the year.

The company uses the straight line method of computing depreciation. Additional details needed for determining depreciation are as follows:

Item	Estimated Trade-in Value	Estimated Life
10-key adding machine................	$ 50	6 yrs.
8-bank adding machine................	50	6 yrs.
Copying machine.....................	100	8 yrs.
8-bank calculator....................	80	10 yrs.
Bookkeeping machine..................	600	8 yrs.
Printing calculator...................	75	8 yrs.

Instructions: (1) Open the following accounts in the general ledger: Office Machines, 121; Accumulated Depreciation — Office Machines, 121.1. As each item is acquired, open an account in the subsidiary ledger, using the form illustrated on pages 265 and 266.

(2) Record the entries in general journal form, posting to the two accounts in the general ledger and to the accounts in the subsidiary ledger after each entry.

(3) Balance and rule the controlling accounts in the general ledger, as of December 31, 1964.

(4) Prepare a schedule of office machines from the subsidiary ledger as of December 31, 1964, using the following columnar captions:

Item	Cost	Accumulated Depreciation	Book Value

Chapter 13

13-1A. The bank statement for Consolidated Freight Company indicates a balance of $6,989.27 on March 31 of the current year. Cash in Bank has a debit balance of $5,493.25 after the cash journals have been posted for March. Comparison of the statement, and the accompanying checks and memorandums, with the books reveals the following reconciling items:
   (a) Checks outstanding total $2,843.54.
   (b) Among the paid checks returned was a check for $83.71 drawn by Consolidated Electronics Co.
   (c) The bank had credited Consolidated Freight for the proceeds of a note left for collection: principal, $800; interest, $30.
   (d) The bank charged Consolidated Freight $2.00 as a collection fee and $1.50 for service charges.
   (e) A deposit on March 31 for $2,065.31 had been made too late to appear on the bank statement.

(f) A check for $260 returned with the statement had been recorded in the books as $235. The check was in payment of a cash purchase of office supplies.

Instructions: (1) Prepare a bank reconciliation.

(2) Journalize the necessary entries. Although the cash journals have already been posted, the books have not been closed.

13-2A. Piedmont Co. has just adopted the policy of depositing all cash receipts and making all payments by check. As of December 31, the close of the past year, all cash owned by the business was on deposit in a bank account. The following transactions relating to special funds were completed in January of the current year:

(a) Jan. 3. Drew Check No. 712 for $100 to Petty Cash to establish a petty cash fund.

3. Drew Check No. 713 for $500 to Cash to establish a change fund.

(b) The following disbursements, each evidenced by a petty cash voucher, were made from the petty cash fund during the month:

Jan. 4. Express charges, $9.00 (Purchases).

7. Postage, $10.30 (Office Supplies).

9. Newspapers, $1.40 (Misc. Gen. Expense).

15. Repairs to display counter, $5.25 (Misc. Sell. Expense).

17. Delivery charges on merchandise sold, $6.10 (Delivery Expense).

23. Office supplies, $3.90.

24. Repairs to cash register, $11.35 (Misc. Sell. Expense).

29. Store Supplies, $4.05.

(c) Jan. 31. Drew Check No. 809 to replenish the petty cash fund.

31. The currency and coins in the change fund total $497.63. Memorandum records of the daily overages and shortages have been maintained but not recorded in the accounts. Drew Check No. 810 to restore the change fund to its original amount.

Instructions: (1) Open T accounts for Cash on Hand, 1112, and Petty Cash, 1113.

(2) Record the transactions of January 3 in a cash payments journal like that illustrated on page 292.

(3) Record the petty cash transactions in a petty cash analysis sheet like that illustrated on page 291.

(4) Record the transactions of January 31.

(5) Post to the two T accounts.

13-3A. Alton Supply Company owns the following notes receivable on June 1. The firm has no contingent liability for notes receivable discounted on this date.

Our No.	Payable By	Payable At	Date of Note	Time	Face	Interest Rate
75	Brooks & Co.	Our office	Mar. 24	90 days	$ 295	—
76	W. S. Hatch Co.	Merchants Bank, City	Apr. 12	60 days	1,500	6%
77	John R. Dana	First National Bank, Troy	Apr. 16	90 days	850	6%
78	Central Corp.	Merchants Bank, City	Apr. 28	60 days	1,200	6%
79	Spencer Shop	First National Bank, Troy	May 8	30 days	600	6%
80	A. L. Murray	Our office	May 22	60 days	900	—

The following transactions affecting notes receivable were completed during June:

June 5. Sent Spencer Shop's note to First National Bank for collection.
6. Discounted the Central Corp. note at Merchants Bank; discount rate, 6%.
7. Received a 75-day, 6% note for $1,800 on account from Byron, Inc. The note is dated June 6 and is payable at Merchants Bank, City.
8. Received check from First National Bank for the principal and interest due on Spencer Shop's note, less a collection charge (Misc. General Expense) of $1.25.
10. Sent W. S. Hatch Co.'s note to Merchants Bank for collection.
12. Received notice from Merchants Bank that W. S. Hatch Co. dishonored their note. Charged the note to the maker's account.
18. Discounted the John R. Dana note at Merchants Bank; discount rate, 6%.
22. Received check from Brooks & Co. for note due today.
25. Received a 30-day, 5% note for $840 on account from Parker Co. The note is dated June 24 and is payable at our office.
29. Received a 60-day non-interest-bearing note for $500 from H. R. Foster on account. The note is dated June 27 and is payable at Citizens Bank, Lima.

Instructions: (1) Open a four-column account for Notes Receivable, 1115, and record the balance of $5,345 as of June 1 of the current year.

(2) Record the notes receivable listed above in a notes receivable register like the one illustrated in this chapter. Assume that the notes were received on the day that they are dated.

(3) Record the transactions in general journal form and make the necessary entries and notations in the notes receivable register.

(4) Post the journal entries to the notes receivable account in the general ledger and determine the balance at the end of the month.

(5) If a balance sheet is prepared as of June 30:
  (a) At what amount will notes receivable be listed?
  (b) What is the amount of the contingent liability for notes receivable discounted?

13-4A. The following transactions are selected from those completed by Moore Industries, Inc. during January of the current year, the first month of operations:

Jan. 5. Issued check for $1,341 to Eastern Fire Insurance Co. in payment of the premium on the following insurance policies, all dated January 3:

Policy No.	Property	Amount	Term	Premium
3865	Building	$50,000	3 years	$702
3866	Merchandise	30,000	3 years	396
3867	Equipment	10,000	5 years	243

6. Issued three checks totaling $2,100 to sales representatives as advances on traveling expenses.
14. Issued check for $1,257 to Acme Casualty Insurance Co. in payment of premiums on insurance policies dated January 13. Details are as follows:

846MB	Delivery Equip.		1 year	$1,104
9375	Public Liability	$100,000	1 year	153

20. Issued check for $213 to Bankers Guaranty Insurance Co. in payment of premium on an insurance policy dated January 18. Details are as follows:

    1447Y   Fidelity $10,000   1 year $213

27. Issued check for $396 to American Fire Insurance Co. in payment of premium on an insurance policy dated January 25. Details are as follows:

    19384   Merchandise $20,000   5 years $396

31. Received reports from the three sales representatives indicating expenditures for travel totaling $1,940. Issued three checks totaling $1,940 to the representatives.

Instructions: (1) Open the following accounts in the general ledger, using the four-column form illustrated in this chapter:

    Advances to Salesmen, 1114   Travel Expense, 6117
    Prepaid Insurance, 1120   Insurance Expense, 7118

(2) Record the transactions in general journal form and post to the accounts.

(3) Record the data in an insurance register like the one illustrated in this chapter. One month is the minimum length of time to be considered in allocating insurance expirations.

(4) Journalize the insurance adjustment as of January 31 and post to the accounts.

(5) Considering only the insurance policies acquired in January:

    (a) What is the total amount of insurance expired during the year?

    (b) What is the total amount of unexpired insurance at December 31?

13-5A. All data necessary for reconciling the bank statement of Carter's Campus Shop as of March 31 of the current year are presented below.

Balance in Cash in Bank as of March 1..................... $7,376.50
Total of Cash in Bank **Dr.** coι. nn in cash receipts journal for
  March... $7,960.40

All receipts are deposited after banking hours twice each week and on the last day of the month. The firm's records indicate the following deposits during March:

Date	Amount	Date	Amount	Date	Amount
Mar. 4	$ 670.20	Mar. 14	$1,184.20	Mar. 25	$ 812.30
7	1,168.70	18	870.40	28	1,260.80
11	629.50	21	958.60	31	405.70

Total of Cash in Bank Cr. column in cash payments journal
  for March... $7,165.30

The numbers of the checks and the amounts recorded in the cash payments journal during March are as follows:

Check No.	Amount	Check No.	Amount	Check No.	Amount
940	$180.70	948	$157.90	956	$375.20
941	72.20	949	128.60	957	78.10
942	416.30	950	275.80	958	212.90
943	3.00	951	510.90	959	228.50
944	24.80	952	758.30	960	703.40
945	598.20	953	54.40	961	501.80
946	452.10	954	131.10	962	147.10
947	322.40	955	283.70	963	547.90

The bank reconciliation for February 28 of the current year is as follows:

Balance per bank statement		$8,023.50
Add: Deposit of February 28, not recorded by bank		720.50
		$8,744.00

Deduct: Outstanding checks

No. 903	$138.70	
920	34.90	
937	491.30	
938	227.20	
939	475.40	1,367.50
Adjusted balance		$7,376.50
Balance per books		$7,379.00
Deduct: Collection and service charges		2.50
Adjusted balance		$7,376.50

Data selected from the bank statement for March are as follows:

Balance, March 1 . . . . $8,023.50

Deposits:

Date	Amount	Date	Amount	Date	Amount
Mar. 1	$ 720.50	Mar. 12	$ 629.50	Mar. 22	$ 958.60
5	670.20	15	1,184.20	26	812.30
8	1,168.70	19	870.40	29	1,260.80

Balance, March 31 . . . . $8,322.80

Bank memos and checks accompanying the bank statement are as follows, with the checks arranged in numerical order:

Bank debit memo for service and collection fees	$ 5.50
Bank debit memo for check returned because of insufficient funds	183.70
Bank credit memo for note collected: principal, $300; interest, $6	306.00

Check No.	Amount	Check No.	Amount	Check No.	Amount
903	$138.70	946	$452.10	954	$131.10
937	491.30	947	322.40	955	283.70
939	475.40	948	229.90	956	375.20
940	180.70	949	128.60	958	212.90
941	72.20	950	275.80	959	228.50
942	416.30	951	510.90	960	703.40
943	3.00	952	758.30	961	501.80
945	598.20	953	54.40	963	547.90

Instructions: (1) Prepare a bank reconciliation for March 31.

(2) Present in general journal form the entries to be recorded in the cash receipts and cash payments journals as of March 31. If errors in recording checks are discovered, assume that such checks were in payment of accounts payable. Assume also that the titles of subsidiary accounts will be inserted later.

Chapter 14

14-2A. The Adair Company has the following unpaid vouchers outstanding as of April 30 of the current year:

Voucher No.	Company	Date of Invoice	Amount	Terms
285	Todd, Inc.	April 14	$ 400	n/30
303	Harper Co.	April 28	1,500	1/10, n/30

The vouchers prepared and checks issued during the month of May are presented below:

Vouchers

Date	Voucher No.	Payee	Amount	Terms	Distribution
May 2	306	Blake Corp.	$1,300	2/10, n/30	Merchandise
3	307	Rush, Inc.	2,100	n/30	Store equipment
5	308–10	Fay Motors, Inc.	3,900	$1,900 down, balance in 2 equal monthly payments	Delivery equipment
10	311	Carson Supply	500	cash	Store supplies
13	312	Pellot & Son	1,500	2/10, n/30	Merchandise
17	313	R. B. Hanson	350	cash	Advertising expense
19	314	Sims & Rowe	280	n/30	Merchandise
24	315	Merchants State Bank	1,010	———	Note payable, $1,000 and interest $10
27	316	Acme Supply Co.	425	n/30	Store supplies
29	317	Daily Gazette	75	cash	Advertising

Checks

Date	Check No.	Payee	In Payment of Voucher No.	Amount
May 5	311	Fay Motors, Inc.	308	$1,900
7	312	Harper Co.	303	1,485
10	313	Carson Supply	311	500
12	314	Blake Corp.	306	1,274
14	315	Todd, Inc.	285	400
17	316	R. B. Hanson	313	350
22	317	Pellot & Son	312	1,470
24	318	Merchants State Bank	315	1,010
29	319	Daily Gazette	317	75
31	320	Rush, Inc.	307	2,100

Instructions: (1) Set up an account for Accounts Payable, Acct. No. 2113, and record the balance of $1,900 as of May 1.

(2) Record the May vouchers in a voucher register with the following amount columns: Accounts Payable Cr., Purchases Dr., Store Supplies Dr., Advertising Expense Dr., and Sundry Accounts Dr.

(3) Record the May checks in a check register with the following amount columns: Accounts Payable Dr., Purchases Discount Cr., and Cash in Bank Cr.

(4) Total and rule the registers, post to the accounts payable account, and bring down the balance in this account.

(5) Prepare a schedule of unpaid vouchers.

14-3A. The Gibbons Company has the following unpaid vouchers outstanding as of March 31 of the current year:

367	Thurman Corp.	$ 800
376	Bell & Hart	2,950
377	Conners, Inc.	480

Vouchers and checks prepared and recorded, bank deposits, and related transactions during April are as follows:

Apr. 2. Check No. 364 to Conners, Inc. in payment of Voucher No. 377.

3. Voucher No. 378 to Landis Co. for merchandise, $1,800.

Apr. 5. Voucher No. 379 to Sabina Bank for note payable, $6,000, and interest, $30.
5. Check No. 365 to Sabina Bank in payment of Voucher No. 379.
7. Check No. 366 to Thurman Corp. in payment of Voucher No. 367, 1% discount. Bank deposit, $7,120 (record check and deposit on same line).
9. Voucher No. 380 to Cooper Supply Co. for store supplies, $51, and miscellaneous selling expense, $21.
12. Voucher No. 381 to Fred Cole Corp. for merchandise, $850.
13. Check No. 367 to Landis Co. in payment of Voucher No. 378, 2% discount.
13. Voucher No. 382 to Modern Outfitters, Inc. for office equipment, $2,500.
14. Adjustment to Voucher No. 381 for merchandise returned, $100.
15. Voucher No. 383 to Ballard Express for freight charges on the following: purchases, $38; merchandise sold (delivery expense), $55; office equipment, $32.
15. Check No. 368 to Ballard Express in payment of Voucher No. 383. Bank deposit, $5,420 (record check and deposit on same line).
17. Voucher No. 384 to Payroll for salary expense, $1,875.
17. Voucher No. 385 to Saxton Corp. for merchandise, $1,125.
17. Check No. 369 to Payroll in payment of Voucher No. 384.
18. Vouchers No. 386 and 387 to Modern Outfitters, Inc. replacing Voucher No. 382, each for $1,250.
19. Check No. 370 to Modern Outfitters, Inc. in payment of Voucher No. 386.
20. Voucher No. 388 to Kemper Publications for advertising, $220.
22. Check No. 371 to Cooper Supply Co. in payment of Voucher No. 380. Bank deposit, $3,355 (record check and deposit on same line).
23. Voucher No. 389 to Conners, Inc. for merchandise, $2,160.
24. Check No. 372 to Kemper Publications in payment of Voucher No. 388.
25. Check No. 373 to Bell & Hart in payment of Voucher No. 376.
26. Check No. 374 to Fred Cole Corp. in payment of Voucher No. 381.
26. Cancellation of Voucher No. 385 by issuance of a note payable.
27. Voucher No. 390 to Fred Cole Corp. for merchandise, $2,015.
27. Voucher No. 391 to Ballard Express for freight charges on the following: purchases, $73; merchandise sold (delivery expense), $138.
27. Check No. 375 to Ballard Express in payment of Voucher No. 391.
30. Voucher No. 392 to Payroll for salary expense, $1,750.
30. Voucher No. 393 to Petty Cash to reimburse the fund for the following disbursements: store supplies: $24; delivery expense, $11; miscellaneous selling expense, $51; miscellaneous general expense, $16.
30. Check No. 376 to Payroll in payment of Voucher No. 392.
30. Check No. 377 to Petty Cash in payment of Voucher No. 393. Bank deposit, $4,593 (record check and deposit on same line).

The bank statement indicates an April 30 balance of $12,392. The numbers of the paid checks returned with the statement are as follows:

358	363	366	370	373
359	364	367	371	375
362	365	369	372	376

Comparison of paid checks returned with the bank reconciliation for March reveals that No. 330 for $23 is still outstanding.

The deposits listed on the bank statement agree with the amounts listed in the check register.

Instructions: (1) Set up a T account for Accounts Payable, Acct. No. 2113, and record the balance as of April 1.

(2) Record the transactions for April, using a voucher register like the one illustrated on pages 310 and 311, a check register like the one illustrated on page 312, and a two-column general journal. Insert the amount, $9,275, in the Bank Balance column of the check register before recording the transactions. Assume that appropriate notations are made in the Paid columns of the voucher register when March vouchers are paid.

(3) Total and rule the voucher register and check register.

(4) Post from the journals to the accounts payable account and bring down the balance.

(5) Prepare a schedule of unpaid vouchers as of April 30.

(6) Prepare a bank reconciliation as of April 30.

14-4A. The Kesler Co. records all vouchers at the net price after deducting cash discounts. Available discounts not taken are recorded in the check register as a debit to Discounts Lost. The following are selected from among the transactions recorded in October of the current year.

Oct. 3. Recorded Voucher No. 1052; payee, Foster Co.; invoice total, $1,800; terms 2/10, n/30, account distribution, Purchases.

8. Recorded Voucher No. 1064; payee, Commerce Realty Co.; amount, $3,200; account distribution, Mortgage Payable, $3,000; Interest Expense, $200.

8. Recorded Check No. 1102 in payment of Voucher No. 1064.

10. Recorded Vouchers No. 1068 and 1069; payee, Allen Construction Co.; amount of each voucher, $2,500; account distribution, Building Repairs.

11. Recorded Check No. 1106 in payment of Voucher No. 1068.

13. Recorded Voucher No. 1078; payee, Petty Cash; amount, $100; account distribution, Petty Cash (to increase amount of fund).

13. Recorded Check No. 1112 in payment of Voucher No. 1078.

14. Recorded Voucher No. 1081; payee, Robert Ford, Inc., invoice total, $2,000; items returned, $300; terms 1/10, n/30; account distribution, Purchases.

16. Recorded Voucher No. 1089, payee, Irving & Sons; invoice total, $700; terms 1/10, n/30; account distribution, Purchases.

17. Recorded return of merchandise with an invoice price of $200 to Foster Co. (Voucher No. 1052).

19. Recorded Voucher No. 1102; payee, Halton Equipment Co., invoice total, $6,000; account distribution, Store Equipment.

22. Recorded Check No. 1122 in payment of Voucher No. 1081.

24. Recorded Vouchers No. 1110 ($2,000) and No. 1111 ($4,000) to replace Voucher No. 1102.

25. Recorded Check No. 1127 in payment of Voucher No. 1110.

28. Recorded issuance of note payable in settlement of Voucher No. 1111.

30. Recorded Check No. 1140 in payment of Voucher No. 1089; discount lost, $7.

31. Recorded Check No. 1142 in payment of Voucher No. 1052, discount lost, $32.

Instructions: Record the transactions in (1) a voucher register similar to the form illustrated on pages 310 and 311 (with amount columns for Accounts Payable Cr., Purchases Dr., and Sundry Accounts Dr. only); (2) a check register similar to the form illustrated on page 312, modified to provide for discounts lost and omitting columns for Bank Deposits and Bank Balance; and (3) a two-column general journal.

Chapter 15

15-1A. A business enterprise pays $3,600 for a three-year insurance policy, effective July 1, 1961. Their fiscal year ends on December 31. Among the many possible methods that might be employed in allocating this cost against revenue are the following:

(a) Charge one third of the premium to expense in each of the following years: 1961, 1962, 1963.
(b) Charge the entire premium to expense in 1961.
(c) Charge 1961 with $672, one half of the cost of the premium on a one-year policy; 1962 and 1963 with $1,344 each, the cost of the premium on a one-year policy; and 1964 with the remaining balance.
(d) Charge the entire premium to expense in 1964.
(e) Report the unexpired premium at the cancellation value at December 31 of each year and charge the decrease to expense of the period. The cancellation values at December 31 are as follows: 1961, $2,800; 1962, $1,700; 1963, $560.

Instructions: Determine the amount of the overstatement or understatement of net income for each of the years, 1961, 1962, 1963, and 1964, that would result from the use of each of the allocation methods listed. (Pro rata allocation of the premium over the life of the policy is the usual and acceptable method.)

15-2A. During its first three years of operations, the D. E. Albertson Co. determined the cost of the merchandise inventory at the end of the period by the first-in, first-out method, depreciation expense by the straight-line method, and bad debts expense by the direct write-off method. The amounts of net income reported and the amounts of the foregoing items for each of the three years were as follows:

	First Year	Second Year	Third Year
Net income reported.............	$40,000	$75,000	$ 90,000
Ending merchandise inventory.....	70,000	80,000	100,000
Depreciation expense............	10,000	11,000	12,000
Bad debts expense..............	500	2,500	4,000

The firm is considering the possibility of changing to the following methods in determining net income for the fourth and subsequent years: last-in, first-out inventory, declining balance depreciation at twice the straight line rate (on new acquisitions), and provision for bad debts through the use of an allowance account. In order to consider the probable future effect of these changes on the determination of net income, the management requests that income of the past three years be recomputed on the basis of the proposed methods. The inventory, depreciation, and bad debts expense for the past three years, computed in accordance with the proposed methods, are as follows:

	First Year	Second Year	Third Year
Ending merchandise inventory.....	$68,000	$70,000	$75,000
Depreciation expense............	20,000	18,000	16,400
Bad debts expense..............	3,600	4,000	5,000

Instructions: Recompute the net income for each of the three years, presenting the figures in an orderly manner.

15-4A. The balance sheet and income statement prepared from the unadjusted accounts of Benton Athletic Supply at the close of the first year of operations are presented below.

Benton Athletic Supply
Balance Sheet
December 31, 19—

Cash....................................	$3,200
Equipment.............................	6,000
L. R. Benton, capital..................	$9,200

Benton Athletic Supply
Income Statement
For Year Ended December 31, 19—

Sales..		$60,000
Purchases....................................		49,000
Gross profit on sales........................		$11,000
Operating expenses		
Salary expense.............................	$10,000	
Rent expense..............................	3,250	
Utilities expense..........................	700	
Advertising expense.......................	450	
Miscellaneous expense.....................	2,400	
Total operating expenses.....................		16,800
Net loss.....................................		$ 5,800

You are engaged to review the accounting methods employed and, if material errors are found, to prepare revised statements. The following information is elicited during the course of the review:

  (a) The business was established on January 2 by an investment of $15,000 in cash by the proprietor. The only transactions recorded have been those in which cash was received or disbursed. The books have not been closed for the year.

  (b) The equipment listed on the balance sheet at $6,000 was purchased for cash on January 10. Equipment purchased July 6 for $2,000 in cash was recorded as "purchases." Equipment purchased on December 17 for $1,000, for which a 60-day non-interest-bearing note was issued, was not recorded.

  (c) Depreciation on equipment has not been recorded. The equipment is estimated to have a useful life of 10 years and a salvage value of 10% of its original cost. (Use straight-line method.)

  (d) Accounts receivable from customers at December 31 total $7,500.

  (e) A total of $11,500 is owed to merchandise creditors on account at December 31.

(f) The merchandise inventory at December 31, as nearly as can be determined, has a cost of $18,000.

(g) Insurance premiums of $790 were charged to miscellaneous expense during the year. The unexpired portion at December 31 is $450.

(h) Rent expense includes an advance payment of $250 for the twenty-fourth month of the two-year lease.

(i) Miscellaneous expense includes $400 of transportation costs on merchandise purchased.

(j) Salaries owed but not paid on December 31 total $370.

(k) Uncollectible accounts are estimated at $800.

(l) The classification of expenses as "selling" and "general" is not considered to be sufficiently important to justify the cost of the analysis.

(m) The proprietor made no additional investments, or withdrawals, during the year.

Instructions: (1) On the basis of the preliminary statements, prepare a trial balance as of December 31 of the current year on an eight-column work sheet.

(2) Record the adjustments and corrections in the adjustments columns and complete the work sheet.

(3) Prepare an income statement, capital statement, and balance sheet.

Chapter 16

16-1A. The Morgan Distributing Co. has nine employees. They are paid on an hourly basis, receiving time-and-one-half pay for all hours worked in excess of 40 a week. The record of time worked for the week ended Saturday, October 28, of the current year, together with other relevant information, is summarized below:

Name	No.	M	T	W	Th	F	S	Rate Per Hour	Bond Deduc- tions	Income Tax Withheld
A	11	8	8	8	8	8	4	$2.00	$3.75	$ 9.80
B	13	6	8	8	4	9	0	2.40		6.10
C	17	8	8	8	8	8	5	2.50	2.50	11.90
D	16	8	8	4	8	8	5	2.20		7.10
E	15	6	8	8	8	8	4	2.00	2.50	11.00
F	19	4	8	8	8	8	0	2.50	3.75	14.10
G	20	8	8	8	6	8	2	2.80	5.00	6.40
H	12	8	6	8	8	8	5	2.20		5.90
I	18	8	8	8	8	8	0	2.40	2.50	8.20

Cumulative earnings paid (before deductions) prior to the current week were as follows: A, $2,900; B, $3,300; C, $4,750; D, $2,950; E, $2,790; F, $4,770; G, $5,110; H, $2,960; and I, $4,730.

C, G, and I are office employees, the others are salesmen. A group insurance deduction of $.60 per week is made from each employee's earnings. The following tax rates apply: F.I.C.A., 3% on maximum of $4,800; state unemployment (employer only), 1.8%; federal unemployment, .4%.

Instructions: (1) Prepare a payroll record similar to that illustrated on pages 352 and 353 of the textbook.

(2) Journalize the entry to record the payroll for the week.

(3) The company uses a voucher system and a payroll bank account. Give the entries in *general journal form* to record the payroll voucher and the payment of the payroll. The payroll checks are issued in the order of the names on the payroll, beginning with Check No. 283.

(4) Journalize the entry to record the employer's payroll taxes for the week.

16-2A. The following accounts, with the balances indicated, appear in the ledger of Everglade Products Co. on December 1 of the current year:

214	Salaries Payable.............................	——
215.1	F.I.C.A. Taxes Payable.......................	$ 254.24
215.2	Employees Income Taxes Payable..............	1,150.70
215.3	State Unemployment Taxes Payable............	174.60
215.4	Federal Unemployment Taxes Payable..........	293.70
216.1	Bond Deductions Payable.....................	440.50
216.2	Hospital Deductions Payable..................	87.50
611	Sales Salary Expense........................	92,400.60
711	Officers Salary Expense......................	39,200.00
712	Office Salary Expense.......................	9,970.40
719	Payroll Tax Expense........................	4,325.76

The following transaction relating to payroll, payroll deductions, and payroll taxes occur during December:

Dec. 1. Prepared Voucher No. 647, payable to Midland State Bank, for $150.00 to purchase U. S. Savings Bonds (4 at $37.50) for employees.

2. Issued Check No. 631 in payment of Voucher No. 647.

14. Prepared Voucher No. 685, payable to Midland State Bank, for the amount of employees' income tax and F.I.C.A. tax due on December 15.

14. Issued Check No. 665 in payment of Voucher No. 685.

15. Prepared a general journal entry to record the biweekly payroll for the period ending yesterday. A summary of the payroll record follows:
Deductions: F.I.C.A. tax, $62.40; income taxes withheld $667.80; bond deductions, $67.50; hospital deductions, $87.50.
Salary Distribution: officers salaries, $1,850; sales salaries, $4,166; office salaries, $640.
Net Amount: $5,770.80.

15. Prepared Voucher No. 691, payable to Payroll Bank Account, for the net amount of the biweekly payroll.

15. Issued Check No. 688 in payment of Voucher No. 691.

16. Prepared Voucher No. 698, payable to Mercy Hospital, for $175 for contributions withheld from employees' earnings during the past two pay periods.

17. Issued Check No. 693 in payment of Voucher No. 698.

29. Prepared a general journal entry to record the biweekly payroll for the period ending yesterday. A summary of the payroll record follows:
Deductions: F.I.C.A. tax, $59.48; income taxes withheld, $628.50; bond deductions, $78.75.
Salary Distribution: officers salaries, $1,850; sales salaries, $3,960; office salaries, $640.
Net Amount: $5,683.27.

29. Prepared Voucher No. 749, payable to Payroll Bank Account, for the net amount of the biweekly payroll.

Dec. 29. Issued Check No. 742 in payment of Voucher No. 749.
    29. Prepared Voucher No. 821, payable to Midland State Bank, for $93.75 to purchase U. S. Savings Bonds (5 at $18.75) for employees.
    30. Issued Check No. 818 in payment of Voucher No. 821.
    31. Prepared a general journal entry to record the employer's payroll taxes on earnings paid in December. Taxable earnings for the two payrolls, according to the payroll records, are as follows: subject to F.I.C.A. tax, $4,062.50; subject to unemployment compensation tax, $2,340. The following rates apply: F.I.C.A., 3%; state unemployment, 2.4%; federal unemployment, .4%.

Instructions: (1) Open the accounts listed and enter the balances shown under date of December 1.

(2) Record the transactions, using a voucher register like the one on pages 310 and 311, and a check register like the one on page 312, and a general journal. After each entry, post all items affecting the accounts opened in the ledger.

(3) Journalize the adjusting entry on December 31 to record salaries for the incomplete payroll period. Salaries accrued are as follows: officers salaries, $185; sales salaries, $390; office salaries, $64. Post to the accounts.

(4) Journalize the entry to close the salary expense and payroll tax expense accounts to Expense and Revenue Summary, post to the accounts, and extend all account balances to the appropriate balance columns.

(5) Journalize the entry on January 1 to reverse the adjustment of December 31. Post to the accounts.

(6) Assume that Vouchers Nos. 865, 866, and 867 are prepared on January 29 for the payment of the liabilities for payroll taxes shown on December 31. List the taxes, the period of time to which each applies, and the amount of each voucher using the following headings:

VOUCHER NUMBER	TAX	PERIOD COVERED	AMOUNT OF VOUCHER

16-4A. The following information relative to the payroll of Spencer Bros. for the week ended December 30 of the current year appears on the payroll record and other records:

Salaries:		Deductions:	
Sales Salaries	$27,600	Income tax withheld	$4,120
Office Salaries	5,800	Bond deductions	500
Warehouse Salaries	4,400	Hospital deductions	200
	$37,800	F.I.C.A. tax withheld is assumed to total the same amount as the employer's tax.	

Tax Rates:
    F.I.C.A., 3%.
    State unemployment (employer only), 2.1%.
    Federal unemployment, .4%.

Instructions: (1) Assuming that the payroll for the last week of the year is to be paid on December 31, present the following entries:

(a) December 30, to record the payroll. Of the total payroll for the last week of the year $11,600 is subject to the F.I.C.A. tax and $4,620 is subject to unemployment compensation taxes.

(b) December 30, to record the employer's payroll taxes on the payroll to be paid on December 31.

(2) Assuming that the payroll for the last week of the year is to be paid on January 2 of the following fiscal year, present the following entries:
   (a) December 31, to record the payroll.
   (b) January 2, to record the employer's payroll taxes on the payroll to be paid on January 2.

Chapter 17

17-1A. The Hamilton Company prepares interim statements at the end of each month and closes its books annually on December 31. On January 31 of the current year the accountant estimates that the property tax assessment for the city's fiscal year ending December 31 will be $5,280. On April 10 a tax statement for $4,908 is received; one half is payable on May 15 and the other half on November 15.

Instructions: Present, in general journal form, the entries to record the following:

Jan. 31. Property tax allocation.
Apr. 30. Property tax allocation (assume that proper entries were made at the end of February and March).
May 15. Payment of first half of the tax bill.
June 30. Property tax allocation.
July 31. Property tax allocation.
Nov. 15. Payment of second half of the tax bill (assume that proper entries were made at the end of August, September, and October).
Dec. 31. Property tax allocation.

17-2A. The state statutes require that retailers collect a sales tax of 4% on all sales to consumers except on certain items such as seeds and fertilizers, and on sales to governmental units such as public schools, the city, and the county. In the event the amount collected is less than 4% of the taxable sales, the deficiency must be borne by the retailer. Quarterly remittances are payable by the end of the month following the quarter.

The balances in certain accounts of Plaza Appliances Co. as of March 31 (after adjustment for tax liability) and June 30 of the current fiscal year (which ends on December 31) are as follows:

	March 31	June 30
Sales Tax Payable....................	$ 4,684.36	$ 5,179.52
Sales.....................................	124,730.60	262,341.40
Sales Returns and Allowances...........	2,147.10	4,465.30
Sales Tax Expense.....................	18.64	18.64

Supplementary records indicate that sales for the second quarter of the year included nontaxable sales of $5,618.20 and that returns and allowances on nontaxable sales for the same period amounted to $342.80.

Instructions: (1) Determine the amount of the liability for sales taxes for the second quarter of the year, presenting your figures in good order.

(2) Present the entry as of June 30 to record the additional liability for sales taxes for the second quarter.

(3) Present the entry on July 31, in general journal form, to record payment of the sales tax liability for the second quarter.

(4) On the basis of the information presented above, determine the amount of the net taxable sales for the *first* quarter of the year.

17-3A. Charles D. West has just completed his first full calendar year of practice as an architect. He is unmarried, under 65 years of age, and has good vision. During the calendar year he contributed more than half of the cost of supporting his brother, who is a student and resides with his parents. The brother's income for the year totaled $550.

Mr. West has maintained a detailed record of cash receipts and disbursements, including those of a personal nature. A summary of his records is presented below.

Receipts

Professional fees..	$39,462
Borrowed from bank (professional purposes)..............	2,000
Inheritance from grandfather's estate.....................	3,000
Dividends on corporation stocks...........................	480

Disbursements

Cost of new automobile (purchased January 10)............	$ 4,800
Office equipment (purchased March 18).................	400
Salary of draftsmen and typist...........................	11,200
Payroll taxes...	557
Fees to collaborating engineers..........................	3,150
Office rent...	3,600
Telephone expense (office)..............................	306
Electricity (office)......................................	174
Insurance on office equipment (1-year policy).............	30
Payment on loan from bank (see above)..................	1,500
Blueprint expense.......................................	618
Office supplies expense..................................	67
Interest on bank loan....................................	75
Automobile operating expenses (gasoline, oil, etc.).........	492
Purchase of Benton Corporation stock...................	1,850
Life insurance premiums................................	620
Contributions to church, university, and United Fund.......	450
Personal and living expenses............................	6,820
Payment on Declaration of Estimated Income Tax.........	5,000

The automobile was used ½ of the time for professional purposes. It is to be depreciated on the straight-line basis, assuming 4 years of life and a trade-in value of $1,000. Allocate ½ of the depreciation and other autombile expenses to professional purposes.

Office equipment was acquired in the previous year at a cost of $2,400. Use a straight-line composite depreciation rate of 10%, taking depreciation for ¾ year on the equipment purchased on March 18 of the current year.

Instructions: Determine Mr. West's taxable income and income tax, presenting the details in good order. Apply the appropriate table of tax rates appearing in this chapter.

17-4A. The preliminary income statement of the Mountain Shadows Gift Shop appearing below was prepared as of the close of the calendar year in which the business was established. You are engaged to review the business records, revise the accounting system to the extent necessary, and prepare a corrected schedule for submission with the income tax return of the proprietor.

Sales...		$86,296
Purchases..		79,324
Gross profit on sales................................		$ 6,972
Operating expenses:		
Salaries..	$8,670	
Rent...	1,500	
Store equipment.................................	4,200	
Insurance..	360	
Utilities..	415	
Fuel...	290	
Advertising......................................	210	
Taxes..	502	
Donations.......................................	77	
Miscellaneous...................................	634	16,858
Net loss...		$ 9,886

The following information was obtained during the course of your examination:

    (a) The preliminary income statement is in agreement with the records of cash receipts and disbursements. Unpaid invoices for merchandise and other expenditures are filed in an unpaid file. Uncollected charges to customers are evidenced by duplicate sales tickets.

    (b) Unpaid invoices at December 31 for expenditures of the past year are summarized as follows:

Merchandise.............................	$5,673
Utilities.................................	39
Fuel.....................................	45

    (c) Uncollected sales to customers on account at December 31 amount to $2,748.

    (d) The inventory of merchandise on hand at December 31 was $21,485.

    (e) The store equipment was installed on March 5. It has an estimated composite life of 10 years and a residual value of $300. Straight-line depreciation is to be claimed for 10 months.

    (f) A total of $270 of insurance premiums was unexpired at December 31.

    (g) Withdrawals of $4,800 by the proprietor were included in the amount reported as Salaries.

(h) Payments classified as Donations were contributions to charitable, religious, and educational organizations.

Instructions: Prepare a statement of income from the business for submission with the income tax return of E. G. Beamer, the proprietor, employing the accrual method of accounting.

Chapter 18

18-1A. On May 1 of the current year James Alton and Arthur Black form a partnership to engage in the retail clothing business. Alton is to invest certain business assets at valuations to be agreed upon, is to transfer business liabilities, and is to contribute sufficient cash to bring his total capital to $38,000. Details regarding the book values of the business assets and liabilities, and the agreed valuations, follow:

	Alton's Ledger Balance	Agreed Valuation
Accounts Receivable............................	$10,000	$10,000
Allowance for Uncollectible Accounts...........	1,000	2,000
Merchandise Inventory........................	24,000	19,000
Store Equipment.............................	4,500	2,600
Accumulated Depreciation — Store Equipment...	2,500	
Office Equipment............................	3,000	800
Accumulated Depreciation — Office Equipment..	2,000	
Accounts Payable............................	6,000	6,000

Black agrees to invest $28,000 in cash.

The articles of copartnership include the following provisions regarding the distribution of net income: interest on original investment at 6%, salaries of $8,000 and $5,000, respectively, and the remainder equally.

Instructions: (1) Give the entries, in general journal form, to record the investment of Alton and Black on the partnership books.

(2) Prepare a balance sheet as of May 1, the date of formation of the partnership.

(3) After adjustments and the closing of revenue and expense accounts at April 30, the end of the first full year of operations, the expense and revenue summary account has a credit balance of $24,500. Present the journal entry to close Expense and Revenue Summary.

18-2A. John King and Joseph Lane are in process of forming a partnership. They have agreed that King is to invest $70,000 and Lane is to invest $50,000. King is to devote one half of his time to the business and Lane is to devote full time. The following plans for the division of income are under consideration:

(a) In the ratio of original investments.
(b) Equal division.
(c) In the ratio of time devoted to the business.
(d) Interest of 6% on original investments, salaries of $4,000 (King) and $7,000 (Lane), and the remainder equally.

(e) Interest of 5% on original investments and the remainder equally.
(f) Plan (d) except that Lane is also to be allowed a bonus equal to 10% of the amount by which net income exceeds the salary allowances.

Instructions: Determine the division of income under each of the following assumptions: net income of $42,000, net income of $30,000, net income of $12,000. Present the data in tabular form, using the following columnar headings:

Plan	$42,000		$30,000		$12,000	
	King	Lane	King	Lane	King	Lane

18-4A. Earl Franklin and Charles Goodman, partners, engage you to review their accounts at the close of their first year of operations, with particular regard to year-end adjustments and division of income. Their fiscal year ends on June 30. During the course of your examination you determine the following facts:

(a) All revenue and expense accounts have been closed to Expense and Revenue Summary, which has a credit balance of $7,440.
(b) The cost of an addition to the building completed in mid-year, $7,000, was charged to Repair Expense.
(c) Expired insurance of $510 during the year was not recorded.
(d) Accrued salaries of $780 at the end of the current year were not recorded.
(e) As a result of the error in (b), depreciation of buildings was understated by $200.
(f) Sales of $3,250 on account on June 30 were not recorded. (The inventory was correctly stated.)
(g) The original capital investments of the partners, dated July 1 of last year, were $30,500 and $17,500 respectively. There were no other entries in the capital accounts during the current year.
(h) Withdrawals during the current year, all of which were charged to Salary Expense, were as follows: Franklin, $250 per month and $4,000 on Oct. 1; Goodman, $400 per month.
(i) The agreement as to division of income is as follows:
  (1) Interest at the rate of 6% is to be allowed on capital balances at the beginning of the year, diminished by interest at the same rate per annum on withdrawals in excess of salary allowances drawn each month.
  (2) Franklin, who devotes half time to the business, is to have a salary allowance of $250 a month. Goodman, who devotes full time to the business, is to have a salary allowance of $400 a month. As general manager he is also allowed a bonus of 10% of the excess of net income over the sum of the interest and salary allowances.
  (3) Any balance remaining is to be divided equally.

Instructions: (1) Present the necessary adjusting and correcting entries as of June 30 of the current year. Reductions and increases in net income should be charged and credited directly to Expense and Revenue Summary.
(2) Prepare the income division section of the income statement.
(3) Prepare a capital statement.
(4) Present the journal entries to close the expense and revenue summary account and the drawing accounts.

Chapter 19

19-1A. Harold Forman and Paul Gilbert are partners sharing income in the ratio of 2:1. After adjustments to asset values as of June 30 of the current year, their proprietary interests in the firm are $20,000 and $16,000, respectively. Alvin Horton is to be admitted to the partnership with a cash investment of $18,000.

Instructions: Record the admission of Horton to the firm, in general journal form, under each of the following assumptions (if fractional dollars are involved, round final amounts to the nearest dollar):

(1) Horton to receive credit for the amount of his investment, which is to represent a one-third interest.
(2) Horton to receive credit for the amount of his investment, which is to represent a one-fourth interest.
(3) Horton to receive a one-fourth interest; total capital to be increased only by the amount of his cash investment.
(4) Horton to receive a two-fifths interest; total capital to be increased only by the amount of his cash investment.
(5) Horton to receive a one-half interest; Forman and Gilbert to retain their present capital balances.
(6) Horton to receive a one-fifth interest; no goodwill to be recorded.
(7) Horton to receive a two-fifths interest; goodwill to be recorded.

19-2A. Earl Kline is to retire from the partnership Kline and Associates as of December 31 of the current year. After closing the books and giving effect to revisions in asset values as of that date, the capital balances of the partners are as follows: Earl Kline, $36,000; John Lanter, $28,000; Herbert Meyer, $20,000. They have shared net income and losses in the ratio 4:2:1.

Instructions: Present the entries, in general journal form, to record the withdrawal of Kline under each of the following assumptions:

(1) Lanter and Meyer each purchase one half of Kline's interest for $24,000, in each case paying him $4,000 in cash and giving an interest-bearing note for $20,000.
(2) Kline receives $12,000 in cash from the firm and a note for $30,000, to be collected over a period of three years. The partnership goodwill indicated by the settlement is not to be recorded in the accounts of the firm.
(3) Kline receives from the firm $9,000 in cash and six $5,000, interest-bearing notes maturing at six-month intervals. The goodwill attributable to Kline's interest is to be recorded in the accounts of the firm.
(4) Kline withdraws $25,500 in cash in full settlement.
(5) Kline receives $8,400 in cash, real estate, and a note for $18,000. The real estate had been included in Kline's original contribution to the capital of the partnership. He had acquired the property for $12,000 (land $1,000, building $11,000); when contributed to the firm it had been valued at $10,000 (land $1,000, building $9,000); and its adjusted valuation at December 31 is $14,000 (land $3,000, building $11,000). The total goodwill of the firm, as indicated by the settlement with Kline, is to be recorded in the accounts.

19-3A. Dalton, Evans, and Foster decide to discontinue business operations as of April 30 and liquidate their enterprise. The firm's post-closing trial balance at that time appears below.

Dalton, Evans, and Foster
Post-Closing Trial Balance
April 30, 19 – –

Cash.	12,000	
Accounts Receivable.	6,000	
Allowance for Uncollectible Accounts.		2,000
Merchandise Inventory.	19,400	
Prepaid Insurance.	800	
Supplies.	700	
Equipment.	5,000	
Accumulated Depreciation — Equipment.		3,800
Building.	23,000	
Accumulated Depreciation — Building.		4,000
Land.	3,500	
Notes Payable.		4,000
Accounts Payable.		3,600
Mortgage Payable.		10,000
P. Dalton, Capital.		18,000
R. Evans, Capital.		15,000
J. Foster, Capital.		10,000
	70,400	70,400

The partners share net income and losses in the ratio 3:2:1. The realization and liquidation transactions are summarized as follows:

(a) Sold the supplies for $500 cash.
(b) Collected $3,800 of accounts receivable; the remainder are worthless.
(c) Sold the merchandise for $10,000 cash.
(d) Sold the equipment for $1,500 cash.
(e) Sold the land and building for $26,000, purchaser paying $16,000 cash and assuming the mortgage. The mortgage holder released the partners from further liability.
(f) Paid miscellaneous expenses in connection with the sale of the assets, $350. (Charge to Loss and Gain on Realization.)
(g) Realized $550 cash from cancellation of the insurance policies.
(h) Distributed the loss on realization to the partner's capital accounts.
(i) Paid the notes payable in full.
(j) Paid the accounts payable in full.
(k) Distributed remaining cash to the partners.

Instructions: (1) Set up T accounts for all of the accounts appearing in the trial balance and for Loss and Gain on Realization.

(2) Record the April 30 balances in the T accounts.

(3) Present entries, in general journal form, to record the liquidation; post to the accounts; rule the accounts.

(4) Assuming a net loss on realization of $36,000, determine each partner's share of the cash remaining after paying the creditors (no entries required).

(5) Assuming a net loss on realization of $42,000, determine each partner's share of the cash remaining after paying the creditors (no entries required).

Chapter 20

20-1A. The net income or loss, after income taxes, of the Madison Corporation for a period of eight years is shown in the table below. During the entire period the corporation had outstanding 1,600 shares of cumulative 5% preferred stock, par $100, and 10,000 shares of common stock, par $10. Each year the board of directors (1) applied earnings to offset any accumulated deficit, (2) declared a partial or full dividend on the preferred stock to the extent of the available current or accumulated earnings, and (3) distributed one half of any remaining balance of current earnings as a dividend on the common stock.

Year	Net Income or Loss*	Preferred Dividends Declared	Total Arrears	Common Dividend Declared	Increase or Decrease* in Retained Earnings	Retained Earnings Balance
1955	$ 6,000					
1956	11,000					
1957	3,000*					
1958	25,000					
1959	32,000					
1960	1,000					
1961	2,000*					
1962	18,000					

Instructions: (1) Indicate the disposition of the net income or loss for each year, using the headings shown above. Use an asterisk to denote deductions and negative items.

(2) Determine the total dividends per share declared on each class of stock.

20-3A. Selected data from the balance sheets of six corporations, identified by letter, are presented below:

A. Common stock, $25 par. . . . . $ 750,000
   Retained earnings. 325,000
B. Total assets $867,300; total liabilities, $410,800; common
   stock outstanding, 10,000 shares, $50 par.
C. Preferred 4% stock, noncumulative, nonparticipating, $50 par. $ 250,000
   Common stock, $5 par. 1,200,000
   Retained earnings. 423,690
D. Preferred 6% stock, noncumulative, nonparticipating, $100 par $ 400,000
   Common stock, $10 par. 760,000
   Deficit. 126,800
   Preferred has prior claim to assets upon dissolution.
E. Preferred 5% stock, cumulative, nonparticipating, $50 par. . . $ 180,000
   Common stock, $50 par. 800,000
   Retained earnings. 52,800
   Dividends on preferred stock are in arrears for 4 years.
F. Preferred 4% stock, cumulative, nonparticipating, $25 par. . . $ 400,000
   Common stock, $10 par. 2,250,000
   Retained earnings. 68,000
   Dividends on preferred stock are in arrears for 6 years. Preferred stock is
   entitled to unpaid cumulative dividends upon dissolution, regardless of
   the availability of earnings.

Instructions: Determine the book value per share of each class of stock for each corporation, presenting the total capital allocated to the class and the number of shares outstanding.

20-4A. Brown, Fisher, and Taylor organize a corporation under the name of Southern Heights Realty, Inc., to subdivide and develop a 700-acre tract for homesites. They expect to build houses for sale, build on a contract basis, and sell lots. The charter authorizes 10,000 shares of common stock with a par value of $25. The corporation completes the following transactions (some stated in summary form) during June of the current year, the first month of operations:

  (a) Received $900 cash from each of the three incorporators, issuing 30-day non-interest-bearing notes.
  (b) Purchased 700 acres of land from Brown. Brown had acquired the land some years earlier at a cost of $34,000. There are delinquent property taxes of $2,250 and a 6% ten-year mortgage of $12,000. It is agreed that the land is to be valued at $45,000 and that Brown is to accept stock, at par value, for his net equity. The corporation assumes the mortgage and accrued interest of $300, as well as the delinquent taxes.
  (c) Paid the delinquent taxes.
  (d) Paid Taylor $250 cash to reimburse him for the incorporation fees that he had remitted with the charter application.
  (e) Received cash for 2,000 shares of stock at par from Fisher.
  (f) Paid Taylor, who is an attorney, $400 cash and 100 shares of stock for legal fees and promotional services connected with organizing the corporation.
  (g) Paid contractor $6,000 for surveying and for grading the roadways.
  (h) Purchased various building materials for $12,000 on account.
  (i) Received cash for 1,800 shares of stock at par from Taylor.
  (j) Paid expenses of advertising the lots, $750.
  (k) Paid the semiannual interest and $1,000 of principal on the mortgage.
  (l) Paid the $2,700 owed to the incorporators.

Instructions: (1) Record the corporation's transactions, in general journal form.

(2) Assuming that there were no additional transactions and no accruals, prepare a balance sheet for the corporation as of June 30. Omit subcaptions for current assets, current liabilities, etc.

Chapter 21

21-1A. The LaSalle Construction Co. was organized on June 1 of the current year with an authorization of 2,500 shares of $100 par, 6% cumulative preferred stock and 15,000 shares of $50 par common stock. Transactions completed during June and July are summarized as follows:

June 1. Received subscriptions to 8,000 shares of common stock at $52.
  1. Received cash for 40% of the subscription price from all common stock subscribers.
  2. Received subscriptions for 1,000 shares of preferred stock at $98.
  3. Paid organization costs of $1,750 in cash and issued 100 shares of common stock to the promoters at $52, in payment for their services.
  10. Purchased equipment for cash, $61,000.
  13. Received cash for 50% of the subscription price from all preferred stock subscribers.
  22. Issued 500 shares of preferred stock for land valued at $9,000 and a building valued at $40,000.

July 1. Received cash for 60% of the subscription price from June 1 subscribers to 4,000 shares of common stock and issued the certificates.
    4. Received cash for 40% of the subscription price from June 1 sub-
scribers to 4,000 shares of common stock.
  10. Received balance due from preferred stock subscribers and issued the
certificates.
  17. Received subscriptions to 5,000 shares of common stock at $53.
  20. Received cash for 50% of the subscription price from all July 17 subscribers to common stock.
  28. Received the balance due from the June 1 subscribers to 4,000 shares
of common stock and issued the certificates.

Instructions: (1) Record the transactions in general journal form and post
to the general ledger accounts. The accounts required are:

111 Cash	131 Organization Costs
113 Preferred Stock Subscriptions Receivable	311 Preferred Stock
	312 Preferred Stock Subscribed
114 Common Stock Subscriptions Receivable	313 Discount on Preferred Stock
	314 Common Stock
123 Equipment	315 Common Stock Subscribed
125 Buildings	316 Premium on Common Stock
126 Land	

(2) Assuming that no other transactions occurred during the period, prepare
a balance sheet in report form as of July 31.

21-2A. The following accounts and their balances appear in the ledger of
the Matson Corporation on September 1 of the current year:

Common Stock Subscriptions Receivable...............	—
Preferred 6% Stock, par $100 (10,000 shares authorized, 6,000 shares issued)...............................	$ 600,000
Premium on Preferred Stock.........................	6,000
Common Stock, no par (200,000 shares authorized, 120,000 shares issued)..................................	2,400,000
Common Stock Subscribed............................	—
Retained Earnings.................................	638,000

Acting upon a plan to redeem its preferred stock with funds to be acquired
by the issuance of additional common stock, the corporation completed the following transactions during the remainder of the fiscal year:

Sept. 1. Holders of the common stock were issued rights to subscribe to additional shares at $25 a share, at the rate of ⅓ share for each share
held. (No entry.)
Oct. 1. Three fourths of the stock rights were exercised and subscriptions
were received for that number of shares at $25, together with a down
payment of 50% of the subscription price.
Nov. 1. Collected the remainder due from all subscribers to common stock
and issued the stock certificates.
    7. In accordance with contract provisions of the preferred stock, the
6,000 shares were redeemed at $105 and retired.
  11. Issued 22,000 shares of common stock at $29, receiving cash.
  30. After closing all revenue and expense accounts for the year and recording income tax payable, Expense and Revenue Summary has a
credit balance of $262,000. Close Expense and Revenue Summary.

Instructions: (1) Open the accounts listed and record the balances.

(2) Record the foregoing transactions in general journal form and post to the selected accounts in the ledger.

(3) Prepare the capital section of the balance sheet as of November 30.

(4) Determine the book value of the common stock as of November 30.

21-4A. The capital accounts appearing in the ledger of Belmont Corporation on January 1 of the current year, together with other accounts that will be needed in the problem, are listed below:

Preferred 6% Stock, par $100 (20,000 shares authorized and issued)...	$2,000,000
Premium on Preferred 6% Stock	40,000
Preferred 4% Stock, par $50 (50,000 shares authorized)....	—
Premium on Preferred 4% Stock.......................	—
Common Stock, par $10 (500,000 shares authorized, 375,000 shares issued).............................	3,750,000
Preferred 4% Stock Subscribed........................	—
Treasury Stock..	—
Premium on Common Stock............................	375,000
Paid-in Capital from Sale of Treasury Stock.............	—
Retained Earnings....................................	1,670,000

During the year the corporation completed a number of transactions affecting the capital structure. They are summarized below.

(a) Purchased 10,000 shares of treasury common stock for $120,000 cash.

(b) Called the 6% preferred stock for redemption and retirement, paying the redemption price of $106.

(c) Sold 4,000 shares of treasury stock for $54,000 cash.

(d) Received subscriptions to 20,000 shares of 4% preferred stock at $52, collecting 50% of the subscriptions.

(e) Issued 25,000 shares of 4% preferred stock at $52, receiving cash.

(f) Sold 5,000 shares of treasury stock for $72,000 cash.

(g) Received balance due from subscribers to 19,000 shares of 4% preferred stock, and issued the stock certificates.

(h) Received balance due from subscribers to the remaining 1,000 shares of 4% preferred stock and issued the stock certificates.

Instructions: (1) Present the entries, in general journal form, to record the transactions. (Use of T accounts is suggested for accumulating balances needed to record particular transactions and for use in remainder of problem.)

(2) Prepare the capital section of the balance sheet as of December 31. Net income for the year, after deducting income taxes, amounted to $872,200. Dividends charged to Retained Earnings during the year totaled $350,700.

Chapter 22

22-1A. The capital accounts of the Conley Company on April 1, the first day of the current fiscal year are as follows:

Common Stock, $5 par (200,000 shares authorized, 125,000 shares issued)......................................	$625,000
Premium on Common Stock............................	125,000
Retained Earnings Appropriated for Plant Expansion......	150,000
Retained Earnings....................................	375,000

The following transactions occurred during the year:

Apr. 5. Issued 25,000 shares of common stock for $225,000 cash.

May 14. Discovered that the merchandise inventory as of April 1 was over-stated by $15,000. Correct through retained earnings.

Sept. 12. Declared regular cash dividend of 50¢ a share on common stock.

Oct. 2. Paid the dividend.

Mar. 12. Declared regular cash dividend of 50¢ and an extra dividend of 25¢ a share on common stock, payable April 2.

    30. Patents with an unamortized cost of $60,000 are considered to be worthless as a result of patents on an improved product obtained by a competing firm. The board of directors authorizes their write-off and directs that the loss be charged to the retained earnings account.

    30. The board directs that the appropriation for plant expansion is to be increased by $100,000.

    31. After closing revenue and expense accounts, including the income tax account, Expense and Revenue Summary has a credit balance of $260,000. Close the expense and revenue summary account.

Instructions: (1) Set up T accounts for the four capital accounts and enter the balances as of April 1.

(2) Journalize the transactions listed above, posting to the capital accounts.

(3) Prepare the capital section of the balance sheet as of March 31 of the current year.

(4) Prepare a retained earnings statement for the year.

22-2A. Selected transactions completed by the Rand Corporation during the current fiscal year are as follows:

Jan. 2. Received final payment from subscribers to 10,000 shares of preferred 5% stock, $50 par, and issued the stock certificates. The cash received was $102,000, which represented the final installment of 20% of the contract price. Earlier transactions related to the stock had been recorded correctly.

Feb. 18. Purchased 5,000 shares of own common stock at $6, recording the stock at cost. (Prior to the purchase there were 200,000 shares of $5 par common stock outstanding.)

May 6. Declared a semiannual dividend of $1.25 on the 10,000 shares of preferred stock, and a 20¢ dividend on the common stock, to stockholders of record on May 18, payable on June 1.

June 1. Paid the dividends.

Aug. 16. Discovered that equipment purchased for $29,000 on January 10 of the preceding year had been charged to expense. The equipment has an estimated life of 10 years, salvage value of $1,500, and is to be depreciated by the sum of the years-digits method. Correct through retained earnings.

Sept. 15. Sold the 5,000 shares of treasury stock at $9, receiving cash.

Nov. 6. Declared semiannual dividend of $1.25 on the preferred stock and 25¢ on the common stock. In addition, a 10% common stock dividend was declared on the common stock. The fair market value of the common stock to be issued is estimated at $9.

Dec. 1. Paid the cash dividends and issued the certificates for the common stock dividend.

    31. The board of directors authorized an appropriation for contingencies of $100,000.

Instructions: Record the above transactions in general journal form.

22-3A. The retained earnings accounts of Meadows Corporation for the current fiscal year ended December 31 are presented below.

Retained Earnings Appropriated for Plant Expansion

Jan.	1	Balance........................				75,000
Dec.	31	Retained earnings..............			100,000	175,000

Retained Earnings Appropriated for Treasury Stock Purchased

Jan.	1	Balance........................				50,000
Dec.	31	Retained earnings..............		15,000		35,000

Retained Earnings

Jan.	1	Balance........................				364,000
Mar.	10	Understatement of depreciation charges of preceding year........		14,000		
	12	Overstatement of income tax of preceding year................			19,000	
Aug.	18	Gain on sale of investments........			125,000	
Nov.	15	Cash dividend..................		80,000		
	15	Stock dividend..................		200,000		
Dec.	31	Organization costs written off....		4,000		
	31	Net income after income tax.......			310,000	
	31	Appropriation for plant expansion..		100,000		
	31	Appropriation for treasury stock purchased....................			15,000	435,000

Instructions: Prepare a retained earnings statement for the fiscal year ended December 31.

Chapter 23

23-1A. The following transactions were completed by Comstock Tools, Inc. during 1961 and 1962.

1961
April 30. Issued $1,000,000 of 20-year, 4½% bonds at 95½. Interest is payable semiannually on April 30 and October 31.
Oct. 31. Paid the semiannual interest on the bonds.
Dec. 31. Recorded the adjusting entry for interest payable.
    31. Recorded amortization of discount on the bonds.
1962
Jan. 1. Reversed the adjusting entry for interest payable.
April 30. Paid the semiannual interest on the bonds.
Oct. 31. Paid the semiannual interest on the bonds.
Dec. 31. Recorded the adjusting entry for interest payable.
    31. Recorded amortization of discount on the bonds.

Instructions: (1) Record the foregoing transactions in general journal form.
(2) State the amount of the interest expense in (a) 1961 and (b) 1962.

23-2A. Over a period of two years Phoenix Corporation completed the following transactions relating to its $2,000,000 issue of 10-year, 5% bonds dated March 1. Interest is payable on March 1 and September 1. The corporation's fiscal year is the calendar year.

1961
Apr. 16. Sold the entire bond issue, receiving $2,033,180 plus accrued interest for 1½ months.
Sept. 1. Paid the semiannual interest on the bonds.
Dec. 31. Deposited $120,000 in a bond sinking fund.
    31. Appropriated $142,000 of retained earnings for bonded indebtedness.
    31. Recorded the adjusting entry for interest payable.
    31. Recorded amortization of the bond premium.
    31. Closed the interest expense account.
1962.
Jan. 1. Reversed the adjustment for interest payable.
    4. Purchased various securities with sinking fund cash at a cost of $116,500.
Mar. 1. Paid the semiannual interest on the bonds.
Sept. 1. Paid the semiannual interest on the bonds.
Dec. 31. Recorded the receipt of $5,240 of income on sinking fund securities, depositing the cash in the sinking fund.
    31. Deposited $165,000 cash in the sinking fund.
    31. Appropriated $200,000 of retained earnings for bonded indebtedness.
    31. Recorded the adjusting entry for interest payable.
    31. Recorded amortization of the bond premium.
    31. Closed the interest expense account.

Instructions: (1) Record the transactions in general journal form. (Carry computations to the nearest dollar).

(2) Prepare a columnar table, using the headings shown below, and present the information for each of the two years:

Account Balance at End of Year

Year	Bond Interest Expense for Year	Bonds Payable	Premium on bonds	Sinking Fund		Appropriation for B. I.
				Cash	Securities	

23-3A. The following transactions relate to certain investments of the Fielding Corporation:

1961
Feb. 1. Purchased $100,000 of Davis Co. 10-year, 6% coupon bonds, dated Jan. 1, 1961, directly from the issuing company for $104,760 plus accrued interest. Davis Co. is an important subcontractor for the Fielding Corporation and it is expected that the bonds will be held until maturity.
Mar. 10. Purchased as a long-term investment 800 shares of Taylor Inc. common stock at 54¾ plus commission and other costs of $400.
June 20. Received a semiannual dividend of $1.00 per share on the Taylor Inc. stock.
    30. Deposited the coupons for semiannual interest on the Davis Co. bonds.

Dec. 20. Received a semiannual dividend of $1.00 per share and a 25% stock dividend from Taylor, Inc.
31. Deposited the coupons for semiannual interest on the Davis Co. bonds.
31. Recorded the amortization of premium on the Davis Co. bonds.

1962
Mar. 20. Sold $50,000 of Baltimore, Inc. bonds at 98½ plus accrued interest of $389. The broker deducted $148 for commission and other costs, remitting the balance. The bonds were carried on the books at $48,700.
June 20. Received a semiannual dividend of $1.00 per share on the Taylor, Inc. stock.
July 15. Sold 250 shares of Taylor, Inc. stock at 53. The broker deducted commission and other costs of $96, remitting the balance.

Instructions: Record the foregoing transactions in general journal form.

Chapter 24

24-1A. The Barnes Co. operates two sales departments: Department A, composed of women's clothing; and Department B, composed of men's clothing. The trial balance at January 31, the end of the current fiscal year, is presented on page 769.

Data for end-of-year adjustments are:

Merchandise Inventories, January 31:
Department A.	$41,364
Department B.	42,948

Supplies used during the year:
Store supplies (charge to Store Supplies Expense).	1,105
Office supplies (charge to Miscellaneous General Expense).	645
Insurance expired.	3,675
Depreciation of equipment.	3,000
Estimated income tax.	4,235

The bases to be used in apportioning expenses, together with other essential information are as follows:

Sales salaries — Payroll records: Department A, $14,000; Department B, $9,100.
Advertising — Usage: Department A, $1,720; Department B, $1,130.
Depreciation of equipment — Book value of equipment at beginning of year: Department A, $11,040; Department B, $7,360.
Store supplies — Requisitions: Department A, $610; Department B, $495.
Administrative and office salaries — Department A, 55%; Department B, 45%.
Rent, heating, and lighting — Floor space: Department A, 5,600 sq. ft.; Department B, 4,400 sq. ft.
Insurance and property tax — Average merchandise inventory.

Miscellaneous selling expense, miscellaneous general expense — Volume of gross sales.

Instructions: Prepare a twelve-column work sheet.

Barnes Co.
Trial Balance
January 31, 19—

Cash.	14,620	
Accounts Receivable.	27,410	
Merchandise Inventory, Department A.	39,708	
Merchandise Inventory, Department B.	11,100	
Prepaid Insurance.	6,700	
Supplies.	3,200	
Equipment.	24,000	
Accumulated Depreciation — Equipment.		4,700
Accounts Payable.		19,810
Common Stock.		100,000
Retained Earnings.		13,189
Sales, Department A.		194,700
Sales, Department B.		100,300
Sales Returns and Allowances, Department A.	4,960	
Sales Returns and Allowances, Department B.	1,320	
Purchases, Department A.	156,765	
Purchases, Department B.	88,945	
Purchases Discount, Department A.		1,712
Purchases Discount, Department B.		892
Sales Salaries.	23,100	
Advertising Expense.	2,850	
Miscellaneous Selling Expense.	1,100	
Administrative and Office Salaries.	16,500	
Rent Expense.	7,200	
Heating and Lighting.	2,800	
Property Tax Expense.	1,620	
Miscellaneous General Expense.	1,405	
	435,303	435,303

24-2A. Federated Specialties, of San Diego, opened a branch office in Fresno on April 1 of the current year. Transactions and adjustments related to branch operations for the current year ended October 31 were as follows:

(a) Received cash advance from home office, $30,000.
(b) Purchased office equipment for cash, $12,000.
(c) Shipments of merchandise received from the home office totaled $220,000, billed at cost.
(d) Purchased merchandise on account, $35,000.
(e) Sales on account, $232,000; cash sales, $38,600.
(f) Paid creditors on account, $26,500.
(g) Received cash from customers on account, $196,300.

(h) Paid operating expenses, $32,800 (all expenses are charged to Operating Expenses, a controlling account).
(i) Sent $175,000 cash to home office.
(j) Recorded accumulated depreciation, $1,750 and allowance for uncollectible accounts, $2,000.
(k) Merchandise inventory at October 31, $62,600.

Instructions: (1) Present the entries on the branch books, in general journal form, to record the foregoing transactions, adjustments, and year-end closing. Post to the following T accounts: Cash, Accounts Receivable, Allowance for Uncollectible Accounts, Merchandise Inventory, Office Equipment, Accumulated Depreciation, Accounts Payable, Home Office, Expense and Revenue Summary, Sales, Shipments from Home Office, Purchases, and Operating Expenses.

(2) Prepare an income statement for the period and a balance sheet as of October 31 for the branch.

(3) Present the entries required on the home office books, in general journal form. Post to a T account entitled Fresno Branch.

24-3A. The adjusted trial balances of the home office of Harris & Barton, Inc. and of its Syracuse branch, as of December 31, the close of the current fiscal year, are as follows:

	Home Office		Syracuse Branch	
	Dr.	Cr.	Dr.	Cr.
Cash.	97,600		19,500	
Accounts Receivable.	82,000		26,400	
Allowance for Uncollectible Accounts.		2,700		1,100
Merchandise Inventory	260,000		74,000	
Prepaid Expenses.	2,300		800	
Syracuse Branch.	78,700			
Equipment.	32,000		15,000	
Accumulated Depreciation.		18,000		3,700
Notes Payable.		16,000		
Accounts Payable.		72,100		8,500
Home Office.				78,700
Common Stock.		200,000		
Retained Earnings.		79,300		
Expense and Revenue Summary.	280,000	260,000	60,000	74,000
Sales.		950,000		360,000
Shipments to Branch.		226,000		
Purchases.	790,000		24,000	
Shipments from Home Office.			226,000	
Operating Expenses.	201,500		80,300	
	1,824,100	1,824,100	526,000	526,000

Instructions: (1) Prepare an income statement and a balance sheet for the branch.

(2) Prepare an income statement for the home office.

(3) Prepare the journal entry to record branch income on the home office books.

(4) Prepare a balance sheet for the home office, giving effect to the journal entry in (3).

(5) Prepare a work sheet for a combined income statement and a work sheet for a combined balance sheet.

(6) Prepare a combined income statement and a combined balance sheet.

Chapter 25

25-1A. A statement of cost of goods manufactured for the Howard Company is presented below:

Howard Company
Statement of Cost of Goods Manufactured
For Year Ended December 31, 1961

Work in process inventory, January 1, 1961..........		$ 50,000
Raw materials:		
Inventory, January 1, 1961.....................	$110,000	
Purchases....................................	322,000	
Total cost of materials available for use...........	$432,000	
Less inventory, December 31, 1961...............	115,000	
Cost of materials placed in production..........	$317,000	
Direct labor......................................	323,000	
Factory overhead.................................	210,000	
Total manufacturing costs........................		850,000
Total work in process during period...............		$900,000
Less work in process inventory, December 31, 1961....		75,000
Cost of goods manufactured.......................		$825,000

Instructions: (1) Prepare journal entries to adjust the work in process inventory and raw materials inventory accounts on December 31, the end of the fiscal year.

(2) Prepare the journal entry to close the raw materials purchases account, the direct labor account, and the factory overhead control account to the manufacturing summary account.

(3) Prepare the journal entry to close the manufacturing summary account.

25-2A. The work sheet for the Mitchell Manufacturing Company, with the adjustments columns omitted, is presented on page 773.

Instructions: (1) Journalize the entries to record the adjustments for inventories, depreciation, amortization of patents, bond interest and premium, salaries and wages payable, and estimated income tax.

(2) Journalize the entries to close the manufacturing accounts and the manufacturing summary account.

(3) Journalize the entries to close the revenue and expense accounts, and the expense and revenue summary account.

(4) Prepare a statement of cost of goods manufactured.

(5) Prepare an income statement.

Chapter 26

26-1A. Selected transactions completed by the Stuart Manufacturing Company during the month of May are summarized below:

(a) Materials and supplies purchased on account..........	$250,000
(b) Materials and supplies requisitioned:	
For production orders...........................	200,000
For general factory use.........................	15,000
(c) Labor used:	
Direct..	320,000
Indirect......................................	40,000
(d) Factory overhead is applied at the rate of 90% direct labor cost	
(e) Repairs and maintenance to factory incurred on account.	$ 50,000
(f) Factory building rental paid.......................	10,000
(g) Products finished and transferred to stock............	350,000
(h) Goods sold on account: cost $240,000; selling price....	400,000
(i) Factory wages paid................................	362,000

Instructions: Prepare entries in general journal form to record the foregoing summarized transactions.

26-2A. The following balances appear in the general ledger of Campbell Manufacturing Company on June 30, the end of the fifth month of the current fiscal year:

Cash..	$ 15,000	
Accounts Receivable.........................	23,500	
Finished Goods..............................	21,500	
Work in Process.............................	16,000	
Materials and Supplies......................	19,000	
Plant Assets................................	150,000	
Accumulated Depreciation — Plant Assets......		$ 60,000
Accounts Payable............................		25,000
Wages Payable..............................		5,000
Capital Stock...............................		50,000
Retained Earnings...........................		26,000
Sales.......................................		400,000
Cost of Goods Sold..........................	280,000	
Factory Overhead...........................	1,000	
Selling and General Expenses.................	40,000	

Mitchell Manufacturing Company
Work Sheet
For Year Ended December 31, 1962

Account Titles	Trial Balance Dr.	Trial Balance Cr.	Manufacturing Statement Dr.	Manufacturing Statement Cr.	Income Statement Dr.	Income Statement Cr.	Balance Sheet Dr.	Balance Sheet Cr.
Cash in Bank	26,000						26,000	
Finished Goods Inventory	40,000						35,000	
Work in Process Inventory	61,000						55,000	
Raw Materials Inventory	27,000						25,000	
Factory Supplies	7,000						4,000	
Machinery and Equipment	280,000						280,000	
Accumulated Depr. — Mach. and Equipment		110,000						135,000
Buildings	152,000						152,000	
Accumulated Depr. — Buildings		45,000						51,000
Land	25,000						25,000	
Patents	10,000						9,000	
Bonds Payable		200,000						200,000
Premium on Bonds Payable		5,000						4,500
Common Stock		100,000						100,000
Retained Earnings		38,000						38,000
Sales		705,000				705,000		
Raw Materials Purchases	95,000		95,000					
Direct Labor	205,000		209,000					
Factory Overhead (control)	160,000		196,000					
Operating Expense (control)	110,000				110,000			
Interest Expense	5,000				9,500			
	1,203,000	1,203,000						
Expense and Revenue Summary					40,000	35,000		
Manufacturing Summary			61,000	55,000				
Manufacturing Summary			27,000	25,000				
Interest Payable								5,000
Wages Payable								5,000
Estimated Income Tax					31,120			
Estimated Income Tax Payable								31,120
Cost of Goods Manufactured			588,000	508,000 / 588,000	508,000			
					698,620	740,000	611,000	569,620
Net Income After Income Tax					41,380			41,380
					740,000	740,000	611,000	611,000

As of the same date, balances in the accounts of selected subsidiary ledgers are as follows:

Stores Ledger

  Material X, $5,000; Material Y, $9,000; Material Z, $5,000

Cost Ledger

  Job No. 501, $10,000; Job No. 502, $6,000

Finished Goods Ledger

  Commodity R, 500 units, $2,500; Commodity S, 4,375 units, $17,500; Commodity T, 1,000 units, $1,500

The transactions completed during July are summarized below:

(a) Materials and supplies purchased on account:

Material X	$14,000
Material Y	5,000
Material Z	1,000

(b) Materials and supplies were requisitioned from the stores clerk as follows:

Job No. 501, Mat. X, $9,600; Mat. Y, $5,000........	$14,600
Job No. 502, Mat. X, $5,000.....................	5,000
Job No. 503, Mat. X, $2,400; Mat. Y, $500........	2,900
General factory use; Mat. Z.....................	800

(c) Time tickets for the month were chargeable as follows:

Job No. 501......................................	$14,000
Job No. 502......................................	6,000
Job No. 503......................................	1,000
Indirect labor...................................	2,000

(d) Factory pay checks for $25,000 were issued.

(e) Cash of $76,000 was received on accounts receivable.

(f) Various factory overhead charges of $8,700 were incurred on account.

(g) Depreciation on factory equipment was recorded, $1,500.

(h) Factory overhead was applied at the rate of 60% of direct labor cost.

(i) Selling and general expenses incurred on account, $8,000.

(j) Payments on account, $42,000.

(k) Job orders completed during the month: Job Order No. 501 produced 10,000 units of Commodity R; Job Order No. 502 produced 5,150 units of Commodity S.

(l) Total sales on account, $70,700. The goods sold were as follows (use FIFO):

  6,000 units of Commodity R
  3,445 units of Commodity S
  400 units of Commodity T

Instructions: (1) Prepare T accounts for the general ledger, materials and supplies ledger, the cost ledger, and the finished goods ledger. Record directly in these accounts the balances listed above, identifying them as "Bal."

(2) Prepare journal entries to record the July transactions.

(3) Post to the T accounts, identifying transactions by letters. When posting to the finished goods ledger record quantities as well as amounts.

(4) Take a trial balance.

(5) Prove the subsidiary ledgers with the control accounts in the general ledger.

(6) Prepare an income statement for the six months ended July 31.

Chapter 27

27-1A. Product X is manufactured in Departments 1 and 2. All raw materials are introduced in Department 1. The output of Department 1 passes through Department 2 where it emerges as finished product X. Inventories are priced at cost by the fifo method.

On May 1 the following balances appeared in the Department 2 work in process and the finished goods account:

Work in Process, Department 2
Balance — 1,000 units, 71% completed.............. $ 7,493.50

Finished Goods
Balance — 1,500 units at $9 a unit................. $13,500.00

During the month of May, 10,300 units of X were completed in Department 2. The following costs were charged to Work in Process, Department 2 during the month:

Materials transferred from Department 1 — 10,000 units
  at $4.. $40,000.00
Direct labor...................................... $26,900.50
Factory overhead.................................. $20,120.25

Inventories on May 31 were as follows:

Work in process, Department 2 — 700 units, 15% completed.
Finished goods — 1,000 units.

Instructions: (1) Determine the following, presenting the computations in good order: (a) equivalent units of production, (b) unit processing cost, (c) cost of goods finished (determine unit cost of goods started in prior period and unit cost of goods started in May) (d) work in process inventory, May 31, (e) cost of goods sold (indicate number of units and unit costs), (f) finished goods inventory, May 31.

(2) Set up T accounts for Work in Process, Department 2, and for Finished Goods. Record the balances at May 1, the transactions for May in summary form, and bring down the balances at May 31. Record the number of units and degree of completion, where appropriate, in the items sections of the accounts.

27-2A. The Bennett Chemical Co. manufactures two products, designated A and B. Raw Material X enters Department 1 where it is ground and partially refined. The output of Department 1 is transferred to Department 2 where raw material Y is added and further refining occurs. The output of Department 2 is Product A. Product B is produced by additional processing of Product A in Department 3. There is some shrinkage in weight in each process; unit costs of the output of each department are therefore determined by dividing the accumulated costs by the number of pounds produced. There are no inventories of work in process at either the beginning or the end of the month.

The accounts in the general ledger and their balances on January 1 of the current year are presented at the top of page 776.

Cash.....................................	40,000	
Accounts Receivable......................	30,000	
Product A (2,000 pounds at $3.00)...........	6,000	
Product B (1,500 pounds at $5.00)...........	7,500	
Work in Process — Dept. 1..................	—	
Work in Process — Dept. 2..................	—	
Work in Process — Dept. 3..................	—	
Maintenance Department....................	—	
Raw Material X (7,000 pounds at $1.00)......	7,000	
Raw Material Y (2,000 pounds at $2.00)......	4,000	
Prepaid Expenses..........................	3,500	
Plant Assets..............................	400,000	
Accumulated Depreciation — Plant Assets.....		100,000
Accounts Payable..........................		30,000
Wages Payable............................		1,000
Common Stock............................		200,000
Retained Earnings.........................		167,000
Sales.....................................		—
Cost of Goods Sold........................	—	
General Operating Expenses.................	—	
	498,000	498,000

The operations for January are summarized as follows:

(a) Raw materials purchased on account: X, 30,000 pounds, $27,000; Y, 12,000 pounds, $21,600.

(b) Prepaid expenses incurred on account, $1,800.

(c) Miscellaneous costs and expenses incurred on account: Department 1, $800; Department 2, $200; Department 3, $1,200; Maintenance Department, $1,500; General Operating Expenses, $8,000.

(d) Material X placed in Department 1 for processing, 25,000 pounds (use FIFO method).

(e) Material Y placed in Department 2 for processing, 10,000 pounds (use FIFO method).

(f) Factory labor used: Department 1, $10,000; Department 2, $10,000; Department 3, $6,000; Maintenance Department, $4,000.

(g) Expiration of various prepaid expenses: Department 1, $400; Department 2, $800; Department 3, $800; Maintenance Department, $200; General Operating Expenses, $600.

(h) Depreciation charges: Department 1, $600; Department 2, $880; Department 3, $370; Maintenance Department, $300; General Operating Expenses, $500.

(i) Allocation of Maintenance Department Costs: Department 1, 50%; Department 2, 30%; Department 3, 20%.

(j) Output of Department 1 was 20,000 pounds, which was transferred to Department 2. There is no work in process remaining in the department.

(k) Output of Department 2 was 24,000 pounds, which was transferred to Product A. There is no work in process remaining in the department.

(l) Product A in the amount of 6,000 pounds was transferred to Department 3 (use FIFO method).

(m) Output of Department 3 was 5,000 pounds, which was transferred to Product B. There is no work in process remaining in the department.

(n) Sales on account: 19,000 pounds of Product A at $4.00, 6,000 pounds of Product B at $7.00 (use FIFO method in crediting finished goods accounts).

(o) Cash received on account, $116,000.

(p) Cash payments: on account, $65,000; wages, $30,200.

Instructions: (1) Set up a T account for each account listed and record the balances as of January 1. Omit dates, writing "Bal." in the space normally allotted to dates.

(2) Record the entries directly in the accounts, using the identifying letters in place of dates. Use the items space for memorandums on pounds, cost per pound, and similar data. Credits to raw materials and finished goods are to be priced in accordance with the first-in, first-out method.

(3) Balance and rule the accounts and take a trial balance as of January 31.

Chapter 28

28-1A. Department heads of the Gilmore Manufacturing Co. were asked to submit estimates of fixed and variable expenses for the coming year, assuming that inventories at the end of the year will be the same as at the beginning of the year. The total of all direct and indirect manufacturing expenses for the year are therefore assumed to be equal to the cost of goods sold. The following report was submitted:

	Estimated Fixed Expense	Estimated Variable Expense (per unit sold)
Cost of goods sold....................		
Direct materials...................	$ 0	$2.50
Direct labor......................	0	3.00
Factory overhead.................	180,000	2.00
Selling expenses:		
Sales salaries.....................	26,000	.30
Advertising......................	0	.35
Miscellaneous selling expenses......	15,000	.40
General expenses:		
Management and office salaries.....	80,000	.25
Supplies.........................	1,000	.05
Miscellaneous general expenses.....	18,000	.15

Selling price of the product is $15 a unit, and capacity output is 80,000 units per year. It is expected that 70,000 units will be sold in the coming year.

Instructions: (1) Prepare an estimated income statement for the coming year. (2) Construct a break-even chart, indicating the break-even point.

28-3A. Condensed budget data for the D. B. Spear Company are as follows:

	January	February	March
Sales.......................	$220,000	$250,000	$280,000
Production costs..................	140,000	154,000	166,000
Operating expenses...............	43,000	47,000	53,000

Of the total monthly sales, 70% are expected to be for cash. All sales on account are expected to be collected in full in the month following the sale. Depreciation, insurance, and property taxes represent $4,000 of the estimated monthly production costs and $3,000 of the probable monthly operating expenses. The remaining expenses in each budget are out-of-pocket costs. Of these costs, 90% are expected to be paid in the month in which they are incurred and the balance will be paid in the next month.

At the beginning of the current year, assets include cash, $35,500, accounts receivable resulting from December charge sales, $50,000, and investments in long-term securities, $45,000. Liabilities, on January 1, consist of notes payable, $32,000, accounts payable, $14,000, and accrued expenses payable, $3,950. The note is non-interest-bearing and is scheduled for payment in January. The other liabilities represent unpaid December production costs and operating expenses, respectively.

Management's future plans include a cash purchase of equipment for $45,000 in March and the declaration and payment of a $50,000 cash dividend in February. It is expected that $1,500 of interest will be received in January and the receipt of dividend checks totaling $1,800 is anticipated in March. Management desires to maintain a minimum cash balance of $30,000.

Instructions: Prepare a monthly cash budget for the first three months.

28-4A. At 100% of plant capacity the yearly income statement of the Kaye Company is expected to be as follows:

Sales.		$800,000
Cost of goods sold.		560,000
Gross profit.		$240,000
Operating expenses:		
Selling expenses.	$70,000	
General expenses.	55,000	
Total operating expenses.		125,000
Net income.		$115,000

An analysis of costs and expenses reveals the following division of costs between fixed and variable:

	Fixed	Variable
Cost of goods sold.	20%	80%
Selling expenses.	40%	60%
General expenses.	60%	40%

The management of the Kaye Company is considering a plant expansion program that will permit an increase of $400,000 in yearly sales. The new facilities are expected to increase yearly fixed expenses by $67,000; the per cent of variable expenses to sales is expected to decrease by 4 percentage points.

Instructions: (1) Compute the total fixed and total variable expenses at present capacity.

(2) Determine the percentage of total variable expenses to sales at present capacity.

(3) Compute the break-even point under the proposed program.

(4) Determine the amount of sales under the proposed program that would be necessary in order to realize the $115,000 of net income which is expected to be earned under existing capacity.

(5) What is the amount of estimated net income that would result from the expansion, assuming sales of $1,200,000?

Chapter 29

29-2A. The comparative balance sheets of Graham Corporation at December 31, 1961 and 1962, are presented below in condensed form:

	December	
Debits	1961	1962
Cash..	$ 56,000	$ 85,000
Notes and accounts receivable (net)..............	110,000	105,000
Inventories...................................	195,000	240,000
Prepaid expenses.............................	6,400	5,800
Investment in stock of Carroll, Inc..............	80,000	100,000
Building and equipment.......................	550,000	620,000
Land...	11,700	11,700
Discount on bonds payable....................	4,000	3,400
	$1,013,100	$1,170,900

Credits		
Accumulated depreciation — bldg. and equip......	$ 100,000	$ 130,000
Notes and accounts payable....................	88,500	104,700
Estimated income tax payable..................	63,400	71,200
Dividends payable.............................	8,750	10,000
Bonds payable................................	100,000	100,000
Preferred stock, $100 par......................	50,000	——
Premium on preferred stock....................	2,000	——
Common stock, $10 par........................	400,000	500,000
Premium on common stock.....................	40,000	60,000
Retained earnings.............................	120,450	145,000
Reserve for bond redemption..................	40,000	50,000
	$1,013,100	$1,170,900

The retained earnings account and other necessary data are presented below:

RETAINED EARNINGS

1962			1962		
Mar. 20	Preferred dividends...	750	Jan. 1	Balance..........	120,450
	Common dividends...	8,000	Dec. 31	Net income......	71,300
21	Retirement of pref. stock...............	2,000			
June 20	Common dividends...	8,000			
Sept. 19	Common dividends...	8,000			
Dec. 19	Common dividends...	10,000			
31	Reserve for bond redemption...........	10,000			

An item of equipment acquired at a cost of $10,000 and on which the accumulated depreciation was $7,000 was sold for $1,000. New equipment was purchased during the year at a total cost of $80,000.

All preferred stock was retired on March 21 at 108.

Ten thousand shares of common stock were issued in October at 12.

Instructions: (1) Prepare working papers for the funds statement. (Allow three lines for retained earnings and four lines for funds provided by net income.)

(2) Prepare a funds statement, including an analysis of changes in working capital.

29-3A. The balances in the accounts of Ungar, Inc., after adjustment at December 31, the close of the current year, are as follows:

Accounts Payable...........................		65,800
Accounts Receivable........................	63,400	
Accumulated Depreciation — Buildings........		31,500
Accumulated Depreciation — Equipment.......		9,600
Allowance for Uncollectible Accounts..........		2,100
Bonds Payable (Due 1970)..................		100,000
Buildings.................................	160,000	
Bond Sinking Fund.........................	50,000	
Cash in Bank.............................	59,600	
Common Stock, $10 Par....................		175,000
Cost of Goods Sold........................	248,300	
Dividends Payable.........................		4,000
Estimated Income Tax Payable...............		29,000
Equipment................................	44,000	
General Expenses..........................	34,750	
Estimated Income Tax......................	29,000	
Interest Income...........................		4,800
Interest Expense..........................	5,200	
Land.....................................	65,000	
Merchandise Inventory.....................	66,800	
Prepaid Insurance.........................	4,200	
Retained Earnings.........................		50,750
Sales....................................		389,100
Selling Expenses..........................	41,600	
Wages Payable............................		10,200
	871,850	871,850

Dividends charged to Retained Earnings during the year totaled $16,000; there were no other charges and no credits to the account during the year.

Instructions: (1) Prepare a combined income and retained earnings statement using the single-step form.

(2) Prepare a detailed financial position form of balance sheet.

Chapter 30

30-1A. Comparative statements of Madison, Inc. are presented on pages 781 and 782.

Madison, Inc.
Comparative Balance Sheet
December 31, 1962 and 1961

Assets	1962	1961
Current assets.	$ 500,000	$ 475,000
Long-term investments.	150,000	300,000
Plant assets (net).	525,000	450,000
Total assets.	$1,175,000	$1,225,000
Liabilities		
Current liabilities.	$ 410,000	$ 360,000
Long-term liabilities.	25,000	50,000
Total liabilities.	$ 435,000	$ 410,000
Stockholders' equity		
Preferred 5% stock, cumulative, non-participating,		
$50 par.	$ 200,000	$ 200,000
Common stock, $5 par.	400,000	500,000
Retained earnings.	140,000	115,000
Total stockholders' equity.	$ 740,000	$ 815,000
Total liabilities and stockholders'equity.	$1,175,000	$1,225,000

Madison, Inc.
Comparative Schedule of Current Assets
December 31, 1962 and 1961

	1962	1961
Cash.	$ 70,000	$ 55,000
Marketable securities.	12,000	10,000
Accounts receivable (net).	105,000	80,000
Merchandise inventory.	305,000	325,000
Prepaid expense.	8,000	5,000
Total current assets.	$ 500,000	$ 475,000

Madison, Inc.
Comparative Income Statement
For Year Ended December 31, 1962 and 1961

	1962	1961
Sales.	$2,120,000	$1,380,000
Sales returns and allowances.	42,000	45,000
Net sales.	$2,078,000	$1,335,000
Cost of goods sold.	1,580,000	975,000
Gross profit on sales.	$ 498,000	$ 360,000
Selling expense.	$ 200,000	$ 155,000
General expense.	174,000	115,000
Total operating expense.	$ 374,000	$ 270,000
Net operating income.	$ 124,000	$ 90,000
Other income.	10,000	5,000
	$ 134,000	$ 95,000
Other expense.	14,000	7,000
Net income before income tax.	$ 120,000	$ 88,000
Estimated income tax.	55,000	43,000
Net income after income tax.	$ 65,000	$ 45,000

Madison, Inc.
Comparative Statement of Retained Earnings
For Year Ended December 31, 1962 and 1961

	1962	1961
Retained earnings, Jan. 1	$ 115,000	$ 100,000
Net income for year	65,000	45,000
Total	$ 180,000	$ 145,000
Dividends:		
On preferred stock	$ 10,000	$ 10,000
On common stock	30,000	20,000
Total	$ 40,000	$ 30,000
Retained earnings, Dec. 31	$ 140,000	$ 115,000

Madison, Inc.
Comparative Statement of Cost of Goods Sold
For Year Ended December 31, 1962 and 1961

	1962	1961
Merchandise inventory, Jan. 1	$ 325,000	$ 295,000
Purchases (net)	1,560,000	1,005,000
Merchandise available for sale	$1,885,000	$1,300,000
Merchandise inventory, Dec. 31	305,000	325,000
Cost of goods sold	$1,580,000	$ 975,000

Instructions: Prepare comparative statements and schedules for the two-year period, presenting the dollar and percentage changes for 1962 as compared with 1961.

30-2A. The comparative statements presented in Problem 30-1A are the principal data for this problem. Other necessary data, taken from the statements of Madison, Inc. for 1960 are as follows:

Accounts receivable (net)	$ 90,000
Long-term investments	300,000
Total assets	1,245,000
Total stockholders' equity (preferred and common stock outstanding same as in 1961)	790,000

Instructions: Determine for each of the two years the following ratios, turn-overs, and other measures listed below, presenting the figures used in your computations:

    (1) Working capital.
    (2) Current ratio.
    (3) Acid-test ratio.
    (4) Ratio of stockholders' equity to liabilities.
    (5) Ratio of plant assets to long-term liabilities.
    (6) Accounts receivable turnover.
    (7) Merchandise inventory turnover.
    (8) Ratio of net sales to assets.
    (9) Rate earned on total assets.
    (10) Rate earned on stockholders' equity.
    (11) Rate earned on common stockholders' equity.
    (12) Earnings per share on common stock.

Index

A

Account, balance, 46; four-column form, 296; mixed, 91; nature of, 45; nominal, 51; real, 51; ruling and balancing of, 104; standard form, 69; T form, 45

Accountancy, profession of, 6

Accounting, defined, 9; importance of, 1; private, 6; public, 6; specialized fields, 2

Accounting cycle, 90; *see also* Periodic summary

Accounting equation, 11

Accounting machines, 297

Accounting reports, scope of, 330

Accounting Research Bulletin, No. 5, 483; *No. 43,* 374, 485, 491

Accounting statements, 15; inter-relationship of, 38

Accounting systems, 3, 280, 305

Accounting Terminology Bulletin, No. 1, 9; *No. 2,* 13

Accounting Trends and Techniques, 14th edition, 338, 447, 647, 661, 662

Accounts payable, 12, 27; schedule of, 173

Accounts payable ledger, 143, 153

Accounts receivable, 14, 26; schedule of, 134, 173; turnover, 679

Accounts receivable ledger, 121, 131

Accrued assets, 221

Accrued expenses, 94, 219

Accrued liabilities, 28, 94, 219

Accrued revenues, 221

Acid-test ratio, 677

Adequate disclosure, 336

Adjusting entries, 91, 101, 174; branch, 540; depreciation, 167; insurance, 166; manufacturing, 559, 567; merchandise inventory, 164, 166; salaries, 167; supplies, 166

Admission of partner, 421; contribution of assets, 423; purchase of interest, 422; with bonus or goodwill to former partners, 424; with bonus or goodwill to new partner, 426

All-inclusive income statement, 494

Alternative cost reports, 632

Amortization, of copyrights, 556; of intangibles, 494; of patents, 555

Analysis of statements, 669

Application of funds statement, 648

Appraisal capital, 483

Appropriation, contractual, 496; discretionary, 486; funded, 487; of retained earnings, 485

Articles of copartnership, 403

Assets, 11; classification of, 25; intangible, 25; tangible, 25

Auditing, 2

B

Bad debts expense, 230; *see also* Uncollectible accounts

Balance, normal, 52

Balance sheet, 15, 100, 172; account form, 29, 30; comparative, 671, 675; consolidated, 659; financial position form, 660, 698, 708, 712; forms, 29; of a manufacturing enterprise, 565; report form, 29, 32; with horizontal analysis, 671; with vertical analysis, 675; *see also* Appendix B

Bank account, 282

Bank statement, 284; reconciliation of, 284

Banker's ratio, 677

Board of directors, 444

Bond discount, 508; amortization of, 509; on balance sheet, 510

Bond indenture, 505

Bond premium, 507; amortization of, 508; extended illustration of, 509; on balance sheet, 510

Bond sinking fund, 511

Bonds, 505; appropriation for, 486, 512; bearer, 505; callable, 506, 513; convertible, 506; coupon, 505; debenture, 506; face value, 505; investments in, *see* Investments in stocks and bonds; redemption, 513; registered, 505; secured, 506; serial, 505; sold at a discount, 508; sold at a premium, 507; term, 505

Bonds payable, 505

Bonus, admission of partner with, to former partners, 424; admission of partner with, to new partner, 427; withdrawal of a partner, 429

Book of original entry, *see* Journal

Book value of stock, 450

Bookkeeping, 4

Branch accounting, 535

Branch financial statements, 543

Break-even chart, 631

Break-even analysis, 630

Budget, cash, 626; flexible, 627; operating expense, 624, production, 623; sales, 623

Budgetary accounting, 3

Budgeting, and management, 621; nature of, 620; procedures, 622

Building, 27

Business entity, 328

By-products, 603

C

Capital, 11, 29; average, 409; corporation, on balance sheet, 452; paid-in, 446

Capital expenditures, 260

Capital statement, 16, 38, 100, 172

Capital stock, 29; *see also* Common stock, Preferred stock, and Stock

Cash, 25; on hand, 290; petty, 290; short and over, 289; special funds, 289

Cash budget, 626

Cash discount, 127; lost, 318

Cash payments journal, 150, 151

Cash receipts journal, 128; posting the, 130

Centralized system of branch accounting, 536

Certified public accountant (C.P.A.), 7

Chart of accounts, 72

Check, 283; payroll, 357

Check register, 311

Closing entries, 102, 104, 175; branch, 540; manufacturing, 559, 567

Common stock, 447; earnings per share, 683

Comparative statements, 647; *see* Appendix B

Compound journal entry, 73

Concepts, development of, 328; need for, 327

Conservatism, 339

Consistency, 336

Consolidated statements, 659

Contingencies, appropriation for, 487

Contingent liability, 203

Contra asset account, 93, 232, 255

Controlling account, 120; for factory overhead, 557

Controls, accounting, 280
Copyrights, 556
Corporate readjustment, 485
Corporate securities, listed and unlisted, 514
Corporation, balance sheet, 520, see also Appendix B; characteristics of, 442; charter, 443; close, 441; defined, 441; earnings, 483; financing, 503; income taxes, 483; nonprofit, 441; open, 441; parent, 659; private, 441; public, 441; records, 473; regulation of, 443; subsidiary, 659; taxed as partnership, 442; working organization, 444
Cost accounting, 3; by-products, 603; joint products, 603; see also Job order cost accounting and Process cost accounting
Cost accounting systems, 575
Cost ledger, 581
Cost of goods manufactured, statement of, 558, 566
Cost of goods sold, 34; in cost accounting, 585
Costs, allocation of, 335; differential, 611, 632; expired, 33; fixed, 610; opportunity, 636; organization, 456; out-of-pocket, 636; semivariable, 610; standard, 611; unexpired, 33; variable, 610
Credit, meaning of, 49
Credit memorandum, 123, 147
Credit terms, 149
Current assets, 25; manufacturing business, 554; schedule of, with horizontal analysis, 672
Current liabilities, 27
Current operating performance income statement, 493
Current ratio, 31, 677

D

Debit, meaning of, 49
Debit memorandum, 147
Decentralized system of branch accounting, 537; illustration of, 539
Deferred charges, 556; see also Prepaid expenses
Delivery equipment, 27
Departmental accounting, 527
Depletion, 555
Deposit ticket, 283
Depreciation, 26; accumulated, 26, 256; composite rates, 268; consistency, 257; declining balance method, 258; functional, 255; nature of, 254; physical, 254; recording, 255; straight line method, 258; sum of the years-digits method, 259; units of production method, 258
Differential cost, 611, 632
Direct labor, 557, 578
Direct materials, see Materials and supplies
Disclosure, 336
Discount, bond, see Bond discount; cash, 127, 149; stock, see Stock; trade, 119
Dividends, 447; cash, 488, 489; extra, 488; in arrears, 489; liquidating, 488; nature of, 488; regular, 488; restriction of, 512; stock, 488, 490

Donated capital, 482
Drawee, of a check, 283
Drawer, of a check, 283
Drawing account, 51

E

Earned surplus, see Retained earnings
Earned surplus statement, see Retained earnings statement
Earnings, computation of, 347; per share, 683
Earnings statement, see Income statement
Efficiency reports, 629
Employee, deductions from earnings, 348
Employee's earnings record, 357
Equities, 11
Equivalent units of production, 601
Errors, correction of, 83, 180; corporation, 492; discovery of, 82; of past periods, 180; reported on capital statement, 181
Expense, 33; apportionment to departments, 529; manufacturing, see Factory overhead; recording interest, 197
Expense and revenue summary, 102

F

Factory labor, 578
Factory overhead, 557, 579; predetermined rate, 580; variance, 613
Federal income tax, see Income tax
Federal unemployment compensation tax, 360; payment, 363
F.I.C.A. (Federal Insurance Contributions Act) tax, 349, 360; payment, 362
Finished goods, 553, 584
Finished goods ledger, 584
Fiscal period, 24
Fiscal year, 663
Fixed assets, see Plant assets
Fixed costs, 610
Fixed liabilities, see Long-term liabilities
Flexible budgets, 627
FOB, 134
Footing, pencil, 46
Funds, application of, 654; sources of, 652
Funds statement, 648, 699, 705; illustration, 653, 658; preparation of, 648

G

General expenses, 35
General journal, 118
Going concern, 329
Goodwill, admission of partner with, to former partners, 425; admission of partner with, to new partner, 427; withdrawal of a partner, 429
Governmental accounting, 3
Gross profit, 13, 34; by departments, 528

I

Income, recording interest, 199
Income statement, 15, 99, 171; all-inclusive, 494; budget report, 625; combined with retained earnings statement, 662, 693, 704, 709; comparative, 673, 676; consolidated, 659; current operating performance, 493; estimated, 624; for a mercantile business, 37; form, 33; of a departmentalized business, 534; of a manufacturing enterprise, 564; single-step form, 661, 700, 704; with horizontal analysis, 673; with vertical analysis, 676; see also Appendix B
Income tax, 379; accounting methods, 379; accrual basis, 380; adjusted gross income, 382; base, 382; capital gains and losses, 388; cash basis, 380; corporation, 483; declaration of estimated income tax, 391; deductions from adjusted gross income, 384; deductions from gross income, 382; dividends-received credit, 390; gross income, 381; payment, 390; personal exemptions, 387; rates, 388; records, 392; returns, 390; standard deduction, 382, 387; taxable income, 382, 387; withheld, 362; withholding of, 349
Incorporation, 443; of proprietorship or partnership, 454
Insurance register, 294
Intangible assets, amortization of, 494; manufacturing business, 555; write-off of, 494
Interest, computing, 194; on the income statement, 205
Interim statements, 110
Internal auditor, 3
Internal control, of cash payments, 305; of cash receipts, 288
Internal reports, 620, 628
Internal Revenue Service, Bulletin F, 257
Inventory, adjustments, 164; 166, see also Appendix A; based on estimates, 567; comparison of costing methods, 241; determining cost of, 238; determining quantities of, 237; finished goods, 554; first-in, first-out, 239; gross profit method, 245; importance of, 236; last-in, first-out, 240; lower of cost or market, 242; materials, 554; partially processed materials, 600; periodic, 237; perpetual, 237, see Perpetual inventory; presentation on the balance sheet, 245; retail method of, 244; returnable containers, 554; tools, 554; turnover of, 680; weighted average, 240; work in process, 554
Investment in stocks and bonds, 514; income from, 517; long-term, 516; sale of, 518; temporary, 515

J

Job cost sheet, 581
Job order cost accounting, 575; summary illustration, 586
Joint products, 603
Journal, 67; four-column, 79; special, 117; two-column, 68; used in merchandise, 118; see also specific titles

L

Labor, direct, 578

Land, 27

Ledger, 45; accounts in, 53; general, 120; stockholders, 475; subsidiary, 120; see also specific titles

Liabilities, 11; classification of, 27

Liquidating dividends, 488

Liquidation, of a partnership, 430

List price, 119

Listed securities, 514

Long-term investments, 516

Long-term liabilities, 28; manufacturing business, 556

M

Management, voucher system and, 320

Management services, 3

Manufacturing accounting, 553

Margin, 13, 34

Marginal income, 634

Materiality, 337

Materials and supplies, 557, 577; cost variance, 612

Merchandise inventory, 26; departmentalized, 528; see Inventory

Merchandise inventory turnover, 680

Minority interest, 659

Minute book, 473

Monetary unit, stability of, 330

Mortgage payable, 28

N

Natural resources, 555

Net current assets, 31

Net income, 13, 35, 36

Net loss, 13, 35, 36

Net operating income, 35; by departments, 528

No-par stock, 465

Note, computing interest on a, 194; determining due date of a, 195; discounting, 199, 200; dishonored, 204; long-term, 514; parties to, 193; proceeds of a, 200; supplementary records for, 293

Notes payable, 27, 193, 196; discounting, 200

Notes receivable, 25, 193, 198; contingent liability on, 203; discounting, 201

O

Office equipment, 27

Operating expense budget, 624

Operating expenses, 34

Opportunity cost, 636

Organization costs, 456

Out-of-pocket costs, 636

Overabsorbed overhead, 580

Overhead rate, 568

P

Paid-in capital, 446, 481

Parent corporation, 659

Partner, admission of, see Admission of partner; death of, 430; investment of, 404; mutual agency of, 402; participation in income of, 402; unlimited liability of, 402; withdrawal of, 421, 428

Partners' capital accounts, statement of, 414

Partners' drawing accounts, 406

Partnership, and federal income tax, 414; balance sheet of, 414; capital statement of, 414; characteristics of, 401; definition of, 401; dissolution of, 421; division of income or loss, 406; formation of, 403; limited life of, 402; liquidation of, 430; realization of assets, see Realization of partnership assets; recording investment, 404; statements for, 413; see also Partnership income

Partnership income, division in arbitrary ratio, 407; division recognizing investment, 407; division recognizing services of partners, 411; division recognizing services of partners and investments, 412

Par value, 450

Patents, 555

Payee, of a check, 284

Payroll, 351; adjustment at end of fiscal period, 364; distribution, 354; paying, 355

Payroll check, 352, 357

Payroll record, 346, 352

Periodicity, 331

Periodic summary, 163; see also Accounting cycle

Perpetual inventory, 568; flow of costs in accounts, 576

Petty cash, 290

Petty cash analysis sheet, 291

Petty cash voucher, 290

Plant assets, 26, 93; balance sheet presentation of, 268; determining initial costs of, 254; discarding, 261; exchange of, 263; manufacturing business, 554; nature of, 253; ratio to long-term liabilities, 679; replacement of, 636; sale of, 262; scrap value of, 257; subsidiary ledger for, 265

Plant expansion, appropriation for, 487

Posting, 70; diagrams of, 71

Pre-emptive right, 447

Preferred stock, 447; cumulative, 449; noncumulative, 449; nonparticipating, 448; participating, 448; redemption of, 472

Premiums, bond, see Bond premium; stock, see Stock

Prepaid expenses, 26, 92, 212

Prepaid transportation costs, 135

Principles, development of, 328; need for, 327

Process cost accounting, 597; summary illustration, 604

Processing department costs, 599

Production budget, 623

Profit and loss statement, see Income statement

Profit and loss summary, see Expense and revenue summary

Property, and business operations, 9; intangible, 372; personal, 372; real, 372; tangible, 372

Property tax, 372; accounting for, 373; base, 372; delinquent, 375; payment of, 373; special assessments, 376; rates, 373

Proprietorship, 11, 28; see Capital

Proxy, 444

Public accountant (P.A.), 7

Purchases, departmentalized, 528; procedures, 141

Purchases discount, departmentalized, 528; voucher system, 317

Purchases journal, 142, 144; posting the, 143; using purchases invoices as, 149

Purchases returns and allowances, 147; departmentalized, 528; general journal entry for, 148; voucher system, 316

Q

Quasi-reorganization, 485

Quick assets, 677

R

Rate earned, on common stockholders' equity, 682; on stockholders' equity, 682; on total assets, 681

Ratio, 677; acid-test, 677; current, 677; owners' equity to liabilities, 678; plant assets to long-term liabilities, 679; sales to assets, 681

Raw materials, see Materials and supplies

Realization of partnership assets, 430, 432, 433; gain on, 431

Receivables, classification of, 229

Receiving report, 578

Reciprocal accounts, in branch accounting, 537; parent and subsidiary, 659

Records, need for, 4

Remittance advice, 319

Remuneration, types of, 346

Research and development costs, 556

Reserve, see Appropriation

Retained earnings, 29, 447, 484; appropriation of, 485; consolidated statement of, 659; on balance sheet, 487

Retained earnings statement, 495, 701, 707; combined with income statement, 662, 693, 704, 709; comparative, 673; with horizontal analysis, 673; see also Appendix B

Returnable containers, 554

Revaluation capital, 483

Revenue, 13, 33; recognition of, 332

Revenue expenditures, 260

Reversing entries, 176, 218, 220, 222

Rounding amounts, 662; see Appendix B

S

Sales, 13, 34; departmentalized, 528; ratio to assets, 681

Sales budget, 623

Sales discount, departmentalized, 528

Sales invoice, 199

Sales journal, 121; posting, 122; using sales invoices as a, 126
Sales procedures, 119
Sales returns and allowances, 123; departmentalized, 528; general journal entries, 124
Sales tax, 376; imposed upon the purchaser, 377; imposed upon the seller, 378
Sales ticket, 119
Schedule of cost of goods sold, with horizontal analysis, 674
Self-insurance, appropriation for, 487
Selling expenses, 35
Semivariable costs, 610
Service department costs, 598
Shareholders' equity, on balance sheet, 482
Shares of stock, 442
Shipments to branch, 539; billed at selling price, 546
Signature card, 283
Slide, 82
Source and application of funds, 648
Split-up, stock, 491
Standard costs, 611; variance, 612
State unemployment compensation tax, 361; payment of, 362
Statement analysis, horizontal, 670; vertical, 674
Statement of financial position, see Balance sheet
Statements, interim, 110
Stock, authorized, 452; book value of, 450; classes of, 447; discount on, 463; investments in, see Investments in stocks and bonds; issuance of, 453; issued, 452; market value of, 452; no-par, 450, 465; outstanding, 452; par value, 450; premium on, 463; redemption value of, 452; stated value of, 450; subscriptions to, 466; treasury, 469; values of, 450
Stock certificate, 467
Stock certificate book, 474

Stock dividend, 488, 490
Stock split-up, 491
Stockholder, 442; limited liability of, 442
Stockholders' equity, 445; on balance sheet, 453; rate earned on, 682
Stockholders ledger, 475, 467
Store equipment, 27
Subscribers ledger, 467, 474
Subscription book, 474
Subscriptions to capital stock, **466**
Subsidiary corporation, 659
Subsidiary ledger, 120; cost ledger, 581; finished goods, 584; equipment, 265; factory overhead, 557
Systems, 280; for branch accounting, 536

T

Tax accounting, 3
Taxes, progressive, 371; proportional, 371; regressive, 371; relationship to accounting of, 371
Temporary investments, 515
Timekeeping, 347
Time tickets, 578
Tools, 554
Transactions, 8; and accounting equation, 11; and accounting statements, 23; and accounting values, 10
Transportation on incoming shipments, 155
Transposition, 82
Treasury stock, 469; appropriation for, 486; classification on balance sheet of, 470; donated, 471; purchased, 470
Trend reports, 630
Trial balance, 59, 77; adjusted, 97; post-closing, 108, 176; proof provided by, 59
Turnover, accounts receivable, 679; merchandise inventory, 680

U

Uncollectible accounts, 230; advance provision for, 231; allowance for, 232; direct write-off of, 230; estimating losses from, 234; recoveries of, 234
Underabsorbed overhead, 580
Unearned income, 28
Unearned revenue, 215
Unlisted securities, 514

V

Variable cost, 610
Variance, factory overhead, 613; labor, 613; material, 612
Vertical analysis of statements, 674
Voucher, 306; adjustment on a, 307; filing of, 313; preparation of, 307
Voucher filing, 310
Voucher register, 309
Voucher system, basic features of, 305; purchases discount under, 317; special problems of, 314

W

Wage rates, 348
Withholding statement, 359
Working capital, 31, 677
Work in process, 554, 581
Work sheet, 95; adjustments columns of, 95; eight-column, 169; for combined home office and branch balance sheet, 545; for combined home office and branch income statement, 544; for funds statement, 650, 656; of a departmentalized business, 532; of a manufacturing enterprise, 560; ten-column, 96

Y

Year, natural business, 663; see Fiscal period

SCHEDULE OF CHECK FIGURES FOR PROBLEMS
ACCOUNTING PRINCIPLES
Eighth Edition
by
Noble and Niswonger

The following "check" figures may be compared with those obtained by the student in solving problems. Agreement between the two is an indication that the solution is basically correct, aside from matters of form and technique.

Prob. No.	CHECK FIGURES	Prob. No.	CHECK FIGURES
1-1	Capital, $360	7-1	Accounts Payable, $4,678.20
1-2	Capital, $8,300	7-2	Cash credit, $10,076; Accounts Payable, $4,297
1-3	Capital, $4,330		
1-2A	Capital, $10,350	7-3	Trial balance totals, $56,234
1-3A	Capital, $4,500	7-4	Trial balance totals, $64,811
		7-2A	Cash credit, $11,220; Accounts Payable, $3,955
2-1	Total assets, $82,360		
2-2	Net income, $27,950	7-3A	Trial balance totals, $57,033
2-3	Net income, $18,980; total assets, $55,840		
		8-1	Net income, $12,250
2-4	Capital, $11,150	8-2	Capital, $18,935
2-2A	Net income, $21,950	8-3	Net income, $7,463.10
2-3A	Net income, $24,000; total assets, $64,160	8-4	Net income, $24,960
		8-5	Capital, $33,330
2-4A	Capital, $12,450	8-1A	Net loss, $3,950
		8-3A	Net income, $8,075.60
3-1	Trial balance totals, $6,500	8-5A	Capital, $30,620
3-2	Trial balance totals, $30,795		
3-3	Trial balance totals, $12,513	9-3	Total cash debits, $8,086.86; total cash credits, $7,197.58
3-4	Trial balance totals, $30,702		
3-2A	Trial balance totals, $31,125	9-4	Total cash debits, $15,491.79; total cash credits, $24,230.67
3-3A	Trial balance totals, $13,077		
3-4A	Trial balance totals, $36,545	9-3A	Total cash debits, $9,230.02; total cash credits, $8,272.90
4-1	Trial balance totals, $7,053	9-4A	Total cash debits, $18,861.22; total cash credits, $24,544
4-2	Trial balance totals, $13,143		
4-4	Trial balance totals, $37,209	10-1	Balance, Expense and Revenue Summary, $27,545
4-2A	Trial balance totals, $13,266.70		
4-4A	Trial balance totals, $36,909	10-3	Net income, $13,350
		10-1A	Balance, Expense and Revenue Summary, $26,610
5-1	Net income, $6,127		
5-2	Net income, $995.54	10-3A	Net income, $14,740
5-3	Net income, $4,815		
5-4	Net income, $13,292	11-1	Balance, Allow. for Uncollect. Accts., $1,200
5-1A	Net income, $7,368		
5-2A	Net income, $962.86	11-2	Inventory: (1) $4,484; (2) $4,162; (3) $4,309
5-3A	Net income, $4,563		
		11-3	Inventory: (1) $130,492; (2) $203,300
6-1	Accounts Receivable, $4,090	11-4	Net income, $20,844
6-2	Cash debit, $26,423; Accounts Receivable, $4,428	11-5	Capital, $34,755
		11-6	Balance, Allow. for Uncollect. Accts., $8,100
6-3	Cash debit, $18,728; Accounts Receivable, $3,414		
		11-1A	Balance, Allow. for Uncollect. Accts., $1,400
6-1A	Accounts Receivable, $4,215		
6-2A	Cash debit, $29,631; Accounts Receivable, $4,522	11-2A	Inventory: (1) $5,704; (2) $5,677; (3) $5,607
6-3A	Cash debit, $18,374; Accounts Receivable, $3,320	11-3A	Inventory: (1) $148,135; (2) $211,131
		11-4A	Net income, $19,616

Prob. No.	CHECK FIGURES	Prob. No.	CHECK FIGURES
12-1	Building, $270,400	21-1	Total capital, $537,400
12-3	Loss on disposal, $490	21-2	Total capital, $3,546,500
12-4	Total book values, $7,598	21-3	Total capital, July 31, $631,750
12-1A	Building, $242,200	21-4	Total capital, $9,449,000
12-3A	Loss on disposal, $697	21-5	Total capital, $520,800
12-4A	Total book value, $7,944	21-1A	Total capital, $833,200
		21-2A	Total capital, $4,664,000
13-3	Notes Receivable, $3,460	21-4A	Total capital, $8,582,500
13-4	Total, Unexpired Premium column, $1,180.10	22-1	Total capital, $1,686,500
13-3A	Notes Receivable, $4,040	22-3	Total retained earnings, $513,000
13-4A	Total, Unexpired Premium column, $1,267.55	22-4	Total stockholders' equity, $2,885,700
		22-5	Total capital, $1,315,300
		22-1A	Total capital, $1,497,500
14-2	Accounts Payable, $3,410	22-3A	Total retained earnings, $645,000
14-3	Accounts Payable, $5,505; Bank balance, $10,391		
14-2A	Accounts Payable, $2,705	23-4	Total assets, $1,494,000
14-3A	Accounts Payable $5,425; Bank balance, $11,392	24-1	Net income after income tax, $31,110
		24-2	Net income from operations, $16,500
		24-3	Net income from operations (combined), $135,500
15-2	Net income, third year, $82,300	24-1A	Net income after income tax, $9,883
15-3	Net income, third year, $26,700	24-2A	Net income from operations, $41,650
15-4	Net income, $15,875	24-3A	Net income from operations (combined), $208,200
15-5	Gain on repossession, $1,200		
15-2A	Net income, third year, $69,600	25-2	Net income after income tax, $51,200
15-4A	Net income, $9,100	25-3	Cost of goods manufactured, $1,320,150
		25-4	Net income after income tax, $99,260
16-1	Total, Net Amount column, $667.97	25-2A	Net income after income tax, $41,380
16-2	Total, Accounts Payable Dr. column, $12,262.29		
16-3	Total, Net Amount column, $1,047.30	26-2	Trial balance totals, $974,450
16-1A	Total, Net Amount column, $744.01	26-3	Total assets, $514,880
16-2A	Total, Accounts Payable Dr. column, $13,277.76	26-2A	Trial balance totals, $630,900
		27-2	Trial balance totals, $596,640
17-3	Balance due, $522.74	27-4	Total increase in unit cost, $.10
17-4	Net income, $13,465	27-2A	Trial balance totals, $615,550
17-5	Balance due, $402 15		
17-3A	Balance due, $644.80	28-1	Estimated net income, $50,000
17-4A	Net income, $17,612	28-2	Net income after income tax: budget, $7,416
18-1	Total assets, $73,000	28-3	Estimated excess: Jan., $1,100; Feb., $800; Mar., $5,800
18-3	Total capital, $69,460	28-4	Estimated net income, $180,000
18-4	Total capital, $66,200	28-5	Total cost of abnormal time, $103.10
18-6	Net income, $45,750	28-6	Total increase in quarterly sales, $18,900
18-1A	Total assets, $72,000	28-1A	Estimated net income, $100,000
18-4A	Total capital, $64,200	28-3A	Estimated excess: Jan., $2,650; Feb., $1,450; Mar., $19,050
19-4	Total assets, $113,920	28-4A	Estimated net income, $240,000
20-1	Retained Earnings Balance, $17,000	29-1	Change in working capital, $20,720
20-2	Total common dividends per share, $9.40	29-2	Change in working capital, $24,450
20-4	Total assets, $118,650	29-3	Retained earnings, $73,200
20-5	Total assets, $383,800	29-2A	Change in working capital, $43,150
20-1A	Retained Earnings Balance, $4,125	29-3A	Retained earnings, $85,800
20-4A	Total assets, $150,140		